D1015508

The Last Thousand Days
of the British Empire

Lancashire and the New Liberalism
Liberals and Social Democrats
The Keynesian Revolution in the Making, 1924–1936
The Keynesian Revolution and its Economic Consequences
A Question of Leadership: From Gladstone to Blair
The Cripps Version: The Life of Sir Stafford Cripps, 1889–1952
Hope and Glory: Britain, 1900–2000

The Last Thousand Days of the British Empire

Churchill, Roosevelt, and the
Birth of the Pax Americana

PETER CLARKE

BLOOMSBURY PRESS

Published by Bloomsbury Press, New York
Distributed to the trade by Macmillan

All papers used by Bloomsbury Press are natural, recyclable products made from wood grown in well-managed forests. The manufacturing processes conform to the environmental regulations of the country of origin.

LIBRARY OF CONGRESS CATALOGING-IN-PUBLICATION DATA

Clarke, P. F.
The last thousand days of the British empire / Peter Clarke.—1st U.S. ed.
p. cm.
Includes bibliographical references and index.
ISBN-13: 978-1-59691-531-2 (alk. paper)
ISBN-10: 1-59691-531-5 (alk. paper)
1. Great Britain—History—George VI, 1936–1952. 2. World War, 1939–1945—Great Britain. 3. World War, 1939–1945—Commonwealth countries. 4. Great Britain—Foreign relations—1945–1964. 5. Commonwealth countries—Civilization. 6. Churchill, Winston, Sir, 1874–1965. 7. Civilization, Modern—British influences. I. Title.
DA16.C56 2008
909'.09712410824—dc22
2007036929

First published in Great Britain by the Penguin Group in 2007
First U.S. Edition 2008

1 3 5 7 9 10 8 6 4 2

Typeset by Rowland Phototypesetting Ltd, Bury St Edmonds, Suffolk
Printed in the United States of America by Quebecor World Fairfield

For my sister Jane
1947 And All That

Contents

PART 3:
Hollow Victories

PART 4:
The Liquidation of the British Empire

Illustrations

Photographic acknowledgements are given in parentheses. Every effort has been made to contact all copyright holders. The publishers will be glad to make good in future editions any errors or omissions brought to their attention.

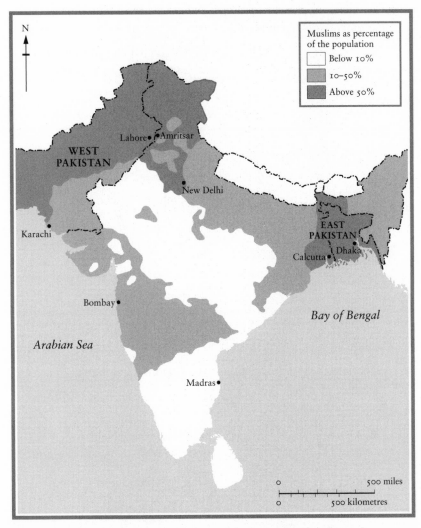

India: communal identity in 1945 and the partition borders of 1947 (largely the Radcliffe Line)

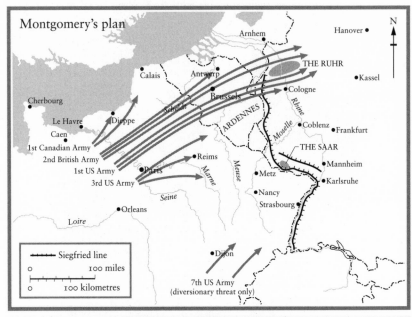

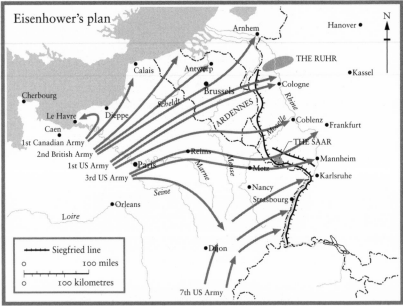

Chester Wilmot's view of the strategic controversy

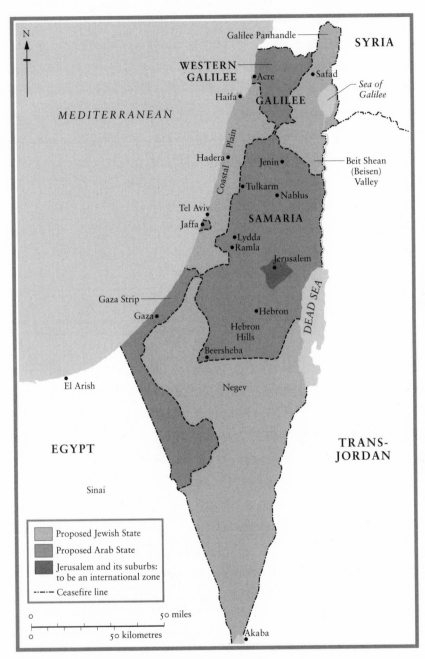

The United Nations Partition Plan, November 1947

Preface

In 1945 the British people were united in believing that they had won the war. The evil of Nazism had been exorcised, not least because the British Empire had stood alone at a crucial hour – its 'finest hour', so people had been led to believe. In the speech that concluded with this famous phrase, Winston Churchill led up to it by posing the stark alternatives: 'if we fail, then the whole world, including the United States, including all that we have known and cared for, will sink into the abyss of a new Dark Age made more sinister, and perhaps more protracted, by the lights of perverted science.' But if only Hitler could be successfully defied: 'the life of the world may move forward into broad, sunlit uplands.'[1] By 1945, victory, which had seemed such an elusive dream to the British in 1940, had been achieved against all odds. After such hardships and such risks, surely their fortitude and sacrifices in the common cause would be duly rewarded?

The Last Thousand Days of the British Empire shows how the British came to be disabused of this idea. It shows how they were surprised to find themselves as much victims as victors after 1945, and how they tried to make sense of this. It tells the story of how the British Empire survived the war only to expire in a post-war world that did not owe the British people a living. Weary and impoverished, they were puzzled to find wartime rationing and austerity succeeded by peacetime rationing and austerity. It was not what they had expected, and one natural reaction was to ask who was responsible. Some blamed the Soviet Union for starting a cold war, some blamed the United States for taking unfair advantage of its loyal ally, some blamed the Labour Government at home. Historians have subsequently argued each of these cases. Few, then or later, blamed Churchill himself for getting the country into this mess in the first place. The abrupt decline of British power nonetheless decisively gathered pace under his wartime premiership. It made what he called 'the liquidation of the British Empire' inevitable; and it happened on his watch.

The six magnificent volumes of Churchill's *The Second World War*, published over half a century ago, still stand proud on many bookshelves. They have provided insights into these events for many people – even those who did not get much further than reading the noble motto at the front:

> IN WAR: RESOLUTION
> IN DEFEAT: DEFIANCE
> IN VICTORY: MAGNANIMITY
> IN PEACE: GOODWILL

The web of words that Churchill spun to good purpose, both during the war and afterwards, created its own tension. It expressed his own views and convictions, but it did so in a way that was intended to have consequences. Thus he represented what was happening in a particular way, so as to generate action that would change the course of events or subsequently to vindicate what was done. And, to some extent, this involved distortion, not always knowingly, and it concealed unpalatable realities – sometimes even from himself.

Today we can move beyond the chivalrous rhetoric and look at what lay behind it. How did a nation that Churchill had inspired to resolution in war, and to defiance in defeat, come to feel cheated of its trusting expectation of magnanimity in victory and goodwill in peace? For the alliance of the English-speaking peoples, on which he set such store, proved itself a rather unequal alliance. The Japanese attack on Pearl Harbor in December 1941 brought the Americans into a war in the Pacific, and Hitler promptly brought them into a war in Europe. The Second World War was a shock to the Americans and the British alike, with two not unimportant differences. First, it made the United States, willy-nilly, into the dominant world power; and secondly, while the Gross National Product of Europe fell by about 25 per cent, that of the United States rose during the war by over 50 per cent in real terms.[2] It was not the first time, nor the last, that Americans claimed to have lost their innocence. They took time to accept the idea of their new international role. Many British people, who had been brought up on quite different assumptions, took time to accept that it was a good idea at all.

This migration of power across the Atlantic was bound to happen, sooner or later. The United States is forty times bigger in area, its population today more like five times bigger than Great Britain's. That is a huge disparity; and though the population gap is now wider than in the 1930s, the British were aware throughout the twentieth century that they were fighting in a league above their natural size. The population of the United Kingdom (including Northern Ireland) was under 50 million just before the Second World War. This compared with 180 million Russians and 140 million Americans, both to become war-time allies of the British, and together outnumbering them by over six to one. The main enemy countries in the Second World War outnumbered Britain by nearly three to one – with the population in pre-war Japan already over 70 million – and vaulting higher than that within the ever-expanding frontiers of Hitler's Germany.

Yet Great Britain, for more than two centuries, ranked as a great power. What made all the difference was the British Empire.

This was what enabled a relatively small country to defy geography and demography alike, in the short run at least. The self-governing Dominions constitutionally comprising the British Commonwealth from 1931 – notably Canada, South Africa, Australia and New Zealand – were of crucial importance in both military and financial terms. India, with a measure of self-government but without independence, stood in a class of its own, with a population breasting 400 million by the 1940s, and with major strategic significance. The Royal Navy symbolized British supremacy over the world's sea routes, with the passage to India guarded by great bases at Gibraltar, Malta, Suez and Aden, stretching imperial sinews across the Mediterranean and what we now call the Middle East. In an empire that was in its heyday built upon free trade rather than protection, the mechanism of the Gold Standard, regulated through the Bank of England, symbolized the international financial dominance of the City of London. This had been a world where – so it was said when Britain returned to Gold in 1925 – the pound could look the dollar in the face.

At the peak of their imperial power, as recently as the 1920s – within the lifetime of old people today – the British controlled a quarter of the world's territory and a quarter of its total population. Much of this was in the Indian subcontinent; but it was only in 1920 that League of Nations 'mandates' over Mesopotamia (Iraq) and Palestine were added, and these mandates – giving effective responsibility for governing the territories – were administered by Britain on familiar imperial lines. All this may have seemed a fitting reward for a country that had emerged bloody but victorious from the First World War. The Empire was also a major reason why Britain had had to fight it, of course, just as it was a major reason for the Second World War.

It is the universal appeal of Churchill's rhetoric that has given it a timeless status. In consequence, it is the democratic passages and sentences that are still so often quoted; the dated imperialist sentiments that are quietly excised. Observe, however, what Churchill had actually said on 18 June in the 'finest hour' speech to the House of Commons, broadcast by the BBC the same evening. It is often wrongly claimed that Britain stood alone after the fall of France. Churchill should not be misquoted to this effect. It was, of course, the *British Empire* that remained blocking Hitler's path – indeed, in his speech Churchill specifically mentioned that Canadian troops had actually landed in France, before being withdrawn. Everything turned on the outcome of what Churchill now called, in a broad sense, the Battle of Britain. 'Upon it depends our own British life,' he said, 'and the long continuity of our institutions and our Empire.' Hence the stance in the peroration: 'Let us therefore brace ourselves to our duties, and so bear ourselves that, if the British Empire and its Commonwealth lasts for a thousand years, men will still say, "This was their finest hour."'[3]

Propagandists in Soviet Russia were not wholly implausible when they characterized this at the time as an 'imperialist war'. They could point to the struggle that had begun in 1939 between the satisfied powers, Britain and France, with empires long established over much of Asia and Africa, and the unsatisfied hunger of the Axis powers – the expansion of Germany, craving *Lebensraum* in eastern Europe, and (from 1940) the opportunist aggression of Italy, still seeking old-fashioned colonial glory in Africa. Admittedly, there was an indecently sudden transformation of this conflict into a 'great patriotic war' against fascism, overnight on 22 June 1941, when Hitler attacked Russia. Americans likewise, from President Roosevelt down, were more open in reproaching the British over their Empire before 7 December 1941, the date of the Japanese attack on Pearl Harbor. Thereafter, American criticisms were often muted in public, but suspicions of British imperialism flourished and festered in private – with a largely unacknowledged impact on policy.

Unlike the First World War, this war did not end suddenly. Long before VE-Day in May 1945, its successful outcome had been widely anticipated. Back in November 1942, when Churchill first sensed 'the end of the beginning' after Allied victories in North Africa, he used that year's Mansion House speech to proclaim Britain's own war aims. 'Let me, however, make this clear, in case there should be any mistake about it in any quarter. We mean to hold our own,' he said. 'I have not become the King's First Minister in order to preside over the liquidation of the British Empire.'[4]

Yet in important respects, as I hope to show, the Second World War was, for the British, an unsuccessful imperialist war. All the European empires in Asia buckled in the face of the initial Japanese assault; the British defended India, where the King–Emperor reigned, but at a price. Like many of the costs exacted by the war, it was to be paid later, after the hostilities were over, when the long-promised spoils of victory were assessed. By 1945 all Britain's enemies had been defeated; but what she owed to her allies, notably the United States, was also part of the reckoning.

What is, I think, still insufficiently appreciated is how intractably Britain's post-war problems were rooted in precisely those wartime commitments that had brought victory. If Churchill was the architect of victory, he was surely to this extent also the author of Britain's post-war distress. The costs of victory were still being counted when he lost power in 1945. Maybe he was simply in denial about the viability of the British Empire. By the time that he wrote his war memoirs, however, the writing was on the wall; we search its six fat volumes in vain for the otherwise often-quoted claim from the King's First Minister about his imperial policy. But the post-war author could also prove apt in his melancholy insights. Little wonder that he called his last volume, covering 1944–5, *Triumph and Tragedy*.

For the essence of tragedy is not simply misfortune, still less mistakes or missed opportunities – awkward corners in history which might have been avoided by an effort of will or an exercise of cleverness. Rather, we often recognize the sense of a tragic destiny unfolding when, despite the best efforts of those trapped in particular circumstances, they reap the bad consequences of actions taken for good motives. We need not attribute blame to the British people or their leaders for their sorry post-war plight. Instead, we simply need to recognize that their finest hour in 1940–41, when the citizens of the British Empire were inspired to resist the Nazi menace at all costs, left bills to be paid later. Defeat would obviously have spelled the end of the Empire. But so did victory, as the British were to discover soon enough.

The outward forms were still maintained and the show went on – for a time. The Official Programme of the Victory Celebrations, held in London thirteen months after VE-Day, on 8 June 1946, gives the flavour. The order of march from Marble Arch to the saluting base in the Mall was led by the representatives of Britain's Allies – from fighting French, gallant Greeks and doomed Poles to improbable Mexicans – with the massed bands of the USA and the USSR together at the head.

It was, however, the Empire that dominated the parade. In pride of place came the Dominions, with bands from Canada, Australia and New Zealand, followed by South Africa, Southern Rhodesia and Newfoundland. India came next: not only the Royal Indian Navy, the Indian Armoured Corps, the Royal Indian Artillery, the Royal Indian Engineers and the Indian Signal Corps but also the band of the Royal Garhwal Rifles leading the Indian Infantry, the Gurkha Rifles, the Indian State Forces and the Royal Indian Air Force. After Burma, the panoply of the colonial Empire was fully represented: ten West African corps from Nigeria, Gold Coast, Sierra Leone and Gambia; then no fewer than twenty-six from East and Central Africa (Kenya, Uganda, Tanganyika, Nyasaland, Northern Rhodesia, Zanzibar and British Somaliland). And so the vast procession marched on – Aden, Bermuda, Ceylon, Cyprus, the Falkland Islands, Gibraltar, Hong Kong, Malaya, the West Indies (Bahamas, Barbados, British Guiana, British Honduras, Jamaica, the Leeward Islands, Trinidad and Tobago, the Windward Islands). Still more to swell the march – from Fiji, Tonga, the British Solomon Islands, the Gilbert and Ellice Islands, Mauritius, North Borneo, Brunei, Labuan, Sarawak, Palestine, St Helena, the Seychelles, Basutoland, Bechuanaland, Swaziland and – last but by no means least in its heroic war record – Malta.

Here was the British Empire, decked out to celebrate its greatest victory, despite everything. The Empire on which the sun would never set. Or would it? It was a thought that had already become inescapable.

At midnight on 14–15 August 1947, a date which Jawaharlal Nehru saluted as marking 'a tryst with destiny', the two new states of India and Pakistan celebrated their independence. It was the end of the Raj, conventionally regarded as 'the jewel in the crown'. The title of Emperor of India was held by King George VI in succession from his great-grandmother, Queen Victoria, revived from the days of the Mughal Empire to crown Britain's now self-consciously imperialist mission. On 15 August 1947, the title lapsed after seventy years of viceregal pomp. The last Viceroy departed Delhi (though Lord Mountbatten continued for a time as Governor-General of the new Dominion of India). 'As long as we rule in India, we are the greatest power in the world,' one of his most pompous predecessors, Lord Curzon, had once claimed. 'If we lose it we shall drop straight away to a third rate power.'[5]

By 1947 such prophecies came home to roost. Though subsequently reinvented simply as the Commonwealth of Nations, the British Empire was now in the hands of the liquidators. Churchill's thousand-year Reich had barely outlasted Hitler's. It all happened so quickly, so quickly . . .

It was less than five years since Churchill's 'end of the beginning'. On that occasion he had stood up in the Mansion House, flushed with the news of the 8th Army's victory at El Alamein, fully determined to make the most of it, free for the moment to ignore the tiresome sermons about India that his friend Roosevelt had been preaching in their correspondence. Churchill had thus defied his critics but not defied history.

It was just short of three years since the Quebec conference of September 1944. Roosevelt and Churchill had met on that occasion, apparently as equals and with a warmth never subsequently recaptured, both anticipating victory with an easy optimism that was quickly overtaken by events.

It was two and a half years since Yalta. Attending this meeting of the Big Three in February 1945 as British prime minister, Churchill sat alongside Stalin and Roosevelt as they made plans to divide and rule the post-war world. Many promises had meanwhile withered on their Crimean vine. Indeed, within weeks of Churchill's departure from office in July 1945, victory turned out to be more costly than even he had imagined.

The Last Thousand Days of the British Empire is in four parts. After Part 1, 'Broad, Sunlit Uplands', which sets out the themes and some historical background, Part 2, 'False Summits', gives a detailed narrative of what happened between September 1944 and February 1945. In the course of these months, it became clear that the British Empire now ceased to exert a dominant influence on a world increasingly polarized between two superpowers, the United States and the Soviet Union. Part 3, 'Hollow Victories', tells a piquant story of how the transition to peace, so hopefully greeted, stored up its own disappointments for the British. Though unreal dreams of parity with the Americans and the Russians were often nurtured, the dynamics of the process were irreversible by VJ-Day.

Finally, Part 4, 'The Liquidation of the British Empire', shows how the United Kingdom limped into the post-war era saddled with financial obligations well beyond its capacity, and beholden to the United States in a way that many British citizens found humiliating. Plainly the stark revelation of military, political and economic weakness had implications for the viability of imperial power. That is why the endgame of empire in India – and also in Palestine – meant playing out a hand that had already been dealt. Clement Attlee, the new prime minister, said as much himself. It was a losing hand; but how Britain played it remains a matter of considerable interest and controversy.

It is no later than the autumn of 1944 that we need to start, with real battles still to be fought, so that we can recapture the mood and perceptions of the end of the war, different in each Allied country. In particular, the military campaign in Europe needs more than cursory mention if we are to understand not only the conflicts between the British and the Americans over strategy and command but also how the war was reported to the public at home. This was how incompatible impressions were generated of who had actually done the fighting and hence who should – and could – determine the shape of the post-war world.

The Quebec conference of September 1944 was the last moment when optimism still reigned about a less troubled peace ahead than that which actually ensued. When the war against the Nazis, which seemed within sight of early victory in the late summer of 1944, turned nasty later in the year, so did relations between the Allies – not as nasty as the war, of course, but enough to give vivid glimpses of peacetime difficulties ahead.

Britain's supposed 'special relationship' with the United States has often been indulgently celebrated in accounts of this period, pre-eminently in Churchill's *Triumph and Tragedy*, which remains a book worth reading. Yet his beatific vision of the 'English-speaking democracies' simply cannot provide an adequate frame for a true picture of the conflicts and competition – as well as the co-operation – between the two countries in the twelve months before VJ-Day.

The transition from war to peace has to be understood, moreover, in another context. As it turned out, Britain's appalling economic situation – which initially seemed to be its main problem – was overlaid by the imperatives of a new cold war that was to shape the world for the next half-century. That the cold war began (and ultimately ended) is a historical fact. Whether it was a historical necessity has often been debated subsequently. Certainly the pattern of its development is more obvious to us than it seemed to contemporaries.

Through a narrative of these thousand or so days, we can recover a sense of how seemingly separate events were locked together by chronology: sometimes reinforcing each other, sometimes checking each other, sometimes occluding each other. How far was the eclipse of British power apparent at the time? How obvious was it that the British Empire would yield to the emergence of what is often called the American empire? How did different people – both rulers and ruled – perceive the course of events?

Looking back, we are privileged by hindsight in our perspectives. Analytically, we have this advantage, and can see some things more clearly than contemporaries could. But there is another perspective that needs to be recovered – that of people living their history without foreknowledge of things that seem obvious to us. What strikes us today as inevitable seemed surprising to many people at the time – but they were sometimes acutely aware of things that we tend to forget, or have pigeonholed separately.

The Big Three conferences, above all at Yalta but also at Potsdam, professionally recorded as verbatim discussions, have dramatic possibilities that often reveal themselves in passing, almost inadvertently. We can sense the fluidity of a situation that only later set into its mould. Furthermore, if we enjoy reading other people's diaries, it is surely because these offer unique opportunities for eavesdropping, recapturing the spontaneity of a moment otherwise lost in time. Old diaries can thus prompt new insights.

We are fortunate that so many participants in these events found the time to write down their experiences. Admittedly, prime ministers are seldom diarists; but one of the peculiarities of Mackenzie King, in his twenty-three years as Prime Minister of Canada, was that he kept an almost daily journal, with a revealing account of his dealings with both Roosevelt and Churchill at Quebec. If Churchill himself, that prolific writer, kept no diary, how lucky that not only his close aide Jock Colville but also his physician, Lord Moran, and his military chief of staff, Sir Alan Brooke, did so (however displeasing publication later proved for the Churchill family). Harry Butcher served in the same candid, mildly embarrassing capacity in recording what the Allied Supreme Commander, General Dwight Eisenhower, really thought, off duty and on.

Other examples are not hard to find. Sir Alexander Cadogan was a Foreign Office mandarin from the top drawer, well used to concealing his own views. Only in his thankfully undiplomatic diary did Sir Alec (as he was known) feel free to reveal his true feelings – as he did one day at the San Francisco conference about a leading politician from a key Dominion: 'Evatt, the Australian, who's the most frightful man in the world; he makes long and tiresome speeches on every conceivable subject, always advocating the wrong thing and generally with a view to being inconvenient and offensive to us, and boosting himself.'[6] This was written in a moment of frustration during the conference which set up the United Nations Organization, in which Australia was in fact playing an impressive role under Dr H. V. Evatt, the Minister for External Affairs, in asserting the rights of the smaller powers. American critics of the British Empire purported to find the separate representation of the Dominions a mere British ruse for exercising a bloc of six obedient votes. Between them, Dr Evatt and Sir Alec suggest how anachronistic such assumptions about imperial unity were by 1945.

The diaries of economists not economizing with the truth – both Lionel Robbins and his colleague James Meade clearly qualify – also help to light up relevant perspectives which are worth developing. When Robbins set down some comments on the role of the respective Dominions in the post-war Anglo-American loan negotiations, he was not afraid to generalize: 'Each delegation true to form – Canada first rate, South Africa debonair and friendly, New Zealand banal, Australia surly and unhelpful.' Some of these instant judgements are as unfairly dismissive as others are indulgently flattering. 'How refreshing these

Canadians are,' he wrote in a benign moment. 'My own private view is that if they rather than UK officials had the lead for the Commonwealth, policy all round would be much more effective and much more intelligent.'[7]

The perspectives of this book inevitably reflect those of the diaries that it uses. Hugh Dalton writes with waspish candour, first as a Labour minister in Churchill's Coalition, craving fuller appreciation from the Prime Minister, and subsequently as Chancellor of the Exchequer, facing what John Maynard Keynes called 'a financial Dunkirk'. Leo Amery, a year older than Churchill and unawed by him ever since their schooldays at Harrow, served as his wartime Secretary of State for India – thanklessly, as his diary makes clear. Harold Macmillan, later a Conservative Prime Minister, was blooded in ministerial office by his roving commission in the Mediterranean, at the heart of Allied disputes over Italy and Greece, and his diary is far from a bloodless account. Of course there is bias; but this is usually self-evident or even self-cancelling, with more than two dozen diarists scribbling and typing away. Archibald Wavell, while Viceroy of India, wrote in his journal with not only unusual insight but also some natural prejudice, notably against Labour's envoy to India, Sir Stafford Cripps; so the obvious antidote is to read the Cripps diary too.

These are all diaries by major figures in government. Likewise, in the United States administration, James Forrestal as Secretary of the Navy, Henry Morgenthau as a long-serving Secretary of the Treasury and Edward Stettinius as a short-serving Secretary of State all confided their feelings and frustrations to their diaries. The fact that the powerful Senator Arthur Vandenberg left revealing traces in his diary of his trajectory from isolationism to internationalism is another boon.

It is not, however, necessary to be a major politician to write a good diary. Two British MPs who never rose to ministerial office – Henry Channon and Harold Nicolson – compensated for their own thwarted ambitions by exploiting their opportunities as privileged observers. The best sources, in short, are those that have the greatest power to illuminate, not simply to record, what was happening. The young Isaiah Berlin drafted despatches from the British embassy in Washington which showed the aptitude for combining political analysis with personal aperçus that later informed his academic writings. When the American writer Robert E. Sherwood published his book *Roosevelt and Hopkins:*

An intimate history (1948), he drew on the vast collection of papers left by Harry Hopkins, Roosevelt's great crony and go-between during the war, and wrote with the proximity and partisanship of someone who had been closely associated with both men. An unimpeachable source? Of course not, but one that I am not alone in finding a perceptive insider view.

The more numerous outsiders, however, were not always less articulate. In Britain, Mass-Observation was a pioneering organization which listened to non-elite voices and its archive at the University of Sussex contains a wealth of material, still too little known, that can help us recapture the feelings of ordinary people at the time.

Frankly, however, archives often tell us things that we should have known anyway, if only we had read through old newspapers. The existence of a digital archive version of *The Times* now facilitates research; but I also relish my hours turning the pages of the often choleric *Daily Mail*, the voice of suburban middle England, or reading the inimitable *Chicago Tribune*, the trumpet of the isolationist Middle West. Such newspapers remain a prime source, not only because of the events that they record, but because that record itself was read by millions of people at the time, whose opinions were often as shrewd as those of ostensibly better-informed persons in top jobs. History is not only made by leaders, however influential or well-informed; and the leaders themselves were not uniquely prescient about coming events.

Almost nobody predicted the rapidity with which Britain's position in the world was to be transformed and diminished – certainly not Churchill. True, some Americans were in a position to know that the great man's hopes for the restoration of imperial power were unlikely to be fulfilled, if only because they themselves were determined to thwart British designs. But few people in September 1944 appreciated that they were about to witness events that precipitated, in little more than a thousand days, the liquidation of the British Empire.

I was born in England during the Second World War. I must have been conceived while my father was on home leave shortly before Pearl Harbor. My earliest specific memory is of the patriotic bunting on VE-Day. Inevitably my own experience shapes my perspective on 'the war', as it was always called when I was growing up. I can now make better sense of things that the grown-ups talked about when I was a boy:

why Uncle Cyril, who had served with the 8th Army, would wryly talk about the contribution of 'the Yanks' to the Italian campaign, then shrug and suddenly break into parodies of Sousa marches; why my older cousin Norman needed to stay with us to recuperate from the 'bad time' that everyone said he had had at a place called Arnhem (before then stumbling into a place called Belsen, which he would not talk about for half a century). I can also make more sense of the fact that Uncle Fred, who was a dyed-in-the-wool Liberal, nonetheless talked with such pride about the good done in the world by that fine institution, the British Empire. Its finest hour was a reality for this generation and they were often puzzled about the way that everything had turned out since.

I hope that reading this book will resolve some such puzzles, just as writing it has done for me. As a professional historian, I had never specialized in imperial history. In tackling this theme, I was reminded, time and again, of the the proposition that all imperial historians are at the mercy of their own concept of empire; and I am obviously no exception.

If the proposition itself has become a cliché, this is a backhanded tribute to the two great imperial historians who first enunciated it over half a century ago. Jack Gallagher and Ronald Robinson – whose pupil I was – were not just considerable players but succeeded in moving the goalposts. They established a concept of 'informal imperialism' which has helped us to understand and debate the international influence exerted by not only Great Britain but later the United States. Gallagher's stimulating and influential revisionist claim about a post-war *revival* of the British Empire is not, however, the perspective of this book, which instead reasserts a more traditional wisdom about the crucial significance of the demise of the Indian Empire.[8]

As a system of power, the British Empire depended crucially upon the Dominions who were Britain's indispensably loyal allies in 1940. There were important differences between them, reflecting the way that the war had developed by late 1944, when this book begins. South Africa remained the least committed and most divided, despite the efforts of its wartime leader, Field Marshal Smuts, once an enemy in the field of the young Churchill during the Boer War, but now the only other prime minister in the Empire in whom Churchill really confided.

Pearl Harbor is chiefly remembered for enlisting the United States from December 1941 as a combatant: not only in the Pacific but in

Europe. But it also prompted hostilities between the British Empire and Japan, making this truly a world war, in which the fall of Singapore soon posed an immediate threat to India and the antipodean Dominions. Australia and New Zealand, accustomed to rely on British assurances that their own defence would be secured, had committed troops to imperial campaigns in North Africa and even Greece; but as the Pacific war developed it quickly became obvious that only the United States could offer them effective defence against Japan. Australia and New Zealand, in short, were simply fighting another war (in Asia and the Pacific) by the time the Italian campaign and D-Day opened a second front against Nazi Germany.

Canada, by contrast, remained committed by geography as much as politics to sustaining British operations in Europe itself. Much the same is true of Newfoundland, since 1934 a bankrupt Dominion, which had reverted to British rule but which in wartime was informally drawn into the orbit of Canada, which it was to join formally, as a province, in 1949.

Canadian troops were stationed in Britain from December 1939; they were ready to participate in the defence of France until the Dunkirk evacuation in the summer of 1940; they were volunteered for the ill-fated Dieppe raid two years later; they served in the 8th Army once it invaded Italy in 1943; and from D-Day until victory the Canadian army fought in northern Europe alongside British troops under Field Marshal Montgomery's command. Meanwhile the Royal Canadian Navy had taken over the vital task of keeping the Atlantic shipping lanes open and became the third-largest Allied navy. In the air, not only did the Royal Canadian Air Force provide key personnel for operations in Europe but the British Empire Air Training Scheme (renamed Commonwealth Air Training Plan from 1942) trained over 100,000 pilots and other crew members, offering safe Canadian skies and – equally welcome – useful Canadian dollars to make this possible. And the fact that Canada, alone in the Empire, could provide dollars, both during and after the war, was a tangible contribution in defraying the costs of victory.

Africa hardly figures in this book. Not because Africa itself is unimportant or uninteresting; not because Britain's African empire and its wartime role is unworthy of attention; above all, not because Britain's continuing imperial role in Africa after 1947 lacks historical significance. Post-war colonial development focused on Africa partly because of the loss of India and is, in this sense, a counter-current to the processes described in this book.

In some senses, then, this was an empire that took a long time dying, certainly far longer than the period covered in this book. The independence of most of Britain's former African colonies was not achieved until the 1950s and 1960s. Residual commitments were retained for even longer. A war was fought with Argentina over the Falkland Islands as recently as 1982. The status of Hong Kong was not resolved until 1997. The territories remaining under British sovereignty at the end of the twentieth century evoke many echoes of distant imperial triumphs: not only the Falklands but St Helena, where Napoleon spent his last days, along with the romantically remote islands of Tristan da Cunha and Ascension Island. Much of this list now reads like an up-market travel brochure: Gibraltar, Bermuda, the Cayman Islands, the Virgin Islands. This is truly imperialism of the last resort, and not the subject of this book.

What *The Last Thousand Days of the British Empire* explores is another story: of how the British Empire survived the war only to find itself a ghost of the great power that had held a dominant position in the world since the fall of Napoleon. It is inevitably the story of how the Americans displaced the British and of their mutual relations. It is likewise the story of the birth of today's world – of the foundation of the great democratic republic of India, now coming into its own as a major economic force too; of its bloody separation from Pakistan, a state created explicitly to assert its Muslim identity; of the triumph of Zionist pressure in Palestine so that Israel was created as a Jewish state, not simply a national home for Jews, leaving the unresolved fate of the Palestinian Arabs to haunt us today. Much of this is the legacy of what happened during the last thousand days of the British Empire.

PART I

Broad, Sunlit Uplands

Prologue

1941–4

'This makes us no longer a client receiving help from a generous patron, but two comrades fighting for life side by side.'

Churchill to Roosevelt after Pearl Harbor

In 1939 Britain had gone to war when Hitler attacked Poland, despite lacking the ability to assist in the defence of its territory. The fact that Stalin was complicit in this attack, gobbling up eastern Poland, further weakened the position of the Western powers. The defeat of their armies in France by June 1940 left the British Empire fighting on – alone indeed for crucial months (though the Axis powers' aggression was to make Greece into an ally that winter). Not until Operation Barbarossa, launched by Hitler against his supposed Soviet friends in June 1941, did Britain enjoy relief from the efforts of a major fellow combatant. Churchill's declared aim of victory at all costs, proclaimed in his speeches of 1940–41, thus seemed an amazing piece of effrontery or at best an enormous gamble.

It was not just that the British bet the farm: they also mortgaged it to the Americans. The United States did not come into the war until December 1941, though its assistance to Great Britain, notably through Lend-Lease, had already made it a co-belligerent in important respects. The economic bond between the two countries thus anticipated the formal alliance between them; and it continued to have a profound effect upon their relationship, one which is often obfuscated by Churchillian rhetoric about the common identity of the English-speaking peoples. Both in paying for the war and in actually fighting it on the ground in Europe, the significant differences between British and American aims, not to mention material resources, need to be understood.

If Britain had its imperial and other interests, for which it fought two world wars, the United States had its own interests too – interests not adequately defined by talk of making the world safe for democracy. Whether the Americans were better served by intervening in these two wars, fomented between internecine European regimes, was obviously for them to decide. An imaginative historian of the First World War vividly conveyed the misgivings that had kept the United States neutral until 1917, resisting high-flown moral appeals from Britain and her Allies:

World Justice makes its appeal to all men. But what share, it was asked, had Americans taken in bringing about the situation which had raised the issue of World Justice? Was even this issue so simple as it appeared to the Allies? Was it not a frightful responsibility to launch a vast, unarmed, remote community into the raging centre of such a quarrel?[1]

The author of this passage was none other than Winston Churchill, in his book *The World Crisis*, which we know to have made a big impression upon at least one influential American reader. Colonel Robert McCormick – he had served in the First World War himself – turned against war and became identified with isolationism, propagating his views as publisher of the *Chicago Tribune*. For him, Churchill remained a larger-than-life hero, as 1940 duly confirmed, but one committed to defending the British Empire, with interests directly opposed to those of the United States. Hence McCormick's strident opposition to any pro-Allied, pro-intervention moves by Roosevelt (whose New Deal the *Tribune* in any case denounced as the road to Communism and dictatorship). The Colonel spoke for the forgotten Americans – those too often forgotten, at any rate, in the afterglow of Allied victory in what everyone liked to think of as a good war.

For McCormick's image of Churchill, though a caricature in some ways, had the virtue of an identifiable caricature in conveying an esssential truth about the King's First Minister. It has long been accepted that Churchill did his political career no good when he staked it from 1930 on a prolonged parliamentary struggle against the liberal consensus of the day on India. He went into the last ditch in opposition to the modest measures of provincial self-government eventually brought in by Stanley Baldwin's India Act of 1935. Little wonder that Churchill's assertion that there was a deplorable failure of will to stand up to Gandhi devalued his subsequent assertion that there was a deplorable failure of will to stand up to Hitler.

For Churchill, however, the two were linked. In May 1932 we find him lecturing a Tory supporter, Lord Linlithgow, soon to become Viceroy of India. 'The mild and vague Liberalism of the early years of the twentieth century, the surge of fantastic hopes and illusions that followed the armistice of the Great War have already been superseded by a violent reaction against parliamentary and electioneering procedure and by the establishment of dictatorships real or veiled in almost every country,' Churchill argued. 'It is unsound reasoning therefore to suppose that England alone among the nations will be willing to part with her control over a great dependency like India. The Dutch will not do it; the French will not do it . . .'[2] He himself had no intention of doing it, then or later.

The British Empire exerted a lifelong emotional pull over Churchill. He had been less than two years old when Queen Victoria assumed the title of Empress of India in 1876; when he eventually retired as Prime Minister in 1955, his final words recorded in the cabinet minutes spoke of 'weaving still more closely the threads which bound together the countries of the Commonwealth or, as he still preferred to call it, the Empire'.[3] Nor was his wartime rhetoric reserved solely for Westminster, the mother of parliaments; it was the Canadian House of Commons that provided the setting for a memorably defiant speech – 'Some chicken, some neck' – on his North American visit soon after Pearl Harbor. Indeed it was in Ottawa that Yousuf Karsh enshrined this moment for posterity, with the portrait known as 'The Roaring Lion', as was recognized at the time. 'Unless we are greatly mistaken,' commented the *Calgary Herald* on 11 February 1942, 'it will be this portrait by Karsh that will go down through the centuries to give future generations their most accurate idea of of the physical appearance of Winston Churchill at the moment when three quarters of the people of the world had their hopes largely based on him.'[4]

In Churchill's greatest speeches in 1940, the imperial dimension is clear and central. On 13 May, immediately after becoming Prime Minister, he declared the policy of his new Government: 'to wage war against a monstrous tyranny, never surpassed in the dark, lamentable catalogue of human crime.' This was a universal aim, pitched in terms which still seem valid in the light of history, and Churchill was both sincere and eloquent in stating it. But it alone was not what made his offer of 'blood, toil, tears, and sweat' seem worthwhile. When asked what was his aim, he gave one simple but daunting answer: 'Victory – victory at all costs, victory in spite of all terror, victory however long and hard the road may be; for without victory there is no survival.' And this logic was more concretely specified. 'Let that be realized,' he intoned; 'no survival for the British Empire; no survival for all that the British Empire has stood for; no survival for the urge and impulse of the ages, that mankind will move forward towards his goal.'[5] The general and the particular were thus yoked together quite openly and explicitly. On 4 June 1940, faced with the enforced evacuation of the British Army from Dunkirk, Churchill's famous exhortations, that 'we shall fight on the beaches' and that 'we shall never surrender', were backed by a final appeal to the fallback strategy: 'even if, which I do not for a moment believe, this Island or a large part of it were subjugated and starving, then our Empire beyond the seas, armed and guarded by the British Fleet, would carry on the struggle, until, in God's good time, the New World, with all its power and might, steps forth to the rescue and the liberation of the old.'[6]

No one was more committed than Churchill to the notion of the English-speaking peoples, whose history he had essayed to write in the late 1930s, a work finally published in the 1950s. Churchill, with his American mother and English father, was characteristically projecting his own identity in world-historical terms. In this sense, or in this mood, or in this extremity, he recognized that one important residue of British power was its cultural legacy, exemplified and enshrined in the English language. A common constitutional heritage, grounded in the common law and the separation of powers, giving rise to common ideals of democracy, was pitted against the challenge of totalitarian aggression. No one could stroke these keys and pull out these stops better than Churchill; no one was better able to find the lost chord or give it the full benefit of the *vox humana*.

Some awkward questions had to be fudged well before the United States entered the war. Churchill showed himself highly skilled in eliding democratic claims with more primitive appeals, especially when the Americans were listening. They obviously were when (prior to Lend-Lease) he had reported an agreement with the neutral United States in August 1940 – offering them the use of imperial bases, accepting their offer of old destroyers – and explained it to the House of Commons. Was it a deal? It looked like a deal, it smelled like a deal – but by no means did Churchill so describe it. 'We had . . . decided spontaneously,' he claimed, to make the one offer. 'Presently we learned,' he went on –

yes, that President Roosevelt was spontaneously making an offer too! And what it meant was that 'these two great organizations of the English-speaking democracies, the British Empire and the United States, will have to be somewhat mixed up together in some of their affairs for mutual and general advantage.'[7] Little wonder that a lot of literal-minded people stayed somewhat mixed up.

It needs to be remembered that the United States never went to war against Nazi Germany. There were all sorts of good reasons why not. The folk-wisdom, for many Americans, was that President Wilson's eventual entry into the First World War had been mistaken, unnecessary, fruitless, unprofitable – and all the fault of British wiles anyway. That war to make the world safe for democracy had apparently fomented dictatorships in defeated countries like Germany while seeing ungrateful allies defaulting on the war debts owing to Uncle Sam (as Britain did in 1934, admittedly in response to defaults by its own war debtors). With the rise of Hitler and Mussolini, Congress tied down the plainly anti-fascist President with legislation designed to stop the United States from being sucked into another European war; this prevented not only him but private US citizens from making commitments to the belligerents. In practice this meant no more open-ended loans to the importunate British.

Churchill and Roosevelt sustained a supposedly personal correspondence throughout the war. It had been initiated by the President, shortly after the outbreak of the European war in 1939, writing to the First Lord of the Admiralty in Neville Chamberlain's Government: a post again held, as it had been in 1914, by Winston Churchill. Then he had been a tempestuous and doubtfully loyal Liberal, chafing for action; now he was a restive and doubtfully loyal Conservative, suddenly restored to office. Then he had been just short of forty and already six years in Asquith's cabinet; now he was to celebrate his sixty-fifth birthday in November 1939, back in the cabinet, with no thought of retirement and with nowhere to go but up. He was obviously pleased to act as the conduit for informal approaches from the White House itself. Protocol was observed by clearing the correspondence with Chamberlain as Prime Minister.

Their extraordinary relationship flourished but it could hardly be an ordinary friendship. Lloyd George, Prime Minister during the First World War and one of Churchill's intimates, had the cynical maxim:

there are no friends at the top. Roosevelt and Churchill were right at the top for most of the Second World War; they came to call each other Franklin and Winston; they often genuinely enjoyed each other's company. 'Our friendship,' Churchill wrote on the eve of D-Day in 1944, 'is my greatest standby amid the ever-increasing complications of this exacting war.'[8] Maybe. But neither allowed mere sentiment to deflect him in his dedication to the national interests of his own country. 'My whole system is founded on partnership with Roosevelt,' Churchill once confided to his Foreign Secretary, Anthony Eden.[9]

If Churchill and Roosevelt nonetheless built a kind of political friendship on these terms, they did so from scratch, with a motivation that was political rather than personal. It was a shrewd move by Roosevelt to cultivate the coming man, whom he remembered meeting while he himself was serving as Assistant Secretary of the Navy in 1918, three years before being afflicted with polio. Churchill, alas, did not remember, as became embarrassingly plain when the two men next met, this time as war leaders, on the cruiser USS *Augusta* in Placentia Bay, off Newfoundland, in August 1941 – despite the unabashed claim in Churchill's war memoirs that in 1918 'I had been struck by his magnificent presence in all his youth and strength.'[10] 'A real old Tory of the old school,' the President remarked privately after the Placentia Bay meeting, deploring the Prime Minister's 'eighteenth-century methods' of running the British Empire.[11]

It is clear that Churchill hardly knew Roosevelt until their wartime meetings established a personal bond; and that the President was the less illusioned of the two. Yet there was an electricity between these two powerful men, positively charged when common aims reinforced personal rapport. The US Secretary to the Treasury, Henry Morgenthau, was to be heartened on a visit to London in 1944 by the affection that Churchill professed. 'Just to hear the President shout "Hello",' Churchill said, 'is like drinking a bottle of champagne.'[12] The voluminous correspondence between the two – it ran to 2,000 communications in five years – was remarkable, but never enough for Churchill. He wrote eloquently and, above all, frequently to his new friend – far more frequently than the cool and canny President replied, always careful to keep his distance.

There was no greater enemy of isolationism than Franklin Roosevelt. He used the term with calculated effect to depict and besmirch his political opponents. Yet he also had to reckon with the power of their constituency within American politics and tailor his own policies to that inescapable reality. Thus the *Chicago Tribune* was a newspaper that Roosevelt could not ignore, as frequent barbed references to it among his circle amply testify. Moreover, the ever-emollient President often found it rather useful to excuse himself to the disappointed British by pleading his political difficulties with Congress – which served the role of Mr Jorkins (in *David Copperfield*), who dwelt unseen in the back office while his law partner invoked his name to excuse his own disagreeable necessity for taking a stern line.[13] It was the discredited Neville Chamberlain, a shrewd reader of Dickens, who had spotted the Jorkins analogy, but Winston Churchill who more often bore the brunt of the stratagem. Furthermore, beyond such tactical games, Roosevelt himself shared many of these common American suspicions of imperialism, which never ceased to influence his own policy and his own view of Churchill.

In particular, there was a lurking dilemma that showed itself on more than one important occasion. The rhetoric of the Atlantic Charter, signed jointly in Placentia Bay in August 1941, depicted two great democracies committed to resisting totalitarianism in defence of liberal values. It was a propaganda gain for the British to be so closely associated with the United States, even though the Americans were still not ready to enter the war. That is why Churchill assented to the Charter's sweeping principles. Its first pledge – 'no aggrandisement, territorial or other' – presented no problem: even the old imperialist could see that the British Empire hardly needed another Iraq, another Tanganyika, and that these were not the broad, sunlit uplands he had in mind. Likewise the pledge of no territorial changes 'that do not accord with the freely expressed wishes of the peoples concerned'. Again, well and good.

The third pledge was 'to respect the right of all peoples to choose the form of government under which they will live', buttressed by the promise that such rights would be 'restored to those who have been forcibly deprived of them'.[14] This too Churchill signed. But the Prime Minister found that it subsequently gave him a lot of trouble. He told the House of Commons that the Charter only applied to European states, like Poland, which had suffered loss of sovereignty, which was 'quite a separate problem' from that of self-government in British territories.[15] The logic was that those who had not been deprived of such

9

rights – because they had never had them in the first place – could not, of course, expect to have them restored. So much for any right to self-government in the Empire.

Though the British Prime Minister might go on telling the House of Commons that it made no difference to the position in India, the Deputy Prime Minister himself had lent credence to the wider interpretation. 'IT MEANS DARK RACES AS WELL,' the official Labour Party newspaper, the *Daily Herald*, had declared on 16 August 1941, reporting Attlee's assurance that, in contrast to Nazi doctrines of racial superiority, the Atlantic Charter had a worldwide application.[16] Roosevelt was of the same view and it reinforced his quiet determination not to pull Britain's imperial chestnuts out of the fire (again). Roosevelt did not need to make a speech saying that he had not become president (for an unprecedented third term) in order to avert the liquidation of the British Empire.

There is little doubt that Lend-Lease was necessary to British survival. This was Roosevelt's masterstroke. It should be remembered that the agreement to set it up in 1941 was made at a time when the British war machine was at full stretch in a last-ditch military resistance to the Nazis – and simultaneously running on empty. Once the seriousness of the crisis was brought home to him, Roosevelt had come up with a brilliant plan of his own, squaring the circle as he did so often in politics. The United States, though still neutral or at least non-belligerent, would again lend to Great Britain – not money this time, but war supplies instead. What it did not lend, it would lease (since leasing escaped legislative prohibition).

The President's vision of Lend-Lease – dreamt up while he sat in a deckchair on a Caribbean cruise in December 1940 – quickly took shape. 'I have been thinking very hard on this trip about what we should do for England' – so Roosevelt explained it to Morgenthau on 17 December – 'and it seems to me that the thing to do is to get away from the dollar sign.'[17] Thus it was a scheme that simply jumped over the hurdles of ancient war debts by refusing to do the sums in the old-fashioned way. As Roosevelt told the American people in a broadcast that same day, it was like freely lending a garden hose to a neighbour facing a fire – a mounting crisis in which it was only sensible to 'get rid of the silly, foolish old dollar sign'.[18] Here was the premise of Lend-Lease: that it was in the Americans' interests to support the British war effort, since their own defence depended upon it.

When the Lend-Lease Bill passed Congress in March 1941, Churchill spoke in the House of Commons of 'our deep and respectful appreciation of this monument of generous and far-seeing statesmanship' which showed that 'the Government and people of the United States have in fact written a new Magna Carta.'[19] The English-speaking peoples were now marching in step – marching to war together perhaps? Churchill's hopes that this was so were encouraged by events, once American ships were deployed guarding the Atlantic shipping lanes and thus open to U-boat attacks – just how the United States had been drawn into the First World War. Roosevelt's Secretary of the Navy, Frank Knox, publicly declared in November: 'We are in this fight to the finish.'[20]

Only a week after Knox spoke, on 10 November 1941, Churchill gave his own annual speech at the Mansion House in the City of London. He gratefully seized on Knox's fighting talk to point to the contrast with the previous year: 'Then we were alone, the sole champion of freedom.' What a welcome change! Not only was the US Navy now in action in the Atlantic, and the two countries more closely aligned against a possible threat from Japan, but the year had also seen a crucial alleviation of Britain's financial plight. 'Then came the majestic policy of the President and Congress of the United States in passing the Lend and Lease Bill, under which in two successive enactments about £3,000,000,000 sterling were dedicated to the cause of world freedom without – mark this, for it is unique – the setting up of any account in money.' Hence the phrase that has lived: that Lend-Lease 'must be regarded without question as the most unsordid act in the whole of recorded history'.[21]

At the time these were not only fine phrases but they also made good political sense. It was not tactful to ask why the British should attribute such unworldly sentiments to Roosevelt's plan when he himself chose to justify it to Congress as a hard-headed assessment of American self-interest in keeping Britain in the war (and the United States out of it still). And nobody in Britain would have called Lend-Lease the most unnecessary act – it was a vital lifeline, irrespective of its motive.

Never did more devil lurk in more detail. Over many months in 1941, the business was settled not only *ad hoc* but *ad hominem*. Difficulties of principle were deferred in favour of immediate working compromises; and the intervention of Harry Hopkins, as Roosevelt's trusted go-between, facilitated eventual agreement. On the British side the key figure was John Maynard Keynes.

Now Keynes liked Americans – on the whole. Whether they liked him was a matter of taste, or at least of style. Soon to be created Lord Keynes in 1942, he was the most famous economist in the world, and knew it. The publication of his magnum opus, *The General Theory of Employment, Interest and Money* (1936), had made an enormous impression in the English-speaking world. Its aim was to revolutionize economic theory by demonstrating that full employment would not necessarily be achieved simply by letting market forces reach their own equilibrium. The relevance of such propositions to the practical proposals of the New Deal for restoring prosperity in the United States was obvious. Keynes, the exquisitely English product of King's College, Cambridge, found that he was a hero to many young American Keynesians, notably in the other Cambridge in Massachusetts, where Harvard University proved particularly receptive to his novel ideas and provided many earnest young New Dealers to serve in Washington.

But not all Americans were economists – Keynes could sound too clever by half to laymen. Not all economists were Keynesians – Keynes's ideas struck defenders of 'sound money' as outrageous nonsense. Not all American Keynesian economists were captivated – the Cambridge house-style, overlaid with an anglocentric Bloomsbury preciousness, was not everyone's cup of tea. Lady Keynes, the former Russian ballerina Lydia Lopokova, tended and protected her now semi-invalid husband; she created her own circle of admirers, while leaving others bemused at her eccentricities. Everyone agreed that they made an extraordinary couple, quite unlike the folk honest Americans were used to doing business with. Although Keynes, working within the British Treasury since 1940 as a special adviser, like a 'dollar-a-year man', had worked his passage in establishing his respectable, pragmatic credentials with ministers and professional civil servants alike, in the United States he had to start all over again, literally on foreign territory.

Keynes first entered the Lend-Lease negotiations near their beginning in May 1941. Henry Morgenthau, he had found, was 'certainly a difficult chap to deal with', but Lydia had intuitively summed him up after sitting next to him at dinner. 'He is a good man,' she decided, 'and will do you no harm *on purpose*.'[22]

The real problem, however, was not personal: it was how to strike a bargain when the rules seemed to keep changing. Like Alice, Keynes found it curiouser and curiouser. The sympathy and magnanimity shown towards embattled Britain, he marvelled, were touching; but how on earth to translate this into decisions? 'There is no clear hierarchy of authority,' he had to explain to the Chancellor of the Exchequer. 'The different departments of the Government criticise one another in public and produce rival programmes. There is perpetual internecine warfare between prominent personalities.' One difficulty was that Washington did not speak with a single voice; another was that the British too often expected it do so. This was a clash of two different cultures of government. Keynes quickly realized that it was no use expecting things to be written down, in the British mandarin tradition of careful minutes, paving the way to agreed conclusions, carefully recorded and faithfully observed. 'Nothing is ever settled in principle,' he ruefully discovered. 'There is just endless debate and sitting around.'[23]

What complicated the whole Lend-Lease agreement, however, as Keynes soon discovered, was 'the question of what is called here "consideration"'.[24] This introduced a new sort of language: that of a bargain in which the Americans should get back something of equal value. Hence Article VII of the agreement, as eventually drafted by the end of 1941, specified that the consideration was to be based on the fourth principle of the Atlantic Charter, as meanwhile signed by Churchill and Roosevelt. This was a pledge that their two countries would ('with due respect for their existing obligations') endeavour to promote equal access to the trade and raw materials of the world.[25] Article VII amplified that this meant not only 'the elimination of all forms of discriminatory treatment in international commerce' but also 'the reduction of tariffs and other trade barriers'.[26] An unimpeachable statement, then, of the general presumption that international free trade benefited all.

The trouble was, as usual, the British Empire. Though Britain, until the First World War, had run its Empire on free trade lines – in contrast to the protectionist American record – the cry for imperial preference in trade had been strong for at least forty years. Joseph Chamberlain had staked his political career on the issue and his son Neville had, as Chancellor of the Exchequer, proudly signed the Ottawa agreements in 1932, formalizing a system of preferential tariffs as imperial policy – obligations by which Britain was still bound. Powerful Conservative newspapers, especially Lord Beaverbrook's *Daily Express*, remained devoted to the cause of imperial preference, as did cabinet ministers like Leo Amery. But they were a minority.

Here is a paradox worth pondering. Imperial preference was often the prime target for American critics of the British Empire, uniting at a stroke visceral Anglophobes and principled free traders. Yet Churchill himself, despite his well-earned reputation as an imperialist, actually cared little for imperial preference. His whole political career testified to this; he had spent twenty years as a Liberal precisely because the Conservatives adopted the Chamberlainite policy. Unlike Amery, Churchill saw as little potential in imperial preference as he did in imperial federation. He was only really committed to the Empire strategically and rhetorically – especially the latter perhaps. If so, one might conclude that he succeeded in arousing disproportionate American suspicion, hostility and resentment about an atavistic stage monster that was already on its last legs.

Churchill, then, regarded the Ottawa agreements as a pragmatic response to the slump, not as a cause to die for; and in this he spoke for his Coalition Government as a whole, as he often explained to Roosevelt. What the British cabinet could not stomach was simply being told by the Americans to eliminate imperial preference because it was discrimination, and to do so unilaterally, as though the Dominions had no voice in the matter. Though the Dominions may have served a Jorkins-like role in this scenario, the procedure undoubtedly contrasted with the sort of international negotiations that would be necessary to reduce, still less eliminate, tariffs. To the ideological free traders now dominating American policy, discrimination was the real evil, yet, to the British, American tariffs were surely as great an affront to the pure doctrine of free trade as the preference practised within the British Empire. On both sides, principle was compromised by prevailing practices and vested interests.

Everyone, it turned out, wanted free trade; it simply depended on what you meant by free trade. And it was not an issue on which the British view was likely to prevail above that of its more powerful ally.

It may well be that the consideration exposed inherent logical flaws in the whole arrangement. Lend-Lease had been offered to Britain in return for a consideration. Yet the title of the bill sent to Congress – 'An Act Further to Promote the Defense of the United States' – proclaimed that its rationale was to serve the USA's own interest, which all members of the Roosevelt administration repeatedly affirmed thereafter. So why was there any need for a consideration? The war effort itself was what the United States got for its money. Great Britain, in the days when it had enjoyed the luxury of getting other countries to do its fighting for it, used to shovel out subsidies to them in just such a businesslike way, but without expecting any consideration.

This is not how it looked through American eyes. In the Mid-West, in particular, common sense spoke differently. How lightly these faraway people were being let off! Did they not understand the nature of a bargain, a deal, a trade? Did they not see that their oppressive structure of imperial taxation, all too reminiscent of King George III, had to go?

In the House of Representatives, the Lend-Lease bill had been carried by 260–165 in February 1941. But out of 124 Representatives from the eleven Mid-West states only 32 voted for: 92 against. Next month in the Senate, the bill had passed by 62–33; but in the Middle West there were only 8 Senators in favour, 14 against.[27] The politics of Lend-Lease demanded that there should be recompense to the United States in some way or other.

Throughout the Second World War, Roosevelt was determined not to be another Woodrow Wilson, losing touch with public opinion. Instead the President set about crafting a policy that made political sense at home. From 1939 to 1941 the United States appeared as neutral as Ireland: that is, much practical support was given to Great Britain but it remained covert and unacknowledged in deference to historic sensibilities about the British Empire, from which both countries were glad to have made good their escape. Running for re-election for an unprecedented third term in 1940, Roosevelt had given his famous pledge in Boston, where the Irish were the backbone of the Democratic Party: 'Your boys are not going to be sent into any foreign wars.'[28] He may have made the mental reservation that an attack on the United States would not count as a foreign war, but Roosevelt's untutored listeners often supposed differently.

That is what those political opponents whom Roosevelt liked to brand 'isolationists' continued to hold against him, long after Pearl Harbor supposedly changed everything. For example, Arthur Vandenberg, Senator for Michigan, commented later that 'all this talk about the "isolationists" is sheer bunk.' It was a label Vandenberg had happily carried himself but he could claim that 'we were perfectly aware they could not and would not "keep us out of war" – and they didn't.' His own position all along, he claimed, was 'that *if* this was *our* war we ought to go in through the front door and not through the back door – and we ought to go in as swiftly and conclusively as possible. But that would not have suited Mr Roosevelt's purposes.'[29]

In saying this, Roosevelt's critics surely had a point. For not only did the re-elected President take open steps to offer material aid to Great Britain in its hour of need – Lend-Lease, above all – but he also sanctioned secret military staff talks during 1941. These American–British conversations (ABC-1) came up with contingency plans, as staff talks will, that covered all sorts of eventualities. The central assumption, however, was that, if the United States were to enter the war, it would be against Hitler and that the strategic priority would be to knock out Germany.

'America First', the slogan of the isolationists, was given political potency through the leadership of the aviation hero Colonel Charles Lindbergh. Philip Roth's novel *The Plot against America* (2004) suggests the dystopian possibilities of the movement and also its potential popular base. America First was a sentiment that recruited widespread support, especially in those states of the Middle West – Illinois, Indiana, Michigan, Ohio – where the *Chicago Tribune* was such a force, with its circulation of over one million. In these four states, the Gallup Poll showed that Lend-Lease attracted less than 40 per cent support, compared with nearly 60 per cent nationally. The *Tribune*'s own poll of its readers in the summer of 1941 asked: 'Shall the United States enter the war to help Britain defeat the Nazis?' Over 80 per cent said no.

Hence the furore when the *Tribune* splashed its great scoop across the front page on 4 December 1941: 'FDR'S WAR PLANS'. Based on a leak of ABC-1 from an isolationist senator, the story told of plans for a joint Anglo-American invasion of the European continent – assuming, of course, that the United States would have entered this foreign war. There was even a suspiciously exact invasion date mentioned in the plans (July 1943) and a specified requirement of a force of 5 million American troops.[30] The political damage to Roosevelt was serious. Alas for the *Tribune*, the timing was such that, within four days, it had to reverse its editorial line completely and support the President in going to war.

For the United States was indeed attacked. On 7 December 1941 a key part of its navy was sunk at Pearl Harbor by the Japanese, obviously locking the two countries into a war in the Pacific. Churchill's recollection was vivid, as usual. He claimed that he heard the news on the radio at Chequers, his official country residence, where he was dining with the US Ambassador, John Gilbert Winant.

Now this seems an odd way for such intelligence to reach the war leader, giving conspiracy theorists leverage for some wild suggestions. It is true that the attack on the Americans was only one part of an amazingly ambitious two-prong Japanese attack, with the British Empire also targeted through an invasion of the Malayan port of Kota Bahru. In the event Kota Bahru was hit several hours before Pearl Harbor without setting the dogs barking at Chequers, or even the phones ringing apparently. At any rate, everyone at dinner that day was well aware that the Prime Minister was already committed to declaring war on Japan 'within the hour' should the United States be attacked. A telephone call to the White House, initiated by Gil Winant, settled the matter. 'It's quite true,' Roosevelt told the Prime Minister, and allegedly added: 'We are all in the same boat now.'[31] What sort of boat was it that contained not only the President but the most notorious upholder of the British Empire, as well as the isolationists of the *Chicago Tribune*, dedicated to its downfall?

Pearl Harbor was a blow for the Americans, a boon for the British. Perhaps it is true that Churchill performed a little jig, as he later told Mackenzie King; certainly he leapt at the opportunity to declare war on Japan in solidarity with the Americans. War was not costless in view of the almost immediate loss of two British battleships off Singapore and the fall of the great imperial fortress itself within weeks. But it had the effect of tying together the two wars, against Japan and against Germany. Roosevelt was spared taking the decision to enter a foreign war only by an extraordinary move on Hitler's part, in himself declaring war on the United States. The President capitalized on this with his usual dexterity by committing the US to his own preferred anti-fascist strategy: Europe First. This implied that the enemy at the gate (Japan) could be kept waiting there until the alliance between the United States, the Soviet Union and Great Britain had dealt with the threat from Hitler and Mussolini.

In this, of course, Roosevelt was at one with Churchill, who could hardly believe the favourable turn of events. Again the latter's war memoirs lost nothing in the telling: 'England would live; Britain would live; the Commonwealth of Nations and the Empire would live.'[32] The Former Naval Person, as he styled himself in their correspondence, received a wonderful telegram from the President, not only reporting the overwhelming majorities by which the Senate and the House of Representatives had passed the declaration of war but helpfully specifying who was aboard. 'Today all of us are in the same boat with you and the people of the Empire,' Roosevelt affirmed, 'and it is a ship which will not and cannot be sunk.'[33]

The Anglo-American alliance was the engine of victory in western Europe just as the alliance with the Soviet Union was the necessary agent of German defeat in eastern Europe. This was what Churchill termed the Grand Alliance and the core of what Roosevelt liked to call the United Nations. In this sense Pearl Harbor marked not only a 'day which will live in infamy', as Roosevelt memorably declaimed, but a day more benignly famous for its effect on European history. Yet in some ways it is easy to exaggerate how much difference Pearl Harbor made, especially upon American perceptions of the war.

American isolationists have had a bad press. They have hardly been ignored, but they have certainly been derided. True, they had to change their tune abruptly after the United States entered the war. Yet their instinct for self-preservation and self-promotion did not suddenly disappear, and strategically the logic of America First was now Pacific First, to defeat Japan. It was largely the means rather than the ends that had changed. American primacy remained their goal, and not theirs alone. Such views did not lose their political clout simply because of Pearl Harbor. One national Gallup Poll in February 1942 asked Americans if their new British allies should actually repay the amount of Lend-Lease aid: yes, said 84 per cent, and later polls told much the same story.[34]

The Allies were fighting different wars in more senses than one. It was not just that the real war was against Japan for many Americans: their alliance with the British could hardly be one of equals. 'If there is to be a partnership between the United States and Britain, we are, by every right, the controlling partner,' the *Chicago Tribune* reasoned on 10 January. 'We can get along without them. They can't get along without us.'[35] One paradox was that British survival depended on American intervention, yet the inexorable effect of American intervention was to eclipse Britain within the alliance: soon outmanned when huge US armies were raised, soon outgunned when American armaments production came on stream and, not least, soon reduced to a degree of economic dependence which threatened the British Empire itself.

For Roosevelt, as for many Americans, it was a grievous inconsistency that India should have been mobilized for war in British interests, at the British behest, and with no clear commitment by the British to the principle of self-determination. At only one point during the war, however, did India move to the top of the political agenda. This was when the Cripps Offer – shorthand for wartime democratization plus post-war independence – was made in 1942. Like the Atlantic Charter, it was sanctioned by Churchill in sweeping terms that he subsequently repented but was not allowed to forget.

The big new fact was that the United States was now formally engaged in the war, giving Roosevelt a clear licence to speak. He needed to show his fellow Americans that their boys were not going to fight in any foreign wars for the British Empire. It was on Churchill's very first wartime visit to Washington, in December 1941, that Roosevelt raised the issue, 'on the usual American lines', as Churchill's war memoirs recount: 'I reacted so strongly and at such length that he never raised it verbally again.'[36] Never orally, perhaps; but the President returned to the topic with unusual verbal profusion only a couple of months later.

The draft of a long message to Churchill, written at the end of February 1942, although 'purely a personal thought based on very little firsthand knowledge on my part', survives as evidence of his continued concern about the European empires in Asia. The old master-and-servant relationship had not been altered by the Dutch, 'nor by you in the Straits Settlements or Burma', Roosevelt asserted, while the people of India, he maintained, felt 'that there is no real desire in Britain to recognize a world change which has taken deep root in India as well as in other countries'.[37]

This draft was not sent, but it was certainly opportune, given the current military threat from Japan. 'We have suffered the greatest disaster in our history at Singapore,' Churchill acknowledged to Roosevelt.[38] Its fall on 15 February was one reason why he reconstructed his government four days later. The big changes were that his crony Lord Beaverbrook was out of the war cabinet and that Sir Stafford Cripps took his place, with the title of Lord Privy Seal. These were ones that Churchill would not have made willingly. Cripps, expelled from the Labour Party just before the war for advocating a popular front with both Liberals and Communists, had just returned from a posting as British ambassador in Moscow, trailing the glory of the Red Army. This helped give him an almost messianic status, as a prophet of high-minded austerity, preaching total effort in a total war, at just the moment when Churchill's authority, for the only time in the war, was seriously shaken. In the early months of 1942, Cripps had unexampled political capital; and he chose to invest it in an attempt to resolve the Indian problem.

Roosevelt was thus pushing on an open door – but giving it a decisive shove nonetheless – when he decided to send a redrafted version of his Indian message to Churchill on 10 March. He knew by then that some move could be expected from London, and pruned his more pointed criticisms, while keeping a lengthy disquisition on the model allegedly provided by the history of the American Revolution in paving the way to independent self-government, replete with many purported parallels with contemporary India. Churchill reprinted this document in his war memoirs in 1951, writing that it was 'of high interest because it illustrates the difficulties of comparing situations in various centuries and scenes where almost every material fact is totally different' – a rare moment when he allowed himself a satirical comment at the expense of the late President.[39] Churchill's reaction in 1942 had been equally dismissive, just more blunt. But he had already, two days before Roosevelt's message, clinched on the suggestion that Cripps should fly to Delhi to try to achieve a settlement on a new basis. The main political parties – not only the Hindu-dominated Indian National Congress but also the Muslim League – should be brought into negotiations to enlist them behind the war effort, on the basis of their immediate participation in the government pending full independence after the war.

This was the essence of the Cripps Offer. Amery was as surprised about it as anyone, but happy at least that India was now the focus of attention. Faced with explaining to the far more conservative Viceroy, Lord Linlithgow, the course that events had taken, he tried to make sense of its knock-on momentum: 'the pressure outside, upon Winston from Roosevelt, and upon Attlee & Co from their own party, *plus* the admission of Cripps to the War Cabinet, suddenly opened the sluice gates, and the thing moved with a rush.'[40] Not mentioned but never forgotten, of course, was another crucial factor: the enemy at the gates of the Empire. Churchill did not make light of the military reverses, publicly commenting on the fall of Singapore: 'Australia is threatened: India is threatened.'[41] He announced the Cripps Mission to the House of Commons on 11 March, three days after the fall of Rangoon. After returning from India, Cripps was to report his eventual failure to the House on 28 April, the day before Mandalay was evacuated.

Perhaps such facts are all that is needed to explain why the Cripps Offer was rejected by the Indian National Congress. The comment of its great mentor, Mohandas Gandhi, was widely reported, that the offer was 'a post-dated cheque', often with the journalistic improvement 'on a failing bank'.[42] Stafford Cripps was the personally honourable individual who found that he was trading in a suspect specie, one which had exhausted its credit in 1942.

The European empires in southern Asia were falling like dominoes in the face of the relentless Japanese advance. The Dutch lost Indonesia, the French lost Indo-China, the British lost the Malayan peninsula and Burma. The collapse of supercilious white imperialists before little yellow men whom they had systematically slighted and disparaged was an object-lesson in Asian nationalism. Faced with the threat of the invader at home, the British had salved their pride with the noble myth of 1940: a nation courageously pulling together with a unity that spanned all classes, in a fitting image of a democracy at war with Nazism. Churchill's timeless rhetoric captured this. Yet faced with the threat of the invader in their Asian empire, the British showed the ugly face of imperialism, leaving a shameful myth of 1942: an army and navy unable to protect the bastions of power, white officials ready to cut and run, saving themselves and their possessions while showing a racist disregard for others, even their own faithful servants. Here Churchill's imperialist rhetoric exposed him as the captive of his own decrepit assumptions.

In India, where Congress leaders seldom thought of Japanese imperialism in any more favourable terms than of British imperialism, they faced an acute dilemma in 1942. Cripps had forged a friendship with Jawaharlal Nehru since the 1930s and well understood Nehru's commitment against fascism, whether in Europe or in Asia. But it was asking too much of Nehru at this moment to trust Cripps: trust him to deliver on making a reality of cabinet government within the shell of the Viceroy's Executive Council. The problem was not really one between Cripps and Nehru. It was that behind Nehru stood the enigmatic figure of Gandhi, responsible only to his own intuitions of right and wrong, and behind Gandhi was the inarticulate phalanx of Congress supporters through-out the country, over whom his charismatic hold was unrivalled and unbroken. And conversely, behind Cripps stood the sinister figure of Linlithgow, conscious that his days were numbered as Viceroy if a settlement were reached, and behind Linlithgow was the brooding presence of Churchill himself, alarmed at any news suggesting that the negotiations were likely to succeed.

Churchill did not stab Cripps in the back. Nor did Cripps exceed his brief in what he offered, intricate in its detail but simple in its thrust. Had Nehru finally committed Congress, as seemed likely at one moment (9 April), the British Government would likewise have been committed and – under a new Viceroy – the 'Indianization' of the government would have proceeded, subject only to British control of military oper-ations. This was the deal that Cripps had brokered, aided latterly by the intervention of Roosevelt's representative in Delhi, Colonel Louis Johnson; and this was the deal that finally collapsed (on 10 April), leaving Cripps without further hope. 'He and Nehru could solve it in 5 minutes if Cripps had any freedom or authority,' Johnson told the State Department.[43] Ironically, it was not Cripps's credentials that con-stituted a difficulty but Johnson's. Fearful that the power of Roosevelt's name was being used to identify the United States with a proposal unacceptable to the British Government, Harry Hopkins, currently visiting London, had played down Johnson's status to Churchill; but the extent of American intervention was actually well appreciated on all sides, not least by Nehru and his Congress supporters.

It was the President himself who finally made this clear. On 11 April 1942 Roosevelt sent Churchill an exceptionally forthright message, no longer coded in terms of eighteenth-century history, not just regretting Cripps's failure, nor just appealing for a further attempt at compromise, but stating the American position in stark terms. He claimed that it was 'almost universally held that the deadlock has been caused by the unwillingness of the British Government to concede to the Indians the right of self-government' and that American public opinion would not forgive the consequences should India be invaded as a result. He con-tinued to press for an interim nationalist government to be set up.[44] Churchill was still talking deep into the night with Hopkins when this message was received in London at 3 a.m. The Prime Minister asserted that he would not countenance any such proposal so long as he held office. 'I should personally make no objection at all to retiring into private life, and I have explained this to Harry just now,' he claimed, with more bravado than plausibility in a draft response, while Hopkins vainly tried to telephone the White House.[45]

No, Churchill did not resign. No, Roosevelt did not enforce a last-minute change in British policy on India. In the very short term, the fact that Cripps had already left India for home gave Churchill room for manoeuvre and Roosevelt time to retreat. Moreover, as the story of the Cripps Mission subsequently unfolded in the press, the reception in the United States turned out to be much more impressed by British good faith in making the offer than Roosevelt had surmised. Once the offer had been made and rejected, 'the inherent difficulties and complexities of the problems' seemed the main point to the New York Times, hitherto a principled supporter of Congress demands: 'It is not simply a question, as many Americans supposed and as some Indian leaders still pretend, of whether "the peoples of India" should be given their "freedom".' The paper now saluted 'the effort of the British to adopt the fairest compromise'; it detected 'a disheartening unreality in the response of some of the Indian leaders'; and it dismissed Congress's reply to Cripps as 'the repetition of slogans that have suddenly lost their meaning'.[46]

The British case was much aided by the fact that Cripps and Churchill closed ranks in blaming Congress for the breakdown. Gandhi's response, in simply calling on the British to 'Quit India', subsequently did little to recruit American sympathy since it so obviously hindered the war effort against Japan – a war mainly fought by the United States, of course. Perhaps it is not surprising that a US poll in April 1943, while showing over 60 per cent favourable to Indian independence, revealed that two-thirds of those in favour thought that independence should await the end of the war[47] – an American endorsement of the post-dated cheque.

The Cripps Offer was not meant to fail. But the demonstration effect of its failure in India provided an immediate propaganda coup and subsequent ideological cover for the British. Moreover, Churchill himself, though almost always truculent when he spoke about India, in fact spoke about it very little, to the despair of his Secretary of State for India, Leo Amery, whose diary bemoaned this paradox at length. For the rest of the war, to a surprising extent, the issue simply went to sleep.

*

Soon after Pearl Harbor, on New Year's Eve 1941, Keynes reminded his Treasury colleagues of his most famous maxim: that in the long run we are all dead. He meant this as a warning against the complacent assumption that things would turn out for the best if only let alone. Writing with reference to the still unresolved fine print of Lend-Lease, he issued a call for the British to wake up and recognize the futility of seeking, as he put it, 'to appease' the Americans: 'What will arouse suspicion will be our agreeing to unreasonable demands against our better judgement and then inevitably having to find some way of slipping out of our ill-advised words.'[48]

Churchill, currently on the North American visit that created the image of the Roaring Lion, evidently read the situation differently. Talking now with the President as an ally in Washington, the Prime Minister refused to reveal exactly what was said but assured Lord Halifax, the British ambassador, that 'with every month that passes the fighting comradeship of the two countries as allies will grow, and the haggling about the lend-lease story will wane. After all, Lend-lease is practically superseded now.'[49]

By no means. Though Congress was sometimes blamed – Mr Jorkins again – Roosevelt showed himself determined to maintain Lend-Lease. The only difference was that it would now become reciprocal, within the framework of a bigger Mutual Aid Agreement, which the British were now asked to sign. The principle of Mutual Aid was that all the Allies should offer such help as they could to each other: the United States to Britain, yes, but also 'Reverse Lend-Lease' by Britain, especially for American forces stationed there.

'Reverse Lend-Lease' showed that the flow of necessary assistance was not all in one direction. In the Pacific war, Australia and New Zealand gave at least as much in Mutual Aid to the Americans as they received from them. Canada (which had refused Lend-Lease) and Britain were likewise to give each other support on a highly significant scale. It was the need to sign the original Mutual Aid Agreement that provoked heated debate in the British cabinet in January and February 1942.

Here is one of the great suppressed crises of the war. We see the impact on a shaken Prime Minister from the surviving documents, notably the text of a telegram, heavily revised by him in red ink.[50] Presented with a tough draft message for his friend the President, he evidently decides to soften its language. 'As I told you I consider situation is completely altered by entry of the United States into the war.' Yes, he agrees with that. But the next sentence? 'This makes us no longer a client receiving help from a generous patron, but two comrades fighting for life side by side' – no, too strong, too choleric: 'client' is amended to 'combatant', 'patron' to 'sympathiser'. The draft continues, striking the plaintive note of ethical superiority with which the British customarily preface their begging letters: 'In this connection it must be remembered that for a large part of 27 months we carried on the struggle single-handed, and that had we failed the full malice of the Axis Powers, whose real intentions can now be seen ['so clearly seen', adds Churchill] would have fallen upon the United States.'

By this time we see Churchill warming to his work. He seems to have forgotten that his task is to tone down such sentiments and instead, persuaded of his own rectitude, he lets his own rhetoric carry an irrefutable argument forward. It is not, he wants Roosevelt to understand, the old argument of protection versus free trade (in which he appeals to his own record): the issue now is 'the inappropriateness in time and circumstance of our being forced to part with our freedom of honourable discussion with you upon an issue, which in certain aspects touches our sovereignty and independence'. It is the client/patron point again. For would not a commitment to end imperial preference, just like that, at the behest of American paymasters, look like acceptance of 'a condition of tutelage'? Hence the final red-ink appeal: 'The key-note of our relations must surely be equality, coupled with rivalry in sacrifice and effort against the common foe, and for the sake of the common cause of liberty and equality.'

This is the clearest statement of the British case ever made by Churchill. In it he stands up to the Americans and tells them that if they want the British Empire as an ally, it must be treated as such on an equal basis, now that they are all in the same boat. But we shall never know Roosevelt's reaction to this insubordinate missive. It was never sent. Churchill contented himself, after a couple of days for reflection, with a deliberately colourless report that the cabinet was resolved that 'if we bartered the principle of imperial prefence for the sake of lease-lend we should have accepted an intervention in the domestic affairs of the British Empire', from which all sorts of bad consequences would flow.[51] Having nerved himself to strike while the iron was hot, he then decided to cool it.

The lion failed to roar. Churchill opted for what Keynes had termed appeasement. Often the best policy when up against hostile odds, it was one upon which he habitually relied in dealing with the United States. In general terms, of course, he saw that the consideration tied the United States to negotiations on multilateral trade, which was to the advantage of all, not a zero-sum game. But when it came to imperial preference, Churchill cowered behind the small print. He was helped by Roosevelt who, as usual, sugared the pill that he nonetheless insisted that the British swallow, sooner or later, in the short run or the long. When critics like Amery berated Churchill over signing up to the American trade agenda, the Prime Minister kept pointing to the 'existing obligations' proviso on which he had insisted. As he assured the House of Commons in April 1944: 'I did not agree to Article 7 of the Mutual Aid Agreement without having previously obtained from the President a definite assurance that we were no more committed to the abolition of Imperial Preference, than the American Government were committed to the abolition of their high protective tariffs.'[52]

All these commitments stored up trouble for the future. Some were eventually enshrined in the convoluted text of the Mutual Aid documents: ambiguous undertakings, cleverly hedged, in the finest British mandarin tradition. Some of them were never written down at all, observing Roosevelt's well-known distaste for a paper trail that would constrain his own freedom of manoeuvre. Two different ways of doing business were united only in papering over cracks that would later reopen amid mutual charges of bad faith. Even sympathetic American negotiators soon began to tire of the endless excuses that the British produced for prevaricating over the consideration. And the British meanwhile relied on whatever it was that the President might verbally assure the Prime Minister.

Lend-Lease, far from being superseded by the Anglo-American alliance, had thus gone from strength to strength. Arguments that no consideration was necessary as between allies went by the board, as did the notion that the other side of the bargain was now fulfilled by the provisions for mutual aid between them. Thus the consideration still remained fundamental to the Lend-Lease agreement. If it really ensured that the Americans would be compensated (twice over, at that) for all their help, it might be a smart deal to strike with a neighbour bereft of a garden hose. Even the backwoodsmen of Congress could understand that, so it was good politics. But when the British people heard Lend-Lease hailed as uniquely unsordid, they entertained expectations of rather more generous treatment.

Yet what was actually done under the auspices of Lend-Lease refutes many airy criticisms with a solid record of achievement. It created a supply line, harnessing the growing might of the American economy to the war needs of the British. In 1941 Germany and the United Kingdom each had about $6 billion in armaments production, well ahead of the USA's $4.5 billion. By 1943, however, although the UK was up to $11 billion, as against Germany's $13.8 billion, the United States was now producing $37.5 billion. American military equipment, manufactured in quantities that the world had never before seen, gave the Allies their cutting edge. Take aircraft production, which decided the control of the skies, so vital in modern warfare. At the peak of production, reached in 1944, the Soviet Union and Germany each produced about 40,000 aircraft, which would have given them parity against each other. Britain and Japan likewise roughly matched in production, albeit in the lower range of 26–28,000. What decisively changed the equation, in Europe and the Pacific alike, was the production by the United States alone of 96,000 aircraft that year.[53]

Lend-Lease did not just mean munitions, however necessary to the British fighting forces. Just as important was the flow of American goods, including foodstuffs. Lend-Lease thus sustained the British people at a standard of living adequate for them to continue fighting, even though their own export trade was deliberately abandoned in the process. It meant too that their own economic production was distorted ever more strongly by the priorities of a combined war effort. British industry was sacrificed to the needs of the war, and manpower mobilized for military purposes.

For Britain, the crucial impact of Lend-Lease was financial rather than economic. It is not as though the British economy was languishing during the war. Gross Domestic Product (at constant 1938 prices) had been as low as £4 billion at the bottom of the slump in 1933, climbing shakily to £5.2 billion by 1939. But it reached £6 billion in 1940, the first full year of war – an increase of 50 per cent over 1933. Levels of output, moreover, remained at least as high as this throughout the war, reaching a peak of £6.6 billion in 1943.[54]

This was a command economy in many ways, subordinating market forces to maximum mobilization and war production. Full employment replaced dole queues as labour shortage became the main problem, with the trade unionist Ernest Bevin, as Churchill's Minister of Labour, using a manpower budget to juggle the needs of industry with the demands of the armed forces. Likewise inflation replaced deflation as the main problem, as Keynes had been quick to realize, and his schemes for restraining domestic demand were adopted and adapted by the Treasury. Everything was sacrificed to the war effort, with maximum production as the urgent priority, here and now, rather than seeking productivity gains that might have better served the long-term need for British competitiveness.

Yet this could only happen because the requirement to export was virtually ignored under Lend-Lease arrangements. The balance of payments for the war years shows that total British exports dwindled to a puny 100,000 US dollars a year from 1941 onward. Meanwhile imports, especially of munitions, zoomed up; in 1944 exports paid for about 1 per cent of total imports. Since these exchanges took place largely between Britain and the United States, and since Britain was responsible for the whole sterling area – mainly the Empire – the main effect can be seen in the accounts for the sterling area, measured in US dollars. It can be seen from the table below that the deficits with the United States during 1941–4 were largely covered by the receipts under Lend-Lease – somewhat offset, though, by the amounts that Britain and other sterling-area countries contributed to the United States in 'Reverse Lend-Lease' (as Mutual Aid was often called). Thus the foreign-exchange deficits in the left-hand column are in effect financed by the net receipts from Lend-Lease in the right-hand column.

Sterling-area balance of payments in US dollars (billions)[55]

	deficit	Lend-Lease	Reverse Lend-Lease	net Lend-Lease
1941	−2.1	+1.1	–	+1.1
1942	−4.4	+4.8	−0.3	+4.5
1943	−6.6	+9.0	−1.8	+7.2
1944	−7.4	+10.8	−2.5	+8.3

Lend-Lease thus solved the problem of externally financing the war, in the absence of anything like sufficient British export earnings, but it did so by creating dependency on the Americans, of a sort that would obviously have to end once the war was won. This may have been a rational division of labour between the Allies but one which inevitably distorted the British economy into supplying purely military needs, whereas the American economy remained more balanced in its huge wartime expansion. For the duration, it might be said, the Americans generously picked up the bills – but also picked off the markets that the British had formerly supplied themselves.

On the eve of peace, Keynes was to summarize the position in all its piquancy. 'The fact that the distribution of effort between ourselves and our Allies has been of this character leaves us far worse off, when the sources of assistance dry up, than if the roles had been reversed,' he wrote in a paper for the cabinet. 'If we had been developing our exports so as to pay for our own current needs and in addition to provide a large surplus which we could furnish free of current charge to our Allies as lend lease or mutual aid or on credit, we should, of course, find ourselves in a grand position when the period of providing the stuff free of current charge was suddenly brought to an end.'[56] Lend-Lease proved itself a wonderful weapon of war; but for the British it was a double-edged sword.

It was only as the end of the war came into sight that some of these rather theoretical arguments became immediate practical problems. For the British, it was a question of providing for themselves in a post-war world in which there would be no Lend-Lease – and perhaps no imperial preference either. For the Americans, it was time to implement a new international economic order with a different centre of gravity, no longer London but Washington. Moreover, Keynes secured British co-operation in this heady enterprise.

Here was the potent brew that made Bretton Woods famous. This charming resort in the hills of New Hampshire was pressed into service in order to avoid the stifling heat of Washington in the summer of 1944. This was a special blessing for Keynes, increasingly plagued by the heart condition that had first hit him in 1937, but still the British Treasury's key player. Lydia Keynes fulfilled the indispensable role of preventing Maynard from overtaxing himself, as well as lightening the proceedings. And he could lean on the intellectual support of Professor Lionel Robbins, head of the Economic Section of the war cabinet, now in his second major transatlantic set of negotiations.

Robbins had experienced much the same learning-curve as Keynes before him. At the Hot Springs conference in 1943 – suddenly called by Roosevelt to steer the United Nations, as he called his allies, towards a common policy on food and agriculture – Robbins had been struck by the differences in Anglo-American institutional culture. In British experience, he mused, if an official was prepared to talk off the record, he could at least predict what line his own side would take. 'With an American – the friendly American of goodwill I mean – it is different,' Robbins thought. 'Quite apart from the matters of discretion, in which they are certainly very lax, they are obviously in the dark concerning the machine they have to handle.'[57]

In some ways, this gave the British a technical advantage, in being able to shape the agenda according to a set plan. The result of the conference was the establishment of a permanent Food and Agriculture Organization (later absorbed into the United Nations Organization as set up in 1945 at San Francisco). 'We have the satisfaction of having saved the proceedings of the conference from futility and lack of direction,' Robbins claimed of Hot Springs. 'And we know that this has been appreciated, not least by the Americans themselves which means that it has been worthwhile – though it is very easy for this kind of advantage to evaporate overnight.'[58]

It was an advantage on which the British hoped to capitalize at Bretton Woods; and it served well enough. The dominating influence over the conference, however, was inevitably that of the US Treasury. Morgenthau had so many more of the chips in this game than anyone else; and he was supported by an extremely able deputy.

This was Harry Dexter White. His forbidding reputation preceded him – 'Of course, normally, Harry is the unpleasantest man in Washington', so Robbins was told[59] – and he came to Bretton Woods as the author of the White Plan, which was to provide the model for a new international monetary system. What was not known at the time was the extent to which White's left-wing outlook made him a committed fellow traveller of the Soviet Union, to which he was actually passing confidential information.

The crux was simple. There was an American plan and there was a British plan. Both were highly professional, both were caricatured by their opponents, both had real merits; but it was no surprise that in the end it was the American plan that prevailed.

The trouble with the Keynes Plan, as published alongside the White

Plan in 1943, was that it had seemed utopian. It proposed to escape from the bad old world of the Gold Standard, which had tied each currency to a fixed gold price, by inventing a new international medium of exchange to lubricate world trade. The new unit – 'bancor' was one name canvassed – could simply be willed into existence and would function like an overdraft facility, leaving each country with its own responsibility for balancing its books. The point was to create the conditions in which full employment could be maintained, rather than allow shortage of gold to impose deflationary policies, with all their attendant evils. It was an elegant conception. 'Personally, I am very attracted by it and if I had my own way, I would go a long way to meet you,' White himself had told Robbins. 'But I know that we can never get it across.'[60]

Politics, then, demanded another approach. The White Plan started with traditional conceptions of central banking, requiring customers to make deposits before they could hope to exercise any drawing rights. It had the ring of sound money, unlike the clever dodges that the British were peddling. 'If we are big enough suckers to swallow the Keynes plan,' wrote a small-town Iowa newspaper, 'we shall be swindled out of everything we have left from the war – and we shall deserve to be swindled.'[61]

It was only a matter of time before the British bowed to the inevitable. They would have to settle for a modified White Plan: banking principles, no funny money – but no rigid Gold Standard either. Instead there would be the chance to set up an international mechanism with a new sort of liquidity in financing trade flows. Keynes had already stood up in the House of Lords, a clear month before going to Bretton Woods, to explain that there would be 'no longer any need for a new-fangled international monetary unit' since the objectives could now be achieved through a compromise involving less radical reform.[62] In a spirit of amity, he now told White that the remaining opponents of their compromise scheme were 'rather dishonestly raising the bugbear of gold, since the mere suggestion that our proposals can be regarded in the light of a return to gold, is enough to make 99 per cent of the people of this country see red'. So the biggest difficulty lay in presentation to two different communities: that the proposals had been 'drawn up on those lines which are most suitable from the point of view of satisfying American opinion, and unfortunately in this case, that means lines which are most likely to provoke opposition in this country'.[63]

31

Bretton Woods proved a triumph for White and Keynes alike. Since the British had already accepted the White Plan as the basis for agreement, a measure of personal magnanimity sealed the pact between them. One participant later commented: 'The happiest moment in the life of Harry White came when he could call Keynes by his first name.'[64] The fact that he was called by his second name – Maynard rather than John – was simply an agreeably eccentric English touch; and he was allowed his moment of glory.

'Keynes was in his most lucid and persuasive mood; and the effect was irresistible,' Robbins recorded. 'At such moments, I often find myself thinking that Keynes must be one of the most remarkable men that have ever lived – the quick logic, the birdlike swoop of intuition, the vivid fancy, the wide vision, above all the incomparable sense of the fitness of words, all combine to make something several degrees beyond the limit of ordinary human achievement.' Bent on reaching a mutually acceptable consensus, building on the solid Anglo-American staffwork that dominated the conference, Keynes's genius was both enrapturing and persuasive on this occasion. 'The Americans sat entranced as the god-like visitor sang and the golden light played around. When it was all over there was very little discussion.'[65]

This was, of course, too good to last. The irony of the conference was that the better the British did, the worse they came out – at least in the eyes of the mainly hostile American press. Even the *New York Times* was suspicious, still hankering after the stability of gold. Two new institutions were to be established: the World Bank, responsible for development, and the International Monetary Fund, responsible for finance. 'The proposals are said to be half-baked and ill-considered; they involve inflation and encourage wasteful internal policies,' Robbins reported on reactions. 'The UK are held up as men of utmost eminence and diplomatic adroitness, whereas their opposite numbers on the American delegation are held up for ridicule.'[66] To some extent the Anglo-American teamwork – with only the Canadians recognized as having comparable expertise – was maintained as a means of avoiding potential disruption from the forty or so other delegations represented.

An acute worry for the British delegation was Keynes's precarious health. He frequently had to transact business lying down in his room, but he lasted the course at Bretton Woods. The conference was able to conclude 'in a blaze of optimism and friendly feeling', as Robbins put it. 'At the end Keynes capped the proceedings with one of his most felicitous speeches, and the delegates paid tribute by rising and applauding again and again.'[67]

For the British, however, the most acute difficulties had been deferred, not solved. They subscribed hopefully to the common ideal for the post-war world but had no idea how to survive the transition to it. Within weeks, therefore, Churchill was to ask Roosevelt personally what on earth would happen to the British economy when Lend-Lease had to stop.

In the British people's mythology of how they won the war, the names of two leaders remained invested with magic long into the post-war era. That of Winston Churchill was obviously the greater, with the successive volumes of *The Second World War* (1948–54) to embalm his own account. But it is generals who actually win battles; and from the time in 1942 that the victory at El Alamein made a full general of him, Sir Bernard Montgomery (as he also then became) ranked with the Prime Minister himself as an emblematic British hero. Montgomery wrote his own memoirs – with a pencil – and their publication in 1958, boosted by the unprecedented publicity given to Sunday newspaper serialization, laid out his version for British readers and for posterity. Whereas Churchill had carefully tailored his story to American susceptibilities, Montgomery managed – not for the first time – to affront his former Supreme Commander, now President Eisenhower, by reviving old disputes between American and British views over military strategy.

Like war itself, this was too serious a matter to be left to the generals. The most serious disagreement between Churchill and Roosevelt, from the time of Pearl Harbor to that of their Quadrant conference in Quebec in August 1943, was over a Second Front. We are all familiar with the idea of D-Day as the opening of a massive Second Front in the west, to squeeze the breath out of the Nazis, pressed as they were against an even more massive eastern front where Soviet advance eventually became relentless. But this sort of inevitability should not blind us to a long-lasting strategic dispute between the Allies that was only finally settled at Quadrant. Until then it was not just that Stalin was unavailingly pressing his Western Allies for a Second Front: Churchill and Roosevelt were themselves at odds on the issue for nearly two years.

Roosevelt had from the first wanted a western front to be opened as soon as possible, for political as well as strategic reasons. He wanted it not only to take some of the pressure off the Soviet Union, but because he also wanted American troops locked into the European struggle, which would seem less and less like a foreign war in the process. Moreover, this was consistent with the American military tradition, favouring the frontal assault rather than indirect approaches. Furthermore, it married with geopolitical strategic thinking which saw control of the European heartland as more important than maritime or peripheral operations. This logic led to the application of overwhelming force on the most direct line of assault on the enemy.

The US chief of staff, General George Marshall, was as indispensable to Roosevelt as Brooke was to Churchill. With towering integrity and formidable executive skills, Marshall saw his job as that of mobilizing a vast army to be landed as soon as possible in France. The trouble was that no such American army existed; the British Empire had far more men under arms than the United States in 1942. And, speaking on the chiefs of staff committee for the US Navy, Admiral Ernest King, with his inveterate scorn for the British, could always be relied upon to plead that the real war was in the Pacific – a predominantly naval war, of course.

The Roosevelt–Churchill partnership had been at its peak in 1942, while Britain still had real military clout within the Alliance. Thus Churchill temporarily got his way in maintaining that the Mediterranean was the key theatre.

This indeed was one of the Prime Minister's longstanding beliefs. For example, he remained immensely proud of the fact that, in the middle of the Battle of Britain in 1940, with German invasion of England a real threat, he had been responsible for sending 'nearly half our best available tanks' to Egypt.[68] There could be no greater measure of his essentially imperial vision, focused on bases like Gibraltar, Malta, Suez and the route to the East. And it was in Egypt and North Africa that he staged the only war in which the British did any serious, large-scale fighting on land during the next three years – until the invasion of Sicily in the summer of 1943, when a further development of the Mediterranean strategy was implemented.

Moreover, in 1942 Churchill had got Roosevelt to support him. Rather than conserve resources to open a Second Front in France in 1943, as Marshall wished, the Americans were induced to invade North Africa themselves, with landings on both the Atlantic and Mediterranean coasts. The Americans would thus challenge Rommel's western flank while the British confronted him in the Western Desert. This plan – the sceptical Secretary of War, Henry Stimson, called it 'FDR's secret baby' – was officially codenamed TORCH.[69] With these landings in November 1942, American troops were committed to what Marshall, surely correctly, saw as an enterprise that would inevitably defer the Second Front. But it had solved the problem, as Roosevelt put it privately, of 'finding a place where the soldiers thought they could fight'.[70] Admiral King, not for the last time, had to reconcile himself to supporting European operations rather than having a free hand in the Pacific, as many Congressmen in middle America would have wished. In June 1942 a fast-rising but as yet unblooded protégé of Marshall, Dwight Eisenhower, had been catapulted into command of TORCH. His fortunes and those of the President were henceforth to be interdependent.

Likewise, Churchill's prestige soon became linked with that of the victor of El Alamein – hitherto an obscure railway halt in the Egyptian desert. In telling the story of the war, or listening to the way that the British people told it to each other, it is impossible to ignore Montgomery's enormous reputation. This was built up, aided by virtually the whole of the British press, and by the reporting of BBC war correspondents, notably Chester Wilmot, originally of the Australian Broadcasting Commission. Wilmot was later author of *The Struggle for Europe* (1952), an influential study not least because it was drawn on by both Churchill and Montgomery in the relevant parts of their own memoirs.

The British and Commonwealth press corps followed Montgomery through the campaign in the North African desert, where he emerged victorious over Rommel's Afrika Korps. The fact that Rommel, uniquely among German generals, acquired not only a formidable but a favourable image among the Allied public was itself a propaganda coup for the British. Churchill had talked in the House of Commons in early 1942 of 'a very daring and skilful opponent', one whom he called 'across the havoc of war, a great general'.[71] Not only did this suggest that the British had a reasonable alibi for their persistent failures against him, culminating in the fall of Tobruk in June 1942, but it also gave the cue for hailing the genius of the British general who finally showed that even the legendary Rommel could be beaten.

It was Monty, of course, who emerged to fill that role. After El Alamein he immediately became a popular hero, with his corduroy trousers, and his jerseys, and his trademark beret, displaying two regimental badges. He did so in the first place in the eyes of his own tatterdemalion army. As well as British troops it contained a division each from Australia, India, New Zealand and South Africa. 'In the Eighth Army,' he liked to claim, 'knit together and fighting side by side, were men from every walk of life and from every part of the Empire; one and all ready to share the toils and burdens of battle so that the rights of man might be preserved.'[72] It was thus represented as both a democratic army and an imperial army, with less frequent mention of its notable reinforcement by Polish and French troops or its material advantage in the two or three hundred American tanks supplied by Roosevelt after the fall of Tobruk.

Whether his own sexually ambiguous nature gave a homoerotic charge to Monty's solicitude for the soldier lads in the ranks was a question not debated in that age of innocence; but their responsiveness to his identification with them is unmistakable. Initially demoralized by Rommel's mystique, they manifested a growing pride in belonging to the 8th Army as it blazed a trail of victories across North Africa after El Alamein, hounding the Afrika Korps into the sea in Tunisia by May 1943. Others might criticize their commander for his caution in not following up his advantage more decisively; but they appreciated his reluctance to risk their lives unnecessarily; and there is overwhelming evidence of Monty's personal popularity with his troops. With his fellow commanders, however, this was not axiomatic. Air Marshal Sir Arthur Coningham, for one, felt that his Desert Air Force was starved of recognition by the press: 'It's always "Monty's Army", "Monty's Victory", "Monty Strikes Again."'[73]

None of this happened by accident. Monty regarded morale as the key factor for a citizen army. Obviously, he was vain, hogging the limelight shamelessly; and, though physically small and unprepossessing in his looks, he made sure that he was projected like a film star in showing himself to his troops before engagements. The film *Desert Victory* (1943) was made by Captain Geoffrey Keating, granted unlimited facilities as head of his film and photographic unit to film Monty. The diary of Eisenhower's head of publicity, Captain Harry Butcher, records the claim genially advanced by Keating, as one professional to another: 'He said that England had no hero so he set out to make one and Montgomery was now "it".'[74]

Just as Monty was what the British public needed by November 1942 – a general who could actually win battles while looking after the safety and welfare of his men – so Churchill needed a victory in North Africa to justify the Mediterranean strategy, on which he had staked so much, and thus shore up his war leadership at its only vulnerable moment. Little wonder that the Prime Minister was fully complicit in building up the legend of 8th Army and its inimitable commander, who had finally bested Rommel. An inveterate late-night movie buff, Churchill sent an early copy of Keating's film to Roosevelt, who responded: 'That new film *Desert Victory* is about the best thing that has been done about the war on either side.'[75] His own generals, however, by now fuming at invidious comparisons with Monty, naturally tended towards the Coningham view.

Fame is often evanescent and intangible. But Montgomery's wartime prominence can now be measured by an exact citation-count in *The Times*. In the period between D-Day and VE-Day (6 June 1944–8 May 1945) he was mentioned nearly 400 times – eight or nine times a week. This was three times as often as Omar Bradley, who became his equal in the Allied command structure, and more often even than Eisenhower, the Supreme Commander – or indeed than Stalin. Churchill, admittedly, was mentioned nearly 1000 times, and Roosevelt over 600.

It is surely significant that Monty's place in the British popular consciousness was now in the same league as that of the Big Three. His name was used even in advertisements. Miss Gladys Storey's Bovril Fund was promoted largely on the strength of his endorsement: 'I want you to know that you, and all who contribute to your fund, have been a definite factor in our success,' he wrote from Normandy, sharing the credit for once; 'the men in our fighting areas, and the sick and wounded in our hospitals, all have a share in the Bovril in so far as it will go round. I must admit that I keep a tin occasionally for myself.'[76]

Churchill took to saying that before El Alamein they never had a victory, and after El Alamein they never had a defeat. Monty thus became the only charismatic figure on the British side to rival Churchill – or rather, not to rival but to complement (and compliment) him. The story circulating at the beginning of 1944 was that Field Marshal Sir Alan Brooke, Chief of the Imperial General Staff (CIGS), told the King: 'He is a very good soldier, but I think he is after my job.' The King replied: 'What a relief! I thought he was after mine!'[77] This iconic status elevated Monty above ordinary criticism in British eyes. To the British public, El Alamein was a triumph – simultaneously a deliverance, a talisman, a myth and a sign.

But sheer numbers count in war, as the British were often uncomfortably reminded. When one of their delegation to the Teheran conference of the Big Three grew weary of endless toasts to Stalingrad, he proposed one to El Alamein, of which the Soviet officers seemed unaware. Asked how many Axis divisions had fought there, he exaggerated by saying fifteen. 'In the Soviet Army, we do not call that a battle,' came the response. 'To us, that is a skirmish.'[78] Another story circulated that the British emissary to Moscow, sent on the eve of war in 1939 to talk about a possible anti-German alliance, had been asked by Stalin how many divisions Britain could put in the field. Two, he had to reply. 'Soviet Russia will have to put in 500,' said Stalin, 'so that will make 502.'[79]

The relative disparity, of course, was not actually so gross; but it was telling. And it told against Churchill. Granted, he had drawn the Americans into operations in North Africa, where their invasion from the west ultimately linked up with the advance from the east of the 8th Army under Montgomery. For a time, too, the prestige of Monty, the victor of El Alamein in 1942, eclipsed the initially faltering efforts of the novice Americans. At El Alamein, Monty had 200,000 men against Rommel's 100,000; and this still outranked the Americans' current commitment in the Pacific, where they had fewer than 50,000 men at Guadalcanal against 30,000 Japanese. The real comparison, however, is with the eastern front, where the Axis had 5 million troops in the field, countered by an even greater number of Russians. Roosevelt may not have known the exact numbers at the time but he appreciated the difference in orders of magnitude. The Americans found it heartening (as well as galling) to have the 8th Army on their side; but they found it indispensable to have the Red Army.

Moreover, though exposing divisions on the American side, TORCH also served to show who was in command: the commander-in-chief, of course, President Roosevelt. 'I pray that this great American enterprise, in which I am your lieutenant and in which we have the honour to play an important part, may be crowned by the success it deserves,' Churchill wrote, more as a courtier than as the power behind the throne.[80] Roosevelt's choice of military strategy may indeed have been political, but it also made good military sense to avoid a premature engagement in northern Europe. An assault on the French coast was doomed in 1942, as the ill-fated Dieppe raid in August, with its massive Canadian casualties, sufficiently indicated; and an attempt to invade in force in 1943 would have held many dangers. One would have been the effect of an abortive invasion on the political fortunes of either Roosevelt or Churchill.

Most arguments against mounting a Second Front, however, had a short shelf-life. The best reason for not doing it in 1943 was that it was better to do it in 1944. Hence the centrality of the issue at the Quadrant conference in August 1943. By this time, Churchill's search for an alternative, outflanking strategy looked increasingly like a diversion of energy from the real Second Front. The ingenious operations he continued to propose had little attraction for the Americans, especially if these plans could be interpreted or represented as part of a deep-laid plot to reassert Britain's great-power status and to prop up its Empire. As an irritated Roosevelt said to his chiefs of staff in late 1943: 'The British look upon the Mediterranean as an area under British domination.'[81] More or less anything in the Mediterranean or the Balkans was tainted by such suspicions, well founded or not. Above all, the Americans were not only paying the bills but providing more and more of the troops with every passing month. By the end of 1943 US forces were to number over 1.8 million in *each* theatre: against Japan and against Germany. Marshall was determined not to be thwarted again in making a reality of a mass cross-Channel invasion in 1944. This was OVERLORD. Like TORCH it was to be American-led, if not by Marshall himself, the obvious American name, then by the ever-eligible Eisenhower.

A popular and approachable figure, everybody's friend, Ike succeeded in making a success of the D-Day landings, beginning on 6 June 1944. Montgomery served under him, with initial amity, as ground commander of all Allied troops, though his failure to take Caen as planned was a source of irritation to the Supreme Commander, still at his headquarters in England. The problem, then, was not so much to secure a bridgehead on the Continent but to make the planned break-out from Normandy to establish a real western front, which had still not been achieved some six weeks later.

More progress was apparent on the eastern front. During the summer Soviet forces, aided by Lend-Lease supplies from the United States, had driven forward, meshing the mobility of modern tanks with the slog,

slog, slog of a war-hardened infantry numbered in millions. By the middle of August the offensive had penetrated deep into the Baltic states, taking the war to the frontiers of the Reich itself in East Prussia, and had swept into southern Poland. It was, of course, the Poles for whom the British had formally gone to war in 1939; the Poles who had established a government in exile in London once their forces had been defeated in the field; the Poles who had endured the extremes of Nazi occupation through five harrowing years; the Poles who took particular sustenance from the pledges of the Atlantic Charter. Had not Churchill and Roosevelt declared their intention 'to see Sovereign rights and self-government restored to those who have been forcibly deprived of them'?[82]

It was not, however, the British or American armies that now stood at the gates of Warsaw but those of their ally, the Soviet Union. This seemed to many in the west a cause for rejoicing. In New York, for example, the tabloid *Daily News* celebrated on 28 July all over its front page:

ENTIRE NAZI EAST FRONT COLLAPSES;

Reds Take 6 Big Enemy Bases in War's Greatest Victory

A British tabloid, the *Sunday Pictorial*, had the same approach on 6 August:

BIG NEWS!

Russians Are Fighting On German Soil –
Montgomery Bursts Through

Even the least observant reader, taking in only headlines two inches high, could not miss these cheering tidings of Allied successes.

Then the Red Army was pushed off the front pages by a bigger, better story nearer home, as British and American newspapers became preoccupied with the advance of their own armies. First there was the American breakout in Normandy from the end of July. After their slow start, the British and Canadian armies in northern France (under Montgomery and General Henry Crerar) achieved gains to match those of the US armies (under Generals Omar Bradley and George Patton), pushing further south and then swinging east towards Paris. 'U.S.

TANKS REACH BREST,' splashed the tabloid *Sunday Graphic* on 6 August, though the British papers generally preferred British headlines, like the next day's *Daily Mail*: 'MONTY SWINGS EAST – FOR PARIS', or the mass-circulation *Daily Mirror* a couple of days later: 'MONTY SENDS IN HIS TANKS'. Allied tanks made striking advances day by day, much as the German Panzer divisions had done in 1940.

Eisenhower was known to share the hope of an early end to the war. Indeed the worry now at Supreme Headquarters Allied Expeditionary Forces (SHAEF) was of premature euphoria. His press aide, Captain Harry Butcher, formerly a CBS executive, was concerned to be told by correspondents as early as 9 August that Montgomery's chief of staff and Crerar himself had talked openly of the war being over in three weeks. 'If the war doesn't end in three weeks – and it probably will not – the public will have been led up a blind alley, and naturally will be disappointed,' he wrote in his diary. 'I told Ike about this superoptimism and he lamented it but said there was little he could do.'[83]

The newspapers for August 1944 show a degree of confidence on both sides of the Atlantic that was benign, verging on benighted. The *New York Times* abandoned its sober and cautious house-style in writing of 'the nemesis that is now rising up against Germany on all her fronts' and of how 'the fighting spirit of the Germans begins to droop under the impact of defeat.'[84] The Allies showered compliments on each other. In London the initial American advance after OVERLORD was lauded by *The Times* as 'a sweep which has had few parallels in its dramatic quality and in its headlong speed', while in New York it appeared that 'acting together with perfect coordination, the Americans, British and Canadians have now set the whole Normandy front in motion . . . General Eisenhower may well make good his prediction that the war in Europe will end this year.'[85]

The division was thus between the optimists and the superoptimists. The *Daily Mail*, its masthead emblazoned every day with the motto 'For King and Empire', ran an editorial on 15 August: 'We stand near a consummation we have scarcely dared to think about through five of the blackest, weariest, and yet most glorious years of our history.' Its banner headline on 19 August read simply: 'FRANCE: WE HAVE WON DECISIVE VICTORY'. Since the Germans were 'irretrievably disorganised', they would 'probably never again be able to organise any sort of a front in France'. A leading article the same day, claiming that 'complete victory in the West has been achieved', gave credit where it was due: 'The people of Britain may this day be proud indeed.'

This tone, triumphant if not triumphalist, was by no means confined to the political right in Britain. In the Liberal paper the *News Chronicle*, its influential columnist A. J. Cummings, a great believer in 'Monty', was scathing about 'sceptics' who said that the Nazis were capable of lasting out for months. There was an unaccustomed gaiety to the paper's reporting of the advance upon Paris: 'AMERICANS SWING ALONG SEINE TO FORM SECOND TRAP'.[86]

By the last week of August the liberation of Paris had been achieved, largely through external American action, but presented in terms that emphasized the role of the Resistance in mounting an internal rising. Thus the London *Evening Standard* on 23 August: 'THE PEOPLE OF PARIS HAVE FREED THEIR CITY', or the *Daily Telegraph* three days later: 'Gen. de GAULLE ENTERS LIBERATED PARIS'. Everyone was caught up in the current mood, listening to the BBC for breaking news or seeing it confirmed in print. 'The news is better every hour,' commented the *Mail*.[87] 'One is dizzy, and too excited to write coherently,' the backbench Tory MP Henry ('Chips') Channon jotted in his diary on 23 August after hearing on the radio about Paris, evoking Proustian memories of good pre-war dinners. 'The news is increasingly wonderful,' he gushed two days later, only to find even more to come: 'The Allies march on to victory, more triumphs everywhere.'[88]

At this stage of the war, so much good news made for mutual magnanimity over the battle honours. In London the *Daily Mail* celebrated 'PATTON'S TANKS 90 MILES FROM GERMANY' on August 28, while in New York the *Daily News* on 5 September enthused: 'BRITISH FREE ANTWERP AND BRUSSELS'. An assault on the Germans' defensive Westwall, emblematically called the Siegfried Line by the Allies, lying in the path of the American advance, was now widely anticipated, and this further success was duly hailed on 16 September by the *New York Post*: '*Official*: SIEGFRIED LINE COMPLETELY PIERCED'. Almost immediately, for British, Canadian and American newspaper readers alike, the agonizing suspense over the fate of the airborne assault on the Rhine bridges in the Netherlands (MARKET GARDEN) was played out day by day.

These were the war stories that people in Britain and North America saw on the front pages throughout August and September 1944. The Red Army had apparently made a mysterious disappearance. Yet it was not all quiet on the eastern front. True, the Red Army paused on the Vistula; but its capacity to reach the greatest city on that river, Warsaw itself, could hardly be doubted. Appeals for an insurrection against the Nazi oppressors were made by Moscow Radio; they were heeded by the Polish Government in London, under Stanislaw Mikolajczyk, which sanctioned action by its undercover Home Army. But Warsaw was not Paris, where it all ended in roses, or at least Gaullism. The Warsaw Rising was undoubtedly heroic; it was also futile. No effective intervention came from the nearby Red Army until the Polish resistance had been brutally suppressed by the Germans. Stalin even prevented American and British aeroplanes, sent to drop supplies, from using Soviet bases for necessary refuelling until September, when it was too late. Meanwhile a rival government was established in Soviet-occupied Lublin, about a hundred miles south-east of Warsaw.

Churchill's protests during August failed to elicit further action from either the Russians or the Americans. Unable to challenge Stalin, unwilling to affront Roosevelt, he decided to shut up, an inglorious decision duly endorsed by the British cabinet. 'I do not remember any occasion when such deep anger was shown by all our members, Tory, Liberal and Labour alike,' he wrote in *Triumph and Tragedy*, leaving his readers with the rueful comment that 'terrible and even humbling submissions must at times be made to the general aim.'[89]

Any terror or humiliation experienced by the British Government, of course, palls besides what Warsovians experienced. Numbering well over a million in 1939, they were reduced to a handful of survivors living as fugitives in the rubble of their former capital. As for their sovereign rights and self-government, the Lublin Poles, loyal to Moscow in denouncing the Rising as a reckless and criminal adventure, competed for legitimacy with the London Poles, who had clearly suffered an enormous setback. The Polish troops serving in the Allied armies, notably those in Italy under General Wladyslaw Anders – who had languished in the Lubianka jail in Moscow between 1939 and 1941, before emerging to command the two Polish divisions in the 8th Army – had increasing reason to wonder exactly what they were fighting for, with such courage and hope.

PART 2

False Summits

I

The Spirit of Quebec

September 1944

'I had no idea that England was broke. I will go over there and make a couple of talks and take over the British Empire.'
Roosevelt in conversation with Morgenthau, August 1944

The perfect time for a visit to Quebec is when the autumn brings its autumnal splendour to the maple trees. Long recognized as a Canadian national emblem, the maple leaf begins to turn its own thrilling shades of amber and russet during September, as the sun gently declines and while memories of a fine summer are still unfaded. It is a time for harvest and thanksgiving; a time for reaping the fruits of past endeavours in hope of a no less bountiful future. So it was in September 1944. With good news from Europe, that the Allied armies were consolidating their spectacular summer advance upon Germany's frontiers, William Lyon Mackenzie King prepared to welcome his important guests.

Mackenzie King was not formally the host at the Quebec conference. As Prime Minister of Canada, a post he had occupied for all but five years since 1921, he was the undisputed master of the federal Liberal Party and his own Secretary of State for External Affairs; but as head of government he deferred constitutionally to the head of state, the Governor-General of Canada, representing King George VI. The Earl of Athlone was not only treated like royalty: he was indeed the brother of the Queen Mother, George V's widow Queen Mary; and his own wife, Her Royal Highness Princess Alice, was a granddaughter of Queen Victoria. The Athlones represented the old-fashioned way of governing the British Empire, extending the imperial tentacles of the royal family over self-governing Dominions, which were soon to throw off this cere-monial subservience by each appointing one of their own citizens as Governor-General. But in 1944 it was Lord Athlone who made his official summer residence, the Citadel, available for a summit conference, as he had done before, formally welcoming the leaders on 11 September and then leaving them to get down to business.

The *Globe and Mail*, the voice of the Ontario establishment, English-speaking and generally Conservative in their politics in those days, was in no doubt about the significance of the meeting. The two distinguished visitors – 'Winston Churchill, the accepted leader of the British Commonwealth of Nations, and Franklin Roosevelt, the chosen leader of the American people' – were presented as equals in their power, in their accomplishments and in their own towering stature. 'The annals of the world can show no more fruitful partnership in a lofty cause,' the editorial claimed. 'Today, as they sit in the autumn sunshine on the historic battlements at Quebec planning the final discomfiture of Germany and her jackal Japan, Roosevelt and Churchill are entitled to feel a glow of satisfaction over the immense achievements of the Allies since they forgathered in Quebec in August, 1943.'[1]

For this was not the first time that the Citadel had been put to service. Its grandeur was indisputable. A former fortress, it had a commanding position in Quebec City, the old French capital, which still bore the distinctive traces of its ancestry in the picturesque buildings hugging the cliff above the St Lawrence River. Simply as an illustration in a tourist brochure, the Citadel had much to commend it. Mackenzie King had chosen it as the venue for the first expedition of an American President onto Canadian soil when Roosevelt had visited in 1936. When it was offered for the first Quebec conference (codenamed Quadrant) in August 1943, the Citadel was quickly put in order to accommodate the disabled President, with ramps specially fitted for his wheelchair to make him comfortable during his stay. This was to prove a good investment in attracting repeat business from a favoured client.

Each of the leaders had his own reasons for holding this conference in Quebec. These reasons were rather more hardheaded than the sentimental version put about at the time. 'Canada should be proud,' cooed the *Globe and Mail* on 12 September, 'to be selected once more as the scene of a meeting, where plans will be matured to deal a final death-blow to the now tottering dictatorial Powers, and to garner such fruits from the coming victory as will offer compensation for the wastefulness, the woe, and the cruel losses of this terrible war.' This was not untrue and all very well for public consumption; but in private it is not surpris-

ing that a meeting of three adroit politicians, each known for his manipu-
lative finesse, should have had its own politics.

That Churchill wanted to meet Roosevelt came as no surprise, since
the Prime Minister felt that they actually met frustratingly seldom. 'What
an ineffectual method of conveying human thought correspondence is,'
he declaimed to a press conference at Quebec.[2] Whenever Churchill, for
all his literary artifice, did not succeed in carrying his point on paper, he
nourished the belief that this was only because of the difficulties of
arranging a face-to-face encounter, where his impromptu rhetoric and
personal vibrancy could have prevailed. Even in *Triumph and Tragedy*
he clung to this theory, writing of his vain pleas for a Balkans campaign:
'I was sure that if we could have met, as I so frequently proposed, we
should have reached a happy agreement.'[3] He was thus always ready to
meet Roosevelt, with or without Stalin, as at Casablanca in January
1943 and at Teheran in November 1943. In each case these were heroic
journeys, both for an elderly Prime Minister with heart problems and
for a wheelchair-bound President; but both men had been prepared to
make the effort.

Roosevelt, however, was not ready to go to such lengths to see Churchill
alone. This was the case even – or perhaps especially – before a Big
Three summit. 'I think that you and I understand each other so well that
prior conferences between us are unnecessary,' Roosevelt shamelessly
wrote.[4] The subtext was that Stalin, once he had mobilized Russia's
huge armies in the field against Hitler, had to be wooed, cajoled and
propitiated – seductive techniques in which Roosevelt had long out-
matched other political leaders, first at home and now abroad. It was
not just that he was not prepared to lavish his attentions upon the
reactionary old imperialist Churchill: Roosevelt did not want to be
seen doing so by their 'Uncle Joe', with his suspicious mind and his
ever-present paranoia about capitalist plots against him.

Anglo-American summits, when they took place at all, meant long
transatlantic flights or voyages by Churchill, with hazards which he
faced robustly in a good cause. Thus he had sailed to Newfoundland in
August 1941, to woo a non-belligerent if hardly neutral President at a
meeting on a warship, producing the Atlantic Charter but not the hoped-
for American declaration of war. He had flown to Washington in
December 1941 as soon as news of Pearl Harbor came through, to seal
an alliance with the United States while passions ran high. He was there

again in June 1942, learning in the White House itself of the devastating loss of Tobruk in North Africa to the Germans; and had gone a third time in May 1943. The first Quebec conference (Quadrant), had been in this pattern in August 1943. For Roosevelt, it was a gentle journey in the luxurious presidential train from his country house on the Hudson River.

By contrast, Roosevelt wriggled out of all invitations to visit wartime Britain. True, the accommodation at Buckingham Palace was measured up by his independent and strong-minded wife Eleanor when she stayed with the King and Queen; but Franklin and Eleanor had long led surprisingly separate lives and a presidential visit was another matter. Churchill tried to bait the hook in July 1944 by suggesting that the Big Three meet – 'It would be better that U.J. came too' – and that Uncle Joe would find it convenient to come to Invergordon in Scotland, 'where each could have his battleship as headquarters besides a suitable house on land', while the King stood by to entertain them, perhaps at Balmoral, the royal retreat in the Highlands.[5]

Stalin's refusal to participate stifled any enthusiasm that Roosevelt had shown and he was warned by his loyal adviser, Harry Hopkins, that a meeting in Britain with Churchill alone would send all the wrong signals, suggesting Russia's exclusion from the cosy Anglo-American partnership of Churchill's dreams. Such a rendezvous of the leaders of the English-speaking peoples would have been as big a political prize for Churchill as it would have been a political burden for a President running for re-election. Trying to keep his New Deal coalition together, as he had since 1932, he was fearful of appearing too sympathetic, in the eyes of mistrustful voters, to the Tory Churchill, or to needy Britain, or to its outmoded Empire, or to the nefarious post-war designs that the scheming British were no doubt cooking up. Bermuda was thought too hot. But the offer of Quebec, which Mackenzie King still held open, was another matter.

Quebec was saturated with historical associations. In 1759, during the Seven Years War, it had been seized from the French by British forces under General Wolfe, who had died a hero on the Plains of Abraham, having won Canada for the Empire – the territory would be formally ceded by France in 1763. Every schoolchild in the Empire knew this – or ought to have done so, in Churchill's eyes. For him, it was a touchstone of imperial sentiment as potent as Trafalgar; and he was a man who wept at Nelson's death every time he saw the film *Lady Hamilton*. 'I should not object if you could introduce a note of patriotism into the schools,' the Prime Minister had suggested to his new and rather bemused Minister of Education in 1941. 'Tell the children that Wolfe won Quebec.'[6]

The trouble was that every francophone schoolchild in the province of Quebec, which used to vote solidly Liberal in Canadian federal elections, was also aware of this great historical event, and in rather different terms. It represented a burning injustice that stoked a natural reluctance to engage in yet another war to prop up the British Empire. This was Mackenzie King's problem in keeping his party together. He had brought Canada, substantially united, into the war in 1939; most Canadians were proud of their troops, now fighting in Italy and France; he wanted to maintain the consensus. Anglo-Canadians in Ontario might noisily clamour for conscription; but he well remembered how inflammatory the issue had been in Quebec during the First World War. While giving himself a free hand in principle, King had refused to use conscription to send Canadians overseas, relying upon volunteers, backed with much-needed financial and supply support for Britain. In fastidiously balancing his war policy, King showed sensitivity to French-Canadian susceptibilities. It was a point that Churchill had well appreciated at the time of Quadrant in 1943. 'The holding of the conference at Quebec is most timely,' he had told King George on arrival, 'as there is a lot of fretfulness here, which I believe will soon be removed.'[7]

The second Quebec conference (Octagon) was likewise a feather in Mackenzie King's cap. Diminutive in stature, with no oratorical gifts or charismatic presence, this ponderous Presbyterian never bestrode the world like a colossus. But in September 1944 he scored his own kind of political triumph when he brought Churchill and Roosevelt to confer in Quebec, albeit as quasi-host, not a full participant. Stalin's absence was inevitable, given his reluctance to leave the Soviet Union at a critical moment in the war; without him, there would be no meeting of the Big Three between Teheran, now ten months past, and Yalta, which was to come five months later. To say that his place was taken by Mackenzie King strains credulity, but King self-consciously basked in his moment of fame, replete with photo-opportunities. This was the Not-So-Big Three.

The agenda for Octagon was conditioned by the war news, which lost nothing in the telling. 'NO SECOND-CLASS FUTURE FOR US!' – so the headline of an editorial-page article proclaimed in the *Daily Mail* on 30 August 1944, showing that to parts of the British press the successful military operations of the summer had revived the nation's glory days. 'We emerge brilliantly victorious, with a Navy and an Air Force of unsurpassed quality,' it claimed. 'Into the bargain, we have become, for the first time in our history, a great military power.' Such comments, reacting against the slights or condescension of more powerful allies, were surely a plea for reassurance from Churchill's natural constituency. 'Was there ever a greater proof of national vitality after the exhausting years of fighting Germany alone?' the *Mail* demanded. 'Surely we should command the admiration of the world? Surely we can feel unbounded confidence in our future?'

As the participants packed their bags for Quebec, a map of operations, showing the advances in northern Europe, hung at 10 Downing Street. The Foreign Secretary, Anthony Eden, told his colleague Leo Amery after a cabinet meeting: 'We shall never see a map like that again.'[8] They shared an infectious elation about the war – 'hopes run high,' wrote Jock Colville, not yet thirty and Churchill's private secretary.[9] For him Octagon had the additional excitement of his first transatlantic trip. For Field Marshal Sir Alan Brooke, the CIGS and Churchill's indispensable military adviser, it was different; but even 'Brookie', a difficult man to please, admitted: 'News very good and every chance of rounding off Boche on Monty's front.'[10]

Obviously Brooke had to attend Octagon, just as he had attended Quadrant the year before. It was during Quadrant that his diary recorded the great disappointment of his whole career, on 'a gloomy and unpleasant day' that saw the President press for OVERLORD to have an American as Supreme Commander – 'and as far as I can gather Winston gave in, in spite of having previously promised me the job!'[11] Brooke remembered all too well how he and the Prime Minister walked up and down on the terrace outside the Citadel, above 'that wonderful view of the St Lawrence River, and the fateful scene of Wolfe's battle for the heights of Quebec', his despair in no way assuaged by Churchill's apparent lack of comprehension and failure to express regret. Not happy memories to bring to the city.

The British Minister-Resident in occupied Italy, Harold Macmillan, did not attend Octagon. Just past his fiftieth birthday, the future prime minister was not yet of an eminence that brought him to summit meetings. But he felt that his experience over the past couple of years, in dealing with Allied rivalries and tensions in the Mediterranean, had given him some insight into Anglo-American relations, as he confided to Leo Amery, an old friend and colleague visiting him at this juncture. 'He thinks we don't understand the Americans,' Amery wrote in his diary, 'and should realise that their Government is much more like that of Charles II, and their ways conversational and suspicious of clear thought out memoranda, but quick decisions regardless of what other American departments may think or say.'[12]

Octagon was like this, but more so. On the British side, too, there was a full complement of courtiers or at least a pervading flavour of crony-ism. The Prime Minister had his trusted scientific adviser, Lord Cherwell, with him, but not for any particular scientific reason. 'The Prof.', with his ministerial sinecure, was there as a court favourite, licensed to stray well beyond his brief, and was to play an important part in discussions of financial policy. Another confidant, one who recorded a good deal of what he heard in his diary – as frequently indiscreet as perceptive – was Churchill's doctor, Lord Moran, much concerned about his patient's health, which had not been good.

It was put about that Octagon would only deal with military matters: how to finish off Hitler and what to do about Japan. The American and British chiefs of staff were there, of course, headed by Marshall and Brooke respectively. But it turned out that the President had suddenly invited Henry Morgenthau, his supportive Secretary of the Treasury since early 1934, much to the latter's surprise. In a sense, he took the place of Harry Hopkins, who had been at Quadrant and whom Churchill sorely missed at Octagon; but Hopkins was a court favourite temporar-ily out of favour. It had seemed acceptable to the even longer-serving American Secretary of State, Cordell Hull, that the American State Department would not be represented – at least until he learnt that his British counterpart, Anthony Eden, was flying out. Hull was currently hosting a conference himself, at the Washington mansion of Dumbarton Oaks, that was to prove seminal for the creation of the United Nations Organization. When the Foreign Office mandarin representing Great Britain at Dumbarton Oaks, Sir Alec Cadogan, was suddenly summoned instead to Quebec, Hull was bound to feel doubly slighted.

The Big Three had met in this way, picking and choosing who was to be privy to their secrets. But at least in London some sense of bureau-cratic decorum prevailed and relevant papers were circulated within government, albeit on a strict need-to-know basis. Not so in Washington. Thus the minutes of the Teheran conference, held in November 1943, had to be winkled out of Eden by Morgenthau when he visited London nine months later. And it was only on the latter's return to Washington that his colleague Hull thereby learned of the agreement to partition Germany after its defeat, as Morgenthau's diary makes plain. 'Henry, this is the first time I have ever heard this,' the American Secretary of State gasped. 'I have never been permitted to see the minutes of the Teheran Conference.'[13] Hull's absence from Octagon likewise revealed Roosevelt as, in all but name, his own Secretary of State.

Now this may be thought an odd way of conducting important discussions. That master of protocol, that drafter of elegant minutes, that author of many a disciplined brief, Alec Cadogan, certainly thought so. On his first full day in Quebec, he noted in his diary that the Prime Minister and the President, with Eden, 'and at intervals Morgenthau and Cherwell, talked – or rambled – on a variety of things. It's quite impossible to do business this way.'[14] Nonetheless it is how the business was done, because it suited both of the principals.

It did not suit Sir Alan Brooke but it did not surprise him. His frustration at Churchill's methods had long filled pages of his own diary. Brookie was admittedly a rather testy Ulsterman, thoroughly the professional soldier, somewhat austere in his habits, prizing order and proper procedure, abhorring late nights and cronyism and the effusions of armchair strategists. The diary was his solace, his consolation, his revenge. When lengthy extracts were later published in Arthur Bryant's *The Turn of the Tide* (1957) and *Triumph in the West* (1959), it was after long deliberations. Even so, great offence was taken by the family and friends of the aged Churchill; but what now seems remarkable is how much Bryant left out.

On the voyage out on the *Queen Mary*, Brooke had wanted the Prime Minister to be fully briefed by the British chiefs of staff. But Churchill seemed 'old, unwell and depressed', following a taxing recent visit to the troops in Italy. 'He gave me the feeling of a man who is finished, can no longer keep a grip of things, and is beginning to realize it,' Brooke remarked, perhaps in a moment of exasperation; but the next day there was evidently another moment of exasperation: 'The tragedy is that in his present condition he may well do untold harm!' (Bryant omitted such comments in 1959).[15] Churchill appeared unable to concentrate:

worse, unwilling to accept advice. 'Here we are within 72 hours of meeting the Americans,' said Churchill, 'and there is not a single point that we are in agreement over!!'[16] Still preoccupied with the Italian campaign, his mind was full of plans for an advance through the Istrian peninsula, at the head of the Adriatic, towards Vienna, in order to forestall the Russians – schemes that were not on the agreed agenda of Octagon because they had already been rejected by Roosevelt. The British chiefs of staff agreed that Italy was no longer the priority, whatever the Prime Minister thought.

For Churchill the Italian campaign, launched on the back of Allied successes in North Africa, was a brilliant plan for striking at what he liked to call the soft under-belly of the Axis. For the Americans, the resources swallowed up in Italy were a symptom of their ally's obsession with playing the great power in the Mediterranean. In September 1944, while his President sat at Quebec, one American naval attaché voiced the common grumble at their 'being taxed hundreds of thousands of lives and billions of dollars to save the British Empire'.[17] Even General Mark Clark, the American commander who had taken Rome in June 1944, complained that autumn: 'We are caught in the British empire machine.'[18] Roosevelt had already repeatedly made it clear that he wanted no diversion from France to the Balkans. Though Churchill later claimed that the Balkans were not his object, and mischievously implied that the President hardly knew where 'the Balkans' were, his own words at Quebec were to show otherwise: he was ready enough to talk to Mackenzie King about the merits of 'the route that Napoleon took with a view to making a drive in through the Balkan States'.[19]

Brookie was well used to shooting down the Prime Minister's wild strategic schemes. 'He knows no details, has only got half the picture in his mind, talks absurdities and makes my blood boil to listen to his nonsense,' he wrote. 'I find it hard to remain civil.'[20] He tried to bite his lip and ignore the tedious old man. The *Queen Mary* too steamed on regardless with its important passengers, outpacing any U-boats. More patient than Brooke – and more junior – Jock Colville, joint private secretary to the Prime Minister, agreed about Churchill's low spirits. For a couple of days he had done nothing but read a Trollope novel, only emerging for dinner with his intimates, Cherwell and Moran. 'The P.M. produced many sombre verdicts about the future, saying that old England was in for dark days ahead, that he felt he no longer had a "message" to deliver,' Colville noted.[21] Churchill's account in *Triumph and Tragedy* merely says: 'As a result of our lengthy talks on the voyage we reached agreement about what we should say to our great Ally.'[22]

Sure enough, on arrival in Quebec, the message was suddenly quite different. To Mackenzie King, sitting opposite him at dinner, Churchill looked 'as fresh as a baby' and 'seemed to enjoy having a chance to take some Scotch as well as a couple of brandies'. It was Roosevelt, by contrast, who seemed the sick man: 'much thinner in his face', 'distinctly older and worn', 'quite drawn and his eyes quite weary'.[23] To Moran, with his physician's eye, this was sinister: 'you could have put your fist between his neck and his collar – and I said to myself that men at his time of life do not go thin all of a sudden just for nothing.'[24] The President's health had become a problem during the last year, with the treatment for his high blood pressure leading to his weight loss and grey pallor. This showed at Quebec, even when the President was simply being wheeled in his chair by his wife, inspecting models of the OVER-LORD equipment. Mackenzie King noticed that 'out of sheer weakness, there was perspiration on his forehead' and that Eleanor 'seemed anxious to get him off to bed for an afternoon rest'.[25] Clementine Churchill, likewise accompanying her husband, thought that Roosevelt could no longer focus on the war for more than four hours a day.[26]

As the conference got under way, Churchill put the best face on the situation, as ever. Over dinner he straightforwardly told Roosevelt 'that he was the head of the strongest military power today', as Mackenzie King noted. 'The President said it was hard for him to realize that, as he did not like it himself.'[27] This was hardly the case; Roosevelt had long insisted on American supremacy for exactly this reason, as Quadrant had shown. Churchill's general survey of the war, with which Roosevelt asked him to open the formal proceedings of Octagon, explained that 'although the British Empire had now entered the sixth year of the war it was still keeping its position, with a total population, including the Dominions and Colonies, of only seventy million white people.' Though this was somewhat unappreciative of the contribution of Indian and other troops of colour to the Empire's forces, his point was that they still had parity with the number of Americans deployed in Europe, and were 'proud that we could claim equal partnership with our great Ally'. But he added, significantly: 'Our strength had now reached its peak, whereas our Ally's was ever increasing.'[28]

This inexorable fact cast its shadow over all the pleasantries exchanged in Quebec. It doomed from the outset Churchill's notion that, if only he could meet the President, he could get his own way on the strategy for finishing the war. Yet he went home at the end a happy man, and not only because his expectations were pitched low. 'What is this conference?' he expostulated to Moran. 'Two talks with the Chiefs of Staff; the rest was waiting for a moment to put in a word with the President. One has to seize the occasion.'[29] It was noticeable how he went about this, often over drinks after dinner. 'To our surprise, we found Churchill and the President and a small party still at the table,' the abstemious Mackenzie King observed one night. 'They had been seated there when I left at 9, and were still seated at half past eleven.'[30]

As for the chiefs of staff, they produced the necessary agreements without much fuss. Churchill's plan 'to give Germany a stab in the Adriatic armpit' seemed to them as logistically unsustainable as it was anatomically improbable.[31] Only Admiral King unexpectedly supported it, probably to keep the British occupied in the Mediterranean while the serious war in the Pacific was concluded without them. For Churchill, conversely, it was top priority that Britain should be conspicuously involved in the defeat of Japan. 'For nearly three years we had persisted in the strategy of "Germany First",' he wrote in *Triumph and Tragedy*. 'The time had now come for the liberation of Asia, and I was determined that we should play our full and equal part in it.'[32] Liberation can mean many things. Indian independence was not what Churchill had in mind. As everyone knew, he wanted Singapore back. Roosevelt was ready to concede, overruling King in the process. The Admiral's apoplectic temperament – according to his daughter, 'the most even-tempered man in the Navy. He is always in a rage'[33] – meant that his infuriated and inarticulate scorn for the idea quickly entered the annals of anecdote. Thus the Americans accepted their ally's offer of assistance in the Pacific from the Royal Navy, once Hitler had been defeated in Europe.

To Brooke, the outcome was satisfactory, the process exasperating, largely because of Churchill. 'He is gradually coming round to sane strategy, but by heaven what labour we have had for it,' he recorded on 12 September, only to find an unreconstructed Prime Minister in full spate at a plenary session the next day: 'According to him we had two main objectives, first an advance on Vienna, secondly the capture of Singapore!' September the 14th was another day: 'Things have gone well on the whole in spite of Winston's unbearable moods.' This time, despite one last-minute alarum, the consensus held and Churchill was content to accept the careful compromises of the combined chiefs of staff. 'The tragedy is that the Americans whilst admiring him as a man have little opinion of him as a strategist, they are intensely suspicious of him,' Brooke wrote. 'All his alterations or amendments are likely to make them more suspicious than ever.'[34]

Mackenzie King, excluded from these working sesssions, was spared such disillusionment. He was content to sit at the same dining table, letting Churchill and Roosevelt dominate the talk. 'What I felt in listening to this conversation and much else is what a mistake I have made in the years in not keeping up with my reading,' he painfully recorded. 'In fact never really mastering history as I should.' For us, of course, his redeeming virtue is that, unlike them, he had the time, energy and inclination to write it all down in meticulous detail, not disguising either the ingenuous vanity with which he recorded their patronizing compliments to him or the rueful humility he felt in their company. 'I am woefully ignorant of questions on which I should be best informed, when associating with the President and Mr Churchill.'[35]

All of the Not-So-Big Three were democratic politicians down to their fingertips. As soon as Roosevelt arrived, he wanted to talk shop. 'He asked me if we were going to have an election,' Mackenzie King recorded. 'I told him that I was not going to have an election till the war was over.' Postponement was a luxury that Roosevelt did not enjoy; under the US constitution he faced re-election (for a fourth term) in November and claimed to be far from sure of the result, worried that soldiers' votes might be excluded in some states. He knew that issues would be made not only of his policies but of his health and his own personality – even of his pet dog Fala, the butt of stories of misuse of public funds, which he dismissed as 'pure fabrication'.[36] Indeed he was subsequently to make his mock-gallant defence of Fala's reputation the keynote of his election campaign.

Inescapably, the course of the war and the shape of the peace had electoral implications in all three countries. The Canadian 1st Army under General Crerar was in action during the conference, news of its capture of the Channel port of Le Havre coming through on 12 September: another opportunity for Churchill to flatter the Canadian Prime Minister. Brooke too was friendly enough when he gave Mackenzie King a briefing and 'spoke in the highest terms of the fighting of the Canadians and of Crerar's leadership'. It was part of the hopeful assessment by the CIGS that King recorded: 'At the present time, victory was wholly certain and he felt it was coming rapidly.'[37] This was a good moment to press for the Canadian forces to be reunited. Some had been sent to serve in the Italian campaign, now winding down, as Octagon confirmed; so they could in principle be transferred to Crerar's command in northern Europe (though it took months for this to happen).

Mackenzie King was quite explicit about his political needs, as befitted a man who served longer than any other Prime Minister in the Commonwealth. When he brought Churchill to meet the members of the Canadian Government's war committee, they heard what they wanted to hear: that the decision to offer naval support in the Pacific meant that the army should not be called upon in the first instance. The Canadian army's European commitment was hard enough to meet without conscription; the last thing that Mackenzie King wanted was to put his Quebec support at risk by any open-ended pledge about the Pacific. It was only once they had been reassured politically that the politicians then brought in the chiefs of staff and 'the question was reopened without mention of a general election'.[38] Brooke gave this pantomime fairly short shrift – 'More of a politeness than anything else.'[39]

Having guided Canada through the war, Mackenzie King could sense that the time was nearer than he had thought to harvest the political gains for himself and for the Liberal Party. He could either call an election 'the moment surrender comes in November or December' or wait and see how Churchill responded.[40] For Churchill too had a problem. His Coalition Government had been formed in the crisis of 1940 simply to win the war against Hitler. Suddenly this objective seemed within reach. At the end of August, Churchill had learned from Attlee, his deputy Prime Minister and leader of the Labour Party, that Labour was against extending the Coalition into peacetime, as Churchill had wished. A few days later, Leo Amery heard 'that Winston was already thinking of an immediate election to follow Germany's surrender, his one remaining ambition being to run an election as Conservative leader'.[41] Churchill's shipboard talk on the voyage out had showed his mixed feelings, as Colville records, even contemplating how he might stoically countenance defeat: 'What is good enough for the English people is good enough for me.'[42] Was it conceivable that Churchill could win the war only to lose a post-war election? What he needed from Octagon was a victory plan, and American co-operation in underwriting it.

'The Conference has been going well from our point of view,' Colville recorded on 14 September, 'and the Americans are being amenable both strategically and financially.'[43] This was exactly what Churchill had told Mackenzie King earlier that day: 'that this conference had been a love-feast; that everything had gone splendidly. No difficulties at all.'[44] Churchill's robust enjoyment of the cut and thrust of political argument was evident to all, and it is pleasant to know that he had found Octagon so agreeable.

That is not how Henry Morgenthau, a more delicate political animal, remembered it. He was described by the acute pen of Isaiah Berlin, then working in the British embassy in Washington, where they had met at dinner, as 'an infinitely shy man, who, if you look at him for more than two minutes on end, blushes automatically and looks for help to his wife'.[45] The fact that Morgenthau had been brought to Quebec – he had never attended an Anglo-American summit previously – was obviously because Roosevelt needed his Secretary of the Treasury at his side on this occasion. Partly this suggested that Britain's finances would have to be discussed, but partly it was because Morgenthau had come up with his eponymous Plan: a drastic proposal for deindustrializing a defeated Germany. The two were linked. His thinking was revealed round the dinner table at the Citadel, with more cronies than high officials to hear him. Churchill took Cherwell along, since he liked to have the Prof. at his side. And both the President and the Prime Minister brought their personal doctors, so Moran's account is full: 'Morgenthau wanted to close down the Ruhr to help British exports, especially steel. The P.M. was against this. He did not seem happy about all this toughness.'[46]

For those who were accustomed to dining with the Prime Minister, a well-known carnivore, his response seemed nothing unusual. Moran records no fireworks. That is not how it struck Morgenthau; and Mrs Morgenthau was not there to protect him from the Prime Minister. 'He was slumped in his chair, his language biting, his flow incessant, his manner merciless,' Morgenthau recalled. 'I have never had such a verbal lashing in my life.' With his long experience of working with Roosevelt, who sat silently observing, Morgenthau could see that he had been led into the lion's den on purpose – 'This was part of his way of managing Churchill.'[47] But the well-briefed Treasury Secretary evidently gave as good as he got, in the substance of his arguments if not in the rhetorical force of their delivery. 'Morgenthau asked the P.M. how he could prevent Britain starving when her exports had fallen so low that she would be unable to pay for her imports,' Moran wrote. 'The P.M. had no satisfactory answer . . . This war, the P.M wound up, could easily have been prevented. The P.M. is never less impressive than when he talks of the future.'[48]

Here, then, was the sort of Anglo-American confrontation that might have disrupted the love-feast. Yet the Morgenthau Plan, though subsequently regarded as rather an embarrassment, was to be accepted by the British. Part of the reason is that, overnight, the disputation over dinner had been left for resolution between the Prof. and Morgenthau. Frederick Lindemann, as he had been before taking the title Lord Cherwell, and Henry Morgenthau both had an émigré German ancestry which gave their discussion some piquancy. Of course, as a Jew, Morgenthau had special reason for animus against the Nazis and his Plan was premised on the need for exemplary punishment. At any rate, the two men hit it off at once.

By noon the next day, the Morgenthau Plan was back on the agenda, as its begetter's diary shows. When Churchill asked for the relevant minutes, 'the President said that the reason we didn't have them was because Henry interspersed the previous discussion with too many dirty jokes, and that sort of broke the ice. So Churchill broke in and said, "Well, I'll restate it", which he did, and he did it very forcefully and clearly.' Still it was not quite right; so Churchill's own secretary was brought into the room. 'He dictated the memorandum, which finally stood just the way he dictated it,' wrote Morgenthau. 'He dictates extremely well because he is accustomed to doing it when he is writing his books.'[49] Morgenthau could afford the compliments since his eponymous Plan had thus been enshrined in Churchill's prose, and the headline word usually associated with it – reducing Germany to a 'pastoral' state – was actually supplied by that versatile wordsmith, Churchill himself.

Exactly why Churchill did this is not documented, and with good reason. His general reasons are obvious – rather too obvious for hostile American journalists, who were quick to imply that Roosevelt must have bribed Churchill.[50] Though there is no evidence of an actual deal, various linkages were established in a process of give and take. It is certainly significant that the Plan emanated from the Treasury, charged with the Lend-Lease negotiations since 1941, and that the State Department had been kept out of the picture. Morgenthau records that, when he had asked Cordell Hull about proposals for post-war Germany, his only answer was: 'I am not told what is going on ... I am not even consulted.'[51] In fact it was when the State Department belatedly exerted its muscles later that the Morgenthau Plan was emasculated, even though agreed at Octagon by both Roosevelt and Churchill.

In Churchill's draft, the Plan was less potent than the original; as with his whisky, he knew how to dilute it to taste. He also knew that implementation of the plan would depend on who controlled the Ruhr. Eisenhower's idea was that SHAEF, that model of inter-Allied co-operation, should be kept in place for the occupation; but, as Harry Butcher noted, Ike suffered 'some repercussions from the Quebec conference' when he found himself overruled and learned that 'Germany is to be divided into areas in which the Russians, Americans and the British are to have control on nationalistic lines.'[52] Since the American armies were in the south, the British in the north, it was agreed that their respective occupation zones would be split likewise, while the Russians would have the east. So how much pastoralization actually happened in the Ruhr would become a British responsibility.

Above all, Churchill was more interested in the welfare of his own people than that of the Germans. In 1944 it seemed to many a straight-forward choice between your friends and your enemies. When Morgenthau had been reproached by a colleague about the potential hardship for displaced German industrial workers, his reply was simple: 'Well, that is not nearly so bad as sending them to gas chambers.'[53] Conversely, Churchill was brought to appreciate that Morgenthau was speaking, not for the first time, as one of Britain's best friends around the table.

Face to face, these two very different figures established a personal rapport. Admittedly, the Prime Minister had long known, through reports on British pleas for financial help as far back as 1940, of the importance of their remaining on good terms with Morgenthau, 'who is such an important means of approaching the President'.[54] But equally, once Lend-Lease was broached, it had fallen to the Secretary of the Treasury to sit on the other side of the table, counting the money with a beady eye, while the British were forced to tip out their pockets to prove their poverty to suspicious isolationists in Congress. 'We cannot always be playing up minor political exigencies of Congress politics,' Churchill had growled at one point in 1941. 'Morgenthau may have a bad time before his Committee but Liverpool and Glasgow are having a bad time now.'[55]

Morgenthau's credentials as a friend in need became more clearly apparent to Churchill as time went by. Less effusive than the personable Hopkins, who would sit up into the small hours drinking for his country at Chequers, Morgenthau too revealed strong pro-British sympathies on his successive wartime visits. 'But the spirit of those people!' he enthused when visiting London in 1944.[56] A fervent democrat as well as a Democrat, a committed New Dealer as well as a Jew, he was a man whose deep hatred of the Nazis confirmed his admiration for Britain's stance against them – and made him wonder who ought to gain most from the peace. It was not just that the British economy might benefit from the hobbling of German industry, in a zero-sum game: Morgenthau was the best person to make the case for helping Britain more directly.

Morgenthau's recent visit to Britain, in August 1944, had been a defining moment. As he reported to Roosevelt afterwards, Churchill was now saying that Britain was broke. 'The President said, "What does he mean by that?" I said "Yes, England really is broke." That seemed to surprise the President, and he kept coming back to it.'[57]

It should not have been a surprise. Since the inception of Lend-Lease, it had been generally assumed that Britain's immediate financial difficulties were over. But the fact that the US Treasury had discretion in monitoring both what was supplied by the USA and what was demanded under Reverse Lend-Lease seems to have escaped proper attention.

The implications, however, were fundamental. For the US Treasury was thus given virtual control over the British balance of payments (since the net amount of Lend-Lease determined the size of the deficit) and hence also over the levels of British currency reserves (since these had to finance any resulting gap). So while British officials continued to worry about the reserves, which mysteriously never seemed to amount to much more than $600 million, they did not apparently realize that Harry White could pull the appropriate levers in the US Treasury, precisely so as to keep the reserves at these minimal levels.

Keynes's back-of-an-envelope assumption was that after the war British exports would need to be 50 per cent above their pre-war level.

This would be necessary partly to compensate for the loss of Britain's capital assets abroad, which had hitherto helped to finance trade deficits. Now in 1938 British exports of merchandise had totalled about 2000 million dollars – twenty times what Britain was collecting in cash for exports under the Lend-Lease regime, as has been seen. The target was a level thirty times higher. Maybe this could be achieved, but not quickly. Given that any transition from the command economy of wartime to the market economy of peacetime would take a matter of years rather than months, how could reserves of only $600 million meanwhile stave off bankruptcy?

This was the picture in the summer of 1944. Now that the war in Europe seemed almost over, so did the need for Lend-Lease to pay for it. In British eyes, of course, this opened the big question of what was to happen to them in that event, and thus reopened the the big issue of who owed what to whom – financially, of course, but also morally.

This was always bound to be part of the British agenda at Octagon. Hardly had Churchill arrived than he seized his chance to paint in some of the essential background at a small luncheon hosted by the Governor-General, with Franklin and Eleanor Roosevelt his guests. It was a fitting context in which to dwell on the Empire's war record. 'Churchill said quite frankly he was sure if Britain had not fought as she did at the start, while others were getting under way, that America would have had to fight for her existence,' recorded Mackenzie King. 'If Hitler had got into Britain and some quisling government had given them possession of the British navy, along with what they had of the French fleet, nothing would have saved this continent and with Japan ready to strike, the President was inclined to agree with him they could not have got ready in time.'[58]

Such reasoning, of course, was long familiar to Roosevelt. The point was that, much as good Americans disliked the British Empire, it was what had stood between them and the threat of Nazi domination; and that they needed to ponder their attitude towards it accordingly. Churchill had cabled Mackenzie King in 1940, confident that the message would reach Roosevelt: 'We must be careful not to let Americans view too complacently prospect of a British collapse out of which they would get the British Fleet and the guardianship of the British Empire, minus Great Britain.'[59] The President had used some similar arguments himself in rousing his fellow countrymen. Indeed the premise of Lend-

Lease was that, regardless of whether the United States was actually at war yet, American security depended on British survival. Still, the United States had not gone to war to save the British Empire. One influential State Department official had speculated in March 1940 that Britain was 'a small country of 45 million population and may not be able to hold a far-flung empire together. Should it go under, it is a very fair question whether the United States might not have to take them all over, in some fashion or other.'[60]

It is not surprising that this still seemed a fair question to the President in August 1944, as Morgenthau's diary testifies. 'I had no idea that England was broke,' Roosevelt repeated. 'I will go over there and make a couple of talks and take over the British Empire.'[61] This was how the two spoke between themselves; it is the equivalent of Henry's 'dirty jokes' and not to be taken literally; but there was a serious issue behind it. Morgenthau felt that he could win the President's support for a policy to replace Lend-Lease, now that this had served its turn. This could be justified not on the rhetoric about preserving the British Empire that the King's First Minister sometimes used, but that of his anti-fascist alter ego who talked so movingly about the broad, sunlit uplands. Morgenthau argued that 'this has to be approached from the standpoint that Great Britain made this fight for democracy. Now we have got to help her. She is a good credit risk, a good moral risk, and we have got to put her back on her feet.'[62]

It was Morgenthau's influence that eased Churchill's financial worries at Octagon. At the same time as agreeing the principles of the Morgenthau Plan, there was agreement too that in principle Lend-Lease should be extended into Stage II of the war – the period between the defeat of Germany and the end of the Pacific war. As the only record – that of a conversation between Churchill and Roosevelt – laconically noted: 'The President indicated assent.' Indicative figures were then mentioned – $3.5 billion for munitions and $3 billion for other supplies. 'The Prime Minister emphasised that all these supplies should be on lend lease. The President said this would naturally be so.' Likewise when Churchill said that Britain must be allowed to re-establish its export trade. 'The President thought this would be proper.'[63]

Laconic perhaps, informal too, and to be implemented only when an ad hoc committee had done its work; but the three American members of the committee, led by Morgenthau, could surely be expected to interpret their brief in generous terms. So it was an agreement that left Churchill well content. 'While going to bed the P.M told me some of the financial advantages the Americans had promised us,' Colville recorded. ' "Beyond the dreams of avarice," ' I said. "Beyond the dreams of justice", he replied.'[64] As usual with Churchill, there are two stories: one noble in its rhetoric, the other vernacular in its bathos. For it is also recorded that, when Roosevelt showed hesitation in signing the text of the Lend-Lease memorandum the next day, Churchill exclaimed: 'What do you want me to do, stand up and beg like Fala?'[65]

Either way, the British went home well pleased but with their fate at the mercy of events. The final full day of Octagon, so Colville wrote, 'was crowned with further successes as far as our desiderata, political, financial and strategic go'.[66] Yet the promised extension of Lend-Lease still needed to be negotiated, and a lot turned on sustaining 'the spirit of Quebec', as Morgenthau kept saying. Moreover, the length of Stage II depended on how long the war against Japan lasted. Churchill had told Mackenzie King 'that the Chiefs of Staff estimated it might last eighteen months. That would bring us until March 1946.' In fact, they meant even longer – eighteen months beyond the victory in Europe.[67]

This was the best working assumption about VJ-Day, just as the current assumption was that the war in Europe would end by December 1944. The massive airborne assault now launched by the Allies on the Dutch bridges over the lower Rhine encouraged this prospect. On the same day that Churchill left Quebec, 17 September, the 1st British Airborne Division landed at Arnhem, the furthest of the three major bridges that had to be taken if the last obstacle to a full-scale invasion of Germany were to be quickly overcome. This operation (MARKET GARDEN) was impressive in its boldness and its use of paratroopers on a scale never seen before. 'SKY ARMY INVADES HOLLAND' was the next day's banner headline in the *Globe and Mail* in Toronto, 'GREAT SKY ARMY OPENS BATTLE FOR RHINE' that in the *Daily Mail* in London.

The *Queen Mary* observed the usual radio silence on its homeward transatlantic crossing, with the Prime Minister in a mellow mood. As it docked on 25 September, Colville wrote in his diary: 'The First Airborne Division has been wiped out at Arnhem.'

2

Setbacks

October–November 1944

'If our dreams of Zionism are to end in the smoke of assassins' pistols, and our labours for its future to produce only a new set of gangsters worthy of Nazi Germany, many like myself would have to reconsider the position we have maintained so consistently and so long in the past.'

Churchill in the House of Commons, 17 November 1944

After Quebec's Indian summer, wintry portents soon appeared. The whole war situation, which had seemed so encouraging for the Allies, steadily deteriorated. The immediate reason was the military check which the Allies met from unexpectedly dogged German resistance. But more deeply rooted causes were not hard to find, disrupting the unity of what Churchill liked to call the Grand Alliance and what Roosevelt called the United Nations: political causes and economic causes too. The difficulties with the Russians initially seemed more obvious. In the hindsight of the cold war, this perspective dominated as historians (not least Churchill himself) focused on the rough intrusion of conflicts with the Soviet Union, contrasted with the smooth path of Anglo-American understanding.

Lend-Lease clearly needed attention after Octagon. Following their mutual accord in Quebec, it was actually Lord Cherwell who initially began talking direct with his fellow spirit Morgenthau. This was a mark of Churchill's increasing inclination to regard the Prof. not just as a scientific expert but as an expert on everything. The British Treasury, however, would not stand for this and business really began after Keynes reinforced (and reorganized) the British team at the beginning of October.

The fact that Keynes had a track record behind him was one reason why he was entrusted with the mission, which in view of its importance might have been thought the job of the Chancellor of the Exchequer himself. The technical data were complex; it was difficult to get answers out of the Americans, especially during a presidential election campaign; but the real problem was that any adjustment to Lend-Lease for 1945 threatened to reopen so many outstanding Anglo-American financial agreements and disagreements, hedged about with past commitments and half-promises. Little wonder that the negotiations were to drag on through October and November, never likely to be concluded until after the US presidential election.

By this time, everyone was talking about the Morgenthau Plan (including Dr Goebbels, who found its draconian ideas useful for Nazi propaganda). But Henry Morgenthau himself knew that his was one of many voices that Roosevelt listened to, and easily agreed with, often on an interim basis and always with bland bonhomie, while he moved in fits and starts towards his own conclusions. That was part of the peculiar way that Washington worked by 1944, as this unprecedentedly experienced President prepared to seek a fourth term in office.

Churchill, meanwhile, had gone to Moscow. Eager as always for summit diplomacy, he knew that the President was preoccupied with his re-election campaign until November; so he determined to take on the job himself. His visit to Moscow in October 1944 was thus a natural follow-up to Octagon, on which Stalin imagined he might receive a first-hand report, or at least proposals from the President's comrade-in-arms. But whether Churchill was dutifully stepping into the breach or presumptuously stepping into the limelight was a matter on which Roosevelt showed himself rather touchy, making it clear to the Russians that the British Prime Minister spoke for himself and himself alone.

'CHURCHILL FLIES TO STALIN,' reported the *Daily Mail*, that reliable cheerleader, on 10 October: 'FIRST TALKS BY THE "BIG TWO"'. When the British mission, including the Foreign Secretary, landed in Italy en route, Harold Macmillan pressed Anthony Eden on its rationale, and 'was able to discover that the visit was: (a) To try to find out the Russian military plans. (b) To try to settle the Polish question. (c) To try to unravel some of the Balkan tangles . . .'[1] On each of these points there was room for American concern about what the Prime Minister might say without the benefit of the President's wise, far-seeing, restraining, conciliatory – and usually ambiguous – counsels. Washington was known to be wary and Roosevelt, with his tendency to over-excitement whenever the B-word came up, was only informed about the first two points. Indeed it seemed to be part of Churchill's agenda, as he had told Colville, 'to discourage any idea that the UK and the USA are very close (as exemplified by the Quebec Conference) to the exclusion of Russia'.[2] He expanded on this theme to Eden on the next leg of the flight to Moscow (so Moran recorded): 'I shall say the President and I have been like brothers, but I don't want the USSR to feel it is just an Anglo-Saxon affair.' This was a magnanimous view to take, perhaps an inflated one for the junior partner among the English-speaking peoples, still aspiring to mobilize the Big Three: 'We can settle everything, we three, if we come together.'[3]

The conference was codenamed Tolstoy. True, it was concerned with war and peace, and was very long, and had many twists in the plot. The reception in Moscow was nothing if not convivial. 'What had we done?' the impatient Field Marshal Brooke expostulated after one long banquet. 'Listening to half-inebriated politicians and diplomats informing each other of their devotion and affection, and expressing sentiments very far detached from veracity.'[4] In private Churchill traded shamelessly on the personal relationship that he thought he had established with Stalin through previous summits, taking chances in the hope of reciprocity.

They were both night owls, accustomed to summoning reluctant minions to midnight parleys. Despite having travelled for sixty hours without proper sleep, Churchill plunged in on his first night. It was all informal, which was a good excuse to exclude the American ambassador, Averell Harriman. The official minutes of Tolstoy taken by Major A. H. Birse, who had acted as Churchill's interpreter in previous meetings, were subsequently censored in the British official copies; and it is easy to see why. Churchill spoke very freely. He made jokes about the Poles – 'Where there were two Poles there was one quarrel.' Stalin came back with his own Polish joke: 'where there was one Pole he would begin to quarrel with himself through sheer boredom.'[5] But Poland was deferred as a topic that night in favour of another defeated ally with whom the British had fought shoulder to shoulder in the early stages of war.

Greece was Churchill's immediate preoccupation. Nor was this a sudden whim. For a time in 1940–41 the Greeks had been Britain's only European allies still in the field, first pitted with success against the Italian aggressors and then matched unequally against the Germans. It had been Churchill's own decision to reinforce Greece in its hour of peril in 1941, even though the British troops concerned were badly needed in North Africa and were being sent to almost certain defeat.

For Churchill this almost quixotic action was a characterisitic mixture of moral commitment, military bravado, strategic motives and a desire to impress President Roosevelt with British resolve. Britain continued to arm the Greek partisans, even though many of them were Communists. The strategic thinking involved was in turn to cause friction with the Americans, who saw it as part of Britain's great-power posturing in the Mediterranean, with one flank in the Balkans and the other guarding the imperial sea-routes through Suez. Indeed the deployment of British troops in Greece in the week before the Moscow conference looked to the Americans, with their republican notions and antipathy to power politics, less like liberation than an attempt to restore the monarchy as a tool of British interests. Even Macmillan, who supported intervention, was worried by his conversation with Churchill during his Italian stopover (as Moran recorded): 'To Winston any king is better than no king.'[6]

Hence the delicacy of raising such issues in the Kremlin, behind Roosevelt's back. 'Britain must be the leading Mediterranean Power,' Churchill said, 'and he hoped Marshal Stalin would let him have the first say about Greece in the same way as Marshal Stalin about Roumania.' It was to be a trade-off, then, as Stalin readily agreed. And it was better, Churchill added, 'not to use the phrase "dividing into spheres", because the Americans might be shocked'. Worse was to follow. Birse's notes state that the Prime Minister produced what he called a 'naughty document' which specified in actual percentage terms – 'the Americans would be shocked if they saw how crudely he had put it,' Churchill said – the extent of Russian or British predominance in five countries. Yugoslavia and Hungary would be fifty-fifty, Bulgaria 75 per cent to Russia. Crucially, in Rumania, Russia would have 90 per cent, the others 10 per cent; while in Greece, Great Britain ('in accord with United States') would have 90 per cent, Russia 10 per cent.[7]

Shocking indeed. Birse's notes were subsequently suppressed by the Cabinet Office on the grounds that they might 'give the impression to historians that these very important discussions were conducted in a most unfitting manner'.[8] Even Churchill blushed. He asked Stalin if they should burn the 'naughty document'. Stalin, who had seen naughtier in his time, was not so squeamish. He said Churchill should keep it – which he did, and even considered reproducing it in facsimile when he came to write *Triumph and Tragedy* (though he had second thoughts in 1953, again Prime Minister by that time; it would be nice to suppose that he was still worried about shocking the historians).[9]

Churchill's anecdote about the document was one of the highlights of *Triumph and Tragedy*, published at the height of tension with Soviet Russia and inevitably read through cold-war spectacles. By then it had become axiomatic that Europe was divided by an iron curtain between the Soviet bloc in the East and the free countries of the West, looking to the other superpower, the United States. So it is important to note that there was no American dimension to the sort of division that Churchill specified in October 1944. 'It is not intended to be more than a guide,' he told his cabinet colleagues, 'and of course in no way commits the United States . . .'[10] Moreover, the whole discussion was premised on frank speaking which simply recognized the realities on the ground. Churchill knew and mentioned – without labouring the point, obviously – that the Red Army was already in a position to control the countries where Russian influence was acknowledged as predominant. In that sense, all he was doing was extracting a reciprocal acknowlegement from Stalin. On Greece, this worked.

Poland was another matter. The fate of the Warsaw Rising had shown Churchill what it meant for the Russians to control the situation on the ground, apparently manipulating it with a breathtaking ruthlessness. No, said Stalin, it was not policy but logistics that had held the Red Army back, but he 'could not admit this failure before the world'. Churchill and Eden were politicians; they could empathize; they knew that it was important how things looked; they understood the impor-tance of not losing face; they knew how tiresome public opinion could be; and accordingly they developed the point further. 'The Prime Minis-ter emphasised how we had entered the war for the sake of Poland although we had no sordid or material interests in that country,' Eden reported home. 'The British people would not understand that she should be let down.'[11] In this perspective, it was important not simply to secure the best deal for Poland with Stalin, as though everything could be settled in a late-night conclave over cigars and brandy, but to secure a deal that would be openly accepted by the London Poles.

As over Lend-Lease, so over Poland. Everyone, it turned out, wanted democracy; it simply depended on what you meant by democracy. And it was not an issue on which the British view was likely to prevail but that of its more powerful ally.

For Mikolajczyk, summoned from London into Stalin's presence, it was disconcerting to find the odds stacked so much in favour of the patently subservient Lublin Poles. The issue at this stage was not really democracy, since the London Poles had no more been elected than the Lublin Poles – or indeed de Gaulle in France, as Stalin intermittently recalled. The issue was legitimacy and territory.

The two were linked. The Russians were intent, for security reasons, on keeping the Polish territory that they had annexed under Molotov's pact with Ribbentrop in 1939; but they did not put it quite like that. Instead they talked of the Curzon Line. This was a hypothetical line drawn on one of the Foreign Office's maps while Lord Curzon was Foreign Secretary in 1919, in order to suggest a settlement to the Paris peace conference; but the Poles had meanwhile taken more and the Curzon Line was then largely forgotten – but not by the Russians, who found it uncannnily close to the Molotov–Ribbentrop line. A happy coincidence for them, of course; but surely rather more than that if the same ethnic considerations underlay the drawing of both lines. In this perspective, the Russians were simply asking to keep what the British had long ago conceded ought to be theirs anyway. At any rate, the Foreign Office in 1944 could still see the logic of the Curzon Line, 'not because Soviet Russia is strong but because she is right', as Churchill and Eden kept telling Mikolajczyk.[12]

Mikolajczyk could not see this logic. He had his own logic, which was that the London Poles would lose legitimacy if they ceded territory on the eastern border on this scale. He was unimpressed by hints of compensation on the western border, at Germany's expense. What Chamberlain had guaranteed in 1939 was not Poland's existing frontiers but its independence; but it had been implied that it was for the Poles to judge whether their independence was threatened. Could Churchill in 1944 guarantee less? The Poles had fought for their frontiers in 1939 and they would fight still – even against Russia, General Anders said.

Churchill sought to turn such arguments around by saying that Britain's support for Poland entitled it to be heard. It then slipped out that the Curzon Line had already been conceded by the Big Three at Teheran. Both parties became angry. 'We will be sick and tired of you if you go on arguing,' Churchill said at one point. Mikolajczyk, already with reason to feel sick, already with reason to feel tired, would not give in. Churchill tried bribery – with other people's money, of course. 'If you acept the frontier the United States will take great interest in the rehabilitation of Poland and may grant you a big loan after this war possibly without interest,' he claimed. 'As to ourselves we shall be poor after the war.' But the real bottom line was not financial. 'Look, what is the alternative?' Churchill beseeched Mikolajczyk. 'You are threatened with virtual extinction, you will be effaced as a nation.'[13]

Churchill could do no more, as he ultimately recognized. He left Moscow on 19 October with Poland in limbo and Russian entry into the Japanese war likewise unresolved, pending a meeting of the Big Three, the real hub of power. But Churchill was pleased with his deal on the Balkans. 'Coupled with our successful military action we should now be able to save Greece,' he told Attlee.[14] Tolstoy had not been the Big Two; it had not really carved up Europe; but Stalin had allowed Churchill his soupçon. In Moran's view, the Prime Minister was simply reconciling himself to the inevitable, admitting: 'it's all very one-sided. They get what they want by guile or flattery or force. But they've done a lot to get it. Seven or eight million soldiers killed, perhaps more.'[15] For Churchill, the peace pragmatist, Tolstoy had been a success.

For Brooke, the war strategist, Tolstoy had been a bore. True, the longueurs were relieved by some sightseeing and – his real balm – some bird-watching. But as Chief of the Imperial General Staff he had to mull over an altogether more serious turn of events in military operations on the western front. These understandably weighed on Brooke more than Tolstoy's debates about the shape of a now receding peace. 'There is some fable,' he wrote in his Moscow diary, 'about some hunters going out to shoot a bear, who on the eve of the shoot become so busy arguing about the sale of the skin and the sharing of the proceeds, that they forget to shoot the bear!'[16] He was especially worried about the impact on Allied prospects of the over-ambitious MARKET GARDEN operation.

'The battle was a decided victory,' Churchill assured Field Marshal Smuts in distant South Africa on 9 October.[17] But even the British press had not bought this line about Arnhem. Six days after MARKET GARDEN was launched, on 23 September, the *Daily Mail* had to modulate the tone of its reporting: 'BATTLE TO SAVE AIR ARMY'.

Three days later, demoted to a single column, the truth was out, with a report that the 'survivors of the glorious action in which the parachutists holding out at the bridge finally went down fighting under waves of German attacks'. Alas, Arnhem had to find its place in the annals of honourable defeats. Thus the *Mail*'s banner headline on 28 September:

SKY MEN TELL GREATEST STORY OF THE THE WAR

8,000 IN – 2,000 OUT

In the armed forces edition the presentation was even starker: 'THE AGONY OF ARNHEM' above photographs of wounded British para-troopers – '230 HOURS OF HELL'. Later figures suggest that of the 10,000 British paratroopers landed, over 1100 died at Arnhem and 6000 were captured (more than half of these already being wounded).

What had gone wrong?

Everyone knew that it was really Montgomery's baby. Belgium and the Netherlands lay in the path of Crerar's Canadian 1st Army and Dempsey's British 2nd Army, which together comprised Montgomery's 21st Army Group. It was a disposition that followed from the fact that on D-Day the British Empire forces landed on the beaches to the left (Gold, Juno and Sword), the Americans on the beaches to the right (Omaha and Utah). This in turn went back to the decision that the British, for obvious strategic reasons, wanted to control the Channel coast and its ports.

But so did the Germans. That is why the cream of the German army was deployed there, initially under von Rundstedt with Rommel responsible to him. So the British and Canadians had the hardest fighting, as they had found when they tried to take Caen, ten miles behind Sword. Though Eisenhower had been privately impatient, he was widely reported in the British press (as he intended) when he said, after Caen had finally fallen: 'Every foot of ground the Germans lost there was like losing ten miles somewhere else.'[18] It was true that Montgomery's plan required the British and Canadians to hold the Germans on the left while unbalancing the enemy with an assault on the less well-protected right. The triumph was that the breakout, when it came, succeeded so spectacularly, with smashing Allied gains that soon put OVERLORD back on track.

These gains, of course, were made initially by the American armies. Under Montgomery as ground commander for OVERLORD, General

Omar Bradley commanded what became the US 12th Army Group, comprising not only the 9th and 3rd Armies but also General George Patton's 3rd Army, which grabbed most of the ground – and the headlines. Even the *New York Times*, far from chauvinist in its support for the Allies, led day by day with the feats of the US forces, with barely a mention of Montgomery. Wheeling round, the American forces were henceforth to the south, the British and Canadians hugging the coast to the north as they too eventually broke through. Suddenly, OVERLORD was ahead of schedule, as Eisenhower subsequently pointed out to critics. In his memoirs he quoted Churchill as telling him, in the course of their arguments over whether a Riviera landing was also necessary: 'I applaud your enthusiasm, but liberate Paris by Christmas and none of us can ask for more.'[19] A SHAEF planning map duly shows the Allies' target for D+270 as roughly the line that they in fact succeeded in occupying by mid-September – so they had taken little more than three months to do what had once been expected to take nine.

At this point the Allied war scenario at SHAEF looked good. Eisenhower had built around himself a staff of both British and American officers, demonstrably loyal to the Allied nature of the enterprise and increasingly to himself as the embodiment of that vision. 'I have often thought,' Butcher once observed before D-Day, 'that the Allied camaraderie at Ike's headquarters is helped a lot by the fact that we have American coffee at our desks around eleven each morning and British tea around five.'[20] The SHAEF chief of staff, General Walter Bedell Smith – usually known as 'Beetle' – was truly Ike's right hand and his buddy: 'the two together forming one of those great partnerships that will be added to the roll of fame in the world's military history'. This florid tribute is the more impressive because it came from the British general whom Beetle had supplanted, Sir Frederick Morgan, who had made the early plans for what became OVERLORD.[21] It is as much a tribute to Eisenhower's tact and charm as to Morgan's magnanimity that the latter was persuaded to settle for the position of deputy chief of staff with a good grace that lived up to the SHAEF ethos. Morgan, the bane of Monty (who disparaged his planning efforts), took to saying: 'There was a man sent from God and his name was Ike.'[22]

Not everyone was so complimentary. Eisenhower's obvious political skills in smoothing over difficulties led to his military prowess being questioned, the more so since Montgomery had fully exploited his position in temporararily commanding all the Allied ground forces for nearly three months after the invasion. Eisenhower's decision to establish SHAEF in France and take direct command himself at the end of August was an obvious reassertion of his strategic control and his personal authority. It did not, however, stem from his own doctrine of Allied harmony. Rather, it facilitated a clearer separation between, on the north flank, the British and Canadian armies, still under the famous Monty, and, to the south, the American armies, each commanded by an American general, as the folks back home would appreciate. It was politically imperative, as General Marshall kept saying from Washington, that the American forces should be given their head, and their due, and their battle honours. Rein in Patton to guarantee success for the British attack? 'The American public would never stand for it,' Eisenhower told Montgomery; 'and public opinion wins wars.'[23]

It was hardly a new problem; and dividing the armies was not a new solution. Much the same thing had happened in Italy when it became clear that, instead of Allied co-operation, competition between the different armies was rife. General Mark Clark's pre-emptive dash to liberate Rome in June 1944, in defiance of agreed plans, was as much an assertion of national identity as of his own vanity. Thereafter, the 8th Army, now under General Oliver Leese, seething with a sense of betrayal, was pointedly allowed (by Field Marshal Alexander as Allied commander-in-chief) to fight its own campaign in a way that did not require American assistance. Supreme Command, in Italy as in France, manifestly required emollience.

Yet Eisenhower's dilemma was more acute than Alexander's had been. Part of the problem was perennial and personal: how to handle Monty. But his was not the only big personality involved. There was one other Allied soldier in the European war theatre with this sort of sheer theatricality. Despite coming into the campaign weeks after the more senior Bradley, George Patton was in the news three times as often (as measured by *The Times*), even though his very presence in Normandy was initially kept secret to mislead the Germans. And in the American press, this was even more true. 'If the correspondents with the Third Army don't mention Patton, apparently the headline writers at home insert his name,' Butcher discovered, realizing that his own efforts to even up the treatment of other generals were of little avail – 'it takes a lot of color in any man to balance Patton.'[24] 'Old Blood and Guts' alone could rival the prominence of Monty, over whom he towered on the rare occasions when they were photographed together. (The only photograph of them in Montgomery's war memoirs shows them sitting down, each looking away, and separated by Eisenhower, who gives the camera a look of weary resolution, as Plate 4 shows.)

Poor Ike. The Supreme Commander went back a long way with Omar Bradley, who had first encountered 'a smiling golden-haired Kansan' as his classmate at West Point, the American military academy.[25] It became known as 'the class the Stars fell on' because so many of them eventually became generals – many of them, like Bradley himself, only to be leap-frogged in rank by Eisenhower, altogether too easily dismissed as simply a nice guy, in the course of his meteoric rise during the Second World War. As with Bradley, so with Patton – and all the more so since his indefensible conduct in publicly upbraiding shell-shocked troops in Sicily in 1943 might have ended his ambitions. Old Blood and Guts knew that he owed a lot to Ike, who first exacted an even more public apology from him and then rescued him for service in OVERLORD.

Patton was in fact five years older than his chief. He was battle-hardened in the First World War as a junior officer in France, where he had been gravely wounded: an experience much like that of Montgomery (who later saw the carnage on the Somme – a cautionary memory for the British). Indeed this is not the only affinity between these two otherwise contrasting figures: one a sexually repressed abstainer from tobacco and alcohol, the other a cigar-chewing, all-American extrovert, with his ivory-handled pistols to match. Visiting the American headquarters at Liège in October 1944, King George VI asked Patton how frequently he used them. 'I personally have killed thirty Germans.' 'How many?' demanded Ike (who told this story to Butcher later). Patton, unabashed, simply replied: 'Five.'[26]

Though Patton had a reputation for tall stories, big talk and reckless-ness, and was regarded by his men with mixed feelings, he was also a focused strategic thinker. Like Monty, he liked to formulate bold plans; unlike Monty, he did not pretend afterwards that his battles had always gone according to plan and he was certainly less fearful of accepting heavy casualties. The fact is that both generals had a capacity to impro-vise in the heat of battle and to pull off victories with a panache and resilience that silenced the critics. Left to themselves, they often proved more likeminded with each other than either did with Bradley (though it is true that they were seldom left to themselves). It is worth remembering that Patton's brilliant breakout in Normandy was achieved under Montgomery, who showed no desire to interfere or intrude. Above all, both had strong ideas on how to win the war – in each case with himself in the van, though each of their hammer-blow plans could have meshed with the other. In each case the real contrast was with Eisenhower's commitment to a broad-front strategy, where everyone could pull together and everyone have a chance to shine – even the lacklustre Bradley.

The personal factor was a largely unacknowledged reason for preferring the broad front. Montgomery's consistently maintained strategic argument for a concentrated assault may have promised a quick end to the war. But his own projected role itself compromised the plan. Though hardly the 'pencillike thrust' that Eisenhower disparaged in his memoirs, it was nothing if not an integrated Allied plan.[27] It thus demanded unity of field command under a single figure. And to make Monty that commander was not among the war aims of the United States, least of all at a time when its military predominance over its British ally was steadily growing.

On D-Day, the British Empire had supplied as many troops as the United States, as Churchill often proclaimed. As the months went by, however, British generals became all too aware of a domestic manpower crisis, and Canadian generals of a mounting conscription crisis, that alike served to deny them adequate reserves. By contrast, under Marshall's mobilization scheme, American reinforcements flooded into Europe. In fact, with the failure to open more ports on the Channel or clear the Scheldt (Antwerp), over 100,000 US troops were queueing up in Britain at some points.[28] At any rate, the Americans could continue to man new armies: not only the 6th US Army Group under General Jake Devers, moving up from its landings on the French Riviera in August, but successively the 3rd Army under Patton, which became operational in August, and in September the 9th Army under William Simpson.

Again, the crux was simple. There was an American plan and there was a British plan. Both were highly professional, both were caricatured by their opponents, both had real merits; but it was no surprise that in the end it was the American plan that prevailed. But just as the White Plan had sought to subsume the Keynes Plan in an ostensible compromise, so Eisenhower's broad-front strategy sought to embrace Montgomery's plan for a concentrated thrust.

It was always Ike's way to soften the blow and to split the difference. He knew that the British press, touchy over any idea that Montgomery was being slighted, needed careful handling. The *Daily Mail* on 1 September was happy to print Eisenhower's tribute to 'one of the greatest soldiers of this or any other war', coupled with the announcement that Montgomery had been promoted to the rank of Field Marshal (though when Patton heard all this on the radio, the necessary compliments stuck in his gorge). Issues of command and of strategy were inextricably intertwined. The vehemence of Montgomery's continued advocacy of a north European thrust to the Ruhr took Eisenhower aback when they met on 10 September, proving too much for even his tolerance. 'Steady, Monty!' he had to say. 'You can't speak to me like that. I'm your boss.'[29]

That Eisenhower really was the boss had to be demonstrated. For while Montgomery's northern strategy – MARKET GARDEN as a first instalment – demanded that the US 3rd Army, the heroes of the Normandy break-out, now sit tight, Patton had simultaneously come up with a rival southern strategy which reversed the roles. 'I hope to go through the Siegfried Line like shit through a goose,' he told a press conference on 7 September, quickly adding: 'That is not quotable.'[30] Constrained nonetheless by Eisenhower's support for MARKET GARDEN, Patton became restive. Third Army's piratical methods, in laying hands on the gasoline they felt unjustly denied, became the stuff of legend, with stories of staff officers posing as 1st Army in order to divert the delivery trucks. The point was that Courtney Hodges' US 1st Army, though reporting to Bradley, was assigned the role of supporting Montgomery in the north.

Patton's connivance in such methods, though blandly denied at the time, was clear enough. Moreover, he plotted with Bradley to slip the leash. The plan was to send out his troops on 'reconnaissance' so as to get them drawn into conflict on the Moselle – at exactly the time that Montgomery was due to attack further north. 'Bradley called to say that Monty wants all the Americans to stop so that he, Monty, can "make a dagger-thrust with the 21st Army Group at the heart of Germany",' Patton fulminated on 17 September. 'Bradley said he thought it would be a "butter-knife thrust." To hell with Monty.'[31]

Not very auspicious circumstances, it might be thought, for a disciplined application of Allied resources to support MARKET GARDEN.

Eisenhower called a conference at Versailles for 22 September in order to determine strategy. Montgomery had been pressing for a month for endorsement of the northern assault. In the midst of the battle to save Arnhem, perhaps his failure to attend the conference in person can be understood. The American generals understood it – as a snub. They were not flattered that the priority of the Ruhr objective was argued instead by Montgomery's more tactful chief of staff, de Guingand. He was pushing at an open door since Eisenhower seemed already persuaded, ready to weigh the military merits of the plan more heavily than its political drawbacks. 'Bradley and I are depressed,' Patton had written on the eve of the conference. 'We would like to go to China and serve under Admiral Nimitz.'[32]

A front of Allied unity was maintained through the Supreme Commander's ingenuity in stretching his broad-front strategy, first this way and then that, with a show of forbearance at which his own staff marvelled. Little dissension got into the press at the time. Butcher, with his responsibility for the Publicity Relations Division (PRD), admittedly concentrated much of his efforts on what appeared in the US forces' own newspaper, *Stars and Stripes*, with its unique ability to reach the front-line troops. A briefing he gave Eisenhower on 24 September, however, suggested that, outside this cocoon, all was not well. 'Ike was shocked to know of the extent of anti-British feeling in American correspondents and was surprised when I reported a somewhat similar feeling in British writers, notably those attached to press camps in Montgomery's sector,' Butcher noted. 'I told him I had discovered, while working with the PRD, that I had lived in an ivory tower with him, and that I was beginning to learn the facts of life.' This was bad enough. It evoked a familiar mordant comment – 'This world and then the fireworks' – that often consoled the Supreme Commander in bearing his lonely burdens. But there was a further twist, more personally wounding. It was now that Eisenhower learned of talk among junior officers in the 3rd Army: 'Ike is the best general the British have.'[33]

If Arnhem proved a failure, it was because MARKET GARDEN illustrated the problems of success. Eisenhower had been persuaded to go ahead with the gamble on the bridges, in order to maintain the pursuit of the Germans while they were unbalanced. But in the process the Allies' own supply lines had been stretched, still bringing in not only food and ammunition but precious oil supplies all the way across France.

The Germans, by contrast, had been forced to shorten their own lines, in spite of Hitler, thereby putting their defences on a better basis. MARKET GARDEN implied a consequent concentration of resources in Montgomery's sector of the front. It was bound to be an unpalatable decision for the American armies, thirsty for victory and gasoline alike. 'Monty does what he pleases and Ike says "yes, sir",' Patton had written in his diary on 15 September.[34]

To succeed, MARKET GARDEN had depended on seizing all three Rhine bridges, first from the air through surprise, then in strength on the ground. Adverse weather fatally hampered the later air drops. Eisenhower, who never shirked responsibility for authorizing the plan, sought no scapegoats, then or later. 'The British 1st Airborne Division, in the van, fought one of the most gallant actions of the war, and its sturdiness materially assisted the two American divisions behind it,' he wrote in his war memoirs.[35] Thus his fellow countrymen's success in holding the Eindhoven and Nijmegen bridges – useful enough in themselves – was not to be contrasted with his allies' failure to retain the final, vital bridge at Arnhem. This was only what he had privately said at the time, reported pungently in Harry Butcher's diary: 'What would be the American reaction if either our 82nd or 101st Airborne had been assigned by Monty to the tough spot given the British airborne?'[36]

The fact was that Monty had failed to deliver the goods. Though in his memoirs he remains MARKET GARDEN's 'unrepentant advocate', he does admit his mistake in not ensuring that the British paratroopers were dropped right on to their target, as the Americans were, taking heavier casualties in the drop so as to achieve the necessary surprise (and also minimize subsequent losses).[37] Moreover, the British ground support seems to have been similarly culpable in its caution. Even Chester Wilmot, the Australian war correspondent who became Monty's redoubtable literary champion, thought so; and he had been there. 'I rather think it is our fault,' one British officer told him. 'We have been slow.'[38] It is tempting to wonder whether Patton might have bludgeoned through if charged with this responsibility.

Perhaps, though, the plan was more fundamentally flawed. To Brooke, whose *protégé* Montgomery had long been, the key point was that the great port of Antwerp, though in British hands since 4 September, was still not operational for supply purposes a month later. 'I feel that Monty's strategy for once is at fault,' Brooke reflected on 5 October, 'instead of carrying out the advance on Arnhem he ought to have made certain of Antwerp in the first place.'[39]

One way or another, Monty's big plan to win the war in 1944 had failed. Perhaps it was already doomed by the end of August, when the British and American armies had divided, pursuing diffferent objectives only nominally reconciled within a broad-front strategy that had the great advantage of keeping all the Allies moderately happy, or at least not immoderately discontented. Certainly hopes of an early victory could not survive the setback at Arnhem in September. If Antwerp still remained to be opened as a major supply port, how could a forty-division assault on the Ruhr be sustained?

By the end of October the writing was on the wall, or at least on the memoranda in Whitehall. Sir Alec Cadogan, back in London after attending the Tolstoy conference, found that the implications of the military stalemate were officially recognized. 'Planners now give earliest date for defeat of Germany as Jan. 31 – latest May 15,' he noted on 30 October. 'All depends on Antwerp – where we're doing fairly well.'[40] There was nothing for it but to settle in for the long haul. Even if it was true that the war was being prolonged because of command issues, so Brooke tried to tell Montgomery when they met on 9 November, this too simply had to be accepted. 'He has got this on the brain as it affects his own personal position, and he cannot put up with not being the sole controller of land operations,' wrote Brooke. 'I agree that the set up is bad but it is not one which can easily be altered, as the Americans now have the preponderating force in France, and naturally consider they should have a major say in the running of the war.'[41]

In Moscow, after Tolstoy, and after more than one false start, Brooke was grateful to have got as far as the airport on 19 October. Stalin was there in person to see off the Prime Minister and his party. They reached Cairo the next day in time for breakfast with Lord Moyne, the British Minister-Resident in the Middle East, and thus responsible for both nominally independent Egypt and Mandate Palestine.

It should be recalled that the British mandate under the League of Nations had stretched from the Egyptian border in the west to the Iraqi border in the east – an area partitioned in 1921 (using a line along the River Jordan, through the Dead Sea and thence to the Red Sea coast). Partition thus created the Arab state of Transjordan, leaving the populated part of Mandate Palestine as the territory between the west bank of the Jordan including Jerusalem (mainly Arab) and the settlements on the Mediterranean seaboard (increasingly Jewish).

Churchill had not travelled well and seemed sour. But a sleep and a bath, as usual, had wonderful restorative powers. And he could look forward to dining with Moyne that night, as he had twelve days previously on the journey out to Moscow. As Walter Guinness, a member of the famous brewing family, Moyne had served as a junior Treasury minister when Churchill became Chancellor of the Exchequer in 1924 and later with him in Baldwin's cabinet. They were old friends who enjoyed each other's company. 'Towards end of dinner,' Brooke observed, 'PM was in great form and produced several gems.'[42] He clearly enjoyed this chance for another stopover, another dinner, another reunion.

Moyne may well have inspired another idea in his friend's always suggestible mind. Churchill knew that the Big Three had to meet again soon. Stalin would not travel (at least not in aeroplanes and not far from the Soviet borders) and Roosevelt could not (at least not until the presidential election was over). But the President was known to have a great fondness for meetings on battleships. Churchill ingeniously put together this fact with a little research on railway timetables, which showed that Stalin could travel on a special train direct from Moscow to Jerusalem, where, he assured Roosevelt on 4 November, 'there are first-class hotels Government houses, etc., and every means can be taken to ensure security.'[43] The warships could lie off Haifa, everyone would be perfectly safe – Lord Moyne could vouch for that – and the Big Three would have their long-heralded meeting in an oasis of peace where the power and prestige of the British Empire still meant something.

It was not to be. A sufficient reason was that Moyne was assassinated in Cairo on 6 November. He had been a moderately well-known and certainly a well-connected figure in British political circles. 'My uncle murdered!' wrote a shocked Chips Channon, whose marriage to Lady Honor Guinness (though now on the rocks) had brought him not only wealth but his safe parliamentary seat at Southend. 'Walter Moyne was an extraordinary man,' he reflected, 'colossally rich, well-meaning, intelligent, scrupulous, yet a viveur, and the only modern Guinness to play a social or political role, being far less detached than most of his family. He collected yachts, fish, monkeys and women.'[44]

This was not what Churchill dwelt on when he came to compose his eulogy. Yet he was plainly moved. 'News of attack on Moyne had, I think, upset P.M.,' Cadogan noted. 'Anyhow he in awful mood.'[45] It was not just that the Jerusalem Big Three was certainly off, nor just personal regard for poor Walter. The assassination had much greater significance, albeit not widely appreciated at the time, and seldom fully recognized later.

Britain was committed to the Balfour Declaration. Arthur James Balfour, the Foreign Secretary (and former Prime Minister) who had framed it in 1917, had been a man of high intellect and deep subtlety, who was known to have published a book in his youth defending philosophic doubt. His eponymous Declaration certainly left a good deal of doubt – philosophic, semantic but above all political – as to its meaning: apparently offering Zionists what they wanted while apparently offering Arabs guarantees that nothing could happen against their wishes. The problem was, of course, that Balfour and Lloyd George wished to propitiate the new force of Zionism while not renouncing the old pledges already given to Arab allies in the region. Hence the joke that Palestine was the twice-promised land.

What British diplomacy under this sort of masterfully ambiguous leadership had achieved in the First World War, American diplomacy largely replicated in the Second World War. Roosevelt's policy on Palestine – whatever it really was – stood directly in this heritage. Faced with a Zionist movement that had committed itself since 1942 to the establishment of 'a Jewish commonwealth' in Palestine, FDR adopted the same formula in his election pledges in 1944, while continuing to ply Arab leaders, notably King Ibn Saud, with private assurances of which Balfour himself would have been proud. It was plainly Roosevelt's intention that, though Britain might still hold the mandate over Palestine, the country's fate should be determined by American power and according to American ideas, rather than along British imperial lines.

This was not at all how leading British Zionists looked at the issue. Their support for the goal of a Jewish national home, or a Jewish commonwealth, or ultimately perhaps a Jewish state, was premised on its compatibility with the finest ideals of the British Empire and Commonwealth as a force for good in the world. That great imperialist Leo Amery had helped draft the Balfour Declaration. Winston Churchill did not see his support for Zionism as leading to the liquidation of the

British Empire but to its perpetuation by new means in the twentieth century.

Churchill's long and friendly association with Dr Chaim Weizmann, the British president of the World Zionist Organization, was conducted on this basis. Weizmann's equally long-serving assistant was no less than Balfour's niece, Mrs Blanche Dugdale, who used her impeccable Tory connections to help permeate the British establishment with Zionist ideas while reporting back privileged information from ministers to Weizmann, as her diary candidly records. What 'Baffy' Dugdale embodied was a traditional British insider strategy of doing good by stealth and by virtue of knowing the right people – such as the Prime Minister, naturally.

Colonel Richard Meinertzhagen, though socially well connected – he was a relative of Beatrice Webb and Sir Stafford Cripps – is less interesting for his influence, which was small, than for his views, which were both expansive and revealing. A former intelligence officer who had in his day served in Palestine and then on Balfour's staff at the Paris peace conference, Meinertzhagen had, by the time he worked for the Mandate authorities in the early 1920s, become a convinced Zionist (unlike his roommate at the Colonial Office, T. E. Lawrence). He was subsequently on good terms with Weizmann, with whose outlook he readily sympathized.

Like his Aunt Beatrice, Meinertzhagen kept a diary: hers full of statist Fabian plans, his redolent of British Zionist dreams. 'The Balfour Declaration is a compromise,' he wrote in April 1944, 'giving with one hand and taking away with the other.' The urgent point now was to make sure that this war brought clarity to the situation – what he sometimes termed 'a final solution of the Jewish problem' – in a way that could not subsequently be undone. The Old Testament was an obvious pointer to where an answer lay. 'The only solution is the gift of Palestine to Jewry,' he argued. 'There would be local trouble for a short time and then peace.' Any slight injustice to the Arabs would be outweighed by this visionary settlement – literally, in the sense of settling the promised land with industrious, progressive Jews in a new form of imperialism. It was simultaneously the right thing to do and the right policy to follow: 'A great injustice will have been righted and the British Commonwealth will gain a corner-stone in the Middle East which nothing can shake and which will rest loyal to British tradition for all time.'[46]

Churchill himself had first exhibited Zionist sympathies nearly forty years previously, championing the Jewish community in his Manchester constituency when he first contested it as Liberal, supporting its fight against immigration restrictions into Britain. In the White Paper that he later sponsored as Lloyd George's Colonial Secretary in 1922, the Balfour Declaration, which committed the British Government to securing a national home for the Jewish people in Palestine, was reaffirmed; but this was in terms that carefully avoided saying 'state' and which precluded 'the imposition of a Jewish nationality upon the inhabitants of Palestine as a whole'.[47] At this time the population of Palestine had been about 90 per cent Arab, predominantly Muslims but including a significant number of Christians. When in 1937, excluded from power, Churchill gave evidence to the Peel Commission on Palestine, he took advantage of his freedom as a backbencher to assert that the British Government had all along envisaged 'a great Jewish State there, numbered by millions, far exceeding the present inhabitants of the country'. This was highly disputable; it was certainly not what the Balfour Declaration had said. 'We never committed ourselves to making Palestine a Jewish State,' as Churchill had to concede under questioning.[48]

The escalating crisis for European Jewry under the Nazis had not created the case for Zionist immigration; it simply reinforced it. And in 1936 the Arab revolt against British rule signalled alarm on the part of Arabs that their community in Palestine would be the one to suffer from a problem not of their making. Traditionalist Arab monarchs, negotiating with Britain about oil as well as immigration, were now paralleled by radical Arab terrorists, deploying the weapons of the street to make their protest against the unreliable British. The Conservative Government of Neville Chamberlain was as guilty of appeasement of the now restive Arabs as it was of the now rampant Nazis, or so it seemed to British Zionists like Churchill and Amery.

There was, admittedly, some difference of emphasis among Zionists. All of them agreed that the effect of immigration into Palestine was to displace some of the existing inhabitants. But for Amery, as he acknowledged in 1938, this was a genuine dilemma in which a lesser evil ought to be chosen. 'There is no real comparison,' he argued, 'between the quite natural resentment of the Arabs at seeing the character of their country changed, though with material advantage to themselves, and the agony of the Jews of Central Europe, for whom there is really no other serious alternative city of refuge.'[49] Weizmann felt much the same. For Churchill, however, the logic of imperialism legitimized the use of immigration to achieve the end of a Jewish state. Thus he could not accept that his scenario for immigration, 'numbered by millions', implied injustice for the Arabs. 'Why,' he asked, 'is there harsh injustice done if people come in and make a livelihood for more, and make the desert into palm groves and orange groves?'[50] In his view, too, British strategic needs would be well served by the establishment of this Zionist idyll.

The Chamberlain Government's 1939 White Paper had been opposed by Churchill (and Amery too). Its crucial proposal was a restriction of Jewish immigration, by certificates, to 75,000 over the next five years. Churchill called it a breach of the Balfour Declaration, meaning that it thwarted his own conception of achieving a Zionist state through a critical shift in the demographic balance. 'What will be the opinion of the United States of America?' he demanded. 'Shall we not lose more – and this is a question to be considered maturely – in the growing support and sympathy of the United States than we shall gain in local administrative convenience, if gain at all indeed we do?'[51]

The point was that Zionist pressure in the United States henceforth focused on immigration. This was obviously understandable given the needs of Jewish refugees, fleeing persecution under the Nazis. But the United States admitted few of them itself. Roosevelt did not choose to affront popular prejudices here; tight controls on American immigration, rationed by quotas, were maintained with little political outcry, even from quarters where it might have been expected. Instead American Zionists made British policy in Palestine the butt of their criticism.

Churchill was in the midst of grappling with Palestine – among other issues, of course – when Moyne was assassinated. Earlier in the year, a proposal to partition Palestine had been discussed, though not agreed, within the Government. This in turn had become entangled in discussions with the Americans about whether Palestine should become subject to international trusteeship – ideas that were to be refined when what became the United Nations Organization was set up – and here too the British Government was split.

Chaim Weizmann, a man of moderation, widely respected as a Zionist spokesman, and one who forthrightly denounced Moyne's assassination, had met the Prime Minister as recently as 4 November. Asked about immigration, Weizmann indicated '100,000 or more Jews a year for some 15 years' as his objective. One and a half million in all, then? Yes, said Weizmann, 'in the beginning'.⁵² The current Palestine population was just over half a million Jews and over twice as many Arabs. But on such arithmetic, it was obviously only a matter of time before there were more Jews than Arabs. There is no indication that Churchill thought any of this alarming. Why should he?

Two days later, as Brooke recorded, there was a difficult chiefs of staff meeting on the morning of 6 November, 'at which we discussed the problems of partition of Palestine for the Jews', and they unanimously decided to try to stall until the war ended. It was later that same day, when Brooke attended a cabinet meeting – 'an exciting one' – that 'the P.M. announced that Lord Moyne had been shot in the neck in Cairo by terrorists!'⁵³

Unnerved, uncertain, unsure as yet whether the shooting had been fatal, the cabinet went from bad to worse. Leo Amery, although often in the past a supporter of Churchill on imperial and Zionist matters, recorded in his diary that he 'had the worst open row with Winston that I have yet had'. As Secretary of State for India he was determined to defend his patch and to support the Viceroy, Field Marshal Wavell, with whom he was currently working on reconstruction policies for India. When Churchill misunderstood this as adversely affecting the sterling balances – debts to India already piled up by British war expenditure – and disparaged Wavell, as he disparaged most Indian reformers, Amery admitted that he 'could not help in the end exploding violently and telling him to stop talking damned nonsense'.

Churchill suggested that Amery should withdraw from the cabinet. Amery stood his ground. 'At the end of the meeting I told Winston that I was sorry if I had used strong language but wished that he would find time to talk to me about these matters and find out how they really stood,' Amery noted sadly. 'It is terrible to think that in nearly five years, apart from incidental talks about appointments etc he has never once discussed either the Indian situation generally or this sterling balance question with me, but has indulged in wild and indeed hardly sane tirades in Cabinet.'⁵⁴

Moyne's death was confirmed and reported in the press on Tuesday, 7 November. This was election day in the United States, with Roosevelt's campaign belatedly making ground for the Democrats. Their hopes of retaining their narrow control of Congress were enhanced by a good finish from the President, not least in adroitly making Fala into a symbolic issue. This helped focus attention on his highly personalized leadership, in contrast to the young challenger, Governor Thomas Dewey of New York, who was in any case thought rather too consensual and simply too eastern by Mid-West isolationists like Colonel McCormick. Those close to Roosevelt – once more including Harry Hopkins, much to Churchill's relief – were already optimistic. Hopkins telegraphed to Churchill's crony Beaverbrook that, should his confident predictions of a triumph come adrift, 'I will underwrite the British National debt and subscribe to the *Chicago Tribune*.'[55]

Election day was the big story on both sides of the Atlantic. In London, it overshadowed the report in *The Times*: 'Lord Moyne Shot'. The headlines in the *New York Times*, in a column well down on the front page, despatched Moyne in its non-sensational style: 'British diplomat is slain in Cairo / Two assassins, not Egyptians, mobbed'. No need for excitement – hardly a last-minute electoral issue, still less top world news.

Roosevelt's victory duly made headlines everywhere on 8 November. Despite the disfranchisement of several million members of the armed forces, Roosevelt had a clear edge over Dewey in votes, an even clearer lead in the electoral college. The *New York Times*, though its support had earlier been uncertain, hailed Roosevelt's re-election 'in a war year as a war President who could promise the country victory in the war and, on the basis of victory, a lasting peace'. It was a point not lost on Arthur Vandenberg, himself spared the need for re-election until 1946 as Senator for Michigan, which he had carried as an isolationist Republican in 1940. Dewey's defeat, honourable as it was, marked the end of a chapter (albeit not of his own politcal career). 'The war was too much for him,' Vandenberg told his Republican ally, John Foster Dulles. 'That's the whole story as I see it.'[56] And it raised the question of whether the Republicans should now move on, shedding the isolationist label that Roosevelt had so successfully hung around their necks, and work with their re-elected President in developing an American international policy that abjured the old-world power politics so typical of their Russian and British allies alike.

In the British papers, too, Roosevelt's re-election was the main news and it was only on 9 November that the Moyne story resurfaced. There were now confessions from the two terrorists. They were Jewish and identified themselves as members of the the the Freedom of Israel Organization. 'The organization in question,' explained *The Times*, 'is the notorious Stern Gang.' Known locally as Lohamei Herut Yisrael, or simply Lehi, it had several hundred members among the Zionist settlers in Palestine – its rival Irgun was bigger – and was openly committed to terrorist methods as the only means of realizing the dream of a Jewish state. It was reported, too, that the entire Jewish press in Palestine condemned the killing; likewise in the *New York Times* the same day, albeit in a small story tucked away on page 4: 'Two Jews admit murder of Moyne.'

Eden confirmed in the House of Commons that the Stern Gang was responsible. On 10 November *The Times* called for the Jewish community to go beyond mere words and actively assist the authorities in taking action against terrorism. 'The Jews have been the principal victims of the Nazi doctrine of the glorification of violence and, as such, have won the eager symapthy of men of good will throughout the world,' its editorial said. 'They would stand to lose all if they seemed to become in the least degree contaminated by the villainies from which they have suffered.'

Nearly everyone could nod wisely and sadly at such sentiments. It was left to the next day's edition of *The Economist*, a long-established but not yet a high-circulation weekly, to strike a more challenging note. It sought to remind people why Moyne might have been seen as a political target. Admittedly, the terrorists had performed 'the greatest disservice to official Zionism, which naturally condemns any deed so wanton and so politically stupid'. But this was not simply because, in striking down a symbolic British office-holder, the Zionists had actually lost a good friend (which is what Churchill had already said in the Commons, the day after the murder). Nor was it just that 'they also created for the British Government a situation in which, for some time to come, any concession to the Zionists will be interpreted as yielding to violence.'[57]

What *The Economist* thought had been overlooked was Moyne's own stance, as revealed in 1942 in a House of Lords speech which had not been forgiven by Zionists. Admittedly, *The Economist* went on to make the incautious comment that such points were too little disseminated through British newspapers because all but one of their Palestine correspondents were Jewish. This was a contention that provoked hot denials from the journalists concerned, who quite reasonably cited the competing pressures for space from war news in the thin British newspapers permitted by paper rationing. But nobody denied that the complexity of the Palestine problem received inadequate attention.

What had Moyne said in 1942? For the speech was indeed cited by the Stern Gang in justifying its action. Moyne had claimed that any proposal 'that Arabs should be subjugated by force to a Jewish régime is inconsistent with the Atlantic Charter, and that ought to be told to America'.[58] This was an interesting line for a former (and future) Conservative minister, especially one who was personally close to the Prime Minister. It was obviously inspired by some pique at Zionist pressure in the United States; and as a debating ploy it nicely turned the rhetoric of the Atlantic Charter back upon those Americans who so tediously kept quoting it.

To Amery, who wrote in 1942 that he pined 'to say what I think about the Atlantic Charter and all the other tripe which is being talked now, exactly like the tripe talked to please President Wilson', it was all a self-inflicted embarrassment. He knew well enough that his fellow Zionist Churchill had even less intention of applying the principles of self-determination in Palestine than he had in India. Amery had had this direct from the Prime Minister himself, only eight days after the Atlantic Charter had been signed. It could hardly be thought, Churchill had explained, 'that the natives of Nigeria or of East Africa could by a majority vote choose the form of government under which they live, or the Arabs by such a vote expel the Jews from Palestine'.[59]

Few Arabs, of course, were claiming any such right; simply that their existing majority in Palestine should not be deliberately undermined by Zionist immigration. Whether the British authorities in Palestine should permit uncontrolled entry to Jews – many of them now likely to be refugees from the Nazis – posed a real dilemma throughout this era.

It was here that responsible British officials like Moyne had given vent to a sense of frustration at the exploitation of 'these most pitiable victims of Nazi abominations' by those bent on furthering their own agenda. 'It is to canalize all the sympathy of the world for the martyrdom of the Jews that the Zionists reject all schemes to resettle these victims else-where,' Moyne had said in June 1942. Indeed he had been ready to turn the anti-Nazi polemic in a different direction: 'If a comparison is to be made with the Nazis it is surely those who wish to force an imported régime upon the Arab population who are guilty of the spirit of aggres-sion and domination.'[60]

Whatever would Moyne's old Zionist friend the Prime Minister make of such comparisons? Churchill paid his formal Commons tribute to Moyne on 17 November. In calling the terrorists' action 'a shameful crime which has shocked the world', he erred on the side of exaggeration; in the United States, barely a dog had barked. But in saying that it had 'affected none more strongly than those like myself who, in the past, have been consistent friends of the Jews and constant architects of their future', he was on surer ground, as fellow members of the House would have appreciated. Hence the real potency of his declaration: 'If our dreams of Zionism are to end in the smoke of assassins' pistols, and our labours for its future to produce only a new set of gangsters worthy of Nazi Germany, many like myself would have to reconsider the position we have maintained so consistently and so long in the past. (Cheers).'[61]

How much difference, then, did Moyne's assassination make? One person who came to think that it had been 'a critical turning point in the entire story' of British policy towards Zionism was Isaiah Berlin.[62] Later a distinguished historian of ideas, Berlin served in the British embassy in Washington during these years: a young but perceptive observer of American opinion, on which he reported to the British Government with a calculated informality which appealed to Churchill. Though now proud to proclaim his British citizenship – especially to American officials baffled as to which country was currently claiming sovereignty over his birthplace, the old Latvian capital of Riga – Berlin, with his Jewish background, was obviously sympathetic to the Zionists whose propaganda activities in Washington he was paid to monitor.

Berlin's own position was delicate. It had become an awkward issue for the British that Zionism was so clearly gaining ground in official Washington in 1943–4: not only previous supporters like Henry Morgenthau in the Treasury, his anti-German sentiments fuelling pro-Zionist even more than pro-British sentiments, but sympathetic recruits in the State Department, notably Edward Stettinius, soon to succeed Cordell Hull as Secretary of State. Hence the sensitivity that had surrounded a leaked story in the summer of 1943, revealing plans for a joint statement by Churchill and Roosevelt on the Middle East, to be issued in the hope of damping down Zionist pressure until the war had been won. The premature leak, especially its publication in the *New York Times,* had scuppered the statement.

Who could have been responsible? Berlin made a great show of retailing his version to the Foreign Office at length, and, in high satirical style, showing that 'the whole story is an almost clinical case of Washington intrigue'. He rounded up the usual suspects, he pointed the finger of suspicion alike at the War Department and at State. He acknowledged that 'the President was a trifle nettled by all this Jewish barrage – after all, what it comes to is the triumph of the Zionist lobby.' It was, he claimed, 'a melancholy thing' that the British Government's efforts had been thwarted in this way. Above all, it was 'an instructive model to those who wish to know how the foreign policy of the United States is sometimes moulded'.[63]

Not the least instructive point, as we now know, is that the leak had come from Isaiah Berlin himself, making sure that Morgenthau was tipped off to beard the President and thereby squash any Middle East statement.[64] That Zionist propaganda went unchecked in wartime Washington was as much Berlin's own doing as that of anyone who featured in his imaginative reports. If this was one token of his own Zionist zeal, another was his subsequent acute distress over Moyne's death, or rather over its side-effects. The news from Cairo had come to Baffy Dugdale as a great shock. As she put it in her diary: 'a dreadful disaster, all the more cruel because it follows on a very satisfactory talk Chaim had with the PM when he lunched with him at Chequers last week.' A couple of days afterwards, she still hopefully recorded what Weizmann had been told in Downing Street, 'that the whole Palestine settlement depended upon the lives of two men – himself and the Prime Minister'.[65] A third life – Moyne's – proved equally fateful, in that his violent death prompted Churchill to withdraw his active support for Zionism, in turn duly exposing the supposed influence of Weizmann as a nullity.

In the United States, of course, Moyne's assassination had barely made the headlines; terrorism seemed simply a fact of life in a bad situation. The incident changed nothing, certainly not the increasing impatience of American Zionists with British excuses. But Churchill evidently meant what he said at Westminster on Friday, 17 November 1944. Of course he could not have foreseen the full consequences for either Zionism or a cause for which he cared even more deeply: the British Empire. It was exactly a thousand days later, on 15 August 1947, that the liquidation of the Empire in India was to take place.

3

Bad to Worse

November–December 1944

'Democracy is no harlot to be picked up in the street by a man with a tommy gun.'

Churchill in the House of Commons, 8 December 1944

The spirit of Quebec was like a fresh country wine: it was exhilarating when drunk in its *pays* of origin but did not travel well and did not keep well. It was difficult to know exactly why – there were so many diverse problems assailing the Allies by the end of 1944, and they all seemed to be interconnected, and to have a cumulatively adverse impact on each other. No sooner did Churchill concentrate his attention on one pressing issue than another popped up, sometimes as a result of previous inattention. 'Very busy all day with civil aviation and Argentine meat,' Jock Colville noted one Sunday in late November, 'while the P.M.'s box is hopelessly overcrowded with more or less urgent papers.'[1] An obvious expedient was simply to leave the papers unread and turn up at cabinet meetings ready to expatiate at large, drawing on rhetorical resources that were just about the only thing not in short supply.

The Prime Minister was a versatile orator, copious too, liable to hold forth as the mood took him. In Washington, DC, it was not his Palestine speech in mid-November that made an impression so much as earlier effusions when he had spoken proprietorially of a region always likely to excite and upset impressionable Americans: the Mediterranean and the Balkans. Henry Morgenthau, ready to balance hatred of the bellicose Germans with indulgence towards the indigent British – an approach apparently endorsed at Octagon – found in mid-November that the President was certainly no longer suffused with what Morgenthau persisted in calling 'the spirit of Quebec'. This was disconcerting. 'These speeches Churchill has been making,' Morgenthau now told Edward

Stettinius, Deputy Secretary of State, 'have ruffled him tremendously.' For this revelation of Churchill's fondness for the royal families of southern Europe – Greek, Italian, Yugoslav – piqued Roosevelt during a sensitive election campaign, with the unfortunate result that he now acted 'as though he had never heard' of the agreements reached at Quebec about the extension of Lend-Lease.[2]

True, Churchill made no secret of his belief in heredity. He himself had been particularly proud to become Chancellor of the Exchequer because his father, Lord Randolph Churchill, had once held the office. He should perhaps have remembered how this sort of thing affronted American democratic sentiments when dealing with men like Roosevelt (whom Churchill first knew as a distant cousin of former President Theodore Roosevelt) or Morgenthau (whom Churchill knew as the son of Henry Morgenthau Senior, American ambassador to Turkey at the time of Gallipoli) or Stettinius (whom Churchill knew as the son of Edward Stettinius Senior, who had been in charge of purchasing American supplies for Britain in the First World War). Churchill had blundered; it began to look as though his weakness for monarchy might threaten his nation's lifeline from the Great Republic before the war was even finished.

'EISENHOWER LAUNCHES HIS KNOCK-OUT BLOW' was the *Daily Mail*'s banner headline on 17 November. He may have launched it, but he did not land it. German resistance had been consistently underestimated during the campaign, notably at Caen and Arnhem against the British; it was the same in the Roer valley and the Saar, now against the Americans. This time Hodges's 1st Army and Patton's 3rd Army bore the brunt. The lesson was reinforced, that the Germans were not yet beaten. It was a real question whether their will to fight on had been strengthened by tougher talk about the kind of victory the Allies would impose: first the insistence on unconditional surrender that Roosevelt had suddenly produced at Casabalanca in January 1943, then the botched proposals in the Morgenthau Plan which had become an electoral issue in the USA. A sensitive Morgenthau was reassured on 17 November by his colleague Stimson at the War Department that the Allied advance had already halted, irrespective of the impact of the eponymous Plan, and that he did not believe that 'the use of the rumor by the Nazi propagandists made any substantial change in the situation whatever'.[3]

Still, the Nazis were plainly not yet defeated. 'It's going to be a *Hell* of a job finishing off the Germans,' Alec Cadogan ruefully acknowledged four days later.[4] The remarkable fact was that the *Wehrmacht* had lost neither its nerve nor its professionalism. Its biggest problem was its commander-in-chief, Hitler, imposing his own erratic whims and hunches upon soldiers who knew better. Not that the Chief of the Imperial General Staff (CIGS) thought things much different at home. On 17 November, Brooke had found at a chiefs of staff meeting that 'Winston was still confused about the system of command in Italy and in the Mediterranean.' It was indeed complicated, with a lot for the Prime Minister to attend to that day: his speech about Lord Moyne and Zionism, unsettling news about Lend-Lease filtering through in despatches from Washington, the troubled situation in Greece, which was continually on his mind. Perhaps the new moves would help, once he understood them. Sir Harold Alexander, even more than Monty the Prime Minister's favourite general, was to be elevated to Supreme Allied Commander in the Mediterranean, which was always close to Churchill's heart as a theatre in which British arms might yet gloriously prevail. Alexander, with his aristocratic graces and his impeccable uniforms, cut a more elegant figure than Monty but did not impress Brooke: 'I cannot imagine that Alex will ever make a Supreme Commander, he has just not got the brains for it.'[5]

This job, even more than Eisenhower's in northern Europe, had a strong political element. Enemy territory would be occupied and allies would be liberated; and whether, after the régime change in 1943 which had replaced Mussolini with a non-fascist government, Italy was the one or the other was itself a conundrum – and one with an American dimension, given the need to court Italian votes in New York and elsewhere. Such puzzles could well be left to the ingenious brain of the Supreme Commander's political adviser, Harold Macmillan, occupying his post as Minister-Resident in the Mediterranean. He got on well with Alexander, whose understated upper-class charm captivated him. He wrote in his memoirs: 'If Montgomery was the Wellington, Alexander was certainly the Marlborough of this war.'[6] John Churchill, first Duke of Marlborough, was a name to conjure with in this Government, as Macmillan well knew, and it is unlikely that he kept this insight to himself during his agreeably relaxed dinners and lunches with the Prime Minister, whose patronage since 1940 had remade Macmillan's career, rescuing him from his outcast status under Chamberlain.

Macmillan had been given a virtually pro-consular role as Minister-Resident. He inhabited it with it a sweep and grandeur, a sense of history and an opportunity for byzantine plotting that suited him better than in any other post he held before becoming Prime Minister himself some twelve years later. Like Churchill in having an American mother, Macmillan relished the sort of inter-Allied politics that went with the job and had his own metaphor for the relationship. 'We are like the Greeks in the later Roman Empire' was how it was retailed to Hugh Dalton. 'They ran it because they were so much cleverer than the Romans, but they never told the Romans this.'[7]

Perhaps Macmillan told rather too many people (for the comment became well known). He now had his own twentieth-century Greeks to worry about. He was well pleased that their exiled government under George Papandreou had, in August, relocated from Cairo to Salerno, south of Naples, and thus near the vast palace of Caserta – bigger than Versailles, Macmillan thought – which was Allied Headquarters. He had a villa nearby, with four British ambassadors more or less responsible to him: not only those accredited to Italy and France but also Yugoslavia and Greece. Having meanwhile helped the Papandreou government to move to Athens, Macmillan flew out of Caserta on 22 November, bound for Paris, en route to London for consultations.

American Thanksgiving, Thursday, 23 November 1944, was celebrated in the Albert Hall, London's largest concert venue, seating thousands. 'Wish people wouldn't think of these things,' wrote Cadogan. 'Poor P.M. there, looking the picture of boredom.'[8] The strain was telling on Churchill, as Leo Amery felt in making an unfavourable comparison with Lloyd George at that day's cabinet: 'Winston neither reads the papers or tries to collect opinions systematically and is a good deal slower on the uptake than Ll.G. with the consequence that when he is not talking himself the thing is rather a bear garden, everybody, himself more particularly, interrupting everyone else, while the whole purpose of the discussion gets lost sight of and confused.'[9]

The following day Brooke found himself even more disenchanted over a worrying lack of grip on events, though this time targeting SHAEF rather than Downing Street. He gave the chiefs of staff his views on 'the very unsatisfactory state of affairs in France, with no one running the land battle'. The further comment in his diary – 'Eisenhower, though supposed to be doing so, is on the golf links at Rheims' – was to cause much offence in the United States when published by Sir Arthur Bryant during the Eisenhower presidency in 1959. Even so, what Bryant omitted was worse: not only a statement that Ike was there, 'detached and by himself with his lady chauffeur', but Brooke's judgement: 'Personally I think he is incapable of running the war even if he tries.'[10]

This is a damning indication, not of Eisenhower's actual capacity, but of the low ebb of confidence in him in the highest British military echelon. Of course the accompanying tittle-tattle was used as the detonator for the heavier charge. The reference was to the attractive British chauffeur attached to SHAEF, Kay Summersby, whom Brooke had recently been surprised to find promoted to the role of hostess at a lunch at Rheims for himself and the Prime Minister. 'We have no secrets from Kay,' Ike liked to say.[11] Maybe not, but whether the two of them had their own secret was naturally a topic on which there was much speculation. Rather against appearances, it seems that there was no sexual relationship; but the conduct of the lonely general, with his often disaffected wife sitting out the war in a Washington hotel, created ripples. In persistently giving Summersby such prominence, Eisenhower provoked questions about his judgement from those who wished to pose such questions anyway.

Brooke, despite having previously urged acquiescence in American control of the campaign, was now sufficiently agitated to support a reappraisal of the command issue. Montgomery flew from Belgium for a meeting on 26 November. The two men agreed on their plan. 'What we want is Bradley as Commander of Land Forces,' Brooke summarized, 'Montgomery, Northern Group of Armies, with Patton's Army in his group – by substituting 3rd Army for 9th Army – and Devers commanding Southern Group.'[12] Not for the first time, Montgomery showed himself in earnest about the appointment of a single land commander by offering to defer to Bradley: a mark of his sincerity but hardly of his judgement since the affable but indecisive Bradley, 'the GIs' general', was so obviously part of the problem that Montgomery specified. What the Field Marshal clearly wanted was for the Patton punch to be delivered within his own northern army group, where it could make a real difference, rather than leave the 3rd Army camping outside a German fortress like Metz, belatedly taken on 25 November.

Two days later Brooke put Montgomery's plan to Churchill. The CIGS failed to make much headway: 'PM evidently beginning to realize that all is not well in France, but incapable of really seeing where the trouble really lies!'[13] Luckily the CIGS was on hand to enlighten the confused old man in a further encounter the next day. 'I said that when we looked the facts in the face this last offensive could only be classified as the first strategic reverse that we had suffered since landing in France,' Brooke told him. 'I said that in my mind two main factors were at fault, i.e. (a) American strategy and (b) American organization.'[14] That certainly put the problem in a nutshell.

Also on 28 November, the argument was developed at an unusual three-hour conference between Eisenhower and Montgomery. News of their meeting – though hardly its true import – was publicized in the press. With the aid of a huge operational map on the wall of the caravan that always served as his tactical headquarters, Montgomery put his now familiar points to Eisenhower: concentration alike of Allied command and Allied assaults. Characteristically, the latter was polite, even in the face of having his subordinate also use the phrase 'strategic reverse', which the Supreme Commander refused to acknowledge; and his politeness was interpreted for the moment as assent. Actually Ike was still Monty's boss and determined to remain so.

There was an agreeable dinner for Government ministers at Downing Street on 29 November. It was the eve not only of the parliamentary session but of Churchill's seventieth birthday: a conjunction that set his mind brooding on his political future. 'He seemed tonight to be fixed in the idea that, as soon as the German war came to an end, it would be necessary to have a dissolution,' the Labour minister Hugh Dalton noted in his diary.[15] But for the moment the spirit of consensus reigned. 'Presently,' Amery recorded, 'Attlee made a nice little speech proposing Winston's health and Winston in an amiable reply dwelling on the virtues of the Coalition proposed that of the Labour and Liberal Parties to which Bevin responded.'[16] Harold Macmillan, having now arrived from his Italian posting, agreed that it was a good speech from Bevin – he and Churchill, though of contrasting social and political origins, were stout companions in more senses than one – and Macmillan's diary catches the mood of nostalgia: 'The whole thing was rather sentimental, like a party of undergraduates at the end of their last university term, pledging themselves to friendship but knowing that their ways will inevitably part.'[17]

Everyone wished the Prime Minister well. Amery had written a birthday tribute for him, published in the *Daily Mail* on 30 November, the actual anniversary. 'Thank you my dear Leo,' Churchill beamed, a red rose in his button-hole. 'I have read every word of it with deep emotion.' Amery did not doubt it, knowing well enough how readily the springs of emotion could be tapped, drily commenting: 'Naturally I did not emphasise the fundamental differences between our two conceptions of Empire and its consequential economics, which have divided us all our lives.'[18] The loyal Colville was worried at the Prime Minister's lack of attention to his duties: 'He has frittered away his time in the last week and has seemed unable or unwilling or too tired to give his attention to complex matters.'[19] The somnolent septuagenarian received an official deputation in bed at 10.30 a.m. on 1 December. 'Excuse me receiving you like this, but this is the morning after the night before,' he apologized. Alec Cadogan, one of the deputation, commented uncensoriously in his diary: 'He must have had a hell of a birthday party!'[20]

Back at work on 2 December, Churchill tried to pick up the threads of the Eisenhower–Montgomery discussions. Their meeting had hardly been a secret. So Churchill had a point in proposing to weigh in himself, despite Brooke's objection that his draft 'was a hopeless one referring to the conversations which Monty has been having with Ike, and which the latter does not even know that Monty has told me about!' But the Prime Minister had at least read the newspapers and knew better. 'It was quite clear,' Brooke noted in his diary, 'that his pride was offended that Monty and Ike had had some lime light turned on them which he had not shared!'[21] Churchill agreed to hold back for the moment. But he obviously realized that, whereas the American Supreme Commander, by virtue of his exalted post, had higher cards in his hand than any other general, including the CIGS, the British Prime Minister might hold some low trumps of his very own – especially if, in the last resort, he could call upon intervention from an even more powerful friend in the White House. The next day he elaborated his thanks for Roosevelt's birthday greetings: 'I cannot tell you how much I value your friendship or how much I hope upon it for the future of the world, should we both be spared.'[22]

It was on Churchill's seventieth birthday, 30 November 1944, that he was finally able to announce the conclusion of the Washington negotiations on Lend-Lease to an indulgent House of Commons. The need to reach a deal was obvious since the supplies were already in the pipeline.

For the British, the need to discuss Stage II – for the period after the end of the European war – had seemed more pressing with every advance on the western front, which is why Lend-Lease had been on the agenda at the Octagon conference in September. But events since then had framed the discussions in a different context, at once less urgent and less benevolent, at least so far as the President was concerned.

On 16 November, Keynes had written a letter to Morgenthau, seeking to break the log-jam. He played – not for the first time or the last – the moral card, appealing to Britain's record in its finest hour. 'We threw good housekeeping to the winds,' he claimed. 'But we saved ourselves, and helped to save the world.' It was an appeal that sought to enlist a sense of solidarity in the common cause, provided it did not actually reproach the Americans for the belatedness of their intervention. So Keynes danced around the point by maintaining 'that financial imprudence may have been a facet of the single-minded devotion without which the war would have been lost. So we beg leave to think that it was worth-while for us, and also for you.'[23]

It was the same song that Churchill had sung at the Octagon conference, a mere two months previously. He and Lord Cherwell had imagined that ongoing Lend-Lease supplies of the order of $6 billion would be made available in the coming year; and the Secretary of the Treasury himself had taken away a similar impression. In London *The Times* of 18 November optimistically reported that agreement was near, covering not only transitional arrangements after victory in Europe but also some resumption of British exports, necessary to escape dependency on American dollars. On the same day, however, closer to the real source in Washington, Morgenthau had his premonition of bad news confirmed from Admiral Leahy, the White House chief of staff: 'the President said he never promised them anything at Quebec, and that we should handle this just the same as any other Lend-Lease operation.'[24] That meant no allowance for a transition to peacetime priorities.

Morgenthau did his best to square the circle, keeping faith with Quebec while keeping his nose clean with the President. Edward Stettinius's diary records an awkward interview at the White House on 21 November, when Morgenthau reported on the Lend-Lease discussions: 'The president could not understand why it was necessary to make any commitment. He indicated he did not wish to receive a written report.' This was vintage FDR: slipping out of an agreement he affected not to remember, making sure that there was no paper trail to embarrass him, asking why things could not simply be let alone. 'Mr Morgenthau pointed out that this would not be following through on the commitment made to the prime minister at Quebec,' Stettinius noted. 'The president indicated that he could straighten that out.' So no commitments; and, just to make sure, no records to suggest any future commitments. As for the expectations of the British, so Roosevelt blandly concluded: 'They must rely on our good will.'[25]

What the British wanted was not an indefinite extension of Lend-Lease but an opportunity to provide for themselves once it ended. And if they were to plan for this transition, they needed to know when it would happen, and how – rather than being left in the dark, dependent on spasms of presidential goodwill. Everyone agreed that Lend-Lease must continue in some form into Stage II, beyond the expected victory in Europe, itself steadily receding. Although Britain would, of course, continue to be at war with Japan, in Europe the key economic issue would be the restoration of an export trade that had deliberately been driven into the ground. Good housekeeping would have entailed financing the balance of payments abroad by maintaining sufficient British exports; instead, the logic of Lend-Lease had required their extinction.

Conversely, if Lend-Lease were to be run down, it was necessary that exports should be cranked up, and the restrictions on doing so relaxed. But allowing the British to fend for themselves in this way was almost as politically fraught as continuing the handouts, or so Roosevelt now thought, worrying that on Capitol Hill politicians were talking about Britain 'getting a jump' in export markets. It was this, Morgenthau concluded after the 21 November meeting, that now made the President reluctant to give Churchill what he wanted: 'the feeling that he could sew the silver lining to the black cloud which has been hanging over England for four years'.[26] The Roosevelt of 1941 had gone out on a limb to succour Churchill the democrat in his hour of need; but the Prime Minister's perceived imperialist recidivism in the Mediterranean had no appeal for the Roosevelt of 1944.

It was left to Stettinius to break the news to Keynes. Neither of them had been at Quebec; there was no sense of personal betrayal; they usually got on well, both priding themselves on their realism, both naturally optimistic. Stettinius records that when he said: 'I didn't think they could get a written agreement', Keynes obligingly answered that they had 'felt all along' that the Americans 'wouldn't be able to give them a firm commitment'. Stettinius offered warm words instead, transparently stopping short of a pledge, a guarantee, a bankable assurance: 'it was our desire that if supplies were available we could and that we would carry through the best way possible. This seemed to satisfy him.'[27]

Roosevelt's tactical manoeuvring was characteristic. He sought to counter any public perception that he was treating Britain too well not only by murmuring to Morgenthau that Lend-Lease must be cut back, but also by loudly talking up its benefit to the USA. The opportunity was the simultaneous publication on 25 November of his own regular Report to Congress on Lend-Lease and a Government White Paper in London. The story was geared towards highlighting Reverse Lend-Lease. 'BRITISH AID TO ALLIES: Mr Roosevelt's Tribute' was *The Times'* headline. 'From the day our first soldiers arrived in 1942,' the President's report told Congress, 'one-third of all the supplies and equipment currently required by United States troops in the British Isles has been provided under reverse Lend-lease.' The report showed that British mutual aid to all countries totalled £1.08 billion, of which the USA received £605 million, while British mutual aid to the USSR totalled £270 million. This was at a time when the pound sterling was worth $4.03, so the value of reverse Lend-Lease to the USA had been about $2.5 billion, with the clock still running. In fact, although the books obviously did not balance in dollar terms, in proportion to the relative size of the two economies, the contributions were closely comparable.

Such perspectives had hardly been common on the other side of the Atlantic. Gallup Poll evidence from 1943 provides instructively contrasting answers to the question: which of the Allies had so far made the biggest contribution towards winning the war? The Russians were named by 50 per cent of the British respondents, putting themselves next at 42 per cent, and the Americans at 3 per cent. In the American sample, 55 per cent said the United States, 32 per cent the Soviet Union and only 9 per cent Great Britain. This is admittedly only a statistical snapshot, taken before D-Day shifted the focus. But it would be naive to think that rooted attitudes were easily changed. 'We are doing virtually all of the fighting in the Pacific and have made virtually all the advances in France,' the *Chicago Tribune* had claimed on 2 August 1944. 'This is an American-made victory and the peace must be an American peace.' And part of any peace, as over 70 per cent of

Americans continued to tell the opinion polls, should be the repayment of Lend-Lease.[28]

The circulation of the President's report in November 1944, much as it cheered the British, was inevitably limited; likewise its impact on American opinion. Nonetheless the facts it presented directly challenged the idea that Lend-Lease was simply an unreciprocated drain on American benevolence. It showed that 31 per cent of all supplies and equipment used by US forces in Europe up to 30 June 1944 had been supplied by the British, without payment. The report claimed that it would have taken 1,000 ships to send these supplies across the Atlantic; instead, the shipping space had been used for direct military purposes. The results were exactly in line with the policy's original rationale: that Lend-Lease enabled a more effective prosecution of the war against Hitler, whether by the United States or others; that it brought the invasion of Europe forward by months; and that it gave the Allied armies their striking power, which had now taken them to the borders of Germany. And Reverse Lend-Lease was its obverse: the face that made it unnecessary to launch a thousand ships.

On the same day that the President's report was published, a telegram from Roosevelt had reached Churchill at Chequers, delivered personally by the American ambassador, J. G. Winant. The substance concerned the conference on post-war civil aviation, currently deadlocked in Chicago. Basically, the Americans wanted free trade in the air, with equal access for all to airfields worldwide – most of them actually in the British Empire, which sought to keep control of its hard-won assets. To James Forrestal, still new to his job as US Secretary of the Navy, it had seemed a good example of the the need to 'create something similar to the British system for co-ordinated and focused government action'. He reasoned that the British were being difficult in the Chicago talks at just the moment when 'Morgenthau was conducting negotiations here to give the British many billions of dollars under Lend-Lease, and that I didn't see that we would be doing anything more than acting in the national interest if we used the one negotiation to facilitate the progress of the other'.[29] The President's telegram merely made a connection that seemed obvious in Washington.

Its tone, however, was what struck Jock Colville, on duty at Chequers that weekend. 'It was pure blackmail, threatening that if we did not give way to certain unreasonable American demands, their attitude about

Lease-Lend supplies would change.' The Anglophile ambassador, Gil Winant, seemed embarrassed, and had to be persuaded to accept hospitality on the strength of Churchill's conviction that 'even a declaration of war should not prevent them having a good lunch'.

There was no escaping the fact, at Chequers as in the White House, that all was not well. 'The Americans are also being tough, and even threatening, about a number of other things,' Colville observed, 'and the P.M. is disturbed at having to oppose them over so many issues.'[30] Churchill wrote to Roosevelt after a few days' reflection: 'It is my earnest hope that you will not bring on this air discussion the prospect of our suffering less generous treatment on lend-lease than we had expected from the Quebec discussions.'[31]

Under the circumstances, it was a blessing that the Stage II negotiations managed to avoid breakdown. On Sunday, 26 November, business concluded, Keynes had a farewell appointment at the White House. He told Stettinius, on whom he called afterwards, that 'the president had been most helpful' and clearly they had adroitly avoided any embarrassment in discussing the Lend-Lease agreement (which was to remain under a press embargo for another four days). 'All in all, Lord Keynes seemed quite happy, very cheerful, and feeling his mission here had been a succcess,' wrote Stettinius (rather formally, not yet in the 'Maynard' league, like Harry White), adding that Keynes 'felt London was relatively happy'.[32]

Keynes left Washington the next day for the friendlier climate of Ottawa, to report and to confer. He arrived in the Canadian capital only to find any other topic overwhelmed by the long-feared political crisis over conscription. Mackenzie King had lost his Defence Minister in a vain attempt to avoid sending Canadian-based conscripts to reinforce Crerar's beleaguered 1st Army, faced with its problems in clearing the Scheldt. The first convoy at last entered Antwerp on 28 November. Belatedly implemented, the measure to send 16,000 Canadian conscripts overseas meanwhile cost King not only a ministerial resignation but a worrying loss of support in Quebec and even the threat of mutiny by the conscripts themselves. But at least the crisis offered Keynes an incidental respite, curtailing any financial discussions. Deeply tired, Maynard sailed home with Lydia, his heart not strong enough for any more transatlantic aviation.

Always the optimist, Keynes made the best of the deal that had finally been struck on Lend-Lease; and always preferring long slow journeys to rapid transit, he reported back to the Treasury on shipboard. He purported to believe that at least it showed who Britain's friends were in Washington. His own informal access to Harry White had been important; as a British civil servant (Frank Lee) confirmed: 'that difficult nature unfolds like a flower when Maynard is there, and he is quite different to deal with when under the spell than he is in our normal day to day relations with him.'[33] Keynes himself singled out Morgenthau as the champion of Britain's cause, albeit one unable to deliver all he wished; and Stettinius, representing the State Department, seemed likewise well disposed (which was the more significant since he was about to succeed an ailing Hull as Secretary of State). By comparison, Leo Crowley of the Foreign Economic Administration (FEA), which actually administered Lend-Lease, struck Keynes as inhibited by the prevailing political difficulties – 'Mr Crowley, though quite well disposed in principle, never attained the same level of consciousness of what it was all about, his ear being so close to the ground that he was out of range of persons speaking from an erect position.'[34]

On 30 November, then, the Lend-Lease agreement was finally announced in Washington as well as London. Stettinius, Crowley and Morgenthau reported a programme of $5.6 billion for shipments to Britain in 1945, about half that for 1944. At face value, this appeared not far short of what the British had asked for, and it was reaffirmed that both Lend-Lease and Reverse Lend-Lease would continue 'until the unconditional surrender of both Japan and Germany'.[35] This much was public knowledge. In practice, everything depended on the administration of the scheme, under Crowley and even less charitably disposed colleagues. The conditions were henceforth much more exacting, both on what could be supplied and how it could be used, reflecting sensitivity to loose talk, both in Congress and in the press, about alleged misappropriation of Lend-Lease supplies. The new signals came from the top. As Christmas approached, Roosevelt was more Scrooge than Santa Claus, telling Stettinius that 'the world seemed to think that we had all the money' and that 'it was about time we began to get tough and not be so liberal with our money'.[36]

The British, often taking their cue from Keynes, ignored such signals, and did so at their peril. They were slow to learn, often reluctant to believe, through practical experience, that the flow of Lend-Lease supplies was steadily drying up. Since the new agreement provided for the reductions to begin before the end of the European war, there was now scope for restriction through discretionary action without further top-level discussion. American officials were licensed – and encouraged – to question the exact military uses of munitions requisitioned by the British, and to take a rigorous view of other supplies in case any of these could possibly be substituted for goods that the British might seek to export subsequently.

For the moment, however, there were cheers for Churchill when he announced the deal in the House of Commons on 30 November. Buoyed up by birthday greetings, he was out to enjoy the occasion. True, he went out of his way to mention the 'changes in the programme of supplies which the American Administration feel that it is proper and right for us to have', telling the House that Lend-Lease came under 'an Act which we must remember is for the defence of the United States, and is strictly limited to what is necessary for the most effective prosecution of the war by the United States and its allies'. But he went on to suggest that the settlement had been a good one. 'If men of good will start out from the same premises of agreed fact,' Churchill intoned, 'they do not necessarily find it impossible to reach the same conclusion. (Cheers).'[37] The voice was the voice of Churchill but the analysis was that of Keynes. It was Dalton, as President of the Board of Trade, who had passed Keynes's briefing notes to the Prime Minister the previous evening at Downing Street.

Whether the deal was too harsh on Britain or too soft was obviously a matter of opinion. The American financier Bernard Baruch, whom Churchill regarded as a friend, was privately contemptuous of the new agreements for giving away too much, too easily, and immediately told Morgenthau so in blunt terms. 'Winston Churchill said that he did not accept a portfolio to liquidate the British Empire,' he recalled, and asked for some explanation of what the Treasury was up to – 'or simple Americans like myself will wonder if this action is of such a nature as to tend to liquidate the American standard of living'.[38] Though true believers in the British Empire, like Leo Amery, often feared that Lend-Lease was being used as a lever to wreck it, by demanding the demise of imperial preference as a *quid pro quo*, clearly there was also room for Americans to harbour suspicions that Lend-Lease was instead propping up the Empire at their expense.

*

The President's promotion of Edward Stettinius to become Secretary of State at the end of November showed that (if spared, as Churchill had piously hoped) FDR would continue to call the shots himself. Everyone agreed on that. If the President had desired otherwise, the formidable Democratic politician James F. Byrnes had been eligible, just as he had been eligible to run as Vice-President – eligible, but twice not chosen. 'I said I didn't think Stettinius would be ideal,' Morgenthau had told Eleanor Roosevelt, 'but I thought he was the best man I could think of from the President's standpoint as the President likes to be his own Secretary of State, and that what he wanted was merely a good clerk.'[39] Stettinius himself had no illusions on this score, recording in his diary that the President had mentioned Byrnes to him as a possible alternative, only to voice doubts about whether they could have acted as a team together. 'In other words,' Stettinius chipped in, 'Jimmy might question who was boss.' Roosevelt replied: 'That's exactly it.'[40]

The rather patronizing view that Stettinius would do nicely was initially shared by the British. *The Times* thought his record on Lend-Lease a good omen. Isaiah Berlin, from his vantage-point in the Washington embassy, drafted a reassuring despatch about the new man: 'young, jovial, energetic, the exemplar of glad-handing, back-slapping, vigorous American executive, he provides the politically much needed contrast with both the "tired old men" and the "Europeanized" diplomats so abhorrent to American people.'[41] Stettinius was above all well-connected, not least with Republican business leaders, whose support for a bipartisan international policy was vital.

Within days the new Secretary of State had a major foreign affairs crisis on his hands. It was not, as might have been expected, about Poland. True, the Polish situation was slipping out of control – out of the control of the increasingly marginalized London Poles anyway, now divided between Mikolajczyk's supporters and a more intransigent faction. It all seemed rather boring to the British Foreign Office. 'Not much news,' Cadogan wrote in his diary on 26 November. 'Mikolajczyk's resignation seems to have been accepted, which wd. be the end of these silly Poles.'[42] Not quite the end – Churchill refused to withdraw recognition – but, as he might have put it himself, perhaps it was the beginning of the end.

The new crisis was not about Poland but about Italy. As Churchill had confided to Stalin – 'off the record' – at the Tolstoy conference, he did not think much of the Italians 'but they had a good many votes in New York State'.[43] The trouble now arose because the British had sought to obstruct the appointment of Count Sforza to a major post in the Italian government. Sforza was a man with obvious political ambitions, influential support among Italian-American voters, and a known antipathy to restoring the King: none of them factors which disposed Churchill favourably. His intervention against Sforza became public knowledge while Macmillan was away from Caserta, on his visit to England, and it did so at virtually the same moment that Stettinius took office. 'Really the P.M. should *not* have interfered so heavy-handedly about Sforza,' Macmillan commented in his diary on 28 November.[44] What looked slightly clumsy in London looked decidedly sinister in Washington. A few days later, Berlin wearily told the Foreign Office: 'the blocking of Sforza allegedly because of his opposition to the House of Savoy which is most unpopular here will merely strengthen our bad name . . .'[45] Well, nothing new about that; perhaps it would all blow over.

Monday, 4 December, was a busy day for the Prime Minister, and a long one, momentous too. First he had the ongoing command crisis in the Allied armies to worry about. He was resolved on appropriate action, if only he could think what it was. He promised Brooke that morning not to fire off any messages pending a further Eisenhower–Montgomery meeting three days hence. Brooke settled for this but was exasperated at Churchill's further comment: 'he did not want anybody between Ike and the Army Groups as Ike was a good fellow who was amenable and whom he could influence! Bradley on the other hand was a sour faced blighter and might not listen to what he said.' To the CIGS, who could also be a sour-faced blighter who refused to heed his master's wilder utterances, this was not the point – 'I could see little use in having an amenable Supreme Commander if he was totally unfit to win the war for him!'[46]

Later the same day, Sforza's name inevitably came up when Macmillan had lunch with Churchill at Downing Street. 'It was a terrible party and P.M. got very cross and bored,' Macmillan recorded. For him the real Italian connection was that of administering and provisioning occupied territory, and its impact upon the shipping position. Why had supply problems become so desperate at this point? 'Partly,' Macmillan noted, 'because the German war was expected to end by 31 December 1944, and partly because of the Germans holding on so long to the French ports, and partly by the large liberated areas to be looked after without the war ending.' Not only had all the calculations gone wrong in Europe: the Americans wanted to divert more shipping to the Pacific war, and the more successfully they waged it, getting nearer and nearer Japan, with longer and longer supply lines, the more ships would be needed. 'It is a vicious circle.'[47]

It was not, however, the supply problem which dominated the Prime Minister's attention over his disagreeable lunch; nor was it his long discussion with Brooke of American generalship, from which he had just emerged; still less was it the recital of Gallic woes that the former French prime minister Paul-Boncour insisted on spitting out (literally) over the table. 'The P.M found him tedious too and spoke in French more execrable than usual, frequently calling upon me to translate,' wrote Colville, also at table, 'and more frequently still turning to address Harold Macmillan in English, which Paul-Boncour cannot understand, about the iniquities of the Communists in Greece and of Sforza in Italy.'

From Churchill's perspective, it was Greece that remained the cockpit of southern Europe, just as it had been when he sat long hours at Stalin's table in October. Now the left-wing guerrillas (EAM) were seeking to translate their wartime resistance into political capital through demonstrations by their political arm (ELAS). Colville observed: 'The P.M. becomes more and more vehement in his denunciation of Communism, and in particular of ELAS and EAM in Greece, so that before lunch Mrs C. had to send him a note begging him to restrain his comments.'[48] True enough, Clementine Churchill wanted her husband to be sure of his facts before denouncing the Greek Communists as not only subversives but cowards too – it seemed implausible in view of their resistance record.

The Prime Minister determined to take direct control himself. It was a story he later enjoyed telling in *Triumph and Tragedy*. He did not reveal whether he had a sleep after his long lunch but this was so much his usual practice that it can be assumed. Refreshed, he stayed up late at Downing Street, closeted with Eden, his Foreign Secretary, who actually favoured a compromise solution under a regency rather than restoration of the King. But they both agreed on a tough line against direct action by the Communists. It was now 2 a.m. and Eden, with no siesta to sustain him, was drooping. 'If you like to go to bed, leave it to me,' said Churchill, just getting into his stride.

The old man's mind went back to the 1880s. At that time, with a Tory government in office, a hot issue had been the Irish administration of 'Bloody Balfour'. One notorious telegram of his had read: 'Don't hesitate to shoot' – which became anathema to British Liberals. By 3 a.m. Churchill had his own form of words for General Sir Ronald Scobie, the British commander in Greece: 'Do not however hesitate to act as if you were in a conquered city where a local rebellion is in progress.' By 4 a.m. the telegram was ready to be sent. Churchill went to bed ruminating on his historic action – ' "Don't hesitate to shoot" hung in my mind as a prompter from those far-off days.'[49]

In *Triumph and Tragedy*, the effect of this account is to overlap three time-periods, almost like a postmodernist novel. Churchill rediscovers an atavistic Tory hero from the days of his youth; the wartime Prime Minister is throwing Britain's (diminished) weight around in settling the affairs of faraway kingdoms; and the author is writing his memoirs during the cold war, with an eye to American approval of his prescience in countering the rising menace of Communism. Both at the time and later, he felt very pleased with himself.

Not everyone agreed. Even the faithful Colville, who had naturally had to stay up too, noted that 'these late hours do not improve the quality of his work.'[50] As private secretary, he thought he had done his own job satisfactorily before eventually getting to bed, in sending off the telegram to the Allied Headquarters at Caserta, where Alexander was Scobie's commander. This was not, however, an Allied operation, far from it; it was a very British show in Greece; the telegram should have been marked 'Guard' so that it would not be shown to the Americans (or Romans, as Macmillan might have put it). But a weary Colville had slipped up; the Americans at Caserta saw what Churchill had written and immediately knew what to do with such an explosive document – don't hesitate to shoot it off to Washington, DC.

Up betimes, after a short night's sleep, the Prime Minister little knew the extent of his difficulties, self-inflicted or not. He had to face the House of Commons that morning. 'The news from Athens is very bad, and something like civil war has broken out,' Harold Nicolson wrote on 5 December; and as an MP who supported the Government line he was well aware that there was also a battle for support at home, fuelled by BBC reports that he thought likely to recruit sympathy for the EAM.[51] Churchill's parliamentary statement that British arms were only being used to ensure that the Greeks had a free choice of government was challenged by Aneurin Bevan and the Labour left. To Brooke, as CIGS, Greece was a distraction, requiring reinforcements that the British did not have, as he now sought to make clear. The Prime Minister kept him waiting for half an hour 'as he was in the House and having a bad time', evidently not much cheered by the implication that at least Bloody Balfour had had enough troops to do the business. 'I found him rather rattled about situation,' Brooke concluded.[52]

Then the situation suddenly got much, much worse. 'Returned to the Annexe,' Colville noted, 'to find that the State Department in the U.S. had published a statement which could be interpreted as nothing but an attack on our Greek and Italian policies. Angry telegram from the P.M. to the President.'[53] What Stettinius had authorized was a statement upholding Italy's right to form a democratic government without influence from outside and extending this pious hope to unspecified territories liberated by the Allies. State Department spin helped the media to report this as a reference to British intervention in Greece. Churchill's telegram of reprimand actually needed another day's gestation before it was ready for despatch to Washington. That evening the Prime Minister first had to go through with one of his periodic meetings with all ministers who were not members of the small war cabinet.

It is a measure of Churchill's fortitude that he carried off the meeting so well, besieged with his mounting crises. To Macmillan, who had sat through Churchill's table-talk already that week, it may have seemed simply like 'a monologue by P.M. on number of subjects'.[54] But to Dalton, a senior Labour minister often disappointed at his lack of access to No. 10, the evening was a treat: 'The P.M. invites us to put questions on anything we like and launches forth into long, discursive and well-phrased replies.' Churchill's *tour d'horizon* was sombre but not despondent. Greece, yes, inevitably top of the agenda that day. 'As soon as possible they shall vote freely on their future Government – monarchy or republic etc. – meanwhile we have kept the King over here and our troops must take steps to keep order.' Belgium and Italy much the same. Then there was Yugoslavia – 'Tito is a Soviet Agent' – which ought to be watched, and Poland too: 'a very tragic picture'. No, the war was not going too well, with a frank need to acknowledge disappointment in the west. 'The American High Command had made a mistake in trying to attack along too long a front,' Churchill said (just like Monty). 'They should have tried battering ram tactics at some selected point.' At this rate, no victory in Europe till June 1945.[55] The subtext is perhaps best captured by Churchill's private motto: 'KBO – keep buggering on'.

What a moment for Stettinius to break ranks! His statement had in fact been brewing for a long time, since there was nothing new about the Americans' discontent with Churchill's stance in southern Europe and the Balkans. They saw too much British politicking, too much sympathy for discredited monarchs, too much hankering after great-power games. Their patience had run out. Hence Italy for the Italians, Sforza and all, was the force of Stettinius's statement, telling 'both the British and Italian governments that we expected the Italians to work out their problems of government along democratic lines without influence from outside'. It was added that the United States would apply this policy 'in an even more pronounced degree' in those countries liberated by its allies. If Stettinius did not mean this to apply to the British in Greece, he was inept in conveying his intention. On 6 December 1944 Churchill cabled Roosevelt. Here was 'the most violent outburst of rage in all of their historic correspondence', as it patently seemed to Robert Sherwood, at the receiving end with Harry Hopkins in the White House.[56]

In fact there were four telegrams that day: Stalin, de Gaulle, anti-submarine warfare, all needed discussion, as did the war situation as a whole; but the rage was reserved for Stettinius. Churchill did not mask his feelings of betrayal. Cordell Hull might have been a sour-faced blighter at times, when his free-trade principles embittered him against the British Empire; but this new man was supposed to be a lapdog, almost in the Fala class. 'I do not remember anything that the State Department has ever said about Russia or about any other Allied state comparable to this document with which Mr Stettinius has inaugurated his assumption of office,' Churchill wrote, with icy disdain. There was bound to be a parliamentary debate, he warned Roosevelt, 'and I hope you will realise that I must have all liberty in this matter.' He confessed himself 'much astonished at the acerbity of the State Department's communiqué to the public'. Above all, he reminded the President 'that on every single occasion in the course of this war I have loyally tried to support any statements to which you were personally committed' and said that he was 'much hurt' at this attempt 'to administer a public rebuke'.[57]

It was thus a day of telegrams and anger in Downing Street. A separate message, unsullied by this sort of unprecedented language, gave Churchill's gloomy appraisal of the war. This brought his mind back from Greece to the Rhine and to the argument about command which he knew Montgomery and Eisenhower would shortly be continuing. Fine tactical victories had certainly been achieved, he told Roosevelt, but 'the fact remains that we have definitely failed to achieve the strategic object which we gave to our armies five weeks ago.' The Riviera landings (which he had not himself favoured) might have helped on the French front, but only by weakening that in Italy and ensuring that Churchill's 'ideas about a really weighty blow across the Adriatic' would come to nothing. This latter point was hardly likely to impress Roosevelt, who had never encouraged his ally's armpit-stabbing Balkan ambitions. Churchill also said that it would inhibit action in Burma, where a forgotten army (or so it felt) was holding off the Japanese: again an issue with imperial overtones that were unlikely to stir Roosevelt.

The real point was what to do next. Churchill listed various discouraging probabilities, in both Asia and Europe, the most immediate being 'a considerable delay in reaching and still more in forcing the Rhine on the shortest road to Berlin'. This contrasted with 'the rosy expectations of our peoples' and needed urgent attention. Failing an early meeting of the Big Three, or an Anglo-American summit on Quebec lines, Churchill asked for a visit from the American chiefs of staff, to confer with Eisenhower.[58]

Roosevelt remained entirely unmoved by these volleys of rhetoric from the Downing Street bunker. He offered no apology, suggested no change of strategy, agreed to no high-level meetings. The prospect of a Big Three summit was put off into the New Year.

Meanwhile the outlook remained bleak as pressure mounted. 'The Greek news is very bad, and so is the Italian,' Macmillan wrote on 7 December, aware that 'in both cases we have drifted apart from our American ally and a great part of British opinion is disturbed and hostile.' He took the opportunity of lunch with the editor of *The Times*, Robin Barrington-Ward, who was emerging as one of the Government's leading critics, to offer his own reproof; and personally remained confident that in Italy at least 'we can shame the Americans into co-operating with us.'[59] His own view was that Churchill and Eden should play down 'the rather silly business that we would not have Sforza as Foreign

Minister', as his friend Amery recorded after they had had a leisurely gossip. Amery, responsible for India, with its own problems in which he could rarely interest the Prime Minister these days, affected lofty detachment: 'All this stage of the war reminds me of the chapters in Thucydides in which he describes the effect of "stasis" in the later stages of the Peloponnesian War.'[60]

'The chief topic is still the Greek crisis,' Colville wrote on 7 December, meaning the current one of 1944. It excited such attention, he thought, because ELAS had the public image of 'a heroic left-wing resistance movement'.[61] It was in this context that Churchill faced – and faced down – his critics through a Commons motion of confidence the following day, with a speech and a demeanour that is worth further examination.

The Government won its vote with only 30 MPs against, though many Labour abstentions. To Cadogan, the loyal Foreign Office man, it was simply an opportunity for 'poisonous mischief-makers' to sound off. That they should do so in the left-wing weekly the *New Statesman* was predictable but 'the swill dished up' in *The Times*, the newspaper of choice of the British establishment, was another matter: 'Barrington-Ward is not capable of running a mussel stall.'[62]

It was a mistake, however, to dismiss the unease over Greece as simply the product of tendentious journalism, still less of left-wing partisanship. The doubts that the critics were voicing in Britain, after all, were shared by a far larger number of Americans, from their President down. They suspected Churchill's motives partly because of his own truculent stance and his own reactionary utterances. Even Colville recorded, in the aftermath of the debate, 'the belief, now current, that we support the monarchies of Europe as matter of principle – whatever the will of the people'.[63] More bizarre, in the smoking-room of the House of Commons, where Churchill was receiving compliments after the debate, he showed what a curious figure he could sometimes cut. Since Harold Nicolson, in his own speech, had mocked Sforza, the Prime Minister insisted on acting out a charade (with Nicolson conscripted into the part of the Count) to demonstrate the body language of their encounter on a recent visit to Naples. 'Winston drew himself up with an expression of extreme disgust and gave me a hand like the fin of a dead penguin,' Nicolson recorded. 'I do not know how my colleagues in the smoking-room interpreted this strange scene.'[64]

It is surely significant that experienced MPs from Churchill's own side of the House had their doubts about the manner of his speech. To Macmillan it was 'a superb Parliamentary performance and its courage magnificent. It was not, however, a very profound speech – that is, I think it oversimplified the problem.'[65] To Nicolson, likewise, Churchill seemed 'to be in rather higher spirits than the occasion warranted. I don't think he quite caught the mood of the House, which at its best was one of distressed perplexity, and at its worse one of sheer red fury.'[66] And to Amery it was 'a very able speech which, however, contained two psychological mistakes from the point of view of its effect on Labour Members opposite'. Not only was there 'an occasional note of flippancy in dealing with this subject on which there is very deep feeling', but it was misjudged in not providing the substantiating detail. In all these repects, Eden's speech, winding up the debate, was widely thought much better and, so Amery judged, 'undoubtedly made it easier for most of the Labour Ministers to vote'.[67]

In short, Churchill surely needed a liberal rather than a conservative apologia for his Greek policy. He needed it in the House, as his supporters were uneasily aware and as Dalton, widely tipped to become Foreign Secretary in any future Labour administration, also perceived. So the fact that the old matador 'rather trails his coat and gives the impression of enjoying the whole thing too much' recruited no support from tender-minded sceptics, 'unduly sensitive to manner, as against substance'; whereas Eden 'makes a much better impression on many than did the P.M. and shows more sympathy and understanding'. Yet Dalton thought 'the P.M.'s general argument is irresistible. It would be wrong for us to hand over Greece to a clash of private armies.' Talking to Sir Stafford Cripps, a Labour minister with a far more left-wing track record than his own, Dalton agreed with him that 'we have, as so often in our foreign policy, done the right thing in the wrong way.'[68]

This may be the reason why Churchill's speech reads better in hindsight, re-edited as a tocsin against totalitarianism, than it went down at the time, tainted with rather too much tawdry majesty. He proudly reprinted pages of it in *Triumph and Tragedy*, spiced with one-liners – 'Democracy is no harlot to be picked up in the street by a man with a tommy gun' – to stud his principled defence of self-determination and his denunciation of terrorist methods.

The speech is notable too for striking another note. This is the cry from the heart by a beleaguered Prime Minister who has discovered the world to be a particularly ungrateful place that week: a national leader finding as little sympathy from liberated territories as from the allies whose beneficence he has always saluted. There is no reason to doubt Sherwood's judgement that 'relations between the White House and Downing Street were more strained than they had ever been before'. At this moment, the great prophet of the English-speaking peoples found himself without honour in his mother's country. In the House, he publicly let the mask slip, hinting that friendship with the United States seemed to be a one-way street. 'Poor old England!' Churchill lamented. '(Perhaps I ought to say "Poor old Britain!") We have to assume the burden of the most thankless tasks, and in undertaking them to be scoffed at, criticised, and opposed from every quarter; but at least we know where we are making for, know the end of the road, know what is our objective.'[69]

If only the long-suffering British had had other allies: more pliant allies, more biddable allies, more humble allies. But not, of course, allies in such humble material circumstances as to render them unable to pay for much of the war through Lend-Lease or to provide most of the manpower for the armed forces. Such allies were not available in December 1944. Churchill knew this. The British and the Americans were stuck with each other as partners – a junior partner and a senior partner respectively.

'How do you feel about the Americans?' was a question that Mass-Observation had been asking since 1941. Though generally known for its in-depth surveys of British public opinion, recording people's responses in their own words, Mass-Observation also used opinion polling to track such questions as this over time. In 1944, 45 per cent of respondents said that their feelings about the Americans were favourable, much the same figure as in 1941 when the USA was lauded for its unsordidness over Lend-Lease and in 1942 when it had fully entered the war as Britain's ally.

But most British people at this time had never actually met an American. Why the approval rating dropped to 34 per cent in 1943 is an awkward question since this obviously coincides with the influx into Britain of American forces, whose numbers reached a total of three-quarters of a million by the end of the year. Yet these numbers doubled by the eve of D-Day in 1944, while favourable views of the Americans rebounded to previous levels. Since 'boastfulness' was cited as the main reason for dislike, perhaps in 1944 it was felt that the Americans had more to boast about by then.

Whereas about half the Britons polled had a favourable view of his countrymen, their President himself ran way ahead of such ratings. No fewer than 85 per cent of those polled held a favourable view of Roosevelt in 1943 and still 76 per cent the following year.[70] These were levels as high as those for Churchill himself. The President was undoubtedly seen as Britain's best friend and his own stereotyping of his political opponents in the USA as isolationists, whom it was his mission to thwart, simply reinforced his own high standing in British eyes. As one respondent summed up this interpretation of history: 'Roosevelt worked up American feeling to come into the war deliberately to fight Fascism.'[71]

The British newspapers maintained a discreet non-partisanship during the 1944 presidential election campaign. Once the results had become clear on 8 November, however, Roosevelt's re-election was openly welcomed across the spectrum: not only in the Liberal *News Chronicle* and the Labour *Daily Herald*, but also in Barrington-Ward's *Times*, which congratulated 'a tried and trusty friend and a great leader and campaigner in the cause of the United Nations'. Significantly, this was echoed also in the Conservative press. Lord Beaverbrook's *Daily Express*, crusading as ever for imperial preference, was nonetheless pro-Roosevelt; so was the solidly respectable *Daily Telegraph*, which certainly would not have supported a British New Deal; and even the *Daily Mail* ('For King and Empire') was also for FDR.

Roosevelt's high prestige in Britain thus stoked up correspondingly high expectations about his supposedly pro-British sympathies. Moreover, it was Roosevelt who promised the new diplomacy and the principles of what was to become the United Nations Organization, which had been hammered out in the international conference at Dumbarton Oaks, concluding at virtually the same time as the Octagon meeting in September 1944. It was Churchill who embodied in his own person the language and perspective of the old diplomacy of power politics, much derided by the centre and left in British politics. In the short term, at least, if he and Roosevelt differed, it was not axiomatic that Britons would simply support their own leader on nationalistic grounds.

Roosevelt and Churchill had both become emblematic figures. It was reported that in the streets of Athens the rebels raised the cry: 'Long

Live Roosevelt!'[72] That the Americans should remain at arm's length from the British intervention in Greece was one thing. They had not been implicated in the 'naughty document' passed across the table at the Tolstoy conference, ceding Britain 90 per cent influence in Greece; and they had long made it clear that they wanted no involvement in any of Churchill's Balkan strategies, which diverted resources like LSTs (landing ship tanks) which the US Navy naturally considered more urgently needed in the Pacific. It came as no surprise to the CIGS that the commander-in-chief of the US Fleet had acted with alacrity to just this effect. 'As I predicted the Americans in the shape of [Admiral] King turned sour about Greece, and ordered their LSTs not to be used for ferrying troops to Greece!' Brooke noted on 11 December. 'However, Harry Hopkins put the matter right by reversing King's order.'[73]

This was true, in effect if not in military protocol. Hopkins, acting as intermediary between an aloof President and an angry Prime Minister, was trying to prevent an open breach. His feeling was that 'while we should keep our troops out of Greece, and let the British do the policing, withdrawing the LSTs was like walking out on a member of your family who is in trouble.' But Hopkins had to advise the British ambassador, Lord Halifax, that further telegrams from Churchill to Roosevelt would not be welcome at this point: 'I told him that public opinion about the whole Greek business in this country was very bad and that we felt the British Government had messed the whole thing up pretty thoroughly.'[74]

There was now a palpable sense that the Americans were fighting a different war from the British, and fighting it in a different way. Germany First remained the agreed policy; the Pacific war would have to wait until victory over Germany. But the way that the European war was concluded was also important. In particular, it was important to the Americans that it should be concluded according to their ideas and not those of the British. The Allied generals were bound to be caught up in the politics of war which so largely determined their strategic priorities.

At their meeting at Maastricht on 7 December, Eisenhower had needed to impose his authority on Montgomery and Bradley. As ever, he sought to craft a compromise on strategy that would satisfy everyone: both a northern assault and a southern assault. But this time it was Bradley who got his way, slightly unexpectedly, by vetoing any idea of his 12th Army group (comprising the 1st, 3rd and 9th US Armies) being removed from his sole command. If that were to happen, he had privately

threatened that Eisenhower would have to replace him. The consequences of such a loss were unthinkable for Eisenhower, who would
have faced not only a breach with an old friend, in whom he still felt
confidence, but a political storm in the United States if it seemed that
Monty and the British were running the war. The Supreme Commander,
accompanied by his personally loyal British deputy, Air Chief Marshal
Tedder, moved swiftly to by-pass Brooke and plead their case with
Churchill himself, face to face in London.

Eisenhower must have realized that any further appeal by Churchill
to Washington was now effectively stymied by the increasingly frosty
relations between the Allies. As reports that week from the Washington
embassy made clear, 'a desire for a brand new 100 per cent American
foreign policy, not tied to Britain's apron strings' was widespread: 'Any
assertion of an independent, emphatically American line, is therefore
exceptionally well received here.'[75] Stettinius's action had thus made
Bradley's job safe – and made Brooke's practically impossible.

It certainly felt hopeless to the CIGS himself on 12 December. 'I have
just completed one of those days which should have been one of the key
stones of the final days of the war and has turned out as utterly futile,'
he wrote with a degree of exasperation unusual even by his formidable
standards. A glance at the *Daily Mail*, might have warned him about
Downing Street's priorities that morning:

ALEXANDER RUSHED TO GREECE

Churchill: 'Deal With the Situation and Report'

11th HOUR MOVE SENDS MACMILLAN TOO

Thrilling stuff; just the sort of adventure that Churchill had always
loved. Brooke tried at 10 a.m. to interest the Prime Minister in Ike's
crucial visit but found Churchill breakfasting in bed, absorbed by Alex's
telegrams rather than Monty's account of the Maastricht conference –
'He was quite incapable of concentrating on anything but his breakfast
and the Greek situation!' And the war cabinet that afternoon was as
bad – Greece again, whether to back the King or support Archbishop
Damaskinos as regent – with little time to prepare for the interview with
Eisenhower at 6 p.m. in the map room.

Eisenhower and Tedder had flown over from SHAEF. They met the

British chiefs of staff (Cunningham for the Royal Navy, Portal for the RAF and Brooke himself), all there to support Churchill, who was Minister of Defence as well as Prime Minister. Here was the only chance to adopt Montgomery's principle of concentration on one mighty thrust across the Rhine. Eisenhower, of course, expounded his alternative of paralleling an advance north of the Ardennes mountains, led by Montgomery, with one to the south, led by Bradley. Brooke found himself without the political support he had hoped for from the Prime Minister. 'He *cannot* understand a large strategical concept and must get down to detail!' was Brooke's chiding comment. 'Ike also *quite* incapable of understanding real strategy.' Tedder supported his chief, as expected. Dinner brought no relief for the CIGS, only the revelation that 'Ike now does not hope to cross the Rhine before May!!!'[76]

Eisenhower won hands down. Brooke was left contemplating resignation, feeling that he had lost not only the argument but the confidence of the Prime Minister – who clearly sensed that he had to put things right. Brooke recorded the next day that 'the situation was far better than I thought' after a disarming chat with Churchill: 'He told me that he had had to support Ike last night as he was one American against five of us with only Tedder to support him. And also he was his guest.'[77] This touching conversation shows that, when he chose, Churchill still had Brookie eating out of his hand – and swallowing whole the most fanciful of excuses. Did they really believe that, if this was the great strategic crisis of the campaign against Germany, the options should be determined by conventions of social politeness and hostly etiquette?

The fact is that one American, if as well placed as Eisenhower, could, by the end of 1944, easily see off a challenge from three or four Britons. And this was so even if the opposition fielded a hamstrung Prime Minister: one with nothing in the bank in Washington and his own mind focused on Athens instead. Roosevelt had reason to be content. On 16 December Harry Butcher reported the news that the President had forwarded Eisenhower's nomination to the Senate as a five-star general: 'The man who always cautioned his family not to expect him to be promoted has risen from lieutenant colonel to a five-star general in three years, three months, and sixteen days – six promotions, one about every six months.'[78] Montgomery's promotion to Field Marshal, three months previously, had been a pretty piece of public relations to offset the fact that he was subordinated to the Americans; Ike's five stars more straightforwardly reinforced Monty's subordinate position for the rest of the war.

Churchill had 'won the debate but not the battle of Athens', Macmillan had written on 8 December. And the next day he had welcomed the decision that he himself should accompany Alexander to Athens – thus escaping from an apparently insoluble supply problem that could only be tackled in Washington. 'The political problem in Athens is probably insoluble also,' Macmillan reflected. 'But the second is human and exciting and in a field where I feel what talents I have will be more useful.'[79]

Churchill might well have said the same about himself. The ministerial boxes of papers piled up at Chequers as public interest in the Greek crisis steadily mounted. 'I think the P.M. and the Government are, quite unjustly, losing stock over Greece,' Colville noted on 11 December; but the next day he stumbled upon the booby-trap he had inadvertently set a week previously. He found Churchill 'incensed, not unnaturally, at the discovery that one of his personal telegrams to General Scobie in Athens had been seen and published by the notorious anti-British American columnist, Drew Pearson'.[80] The *Washington Post* had been given a leaked version and had splashed the story. The in-house *post mortem* was soon settled; Colville soon realized that it resulted from his error in sending the unguarded telegram to Scobie; he confessed to Churchill, who took it kindly and said it was his fault for keeping such late hours (without, however, promising to amend his habits). The political damage, however, had been done.

Critics on both sides of the Atlantic could now see for themselves how the ghost of Bloody Balfour had come back to haunt the British Government, with its unregenerate foreign policy. This was a sensitive issue for the Labour Party, which was currently holding its party conference, postponed because of D-Day and the V2 attacks on London. Churchill had long been a bogeyman for many ordinary members of the Labour Party, who remembered (or sometimes misremembered) his long record of hostility to the labour movement and his reputation as a man of the right. The paradox was that the Coalition he had formed in 1940 had made him a hero to many on the anti-fascist left – Dalton talked of 'this Churchill–Labour Government'[81] – at a time when many Conservatives, conversely, still hankered after Neville Chamberlain. On domestic policy, admittedly, there were some strains, especially after the Beveridge

Report of 1942 had made plans for a post-war welfare state into a big issue. But Labour had had few qualms about the Government's foreign policy, mainly because this centred on one simple (but difficult) aim – victory at all costs.

Greece changed all that. The potency of Roosevelt's name over the centre and left in British politics was never more clearly displayed. If he did not approve of what was happening in Athens – and Stettinius was surely his master's voice – what was Churchill up to? It was a question now being asked in the British press, not only the liberal *Manchester Guardian* but *The Times* and *The Economist* – hardly organs of the Communist Party. Leo Amery gathered from his son Julian, who was smuggled into the Labour conference, an impression of the 'thoroughly bourgeois appearance of nine-tenths of the gathering and their quite uncomprehending, good natured sentimental outlook on the affairs of fierce Balkan Parties'.[82] Some of these troubled people began to wonder how long Labour should support a Churchill government.

On 11 December, conference readily agreed to stay in the Coalition Government until the end of the German war, but then to pull out. This was what the leadership – Attlee, Morrison, Bevin, Dalton – wanted to hear. But Dalton was worried about the debate on Greece, scheduled for 13 December, by which time the *Washington Post*'s leak had further inflamed feelings. The flames were checked, first by clever drafting of a resolution that avoided any censure on Government policy and secondly by lining up the block votes of the trade unions behind it – familiar manoeuvres of party management in which Ernest Bevin, Churchill's Minister of Labour but still a pivotal figure with the unions, exerted his normal potent influence.

Moreover, Bevin was induced to speak himself. According to Dalton, 'it was like persuading Tetrazzini to sing.' And sing he did, with unique effect: 'a most powerful and persuasive speech in defence of the Government policy. He has very great power in this Conference.'[83] Here was a street-fighter who had long ago seen off the Communist threat in his own union and was quite unimpressed by fierce Balkan parties. Overweight, ungainly, lacking physical grace as much as he lacked formal education, Bevin nonetheless radiated power and seized intuitively on the crucial issue and how to present it. 'These steps which have been taken in Greece are not the decision of Winston Churchill,' Bevin asseverated above hostile barracking, 'they are the decision of the Cabinet.' On that basis he defended a policy of ensuring that democracy could flourish through free elections, defying interventions from the floor – 'What did Churchill think?' – which sought to polarize the issue quite differently. 'I do not care what Churchill thought,' Bevin shouted back – they must be responsible for honouring their own agreements.[84]

The impact of the Greek issue, though still potentially explosive, became redefined. Churchill detected a more 'kindly tone' in Roosevelt's telegrams and told him of the all-party support he was now receiving: 'Ernest Bevin's speech to the Labour conference won universal respect.'[85] But in Washington, British foreign policy continued to excite unfavourable attention. The Prime Minister's attempt at shaming the Americans into displaying more loyalty was (Berlin suggested) 'appreciated by the State Department but nowhere else'. Churchill's robust line in Greece won some admirers from quarters alert to the Red menace, like the Hearst chain of newspapers, but more general support was inhibited by 'a very general conviction that British Government (and more particularly the Prime Minister) is firmly resolved to effect restoration of King George of Greece as well as of other southern European monarchs which is repugnant to traditional sentiment of all shades of American opinion from most conservatives to most radical'.[86] The leaked telegram obviously encouraged such a reading; and reports of the Labour Party conference similarly suggested that British opinion was divided. Moreover, the really worrying thing was that the anti-British contagion might spread to hitherto friendly supporters of Lend-Lease.

This kind of knock-on effect was promptly demonstrated. On 14 December it fell to the Prime Minister to prepare yet another parliamentary speech, this time on Poland. 'He couldn't think of anything new to say on the subject and so inserted long quotations from his own earlier speeches,' admitted Colville, who was later aggrieved to find that Eden had scuppered a plan to let Churchill off making the speech at all – 'as a speech is unnecessary and the P.M. is very tired.' But the draft was jobbed together regardless in an hour and a half the next morning, just before its delivery. It went well enough ('in spite of his interposing an imaginary clause from the Atlantic Charter'), at least in his private secretary's opinion.[87]

More demanding transatlantic critics, however, were less forgiving. Churchill had stumbled in one section, adulterating the Charter's pure principles over territorial changes with an implication that this could be overridden by mutual agreement; and in the current climate in Washington this was interpreted as a reference to secret agreements over Poland between the great powers. Hopkins, almost as weary as his highly placed but now accident-prone British friend, cabled him the next day: 'Public opinion here is deteriorating rapidly because of Greek situation and your statement in Parliament about the United States and Poland.'[88] Stettinius told Lord Halifax that 'this whole activity in Greece and Poland was causing great resentment in this country.'[89] There was even talk of leaving the European war to the British and the Russians and of turning instead to the Pacific.

The report that Isaiah Berlin drafted in Halifax's name from the British embassy confirmed the point. It suggested that the previous week's indignation had given way to 'a kind of disgruntled and disenchanted cynicism' with Britain and Russia alike. Churchill's speech had thus precipitated both a geographical and an ideological shift, as attention turned from Italy and Greece to Poland: 'it threw the two groups, the Russophiles and the Russophobes, into a kind of schizophrenia – the Russophobes who were pleased by our line on Greece could not stomach the "betrayal" of Poland, while those liberals who look on London Polish Government as a reactionary clique little better than Fascists, could not forget events in Athens.'[90] Since Russophobia and Russophilia both contributed to the current Anglophobia, this did not make consoling reading, though there were a few centrist newspapers, notably the *New York Times*, which contrived to find understanding words for their errant British ally.

In Athens, from 11 December, Macmillan found himself in the front line. Holed up in the British embassy, he made the case for a regency (under the Orthodox Archbishop Damaskinos, regarded as non-aligned). To Churchill, he suggested that this would help the Greek politicians rally support; to the Greek leaders he hinted that it would shore up Churchill's own position, attempting to persuade Papandreou to accept a regent. 'Mr Churchill had carried the day by his prestige,' he argued on 15 December. 'But there was great and growing criticism at home, and this move would help H.M.G. enormously.'[91] Of course this did not mean that the Churchill Government was actually tottering, just flummoxed by the obstinacy with which a compromise solution was resisted, especially by the King.

Virtually nobody in Britain now talked of the collapse of the Coalition until the war in Europe was over. And that was a date that stretched further and further into the future. Monty cheekily sent a reminder that he had long ago bet his friend Ike five pounds that the war would not be over by Christmas 1944; and, as Butcher recorded on 16 December, the Supreme Commander agreed to pay up, but not until Christmas Day dawned – 'after all, Ike said, he still has nine days.'[92] Eisenhower well knew by now that even nine weeks would not suffice and, caught napping by his earlier optimism, played very safe in his official predictions, which had been broken to a special meeting of the British cabinet by the CIGS three days previously. 'The date of May for the crossing of the Rhine had a profound effect on the Cabinet,' Brooke wrote. 'However it has cleared the air well, and the Cabinet now know what to expect, which is a good thing to counter the over optimistic attitude of the newspapers.'[93]

If it was reasonable to expect that the Nazis would sit out the winter behind the Rhine, it was also reasonable to suppose that their final collapse would be deferred until the summer of 1945. Rational expectations, however, are always at the mercy of the unexpected, especially when a degree of irrationality intrudes to upset them.

4

Battles of the Bulge

December 1944–January 1945

'It is team-work that pulls you through dangerous times; it is team-work that wins battles.'

Field Marshal Montgomery, 7 January 1945

'THIS MAN IS MAD,' ran the headline of a front-page story in the *Daily Mail* (17 November 1944). Below were six photographs of a man with a toothbrush moustache and a distinctive slick of black hair, his facial contortions complemented by his wild gesticulations. The accompanying report cited an analysis by Dr Wiliam Brown, Reader in Mental Philosophy at Oxford University, of the text of the proclamation that the Nazis' leader had recently composed for their annual commemoration in Munich of the beer-cellar Putsch. 'But I think he went mad before he could deliver it,' Brown commented. 'It is my view that he is now probably being kept under restraint physically and politically.'

Not quite. The Führer was alive and, though far from well because of chronic stress-related illness, far from restrained. The contention that Hitler was mad, of course, had long been a staple of Allied propaganda. Yet the fact was that, over the years, many of his mad plans had worked. The latest one, hatched on his sickbed in September, aimed to repeat the striking success that the German Panzer divisions had achieved in 1940 in their offensive through the Ardennes, hitherto regarded as an impenetrable mountain barrier separating Germany from Belgium and France. There was a difference. In 1940 the Germans had followed the best routes, which ran south-west, in good spring weather; in 1944 they would have to advance even more speedily, against the grain of the land, moving north-west, under severe winter conditions. It was an amazing gamble that appalled the rational minds of the German general staff, not least because it would scrape together resources badly needed on other fronts and stake everything on one long shot against all odds. 'If it doesn't succceed,' Hitler had admitted, 'I see no other way of bringing the war to a favourable conclusion.'[1]

The Führer had laid out his objectives in mid-September. He wanted to exploit the seasonal bad weather, which would ground Allied planes, to split the Allied forces, and to take Antwerp, 125 miles away. This was the task that faced von Rundstedt, himself capriciously dismissed as commander-in-chief in the west in July, capriciously reinstated since September. After some delays, the date for the offensive was finally fixed for 16 December. Meanwhile Hitler briefed his commanders, stressing Allied disunity: 'if a few really heavy blows were inflicted, it could happen any moment that this artificially sustained common front could suddenly collapse with a huge clap of thunder.'[2]

Initially, the Germans' assault bit deep against fairly token resistance, exploiting surprise. They gained ground on the relatively weakly defended sector of the American front covered by Bradley's 12th US Army Group. Within it, the Americans' strengths were with Simpson's 9th Army to the north and Patton's 3rd Army to the south, with Hodges' 1st Army between them, straddling the path of the German advance. Bradley's own tactical headquarters were at Luxembourg, well to the south, which he maintained because this was convenient for liaison with Patton. If the German advance succeeded in splitting the Allied front, however, Simpson would obviously be left isolated from his commander and his fellow Americans – but adjacent to Montgomery's 21st Army Group, with its British and Canadian forces. And communications with Hodges were also impaired. Whether Bradley was guilty of negligence in his disposition of forces over a 200-mile front – Eisenhower had recently noticed how thinly defended the Ardennes section was – inevitably became an issue; and Bradley's subsequent claim to have taken a calculated risk hardly carried conviction in the absence of any contingency plan.

The bad news reached London on 18 December. 'German offensive not too pleasant,' was the terse comment from Cadogan, brought up to believe that the battle of Waterloo (all too close to the front now) had been won on the playing fields of Eton, naturally his old school.[3] Equally upper-crust but less stiff in the upper lip, Harold Nicolson admitted himself frankly worried about von Rundstedt's 'startling offensive' with its reported gains of as much as twenty miles: 'The optimists say that this is the last suicide fling: the pessimists say that there is nothing to stop him getting to Paris or at least to Liège.'[4] To Brooke's professional if hardly impartial eye, the situation was similarly ambiguous, since the Americans hardly ought to fail, and the opportunity of a counter-attack would then offer itself. 'But I am not certain whether they have the skill required,' he pondered, 'I doubt it.' If the situation were mishandled, he reckoned, 'it may well put the defeat of Germany back for another 6 months.'[5] And when Nicolson asked Eden the next day: 'Is it serious?', the answer was: 'yes, it's bad, very bad indeed.'[6]

The Germans' breakthrough, though quickly falling short of their own ambitions, exposed the weakness of the Allied line. This had been established on an offensive basis, in order to sustain a broad-front strategy. Suddenly thrown onto the defensive, in a way that none of the Allied generals had predicted, their position disclosed an obvious lack of reserves to man defences in depth. Montgomery, now the most alert to the danger, promptly moved troops to defend the bridges on the Meuse to the rear of the fighting. This was not only an essential step in itself but his main strategic contribution to the battle, freeing the Americans to commit their reserves; though it was not a promising sign that it was interpreted at Bradley's headquarters as a British retreat.

The brunt of the battle was necessarily borne by the Americans. It was just as well, at this sensitive moment, that Montgomery did not attend the crucial meeting summoned by Eisenhower for the morning of 19 December at Verdun – a name with both thrilling and chilling echoes of one of the bloodiest defensive actions of the First World War. The American high command were abruptly faced with their responsibilities in an action where the fighting qualities of their own troops would prove decisive.

Luckily the situation brought out the best in both Eisenhower and Patton. The tone was set by the Supreme Commander, fully living up to his responsibility in meeting the challenge. As Butcher recorded the story a few days later, 'Ike opened the conference, saying, "I want only cheerful faces."'[7] One of the most cheerful was that of Patton, quick to appreciate that, although his own planned offensive in the south was now pre-empted, his 3rd Army could take on the heroic task of swinging north to relieve a situation with which Hodges' 1st Army was not coping well, its commander not only isolated but demoralized. Patton electrified the conference with a plan, which he had already devised, to swing three divisions through ninety degrees to reach the strategic crossroads at Bastogne, its American garrison threatened by the developing bulge in the German line.

The Battle of the Bulge, as it soon became known, turned on exploiting the Germans' vulnerability by blunting their knife-edge calculations. Already short of supplies to fuel their motorized push towards the Meuse, they had to be denied the breakthrough that would give them access to Allied stockpiles behind the lines; and in the process their salient had to be contained at its shoulders so that their own advance would make them vulnerable on the flanks. This is how Patton immediately saw it, as his admiring staff told Butcher. 'Fine,' he said. 'We should open up and let 'em get all the way to Paris. Then we'll saw 'em off at the base.'[8] Patton said much the same at the Verdun conference, evoking not only laughter at his combative words but also Eisenhower's sober comment that the *Wehrmacht* must not be allowed past the Meuse. Rhetorical excess aside, this strategy – to concentrate on holding and pinching the flanks, with patience rather than panic – was the essence of Montgomery's response too. It was Bradley who appeared to lack a plan in this crisis.

A crisis it certainly appeared, especially in the reports that Montgomery fired off to London. The CIGS read them with understandable alarm. 'American front penetrated, Germans advancing on Namur with little in front of them, north flank of First American Army in state of flux and disorganisation, etc. etc.,' Brooke noted on 20 December. 'Also suggesting that he should be given command of all forces north of the penetration.' Montgomery's distinctive methods in using his own liaison officers to gather personal intelligence reports gave him an immediate sense that he was more in touch with what was happening than the American generals – certainly more than Bradley, back at his Luxembourg headquarters, or indeed Eisenhower, now with SHAEF at Versailles. And it was little surprise that Montgomery found the lesson about fragmented, remote, ineffectual command of Allied ground forces so obvious. Brooke went into action himself, with an appointment to see the Prime Minister at 3.30 p.m. that afternoon: 'I found him very much the worse for wear having evidently consumed several glasses of brandy at lunch. It was not very easy to ensure that he was absorbing the seriousness of the situation.'[9] Nonetheless, a phone call to Ike was hurriedly arranged in order to plead Monty's case for an emergency change of command.

All this certainly had a familar ring. The British were yet again reopening the command issue, finding in their ally's moment of embarrassment a new opportunity to do so. How this was likely to go down at SHAEF can be estimated from the reaction of Bedell Smith to a similar entreaty in the middle of the previous night from two staff officers. Roused, angered, Beetle had rounded on these disloyal Limeys; but on reflection he had come to appreciate the logic of their suggestion and promptly apologized to them in good SHAEF style. It was crucial that Beetle, as an American, now made the case to Ike for a transfer of command, on a temporary basis, of the 1st and 9th Armies to 21st Army Group on the north flank of the salient. Even Bradley, on his own admission, understood the case for doing this – if only it had been a matter between two American generals. The fact was that he had lost touch with Hodges and Simpson, whose armies Eisenhower put under Montgomery's command on the morning of 20 December, despite telephone protests from his old friend that he could not be responsible to the American people for such an outrage. 'Well, Brad, those are my orders,' said Ike, leaving no one in doubt where the buck stopped.[10] By the time the Prime Minister came on the line that afternoon, the matter had already been settled.

Montgomery was now responsible for containing the northern flank of the bulge. He acted in character in insisting on coherent plans to 'tidy up' the disposition of forces, taking steps to straighten the defensive line, with adequate forces held in reserve; and, as in Normandy, he gave the American generals responsible to him considerable latitude in the implementation of his orders. The change of command was kept secret, if only because Eisenhower did not want to alert the *Wehrmacht*. Such was Bradley's bad grace that he covertly kept in touch with Hodges and Simpson, encouraging their inclination to see some of Montgomery's defensive measures as defeatist and hence to resist orders for tactical withdrawals as un-American. In some cases, American troops successfully held positions that Montgomery would have yielded; in others he was undoubtedly responsible for preventing pointless sacrifice of American lives. Bradley's ostensible point, or excuse, was that the change of command was an insult to his troops. The impact on them of their being anonymously commanded for a month by a British Field Marshal hardly seems to have been one of their major considerations at the time.

They had bigger problems to face. The Battle of the Bulge tested the mettle of the US Army in a brutal struggle from which, in a matter of days, it emerged as a match for the much-vaunted fighting prowess of the *Wehrmacht*. The great symbolic incident came in the defence of Bastogne, where the besieged American garrison under Brigadier Anthony C. McAuliffe was resisting acute pressure and encirclement. Under the news blackout, the story did not get into the newspapers for a fortnight, by which time everyone knew that Patton's relieving column had finally reached Bastogne through the snow on 26 December. Thus it was not until 3 January that the London newspapers could print the full story.

The front page of that morning's *Daily Mail* was to the fore in celebrating McAuliffe's inspiriting defiance, now that he was in a position to be quoted. 'The Germans sent in a major and a captain to demand our surrender,' McAuliffe said, recounting the crisis he had faced on 22 December. 'I read the note they brought and remarked, "Oh nuts".' And it was in this form that the official response was made to the German commander, whose efforts to take the town were duly thwarted. The 'Nuts' story had legs: not only literally true but pithy, gutsy and – by the time it could be told – gloriously justified by events.

The Battle of the Bulge swiftly acquired mythic status for the Americans. As for the British at El Alamein, it was a deliverance; but this time with the narrative speeded up, all in one battle, with a vivid sense of an initial peril from which our boys had then blessedly been released by their own dogged efforts.

Eisenhower later joked to journalists that 'he had not been afraid during the breakthrough until two weeks later, when he read the American newspapers.'[11] To some extent this was a problem that he had made for himself – though it eventually made the good tidings all the more dramatic – because a forty-eight-hour news blackout was imposed. So the early *Daily Mail* reports were bleak: '25-MILE GAP IN ALLIED LINE' on 21 December and two days later: 'RUNDSTEDT'S PANZER THRUST IS 30 MILES FROM SEDAN'. The paper's special correspondent on the western front, Alexander Clifford, commented that 'it is virtually certain that things must get worse before they can get better.' This was a message that the British had got used to hearing. Sensitive to the further implications, Butcher warned Eisenhower the same day that 'London papers were vaguely hinting at Monty's new responsibility and inferring that when the Americans got in trouble, Monty had come to the rescue.'[12] The problem was that they were not only inferring it but implying it.

It was not Monty's way to stop at vague hints to this effect. His whole demeanour spoke his real feelings even when his lip was buttoned. On assuming command on 20 December, he had seized the initiative by driving over at once to the 1st Army headquarters, only an hour away – Bradley had not visited from Luxembourg since the fighting began – for a conference with the American generals. One of his own officers told Chester Wilmot that 'the Field Marshal strode into Hodges's H.Q. like Christ come to cleanse the temple.'[13] It was a delicious moment of triumph for him, ill concealed and storing up further ill-feeling for the future. That it was predictable is shown by the fact that Brooke evidently had a premonition and sent a word of warning the very next day: 'Events and enemy action have forced on Eisenhower the setting up of a more satisfactory system of command. I feel it is most important that you should not even in the slightest degree appear to rub this undoubted fact in to anyone at SHAEF or elsewhere.'[14]

In a counter-factual scenario, the Battle of the Bulge would have shown a touching reconciliation between the Limeys and the Yanks in the last reel. The courage and tenacity of the ordinary GIs would have dispelled sour suspicions that the Americans were simply glory-hunters who had never had to face the real strength of the *Wehrmacht*, as the British and Canadians had. The measures of co-operation that Montgomery induced between his 21st Army Group, on the one side, and the 1st and 9th US Armies, on the other, would have shown the practicability of a genuinely joint Allied assault on Germany. Goodwill between the Allies would have been replenished by their own success in ensuring that victory, bloody but strategically decisive, had been snatched from Hitler's wild attempt to cheat his fate. The confidence that Eisenhower had placed in his loyal comrade Montgomery would have been vindicated and reciprocated. Monty would have taken special pains to conciliate Brad, all under Ike's indulgent eye . . .

A Hollywood happy ending was not to be. Instead Eisenhower, as usual, had to salvage what he could from a situation in which it often seemed that only he had both the will and the skill to keep his team together. With Bradley still sulking, stinging with every slight from Montgomery, real or imagined, and with Patton made more hungry rather than more content by his taste of victory, the dysfunctional nature of the Allied high command was more apparent than ever.

On 28 December the Supreme Commander left his Versailles head-quarters, under restrictive security arrangements because of fears of assassination by undercover Nazis, and had a secret meeting with Mont-gomery on a frozen train at Hasselt station in Belgium. It was another replay of the command crisis. The two men met alone. Each took away a different impression of what had been agreed. Montgomery thought that he would be given authority over Bradley; Eisenhower thought that he had simply been civil and was sticking to his own plan for power-sharing. When he received a letter two days later restating Mont-gomery's uncompromising position, it was time for a showdown.

Saturday, 30 December 1944, with the Battle of the Bulge now steadily coming under control, thus saw the Allied generals, on the brink of victory, turn to a second battle – between themselves. In London, Brooke did not like what he heard. 'It looks to me as if Monty, with his usual lack of tact, has been rubbing into Ike the results of not having listened to Monty's advice!' he wrote, all too far away but all too near the truth. 'Too much of "I told you so" to assist in creating the required friendly relations between them.'[15] Montgomery's trusted chief of staff, de Guin-gand, sensing trouble, urgently contacted Bedell Smith, his opposite number at SHAEF, and saw that he must get to Paris as soon as he could to rescue Montgomery's career. Eisenhower had in fact already drafted a cable to Washington, with the intention of forcing the joint chiefs of staff to make a choice between himself and Montgomery. To this there would have been only one answer – and de Guingand not only saw it immediately, once he got to SHAEF, but used all his own credit with Beetle to get a twenty-four-hour reprieve from the impending sentence.

When his chief of staff returned hot foot from SHAEF, Montgomery was faced with his own moment of truth. He listened to de Guingand, appalled. He took in the fact that if he went, there was indeed a possible successor as commander of 21st Army Group – Alexander, a sort of upper-class British Ike. Monty realized now that he was beaten, that his worst enemy was not the *Wehrmacht*, not even SHAEF, and certainly not its American Supreme Commander, but perhaps himself. 'Dear Ike,' he wrote on New Year's Eve, virtually at de Guingand's dictation, in a cable that effected a personal retreat on more than a tactical scale. He offered assurances that he could be relied on 'one hundred percent' to make Ike's plan work – 'and I know Brad will do the same'. It was a total and unconditional withdrawal. 'Very distressed that my letter may have upset you and I would ask you to tear it up. Your very devoted subordinate, Monty.'[16]

The Prime Minister had just returned home from Athens, his own battleground. It was not where he had been expected to spend Christmas, but having previously sent Alexander there, and then Macmillan too, he had taken the remarkable step of going himself with the easily agitated Eden. There had been one or two warning signs for Eden-watchers. On 16 December, Cadogan had tried to calm down the Foreign Secretary at the end of the day, 'while he was flapping about the room collecting hat and coat. What a madhouse!'[17] And, after brooding overnight, Eden came up with the idea that he too should go to Athens, exposing him, thought Cadogan, to the obvious charge that he would be seeking to dictate an internal remedy for another country: 'It's his old trouble – the urge to do something, irrespective of the sense of it. V. dangerous.'[18]

After all, what could actually be done by any British minister in Athens? Macmillan had had an exciting first week, reporting back to Churchill that a political not a military solution was needed; but the second week, virtually under siege in the British embassy while the street-fighting continued, was another matter. True, he had agreeable hosts in the like-minded ambassador, Rex Leeper, and his resourceful wife Margaret, who helped to maintain morale. A publisher by profession and a bookish man by inclination, Macmillan raided the embassy library and kept up his diary at unusual length. He reported finding a short history of modern Greece, which was certainly useful background reading, and a book on the Eastern Church, which might save him from making a *faux pas* with the Archbishop; and he also found some novels by George Meredith, an author whom he thought well worth re-reading when he had time on his hands – as he found he did, rather to his surprise, since there was little to do but wait for the British forces to get a firmer grip on security by confronting the challenge from EAM guerrillas.

'After luncheon, wrote the diary and read some English newspapers, which have just arrived,' Macmillan wrote on 19 December. 'I am horrified to see that I am expected to "settle" this affair.' On a rare trip outdoors, he called on Papandreou, now established at the Hotel Grande Bretagne with his government, only to find that, instransigently anti-Communist, he too was expecting Macmillan to work wonders (or perhaps just to work). 'But I don't think he has any idea of our military difficulties or of the dangers on his northern frontier,' Macmillan noted. 'We do not wish to start the Third World War against Russia until we have finished the Second World War against Germany – and certainly not to please M. Papandreou.'[19]

Churchill was not altogether pleased with Macmillan. Partly he was blaming the messenger for the discouraging news of intractable Greek difficulties, not easily resolved by the methods of Bloody Balfour. Partly he was in disagreement with Macmillan about the desirabililty of installing Damaskinos, who might turn out, Churchill kept saying, to be a clerical dictator rather than a conciliator. And partly the Prime Minister was annoyed at one of his own ministers for pointing out the all too obvious political difficulties which the Greek issue excited both at Westminster and in Washington. He was having to speak almost daily in the House, and not doing it well, as Colville sadly recorded on 19 December: 'The Chief Whip says it is the first time he has seen the House really irritated and impatient with him.' The next day Colville was relieved that Churchill's intention to make 'a short, gay and impromptu speech' on Greece yielded to wiser counsel since he was already so hard-pressed – 'there is so much happening, Greece, Poland, a powerful German counter-attack on the Luxembourg frontier . . .'[20]

It was Eden who took the lead in this further Greek debate on 20 December. Afterwards Nicolson tried to lend him the sympathy that he obviously craved: 'But he is tired, tired, tired, after a long month of incessant House of Commons debate, great public worry, and nerve-wracking Cabinet meetings.' The only real comfort, as it seemed to Eden that evening, lay in the Soviet response – or lack of response – to the Greek imbroglio. 'He has a real liking for Stalin,' Nicolson recorded. 'He says that Stalin has never broken his word once given.'[21]

On that, at least, Eden and Churchill were in agreement. In *Triumph and Tragedy* there is a pointed passage, making an unfavourable contrast between the strictures of both *The Times* and the *Manchester Guardian* upon Churchill's policy and the silence of *Pravda* and *Isvestia*. As Churchill reassured Mackenzie King, sensitive to Canadian public opinion on the Athens confrontation: 'Although Communists are at the root of the business, Stalin has not so far made any public reflection on our action.'[22] Nor did Mackenzie King, which was a solace, if a smaller one.

Yet Churchill found himself virtually isolated within his own cabinet over the idea of a regency. This alone offered a way of defusing the historic republican–monarchist split in Greece. Not only the Labour members but Macmillan and Eden too were in favour of appointing Damaskinos as Regent, whether or not the King could be brought to agree. Macmillan argued privately in a letter to Eden 'that a moderate, reasonable, progressive policy could detach the vague, radical element from the hard, Communist core'.[23] By polarizing the situation around the monarchy, Churchill's intransigence threatened to ruin the democratic cause he claimed to uphold.

And his colleagues saw his folly. This became embarrassingly clear to Cadogan, in attendance at the cabinet meeting called for 5.30 p.m. on 21 December. 'Too awful,' he wrote. 'P.M. rambled on till 7, stating with vehemence opinions based on no ascertained facts.' When Churchill said: 'I won't install a Dictator', what he called 'a Dictator of the Left', the normally disciplined Deputy Prime Minister could tolerate no more. 'We often heard you say that,' Attlee intervened, 'but you haven't produced a scintilla of evidence in support of your thesis.'[24] Eden felt the same, putting his authority as Foreign Secretary on the line and demanding whether he had the cabinet's confidence. 'W. rejoined rather mournfully for him, that there was no doubt of the Cabinet's support of Foreign Secretary,' Eden wrote in his own diary. 'What was in doubt was Cabinet's confidence in him.'[25] The awkward pause that ensued may not have signalled Churchill's capitulation; but even to imagine such a scene earlier in his premiership would have been impossible.

'Poor Winston!' Macmillan wrote the same day in Athens. 'What with Greece, Poland and the German breakthrough on the western front, this is going to be a grim Christmas.'[26] But it was not until three days later, on 24 December, that Macmillan got the first hint that they might be spending this grim Christmas together. Jock Colville naturally heard sooner, though not until the evening of 22 December, when he recorded that Churchill talked 'interminably after dinner about his differences of opinion over Greece with Eden, his intention of flying to Athens to settle the matter, and the fact that the English people throughout their history have always turned on those whom they thought had served them well in hard times (e.g. Marlborough, Wellington, Lloyd George)'.[27] The following day, as private secretary, he rather disbelievingly made the necessary arrangements for the Prime Minister to make a journey to Athens on Christmas Eve. But it was true; they were to be off the next night.

Sunday, 24 December, was Christmas Eve, and Mrs Churchill had been looking forward to a quiet family Christmas at Chequers. It was not until 5.30 p.m. that her hopes were finally dashed. Her husband made for the telephone, informing the King, Attlee, Bevin and Beaverbrook that he was off to Athens. Only a very small group was to accompany the Prime Minister: no other minister besides Eden, none of his own officials except Colville, none of Eden's except Pierson Dixon from the Foreign Office, plus two secretaries from No. 10 and Churchill's indispensable valet, Frank Sawyers.

It was nothing if not a hazardous venture: not only because they would have to fly, skirting the war zone in Europe, and to land in a militarily contested city, but also because the Prime Minister was a man of seventy who had had two heart attacks and a nearly fatal bout of pneumonia. So another call went through to his doctor, reaching a totally unprepared Lord Moran at his country cottage.

It was one of Churchill's eccentricities to dress in the uniform of an Air Commodore, a rank to which he had a rather tenuous claim. He evidently thought this fitting attire for Greece, and Sawyers was there to buff it up for the occasion. Colville, who had actually served in the RAF for two years before being plucked back to Downing Street, had his uniform as a pilot officer sent down accordingly. Moran had had more difficulty in packing; it was not until he reached Chequers that he knew that Greece was the destination. As they all waited for the plane, Churchill chided Dixon for letting his now famous telegram go off through the Foreign Office to General Scobie. 'Of all the telegrams I have written in this war,' he told him, 'it is the one I least liked after I had written it and the only one that has ever been published.'[28] It was good news for the Foreign Office that Bloody Balfour was no longer the hero of the hour. Perhaps the Prime Minister might instead talk more persuasively about democracy, reaffirming his Commons declaration that it was 'no harlot to be picked up in the street by a man with a tommy gun'.

Macmillan met the incoming plane at the Kalamaki airfield on the afternoon of Christmas Day. Alexander had joined them from his headquarters at Caserta. It was bitterly cold and Churchill was persuaded to confer initially on his well-appointed plane. 'I had expected rather a difficult time – but Winston was in a most mellow, not to say chastened mood,' Macmillan recorded. 'After two hours (in which Alex was most helpful and Anthony also) the whole strategic, tactical and political problems were reviewed and general agreement reached.'[29] This meant that the plans cooked up between Macmillan, Alexander and Leeper had found favour: that there would be a conference of the Greek political parties, convened by the British Prime Minister. Signs of Churchill's amenability came as a considerable relief to Macmillan. 'The truth is,' he told Moran, 'he has no solution himself.'[30]

Indeed Churchill went on to display little short of a *volte face*. He accepted not only the desirability of a political solution and the necessity of seeking compromise but also a procedure in which the hitherto demonized Damaskinos would have a prominent role. What clinched it for Churchill was an actual meeting later that day with this imposing figure: not only tall and dignified but also, as it emerged, anti-Communist and politically astute. 'The Archbishop impressed the Prime Minister as much as he had the rest of us,' wrote Colville, 'and we are now in the curious topsy-turvy position of the Prime Minister feeling strongly pro-Damaskinos (he even thinks he would make a good Regent) while the S. of S. [Eden] is inclined the other way.'[31]

The conference was summoned for the afternoon of Boxing Day, 26 December. Churchill, who had spent the night on HMS *Ajax*, anchored off Piraeus, set out for the British embassy in an armoured car with military escort. As is obvious from his account in *Triumph and Tragedy*, he was loving every minute. 'Where is your pistol,' he asked Colville, and reports scolding him for not having one – 'for I certainly had my own.' Colville quickly reappeared with a tommy gun (perhaps of the sort used to pick up harlots in the streets of Athens) and explained that he had borrowed it from the driver. 'What is he going to do?' 'He will be busy driving.' 'But there will be no trouble unless we are stopped,' Churchill persisted, 'and what is he going to do then?' This was already shaping up as one in a very long series of Churchillian anecdotes of martial adventure, lovingly burnished in his memoirs: 'Jock had no reply. A black mark!' They reached the embassy safely, with time to confer with Churchill's new friend, the Archbishop, and also to send a telegram to his old friend, the President of the United States: 'I count on you to help us in this time of unusual difficulty.'[32]

The big question was whether the representatives of ELAS, who had been offered a safe conduct through the British lines, would attend. As the hours passed, prospects dimmed. The postponed start had a beneficial side effect since Churchill and Damaskinos were meanwhile cooped up in the embassy, talking over their objectives, having their photographs taken, and generally building mutual confidence. As 5 o'clock approached, it was decided to begin anyway. Through streets still beset by the threat of snipers, the delegates assembled at the Foreign Ministry: not only Papandreou's government from the Hotel Grande Bretagne and assorted Greek politicians but also the Soviet military representative, the French minister and – most significant of all – the American ambassador, Lincoln MacVeagh. 'This is rather a coup for us and should help,' Macmillan noted.[33]

Since the electricity was cut off, the large oval table was lit only by hurricane lamps, as photographs of the scene testify. Still no word from ELAS, so the decision was taken to begin regardless. Damaskinos presided, resplendent in his flowing ecclesiastical robes, with Churchill on his right. They opened the conference with sonorous speeches, each waiting for translation, which seems to have enhanced the effect rather than otherwise. Churchill had hardly got into his stride, in this gothic setting, when a knock on the door heralded the arrival of three ELAS delegates in British battledress – 'three shabby desperadoes', as Colville called them, whose weapons were handed over, with some reluctance, and deposited for safe keeping.[34] Everyone stood, except for Papandreou and his colleagues. Here was the visible intrusion of the guerrilla struggle into the conference hall, making an indelible impression upon Moran, who sat observing the spectacle: 'The suppressed vitality of ELAS contrasted strangely with the gaunt, grey, weary faces of the Greek Government.' Churchill, his Air Commodore's uniform suddenly quite in keeping with the occasion – had he too been asked to turn in his pistol? – began his speech again, this time directing his remarks largely in the direction of the hard men from the hills. 'We came here because we were invited by all parties in Greece,' he said pointedly.[35]

Macmillan thought Churchill's speech very good: 'He left no doubt in the minds of ELAS on the one hand of our military power. On the other hand, he made it clear to the politicians that he did not mean us to be used for a reactionary policy.' Churchill evidently tried to present a front of Allied unity, as indeed was only proper under the eyes of the

Soviet and American representatives. 'He made it clear that Stalin had agreed to British intervention,' Macmillan noted, adding in his diary his own parenthetical comment on Churchill's public statement that Roosevelt had also given approval back in August – 'the President has let us down badly, and Winston is very hurt about it.'[36]

Churchill thus delivered his oration, like Demosthenes, in the best tradition of Athenian democracy. The Archbishop asked if there were any questions. Eventually, after some whispering between the ELAS delegates – who comprised a soldier, an apparatchik and a professor – they decided to put forward the professor, to present their smoothest face. This was Dimitrios Partsalides, and all accounts agree that he seized his moment effectively, beginning with a glowing tribute to Churchill, responding to the dialogue that the latter had begun. 'The Greeks rose as one man,' the professor declaimed, 'because they believed in the destruction of Fascism, in the right to live free upon the basis laid down in the Atlantic Charter.'[37] As he spoke, he warmed to his own eloquence, and, as Colville described it: 'he raised his eyes which flashed in the lamp-light and spoke with such speed and vehemence that the interpreter was unable to get a word in edgeways and was obliged to give up the unequal task.'[38]

It did not matter. The Prime Minister was much moved by the whole performance anyway. 'We have begun the work,' Churchill told the conference. 'You must finish it!'[39] The final act in this piece of political theatre came as the British delegation now followed Churchill out of the room. He passed down the table, shaking hands with all the members of the Greek government, and pausing when he came to ELAS. 'He had vowed that he would not shake hands with these villains,' Moran observed. 'What was he going to do?' The answer, of course, flowed from the dynamics of the encounter, from the success of the oratorical exchanges that he had himself begun. It was by now unthinkable to snub his Periclean respondent. 'Who,' Churchill asked, 'will introduce these gentlemen to me?' He then shook hands with Partsalides and his colleagues in turn, with Moran watching intently: 'And now for the first time the expressionless features of ELAS came to life, and a look of pleasure crossed their faces. They wrung Mr Churchill's hand with slight, stiff bows.' And to a Prime Minister who had been subjected in Moscow to meeting the despicable Lublin Poles, the Athens Communists seemed a wholesome contrast. 'They had impressed him,' he told

Moran, and anyone else who would listen afterwards. 'He felt that if the three Communists could be got to dine with us all difficulties might vanish.'[40]

The problem now was to restrain Churchill's enthusiasm, not least by preserving him from a glorious death on active service. After another night on HMS *Ajax*, he started proposing expeditions to get closer to the fighting, much to the alarm of General Scobie and Admiral Mansfield, who thought it their duty to protect the Prime Minister, and his to keep himself alive. But he could not be stopped going ashore again for further meetings. 'I do wish he'd let me do my own job,' Eden told Moran, wearily.[41]

They all had lunch in the virtually unheated British embassy, still prone to stray bullets from the street fighting. The Ambassador was there, of course, and Margaret Leeper, whose infectious fortitude, indomitably providing sustenance for all in her fur coat, was much admired throughout. Jock Colville sat between her and the new press attaché, the cartoonist Osbert Lancaster, who no doubt stored up raw material for future use, perhaps visualizing how Maudie Littlehampton might have muddled through in a fur coat. 'After lunch,' Colville noted, 'the P.M. saw MacVeagh, the American Ambassador, and gave him a piece of his mind about the very inadequate support the U.S.A. have given us in this affair.'[42] Churchill may not yet have seen Roosevelt's conciliatory message, not only endorsing his own ambassador's participation but adding: 'I hope that your presence there on the spot will result in achieving an entirely satisfactory solution.'[43]

At 4.30 that afternoon the Archbishop arrived. He had already debriefed Macmillan and Leeper that morning, telling them about the debate that had ensued after their departure the previous evening, himself going back for a resumed session of another five hours. Now he wanted to bring Churchill up to date, with any suggestion that they might retreat to the safety of the basement adamantly rejected. The encounter made a lasting impression on Macmillan: 'the Archbishop, with his great head-dress and robes, and Churchill in his uniform, reclining on the sofa, pushed back against the far wall of the Ambassador's study, which was believed to be out of the line of fire'.[44] The upshot was that only a regency under Damaskinos offered an acceptable compromise for all parties and that the British Government would put all pressure on the King to secure his acquiescence, however grudging.

Papandreou would resign accordingly; a broad-based government, including the EAM, would be formed.

This was the best outcome that anyone could expect for the moment. It certainly left the situation more hopeful than when Churchill had arrived, not least because of an important shift in his own position under pressure. Not only had he shaken hands with the Communists, he was strongly tempted that afternoon to accede to a request from ELAS for a private interview. 'Winston was very inclined to see them,' Macmillan noted, 'but I persuaded him (and Anthony agreed) that if we were going to put our money on the Archbishop, we must let him play the hand as he thought best.' Predictably, Damaskinos argued strongly against such a meeting, no doubt fearful of how the Prime Minister's vanity might be exploited. Less predictably, Churchill backed down. That he was prepared to accede to such advice – 'Winston is more and more delighted with the Archbishop,' Macmillan observed[45] – marked an important stage in his education about the realities of current Greek politics.

On 28 December, Churchill left Athens. He had last-minute qualms about leaving the conference unresolved, he hankered after the idea of meeting with ELAS, he toyed with summoning another session to secure peace, or at least a truce. It took all Macmillan's energy to keep the issues in focus: 'I argued strongly in favour of his immediate return *to secure the regency*.'[46] For the stumbling block to this objective – the King's obduracy – was one which could only be removed in London, not in Athens. So Churchill flew out that afternoon, accompanied by Macmillan, down the Gulf of Corinth towards Naples, where Alexander's headquarters, with hot baths available, provided an unwonted interlude of comfort and joy after the rigours and alarums of the festive season in Athens.

Not that London was any warmer, with the coldest Christmas weather for over half a century. Still, the end-of-year perspective encouraged Harold Nicolson to find twin gleams of comfort when he came to write his diary on 30 December: 'It really does look as if the Rundstedt offensive has been snapped. The King of Greece has agreed to appoint Damaskinos Regent. Good work for Anthony and Winston.'[47] Indeed Churchill's first task on his return to London the previous day had been to browbeat King George of Greece into sanctioning this step. Pausing only to secure the authority of the members of his war cabinet at 6 p.m

– hardly difficult since it was the Prime Minister who had meanwhile been converted to their policy – he and Eden then spent most of their first night back closeted with the King. Facing him with their threat to transfer recognition to a Regency otherwise, they secured his reluctant consent by 4 a.m. This cleared the way for the appointment in Athens of a new government, nominally monarchical but actually under the republican General Plastiros (though fighting continued).

This step helped to redefine the Greek issue in a way that no longer axiomatically identified the British Government with monarchism against republicanism. As Berlin reported from the Washington embassy, Churchill's dramatic shuttle to Athens had been generally seen through American eyes 'as striking evidence of "gallantry", political imagination and a "flexibility" which did a good deal to dissipate the impression of Prime Minister – a compound of Lords Chatham and North – as a crusted and unbending eighteenth-century Tory which had undoubtedly been gaining ground during recent weeks'.[48] The fact that the recalcitrant King George continued to play a double game may have been exasperating for the British Foreign Office – 'These Kings!' snorted Cadogan[49] – but this was not in itself bad news for Anglo-American relations. To Macmillan it was an obviously welcome first step, though more were needed. 'Until we can clear up this Greek position it is like a running sore,' he noted on 31 December. 'It drains away both our military strength and our political prestige at home and abroad.'[50]

Never out-jaundiced in his views, the CIGS was appalled at the military implications, with 80,000 British troops now committed. 'And what are we to get out of it all? As far as I can see, absolutely nothing!'[51] The manpower crisis obviously weighed upon Brooke, with his professional responsibility not only to finish off the Italian campaign – directly drained by Greece – but also to fill up the breach in the Ardennes, and not just with Churchillian rhetoric. The Prime Minister had said on 21 December (so Hugh Dalton recorded) that the 'time has come to play a strong hand', meaning a response to the Battle of the Bulge by reinforcing the British army with 250,000 extra troops, which would 'stimulate our Allies and probably lead to the Americans undertaking to reinforce by a million and redress the balance, now inclined to be seriously tilted towards the Pacific'.[52] All this was easier said than done.

Meanwhile, all other problems were left to simmer on the back burner – India, for example. It was India that had dominated Churchill's career in the early 1930s. It was the menace of Gandhi to the British Empire that had become almost an obsession for him (until displaced by the menace of Hitler to the British Empire of course). Yet Leo Amery, as an old friend and colleague, was reconciled to the fact that it had now become almost impossible to interest the Prime Minister in the subject. Amery had spent Christmas proudly polishing his latest proposals for constitutional reform and wanted the Viceroy home to discuss them, proposing an early date. On 28 December, however, the India Office found out from Attlee, deputizing for the Prime Minister in his absence, that 'we really cannot answer till Winston gets back from Greece.' Little wonder that Amery took a dim view of this distracting Athens adventure, frustrated at being reduced to giving his draft the sort of cosmetic touches that 'might even help to get it looked at by Winston'.[53] India, like much else, would have to wait.

It was now clear that the war in Europe was going to consume much more attention, and many more resources, and for much longer, than the expectations formally minuted at Quebec in September. True, the position had already become less hopeful before Hitler's extraordinary Ardennes offensive, but there was no denying its impact. As Cadogan acknowledged on 27 December: 'the Germans have attained their objectives in upsetting our plans' and the moral was clear: 'This may indeed prolong the war.'[54]

When Lionel Robbins had left the Cabinet Office to return to the London School of Economics in November, his close colleague James Meade succeeded him as Director of the Economic Section. For Meade the pressing problem was how to revise economic plans that had assumed victory in Europe by 31 December. 'The immediate task,' Meade wrote in his diary, as that now inoperative date was reached, 'is to get our Economic Survey completely rewritten on the new asumption that the German war will end in the middle of 1945.'[55] And this new date for the end of Stage I of the war implied that, for Lend-Lease purposes, the recently negotiated arrangements for the transitional Stage II would last from then until the end of 1946.

In Washington, Isaiah Berlin's end-of-year appraisal, though far from unclouded, hunted for any silver linings. 'The reverses on the Western Front have had a profoundly sobering effect on American public opinion,' he wrote, detecting a diversion of attention from inter-Allied squabbling to the immediate threat faced by the US Army: 'The fact that British generals can scarcely be blamed for latest developments (very few, including [Drew] Pearson, imply that fault is partly ours), has inhibited what might otherwise have caused streams of vituperation in the irresponsible press.'[56]

No doubt each newspaper reader has a personal view of the difference between the responsible and the irresponsible press. In London *The Times* stood on a pedestal, often respected as the semi-official mouthpiece of the British Government; yet this was a view more widely entertained abroad than nearer home. It was a view no longer given house-room at 10 Downing Street by one angry old reader who thought that under Barrington-Ward the paper had taken leave of its senses. The Marxist historian E. H. Carr, on *The Times*' staff since 1941, was often identified as a malign influence; but on Greece most of the leaders were written not by Carr but by Donald Tyerman, recently recruited from *The Economist* (which he was later to edit himself).

It was *The Economist* that now enjoyed its moment of untoward fame. A long-established weekly, *The Economist* had a reputation for dispassionate analysis and, under its editor, Geoffrey Crowther, introduced an American section that was widely read in the United States. The fact that the periodical was jointly owned by Brendan Bracken, currently Minister of Information, and that 'dear Brendan' was a court favourite of Churchill, gave it added prominence. Hence the interest excited by its editorial of 30 December 1944 – not least in the United States, among (as Berlin put it) 'those who look on the *Economist* as a liberal, serious, fairminded and, on the whole, pro-American publication'.[57] Readers on this occasion included the President and the Secretary of State.

It remains easy to see why it created a stir. The editorial was provoked by recent American criticism of Britain: not only over Sforza, and then Greece, and next Poland, but also the revival of old complaints about Britain's readiness to exploit Lend-Lease or its unreadiness to fight the Japanese – 'it is even a subject of complaint that Rundstedt did not select the British-held front for his break-through.' But the tone did not remain light and satirical, still less forbearing about any 'tail-twisting'. Instead there was a stinging forthrightness in its comments on Britain's indispensable ally that was just the sort of thing that the Minister of Information was paid to keep out of the newspapers, especially those owned by himself.

'What makes the American criticisms so intolerable is not merely that they are unjust, but that they come from a source which has done so little to earn the right to postures of superiority,' *The Economist* claimed. 'To be told by anyone that the British people are slacking in their war effort would be insufferable enough to a people struggling through their sixth winter of blackout and blockade and bombs, of queues and rations and coldness – but when the criticism comes from a nation that was practising cash-and-carry during the Battle of Britain, whose consumption has risen through the war years, which is still without a national service act – then it is not to be borne.'

Who were these people to say that the British were betraying the Atlantic Charter in Greece and Poland? Such accusations came from a country where 'both political parties were ready to promise, in the hope of securing the electoral vote of New York State, that they would force a wholly Jewish state on the Arab majority in Palestine.' It was also being said that the British offered neither gratitude nor repayment for Lend-Lease – 'yet the Lend-Lease Act itself declares that nothing shall be given that is not necessary for the defence of the United States.' Little wonder that, taunt by taunt, 'the ordinary Englishman gets one degree more cynical about America's real intentions of active collaboration, and one degree more ready to believe that the only reliable helping hand is in Soviet Russia.' E. H. Carr himself could not have put it better.

The tone as well as the substance of these points still carries a charge. Geoffrey Crowther had once advised the Foreign Office that, in dealing with Americans, 'reserve can easily be seen as superior disdain.'[58] That was hardly the problem this time. The article was written, so Berlin discovered, not by the editor himself but by his thirty-year-old assistant, Barbara Ward, already well known to BBC listeners as a panel member of the popular programme *The Brains Trust*. Berlin subsequently judged that the effect of the piece was to have 'shaken the reputation of *The Economist*, which is now regarded as an excusably but nevertheless markedly nationalist journal'. What this 'hysterical and naive girl' (as he dubbed her) had done was to let the cat out of the bag and the genie out of the bottle.[59] For this was not just rhetorical vituperation but a pointed political critique of a relationship of dependence, fostered and concealed by bonhomie and dissimulation: one that traded in a specie of fine promises rather than cash-down delivery. The question was: 'Just how much British safety can be gambled on American good will?' Friendship and co-operation, by all means, wrote Ward. 'But let an end be put to the policy of appeasement which, at Mr Churchill's personal bidding, has been followed, with all the humiliations and abasements it has brought in its train, ever since Pearl Harbour removed the need for it.'[60]

There is no doubt that this article triggered a wide reaction on both sides of the Atlantic, provoking quotation and comment in newspapers more widely circulated than *The Economist* itself. Even the President was asked about it and 'gently pointed out that some things are better not stated' – a Rooseveltian answer which, of course, was exactly a part of the problem, as Ward saw it. Berlin reported the general American reaction: that 'although the British attack was not unprovoked and the British cannot have been expected to take the flood of criticism poured by the United States press and radio lying down, yet the British are surely much too touchy and the tone of their retort is much too harsh.'[61] This was certainly the note struck in the *New York Times*, determinedly pro-Allied in its outlook. Its London correspondent, Raymond Daniels, reminded readers just how long 'the people in this island suffered in silence the privations, the hardship and the horrors of war'.[62] Hence the recent outburst of suppressed feelings, with an impulse to 'blow Britain's horn' fed by the Government's White Paper on the war effort, published on 1 December, which had claimed Britain's contribution to victory as proportionately the largest of any ally.

This much was widely accepted. As Berlin was able to report: 'Even the greatest of all the trouble-breeders, Drew Pearson, in his Sunday column begged readers to distinguish between the good democratic British people and the "outgrown imperialism" of the Prime Minister, and went on to recite the sacrifices made by the British people in the course of the war, demonstrated by the British White Paper: this, as compared with the easier life of the American people.'[63] But such references cut both ways. Should the democratic British be forgiven their great leader's atavistic posture or did this actually reflect their own outlook? 'The empire is all the British have left,' Raymond Daniels's piece commented, 'and they must preserve it to remain a peer among the nations associated with them.'[64] In that case, of course, it was an intractable issue, since the preservation of the British Empire was not the reason the United States was fighting this war: quite the reverse.

For the Anglo-American alliance, it had to be admitted, this was hardly a happy new year. It was not just the acerbic highbrows on *The*

Economist – 'The year 1945 is opening gloomily for the Allies'[65] – but the British popular press too that had become disillusioned, as an editorial-page article in the *Daily Mail* confirmed on New Year's Day. 'Rundstedt's offensive has left our rose-tinted spectacles in splintered fragments at our feet,' it acknowledged. 'The shock to our eyesight is the greater in that we hardly realised we were wearing them at all.' The impact on the United States, in provoking depression and even reviving isolationist sentiment, elicited special comment: 'We see that her nerves are on edge, that her magnificent self-confidence has been temporarily shaken; and it is to this that we attribute the orgy of tail-twisting in which her Press and politicians are now indulging at our expense.' In the liberal *News Chronicle* on the same day the cartoon by Vicky, the most biting satirist of his era, showed a toddler representing '1945 Year of Victory', menaced by the outstretched claw-like hand of a dark, sinister figure labelled 'Allied political disunity'.

George Creel was an American journalist who was known to have the President's ear. His column in *Collier's Magazine* had been used in the past to fly kites for Roosevelt, which was precisely why the *Daily Mail* used him on 2 January to supply a Washington angle on the current debate about the Alliance. He made no bones of the fact that American policy had changed and was no longer content to accept strategic decisions tailored to the political needs of its Allies: 'According to Washington's authoritative voices the rapidly changing conditions now call for plainer, blunter speech.' Hence the pointed questions, following the Tolstoy conference, about how British and Russian talk of 'spheres of influence' in the Balkans squared with the Atlantic Charter. Creel quoted an unnamed Senate leader: 'Mr Churchill and Marshal Stalin must be made to understand our domestic situation. In the United States there is no such control of public opinion as in Russia, and the voice of America, unlike that of Britain, speaks in many tongues.'[66] Here was an informed reminder that American electoral politics were bound to be an important factor in how a democratic nation waged war. It was one reason why the mangy British lion, with its temptingly twistable tail, found itself pitted against the soaring American eagle, proudly careless of any ruffled feathers.

It would be an illusion to suppose that the armies in the field were insulated from politics and public opinion in their home countries. True, many ordinary soldiers saw themselves as passive and hapless, as victims of political happenings that were happening elsewhere. 'The regiment has been to hell, was sent to hell, and only part of it got back,' wrote Farley Mowat, later a well-known Canadian writer but in December 1944 a 23-year-old lieutenant, mired in the last phases of the under-manned Italian campaign. 'As for the reinforcement situation – we hear the news,' he wrote home. 'Stories in papers from home such as "Conscripts stage mutiny and are warned they will lose their pay and allowances for the time they refuse duty" and "Conscripts tear down the Union Jack and burn it and are fined $11.00 each".'[67] The American military historian Charles B. MacDonald, who was caught up in the Battle of the Bulge as a 22-year-old company commander, later reminded his readers that, when cold, wet, hungry young men were fighting for their lives, 'down in the foxholes, nobody read newspapers other than the *Stars and Stripes* (usually a day or so late) and nobody had radios.'[68]

Their generals, however, had all too much time and inclination to read the newspapers. They did so with an acute sensitivity as to how their own doings were reported and how their own career prospects were thereby affected. 'The rumblings in the press, particularly in London,' wrote Butcher on 1 January, 'have now grown to a roar of demand that there be a British deputy commander for all of General Ike's ground forces.'[69] Despite the dark suspicions in Bradley's camp, it is not true that this was a campaign that could be turned off like a tap once Montgomery himself had capitulated to the Supreme Commander, as he had the day before.

The widely read column 'Spotlight', by A. J. Cummings in the *News Chronicle*, was often a thorn in the side of Allied commanders who resented interference. Cummings was nobody's poodle and on 5 January he tactlessly rekindled the whole argument under the headline: 'MONTY SHOULD BE DEPUTY C.-in-C'. This was not in itself an anti-American line. For the previous two days the paper had splashed the achievements of Patton all over its front page in generous terms and had run a leader on 4 January deploring the fact that 'in the political sphere, America and Britain are not working harmoniously together.' Yet Cummings had to acknowledge the spillover effect from politics into military affairs, concluding that Ike probably knew that neither his own generals, nor the War Department in Washington, nor the American public would acquiesce in Monty's appointment.

Churchill set out on 3 January to visit both Ike and then Monty at the front. He had had only three full days at home since his return from Athens, yet here he was, embarking again through the blizzards to get as near the action as possible. It was a highly personal visit, idiosyncratic in both method and personnel, with nobody from his private office, not even Colville, rather to the latter's surprise. This meant that the accompanying party was pared down to the three members of staff whom Churchill evidently considered absolutely essential: Tommy Thompson, his naval ADC; Patrick Kinna as a clerk for shorthand, since the trip was thought too perilous for women; and, of course, Sawyers, his valet.

Naturally Brooke had to go as CIGS. A hardened traveller, he had fresh memories of their last trip to France some six weeks previously. On that expedition, Churchill had been visiting the French Army, now fighting with distinction in the Vosges, as part of his charm offensive on de Gaulle, and had hit upon the idea that his favourite Air Commodore's uniform would match the occasion, as he prepared himself to meet the French generals. While they had stood patiently outside his train in an unseasonable snowstorm, a guard of honour at the ready, the Prime Minister preened himself in the glass while Sawyers handed him the appropriate belt. 'Sawyers you damned fool, why have you not removed that bastard!!' Brooke recorded. 'You know I never want that bastard around me again! Cut off the damned thing!'[70] Yes indeed, the CIGS knew all about the difficulties experienced by Sawyers as he tried to serve a master who was at once so peremptory in his demands, so mercurial in his moods, so jealous in his vanity, and so unappreciative of the expert assistance that alone concealed all this from an admiring world.

The day before they left, on 2 January, the CIGS had had to listen to the Prime Minister while he 'propounded the wildest of strategy, which was purely based on ensuring that British troops were retained in the lime light if necessary at the expense of the Americans and quite irrespective of any strategic requirements!'[71] Nothing came of this, of course; nor of most of Churchill's projects that day. 'The P.M. composed a crushing letter to Barrington-Ward about *The Times'* attitude on the Greek question,' Colville recorded, 'but after consultation with Eden, Brendan, etc., decided not to send it.'[72] Moreover, after sitting through that evening's cabinet, Amery deplored the couple of hours wasted before the proper agenda was even reached: 'Most of the time taken up in a rambling discussion on the iniquities of the BBC in connection with Greece and the still greater follies of Reuter's in sending to the troops that obnoxious fellow Cummings's notes in the *News Chronicle*.'[73]

Churchill talked with Eisenhower at SHAEF headquarters in Versailles on 3 January and, after finding himself snowed in on 4 January, reached Montgomery's headquarters on 5 January. He came back from the front, Colville noted, 'confident about the position on the northern flank of the German breakthrough, where Monty is in command, but less sure of the southern sector'.[74] Brooke's main consolation from the visit was that, at the end of a late-night session at SHAEF, some strategic enlightenment seemed belatedly to have dawned upon the Prime Minister: 'He said that he was beginning to see that any operation from Italy towards Vienna had little prospects! This is the result of many patient hours winning him away from this venture!'[75] It was now that Churchill first broached the idea of bringing in Alexander in place of Tedder as Deputy Supreme Commander. During encounters with Eisenhower, Brooke had deliberately refrained from again raising the command issue: that simmering cause of so much inter-Allied friction and personal aggravation between the ever-sensitive generals. Everyone was on their best behaviour, determined to keep calm. It was, however, the calm before the storm.

'HODGES' PUSH GOING WELL: OUR "PINCERS" 13 MILES APART'. This was the banner headline in the *Daily Mail* on the morning of 5 January, reporting that the Allied strategy of pinching the flanks to contain the German advance was well on the way to success. By the time that the tabloid *New York World-Telegram* was published that evening – in a time-zone six hours behind wartime Britain – there was a further twist to its story, taken from the United Press agency: '2 ARMIES SLUG AHEAD, MONTGOMERY IN CHARGE'. Thus the change of command was now in the public domain. Eisenhower's decision to confirm it officially had been precipitated by a leak in *Time* magazine after its reporter had returned to Washington and thus escaped the SHAEF censorship; and UP had then put the news on the wires.

The British press on 6 January went to town. 'MONTY, WITH BIGGER COMMAND, CUTS THREE MILES INTO SALIENT,' splashed the *News Chronicle*, and the *Daily Mail* went even further:

MONTGOMERY: FULL STORY OF BREACH BATTLE

British Halted Drive to Meuse Line

This was summarized in the continuation on the back page: '"MONTY" INTO THE BREACH'. There was a picture the full width of the front page showing Monty flanked by 'the generals under his command', namely Dempsey of the British 2nd Army, Hodges of the US 1st Army, Simpson of the US 9th Army and Crerar of the Canadian 1st Army. The *News Chronicle* carried a leader, simply headed 'Monty'. 'The news that "Monty" is in command will be welcomed, not because he is British,' it claimed, stretching credence, 'but because he understands, better than anyone else, how the Germans fight and how they can be beaten.' In this the Conservative *Daily Mail* was at one with its Liberal contemporary: 'The British people will learn with satisfaction that Field-Marshal Montgomery has been given command of all the Forces, both British and American, north of the Ardennes salient.' The paper also deplored the belated release of the information that some British troops had now joined the battle.

This barely concealed chauvinistic tone was just what SHAEF had dreaded in keeping the change of command quiet. The *New York Times* made a determined effort to put the right Allied gloss on the news, with a front-page report from its correspondent, Drew Middleton: 'Dough-boys and Tommies fighting shoulder to shoulder on a twenty-one mile front fought their way into the northern flank of the German salient in Belgium as the great Battle of the Bulge neared its climax.' Its editorial defended the shift of command and cited Middleton's reports to show that American soldiers respected Monty. In New York, as in London, however, there was no explicit statement that giving Montgomery command had been a strictly temporary expedient. Instead, it was sometimes simply called 'his promotion'. Even the *Stars and Stripes* was puzzled as to what Bradley was left commanding – an apparent slight not lost upon him.

The fact that the *Daily Mail* had its own correspondent, Alexander Clifford, at Montgomery's headquarters gave its reporting a special impact, a special immediacy and, not least, a special bias. It was an almost inevitable feature of war reporting – Butcher was acutely aware of this problem in trying to manage the news – that correspondents would acquire an active partisanship in favour of the generals to whom they were accredited. They shared the same physical dangers, saw things literally from the same viewpoint, heard what they were meant to hear on a necessarily incomplete basis, and all too often came to perceive that their own prominence within their own newspapers varied directly with the news value of their own general. It was thus only natural that most of the journalists attached to the 21st Army Group were from British newspapers and only natural that they thought Monty front-page news. To be sure, a few correspondents triumphed over this deformation of perspective. Reading Chester Wilmot's *The Struggle for Europe* (1952), the remarkable thing is not that this masterpiece presents Montgomery's view of the campaign but that it presents it with such historical objectivity, only six or seven years afterwards. Clifford, however, was no Wilmot: he was a newsman filing a story against a daily deadline.

The *Mail* did not simply report the news: it wallowed and gloried in it. 'Alexander Clifford last night cabled the first full story of one of the most sensational secrets of the war – the placing of two U.S. armies under Field Marshal Montgomery's command and the part Montgomery and British troops played in stopping Rundstedt's drive to the Meuse,' the breathless front-page summary ran. According to Clifford, the German breakthrough had 'faced Montgomery with one of his toughest problems, and his success may rank as one of his greatest defensive battles'. There was admittedly a tribute to 'the really magnificent fighting qualities of certain American divisions' as being indispensable, but it was Montgomery's contribution that was highlighted. 'Men of the Desert Army remembered the two perfect defensive battles he had fought there – Alam el Halfa in September 1942 and Medenine in March 1943,' Clifford rhapsodized. 'They breathed a sigh of relief – and wondered how the Americans would feel about it.'

It was a good question. The short answer is that they felt highly sensitive, with pride over their achievement in halting the German armies made the more poignant by consciousness of the price paid by their own soldiers. This was no clash of high technologies, clinically determined at arm's length, but a brutal struggle in the snows of the Ardennes, reminiscent of the First World War (or the eastern front) in the horrific casualties on both sides. Estimates vary, depending partly on how the battle is defined, in time and area. Older figures suggest that 20,000 troops died, most of them Germans but with the American dead totalling

8,500 (and British casualties simply not on a comparable scale at all, with about 200 dead). More recent estimates give the American dead (between 16 December and 28 January) as over 10,000, with their total casualties at 80,000.[76]

Montgomery could not have had any exact figures at the time but he was undoubtedly aware of the relative orders of magnitude. This should have made him humble in anything he said at this point about the battle as a whole, as well as heedful of the warnings not to rub it in about the temporary shift in command to himself from the discomfited Bradley.

On 7 January 1945 Montgomery held a press conference. 'This incident,' Eisenhower says in his war memoirs, 'caused me more distress and worry than did any similar one of the war.'[77] Montgomery covers the Battle of the Ardennes in a nine-page chapter of his own memoirs, of which no fewer than five pages are devoted to the press conference. Given his proud claim to have written every word of the book himself, the incident's significance in his eyes is clear. Though Bradley's two attempts to write autobiographically both required ghostly assistance, his view of the notorious press conference is true to form: 'It did more to undermine Anglo-American unity than anything I can remember.'[78] Yet the reason for such reactions is not self-evident; and all these comments are retrospective; so a closer appreciation of the contemporary context is plainly necessary.

The event certainly made an immediate impact. Churchill had approved the idea that Montgomery talk to the press, with the aim of stressing Allied friendship at all levels. Montgomery's notes show that he followed this agenda – in his own characteristic style. First he offered information on the battle. Rundstedt had attempted to drive a wedge. 'The situation looked as if it might become awkward,' Monty commented, before dilating on his own role – 'I took certain steps myself . . . I carried out certain movements . . . i.e. I was thinking ahead.'[79] The verbatim report by Reuters news agency, which was run on 8 January by both *The Times* in London and by the *New York Times*, prints Montgomery's script, almost word for word. The story ran that 'the whole allied team rallied to meet the danger; national considerations were thrown over-board; General Eisenhower placed me in command of the whole Northern front.' The *New York Times* prefaced its full report with the benign summary: 'Field Marshal Sir Bernard Montgomery today declared that Allied teamwork and especially the inherent "courage and good fighting quality" of the American troops had halted the German drive into Belgium.' Its own sub-heads give the narrative line:

> Battle 'Most Interesting'
> Says Von Rundstedt Failed
> Says Americans Stopped Foe
> Calls for Allied Solidarity
> Praises US Air Troops
> Cites Heavy German Losses.

This was, in tone and import, almost exactly how *The Times* presented its account in London: 'THE AMERICAN SOLDIER: Sir B. Montgomery's Tribute'.

Montgomery had said at the beginning of the press conference that, in offering information, he wanted a *quid pro quo* from the assembled journalists. It was that they should highlight his final exhortation: 'It is team-work that pulls you through dangerous times; it is team-work that wins battles.' All this was duly reported. Moreover, he sought to dispel any mischievous doubt as to whose team it was. 'Let me tell you that the captain of our team is Eisenhower,' he said. 'I am absolutely devoted to Ike.' Not only was this, too, prominently reported but Reuters also carried his explicit censure on negative articles about Eisenhower in the British press. The only omission, compared with Montgomery's own notes, was his direct plea to the journalists concerned – 'let us all rally round the captain of the team and so help to win the match.'

At the time, in fact, Montgomery's remarks got a generally good press in the United States. Admittedly, a pro-Allied response might have been expected from the *New York Times*. Its editorial on 9 January – 'Message from "Monty" ' – was appreciative of the tribute to the American soldier and wholly supportive of his general theme: 'As head of a joint American and British army he was saying to his people at home what only a Briton could say to Britons.' Any resentment over the shift of command was distinctly muted. 'Montgomery's new post was moderately well received,' judged Berlin, 'and the Prime Minister's and Montgomery's warm references to United States soldiers are very widely appreciated.'[80]

This reaction brought some relief in high quarters in London. On the night of 8 January Brooke had been summoned to Churchill's bedside, where he was seeking to ward off a cold – it was 'attacking on a broad front', as he told Colville the next day[81] – with the usual remedy of brandy and cigars. 'We then discussed all the evils of Monty's press interview, which resulted in a call to Eisenhower and the sending for Brendan Bracken,' Brooke noted. Eisenhower told Churchill that Bradley was seriously upset; the solution seemed to be some sort of decoration to cheer him up, and perhaps a personal message from the Prime Minister. Later, a telegram to Roosevelt was drafted, to follow up the encouraging account Churchill had already given the previous day of the unity that prevailed at the front. But this telegram proved less easy to dictate, as an impatient Brooke, anxious to get to bed himself, observed. 'Then the red stylo-pen was lost, Sawyers sent for, new pen was brought followed by old one being found inside bed etc. etc.'[82] Yet in the morning, when they compared notes, the CIGS said he was surprised at Monty's good American press. 'So was I,' replied the Prime Minister. 'I do not think it is now necessary for me to call up Bradley.'[83]

Why so much fuss? Was this second battle simply between the bulging egos of self-obsessed generals? There is a complacent Montgomery version that turns on there having been a misrepresentation of what the Field Marshal had actually said, as it was relayed to a suspicious Bradley, still holed up in Luxembourg, licking his wounds. It is true that Wilmot, who had attended the press conference for the BBC, discovered that his report was recycled in a deliberately anti-American form by Goebbels's propaganda broadcasts, picked up in Luxembourg.[84] It is also true that, in the claustrophobic atmosphere of Bradley's headquarters, there were staff officers already primed to take offence and stubbornly remaining, as one of them put it years later, 'certain that the BBC blamed it on the Germans only after it had become too hot to handle'.[85] True but trivial is surely the right verdict on such stories, if they are asked to bear the main weight of interpretation in explaining a major crisis, which is certainly how it now appeared to a distraught Eisenhower.

Bradley, convinced that he had been slighted by Montgomery, insisted that he too must give a press conference. Eisenhower had meanwhile engineered the award of the Bronze Star in his quest 'to find a peg on which the press might draw attention to the fine work of General Bradley', as Butcher put it.[86] And Churchill duly sent congratulations. Bradley pointedly proclaimed to the newsmen that Montgomery's command of the two US Armies had been on a temporary basis – true, as it turned out, of the 1st but not of the 9th Army, which was to stay with Montgomery. And this was as much as could be done for Bradley, who really had very little else to say to the press (though what he did say still managed to annoy the *Daily Mail*) and his line that he had taken 'a calculated risk' in the Ardennes might have been better left unsaid. What was really gnawing away at him could not be said at all in public since it was not the result of any specific piece of misreporting: it was an invidious comparison with an ever-present rival who was having a good war. As his ADC, Major Chester Hansen, later the ghost-writer of Bradley's memoirs, wrote in his diary about Montgomery, the day before the latter had even met the press: 'He is the symbol of success, the highly overrated and normally distorted picture of the British effort on our front.'[87]

The trouble was that Monty was irrepressibly Monty. As has been seen, it would be wrong to suppose that his performance at the press conference was simply inept or below par or only fit for British consumption. One of the most sympathetic reports was by the special correspondent of the famous Melbourne newspaper, the *Age*, its war reporting still concentrated closely on events in the Ardennes rather than those geographically nearer to Australia. 'The Field Marshal was at ease with his audience,' the *Age* correspondent reported. 'There was none of the feeling of "talking down" to the press, and therefore to the people to whom we pass on his words.' Moreover this favourable impresssion was not marred by any sense of scoring points against the Americans: far from it in the passage on Eisenhower, where there was 'something simple – certainly not of the art of the practised politician – in the almost emotional way he spoke of his chief'.[88]

Yet, even as he strode into the press conference, many of his best friends had blenched. His own chief of staff, de Guingand, whose tact had so recently saved his commander's skin, was away sick. No one else would be heeded, as Brigadier Edgar Williams, his chief of intelligence and later an Oxford don, found when he had tried to tackle Monty. 'Oh God, why didn't you stop him?' the *Daily Express* correspondent, Alan Moorehead, had reproached Williams, who surely put his finger on the problem: 'The text in a sense was innocuous; the presentation quite appalling.'[89] The language and the body language told different stories as Monty congratulated the GIs while preening himself as their new commander. It is clear that, after delivering his prepared text, Montgomery then spoke extempore, which offered a further chance for egotism to intrude. If this display appalled journalists as sympathetic to

Montgomery as Moorehead, his first biographer, and Wilmot, his most cogent military apologist, it is obvious that the Field Marshal had failed to make the best case for himself. And it appeared much the same in Downing Street, as Colville recorded: 'Monty's triumphant, jingoistic and exceedingly self-satisfied talk to the press on Sunday has given wide offence.'[90]

In short, this super-charged occasion had inevitably tempted Monty to play to the gallery, with the press gallery in Britain equally inevitably to the fore. The press itself, moreover, was already sensitized on the touchy subject of Anglo-American relations by everything that had happened, and everything that had been published, during the month since Stettinius had gone public about Allied political differences in southern Europe. It is not as though Allied military differences in northern Europe had thereby been created – they were long-standing in private – but the powder trail that was laid, starting with the Sforza affair, now made them infinitely more combustible in public.

The *Daily Mail* disclosed its own politicized agenda by sending its political correspondent, Wilson Broadbent, to reinforce Alexander Clifford in its coverage. On 8 January the banner headlines staked out the story:

MONTGOMERY FORESAW ATTACK

HIS TROOPS WERE ALL READY TO MARCH

ACTED 'ON OWN TO SAVE DAY'

According to Broadbent's summary, the situation had been so desperate that Montgomery, 'using his own initiative, threw in all his weight and authority and asserted his leadership' and thus 'set in motion new strategy, and undoubtedly saved a critical situation'. His colleague Clifford supplied more detail, clearly drawing on information that he had gleaned himself. When he revealed that Montgomery's 'liaison officers were getting arrested as spies and generally being asked not to interfere', it was pretty obviously the Americans who were at fault for obstructing the agents of their own salvation. In an editorial the next day the threads were drawn together with the smug reflection that 'it is hard to think that at any future date we shall once again be caught on one foot as we were in Belgium half-way through December' and that

Montgomery had 'once again shown himself to be one of the outstanding generals in any Army'.

If journalism is a first draft of history, the *Daily Mail* of early January 1945 left plenty of scope for subsequent historical revisions. It was, however, the draft that millions of British people were fed with their meagre wartime breakfasts, day by day. Moreover, it was still the Monty version that many of them continued to accept implicitly in later years when they kept congratulating themselves on how they had won the war, as the best-seller status of the Montgomery memoirs testified as late as 1958. Distance simply lent nostalgia to a view already well established at the time. As Major Hansen wrote in his diary on 6 January 1945: 'Monty is the symbol of the British effort on the Western front.'[91] None of this eased Eisenhower's task as Supreme Commander: unable to acknowledge Bradley's deficiencies because of American public opinion, unable to discipline Montgomery because of British public opinion, unable to heal the feud between them, partly for personal reasons, but partly also because their rivalry fed upon pre-existing Anglo-American tension. This is surely why the Battle of the Bulge was fought so fiercely, not only against the *Wehrmacht* but between the Allies themselves.

5

Awaiting the Big Three

January–February 1945

'*I repulse these challenges, wherever they come from, that Britain and the British Empire is a selfish, power-greedy, land-greedy, designing nation, obsessed with dark schemes of European intrigue or colonial expansion. I refute these aspersions whether they come from our best friends or our worst foes.*'

Churchill in the House of Commons, 18 January 1945

The first meeting of the Big Three had taken place in Teheran at the end of 1943. Since then, of course, Churchill had succeeded in getting Roosevelt to Quebec for the Octagon conference in September 1944 and had himself gone to Moscow for the Tolstoy conference with Stalin in October. But Churchill had no further success in his proposal of a Jerusalem Big Three – an idea that expired with Lord Moyne – still less in getting FDR alone for an Anglo-American summit, without their Uncle Joe. The President, increasingly wary of entrapment in British imperial designs, instead insisted that he must first be inaugurated for his fourth term in January, which, as Churchill had told him in November, destroyed 'the hope which we had cherished that you would now pay your long-promised visit to Great Britain, and that we two could meet here in December and ask U.J. to send Molotov, who would be an adequate deputy'.[1] Another cosy conference on Quebec lines, signalling the unique partnership of the English-speaking peoples to an ever-suspicious Stalin, was simply not what Roosevelt wanted. If he had to travel, it would only be for a meeting with Stalin; and this, it became clear, would have to be on Soviet terms and on Soviet territory.

Hence the eventual plan for a Big Three meeting at the Crimean resort of Yalta at the beginning of February. Churchill also secured Roosevelt's grudging assent for a preliminary Anglo-American summit at Malta en route. This master of English prose composed a New Year telegram to the President: 'No more let us falter! From Malta to Yalta! Let nobody alter!'[2]

The Foreign Office nurtured a professional scepticism about what the Big Three could achieve in any event. 'They dine and wine, which is all very well,' Cadogan noted on 4 January, 'but nobody (least of all themselves) knows what, if anything, has been settled.'[3] Churchill naturally took a more optimistic and ambitious view of what could be brought about, if only he were able to instil the Americans with his own sense of priorities. But the signs were not good and his bad cold did not help matters. 'The P.M. remained in bed,' Colville recorded on 10 January. 'He is disgusted that the President should want to spend only five or six days at the coming meeting between "the Big Three" and says that even the Almighty required seven to settle the world.' Corrective reference to the exact chronology in the first chapter of the Book of Genesis failed to put the Prime Minister in a more constructive mood. More cheering news reached Downing Street the following day from Athens, where ELAS had at last submitted to a settlement. Echoing his master's voice, Colville happily noted: 'It looks as if our policy in Greece is going to triumph, to the discomfiture of critics here and in the USA.'[4]

This policy – certainly the analysis behind it – was as much Macmillan's as Churchill's. To Macmillan, watching the situation from Alexander's headquarters at Caserta, the real trouble came from the outdated feuds between the traditional republicans (most of them pro-British) and the supporters of the slippery King (many of them historically pro-German). It was 'an obsolete question' that split them: 'The issue of the second half of the twentieth century will not be monarchism *v.* republicanism, but a liberal and democratic way of life versus the "proletariat dictatorship of the left" and the police state.' Macmillan saw his opportunity for adroitly co-opting the prestige of the Allied Supreme Commander in the Mediterranean – 'if Alex and I continue the technique we have devised' – behind his own tactics, presented always as joint recommendations to London.[5] This was an essentially political rather than a military approach, as Alan Brooke quickly spotted, perceiving that Alexander himself had not come up with these plans. 'I do not believe that he has a single idea in his head of his own!' he wrote on 12 January; and six days later later, in a backhanded tribute, called Macmillan the real Supreme Commander. 'It is too depressing to see how Alex's deficiency of brain allows him to be dominated by others!!'[6]

Still, the policy seemed to be working, no matter who was really pulling the strings.

The Prime Minister's recent performance in cabinet had not been impressive. Cadogan and Amery, both caustic Winston-watchers when provoked (which was quite often these days), agreed on that. Cadogan's estimation was that it now took two hours to do twenty minutes' worth of business. 'Winston at his worst, possibly aided by a cold,' was Amery's judgement on 9 January. 'The first two items need not have taken five minutes, but we spent an hour and a quarter mainly because Winston had not looked at the papers and had no idea what they were about but talked away at large and would not hear when things were explained to him.' But the good news about Greece also turned out to be good news about India so far as Amery was concerned, as he noted three days later. Attlee had finally been able to secure the Prime Minister's consent to bringing the Viceroy, Lord Wavell, home for consultation towards the end of March, by which time the pending Big Three meeting would be out of the way. 'Wavell will not like this postponement,' Amery noted, 'but I am sure there is little chance of Winston's paying any attention to Indian problems before that or even of the India Committttee really getting down to the job.'[7]

The fact was that everything now awaited the conference that Churchill and Roosevelt were to attend as Stalin's guests at Yalta. In Washington, James Forrestal found that it was the same story when he attended a cabinet meeting at the White House on 11 January. 'The President added that he was considering calling a preliminary meeting of the United Nations sometime after "the Big Three" meeting, possibly in March,' he noted. 'The Secretary of State [Stettinius] had suggested that this might be held somewhere in Midwest United States, possibly at French Lick.'[8] It is an arresting thought that this small spa town in southern Indiana might, like Bretton Woods or Dumbarton Oaks, have hosted a great international conference that snatched its name from obscurity and made it synonymous with plans to remake the post-war world.

Roosevelt's determination to use Yalta as a stepping-stone, to convert the United Nations from an alliance into a world organization, remained central to Stettinius's brief. Moreover, an important speech by Senator Vandenberg the previous day had significantly altered the political context in which these proposals were to be discussed. Vandenberg was a totemic figure in the Republican Party. His isolationist stance had clearly reflected his constituency as a prominent senator from the Middle West. In his mind, however, the argument had moved on after the 1944 presidential election returns had finally despatched the controversy about the war's origins in favour of a new issue: the war's aftermath. His speech of 10 January, delivered in the Senate on the natural assumption that Roosevelt would be in power for another four years, was carefully judged. The context is sufficiently indicated by a US opinion poll that Stettinius had drawn to Roosevelt's attention, asking (somewhat tendentiously) about relations with their allies. 'Are others taking advantage?' was one question, to which 24 per cent had said yes six months previously, 32 per cent three months previously, and 39 per cent currently.[9] Vandenberg now spoke in broadly sympathetic terms of the President's recent State of the Union message on foreign policy. But he added his own comment on Roosevelt's acknowledgement of the danger of disputes between the victorious Allies: 'I frankly confess that I do not know why we must be the only silent partner in this grand alliance.'

Vandenberg, though an outspoken anti-Communist, did not simply have the Soviet Union in his sights. 'There seems to be no fear of disunity, no hesitation in London,' he complained, 'where Mr Churchill proceeds upon his unilateral way to make decisions often repugnant to our ideas and our ideals.' Clearly Greece was a major issue here. With Bevin as well as Churchill serving as the butt of Vandenberg's reproaches, the implication was that Roosevelt needed to distance himself from such allies if there were any question – in India or Poland as well as Greece – of diluting the principles of the Atlantic Charter. 'These basic pledges cannot now be dismissed as a mere nautical nimbus,' Vandenberg declared. 'They march with our armies. They sail with our fleets. They fly with our eagles.'

So far, so rhetorical. The meat of the great isolationist's speech came with his declaration of his own position. No such phrase as America First, of course, but instead the lightly coded preface that 'I have always been frankly one of those who has believed in our own self-reliance.' But since Pearl Harbor, he stated, no nation could rely on its own actions and power. In the name of American self-interest as well as of principled support for international law, he now committed himself to 'maximum American cooperation' in implementing the ideas for an international organization that had come out of the Dumbarton Oaks international conference some three months previously. Moreover, he coupled this general commitment with a specific proposal for an immediate treaty between the Allies guaranteeing their future security by a mutual commitment to keep Germany and Japan disarmed.[10]

It was this proposal that dominated the immediate headlines. What gave the speech such resonance, however, was its confessional tone about the broader framework of international relations. There were no novel insights in what was said; the novelty lay in the saying. It was a 'spectacular move', as Isaiah Berlin put it to the Foreign Office, meaning that the 'spectacle of an ex-isolationist Senator calling for what in effect is a most entangling alliance is surely cause for wonder and gratification'.[11] In the world of January 1945, then, Vandenberg's speech went far towards giving the President's internationalist policy a new kind of bipartisan authority. This had two effects. Of course, it manifestly strengthened Roosevelt; it freed him from fear of the sort of repudiation at home that had politically crippled President Wilson over the League of Nations (even before Wilson's physical collapse in his final months in the White House). But conversely, it was not a blank cheque. Bipartisanship also constrained Roosevelt, making him even more attentive to the ingrained prejudices of former isolationists, who were now part of his coalition, but who were still wary of allies in general, especially those whose policies seemed 'repugnant'.

If Roosevelt needed further incentive to keep the United States clear of the machinations of the British Empire, he had it in the weeks before Yalta. In this context, the submerged issue of 'trusteeship' had a new salience. In order to take forward the Dumbarton Oaks proposals for a world organization, a policy on colonial possessions was necessary, if only because the existing League of Nations mandates – Palestine, for instance – would be left in limbo once the League was replaced by a successor organization. What then? The official British view was that its mandated territories were part of the British Empire, with British sovereignty as the default position. The official American view was that sovereignty was intrinsically vested in the international body itself, hence trusteeship of these territories meant international accountability. It should not be thought that policy on dependent territories was of no interest to the United States simply because it had relatively few of them (Puerto Rico, the Philippines or Hawaii, for example). On the contrary, the relevant committee in the State Department held ninety-six meetings over three years. On this matter at least, the United States was to be much better prepared at Yalta than the United Kingdom.

As with many awkward wartime problems, the British simply hoped that it would go away if they shut their eyes tight, or at least kept smiling and nodding whenever the Americans raised the subject. Sir Alec Cadogan had represented the Foreign Office through earlier discussions, notably at Dumbarton Oaks, and had dealt suavely with the State Department on the basis that 'we were asking them to "underwrite" the British Empire and that from their point of view it was natural that they should expect to have some say in how the British Empire was run.'[12] With Eden's full support, understandings were reached with the State Department that full trusteeship should apply only to former League mandates but that the principle of international accountability would be applicable, albeit somewhat less rigorously applied, in British colonies – and why not if, as they kept saying, they had nothing to hide? To the Foreign Office, this was obvious pragmatism.

To the Colonial Office, it was abject appeasement. The Colonial Secretary, Oliver Stanley, visited Washington in mid-January 1945. His father, the Earl of Derby, had been British ambassador to Paris at the time of Roosevelt's European visit as Assistant Secretary of the Navy, as the President remembered. He had met the father and knew how to size up the son, a bland and affable figure. 'I liked Stanley,' the President told his State Department minder, Charles Taussig, after their meeting on 16 January, adding that 'Stanley was more liberal on colonial policy than Churchill.' Admittedly, this set the bar very low. The implied compliment was, however, well deserved since Stanley acquitted himself in great style on this occasion, giving as good as he got in the sort of exchanges where Roosevelt normally excelled. 'I do not want to be unkind or rude to the British,' the President said, 'but in 1841, when you acquired Hong Kong, you did not acquire it by purchase.' Taussig recorded Stanley's instant rejoinder: 'Let me see, Mr President, that was about the time of the Mexican War.'[13]

Stanley was perfectly ready to carpet the Americans too for land-grabbing but, back at home, he found the rug pulled from under him. The Foreign Office prevailed in determining the British line on trusteeship, selling the pass, as the Colonial Office saw it. Churchill had not read the small print and simply dealt in headlines on this issue. 'There must be no question of our being hustled or seduced into declarations affecting British sovereignty in any of the Dominions or Colonies,' he had minuted on 31 December. 'Pray remember my declaration against liquidating the British Empire.' He freely acknowledged that the Americans should be given a free hand in taking those Pacific islands (previously under Japanese mandates) from which US forces had now displaced the Japanese through conquest. 'But "Hands off the British Empire" is our maxim and it must not be weakened or smirched to please sob-stuff merchants at home or foreigners of any hue.' To which Eden blandly replied on 8 January: 'There is not the slightest question of liquidating the British Empire.'[14] Between the Foreign Secretary's silky finesse and the Prime Minister's instinctive prejudices, there was only one common element: a vain hope that the Americans would not reopen such questions at Yalta.

The Presidential inauguration was on Saturday, 20 January 1945. Roosevelt attended the reception for 2,000 people in the White House despite having just suffered an angina attack, which he tackled with a half-tumbler of whiskey and his customary fortitude. Mrs Woodrow Wilson, who had been invited, noticed the difference. 'Oh, it frightened me,' she told a cabinet member. 'He looks exactly as my husband did when he went into his decline.'[15] Two days later the President sailed in the USS *Quincy* from Newport News, Virginia, bound for Malta, where he was due to meet Churchill on 1 February before they would each fly on to Yalta. It was a much-needed break on the kind of long sea voyage he always enjoyed; just the thing to revive his spirits and his health. He celebrated his sixty-third birthday on board. His daughter Anna, accompanying him to Yalta, produced five birthday cakes, one for each of his four presidential election victories plus a small one iced with the date '1948?'

In London, the seventy-year-old Prime Minister was kept busy throughout January. He wanted to capitalize on the good news now coming out of Greece by holding a parliamentary debate to celebrate it. He had been bursting to chastize his critics, especially *The Times*, and also proposed to use the occasion to mend fences with the American forces in the wake of Montgomery's press conference. He was content that the situation in the Ardennes was now under control and he already knew that Stalin was preparing to launch a new offensive on the eastern front, where the Red Army had remained camped outside Warsaw since the summer.

Indeed Stalin purported to have brought forward his attack to 12 January in order to take the pressure off his Western Allies, though the planned date in fact changed little and it is equally plausible to argue that the Red Army was the beneficiary since the Ardennes both diverted and depleted German resources that could have been better used in Poland.

The Russian move was sympathetically reported in London. 'STALIN IS FORCING SWITCH' was the *Daily Express* headline on 16 January. 'More than ever before, it looks as though we are going to feel the effect of the Russian attack on this front,' reported Alan Moorehead from Montgomery's headquarters. 'There is already a possibility that German units are being moved to the East.' This indulgent view, consistent with Beaverbrook's wartime stance in championing the Soviet Union, was fairly conventional at the time, and not just churned out for public consumption. 'Russian news marvellous – they're tearing the guts out of the Germans,' Cadogan wrote in his diary on 17 January. 'Warsaw has fallen.' But he well knew that, with the recent Soviet recognition of the Lublin Poles, this was piquant news for the London Poles. 'It's no triumph for *them*,' he acknowledged, 'and *they* won't get back. What a tragedy!'[16]

What was not said, at least not in public, was that Warsaw might have been liberated months earlier, at the time of the rising. Most people in Britain were simply glad that the Red Army had now resumed its bloody progress against the bloody Nazis. Here were the Russians playing their full part in the Alliance, applying a squeeze on the eastern front that helped our boys on the western front, just like after D-Day. And it was not the Russians who were thwarting British action in Greece – far from it; perhaps Mr Stettinius could have taken a lesson from Mr Molotov in the virtues of silence. Admittedly, what Isaiah Berlin called 'the orgy of recrimination between the American and British presses' seemed to be cooling.[17] Even the *Daily Mail* was now determinedly pro-Allied in its stance – at least in the case of the Soviet Union. 'Soviet Blow Was Timed With Allies,' it reported on 19 January, giving as much news as it could muster (through Stockholm sources) on the now clearly successful advances by Soviet tanks, joyfully splashed across the front page under the banner headline: 'RED ARMY ENTER GERMANY'. This even relegated the report of Churchill's much-heralded parliamentary speech to two adjacent columns.

The Prime Minister was on top form, oratorically if not physically. Moreover, his words were uttered in a more benign context than for many months past as he rose to give his war review to the House of Commons on 18 January. That morning's *Daily Mail* had evidently already been briefed on part of his agenda: 'The PM To Praise US Heroes' was the headline on a front-page column by Wilson Broadbent, the same political correspondent who only ten days previously had covered Montgomery's press conference in such egregious terms. 'It will be no ordinary tribute,' Broadbent now explained, with tacit penitence, 'for Mr Churchill believes that the American soldiers proved themselves to be men of great military prowess. Their resistance prevented a crisis, and he is determined to give them full credit and the major part of his war speech.' This was orchestrated as part of what Harry Butcher called 'an effort to pour oil on troubled Allied waters' which also saw a press conference at SHAEF the next day, when not only did Bedell Smith talk to reporters but, crucially, his British deputy, General Sir Frederick Morgan, 'spoke feelingly about the teamwork of the Allied Command, praised General Ike to the skies, and said that we simply must stick together'.[18] This was, of course, more or less word for word what Morgan's *bête noire* Monty had said in his press conference. As with Vandenberg's speech, everything turned on who said it.

What Churchill said in the Commons was just what was needed. Colville thought that 'rhetorically, it was the best effort I have heard him make since 1941 or even 1940.'[19] In his speech there was an eloquent and generous passage, duly reproduced in *Triumph and Tragedy*, rejecting any description of the Battle of the Bulge as an Anglo-American battle, instead stressing that 'the United States troops have done almost all the fighting, and have suffered almost all the losses' and asking the House not to forget 'that it is to American homes that the telegrams of personal losses and anxiety have been going during the past month'.[20] No hint of any reprimand to Monty, of course.

This was not, however, the main thrust of the speech. It became a great parliamentary occasion because of what Churchill said about Greece – and how he said it. The words in the columns of Hansard convey this less effectively than the first-hand reactions of those who heard them. 'He started by telling us that he had a bad cold in the head – and in fact he was pink about the nostrils and somewhat hoarse – but he spoke for two hours with immense vivacity, persuasiveness and humour,' Harold Nicolson wrote. 'He made a terrific attack on *The Times*, which was greeted with cheers such as I have not heard since that unhappy Munich morning.'[21] Admittedly, Nicolson was not only a personal supporter of Churchill but actively committed to his policy on Greece; so his testimony might be thought biased.

This parliamentary demonstration was also recorded in the diary of the editor of *The Times* himself. Barrington-Ward had been sitting in the press gallery and thus heard for himself – perhaps helped through his presence to provoke – the remarkable response to Churchill's barbs. 'How can we wonder,' the Prime Minister demanded, 'still more how can we complain, of the attitude of hostile and indifferent newspapers in the United States when we have in this country witnessed such a melancholy exhibition as that provided by our most time-honoured and responsible journals . . .' Barrington-Ward wrote of the uproar that now intervened: 'This – a direct and obvious reference to *T.T.* – immediately touched off the loudest, largest and most vicious – even savage! – cheer that I have heard in the House. It must have lasted a full minute or more.'[22] Churchill long relished the moment, later telling Lord Moran that the cheering, such as he had not heard in years, came from all parts of the House: 'Barrington Ward [sic] was in the gallery. Members looked up at him.'[23]

There was a pent-up passion behind this reponse, as Barrington-Ward recognized. But he probably flattered himself in taking it so personally. Nor was it just the release of Conservative MPs' anger that their own house-organ, which had once offered them such dependable support, had proved itself so subversive. Neither was the discomfiture of the parliamentary left-wingers enough to explain it, though this was certainly relished by those who thought that the Coalition pandered too much to Labour backbenchers. 'The effect of the speech on Labour as a whole was devastating,' the parliamentary correspondent of the *Daily Mail* gleefully reported. 'In many years of parliamentary reporting I have never seen an Opposition so nonplussed, so clearly left without a shot in the locker.' But given that the leading Labour ministers in the Government, notably Bevin, were closely identified with its Greek policy, pure partisanship only explains so much; and it is clear that Churchill was right to think that not only the Tories cheered.

What was also at work here was surely the proxy effect. The offence of *The Times* was to represent views that were not only left-wing, and not only wrong-headed, but also tainted with unbearably smug American connotations. Oliver Stanley was not the only MP whose impatience at sermons about British wrongdoing prompted him to think of the skeletons in American closets. In the current state of the news, British military intervention in Greece appeared as something that could be celebrated in its own right, the more so since it was upholding the actual principles of democracy more effectively than were the tiresome verbal interventions of democracy's self-righteous and self-appointed transatlantic champions.

Churchill spoke to this otherwise unspoken agenda as openly as he dared. Thus he stated British aims in familiar words: 'Government of the people, by the people, for the people, set up on a basis of free and universal suffrage elections, with secrecy of the ballot and no intimidation.' That the words were plagiarized from Abraham Lincoln made his point, as did his terse assertion: 'That is our only aim, our only interest, and our only care.'[24] He did not ask, who but the State Department would ever have supposed otherwise? Not once did he reproach the Americans – indeed his tribute to their troops was an integral part of his speech – and still less did he suggest that he differed from their President, whose disparagement of 'power politics', as a misuse of power, he happily endorsed. In private, his feelings had been more pungent, demanding that the British ambassador in Washington, Lord Halifax, ask Stettinius for a definition of this loaded term, so freely employed against the British. 'Is having a Navy twice as strong as any other "power politics"?' was one of Churchill's list of rhetorical questions, seeking to put the United States on the spot: 'Is having all the gold in the world buried in a cavern "power politics"?' By contrast, he wanted to ask Stettinius: 'Is holding the ring in Greece to enable the people to have a fair election "power politics"?'[25]

Churchill's speech to the House of Commons put his points in parliamentary language, talking up the Grand Alliance. It was now that he publicly welcomed Roosevelt's recent announcement that the Big Three were soon to meet. But he now also reached out to the deepest feelings of his own countrymen about the enterprise on which he had invited them to join him since 1940. Hence the echoes of his greatest war speeches, which had been pitched in the same register, sombre but uplifting. 'We have sacrificed everything in this war,' he told them. 'We shall emerge from it, for the time being, more stricken and impoverished than any other victorious country. The United Kingdom and the British Commonwealth are the only unbroken force which declared war on Germany of its own free will.' Honourable Members could work out for themselves that the Soviet Union had not done so, the United States had not done so.

This was the moment, then, to remember who had done what to secure the victory that now lay ahead. 'After the defeat of France in June 1940, for more than a year we stood alone,' Churchill declaimed. 'We kept nothing back in blood or effort or treasure for what has now become the common cause of more than thirty nations.' It is unlikely that his immediate listeners needed any reminder of this point, since they had never forgotten it, but it certainly challenged any assumption that the common struggle only began with Lend-Lease. Then the Prime Minister, having pleaded for his country's just deserts, vented its just wrath against false imputations upon its motives. 'Our actions are, no doubt, subject to human error, but our actions in small things as in great are disinterested, lofty and true,' he continued. 'I repulse these challenges, wherever they come from, that Britain and the British Empire is a selfish, power-greedy, land-greedy, designing nation, obsessed with dark schemes of European intrigue or colonial expansion. I refute these aspersions whether they come from our best friends or our worst foes.'[26]

It was in this mood, and with the cheers still ringing in his ears, that Churchill was to go to Yalta, buoyed up by a sense of renewed public support and approval for his leadership. Insiders, it must be admitted, were more equivocal. It was not just that the CIGS, jealous of the reputation of the chiefs of staff committee, felt that it had, notwithstanding Churchill's long speech, been accorded none of the credit for the improvement in the fortunes of war. As Brooke observed mordantly on 20 January: 'Any lime light for it could not fail to slightly diminish the PM's halo!'[27] What is remarkable is that Churchill's conduct of government as a whole, and his own performance in cabinet, were now criticized in direct and unprecedented terms, articulated by his own Deputy Prime Minister.

It was on this same day that Colville, as the Prime Minister's private secretary, recorded the receipt of a blunt letter, typed personally by Clement Attlee so that its extraordinary contents would not be seen by his own staff. In it he pointed to the amount of patient committee work that was needed to win consensus within the Coalition before agreed conclusions were presented in cabinet papers. And then? Not only was it 'very exceptional for you to have read them' but increasingly often 'you have not read even the note prepared for your guidance', leading to a waste of time while points were explained orally. 'Not infrequently,' Attlee continued, 'a phrase catches your eye which gives rise to a disquisition on an interesting point only slightly connected with the subject matter.' Moreover, instead of accepting expert advice, Churchill was accused of according undue influence to favourites like Bracken and Beaverbrook.[28]

Churchill was simply not used to being reprimanded like this. His response was explosive, with drafts of a sarcastic reply vehemently dictated and copiously revised, replete with accusations of a socialist conspiracy. It was one thing, however, to rebut calumnies, another to deny the truth. 'Greatly as I love and admire the P.M.,' Colville conceded, 'I am afraid there is much in what Attlee says, and I rather admire his courage in saying it.'[29]

The truth is that Attlee, a strict constitutionalist, was clearly acting here as Deputy Prime Minister not as Leader of the Labour Party. Conventional and conservative in all except his political views, Attlee too admired Churchill's charismatic gifts and respected his unique contribution to ensuring Britain's survival since 1940. So though he obviously differed in his partisanship from Leo Amery, Field Marshal Brooke or Sir Alexander Cadogan, all of them natural supporters of the Conservative Party, this was not the point at issue. Had Attlee read their diaries he would have found ample corroboration for what he had reluctantly summoned his own inimitable headmasterly authority to tell the Prime Minister.

Churchill slept on this rebuff. He had gone to bed late, gaily insisting that his staff 'not bother about Atler or Hitlee'. The next morning, though snow was lying deep, the sun was out, and, when he awoke at 11.30, he told his private secretary that 'he felt recovered and that life had returned'. Colville himself took the opportunity for a walk in St James's Park with Clementine Churchill, 'who says that she thinks Attlee's letter of yesterday is both true and wholesome'. It turned out that Beaverbrook himself (whom she mistrusted) thought it a good letter, even though it had been partly directed against him. The Prime Minister, having digested all this and, as Colville observed, 'still sorely piqued but probably in his heart of hearts not unmoved by the arguments', jettisoned all the earlier drafts in favour of a two-line reply, eloquent only in its taciturn dignity. 'You may be sure I shall always endeavour to profit by your counsels,' he wrote to Attlee on 22 January.[30]

The efficacy of these endeavours, the extent of this profit, and the impact of these counsels, were all to be tested that very evening. 'At 5.30 pm War Cabinet, drawn out by the usual endless statements by Winston,' recorded Brooke, attending as CIGS. 'My God! How I loathe these Cabinet meetings! The waste of time is appalling.'[31] News of the spectacular advance by the tanks of the Red Army under Marshal Zhukov – now believed to be only 165 miles from Berlin – was on everyone's minds. This was simultaneously welcome and ominous. 'During the Cabinet Winston asked Brooke for the number of Russian Divisions, and when he said 500 one could feel the shudder going through the Cabinet,' Amery wrote. 'On this theme Winston spoke very earnestly on the fact that we had at any rate tried, and probably succeeded, in saving Greece from the flood of Bolshevism.'[32] That was the more optimistic way of putting it. Churchill spoke more freely to Colville the following day: 'Make no mistake, all the Balkans, except Greece, are going to be Bolshevised; and there is nothing I can do to prevent it. There is nothing I can do for poor Poland either.'[33] Six days later Churchill set out to meet Roosevelt and Stalin.

We usually think of Yalta as signalling the end of the Second World War. True, even at this point the German army retained an all too effective fighting capacity, both on its eastern and on its western fronts, postponing the Nazi surrender by months longer than had been expected. Yet the agenda of the Big Three meeting was manifestly geared to a transition from war to peace. What was to be the fate of the liberated or occupied territories, especially Poland? How could an international organization be shaped so as to guarantee national security and maintain world peace? Such issues were central at Yalta precisely because the war was, inexorably and inevitably, coming to an end.

In one important respect, however, this war was only just beginning – or at least changing its nature. The British, in their unimaginative but practical way, simply talked about 'the war' – and continued to do so, without serious danger of being misunderstood, for the rest of the century. President Roosevelt, for good reasons of his own, started referring to 'this Second World War' from early 1941, at a time when

Lend-Lease was being implemented but before the United States was itself a belligerent.[34] Such talk paved the way for his country to play its part in a worldwide ideological struggle, rather than simply to concentrate on countering Japanese aggression should a Pacific war begin, as it did after Pearl Harbor. Roosevelt's strategy in such a contingency was already for Germany First. Not until Hitler had been defeated would the United States turn its full might to the Pacific war against the Japanese. In this conflict, of course, it had since December 1941 been allied with the British Empire, which certainly had its own military problems in Asia, symbolized by the fall of Singapore. But with the Big Three about to meet, and with the Soviet–Japanese neutrality pact of 1941 still in force, a big question arose: when would Stalin agree to enter the war against Japan? Only once this happened, and the Allies at last granted the Pacific first priority, would the Second World War fully deserve its name.

Nobody was more conscious that the war in Asia did not have first claim on Churchill's attention than Field Marshal Lord Wavell, Viceroy of India since October 1943. He had come to the post rather unexpectedly, capping a distinguished military career, though one blighted by his serious disagreements with the Prime Minister. Archibald Wavell was a man of few words, though they were often extremely well chosen. Not only had he recently published an anthology of his favourite poems, *Other Men's Flowers* (1944), but he was currently keeping a journal that gives a persuasive and perceptive account of his Viceroyalty, winning him more plaudits posthumously than he received at the time. As a soldier, he had prided himself on giving good advice to the Prime Minister, notably not to commit the British Empire forces in North Africa prematurely against Rommel. After his advice was ignored, the outcome simply confirmed Wavell's view that Tobruk need not have been imperilled but for Churchill's impetuousness. Wavell's own failure lay in not being prepared to argue his case, in the cut and thrust of Churchillian debate, when he had the opportunity to do so in person. Instead he retreated into taciturn submission – an instructive contrast with Brooke's more successful war of attrition against the Prime Minister's wild plans.

Wavell often reflected that he was not the ideal Viceroy. 'Even if I manage to hold down this job for my full five years, I could make little impression on the situation,' he wrote on the last day of 1944.[35] But that was partly a measure of the daunting challenges that faced him. In one respect, at least, his successive service as British commander-in-chief in the Middle East and then as British commander-in-chief in India prepared him well. In each case, and again as Viceroy, he was given vast responsibilities for defending the overstretched British Empire, and was expected to do so with resources plainly inadequate to the task. It is not quite true to say that he carried on without complaint, just that the complaints he made, whether as soldier or Viceroy, were generally ignored by a Prime Minister who was better at willing the ends than providing the means.

In 1942 the Cripps Mission had failed in Delhi but scored a tactical success in Washington. Instead of challenging Churchill's premiership, Stafford Cripps's role turned out to be that of insulating it for the rest of the war against further American intervention in Indian affairs.

This was the situation that Wavell inherited when he succeeded Linlithgow in 1943. True, at the Teheran conference later in that year Roosevelt could still confide his feelings on India to Stalin: 'that the best solution would be reform from the bottom, somewhat on the Soviet line'.[36] This was hardly what the new Viceroy had in mind. He soon realized that the suppressed reforming instincts of the American President were less trouble to him than the recalcitrant obduracy of his own Prime Minister. The Viceroy in fact came round to seeing more merit in the strategy of the Cripps Mission for immediate democratization than he had at the time of its negotiations in Delhi, when Wavell had been involved only as commander-in-chief. 'Wavell's idea is to renew the Cripps offer as regards the interim period,' Amery noted in his diary as early as September 1943.[37]

Now Wavell had been put in by Churchill as a military Viceroy, to clamp down India for the duration of hostilities. It is a mark of his own integrity that he came to take a wider view of his responsibilities, inevitably political therefore, and showed himself far more flexible than his hidebound predecessor, Lord Linlithgow. But it is a sign of Wavell's limitations that he not only despised politicians as a class but himself lacked essential political skills. His capacity for easy face-to-face relations may not have been enhanced by the disconcerting fact that he had only one eye; but he certainly tried to keep it on the ball, so as to seize any favourable opportunities of improving a bad situation.

Such opportunities were few, the obstacles in his path many. 'In Whitehall there is ignorance and prejudice to overcome,' the Viceroy reflected in his diary, 'it is curious how little they seem to know or to care about India and her problems.'[38] This was fair comment, only unfair in not excluding from this general stricture the two or three cabinet ministers who knew enough and cared enough to keep battling against a blinkered bureaucracy and, above all, against a truculent Prime Minister. Leo Amery, as Secretary of State for India, could be found, month in, month out, tirelessly seeking to use the India Committee of the cabinet to enlist more attention for the problems of the subcontinent. Moreover, Amery's impeccable imperialist credentials consorted with an unexpected open-mindedness about reform, basically on the ground that almost anything was worth considering if it might help to keep India within the Empire, or at least within the Commonwealth as a self-governing country.

Yet it often seemed that nobody was listening, least of all Churchill, who preferred the sound of his own voice in cabinet meetings. Any initiatives, then, were successively stalled until Amery himself set the ball rolling again over Christmas 1944. His first task was to gain the Prime Minister's attention. Now that Amery had come up with his own reforming plans, he was particularly irritated that India had to wait while the Prime Minister hopped off to Greece, and then wait again until his return from the Big Three.

By 28 December Amery had prepared a memorandum of 6,000 words. 'Its main conclusion is the inversion of the Cripps offer,' he proudly recorded, 'viz. give India freedom from Whitehall first and let her work out her permanent constitution at leisure – a superficially daring but really cautious and practical policy.'[39] To Cripps, his only reliable ally on the India Committee, the right procedure naturally seemed the other way around: Indian freedom, by all means, but with prior democratization of Indian government. And Wavell's own experience led him to the same conclusion as Cripps, hoping that an interim coalition might be possible between Congress and the Muslim League, led by Mohammed Ali Jinnah and professing the goal of a separate Pakistan. Thus not only the Secretary of State but also the Viceroy had a plan of his own.

The real problem, of course, was not to choose between a revised Cripps Offer and an inverted Cripps Offer: it was to overcome the calculated inertia which it suited Churchill to maintain. When Amery had an opportunity to consider Wavell's plan on 15 January 1945, he gave it little chance of persuading the India Committee or the cabinet, though conceding that 'personally I have little doubt that it would succeed if it were accompanied by the kind of declaration of India's independence under her present constitution which I should like to make.'[40] The following day he was pleasantly surprised at the India Committee's reaction, which helped steel him to action.

An important *démarche* followed. Hitherto, Cripps had played only a modest role in the work of the India Committee since the failure of the eponymous mission, understandably reserving his energies for his huge task as Minister of Aircraft Production. He had been on cool terms with Wavell since their uneasy encounter in Delhi, and the Viceroy in turn was dismissive of Cripps, claiming that he would not stand up to Churchill. Amery, who did so in cabinet with more courage than effect, had likewise taken time to appreciate how much common ground he had with his left-wing colleague. Separately, these three reformers were easily stalled; together they suddenly became a formidable combination. 'Long talk with Cripps about the Indian situation,' Amery recorded on 19 January. 'We both felt that there is a real danger that Winston may drive Wavell into resignation and in that case neither of us could stay.'[41]

The Wavell–Amery–Cripps nexus ensured that Indian reform could no longer be ignored by the British Government. It had no other rationale, not even an agreed programme, as is clear from Wavell's jaded comment: 'Meanwhile I have to cope with a curious (Stafford Cripps called it "startling", Amery says) proposal which S. of S. has evolved and put to War Cabinet.'[42] Conversely, Amery did not imagine that it was his own proposal, but some version of Wavell's, that would constitute the way forward. Only as a last resort did he and Cripps contemplate resignation, knowing that it would mean 'a desperately serious breach in the ranks of the Government and might even bring it down'.[43] Nonetheless, the fact that they were now fighting together in the India Committee to give reasonable consideration to Wavell's proposals gave these a wholly new salience.

The point was that the Prime Minister would no longer be able to avoid discussions on India. Not as soon as had been hoped, admittedly; but the Viceroy acknowledged the prior claim of the Big Three meeting, writing benignly in his diary on 25 January: 'I wonder if P.M., who is the biggest man of the three, will still be able to assert his dominant personality. A great triumph if he can, the oldest man of the three with the weakest hand to play.'[44]

What Wavell did not know was that, en route to Yalta, the Prime Minister's mind would at last focus on India. When, confined to bed for a day, he read the rather cynical book *Verdict on India* (1944) by the journalist Beverley Nichols, it made Churchill depressed, with a feeling of despair about the British connection. 'Meanwhile we are holding on to this vast Empire,' he wrote to his wife, 'from which we get nothing, amid the increasing criticism and abuse of the world and our own people and increasing hatred of the Indian population, who receive constant and deadly propaganda to which we can make no reply.' Why, then, keep an Empire that was of so little benefit? Why endure the criticism? Perhaps Wavell's plans for reviving the Cripps Offer, or even Amery's for quickly working himself out of a job, might appeal to the Prime Minister? But no, the old reflexes were still there when Churchill nonetheless affirmed 'a renewed resolve to go on fighting on [sic] as long as possible and to make sure the Flag is not let down while I am at the wheel'.[45]

By the time the Big Three met, the eyes of the world were fixed on the Soviet Union. Not, however, on the Crimea, where tight security restricted reporting at Yalta. It was, of course, a deliberate decision that the press should be excluded and likewise, as Churchill had proposed to Roosevelt, 'that each of us should be free to bring not more than three or four uniformed service photographers to take "still" and cinematograph pictures to be released when we think fit'.[46] Only on 13 February, at the end of the conference, were the famous photographs of the Big Three published: Roosevelt in his cape, Churchill in his 'British warm', Stalin in his Marshal's uniform. Until then, what grabbed attention were the feats of the Red Army on the eastern front. As far away as Melbourne, the *Age* led the front page, day by day, with news of the Soviet advance – 'RUSSIANS RACING ON TO BERLIN' (1 February).

The immediate war situation thus endowed Stalin with enormous prestige and influence in settling the affairs of Europe. Harry Butcher, in charge of news dissemination at SHAEF, had his own narrower concerns. He had become worried about whether he had the right aircraft to transport the press corps, given that, as he recorded on 27 January, leapfrogging rumours at one moment put the Russians 94 miles, or a few minutes later 91 miles, from Berlin – 'nine miles', so his secretary satirically claimed to have heard. 'All of our plans stress the use of these aircraft for first coverage of Berlin,' her agitated boss wrote. 'If they are not ready, our names will be mud.'[47] In Butcher's line of business, this was a big issue at that moment since the logistics of modern warfare had to allow for the importance of media communications: not to create the news, perhaps, but – given that the fall of Berlin would inevitably be the biggest news of the war – to create the conditions under which it would be reported. Would it eclipse the Big Three meeting?

Berlin had a psychological as much as a strategic importance. Eisenhower might entertain notions, encouraged by Goebbels's propaganda, that the Nazis would nonetheless fight on, perhaps in their fabled national redoubt in the south German mountains. But if the Russians got to Berlin first, as had always been likely and now seemed imminent, it would give them obvious power on the ground. It would also be seen as further evidence of their prowess, in contrast to the reverses the Allies had suffered in the west, notably in the Battle of the Bulge. Moreover, the Soviet push to Berlin was widely seen, not as a move to undermine their Western Allies through a selfish pre-emptive strike, but as a chivalrous rescue effort to take the pressure off the western front. So if and when Berlin fell, SHAEF as usual wanted it reported as a co-operative Allied success, not as a competitive Russian triumph. Actually, Butcher was right to conclude, in a calmer moment, that the Russian advance, like the Allied advance across France in the summer, had now racked up exaggerated expectations of the speed of the German demise, and that supply problems would catch up with even the awesome Red Army. This indeed began to happen while the Big Three were conferring, though Stalin naturally still talked up Russian prospects.

One way or another, it was undeniably the Soviet Union that held the initiative as the British and American leaders converged on Malta for their own preliminary meeting at the end of January. Harry Hopkins, sent ahead to Europe by Roosevelt in lieu of his Secretary of State, visited Churchill in London and spent three nights in his company. If the congenial Hopkins found the Prime Minister 'volcanic' (as his friend Sherwood reports) it perhaps suggests that he was being used to absorb some of the long-suppressed primal frenzy that might have poured forth even more violently had Stettinius himself been subjected to Churchill's views on the Americans' handling of the Greek episode. As it was, Churchill vented his surplus wrath on the choice of Yalta, for which he took delight in blaming Hopkins personally: 'We could not have found a worse place for a meeting if we had spent ten years on research.'[48]

Then Hopkins, though far from well, visited SHAEF. 'Harry said that the big issue at Malta will be the Pacific versus the European war,' Butcher recorded. 'It will develop between General Marshall, whose heart is in completing the war against Germany first and with all possible support, and Admiral King, who, in the tradition of the Navy, has his heart in the Pacific.'[49]

The American chiefs of staff, led by Marshall, and the British chiefs of staff, led by Brooke, were the first to meet at Malta. The official minutes show an incredible picture of unity between the Allies. In particular the agreed report from the combined chiefs of staff on operations in north-west Europe informed the President and the Prime Minister that 'complete agreement had been reached on this question'.[50] Incredible indeed, since the British plan was still to concentrate the Allied assault, the American plan to sustain Eisenhower's broad-front compromise. Rather more credibly, Sherwood records Hopkins's view that the chiefs of staff 'had been engaged in the most violent disagreements and disputes of the whole war', and that these quarrels 'reached such a point that Marshall, ordinarily one of the most restrained and soft-spoken of men, announced that if the British plan were approved by the Prime Minister and President he would recommend to Eisenhower that he had no choice but to ask to be relieved of his command'.[51] It is true that Eisenhower's competence was inevitably an issue after the initial success of the German offensive. Shaken by the experience, and still with plenty on his plate in the Ardennes, he did not go to Malta himself. Eisenhower's case did not go by default, however, since, on top of briefing Marshall in France, he was ably represented in Malta by Bedell Smith – more persuasive than Eisenhower himself in the British view. 'We decided to adopt Bedell's statement and ignore Ike's appreciation' was how Brooke put it on 31 January.[52]

In fact the nub of the chiefs of staffs' differences lay in the familiar conflict between British and American views. Should Eisenhower abandon his broad-front strategy? Did he need a ground forces commander to run operations? The British insistently said yes; the Americans adamantly said no.

There were two new twists. On strategy, even Churchill had belatedly conceded that a measure of withdrawal from Italy was inevitable. This would allow Allied troops to be pulled out of a now fruitless campaign and instead reinforce the north-European front. Rather surprisingly, the Americans proposed that these transferred forces should all be British or Canadian, leaving Mark Clark's 5th US Army intact in Italy. In practice this meant that the two Canadian divisions would have priority in the transfer, thus fulfilling the hope expressed at the Quebec conference that all Canadians fighting in Europe could be unified within Crerar's 1st Army in Belgium and the Netherlands. Given the crisis in Canada over conscription, this was politically helpful to Mackenzie King as well as grimly welcome to Canadian soldiers (like Farley Mowat) who felt that they had languished too long on the barren and bloody Italian front.

On strategy, then, the British lived up to their own rhetoric about concentrating resources on a single north-European push. But even Bedell Smith's capable and conciliatory phrasing could not disguise the fact that Eisenhower himself remained wedded to a broad front which would include closing up to the Rhine in the south as well as giving priority, at least nominally, to an effort to cross it in the north, and thus threaten the Ruhr. The latter, of course, was Montgomery's sector of the front; and everyone realized how closely the strategic and command issues were intertwined. So the other new ploy by the British was that, instead of making the case for Montgomery, they proposed replacing Air Marshal Tedder as Deputy Supreme Commander at SHAEF. This was a means of reviving Churchill's idea of transferring Alexander, always his favourite, into such a role, now that Mediterranean operations were being stepped down (except in Greece).

Why on earth should the Americans mind if the British juggled one of their men out and another in? But Tedder, of course, was an airman, Alexander a soldier like Eisenhower; so the effect would be a real delegation of operations to a British field commander. Indeed that was privately why Brooke, despite his scathing private assessment of Alex's deficiencies, went along with the idea. If only because Alexander was actually present at the Malta conference, this plan was discussed on an informal basis, with a major effort to nobble Marshall, who went no further than agreeing to think it over (which itself came as a betrayal to Eisenhower when he learned this later). But little was really settled at Malta, so a rather messy compromise prevailed on strategy, with Brooke simply agreeing to 'take note' of the American position, which, as he observed on 1 February, 'allowed Marshall to express his full dislike and antipathy to Montgomery!'[53]

Monty was the ghost at the feast so far as the American chiefs of staff were concerned. He was certainly (though incorrectly on this occasion) blamed by Eisenhower for fomenting and perpetuating the internal strife that the Allied generals seemed incapable of escaping. It was a piquant touch that all the meetings of the combined chiefs of staff that Marshall and his colleagues had to attend in Malta were held in a building called Montgomery House. In the US Army photograph of the first meeting, the room where they met looks bare and unprepossessing, with the top brass on each side confronting each other, glum and intent.

The Prime Minister had flown out to Malta on the night of 29 January, accompanied by his daughter Sarah. It was another perilous trip. A subsequent plane, in which Colville would have travelled but for a last-minute decision to keep him in London, crashed near the island of Lampedusa, killing most of the passengers, including Brooke's ADC (Churchill's other private secretary, John Martin, was on the Prime Minister's plane). The problem was the weather as much as enemy action, for Malta had now survived its wartime ordeal of blockade and bombardment, which arose from its strategic position athwart Mediterranean shipping routes. Arguably it was British control of Malta, however tenuously maintained, that in the end condemned Rommel to defeat at El Alamein, because of the vulnerability of Axis supplies for North Africa. All of this had taken its toll on the island, with its magnificent harbour of Valletta showing the scars of long, bitter and recent conflict. It was here, aboard HMS *Orion*, that Churchill established his temporary headquarters while he awaited the arrival of the virtually convalescent Roosevelt, still at sea aboard USS *Quincy*.

Churchill did not arrive in much better shape himself. Lord Moran, always at hand on these occasions, had tried to sleep on the plane but was awoken by the equally indispensable Sawyers. His master was running a temperature and confidently offered his own view that Moran's pills were to blame. Brushing aside this assured but unfounded diagnosis, Moran was nonetheless worried about his patient. 'He has developed a bad habit of running a temperature on these journeys,' he noted. 'It is not the flesh only that is weaker. Martin tells me that his work has deteriorated a lot in the last few months; and that he has become very wordy, irritating his colleagues in the Cabinet by his verbosity.'[54] Incorrigible in all things, Churchill at first slept on the plane at the airfield, feeling sorry for himself and calling out for his wife; but he rallied as usual and later went aboard *Orion*, already set on taking charge.

'What a man!' wrote Cadogan, who had flown out earlier with Eden. 'But it bores Anthony frightfully, of course, taking the wind out of *his* sails.'[55] Churchill insisted on entertaining a party including Averell Harriman, the American ambassador to Russia, for dinner that night. While Cadogan and Eden were happy to leave *Orion* for their own ship, HMS *Sirius*, at 10.30, thinking it a relatively early night, the Prime Minister was only just getting into his stride. Moran, also present at dinner, ruefully observed that 'Winston is a gambler, and gamblers do not count the coins in their pockets. He will not give a thought to his waning powers.'[56] Hence the gambler, at nearly midnight, settled down to play bezique with Harriman, who shared his passion for the game (and his longevity, as it turned out).

Churchill did spend much of the next two days in bed; but then he often did, so this was less on doctor's orders than on his own whim. It was actually the best place for him since, apart from recuperation, it kept him from getting closely enmeshed in the chiefs-of-staff vituperations, now moving towards their conclusion. It also spared him from too much intimate contact with Edward Stettinius, who arrived with Harry Hopkins on 31 January. They had been met at the airfield by Cadogan and Eden, evidently without friction – 'we brought Ed. and Harry to this ship, where they are staying, and gave them tea and a chat,' Cadogan noted. He found much the same the next morning: 'discussion with Ed. and two of his henchmen. We got on very well and I don't think we're going to have any serious differences with them.'[57] The CIGS was invited to lunch on the *Sirius* at the end of this amicable session and recorded: 'I sat next to Stettinius and found him pleasant and easy to talk to.'[58]

No shadow over Anglo-American relations, then, and no perceptible friction between the small party assembled that night on the *Orion* – 'P.M., Ed., Anthony, Harry Hopkins and self,' Cadogan noted. 'P.M. seemed to be in good form and there was a spate of rambling talk on most subjects.'[59] Stettinius did not wholly escape the retribution that had been mounting up for him since the first week of December. 'The prime minister was rather outspoken to me regarding Greece and Italy,' he observed in that night's diary, which is certainly borne out by the undiplomatic terms in which Count Sforza is described: 'Churchill said he was a no-good bum.' But, having got this overdue harangue off his chest, the Prime Minister became distinctly cordial, leaving the apprehensive Secretary of State much relieved – 'I have had a closer association with him than ever before.' He found the old man depressed, as he sat over dinner, about the outlook for a world in which 'there were probably more units of suffering among humanity' than at any point in history. 'He said everything depended on Britain and America remaining in close harmony together at all times.'[60]

At 9.35 a.m. on Friday, 2 February, with the sunshine already warm, the USS *Quincy*, 4883 miles out of Newport News, steamed into Valletta's Grand Harbour. 'The President was on deck as we entered port,' the log recorded. 'From the very large crowd evident, it appeared that all Malta was out to greet him.'[61] It was a stirring moment, some thought historic. From the *Orion*, Moran recorded that the *Quincy* passed slowly by: 'The President, in a cloth cap, sat scanning our ship for Winston, who was on the quarter-deck raising his hat in salutation.'[62] There was lunch on the *Quincy*. The Prime Minister was touched to find a small candle by his place, so that he could light his cigar, and attributed its provision to the President himself (rather than an attentive butler, like Sawyers, perhaps). 'The President's very friendly,' he repeated when he got back – 'half to himself', as Moran thought.[63]

Friendly as the lunch was, no business was done at it, so a dinner that evening was arranged. No business was done at the dinner either. The result was that the only working meeting for the President and Prime Minister was sandwiched between these essentially social events, when the chiefs of staff began assembling at 5.30 p.m. in preparation for a plenary meeting on the *Quincy*. It was now that Admiral King, who had last seen Roosevelt at the Inauguration, became alarmed by the serious deterioration he now detected in the President's health.

The four days of meetings by the combined chiefs of staff had resulted in a short and businesslike document summarizing their agreed conclusions, so far as agreement had proved possible. It set a planning date for the end of the European war within the period 1 July to 31 December 1945, thus moving it as much as a year later than had been anticipated at the Octagon conference in Quebec, with the end of the Japanese war still another eighteen months after that. At worst, what we now call

VJ-Day could have been as late as July 1947. Plainly these were very conservative estimates. In London at this point Dalton recorded the opinion of Albert Alexander, the First Lord of the Admiralty, that 'he couldn't see how the German war could go on more than about two months longer', and Attlee's reponse: 'I'm inclined to agree with him, but I don't say so to anybody.'[64] The difference was obviously that the chiefs of staff, already caught out once for being too optimistic, were now hedging their bets.

The plenary meeting, at 6 p.m. on 2 February, was crucial, at least so far as the British were concerned. It was their last chance to mobilize a well-briefed Prime Minister for a last-ditch appeal to the President over the heads of the military. In particular, since the British had been asking for a modification of the broad-front strategy in northern Europe, the status quo would obviously prevail unless a clear decision were taken the other way. This did not happen. 'Winston as usual had not read the paper although he had had it since this morning!' Brooke noted. 'He made the most foolish remarks about it which proved he had not read it, and altogether did not come out very well!'[65]

The official record does not put it that way. There are indeed some fairly specific references minuted. 'The Prime Minister, referring to paragraph 6f., thought that great efforts should now be made to pass supplies to Russia via the Dardanelles.' Any reference to the Dardanelles, of course, excited Churchill, his career almost destroyed thirty years previously by the Gallipoli fiasco. 'The Prime Minister questioned the meaning of the words "to close the Rhine" which occurred in paragraph 10 of the report.' Yes, it was just Ike's way of saying that his troops would move up to the Rhine all the way along its length rather than concentrate in the north. 'The Prime Minister inquired whether paragraph 18 meant that there would be no help from United States air forces in operations in the Kra Peninsula, Malaya, et cetera.' Whether the United States would be exerting itself to restore the British Empire in these areas of Japanese-occupied south-east Asia was a good question, though not one on which any specific commitments were forthcoming, then or later.

Churchill bluffed through, fortified by his own self-confidence and long practice. Not for nothing had he been attending such briefings since he first entered Asquith's cabinet thirty-seven years previously; and his facility for picking up points extempore had not deserted him. It may well be, too, that what he actually said at the time subsequently benefited in these minutes from the sort of expert drafting that habitually created order out of incoherence, especially by tidying up vague or inaccurate citations. What even the official minutes cannot conceal is the lack of any challenge to the fudged formulations of the conclusions reached by the chiefs of staff. 'Summing up,' as the minutes state, 'the Prime Minister said that he was glad to see that such a great measure of agreement had been reached.'[66] Smiles all round at this point, no doubt, while an exasperated Brookie pretended to look hard at his papers. Then the friendly dinner to round off proceedings. Before it, there was time for him to join Marshall, Roosevelt and Churchill in a word about the proposed Tedder–Alexander switch. 'The President and Marshall considered that politically such a move might have repercussions in America if carried out just now,' Brooke noted later. 'It might be considered that Alex was being put in to support Ike after his Ardennes failure!'[67] Just so; even Alex's tiny brain could have worked that out. The plan was stalled, and later dropped.

Like the love-feast at Quebec three months previously, the show of unity was less benign than it outwardly appeared – at least, so far as satisfying British demands was concerned. The strategic issue, which was in essence very simple, had proved susceptible of an equally simple resolution at Malta. Between the lines of the bland and deliberately uninformative formal record, the realities of the position can be inferred from the outcome. The issue was that, since the Americans were so clearly preponderant, they wanted to fight the war as they chose – as Marshall chose and, by extension, as Eisenhower chose. Moreover, given that there was conflict within the combined chiefs of staff, and knowing that Roosevelt supported Marshall, Churchill simply accepted what the Americans decided. This was the inexorable price to be paid for American support: both the military price and the political price for giving the defeat of Germany a degree of priority over the Pacific war that many Americans had all along been reluctant to accord it. In the end, it appeared, Germany First was yet another way of saying America First.

The final dinner aboard the *Quincy* was cordiality itself. 'There was much joking and talking about the unsigned Atlantic Charter,' Stettinius recorded, with Churchill claiming pride in his share of it, maintaining that he 'still stood for what the Atlantic Charter said'. Then the frivolity gave way to a more serious note as Churchill probed Roosevelt on his famous aspiration about Four Freedoms, declared in January 1941, and later that year serving as a rough draft of the Charter. Freedom from fear struck the Prime Minister as crucial, leading him to declare in a highly emotional way: 'As long as blood flows from my veins, I will stand for this.'[68] This was excellent for bonding the American and British delegations, less useful in focusing them.

The aircraft for Yalta were even now preparing to leave, with flights scheduled from midnight onward. Yet the opportunity for serious attention to business had slipped away. Little wonder that the British Foreign Secretary, ever the well-prepared diplomat, was restive about going into a decisive conference with so little coordination. 'George III has a lot to answer for,' he noted privately. 'He still bedevils Anglo-American relations!'[69] Eden had a point, on the premise that a joint Anglo-American front needed to be agreed in advance, in order to confront the Soviet Union with a Western view on how peace should be declared. Whether that was how Roosevelt saw the problem, however, is open to doubt.

Churchill whiled away his last few hours in Malta in his own way. First there was a bizarre family row with his son Randolph, present aboard, about whether he too, as well as Sarah, should have been invited to Yalta, and then there was time for a courtesy visit to the bar of the *Orion*. Here, among the ship's company, the Prime Minister relaxed and spoke freely, if allusively, about the cursory nature of this Malta conference: 'He talked about the delay caused by a certain late arrival,' one of his secretaries wrote in her diary, adding that he then launched into the old music hall song, 'There was I – waiting at the Church . . .'[70] It is a good question: why had Winston been stood up in this way by his friend Franklin? Roosevelt must have realized that, in allowing only a few hours for his stopover in Malta, he was reducing the Anglo-American summit to a charade, albeit a friendly one so long as no serious business was broached.

6

Yalta

February 1945

'It must not be forgotten, however, that Great Britain had gone to war to protect Poland against German aggression at a time when that decision was most risky, and it had almost cost them their life in the world.'

Churchill at Yalta, 6 February 1945

The first of the promises of Yalta to be broken was about the size of the British and American delegations. These would be small, perhaps thirty-five each, so the Russians had initially been assured. 'All night planes have been taking off from the large airfield,' wrote Lord Moran on 3 February, 'to carry our party of seven hundred across the Aegean and the Black Sea to the Crimea, fourteen hundred miles away.' The landing that morning at Saki was bumpy, the airfield snow-covered, as Roosevelt was disembarked from the *Sacred Cow*, the luxurious presidential aircraft with its new lift, into a jeep on the runway, to inspect the guard of honour. Curiously, Churchill did not sit beside him in the jeep. 'The P.M. walked by the side of the President, as in her old age an Indian attendant accompanied Queen Victoria's phaeton,' Moran observed, and, like others, he also observed Roosevelt's appearance. 'The President looked old and thin and drawn; he had a cape or shawl over his shoulders and appeared shrunken; he sat looking straight ahead with his mouth open, as if he were not taking things in.'[1]

The eighty-mile drive from Saki to Yalta took four hours or more. It was worth it if only because the weather on arrival was so much milder. Throughout the conference the temperature stayed around 40°F or 5°C, feeling warmer in the sun because of the shelter of the mountains to the north. Its benign climate had made Yalta the favourite Black Sea resort for the Russian aristocracy, whose former villas had hurriedly been converted from state-run convalescent homes into conference chambers.

Signs of German occupation remained. 'We are also much more comfortably established than I had ever hoped for,' Brooke noted. 'This house was occupied by the German commander of the Crimean forces, and he had been promised the house as a gift after the war.'[2] This was exceptional; the CIGS was lucky to pull rank and lucky to have a decent room in Field Marshal von Mannstein's former trophy mansion, now the British headquarters. It was another story, and not only of predictable overcrowding, for many of the 700 in this new Crimean war against bugs; but theirs was not to reason why.

Brooke was thus housed, along with the Prime Minister and his immediate staff, in the vast mock castle about fourteen miles south of Yalta, originally built for Prince Vorontsov, a Tsarist ambassador to London. Queen Victoria herself might have been amused at its mixture of Scottish gothic and Moorish architecture, with great marble staircases and imposing reception rooms but only two baths in the whole house. 'It's a big house, of indescribable ugliness – a sort of gothic Balmoral – with all the furnishings of an almost terrifying hideosity,' wrote Cadogan, privileged to share the Foreign Secretary's private bathroom. 'But it's well warmed,' he admitted. 'The food is good and the place is manned by Royal Marines and innumerable Russian waiters.'[3] The servants' bedrooms were now filled with air marshals, generals and admirals, trying to find anywhere to wash or shave. Yet the Russians had gone to exotic lengths in providing amenities from Moscow, with an opulence inappropriate alike to the exigencies of warfare or the ideology of Communism. Only the bedbugs remained undefeated by the Red Army. 'In this palace, with its gilt furniture, its lashings of caviare, its grand air of luxury, there is nothing left out but cleanliness,' Moran noted. 'The P.M. sent for me this morning because he had been bitten on the feet.'[4]

After lunch on the first full day, Sunday, 4 February, Stalin called at the Vorontsov villa and spent an hour with Churchill. It was now, as he later explained in *Triumph and Tragedy*, that Stalin suggested that the British forces in Italy might strike towards Vienna: 'Here they could join the Red Army and outflank the Germans who were south of the Alps.'[5] This is consistent with Churchill's efforts to show that an attempt to take Vienna through the Ljubljana Gap was still a possibility; but it is not consistent with what had already been decided at Malta by the British and American soldiers who would actually have had to mount any armpit-stabbing initiative. 'There was now no question,' as Brooke had explained to the combined chiefs of staff five days previously, 'of operations aimed at the Ljubljana Gap and in any event the advance of the left wing of the Russian Army made such an operation no longer necessary.'[6] Little wonder, then, that when he was told by Eden what had passsed between Churchill and Stalin, Brooke was unenthusiastic: 'This is a bore as we had been killing that idea and banking on transferring troops from Italy to France instead and have got all agreed with the Americans.'[7] In any event, it is worth noting that the suggestion, however impracticable, came from Stalin. And even as described in Churchill's scenario, the Russian advance from the east was envisaged less as a threat, needing to be forestalled, than as a promise – one flank of a combined Allied assault on Germany.

Cold-war perspectives, in short, are premature. Instead, the premise of Yalta was that the Grand Alliance was united in its military strategy. Only on this basis could the Big Three expect to sustain a united approach towards the consequent problems of peace.

A cordial beginning was made. An hour after seeing Churchill that Sunday afternoon, Stalin arrived at the Livadia Palace, the American headquarters, only a couple of miles outside the town. This was the former summer palace of Tsar Nicholas, one of whose many bedrooms the President occupied. General Marshall was in the Tsarina's bedroom, which was fitting, given his status; but the running gag among the Americans was that the irascible Admiral King had been put in the Tsarina's boudoir, replete with a special staircase for visits from Rasputin. The setting was thus as conspiratorial as the atmosphere was comradely.

Roosevelt exerted his famous charm on a man famously not susceptible to cajolery. He had staked a good deal on his ability to deal directly with Stalin and thus square the diplomatic circle in the making of the peace, just as he had so often squared it in the politics of the war. Obviously below par, he reached out with all his familiar techniques – the bonhomie and informality, the dissimulated agreement with everyone, the calculated indiscretions and confidences, the winks and nods and grins – though perhaps with some loss of the old finesse. This even permeates the minutes kept by Charles Bohlen, a young State Department official, who had accompanied Hopkins to Europe en route to Yalta. In Washington, Chip Bohlen was well known to Isaiah Berlin, who had advised the Foreign Office that 'he is not only nice and intelligent but is very genuinely a key man just now, as liaison between the State Department and the White House.'[8] Bohlen's minutes are our second-best source – the notes of his colleague Alger Hiss are in some ways better – on what was actually said at Yalta, starting with the Roosevelt–Stalin *tête-à-tête*.

Of course they began by agreeing how much better the military situation was compared with that at the time of their only previous meeting at the Teheran conference. Roosevelt said 'that he had made a number of bets on board the cruiser coming over as to whether the Russians would get to Berlin before the Americans would get to Manila.'[9] Since the President was fully aware that the US forces were just about to capture Manila, which actually happened the following day, this suggests not only that he may have shared the current exaggerated view of Berlin's vulnerability, and not only that the comparison was intended to flatter Stalin, but also, of course, that it was intended to remind everyone that there was another war going on in the Pacific: a war in which the Soviet Union was not yet participating.

This was very much a meeting of the Big Two. Carefully uncompromised by prior collusion with Churchill, Roosevelt talked to Stalin as an equal – his only equal. The President thus confided that 'the British had wanted to make a major crossing of the Rhine on the north sector in Holland, but since we had four times the number of men in France than the British had we felt we were entitled to have an alternative, which would be either through Holland or in the region of Mainz.' And as for the tiresome French, a few dismissive comments about the intransigence of de Gaulle, and especially his effrontery in expecting an invitation to Yalta, helped seal the complicity of the two leaders. 'The President said that he would now tell the Marshal something indiscreet,' Bohlen recorded, 'since he would not wish to say it in front of Prime Minister Churchill, namely that the British for two years have had the idea of artificially building up France' – clearly so as to resume their traditional policy of sheltering behind the French Army, after this war as after the last. Roosevelt commented that 'the British were a peculiar people and wished to have their cake and eat it too', and cautioned that 'he had had a good deal of trouble with the British in regard to zones of occupation.'[10] Perhaps Roosevelt felt that Stalin, leading his sheltered life in the Kremlin, needed a friendly warning against such wily allies.

With three minutes to spare, the Marshal and the President made their way into the ballroom for the first plenary session. They need not have rushed; it was hardly likely to have begun without them. Round the table were ten Americans (including Bohlen to take the minutes, but not Hopkins, who was ill), ten Russians (including Maisky, their former ambassador to Britain, to interpret) and eight Britons (including Major Arthur Birse, who had done such a good job as interpreter at the Tolstoy conference). Roosevelt was asked to take the chair, as he had done at Teheran. The natural starting point was the military situation, where Roosevelt offered the fulsome claim that 'when the Red Armies advanced into Germany 25 kilometers, it was doubtful whether the Soviet people were more thrilled than those of the United States and those of Great Britain.'[11] This was the cue for General Antonov, the Soviet chief of staff, to report. 'He gave an excellent and very clear talk, but not much that we did not know,' Brooke commented. 'Marshall then described the situation on the Western Front.'[12] The CIGS declined an invitation to add anything himself, knowing that his turn would come the next day, when the chiefs of staff of the three powers commenced their own talks.

In fact, Brooke found himself invited to chair the tripartite military meetings. This can be seen either as a personal tribute to him or as an obvious way to avoid determining precedence between the men with the big battalions, Marshall and Antonov. These military meetings at Yalta were much less contentious than those at Malta. Again this can be read in two ways: either that the Russian presence solidified Anglo-American unity or that neither disagreed with the Russians as much as they did with each other.

The first tripartite military meeting on 5 February set the tone. Brooke started by expanding on Marshall's statement at the previous day's plenary, candidly revealing that it was planned to cross the Rhine during March. All relevant operational dates were openly given. As he put it in his diary that day: 'we hoped that the Russians would find it possible, in spite of the thaw and their long lines of communications, to continue their offensive through March and if possible April.'[13] The objective for the Red Army was obviously Berlin; of course they agreed to continue. Conversely, when Antonov renewed the Russian suggestion of a push through the Ljubljana Gap, Brooke at once jumped in from the chair with all the objections. The military discussions clearly showed that neither the Americans nor the British were thinking in terms of a race against the Russians for Berlin, still less for Vienna. Not only did they encourage the Russians to get to Berlin: they refused Russian invitations to try themselves to get to Vienna.

The President had hosted an opening dinner for the Big Three and their top political advisers in the Livadia Palace on Sunday, 4 February. Roosevelt was supported not only by Stettinius but also by James Byrnes, soon to become the next Secretary of State. Byrnes was a seasoned political operator, all the more influential in the intermittent absences of the ailing Hopkins, though initially less well prepared on foreign affairs – a deficiency which he felt could have been remedied had the presidential party made more effective use of their long sea voyage to study the papers together. Churchill had Eden with him at the dinner. The ambassadors to Moscow of both the United States (Averell Harriman) and of Great Britain (Sir Archibald Clark Kerr) attended. Harriman, a patrician like Roosevelt and Churchill, was used to sitting at the best tables and, like them too, had brought his daughter to Yalta, reinforcing the sense of a big and stylish house-party, with the prospect of a little bezique to relieve any tedium. Stalin had with him Molotov, Vyshinsky and Gromyko: a bevy of hatchet-faced men who soon became familiar for their negative stance at a string of international conferences.

These were the men of Yalta. Meeting frequently, usually with Bohlen, Birse and the Russian Pavlov as interpreters, they formed a core decision-making group – not much bigger than that around the table at the Last Supper, and equally undependable in some cases. Of course, they did not all carry equal weight in this process, since some animals were manifestly more equal than others, and even to talk of the Big Three is arguably an exaggeration by the order of 30 per cent.

The President's dinner was hardly a great success. As Churchill later reported to Brooke: 'Stalin showed great reluctance to propose the King's health stating that he was a republican, Americans failed to take our part in this connection!'[14] Everyone agreed that the President seemed to have lost his touch. Even Churchill, loyally reticent in this regard, went so far as to tell Moran of how Roosevelt blurted out to Stalin: 'We always call you Uncle Joe.' Admittedly, some diverting ploy was needed to retrieve a flagging dinner party. Not this one, however. 'Stalin did not appear a bit amused; he said that he ought to have been told this before or not told now,' Churchill reported. 'Byrnes attempted to pacify him by saying that Uncle Joe was no worse than Uncle Sam.'[15] Again, no good; it was simply not an in-joke that the Marshal found at all funny in translation, as he made clear by asking pointedly how long he was expected to sit at table.

Bohlen did not record these exchanges in the official US minutes – a prudent career move – but he did reveal that Churchill responded by proposing a toast to 'the proletariat masses of the world'.[16] Indeed, as Moran learned at breakfast the next morning: 'Winston was in great form at the President's dinner last night.' Hardly impartial testimony, of course, but certainly vehement and not entirely without insight. 'In the White House, I'm taken for a Victorian Tory,' Churchill observed to Moran, accurately enough, since this is exactly how the President talked of him. Churchill showed adroitness in picking up the partisan label to yield a democratic message: 'Stalin and the President can do what they like, whereas in a few months' time, I may find myself in the street.'[17]

The inaugural dinner, then, showed that Churchill was ready to go on to the offensive in the face of an emerging American–Russian front. What with all the cant he had to endure about whether pure republican democracy or proletarian democracy was the way the world was going, this veteran electioneer evidently thought that an ounce of experience was worth a ton of theory, as he began musing on his dozen or so adventures on the hustings. To Stalin's rather sour post-prandial banter about the Prime Minister's apparent fear of the forthcoming elections, Churchill replied 'that he not only did not fear them but that he was proud of the right of the British people to change their government at any time they saw fit'. Bohlen heard this, and also the *mot* which Churchill produced in their table-talk about how far the Big Three should seek to control smaller nations: 'The eagle should permit the small birds to sing and care not wherefor they sang.'[18]

The smaller birds at the conference were not fed at the President's table. Moran dined that night with the British top brass and absorbed their concerns. 'Stalin expressed pleasure when he heard our main drive was planned to begin in a month's time,' they told him. 'But what we do or do not do is no longer vital to the Russians.' What of the other members of the Big Three? The chief of the air staff, Sir Charles Portal, retailed the malicious comment 'that the P.M. will fight to the last ditch but not in it. He does not like making decisions.' To Moran's surprise, Field Marshal Alexander broke in: 'And he will not listen to evidence.' This led to a comparison with Roosevelt, with agreement that he liked to wait for situations to develop before intervening himself, which led to a discussion of his performance at the first plenary session, which led to a discussion of his health. Again there was agreement, this time that 'the President had gone to bits physically', with questions naturally sought as to why.

It was a topic on which everyone at Yalta seems to have had a view, varying only in the degree of shock or dismay evinced. Moran had, of course, first noticed Roosevelt's loss of weight at Quebec and drawn serious conclusions about the future. Now the signs were of more pressing afflictions that could no longer be held at bay. 'He intervened very little in the discussions, sitting with his mouth open,' Moran recorded – an image that is reinforced by many of the Yalta photographs. Granted, if Roosevelt was lacking in specific preparation for the conference, so was Churchill; and, like him, Roosevelt was known for his ability to cover up and to trade instead on his vast experience and his uncanny talent for seizing on the salient point. 'Now, they say, the shrewdness has gone and there is nothing left,' Moran concluded. 'I doubt, from what I have seen, whether he is fit for his job here. Stalin doesn't seem to be taking advantage of the situation.'[19] These were, however, early days.

What we ought to ask in hindsight is not only how ill was Roosevelt at Yalta but also how much it mattered in shaping the political outcome. On the first question, Moran was an expert. He was one of the leading physicians in Britain; his professional opinion was obviously worth having; he had a superb diagnostic intuition, as testified by his ability to keep a septuagenarian Prime Minister going; that is why he was there and why he had attended earlier summits at Casablanca, at Teheran and at Quebec. Moran was drawing on his own close observations of Roosevelt over a couple of years; and what he saw at Yalta alarmed him. 'To a doctor's eye, the President appears a very sick man,' he eventually concluded. 'He has all the symptoms of hardening of the arteries of the brain in an advanced stage, so that I give him only a few months to live.' Moran wrote this on 7 February, after five days' opportunity to watch the President. He did so although he well knew that 'the Americans here cannot bring themselves to believe that he is finished.'[20] He well knew that Anna Roosevelt Boettiger, the President's daughter, did not believe it; he well knew that Dr Howard Bruenn, the President's doctor, did not believe it.

Nonetheless, FDR had little more than two months to live. If Moran was right about Roosevelt's health, however, it does not mean that he was equally good at assessing its impact on policy. In the metaphor that recurs in talk about Yalta, Roosevelt had so many cards in his hand – as did Stalin in his – that the game was always likely to come out much as it did. The President's lapses in concentration may have meant that he missed a few tricks but did not stop him from taking those he really wanted to win, with much of his old aplomb and his old inscrutability.

Slowly the conference cranked up. The pattern was that the tripartite chiefs of staff usually met in the late mornings, the Foreign Ministers every day around lunchtime, usually at 12 noon, and that the plenary meetings of the Big Three took place daily in the afternoons, usually at 4 p.m. This was a good routine for Churchill, never a morning person, and much happier to resume business following a sleep after lunch. Given Roosevelt's apparent failings, it might be supposed that a great deal would depend upon Churchill, if Stalin were to be prevented from simply getting his own way on a range of crucial issues. Whether the British Prime Minister would be permitted to play a major role by the American President was in any case doubtful, but at least he could try.

Moran gives a graphic impression of exactly how Churchill kept buggering on (or at least about):

All morning the P.M. has been losing things

'Sawyers, Sawyers, where are my glasses?'

'There, sir,' said Sawyers, leaning over his shoulder as he sat, and tapping the P.M.'s pocket.

At last, when the P.M. was getting ready for his afternoon sleep, he cried out irritably:

'Sawyers, where is my hot-water bottle?'

'You are sitting on it, sir,' replied the faithful Sawyers. 'Not a very good idea,' he added.

'It's not an idea, it's a coincidence,' said the P.M., enjoying his choice of words, and without a trace of resentment.[21]

If only the fate of the world, or at least of the British Empire, could have been so easily settled by an apt choice of the right word, the Prime

Minister would have come back from Yalta garlanded. As Wavell had noted, Churchill had the weakest hand to play; his position was thus the converse of Roosevelt's; and again it was this brute fact that settled the outcome.

Serious work began on Monday, 5 February. The plenary that day focused on the treatment of Germany. There was a lot of vague talk about 'dismemberment' but the more concrete discussion was about whether France should be an occupying power. Churchill, a great supporter of the French, however badly he was exasperated by their leader or however badly he mangled their language, made the case for them to play an important role. After all, they would have a strong army in Europe – unlike the Americans, who, Roosevelt disclosed, were unlikely to stay for more than two years. Stalin went no further than agreeing to a French zone of occupation if it were carved out of the British or American zones, with the French represented by the British on the control commission. Eden, who could all too vividly imagine de Gaulle's response to this patronizing suggestion, pointed out that 'they would not accept a zone subordinate to British control.'[22] But since Roosevelt seemed to share Stalin's view, there was impasse.

The position, however, was not irretrievable. It turned out that Harry Hopkins, not for the first time, was himself privately supporting the British case. Now chronically ill, he spent the conference gravitating between his sickbed and the plenaries, where he sat behind the President, periodically passing him brief notes, inscribed with invariably terse and often shrewd suggestions. 'Hopkins is, of course, a valuable ally, particularly now, when the President's opinions flutter in the wind,' Moran noted at this point. 'He knows the President's moods like a wife watching the domestic climate. He will sit patiently for hours, blinking like a cat, waiting for the right moment to put his point; and if it never comes, he is content to leave it to another time.'[23] On this issue, the British were right to think that the battle was not lost. Hopkins eventually prevailed, Roosevelt belatedly changed his mind, Stalin was quietly squared.

Thus full French participation as an occupying power in Germany was finally agreed, despite the initial deadlock. But a second German issue, also broached at the second plenary, proved more intractable. The Russians demanded heavy reparations after the war. The British and

Americans, by contrast, had had enough of this kind of thinking in view of their experience after the First World War. At that time reparations were blamed – initially by Keynes, later by nearly everyone – for destabilizing the fragile peace. Keynes's argument in his famous book *The Economic Consequences of the Peace* (1919) was not so much that reparations were unfair in principle as that in practice such large sums of money could not easily be transferred from country to country; and what was technically known as the 'transfer problem' was well recognized by sophisticated Keynesian policy-makers in London and Washington. The simple, non-technical conclusion was that war debts had polluted international relations for two fatal decades, without any of the Allies really seeing the money anyway. Lend-Lease was itself conceived by FDR as one way of avoiding such errors in future.

The Russian twist now was to talk of reparations in kind. If money payments had created such difficulties, why not simply let the victors seize the spoils – as Maisky put it, 'the removal from the national wealth of Germany of plants, machine tools, rolling stock, etc.'? It was one part Morgenthau Plan (pastoralization), one part reimbursement, and another part vengeance. Annual payments, perhaps for ten years, could also be made in kind. The total amount of reparations was not specified but Maisky said that the Soviet share ought to be 10 billion dollars.

This idea did not go down well. There was no Morgenthau at the table, as at the Octagon conference, and his eponymous plan was now virtually a dead letter. Instead, Bohlen's minutes record general unanimity between Churchill and Roosevelt, not only in substance but in tone. Neither now warmed to the Russian approach, which, like Morgenthau, implied a zero-sum game. In Morgenthau's version at Quebec, a poorer post-war Germany invitingly implied a richer post-war Britain: that had been its attraction to Cherwell, and, through him, temporarily to Churchill. In Maisky's version at Yalta, a richer post-war Russia necessarily implied a poorer post-war Germany.

Both Roosevelt and Churchill had had second thoughts between Quebec and Yalta. They had both lived through the making of the last peace. Churchill spoke now of the futility of the reparations approach and Roosevelt simply commented that 'he remembered very vividly that the United States had lost a great deal of money.' But he added that 'just as we expected to help Great Britain expand her export trade, we would also help the Soviet Union retain the reparations in kind which she required', provided the Germans did not starve as a result. This was thought-provoking in its implication for the British, who did not expect to get reparations from Germany, since it suggested that for them the equivalent would be American aid in rebuilding exports. Rather than the zero-sum Morgenthau arithmetic, this suggested a Keynesian arithmetic of rebuilding prosperity all round, in a sort of international New Deal. The proviso was that everyone agreed with the Russians that post-war Germany should not enjoy a higher standard of living than themselves (or than the British of course).

Maisky's reply had a piquant intellectual interest. It showed that at least everyone was talking the same language here, for he responded to the citation of experience after the last war by explicitly mentioning 'the transfer problem which was the rock on which the reparations policy foundered'.[24] Even in Moscow, it seemed, Keynes provided the concepts for this argument, and the Russian proposal, apparently so crude, could also be more subtly viewed, as a way of outflanking the transfer problem. Such fastidious distinctions, of course, did not inhibit the actions of the Red Army in the gigantic exercises in looting, both official and unofficial, which were already well under way on the eastern front while the discussions in Yalta meandered on.

There were eight plenary meetings in all, held at the Livadia Palace every day from Sunday, 4 February, to Sunday, 11 February. In the end, then, Roosevelt was induced to labour for more than the six days of Genesis and, unlike God, not to rest 'from all his work which he had made' until the ninth day, when he quitted Yalta, exhausted. Meanwhile, it had taken time to focus the discussions. 'It's always the same with these Conferences: they take *days* to get on the rails,' wrote Cadogan on 6 February. 'The Great Men don't know what they're talking about and have to be educated, and made a bit more tidy in their methods.' At that day's plenary session, he had taken a close look at the President in the chair. 'He looks rather better than when I last saw him,' he noted. 'But I think he is woollier than ever. Stalin looks well – rather greyer – and seemed to be in very good form.'[25]

This was the third plenary and the first to turn to Roosevelt's top priority: proposals for an international security organization as developed during the Dumbarton Oaks conference. It was also the first plenary to be serviced not only by Chip Bohlen but by another of the American delegation: a charming, gifted diplomat, just forty years old, called Alger Hiss. We now know him as a Soviet agent. At the time his high-flying career in the State Department, in which he had special responsibility for the emerging United Nations plans, made him one of the officials who were privileged to sit around the table with the Big Three, busily making pencilled notes of this heroic confrontation. Was Stalin actually a bigger hero than Roosevelt? Was Roosevelt guided into some decisions more favourable to Soviet than to Western interests? Frequently abbreviated and ungrammatical, Hiss's notes provide only cryptic answers to such questions; but they often capture the timbre of the exchanges with an immediacy lost in Bohlen's more polished minutes.

What Hiss observed was the almost offhand way in which Stalin dealt with the revised American proposals. At Dumbarton Oaks the sticking point for the Soviet Union had been the suggestion that it might be subjected to the decisions of an international body containing not only potentially hostile powers but a host of small countries. This was what made the arcane topic of voting procedures crucial. The Soviet Union had talked of its sixteen constituent republics also having votes in the General Assembly and had insisted on itself having a veto in the Security Council, so as to prevent issues vital to its own interests from being raised at all. At this third plenary, the British delegation watched apprehensively as Churchill lumbered and growled around the issue. 'I was terrified of what the P.M. might say, as he doesn't know a *thing* about it – he has always refused to look at it – and here he was plunging into debate!' Cadogan privately confessed. 'However, after a few flounderings, he really did fairly well.'[26]

One reason was that his lack of preparation put him at no relative disadvantage, compared with the other members of the Big Three. So his remarks picked up their own momentum as he explored the issue. 'It might look as if we were claiming to rule the world – we 3,' Hiss recorded; and his busy pencil then sought to follow Churchill's undeniably confusing hypothetical case of how Hong Kong might be affected.[27] It showed at least that the British leader, from a slow start, was grappling with the concepts and procedures at stake, modifying his earlier scepticism about the Dumbarton Oaks mechanism in the light of the American draft now before them. Stettinius, who had helped Eden with some private coaching before the session, was gratified to receive Churchill's congratulations during an intermission, coupled with the admission that 'not only Stalin but he himself, the prime minister, now really understood it for the first time'.[28] And the Soviet leader himself? 'I must apologize' – so Hiss's notes give Stalin's official response – 'I was real busy other matters & not chance study this q in detail.'[29]

So much for the prime objective on which Roosevelt had set his sights at Yalta. Little wonder that James Byrnes was put out to discover that 'two months after Washington had sent Stalin a proposal about voting in the Security Council, he had not even read it', as Moran recorded later that day; and recorded too Harry Hopkins's comment: 'That guy can't be much interested in this peace organization.'[30] Hopkins's comment pithily summed up the immediate problem: not so much that Stalin would not agree to some form of international body but that he did not regard it as the effective means of protecting Russian security. What he wanted was the evisceration of Germany plus buffer states in eastern Europe under Russian dominance. Hence his readiness to do the deal about 'spheres of influence' with Churchill at the Tolstoy conference.

There was to be no such 'naughty document' at Yalta. But an implicit deal was nonetheless done between the two superpowers, giving each what it most wanted at that point. Roosevelt got Dumbarton Oaks, albeit hedged for the sake of agreement with face-saving formulae for the Soviet Union; and Stalin got eastern Europe, similarly hedged with fine promises about democracy. What Churchill got was little more than the opportunity to tell anyone who was listening what a fine institution the British Empire was.

It was at the fourth plenary on 7 February that the log-jam was broken. Molotov, who evidently found the time and patience actually to read the circulated papers about the United Nations, came back with general acceptance of Stettinius's proposals, though also with reiteration of the case for at least two extra Soviet votes (for the Ukrainian and White Russian republics). This gave Churchill his chance to expatiate, as Hiss's notes show, on the constitutional position of Dominions, which for twenty-five years had been recognized as fully independent, even though in 1939 'all without hesitation sprang into the war when we declared it though they knew how weak we were.' This no doubt needed saying; but it also led the Prime Minister to ponder how 'a nation so great with 180,000,000 people would perhaps have cause to look at our British org with a questioning eye if they had but one vote when their nos. far exceed our own, speaking of whites.'[31]

It is all very Churchillian. At once the Dominions are wholly independent countries; and thus each like the Soviet Union presumably; and thus no less entitled to a vote each in the United Nations Assembly. Yet in the next breath they are part of a united, whites-only British Empire – also like the Soviet Union, which is thus presumably under-represented if it has fewer UN votes. So much for the independence of large Commonwealth countries like Canada or Australia! Little wonder that Molotov, in a subsequent foreign ministers' meeting, inquired if Canada and Australia were part 'of the United Kingdom', only to be quickly corrected by Stettinius, who had to tell him not so: 'of the British Empire'.[32]

These were time-warp arguments that had been rehearsed to death when the League of Nations was set up at the end of the First World War. It was at that point that separate Dominion representation had been established: a principle that hardly ought to have been reopened twenty-five years later, least of all by a British Prime Minister. Yet he himself remained caught in the time-warp, as is shown by some of the phrases he chose to reproduce in *Triumph and Tragedy*. Not only was it a question of 'our having more than one voice in the Assembly', which suggests that he used the term British Empire in a very proprietorial sense, but 'our' position was disclosed in imperial rather than democratic terms. 'For us to have four or five members,' Churchill telegraphed the war cabinet, 'six if India is included, when Russia has only one is asking a great deal of an Assembly of this kind.'[33]

India, yes, India: non-independent India, the British Raj that Churchill had no intention of ending, was thus the implicit pivot of this argument. And the Americans were co-opted into going down this road. There is a wonderful irony in finding that Alger Hiss, of all people, subsequently had to find arguments to justify telling the Russians that British India 'is generally regarded as having more of the attributes of separate nationhood than the Soviet Republics'.[34]

In fact, the soft option was to by-pass the Soviet Union's nonsense about the purported independence of its constituent republics by inventing a counter-claim that the United States too should have three votes. This fatuous proposal, undercutting the very principle of equal representation in the Assembly, was finally broached in an exchange of letters between the Big Three at the end of the conference. The political trouble that it duly brought down upon Roosevelt can be seen as the foreseeable result of following Churchill's lead when he extemporized at Yalta on 7 February. Yet the British, who had to suffer so many unjustified American imputations about their imperialist proclivities, were rarely held to account for their red-handed guilt on this particular score. Indeed, no sooner had they gone home than, with breathtaking effrontery, they started blaming the Americans for selling the pass over United Nations representation.

At this fourth plenary, Roosevelt found Churchill wanting for rather different reasons. When the Prime Minister started asking for more time to consider the United Nations proposals, his trip down memory lane plainly started to irk a President – 'My motion was a little different' – whose plan for an early meeting of the United Nations at San Francisco now seemed imperilled. The idea that this could be convened in as little as a month's time exposed a rift between them as the Prime Minister conjured up implausible objections: 'Will always do our best to comply with the Pres. wishes but I feel it absolutely nec. to put on record the very great diff. which I see, practically,' noted Hiss, trying to make sense of what was going on.[35]

Why was Churchill flannelling and fudging in this way? At this point Hopkins passed Roosevelt one of his scrawled notes: 'There is something behind this talk that we do not know – of its basis.' The President's reply seems to have been: 'All this is rot!' – but then 'rot' was crossed out in favour of 'local politics'. Hopkins assented to this interpretation, supposing that Churchill must be worrying about an impending General Election.[36] To the appalled British delegation, however, it was perfectly obvious what had happened. 'Silly old man,' wrote Cadogan, conscious that Churchill had launched off, unbriefed, on a tack that he suddenly imagined could be used for courting Stalin's favour. 'The worst of it was that what he said was completely contrary to the line already agreed with the Americans!'[37] It was accordingly necessary to mend fences between the British and American diplomats after this session.

By this stage, the President was on the point of achieving one of his prime aims at Yalta, and was prepared to pay for it in a give-and-take game with the Russians. Hence, perhaps, his reaction to Churchill's unexpected support for giving the Soviet Union extra votes. As Hopkins told Moran the next day, the President 'came to Yalta apparently determined to oppose any country having more than one vote, but when the P.M. came out strongly in favour of Stalin's proposal Roosevelt said he, too, would support Stalin at San Francisco'.[38]

The projected conference to kick-start the United Nations was no light matter. For Roosevelt an early meeting at San Francisco – now definitely superseding Stettinius's notion of French Lick – was a vital objective, if not as soon as mid-March then certainly in late April. By Thursday, 8 February, the fifth day of the conference, this had been agreed by the foreign ministers. A note written that day survives among Hiss's papers, again in pencil but this time in Stettinius's writing, listing the delegates whom the President proposed to invite to represent the United States.[39] The list included the name of Senator Arthur Vandenberg: a clear indication of the bipartisan nature of the enterprise. It marked Roosevelt's success in steering his country out of isolation and into the post-war world beyond Yalta that now happily beckoned. As Hopkins told his friend Sherwood: 'We really believed in our hearts that this was the dawn of the new day we had all been praying for and talking about for so many years. We were absolutely certain that we had won the first great victory of the peace – and by "we", I mean *all* of us, the whole civilized human race.'[40]

It is not surprising that both Churchill and Roosevelt seemed to be making up policy on the hoof, without a concerted strategy. It was only the British who had thought in terms of a two-stage process: Malta to hammer out the Anglo-American position, Yalta to hammer it home. 'Winston is puzzled and distressed,' Moran noted on 7 February. 'The President no longer seems to the P.M. to take an intelligent interest in the war; often he does not seem even to read the papers the P.M. gives him.' Perhaps Mr Attlee ought to have addressed a copy of his recent missive to the White House. Churchill was plainly disappointed that Roosevelt's troubles with Congress – Lend-Lease hearings were currently in progress – seemed to bulk so large in his handling of issues. Yet the Prime Minister remained indulgent, tolerant, hopeful and understanding about American difficulties, as conscious of how much of the war effort they were bearing in the west as he was of how much the Russians were doing in the east. He was obviously reluctant to utter dissent in private, let alone in public. As Moran observed: 'though we have moved a long way since Winston, speaking of Roosevelt, said to me in the garden at Marrakesh, "I love that man", he is still very reticent in criticism. It seems to be dragged out of him against his will.'[41]

The facade of unity among the Big Three was maintained, partly because there was no question of Roosevelt and Churchill ganging up. Stalin, with victories already under his belt and more to come, proved relatively easy to deal with on a personal level, saying little himself but displaying signs of amusement, not least at Churchill's irrepressible interventions, in public and in private. When the Marshal, on a tour of the map room in the British headquarters, made a barbed joke of his own about the possibility of the British seeking a separate armistice, Churchill started singing: 'Keep right on to the end of the road', while Roosevelt said with a grin to the interpreter: 'Tell your Chief that this singing by the Prime Minister is Britain's secret weapon.'[42] Stalin treated Churchill like a good turn at the circus, or an exhibit in a museum of bourgeois oratory.

Above all, Stalin got most of what he wanted, which obviously kept him in a good mood. As at the Tolstoy conference, he insisted that both the frontiers and the government of Poland should be settled on a basis agreeable to Russia. The Curzon Line, as Poland's new frontier with Russia, was by now a *fait accompli*. The only question was how much territory in the west Poland would gain from Germany in compensation for its loss to Russia in the east. On this there had been little real dissension at the third plenary session (6 February). 'It must not be forgotten, however,' Churchill had said, 'that Great Britain had gone to war to protect Poland against German aggression at a time when that decision was most risky, and it had almost cost them their life in the world.' It was thus a question of honour, not of any British material interest. It was 'the earnest desire of the British Government that Poland be mistress in her own house and captain of her soul'. The Lublin Poles, of course, had now been recognized by the Soviet Union; Stalin accordingly called them the Warsaw Poles, while trying to identify the London Poles as *émigrés*, a usage to which Churchill and Roosevelt objected. Would not the inclusion of Mikolajczyk and some of his former London colleagues, Churchill suggested, be possible within a new provisional government that all the Big Three could recognize? Indeed he went further, asking 'whether there might be some possibility of forming a government here for Poland which would utilize these men'.[43]

Stalin was granted a ten-minute break at this point. He then spoke in measured terms. 'It is not only a question of honour for Russia,' he reminded Churchill, 'but one of life and death.' He insisted on the

Curzon Line, unmodified by any concessions, taunting the British (and the absent French) with its pedigree: 'Should we then be less Russian than Curzon and Clemenceau?' This, however, was no longer the crux of the argument, as everyone surely realized, for it now turned not on frontiers but on the sort of government necessary to guarantee Poland's integrity. Hence the magisterial condescension with which Stalin offered a rebuke to Churchill – 'I am afraid that was a slip of the tongue' – for his suggestion that a Polish government could be created in Yalta, without the participation of the Poles. 'I am called a dictator and not a democrat,' Stalin confided, 'but I have enough democratic feeling to refuse to create a Polish government without the Poles being consulted – the question can only be settled with the consent of the Poles.' He concluded this part of his argument with his usual swipe at the French: 'I must say that the Warsaw government has a democratic base equal at least to that of de Gaulle.'[44]

This was hard for the British and Americans to counter without simply alleging bad faith against their ally, the valiant Marshal. After all, if he now controlled the ground in liberated Poland, so did they in liberated France. Roosevelt may have delayed recognition of de Gaulle's government until late October, after French public support for it had become unmistakable; and the British, more well-disposed towards de Gaulle but trying to keep in step with the United States, had almost been wrong-footed when the President suddenly agreed to do this. The fact was, however, that recognition had been granted to a provisional government that had moved into France on the heels of the Allied victories, and it had been granted without prior elections, understandably enough for a country that was still in the war zone. What was so different about what Stalin now proposed in Poland? Moreover, the fact that the Soviet Union had no direct presence in France did not become a major issue. Nor did it in Italy, also run by the British and Americans. Nor, for that matter, in Greece: a point which did not escape Stalin's attention when the Big Three returned to the Polish question.

Poland occupied more of the time of the Big Three at Yalta than any other topic. Their plenary meetings dragged on each day for four or five hours at a time, and these were often about Poland, the one issue that was equally sensitive for each of them. Life and death for Russia, as Stalin had said without contradiction. Honour for Great Britain, as Churchill had said, well aware of how the outcome would be judged at home by his countrymen, fed for years on his rhetoric about the rectitude of the British cause in going to war. As for the Americans, Poland was hardly less sensitive, even though Roosevelt had preferred to dwell on how distant it was from the United States, in order to stress the advantage in viewing issues from a distance. He knew, however, that there were Polish votes to be cast in American elections, if not in Polish elections as yet. Above all, he knew how much this was a test case for his own principles of self-determination as enshrined in the Atlantic Charter.

Yet, reading the extensive minutes of these debates, it gradually becomes evident that the argument did not really progress beyond that first Churchill–Stalin encounter. The issue most easily settled was that of the frontiers. Here, agreement could be declared on the Curzon Line in the east while the exact nature of compensation in the west was not to be specified. At the third plenary, Churchill expressed his hesitation over how much German territory should be ceded to the new Poland: 'Great pity to stuff Pol. goose so full of Ger. food that he died of indigestion', as Hiss heard it.[45] The Prime Minister was pleased with his epigram. At the seventh plenary, revisiting the question for the final communiqué, he objected to stating that Poland should receive East Prussia simply on the grounds that this was a return to the ancient frontier. Laughing, the President quipped to the Prime Minister: 'Perhaps you would want us back?' 'Well,' Churchill responded, 'you might be as indigestible for us as it might be for the Poles if they took too much German territory.'[46]

It was the sort of moment Churchill enjoyed, though the Yalta agreement on Poland was to give him some distinctly more awkward moments later, much as he had envisaged. What was finally declared by the Big Three was that of course democracy should prevail throughout liberated Europe. There was a 'common desire to see established a strong, free, independent and democratic Poland'. There should be a more broadly based government of national unity, to be formed in the first instance in Moscow under the eyes of Molotov, Harriman and Clark Kerr, and it should be 'pledged to the holding of free and unfettered elections as soon as possible on the basis of universal suffrage and secret ballot'. One catch came in the qualifying sentence: 'In these elections all democratic and anti-Nazi parties shall have the right to take part and to put forward candidates.'[47] None of this wording was innocent; it was always appreciated that the Soviet Union had a peculiar talent for sniffing out the 'objectively pro-fascist' tendencies harboured by political opponents and rivals. Thus the *émigré* London Poles, and their shady supporters in the Polish resistance movement, were already being identified as saboteurs of the Red Army's exercises in liberation. A lot depended on the good faith of Stalin himself, then, the man whose signature on the trilateral documents, alongside those of Churchill and Roosevelt, would stand to back the Yalta pledges.

The fifth plenary on the afternoon of Thursday, 8 February, was decisive. It had already rubber-stamped the accord on the United Nations and San Francisco; so the Western Allies, especially the Americans, were well pleased. Then Poland again. Churchill duly warned that 'it would be charged in London that we are forsaking the cause of Poland' unless there were better assurances that a properly elected government would ensue. Stalin responded predictably, comparing the Lublin Poles favourably with de Gaulle. 'If we do not talk to them they would accuse us of being occupiers and not liberators,' he concluded. Asked directly by Roosevelt when elections could be held, Stalin replied: 'In about one month unless there is a catastrophe on the front and the Germans defeat us.' And at this point, smiling, he added: 'I do not think this will happen.'

This was the moment of truth – or what went for truth at Yalta. Churchill, like Roosevelt, admitted that he did not really know what was going on in Poland; that was the cause of their anxiety. 'Free elections would of course settle the worries of the British government at least,' Churchill responded, conceding that 'if it is possible to learn the opinion of the population in Poland in one or even two months no one could object.' After all, this was no more latitude than he had himself asked his allies to grant him in Greece, eliciting more understanding from the Russians than from the Americans. Just in case anyone missed these implicit connections, Stalin raised Greece as one of 'two small questions' at the very end of the plenary. 'I have no criticism to make but I should like to know what is going on,' he said, without a smile this time. Churchill obliged with a short report. 'I thank the Marshal for his help,' he concluded. 'On Greece I only wanted to know for information,' Stalin replied to him. 'We have no intention of intervening there in any way.'[48]

This is where the personal became political. Both Churchill and Roosevelt simply had to decide whether they could trust Stalin. They each appear to have decided, in the end, yes – but for slightly different reasons. 'The Russians had proved that they could be reasonable and farseeing,' Hopkins later told Sherwood, 'and there wasn't any doubt in the minds of the President or any of us that we could live with them and get along with them peacefully for as far into the future as any of us could imagine.'[49] For Churchill, it was slightly different. He had gone out on a limb over Greece; he had made a deal with Stalin and the deal had stuck; so his trust had been vindicated. Why not over Poland too? And while he may have boldly sanctioned British intervention to protect democracy in Greece, British intervention in Poland was unthinkable. 'Our hopeful assumptions were soon to be falsified,' as he later put it in *Triumph and Tragedy*. 'Still, they were the only ones possible at the time.'[50]

An hour after the plenary broke up on 8 February, there was a banquet at the Yusupov Palace, the Russian headquarters. It was the high point of the conference. Thirty guests attended, according to Bohlen's list; but this can hardly be correct since it includes Sir Alec Cadogan, who was well pleased to have been squeezed out. 'A great mercy, as I am tired of these silly toasts and speeches,' he wrote, glad to get an early night, while admiring the superior stamina of his leader: 'P.M. seems well, though drinking buckets of Caucasian champagne which would undermine the health of any ordinary man.'[51] Bohlen's lapse in accuracy can be excused since he also records that there were forty-five toasts, though after about thirty there is an obvious difficulty in keeping an exact count. Brooke, despite his distaste for such occasions, was impressed: 'Stalin was in the very best of form, and was full of fun and good humour and apparently thoroughly enjoying himself.'[52] It helped that nobody tried calling him Uncle Joe.

Stalin's toast to Churchill that night was one of the most memorable incidents of Yalta. It may seem odd that the version given in *Triumph and Tragedy*, though flattering enough, omits the most telling phrases; but then, as we now know, little in the volume's treatment of Yalta actually comes from Churchill's own pen. According to Bohlen, what Stalin said was that 'due in large measure to Mr Churchill's courage and staunchness, England, when she stood alone, had divided the might of Hitlerite Germany at a time when the rest of Europe was falling flat on its face before Hitler.' Given the Marxist orthodoxy about the unimportance of great men in determining major events, it was a remarkable tribute with which Stalin concluded: 'he knew of few examples in history where the courage of one man had been so important to the future history of the world.'[53]

Naturally Churchill became sentimental and emotional. One measure of this is that he resuscitated a familiar oratorical trope: none other than those 'broad, sunlit uplands' that he had first espied in his great speech of 18 June 1940, and had glimpsed again in a radio broadcast on 14 July 1940 (when he had enjoined that 'while we toil through the dark valley we can see the sunlight on the uplands beyond').[54] Admittedly, as time goes by, a sigh is just a sigh, a cliché just a cliché. But the fact is that, through the mixed fortunes of nearly four years of war, Churchill had kept his silence on celestially illuminated topography, at least until 26 March 1944, when the coming offensive licensed him to claim, again over the BBC, that his government was leading the nation and the Empire 'back on to the broad uplands where the stars of peace and freedom shine'.[55] In short, the uplands were revisited only when Churchill felt sanctioned by his own optimism about the future.

Something about the Yalta banquet again triggered this metaphor – perhaps the buckets of Caucasian champagne as much as Stalin's words. At any rate, Bohlen heard the Prime Minister, in buoyant vein, declaiming that 'in the modern world the function of leadership was to lead the people out from the forests into the broad sunlit plains of peace and happiness.'[56]

It may be significant, too, that Stalin saluted Churchill as a great historical figure. It showed goodwill, it showed generosity, it acknowledged the difference he had made; but it also looked backward rather than forward, envisaging no such future role for the British Prime Minister or the British Empire in a world henceforth dominated by two superpowers.

It was this subtext, elegiac if not dismissive, that Churchill could not accept. This was well illustrated the next day at the sixth plenary when Stettinius blithely started explaining how the concept of trusteeship would be applied by the new United Nations body. The gist was that it would not be used as a lever to prise colonies away from their existing masters, simply to replace and rename the old League mandates. All of this had been cleared with Eden and Cadogan, both at Malta and Yalta, but they had not fully briefed the Prime Minister on the detail, not wishing to excite him unnecessarily. Hence Stettinius was walking innocently into a minefield when he spoke. Churchill erupted; then he interrupted. Bohlen's official minutes draw a veil over what happened next, saying only that the Prime Minister 'continued in this vein for some minutes'.[57]

Luckily we have a note of Churchill's exact words – or rather, his inexact words. James Byrnes possessed not only good shorthand but the presence of mind to make his own record. 'I absolutely disagree,' Churchill began. 'I will not have one scrap of British territory flung into that area. After we have done our best to fight in this war and have done no crime to anyone I will have no suggestion that the British Empire is to be put into the dock and examined by everybody to see whether it is up to their standard.' At last the President was able to get a word in from the chair: 'I want Mr Stettinius to finish the sentence he was reading because it does not refer to the matter you have been speaking about.' The Secretary of State duly confirmed that it was not proposed that trusteeship should be applied to the British Empire. The Prime Minister was unappeased, uncomprehending, unstoppable. 'So far as the British Empire is concerned, we ask for nothing,' he banged on. 'We seek no territorial aggrandizement.'[58] Nobody had suggested this in the first place. What Hiss recorded, and what everyone present remembered, was Churchill in his seat still mumbling: 'Never, Never, Never.'[59]

This was magnificent theatre, rather less clever diplomacy. Stalin loved the show, walking round and breaking into applause at intervals. When the session adjourned for half an hour, Hiss scribbled a drafting note and got the President and the Prime Minister together with Eden and Cadogan to approve it. Trusteeship would apply to any particular territory by voluntary agreement, to enemy territories as a matter of course, and also to existing mandates of the League of Nations. The last point was crucial. Stettinius and Roosevelt may have thought it agreed already; Eden and Cadogan may have thought it inevitable; but what Churchill was agreeing, in a hurried confabulation over a scrap of paper pencilled by a man who later turned out to be a Soviet agent, was that British mandates would be 'put into the dock'.[60] This meant, in due course, that the administration of Palestine would be accountable to the United Nations Organization.

Churchill's outburst spoilt the Foreign Office plan for keeping mum about the British Empire. 'This sort of thing does harm, of course,' wrote Moran, who got his version hot from Harry Hopkins. 'When

Winston talks big about the British Empire the President gets very restive; he has a bee in his bonnet about our colonies.'[61] Whose bee, and whose bonnet, was a matter on which there was room for different opinions, of course. What should not be underestimated is the way that a pejorative image of imperialism informed Roosevelt's thinking and accordingly affected his judgement of both Churchill and Stalin. As Chester Wilmot pointed out long ago, there is little reason to doubt Mikolajczyk's statement of what the President told him in Washington months before the Yalta conference: 'Stalin is a realist', and though inexperienced in international relations, 'of one thing I am certain, Stalin is not an Imperialist.'[62] It was axiomatic that the President of the United States did not think of himself as an imperialist; so that was two of the Big Three not guilty.

That left only Churchill. Here Moran showed some detachment as well as perception in thinking that Churchill had really meant it when he made his famous declaration about not presiding over the liquidation of the British Empire. 'The President knows this side of the P.M., but he cannot leave the Empire alone,' Moran concluded. 'It seems to upset him, though he never turns a hair when a great chunk of Europe falls into the clutches of the Soviet Union.'[63] In the doctor's amateur political diagnosis, the combination of Roosevelt's antipathy to the British Empire with the deference accorded to the President by Stalin carried the worrying implication that a wedge was successfully being driven between the two democracies. Thus the British could not effectively enlist the Americans behind their own forebodings about the Soviet Union precisely because of the British Empire: a declining force in the world, no doubt, but still capable of exciting disproportionate suspicions.

The military side of the conference had been easily concluded. True, Russian entry into the Japanese war remained to be settled until the last moment, essentially between Roosevelt and Stalin personally. But the war against Hitler was already under control.

On the eastern front, the Russian advance was continuing despite fierce and frenzied German oppostion. This raised an alarming possibility about the proposed zones of occupation, as pencilled on the State Department maps, showing the boundary of the Soviet zone running south from the Baltic port of Lübeck. The line of the Elbe was thus between this boundary and Berlin, and Berlin about halfway to the Polish frontier. But the momentum of the Red Army was the new reality.

As Stettinius put it in his record of the State Department briefing for the President on 4 February: 'the Russians may soon reach and cross their zone and they might then say that since there was no formal agreement they would not restrict themselves to their zone.'[64] This seemed the more plausible since the size of the Soviet zone would be reduced by the Polish annexation of eastern German territory that was now envisaged. Might Stalin claim other parts of Germany if the Red Army got there first? The zone boundaries were thus agreed at Yalta so as to override such possibilities: no matter whose armies got to – or beyond – Berlin first.

On the western front, the British and American chiefs of staff had papered over their differences at Malta. So Brooke found that the main business of his tripartite meetings concerned coordination between the two fronts. 'The difficulty had been not with the Russians,' Marshall reported to his President, 'but with the British who wish to effect the liaison through the Combined Chiefs of Staff.'[65] This was plainly to prevent Eisenhower from dealing directly with the Red Army. Again the issue was papered over. This left the chiefs of staff free to go home after a final Anglo-American report to Roosevelt and Churchill on 9 February. 'A satisfactory feeling that the conference is finished,' Brooke noted with relief, 'and has on the whole been as satisfactory as could be hoped for, and certainly a most friendly one.'[66] He meant with the Russians, of course.

A final cause, or at least demonstration, of Anglo-American differences was reparations. The British war cabinet had been kept informed of Churchill's negotiations; on all other issues, they had accepted his judgement; but on reparations they were adamant that the Russian proposals were unacceptable. Transfer in kind did not really change much since there was still a transfer of real resources, whether of plant or production; and the removal of capital goods simply reduced Germany's capacity to make the payments. If the Soviet share was set at 10 billion dollars, and this was to be half the total, the total reparations bill would obviously reach the total of 20 billions, all to be paid 'by a Germany which has been bombed, defeated, perhaps dismembered and unable to pay for imports'.[67] Who would end up feeding the Germans? As an occupying power which lacked Russian ruthlessness, the British suspected that it might be themselves, out of their own reduced resources.

In London such arguments seemed conclusive. In Yalta, however, when Churchill read out the war cabinet's telegram at the final working plenary on 10 February, it merely inflamed Stalin for the only time in the conference. He insisted that specific figures be presented to the proposed Reparations Commission in Moscow; Churchill insisted that he had no authority to agree to this. It was a deadlock worse than that over the status of the French as an occupying power, solved earlier in this same session, when the President had reported that he had changed his mind and the Marshal obligingly reported that he would accept this. So the British had won that one, as Hopkins well realized since he had brokered the deal; yet now he saw them at it again, never satisfied, over reparations this time, visibly upsetting the poor Russians. He scribbled one of his notes for the President, in the chair as usual. 'The Russians have given in so much at this conference that I don't think we should let them down,' it read. 'Let the British disagree if they want to – and continue their disagreement at Moscow.' Which is how the issue was shelved: a specific British caveat on reparations in the final protocol but the Soviet proposal as 'a basis for discussion' in Moscow.[68]

By Saturday, 10 February, both Roosevelt and Stalin had secured most of what each most wanted. This included a secret agreement that the Soviet Union would enter the Japanese war after Hitler was defeated, always a major American objective at Yalta, but not something that entered the formal proceedings of the conference. This deal was done behind closed doors – closed on the British, in particular, though the final document was presented for Churchill's signature. In the end, this suited him well enough, since it meant that he could distance himself from an agreement that later became controversial because it promised the Russians so many gains, mainly at Chinese expense. Thus in *Triumph and Tragedy* he claimed that it was 'an American affair' and that 'we were not consulted' about commitments that primarily affected them.[69] At the time, he was ready enough to sign what was put in front of him by the Big Two. Churchill was as ready as Roosevelt to sacrifice Chinese interests if it ensured the early defeat of Japan and certainly unready to pick a quarrel on such an issue.

With Japan's fate settled, Roosevelt's agenda was fulfilled. Accordingly, at the end of the seventh plenary on 10 February, he casually let slip, almost as though it were inadvertent or at least insignificant, that the conference was over so far as he was concerned. Bohlen's laconic minute captures the moment: 'The President then remarked that he would have to leave Yalta tomorrow at three o'clock in the afternoon.'[70]

He was off to meet the reigning monarchs of Egypt, Saudi Arabia and Ethiopia.

Not only Stalin was manifestly shocked: so was Churchill. Yet this is puzzling since Byrnes left a circumstantial account of how Roosevelt had explained the planned visit to Churchill aboard the USS *Quincy* in Valletta harbour more than a week previously.[71] Moreover, the plan had been discussed with Eden by Stettinius, who had been working on it for weeks. Within days of his appointment as Secretary of State he had been told of the President's idea of such a visit, as a means of heading off political difficulties with Zionists in Congress: 'I want to see if I can't unravel this whole situation on the ground.' Yet, according to Hopkins, no advance warning had been given to Churchill, who was 'flabbergasted' at the news.[72]

Churchill certainly acted as if it were the first he had heard of the President's peremptory schedule. Moran's version came from the British ambassador. 'But Franklin, you cannot go,' Churchill had implored. 'We have within reach a very great prize.'[73] The elusive prize was evidently a just peace; but equally evidently, Roosevelt thought that he had already won it. Stalin too chimed in that more time was necessary and suggested the cancellation of that night's dinner, to be hosted by the British at the Vorontsov Villa. This extremity was avoided by using the dinner partly as a final drafting session, which still did not seem adequate to Stalin's sense of how important business should be conducted. The President's insouciant response was simply that he had three kings waiting for him, though he agreed to a minor adjustment in his timetable. It was later that night, as Hopkins noted, that Churchill 'sought me out, greatly disturbed', and was far from reassured to hear that the President intended to talk to King Ibn Saud about the Palestine situation: 'Nothing I said, however, was comforting to Churchill because he thought we had some deep laid plot to undermine the British Empire in these areas.'[74] Churchill soon decided that he too would have to go to Egypt, to try and hold the thin red line.

None of this put the Prime Minister in a good mood at breakfast the next morning. 'The President is behaving very badly,' he told Moran. 'He won't take any interest in what we are trying to do.'[75]

The final meeting of the Big Three started at noon. They set about and sat about agreeing the communiqué. 'Nazi Germany is doomed,' the first section said, with full agreement of all. Other sections were more contentious, papering over practical differences with the exalted language of high principle, especially in commending the attached Declaration on Liberated Europe. This committed the Big Three to assist in installing interim authorities that were 'pledged to the earliest possible establishment through free elections of governments responsive to the will of the people'. It also provided for the three powers to consult on how 'to discharge the joint responsibilities set forth in this declaration'.[76] All this could work. Would it?

While the drafting progressed, phrase by phrase, Churchill relieved his frustrations in characteristic style. According to Moran, Roosevelt was gravely asked what was meant, reverting to the Four Freedoms, by 'Freedom from want', with the Prime Minister musing: 'I suppose the word "want" means privation and not desire.' An innocent enough exchange, of course, but surely fuelled by more than a disinterested spirit of etymological inquiry. No matter: the inveterate wordsmith came back to the villa that afternoon a happier man. They had signed the communiqué over lunch in the Tsar's old billiard room. 'I'm so relieved to get that bloody thing off,' Churchill told Moran, and proved it over dinner by twice bursting into old music hall songs, with a rendering of 'The Soldiers of the Queen', very flat.[77]

Churchill was not the only one to exhibit signs of cheerfulness. The American delegation left in high spirits, of course, with Hopkins reflecting a general optimism about relations with the Soviet Union. Perhaps more striking, Sir Alexander Cadogan, nothing if not a case-hardened British diplomat of conservative views, also proved susceptible. 'I have never known the Russians so easy and accommodating,' he wrote that final day. 'In particular Joe has been extremely good. He *is* a great man, and shows up impressively against the background of the other two ageing statesmen.'[78]

The rather bleak views conveyed in the diary of Lord Moran, some of which are occasionally projected onto his eminent patient, seem to be the exception here. 'Stalin isn't going to butt in in Greece,' Churchill assured him, content that the 'naughty document' seemed to count for something. 'I find he does what he says he will do. It isn't easy to get him to say he will do it, but once he says something, he sticks to it.' On that reading, Yalta was a success, with the hard bargaining for long hours in the Livadia Palace now published to the world in documents that would themselves constrain future Soviet conduct. In acknowledging that 'Stalin and the P.M. are working together more smoothly than ever before,' Moran drew a contrast with Churchill's relations with Roosevelt, a deterioration for which the Greek crisis had only partly prepared him: 'The President's decrepitude has filled him with grief and dismay.'[79] As Churchill later wrote, in a draft comment on FDR omitted from *Triumph and Tragedy*: 'I was in fact talking to a friendly but darkening void.'[80]

There was no solemn or portentous parting on Sunday, 12 February, but an improvised getaway. The President, best prepared since he alone had known his own schedule, got away first. The Marshal simply disappeared, leaving not even a puff of smoke. The Prime Minister, it was understood, would stay another night, having left the Livadia Palace late that Sunday afternoon. By the time he had been driven the twelve miles back to the Vorontsov Villa, all plans had changed, as his entourage were to discover as soon as he swept in. 'We leave at five o'clock', Moran was told, as surprised as the rest. 'Sawyers! Where is everyone?'[81] Churchill's daughter Sarah was currently obtaining a divorce from Vic Oliver, an Austrian-American comedian well known for his mordant throwaway lines, so perhaps she felt well prepared for such scenes. She observed Sawyers, surrounded by half-packed suitcases, putting in a sponge-bag and taking it out again, and saying with tears in his eyes: 'They can't do this to me!'[82]

In haste rather than in style, the British delegation left Yalta. After a night at anchor off Sebastopol, there was time for recreation. During the week, Brooke and Moran had already had sufficient time off from their respective duties to tour the Crimean battlefields. The Prime Minister now had a day to catch up with what he had missed: the Crimean War and the present war equally on his mind, with the Russians, once Britain's enemies, now allies. 'I have been studying their faces, Charles,' he told Moran that evening. 'There is pride in their looks. They have a right to feel proud.'[83] All the evidence is that the Prime Minister, on leaving the Crimea, felt fairly proud of himself too.

The Teheran and Yalta conferences were the only occasions on which Roosevelt, Stalin and Churchill met together. They were so readily called the Big Three not simply because they represented the three major Allies – though from 1941 onwards the largest share of the fighting against the Axis was done by the Soviet Union and (increasingly) the United

States and (decreasingly) the British Empire. The term caught on because these were indeed big leaders with big ideas, for good or evil: Stalin forceful and ambiguous; Roosevelt ambiguous and eloquent; Churchill eloquent and as forceful as he was permitted by reduced circumstances. The image that persists is that of Stalin, Roosevelt and Churchill sitting together as equals. That Churchill retained this degree of prominence was, by 1945, not really a function of his country's actual power.

Yalta put his own position within the Big Three into a sobering perspective, as he realized. This was not a sudden epiphany but a reinforcement of a metaphor that kept stealing into the Prime Minister's conversation, one of his stock of expansive insights with which he tinkered at odd post-prandial moments. 'When I was at Teheran,' Churchill had put it in August 1944, 'I realized for the first time what a very *small* country this is. On one hand the big Russian bear with its paws outstretched – on the other the great American Elephant – & between them the poor little English donkey – who is the only one that knows the right way home.'[84] Back at Chequers, a fortnight after Yalta, Colville duly records the Prime Minister producing another version – not perhaps his best – at a lunch for President Benes of Czechoslovakia: 'a small lion was talking [or walking, perhaps] between a huge Russian bear and a great American elephant, but perhaps it would prove to be the lion which knew the way.'[85]

The metaphor varied, the story was the same. Always the insistence that it was the donkey (or more grandly, the lion) that knew the way home; but even this was a double-edged comment, suggesting that superior knowledge was not enough to persuade the elephant, or to coerce the bear, into taking the right path. As Moran concluded the long entry in his diary on their last day at Yalta, the Prime Minister's hopes were tinged with sombre feelings that he found it increasingly difficult to suppress: 'Far more than at Teheran he is conscious of his own impotence.'[86] And, far more than at Quebec, five months previously, wary of false summits.

False summits, then, in a double sense: not only that these meetings of great leaders might prove delusive in their promises, but that the hopes engendered about the war might also be successively disappointed, as the ascent of each ridge simply revealed the next daunting challenge. The Octagon conference had held out the benign expectation of an early end to the war in Europe. For the British, this promised victory with their own forces in the van; it promised a pre-emptive advance on Berlin; it promised a happy release from the mounting costs of the European war, yet it also promised continued support from the United States through the long transitional period before victory over Japan was also achieved.

With every month, the costs of the war mounted, in blood and treasure. If it had indeed all been over by Christmas (and Eisenhower had won his bet with Montgomery) these costs would thereby have been minimized. The British would have been less deeply mired in debt. More important, the killing would have stopped sooner: of GIs in the Battle of the Bulge, of civilians in London from V2 rockets, of refugees in Dresden from fire-bombing, of Jews in the gas chambers of eastern Europe – with the total victims of the war perishing, every month that passed, at a rate well into six figures. Gruesome counter-factual arithmetic of this toll is unnecessary since the tragic reality is that the expectations underlying the benign Quebec scenario were thwarted. Arnhem, the Ardennes, Athens – this can begin an alphabet of alibis, symbolizing the interlocking crises that simultaneously stalled the military momentum and fostered discord in the Anglo-American alliance.

Churchill went to Yalta, therefore, weaker than ever before. The summit-before-the-summit at Malta – in the cursory form that Roosevelt engineered – was itself a warning that the British were no longer taken quite so seriously. If Roosevelt was a sick man in a hurry at Yalta, he wasted little time on pandering to Churchill, a vaudeville act with which he was becoming bored. Instead, the President summoned his energies to strike terms with Stalin on the shape of the post-war world. After FDR's New Deal, this was to be FDR's Last Deal. The British Prime Minister found himself playing no very significant role, kept at arm's length by the President, no longer quite sure what his old friend Franklin was up to. But Churchill hoped for the best, if only because he was ineluctably faced with Soviet control of eastern Europe; and Britain's decision to go to war for the sake of Poland was now an embarrassment rather than a pledge that could easily be honoured. Churchill clung – rhetorically, sometimes comically – to his line that at least the British Empire, once its enemies were defeated, should not suffer at the hands of its allies.

A British Prime Minister with a more realistic appreciation of his country's size and weight and power would have suffered less disillusionment in 1944–5. The cards in the hand of a well-briefed and prudently calculating leader would have shown what limited options were realistic – for the King's First Minister as merely a titular member of the Big Three; for Great Britain as a bantam in a heavyweight league; for the Anglo-American alliance as an expedient relationship premised on subordination; for the dilapidated British Empire as an anachronism in the phase of world history that dawned at Yalta.

Not, however, Winston Churchill. And had he been otherwise, everything would have been otherwise. Had he not been Churchill, he would not have pitched the British Empire into an all-or-nothing gamble to defy Hitler in 1940, with little support from the United States and none at all from the Soviet Union, by offering the British people his simple policy: victory at all costs.

PART 3

Hollow Victories

7

Faltering and Altering

February–March 1945

'Berlin, Prague and Vienna were needlessly yielded to the Soviets. Here may be discerned the Tragedy in our hour of Triumph.'

Draft for Churchill's *The Second World War*

After leaving Yalta on Sunday, 12 February 1945, the Prime Minister and his party were accommodated aboard the SS *Franconia*, a former troopship, luxuriously reconverted to civilian use, and anchored off Sebastopol. Here they continued to revel in the sort of upper-crust luxury to which Communism had recently accustomed them. Only the bedbugs were missing. All conveniences were supplied and communications were good. The British morning newspapers were available by the evening each day. 'The report of our Crimean Conference seems to have had quite a good reception in the Press,' wrote Sir Alec Cadogan on Monday, 13 February.[1]

The Big Three stole all the front pages as the harbingers of good news. That morning's *Daily Mail* splashed the news of their communiqué under the banner headline: 'GERMANY'S FATE: OFFICIAL'. In the accompanying photograph of the Big Three, all seated, a fur-hatted Churchill looks benign and well satisfied, a fully uniformed Stalin leans across genially, and a gaunt but alert Roosevelt sits centre-stage in his double-breasted suit and cape. 'At Marshal Stalin's suggestion,' it was explained, 'it is to go down to history as the Crimea Conference.'

So much for confident prophecy. It was 'Yalta' that was to be re-membered, and it came to stand for betrayal of Poland, for unwarrant-able secret concessions at China's expense in the Far East, and for botched constitutional proposals about the United Nations, all wrapped up in a general charge about appeasement of the Soviet Union. Some of this was to become apparent sooner rather than later, but not suddenly, and not all at once.

In February 1945 the one thing that everyone still told each other was that there was a war on. On the western front, Allied soldiers remained embattled, only just recovering from the Ardennes campaign. On the eastern front, the last-ditch German resistance was prolonged, even against the famous Red Army – indeed especially against the infamous Red Army. The contemporary perspective was that of a European war that still had to be won, and the focus was understandably on Germany itself. This was what the press picked up from the from the Big Three communiqué.

'The shape of the new Europe after the defeat, occupation, and all-time demilitarisation of Germany' was thus the *Mail*'s theme; and it identified six salient points. First was that the Nazis were doomed. Second that unconditional surrender was affirmed. Third that Germany was to make good 'in kind' for war damage – no use of the word 'reparations'. Fourth that denazification – the concept but not the word was already there – would take place. Fifth that there would be three zones of occupation, with France invited to take a fourth. Finally that the 'close working partnership' of the chiefs of staff would continue to the end of the war. In a longer list, perhaps Poland would have made seventh place, maybe with the United Nations eighth, but certainly the secret agreement for Russia to enter the Japanese war could not have been reported at the time.

Insiders invariably knew more but not invariably better. The British participants, notably Churchill and Eden, but also Cadogan and Brooke, had come away with a sense of satisfaction: not of course at a perfect agreement but at a *modus vivendi* that they hoped would prove robust. After reading the records of the conference, which had reached him in London, Colville shared this view. 'We seem to have won most of our points and the P.M. has won another great personal success,' he noted. 'He was tireless in pressing for this conference, in spite of Roosevelt's apathy, and deserves most of the credit for what has been achieved.'[2]

Poland, however, was at best a submerged problem. To Leo Amery, learning of the Big Three's decisions at a full cabinet meeting in London, the devil was in the detail. 'I am afraid the Polish settlement, even if inevitable, will be a great shock to many, for it leaves out the legitimate Polish Government entirely and only refers to Polish elements in Poland

1. 'The Roaring Lion', Churchill in Ottawa, December 1941, by Yousuf Karsh

2. Churchill greets Roosevelt and his son Elliott (*centre*) at their first wartime meeting, August 1941, when they signed the Atlantic Charter

3. Churchill, Hopkins and Cadogan aboard HMS *Prince of Wales*, August 1941

4. Patton, Ike and Monty, taken after the invasion of Sicily, August 1943

5. The Not-So-Big Three. Roosevelt, Churchill and Mackenzie King at the Quebec conference, September 1944

6. Churchill and Alexander – his favourite general – summer 1944 in Italy

7. Field Marshal Sir Alan Brooke pondering war strategy, by Karsh

8. Cripps and Nehru, at the time of the Cripps Offer, 1942

9. The Big Three at Yalta, February 1945

10. Truman adjusts his vision, taken by Karsh before Roosevelt's death in April 1945

11. The Athens conference: Churchill and Archbishop Damaskinos by lantern-light, December 1944. Alexander and Macmillan to the right of the Archbishop

12. Three British officers crossed the Rhine: Churchill, Brooke and Monty, March 1945

13. German surrender, Lüneberg Heath, 4 May 1945. Chester Wilmot to the right of the flagpole at the back

14. 'Jane' on VE-Day, *Daily Mirror*, 8 May 1945

15. Attlee at San Francisco, May 1945, by Karsh

16. In Washington Lord Halifax (*right*) once whispered to Lord Keynes (*left*) ... September 1945, before the Loan negotiations

17. A special relationship: Churchill's Fulton speech, 5 March 1946

18. Two vegetarians seek to avert bloodshed: Gandhi with Cripps

19. Queuing for rationed food, London, 1946

20. Explosion at the King David Hotel, Jerusalem,
22 July 1946

21. Liaquat Ali Khan (*centre*) with Jinnah (*right*) at the London conference, December 1946

22. Marshall (*right*) and Bevin – all smiles

23. Edwina Mountbatten and Nehru share a joke behind the Viceroy's back

or elsewhere being added to the Lublin Government,' he remarked. 'I wonder whether the Polish divisions and other forces who have fought so gallantly will accept the position.'[3] General Anders, still under Alexander's command with the Allied forces in Italy, was yet to have his say. Did the Yalta agreement fulfil the pledges that Britain had given to Poland in 1939? Had Britain gone to war for this?

Alexander himself, still aboard the *Franconia* in Sebastopol, heard the Prime Minister's current views on such delicate issues. Alexander, always the soul of courtesy and honour, tried to seize the opportunity over lunch on 13 February to plead for better sustenance of the liberated Italians, arguing that 'after all, that was more or less what we were fighting this war for – to secure liberty and decent existence for the peoples of Europe.' As Cadogan recorded, a boisterous Churchill simply riposted: 'Not a bit of it: we are fighting to secure the proper respect for the British people!'

The Prime Minister's mood, it often seemed to those who travelled with him, determined his whims, and his whims determined all their travel plans. As usual, the plans kept changing. Churchill wanted to get to Alexandria, to check up on Roosevelt and his three kings, which apparently left Eden free to fly to Athens with Cadogan. 'But the P.M. evidently had second thoughts about allowing Anthony to go gathering laurels on his own,' Cadogan noted, 'and announced that he would come with us tomorrow – to Anthony's rage and horror. It's rather like travelling about with Melba and Tetrazzini in one company!'[4] It was a remark that he was pleased with, and had tried out on Moran the night before as they were retiring after a spirited dinner where the Prime Minister, always the prima donna, had been performing to a captive audience.

It was Greece that chiefly exercised Churchill, with a lot of talk about teaching the Communists a lesson. 'The P.M. wanted to visit Athens to ginger up the Greek Government and the Archbishop so that they might take a firmer line,' wrote Moran, impressed by the way the issue had 'entered into his soul' and by his animus against his political critics at home. 'It was only when the P.M. had exhausted the topic of his crusade against Communism in Greece that he reverted to the natural conversation of old age, with its dislike of change.'[5]

What was Stalin, likewise fresh from the accord of Yalta, saying at dinner that night? Was he correspondingly dwelling on how he would crush the opposition in Poland? At any rate, Churchill clearly felt licensed to intervene personally, however much it visibly upset Eden, who had to be content, much like Stettinius, with acting as his master's voice. When Churchill commended Macmillan, and revealed that he had him in mind for the War Office, Eden said: 'He wants the F.O.' Moran caught Churchill's dry response: 'There isn't a vacancy at the Foreign Office.'[6] This faint praise from Melba was the only bouquet that Tetrazzini was going to receive.

On the morning of Wednesday, 14 February, the Prime Minister flew to Athens. Harold Macmillan had been there for four days already, anxiously wondering whether, as he hoped, the Prime Minister would come himself. The negotiations between the parties had been dragging on, with the Communists keeping one eye on the Big Three meeting. 'They seem persuaded that Stalin will do something to help them,' Macmillan had written on 5 February. 'For my part, I feel sure that he will try to bargain Greece against Poland.'[7] This was a shrewd hunch. Moreover, his own talents as a negotiator played a part in securing agreement to a treaty between the political parties, signed in the small hours of 12 February, only two days before Churchill and Eden arrived themselves from snowy Saki into the brilliant Greek sunshine.

In Marlowe's words (later applied to Churchill by Isaiah Berlin) it is passing brave to ride in triumph through Persepolis. Such visceral feelings were innate in Churchill, and his progress through Athens on 14 February left nothing to be desired. 'On landing, we went in cars straight to the Royal Palace, through streets lined with cheering Greeks,' wrote Moran. 'In the vast square the crowd was packed so tightly that they could just throw up their hats without much chance of recovering them.'[8] The Prime Minister drove in an open car, side by side with the Regent, Archbishop Damaskinos. Unlike previous demonstrations, there was no competitive chanting between the EAM and the royalists. 'It was a *democratic* crowd, applauding in the Archbishop and Churchill democratic leaders,' Macmillan enthused, and went on to draw the obvious contrast with the Christmas visit – 'cold, dark and armoured cars or tanks. And now, peace signed; glorious warm sun (so that Athens was really "violet-crowned" today), and a procession in open vehicles, like a football match or a race-meeting in peace-time.'[9] His considered estimate was of a crowd of 40,000.

'Speeches of course, which Winston enjoyed enormously,' wrote

Cadogan, equally impressed, but adding: 'Poor Anthony! All this would have been his if the P.M. hadn't butted in.'[10] Yet this would hardly have been the case. The vast crowd may have wanted to demonstrate for democracy but also wanted to see this extraordinary figure, this fabled celebrity, this warrior hero, Winston Churchill, fresh from the Big Three, waving his cigar, weaving his oratorical spell, to be cheered whether or not they understood his actual words, with his florid compliments to their nation, his confident hopes of the future. 'Let right prevail. Let party hatreds die. Let there be unity. Let there be resolute comradeship.' All this delivered extempore in reply to the Archbishop, with intervals for translation and for honing the succcessive phrases, building to the peroration: 'Greece for ever! Greece for all!'[11]

'I have had great moments in my life,' Churchill later told Harold Nicolson, 'but never such a moment as when faced by that half-million crowd in Constitution Square.'[12] No doubt it felt like half a million. That night there was dinner for thirty-six people at the embassy. Churchill was understandably elated and Eden ready to grant him his personal success. Macmillan was appreciative of their (well-merited) compliments to himself. 'The Crimean conference has put them all in a good humour,' he recorded. 'The whole atmosphere seems to have been very good; the Russians have shown more candour and friendliness than ever before.'[13]

After dinner, many of the guests went to the Acropolis. The floodlights were turned on, for the first time in four years, with dramatic effect, albeit only for a few minutes because of power shortages. Churchill preferred to sit at table in the embassy, holding forth until well gone midnight. On returning from the Acropolis, Moran found the Prime Minister still rehearsing his handling of the Greek crisis and his parliamentary annihilation of *The Times*. But a sunlit Greek triumph was one thing; the tragedy of his own country's impending plight another kind of problem, one less susceptible to solution through the exercise of charismatic powers. 'Once more he spoke gloomily of England's financial position after the war, when half our food would have to be paid for by exports,' Moran noted, with an uneasy sense that the old magic was fading. 'For nearly four hours a figure out of history had talked to us without reserve, and yet those who heard him appeared half asleep.'[14]

Neither Yalta nor Athens was the main news story in the London *Evening Standard* on 14 February. 'THE BLASTING OF DRESDEN' was the banner headline: '1350 Forts and Liberators Over Germany

To-day After Night Attack by 1400 'Planes of RAF Bomber Command'. This was, of course, a devastating attack, with an aftershock felt to this day. It was not simply revenge for the 180 V-rockets that fell on England that week but instead a result of the coordination of Allied attacks agreed at Yalta. The common sense of this, albeit not the specific agreement, was duly reported that day: 'The raids were in support of Marshal Koniev's troops who are less than 70 miles away.' That much is correct, so far as it goes. The *Standard* speculated further: 'The Germans may be using Dresden – almost as large as Manchester – as their base against Koniev's left flank.' This was what Russian intelligence claimed; and it is true that there were signs of unusually heavy transit through the city, an important communications centre. What was actually happening, however, was not the deployment of military reinforcements eastwards but a vast influx of hapless refugees moving westwards. That is not how Dresden was reported on the day. Only later, and gradually, did a different picture emerge.

While Dresden burnt that night, Churchill slept in his plane on the airfield in Athens. Next morning he flew to Alexandria for a farewell meeting with Roosevelt aboard USS *Quincy*. Dresden did not preoccupy them; they had other problems.

The President had meanwhile received his three kings, whom he sent away bearing gifts. For King Ibn Saud, no great walker and an admirer of the amenity provided by the presidential wheelchair, there was not only an aircraft but several wheelchairs too. What Roosevelt got in return, however, was less appealing.

The Great Bitter Lake was the venue for this exotic meeting and the outcome too was fairly bitter. Roosevelt's optimistic agenda could be seen as inspiring: to do something for the Jews, who had suffered so appallingly in this war, by unlocking the doors to mass immigration, so that those who wished could move to a safe haven. Not, of course, the doors of mass immigration to the United States, but to Palestine. Roosevelt had told Stalin at their last dinner in Yalta that he was a Zionist and seemed to have evoked a favourable response.

That would have made all the Big Three Zionists of some kind. Churchill had been a believer, but one constrained during wartime by political pressures against lending support to the Jews – and perhaps a lapsed believer following Moyne's assassination. Roosevelt's position was different; insofar as he was a Zionist, this was demanded by domestic political considerations, electorally in states like New York and now pressingly on Capitol Hill.

The President had laid out his plan at a meeting on 2 January with his Secretary of State, as the latter solemnly recorded in his diary. 'The president said he desired to take with him a map showing the Near-Eastern area as a whole and the relationship of Palestine to the area and on that basis to point out to Ibn Saud what an infinitesimal part of the whole area was occupied by Palestine and that he could not see why a portion of Palestine could not be given to the Jews without harming in any way the interests of the Arabs with the understanding, of course, that the Jews would not move into adjacent parts of the Near East and Palestine.'[15] Apparently, this could be expected to do the trick: first, the map, which would perhaps strike the King, who had fought over virtually every mile of its territory in his time, with the same force of novelty as it evidently had the President, and then the helpful suggestion of a solution, which even a child could appreciate.

Thus Roosevelt blithely confronted King Ibn Saud. However, as Hopkins reported: 'when the President asked Ibn Saud to admit some more Jews into Palestine, indicating that it was such a small percentage of the total population of the Arab world, he was greatly shocked when Ibn Saud, without a smile, said "No".' This came as a surprising answer only to Roosevelt himself, who 'seemed not to fully comprehend what Ibn Saud was saying to him for he brought the question up two or three times more', before the full force of the King's increasingly forthright objections sank in.[16] Suddenly the Arabs seemed much less easy to satisfy with easy words than was the Zionist lobby in Washington.

Churchill heard about this curious encounter at lunch aboard the *Quincy* on 15 February. He was to have his own meeting with Ibn Saud a couple of days later. To Western eyes, it was as exotic as Roosevelt's, and to Zionist ears as unpromising. Churchill and Ibn Saud conferred at a hotel on a lake in the Egyptian desert. The gifts proffered by the British were less munificent than those of the Americans, a cause of some embarrassment at the time and a symbol of the two powers' relative influence in the Middle East in the future. Moran observed that the King 'has led armies in the field with unfailing success and is the master of the Arab world; he was not in the least overawed now by his English visitor, whose Zionist sympathies were no doubt known to him.'[17] They were indeed; and the Prime Minister's defiance of his own resolution not to mention Palestine was likewise predictable, as was the King's refusal to be budged. It was only after this parley in the desert, and a day's rest, that the Prime Minister was to return to London, which he had left nearly three weeks previously.

Churchill and Roosevelt had had their first wartime meeting aboard an American warship in August 1941. On that occasion, off the New-foundland coast, they had signed the Atlantic Charter as an indication of their increasingly convergent views on the war. Their last meeting was also on an American warship, this time off the Egyptian coast, but with no document to record their increasing divergence. Lunch was agreeable, with the President always a personable host, the Prime Minis-ter always ready to sit at table and seize his chances for informal diplo-macy. Afterwards they talked confidentially, joined only by Hopkins, so long their mutually esteemed go-between, about the possible develop-ment of atomic bomb research in Britain after the war.

'The President seemed placid and frail,' Churchill wrote in hindsight. 'I felt that he had a slender contact with life.'[18] Gravely ill himself, Hopkins was hardly in better shape, and was to leave the ship at Algiers, creating an untoward final breach with the President, whom he never saw again. Whether he really sensed it or not, Churchill was living on borrowed time politically as much as was Roosevelt more literally. Their wartime relationship had been talked up as a matter of course by both men when it suited them: some of the time by Roosevelt, almost all of the time by Churchill, who went on to give a shamelessly romanticized view of a virtually unclouded friendship in his war memoirs. True, especially with Hopkins around at awkward moments, the British Prime Minister had been granted some extraordinary favours, though few of them recently. His days of privileged access to the presidential court ended as the *Quincy* steamed out of Alexandria.

The immediate reactions to Yalta were almost all favourable; and not only in Britain but also in the United States. Isaiah Berlin reported on 11 February, at a time when it was known that the Big Three had met but not what they had decided, a widespread belief that Vandenberg's 'almost universally acclaimed' speech a month previously, precipitating overt manifestations of Senate support for Roosevelt's handling of foreign policy, had strengthened his hand in 'the Black Sea parley'. Berlin wrote of 'the conviction that in President Roosevelt alone lies the last chance of ensuring a just peace settlement within the framework of the Atlantic Charter', but added: 'British and Russian need for American economic assistance in the post-war period is cited as the main hope for a compliant attitude towards American moral demands.'[19]

The assumption here was not that of a unique English-speaking partnership, but instead that Britain, no less than Russia, had to be bullied into doing the right thing. These were the spectacles through which the fine print of the Big Three communiqué was first read by many Americans. A focus on Poland, and a concomitant Anglo-American concern over Russian intentions, which to us seem the obvious crux of Yalta, bled into a public political debate where other issues, other countries, were initially more prominent.

American suspicions of Great Britain in February 1945 continued to be fed by continuing conflict over the Mediterranean. The fact that it was still under British supreme command itself heightened these suspicions. 'I do not understand the flow of abuse and accusations against alleged British policy towards Italy which is coming from every American source,' Macmillan admitted, as the man on the spot. From his perspective, it was 'the insatiable claims of the Pacific War' that were obviously hogging the shipping space needed to provide more adequate rations for the Italian people; and he was inclined to see the manifold problems of governing Italy purely in American electoral terms. 'Such absurd and impossible promises about Italy were made to get Roosevelt that vote at all costs, that they must now account for the failure to implement them. The easiest way is to "blame" it on the British.' Having successfully exonerated himself to himself, and slept on the matter, he added the next day: 'They are also very sensitive about the Greek affair. If only we can pull off the peace, it will irritate their guilty consciences even more.'[20]

In Washington it all sounded so different. As Berlin put it: 'nothing will shake average American's conviction that Great Britain is determined to reduce Italy to virtual status of a British dependency and that only hope of "democratic" Italy resides in support that United States of America may be able to afford her.' And if this illustrated the effectiveness with which Italo-American politicians had made their case, he reflected that 'one can only compare the results achieved with what the large Polish-born element in this country might have succeeded in doing for their mother country had they possessed anything approaching Italian flair.'[21]

This was how it looked before the American public knew anything of what the Big Three had actually decided (and long before they knew everything). The release of the communiqué had a generally favourable reception. James Byrnes had been sent back to Washington early, so that an American voice rather than that of Churchill would break the news. Byrnes's press conference in the White House on 13 February, following up on the communiqué's release the previous day, brought him gratifying coverage. Yalta was the 'greatest United Nations victory of the war', according to the Philadelphia *Record*; it was 'another great proof of Allied unity, strength and power of decision', according to the *New York Herald Tribune*; while to Henry Luce's influential *Time* magazine, with its national circulation: 'all doubts about the Big Three's ability to co-operate in peace as well as in war seem now to have been swept away.'[22] Support came from Republicans like former President Hoover, Senator White (the minority leader in the Senate), John Foster Dulles (a decade later, Eisenhower's Secretary of State) and, above all, Senator Vandenberg, who was quoted as saying that it was 'by far the best communiqué issued from any major conference'.

Vandenberg had simultaneously been named as one of the carefully balanced United States delegation to the San Francisco conference. Berlin thought that he remained 'the great enigma and is manifestly enjoying the spotlight which is now always upon him'. For a couple of weeks he wrestled with his conscience over whether to accept, determined not to spare the public, and particularly pressmen, such an edifying spectacle. At one moment he was saying coyly that no official invitation to act as a United States delegate had been received, and at the next that his acceptance was 'what the President calls an iffy question'.[23] As Senator for Michigan, Vandenberg had a large Polish constituency, whose views on the iniquity of the Curzon Line he shared and had publicly represented. Polish groups were already publicly denouncing Yalta for this reason. Vandenberg was obviously open to taunts about his own position, given his inclination to become a delegate.

One simple question – 'what can we do about it?' – now put the Senator in the President's shoes, and thus in his hands too. 'Manifestly America will not go to war with Russia to settle such an issue – particularly when the President of the United States has endorsed the settlement,' Vandenberg had written in his diary on 13 February. 'In the final analysis, we could not afford to upset our postwar peace plans on account of this issue.'[24] It is thus a mark of his realism about the politics of Yalta as much as of any idealism about world peace that he began his own negotiations over the San Francisco conference with the seaborne President: to attend but not to be tied. 'I cannot go to this conference as a stooge,' Vandenberg told Dulles on 17 February.[25]

As the days passed, then, euphoria over the fact that the Big Three were in agreement was somewhat clouded by an uneasy awareness that they were in agreement not only to dismember Germany for the sake of Poland but to dismember Poland for the sake of the Soviet Union. For Vandenberg, an acid test of good faith would be the status and fate of General Anders. Macmillan had the benefit of the latter's views at first hand at dinner on 17 February at Alexander's headquarters at Caserta.

It was an uncomfortable evening for all concerned. If it was most deeply distressing for Anders, he at least had a clear conscience and a licence to vent his bitterness, which Alexander respected. 'A rather painful discusion – or rather monologue – in which General Anders said that Poland was finished, betrayed by her allies,' wrote Macmillan. He thought Anders 'a fine man', eight times wounded and two years in a Russian prison, having subsequently led his Polish soldiers on their extraordinary march from Russia, through Turkestan, Palestine and Egypt, now to Italy, where two divisions had taken a notable share in the fighting. A glorious page in Polish history, but history just the same. 'I am very sorry indeed for him,' Macmillan wrote. 'But I cannot see what else we could do.'[26] His reaction was the more significant in view of his own anti-appeasement record, stretching back to the 1930s.

Harold Macmillan was MP for Stockton-on-Tees. An industrial constituency much plagued with pre-war unemployment, this was a highly unusual seat for a Conservative to have held; but the young Macmillan had been a highly unusual sort of Conservative. Not only had he rebelled from his own party over unemployment, espousing instead the views of Keynes, whose publisher he had been, Macmillan had also added rebellion over the policy of appeasement. On Guy Fawkes night, 5 November 1938, just after Munich, the effigy burnt on the bonfire at Macmillan's country house was said to bear a distinct resemblance to Neville Chamberlain. Neither Churchill nor Eden had a better record as an opponent of appeasement: one reason why Macmillan had been snatched from the backbenches to join them on the front bench of the Coalition Government that overthrew the Chamberlain regime in May

1940. The parliamentary reception of Yalta was now likely to be a defining moment, as much as Munich had been.

Members of the House of Commons were already hearing evidence from Poles who had escaped from Soviet-occupied territory. '1,230,000 Poles have been deported and only 9 per cent of them have got away afterwards,' Harold Nicolson retailed in his diary on 15 February, saying: 'All this is convincing and profoundly disturbing.'[27] This was the background to the exercise in persuasion mounted by Churchill and Eden, on their return to England four days later. They had already been warned of trouble brewing on their own backbenches. Their plane had to be diverted to RAF Lyneham in Wiltshire, then no less than four hours' drive south-west of London, so when Colville finally caught up with the returning Yalta party at Reading en route, he found himself wedged in the back seat of the official car between Mrs Oliver (Sarah Churchill) and the Foreign Secretary. 'Eden said that he thought the Tories had no right to complain about Poland,' he noted. 'The P.M. had not sold the pass.'

On the bumpy ride back to central London, the official British defence of Yalta was rehearsed for Colville. So far as Poland was concerned, it rested on the assertions that the Curzon Line was a just boundary in the east; that the boundary in the west was still to be agreed; and that a new Polish government would be recognized 'if and when we were satisfied with its composition'. This was pretty faithful to the proceedings of the conference. So far as the United Nations proposals were concerned, Eden spun an imaginative defence of the Prime Minister, claiming that 'the Russians would have been quite happy to agree to none of their constituent states belonging to the Assembly, had not the Americans foolishly acquiesced.' This was, of course, patently at odds with the records of what had actually taken place, attributing the endorsement of the case for three Soviet votes to American folly instead of to Churchill's imperialist musings. But Eden had not finished. 'Finally the Americans had been very weak,' so Colville recorded. 'The President looked old and ill, had lost his powers of concentration and had been a hopelessly incompetent chairman.'[28]

Arriving at 10 Downing Street, the Prime Minister was met by the small war cabinet. They followed him into the cabinet room for some first impressions of Yalta. On his first full day back, Tuesday, 20 February, he was received with cheers at Prime Minister's questions in the Commons.

'The P.M. and Anthony are well satisfied – if not more – and I think they are right,' wrote Cadogan the same day. 'Of course Poles in London, and extreme right-wing MPs, criticise and grumble.' He had first-hand experience of what to expect from both these groups, having just attended Eden's briefing of Mikolajczyk and others, who 'of course exhibited no gratitude, and were merely critical and unconstructive – like all Poles'.[29]

If this was a tough session, Churchill did not blench from a tougher one the next day. General Anders arrived in Downing Street, as Colville observed when he showed him in, 'black with gloom about the Crimea Conference decision like most of his fighting compatriots'.[30] Cadogan, who was again in attendance, thought the two and a half hours they spent together excessive, since there was so little to say. 'Both rather lost their tempers at first, but calmed down later.'[31] For once, Churchill's dilatory methods may have been appropriate, in dealing with an issue that needed time for emotional adjustment rather than a curt, take-it-or-leave-it exposition.

The Prime Minister's cabinet colleagues had received an encouraging assessment of Yalta. Yet his initial assurance that Stalin 'meant well to the world and to Poland' was also hedged with prudent references to alternative strategies, especially after Churchill's session with Anders, whom he had promised – 'in the last resort' – British citizenship for all his troops if they found themselves in exile. Churchill's 'own feeling was that the Russians would honour the declaration that had been made', he told the war cabinet, 'but the acid test of the[ir] sincerity in this matter in the immediate future would be whether any objection would be raised to M. Mikolajczyk returning to Poland.'[32]

These were Churchill's own words, or rather, among Churchill's own words – there were so many of them. Cadogan, in attendance at the cabinet on 22 February, found it all very familiar, as the clock ticked on and on: '*How* have we conducted this war, with the P.M. spending *hours* of his own and other people's time simply drivelling, welcoming every red herring so as only to have the pleasure of more irrelevant, redundant talk.' It was in this context that Cadogan wrote: 'I *long* for poor old Neville Chamberlain again.'[33]

Such sentiments, however, were suddenly more widespread: if not a professed longing for Chamberlain, at least a sense that perhaps his great dilemma over appeasement had for years been too easily scorned.

It suddenly became a live issue, whether what Churchill asked his followers to believe about Stalin in 1945 was intrinsically different from what Chamberlain had asked them to believe about Hitler in 1938.

This awkward question was already in the Prime Minister's mind when he addressed all those ministers who were outside the small war cabinet at noon on 23 February. Hugh Dalton always loved these occasions, in bringing him closer not only to the real seat of power, for which he thirsted, but also to Churchill himself, for whom he had a deep and unrequited admiration. The Prime Minister, always the trouper, regaled them with his Malta-to-Yalta ditty, which went down better than it had with Roosevelt. He told his anecdotes of Yalta, already becoming something of a stock in trade: the opulence of Russian hospitality, the considered magnanimity of Stalin, the dramatic confrontations over Poland. 'No one could tell whether the pledge to make a truly free and independent Poland would be honoured by the Russians or not,' Churchill claimed. 'We and the Americans would do our best to see that it was.' Dalton inserted in the margin another comment, possibly not part of the Prime Minister's address but an informal remark later: 'Poor Neville Chamberlain believed he could trust Hitler. He was wrong. But I don't think I'm wrong about Stalin.'[34]

It was the same story when the Prime Minister spent that weekend at Chequers, with Colville on duty as private secretary. 'The P.M. was rather depressed,' he recorded, 'thinking of the possibilities of Russia one day turning against us, saying that Chamberlain had trusted Hitler as he was now trusting Stalin (though he thought in different circumstances), but taking comfort, as far as Russia went, in the proverb about the trees not growing up to the sky.'

One dinner guest was Air Marshal Sir Arthur Harris, as fresh from his triumph at Dresden as Churchill was from his in Athens. But 'Bomber' Harris was the more confident and satisfied of the two, whereas the 'shadows of victory' were more apparent to the Prime Minister. 'In 1940 the issue was clear and he could see distinctly what was to be done,' Churchill ruminated, demanding what would happen when Harris had finished destroying Germany: 'What will lie between the white snows of Russia and the white cliffs of Dover?' And after the war, he intoned, 'we should be weak, we should have no money and no strength and we should lie between the two great power [sic] of the USA and the USSR.' At lunch on Sunday, 24 February, attended by the Prof and Gil Winant, the American ambassador, there was some shift in register. 'After lunch the PM said that he would like to make many bitter remarks about the Government if he were not head of it.' And by dinner that last night at Chequers, 'very gay and cheerful, the PM being at the top of his form'.[35]

It was in this frame of mind – cheerful and depressed, confident and mistrustful, resolute and vacillating – that the Prime Minister composed his speech on Yalta for the House of Commons. And he was pitching his arguments at MPs similarly torn in what they kept telling each other about Yalta: that we were lucky to get such a good agreement; or rather that it was the best we could get in the circumstances; or at least that we had no choice but to agree to it; and that anyway it was the Americans' fault for giving so much away.

Harold Nicolson, MP for West Leicester, sat in the Commons as 'National Labour'. Some seven strong (or weak), this faction was the rump of the support that Ramsay MacDonald had taken with him from the Labour Party into the National Government, formed to face the financial crisis of 1931; by 1945, the term was an eccentric euphemism for 'Conservative' and it was little more than a joke that the fastidious Nicolson should claim these unlikely proletarian credentials. With an open marriage to the novelist Vita Sackville-West, unforgivingly aristo-cratic (as she let nobody forget), Nicolson pursued his wayward political career and his homosexual affairs with equal lack of discretion. He was so wonderfully well-connected, so much accepted as one of the inner core socially, that he could never get over his actual political exclusion from government office. But at least, as a connoisseur of the higher gossip, he had the satisfaction of always being in the know, which gives his diary its enduring fascination.

Nicolson had heard all about Yalta from one of his many old friends in the Foreign Office, the diplomat Gladwyn Jebb, sporting campaign medals from the Crimean war against the bugs. 'He says that President Roosevelt was an utterly changed man since he had last seen him. Not only did he look twenty years older, but he was scarcely able to speak.' Eden, Cadogan, Jebb – everyone who was anyone in the FO – were putting about the same story on this count, which obviously had some element of alibi for the British as well as medical diagnosis. The gossip was, too, that 'Winston had repudiated all our pledges to both the French and to the Jews' and that Palestine was to be placed under United

Nations trusteeship. Nicolson knew that 'the diehard Tories' were going to oppose Yalta 'as a matter of principle', though the National Labour vote was solid with no question of Nicolson himself failing to support his hero Churchill or his friend Eden, with both of whom he had identified himself since Munich days.[36]

At Westminster, as the Yalta debate opened that day at noon, the fact that the war was going well took the immediate pressure off the Government but also created space for introspection and stricture. The Commons was packed to the doors in its temporary accommodation in the House of Lords chamber, in use since the destruction of their own chamber by bombing in 1941. The Prime Minister covered various topics, in two instalments, both before and after lunch; but Poland was the crux. He spoke confidently of Poland's being able to enjoy its independence, though the revelation of his offer of British citizenship to Polish soldiers sat rather oddly with this line of argument.

An early attack on the Yalta settlement came from Lord Dunglass, heir to the Earl of Home and later, as Sir Alec Douglas Home, to become a Conservative Prime Minister himself. Before the war, young Dunglass had, like his colleague Chips Channon, been a fervent Chamberlainite – indeed Channon wrote in 1939: 'He admires Neville so much that he has even come to look like him.'[37] Dunglass's tone in now addressing the House was somewhat different, appealing to stark moral imperatives: 'In 1939, when the people of this country had to make a choice between peace and war they chose war because they were convinced to the point of certainty that so long as appeals to force were the rule in international affairs, there could be no peace, nor progress.'[38] Yalta failed this test.

For Nicolson, the Yalta debate was one of the high points of his political career (albeit one marked by many low points, some tragic, most of them comic). He records that, after making his own speech, the Prime Minister joined him for a drink. 'Collins,' Churchill said to the barman, 'you will give me a large brandy. I deserve it.' As the fluid worked its usual magic, points that he had been unable to state openly in debate – 'I decline absolutely to embark here on a discussion about Russian good faith,' he had said – were explained in rather more pragmatic terms. 'Not only are the Russians very powerful,' Churchill told Nicolson, 'but they are on the spot; even the massed majesty of the British Empire would not avail to turn them off that spot.'[39] And why provocatively assume that they would behave badly, especially after Greece?

Everyone was conscious that such arguments, public professions and private reservations alike, were an uneasy replay of the debate over pre-war appeasement. Churchill had wanted to tell the Commons: 'Soviet Russia seeks not only peace, but peace with honour.' The attentive Colville, also a Chamberlainite in his time, had advised him to omit it – 'Echo of Munich.'[40] And Colville noted after the speech (to which he himself, perhaps queasily, chose not to listen): 'He is trying to persuade himself that all is well, but in his heart I think he is worried about Poland and not convinced of the strength of our moral position.'[41] Nicolson, like Churchill, carried no taint as an 'appeaser' of Hitler, as they implicitly reminded each other: 'Winston is as amused as I am that the warmongers of the Munich period have now become the appeasers, while the appeasers have become the warmongers.'[42]

This was a telling point – but which way it told was just what the two sides could not agree. 'All afternoon at the Commons, the supreme debate,' wrote Chips Channon as proceedings resumed on the second day, 'the conscience of the gentlemen of England and of the Conservative Party has been stricken by our failure to support our pledged word on Poland.' He meant the speeches by his friend Dunglass and others, which he found as moving as he found the official line from Churchill and Eden unconvincing and ignominious. 'I am horrified by the inconsistency of some Members of Parliament, members of society, who went about abusing Mr Chamberlain about appeasement in 1938 and 1939, and now meekly accept this surrender to Soviet Russia.' If Channon did not join the rebels, it was only because of his own pragmatic judgement that 'there seemed little use in trying to fight the inevitable.'[43]

Few argued Yalta as an open-and-shut case. Nicolson's big moment approached as he wound himself up for his speech. 'But I was not quite clear where my conscience was,' he told Vita Sackville-West. 'Emotionally I feel for the Poles very deeply.' He smoked too many cigarettes as he tussled with the issues, thereby impairing the delivery of his speech, as Churchill apprised him afterwards, doubtless through his own cigar smoke. But what Nicolson told fellow Members was well received, surely because it picked up their doubts and wove them into a justifying argument for what they knew had to be done anyway. As Nicolson put it to his wife: 'I really do believe that Winston and Anthony did save Poland from a fate far more terrible than might otherwise have been hers. I was absolutely sure in my own inner heart and mind that the

Yalta decisions were not expedient only, but ultimately to the benefit of of the Poles and mankind.'[44] In just such terms had pre-war appeasers explained that Chamberlain was preventing the horror of a general war, thereby saving Czechoslovakia.

There was no chance of the Government sustaining anything more than a moral defeat. In the end, twenty-five MPs voted on an amendment regretting the transfer of Polish territory to Russia: not really the issue that most upset the rebels but their best proxy in expressing doubts about Soviet intentions. On the substantive vote, the Government won by more than 400 to nil. This implied about thirty, mainly Conservative, abstentions – 'who presume to criticise,' as Cadogan judged them, 'while confessing they know not what else to suggest'. He was not short of words to characterize them – 'ambition, prejudice, dishonesty, self-seeking, light-hearted irresponsibility, black-hearted mendacity' – less on account of Yalta in particular than simply because they were politicians.[45] He would not, of course, have contested the conventional description of politics as the art of the possible, but instead disparaged moral gestures made without responsibility for the practical consequences.

Yalta thus reopened the file on Munich, as it were, backwards. For Chamberlain did not spontaneously decide to appease Hitler at Munich; instead, he had to choose between various bad options. Moreover, his judgement in 1938 was informed by both hope and fear. The case for hope was that, since a reasonable case could be made for the revised Czech frontier as ethnically just, it was indeed right as well as expedient to agree to it, as Hitler had himself argued, and reasonable to suppose that the Führer's promises could be trusted. This view was, at best, a high-minded risk or, at worst, a delusion. The case from fear was that, in any case, Britain was quite powerless to intervene, far from home against overwhelmingly stronger forces on the ground. This view was, at best, *realpolitik* in the face of unpalatable facts or, at worst, capitulation. One way or another, in 1945, with Poland substituted for Czechoslovakia, and Stalin for Hitler, the British case for accepting Yalta was all too similar. Ultimately, it was based on a pragmatic judgement rather than a moral imperative. Thus British politicians were simultaneously very sorry indeed for the Poles, and felt deeply for them, but were unable to see what else they could do.

Poor old Poland, poor old England, and, one way or another, a rather sorry English line of argument. Moreover, if this was an awkward, uneasy acknowledgement on British lips, to American ears it had further implications. The British had held the high moral ground since 1940, as they had at intervals sought to remind the world. Thus their stand in the war, heroic and just, should be rewarded when peace came. Admittedly the moral card had rarely carried as much weight with the Americans as the British had persuaded themselves it rightly should; but it was not until 1945, in the aftermath of Yalta, that it was decisively devalued. When the Poles were advised to accept the brute facts of a cold, hard world and to stop boring everyone with their tales of valiant endeavours in a righteous cause, perhaps the British were making a stick for their own backs.

Nobody put it quite like that in the immediate, hopeful aftermath of Yalta. Instead the same old template was often applied to the new situation, suggesting that the exalted expectations that had been sustained since 1940 were about to be fulfilled. Perhaps it was time for the Churchillian rhetoric to be quietly scaled down at this point, in the face of the pragmatic realities of the post-Yalta world, so as to let such hopes down lightly. The Prime Minister's address to the House of Commons was all the better for not pulling out the *vox humana*, instead striking a register of caution and restraint. 'We are now entering a world of imponderables, and at every stage occasions for self-questioning arise,' he reflected. 'It is a mistake to look too far ahead.'[46] In the other chamber, however, the Leader of the House of Lords, Viscount Cranborne, welcomed Yalta with less inhibition, claiming that 'as a result the foetid atmosphere had been in some way cleared and we could see our way a little further ahead.' His peroration came back to familiar territory: 'Perhaps sooner than we might expect we should be able to view afar off the peace and security of the sunny uplands.'[47]

The newspapers in the week before the parliamentary debate on Yalta were full of the most optimistic war news since the Quebec summit. The *News Chronicle* on 23 February had a banner headline reminiscent of those at the time of the assault on Arnhem:

SIX THOUSAND PLANES ATTACK
Grand Offensive in West may be Opening: Nazi General

In fact, since early February, a big push on a broad front had been getting under way, but generally unreported. As Eisenhower later complained to the press (once he was able to voice his feelings after successfully crossing the Rhine in March), the impression had been given that von Rundstedt's offensive had succeeded in immobilizing the Allies for up to three and possibly six months – 'that is what the headlines said.' Initially Allied action was concentrated in the north, seeking to clear the Rhine, though frustrated at delays while the floods in the Roer valley subsided. As Eisenhower was to admit: 'those were the two most anxious weeks I have spent in this campaign.'[48] Whether Montgomery's 21st Army Group was doing enough, which Patton and Bradley naturally doubted, or whether the American generals were woefully lacking in their appreciation of how much was nonetheless being done, created the usual tension at SHAEF. This told on Eisenhower, and his obvious reliance for emotional support on Kay Summersby fuelled damaging gossip.

Montgomery was, with his usual mixture of celibacy, confidence and patience, preparing for a decisive battle. He was able to deploy Crerar's Canadian 1st Army in a prominent role. In belated fulfilment of the decision at Quebec, this reunited all the Canadian troops, who made a significant contribution to operations. They were supported not only by Dempsey's 2nd British Army but also by Simpson's US 9th Army, which remained under Montgomery's command rather than being returned to the US 12th Army Group – much to Bradley's chagrin, as the Supreme Commander knew all too well. '12th Army Group was getting as difficult to work with as 21 Army Group,' Ike let slip at one point.[49]

The problem for SHAEF was not only how to make the news but also how to break the news. Eisenhower put on a brave face and skilfully reasserted his personal authority when he appeared on 24 February at his first press conference since November. The fact that his headquarters were now being moved nearer the front, from Versailles to Rheims, spoke for itself. Everyone agreed that, despite fatigue, he seemed fit and handled the questions well, talking freely and frankly, with no gaffes. Asked by the journalists about Monty, the Supreme Commander simply launched into an affable lecture on the nature of operational command. He was quoted across the front page of the *Sunday Express* the next morning: 'WE EXPECT TO DESTROY EVERY GERMAN WEST OF THE RHINE'.

Such public confidence was privately backed by the intelligence reports that the Allies were now receiving on German morale. One deserter from 12th SS Panzer told his captors: 'You could walk through to

Cologne if you wanted. There is nobody to stop you.'[50] True, for much of the *Wehrmacht*, the real battle was now in the east against the unspeakable Russians, not in the west against the naive Americans and their misguided British henchmen. 'U.S. ARMOUR BREAKS THROUGH 10 MILES FROM COLOGNE: Germans Rush to Surrender: "No Organised Defence",' proclaimed the *Daily Mail*'s front page on Tuesday, 27 February.

Eisenhower was a sadder and a wiser man after the Ardennes: sadder about the feuds between his generals, wiser about handling the press so that Anglo-American differences did not become the story. The policy of saying little himself and trying to damp down Monty had been a failure. His own press conference, by contrast, had been a huge success. The Supreme Commander accordingly switched, not his strategy but his press strategy at this point. Prodded by Marshall, he determined to show the folks back home how much the Americans were doing.

Eisenhower's perfectly reasonable point was that American troops should receive their due share of publicity when they deserved it, as they clearly had during the Battle of the Bulge, before Monty grabbed the headlines. The 101st Airborne Division was the model here, not only in its actual exploits at Bastogne but also in creating the inspiring legend of 'Nuts'. Ike wanted more of this. 'Our problem is much more difficult than it is in the British service and press,' he wrote in a memo to Bradley and Devers on 14 March, 'because we do not have the historical names of regiments and the concentrated interest based on geographical recruiting at home.' Of course he also reminded them to be careful not to disparage their allies and was obviously wary of sparking overt competition. Balanced as his remarks were, they sent a clear message: 'I do not want to be interpreted as saying that we are fighting this war for headlines, but proper publicity does have an effect on troop efficiency.'[51]

The Supreme Commander did not copy this memo to Patton. He had no need. 'PATTON'S MEN REACH RHINE', in bold black type an inch and a half tall, took up nearly half the front page of the tabloid *Daily News* for 8 March, with its daily circulation of over 2 million in New York. In fact it was not Patton's 3rd Army, pressing to the Rhine in the south near Coblenz, that actually deserved most attention at this point but Hodges' US 1st Army, which, on the previous day, had boldly exploited a fortuitous opportunity at Remagen to capture a Rhine bridge, if not intact then still in a usable state. After twenty-four hours of publicity blackout, the news was released by SHAEF on 8 March at 6 p.m. in Paris, which was 10 a.m. in Vancouver, where the same day's *Daily Province* was able to hit the streets with its scoop of this 'sensational news': '1st ARMY CROSSES RHINE; HOLDS FIRM BRIDGEHEAD; "Great Victory Shaping Up"'.

This was all the better news for being unexpected. Throughout history, the mighty Rhine had been a formidable natural defence: the real frontier of Germany, or so the French had often thought (and hoped). Even in this war of rapid transit it was still a barrier to further advance into western Germany, whereas in the east the Russians had recently turned winter ice to their advantage in crossing frozen rivers. Remagen was thus a real coup, giving the Allies a bridgehead nearly twenty miles south of Bonn – and nearly a hundred miles south of Wesel, where Montgomery was laboriously completing preparations for what had been planned as the first Rhine crossing, scheduled for a fortnight later.

There was thus an operational decision to be taken when the generals first learnt about the bridge. For Bradley, in whose sector Remagen was located, this was pure joy, showing him in a better light than his inert response in the Ardennes. Still, it was not part of the plan, as the SHAEF representative was pointing out, and Rheims was quickly contacted by telephone. Harry Butcher heard Eisenhower's side of the conversation, sitting in the next room amid an interrupted dinner. 'Brad, that's wonderful.' A pause to take in the implications: whether to commit more troops. 'Sure, get right on across with everything you've got. It's the best break we've had,' Ike continued, now resolved to make the most of it, and crucially adding: 'To hell with the planners.'[52]

Bradley thus had sanction to back Hodges in holding the Remagen bridgehead. The incident brought out his combative instincts, not only against the once-feared might of the *Wehrmacht* but in competition with the privileged claim of the great Monty to cross the Rhine first. For Patton, the issue was a pointed spur to action himself – why should Hodges, whom he personally despised as much as he did Monty, get all the glory?

It was all the sweeter for the Americans to pre-empt Monty because, within the 21st Army Group, the troops of Simpson's American 9th Army were seen as victims of an effort to relegate them to a minor – or at least inconspicuous – role in the planned assault. This tallied with an uncharitable impression that Montgomery was mired in dilatoriness, rather than simply in the mud of the territory flooded as part of the German retreat. Still, there was room for an abiding clash of perceptions and judgements on how much was possible, and how quickly. Montgomery, also thrilled by news of the Remagen crossing, welcomed it with a generosity not often remarked. But once it had happened, the fact that he had restrained Simpson from crossing the Rhine himself between Duisburg and Düsseldorf, because it was in the wrong place and not according to plan, seemed less clever. For his decision here even Wilmot's *Struggle for Europe* offers no apologia, saying instead: 'The master of the set-piece assault and the "tidy battle", he did not appear to realise that American "untidiness" and improvisation, however dangerous when the enemy was strong, could now yield great dividends.'[53]

As with the Battle of the Bulge in December, military developments were not insulated from cultural and temperamental differences between the Allies. This time, however, the Americans certainly received the credit due to them and could hardly complain that the British response lacked magnanimity. Rejoice – the injunction of a later Prime Minister – was the simple watchword even for normally imperturbable observers. 'Americans are across the Rhine tonight!' was Cadogan's reaction, and Colville's: 'The war goes better and better: the Americans are over the Rhine . . .'[54] The British tabloid the *Daily Sketch* headlined it on 9 March as an Allied success: 'WE ARE OVER THE RHINE'. But the way its report began was clear about who actually did it: 'American troops of General Hodges's First Army have crossed the Rhine at Remagen, between Bonn and Coblenz.' Its statement was that 'the Americans won a dramatic race for the river with the Germans, whose defences had collapsed like a pack of cards', with no hint of any other race or mention of Monty. Next day's *News Chronicle*, 'RHINE BRIDGEHEAD IS FIVE MILES DEEP', brought Patton into the story too, with a release from his headquarters stating that his forces had linked with those of Hodges. Everyone, it seemed, wanted to get into the act, not least a former British Army subaltern and naval person who, it was revealed, had himself ventured onto German soil.

It was true; the Prime Minister had been on his travels again. He had left London on 2 March for a four-day visit to the Allied forces on the German frontier. Not all of his doings were reported by the press. On leaving Simpson's 9th US Army headquarters, he asked that the cars should stop at the Siegfried Line, so that he could get out and ceremoni-ously piss on it. It was the sort of shameless infantilism that seemed engaging, even to more staid participants like the CIGS, in its unabashed directness and visceral energy: more engaging, at any rate, than the similarly infantile excesses of his racist responses over India. But, as those closest to Churchill had best cause to appreciate, he had to be taken as a whole, all of a piece, in the round, whether he was relieving himself or his feelings. 'Winston fretted because he was not allowed nearer the front,' recorded Brooke, 'and trying to make plans to come back for the operations connected with the crossing of the Rhine!'[55]

The visit was plainly good for morale, his own not least. 'The battle is going wonderfully well,' Brooke noted while at Montgomery's head-quarters, 'and there are signs from all sides of decay setting in in the German army.'[56] Colville was left in Brussels, gathering some less favour-able impressions. Monty was 'the most egotistic man he had ever met', according to Air Marshal Coningham: 'He aped the Americans who loathed him.'[57] It was not much different when Brooke accompanied Churchill to Rheims for talks with Eisenhower. 'His relations with Monty are quite insoluble,' Brooke noted sadly, 'he only sees the worst side of Monty and cannot appreciate the better side. Things are running smoothly for the present, but this cannot last and I foresee trouble ahead before long.'[58] At least the CIGS saw for himself that inserting Alexander as Deputy into the SHAEF command structure was not worth pressing, certainly not against Eisenhower's wishes, and especially since the end of the war was in sight (again).

The Prime Minister returned to London uninjured, with nothing worse than laryngitis to impair his verbal contributions to the war effort. On 12 March the cabinet, its meetings now shifted to mornings, was there-fore chaired by Attlee. 'The result was that we got through our business in less than three quarters of an hour,' noted Amery.[59] Three days later, Churchill was back in the chair, literally. He was carried in it backwards by three marines, upstairs from the underground cabinet war rooms, where the meetings now took place because of V2s. 'The Cabinet trail behind,' Colville observed, 'and the general effect of the procession is utterly ludicrous.'[60]

In the White House, meanwhile, President Roosevelt was defying his doctors by working full days. Mackenzie King found him 'looking more like President Wilson' when the Canadian Prime Minister was entertained to dinner on 20 March (but was less entertained to be retailed the same two anecdotes over dinner that the President had told him before it).[61] Fortunately, by this time things were even worse in the bunker under the Chancellery in Berlin.

The Allied forces were now tightening their grip, tautening their sinews. 'News good, but not sensational,' Sir Alec Cadogan thought on 12 March.[62] The next day Harold Nicolson wrote: 'The Americans seem to have exploited with skill and daring the bit of luck given them by the capture of the Remagen bridge. Above all, Patton's three-pronged drive into the Palatinate would seem to put the German forces in the Saar in a very awkward position.'[63] Only the false summits of past hopes instilled caution. This did not prevent Churchill, when he rose from his chair in the afternoon of 15 March in order to address the Conservative Party conference, from speaking of victory as 'certain and perhaps near'. These words, amplified and simplified by distance, went around the Empire; the front-page headline in that day's *Vancouver Sun* was printed white on black for bolder effect: 'VICTORY BY SUMMER'.

The political subtext was as difficult to miss as when an earlier Prime Minister, Lloyd George in 1918, was hailed as 'the man who won the war' before going on to win a landslide victory in a post-war General Election. Colville was told by one of his colleagues in the private office, Leslie Rowan, of his opinion that 'the P.M. is losing interest in the war, because he no longer has control of military affairs.' His strategic interventions sidetracked, Churchill was now 'by force of circumstances little more than a spectator. Thus he turns his energies to politics and the coming General Election, varying the diet with occasional excursions into the field of foreign politics.'[64]

A final excursion to the battlefield was the immediate objective. 'Tomorrow I start off with PM on this visit to France for him to see operation connected with the Rhine crossing,' Brooke wrote in his diary on Thursday, 22 March, with his usual disdain. It was clear to him that the Prime Minister 'has *no* business to be going on this trip'; equally clear that the CIGS would naturally have to accompany him. 'All he will do is to endanger his life unnecessarily and to get in everybody's way and be a damned nuisance to everybody. However nothing on earth will stop him!'[65]

Many of these prophecies were fulfilled, certainly the last. 'The war cannot last much longer now,' Chips Channon wrote the next day, with the Prime Minister's party already en route, their ringside seats booked for the finale.[66] The entourage numbered, as well as the CIGS, and the habitual presence of his security man, Tommy Thompson, 'the inevitable, egregious Sawyers (the valet)', as Colville noted – himself at thirty flushed with the same youthful enthusiasm as the Prime Minister.[67] Even the disaffected Brookie cheered up after a good flight over the Channel as far as Brussels. 'On arrival there,' he noted, 'we reduced the party to 4 (PM, Tommy, Sawyers and self) and drove to Monty's HQ which is close to the aerodrome. We found Monty there, very proud to be able to pitch his camp in Germany at last!'[68]

As usual, the Field Marshal retired early that night into his caravan. This was now parked in a former riding school in the middle of a pine forest at Venlo, within earshot of the preliminary artillery bombardment, as troops prepared for the overnight crossings of the Rhine. Churchill had two caravans, one for working and one for sleeping, but spurned them for the moment, instead taking Brooke for walk in the moonlight. Naturally, Churchill was prompted to reminiscence about their co-operation and 'our early struggles', as Brooke recorded. 'He was in one of his very nicest moods and showed appreciation for what I had done for him in a way in which he had never before.'[69]

This was a big moment for all of them: for the war leader who had promised his people victory against Hitler, for the Chief of the Imperial General Staff who had spent weary hours in staff work to organize the means of delivering victory, for Field Marshal Montgomery with his long-nurtured plan to make Saturday, 24 March 1945, an historic day for British arms. Harry Butcher, sitting with the war correspondents in Paris the following morning, found them chuckling that, in the meantime, 'Patton had slipped around right end. *He was across the Rhine.* His Third Army troops had quietly crossed in small boats in the darkness of Thursday night.'[70]

The Allied operations, in their different ways, were as successful as could reasonably have been hoped. True, casualties were heavy in the airborne assault, where gliders proved as vulnerable as at Arnhem and were never to be used again. The troops making the actual river crossing, however, escaped more lightly, perhaps justifying Montgomery's characteristic reliance on massive artillery bombardment and smoke, reducing surprise and casualties alike on this occasion. On 25 March, Palm

Sunday, all the British top brass attended a church parade in thanksgiving. 'I think it is the first time I have known the P.M. go to church,' Colville observed.[71]

After thanking the Almighty, it was time to meet the almighty Americans. In his war memoirs, Eisenhower recalls standing with Brooke on the banks of the Rhine, watching the crossing by troops of the US 9th Army and the British and Canadian troops of the 21st Army Group. 'Thank God, Ike, you stuck by your plan,' so Brooke's words are recorded. 'You were completely right and and I am sorry if my fear of dispersed effort added to your burdens.'[72] This handsome apology, when it was published in 1948, made a fine impression – unfortunately spoiled by the publication a decade later of Alanbrooke's riposte, in which he repudiated it. The most that his own diary suggests is that, in the new situation, he could endorse Eisenhower's future strategy: 'I told him that with the Germans crumbling as they are the whole situation is now altered from the time of our previous discussions.'[73] This is actually how Butcher, a few days later, also recorded Eisenhower's impression of what Brooke had 'generously told him': that Ike 'was right and that his current plans and operations are well calculated to meet the current situation'.[74]

The Prime Minister was becoming restive. He did not take kindly to the advice of General Simpson, that exposing himself to sniper fire was a bad idea; and his heart had plainly not been in it when, on the previous day, Colville had to be reprimanded by Montgomery for crossing the Rhine in a small boat. The Field Marshal was less testy and less fearful, more benign and more foolhardy, on that triumphant Sunday. Churchill said to him, once the Americans had departed: 'Why don't we go across and have a look at the other side?' As he told the story in *Triumph and Tragedy*, he was somewhat surprised that Montgomery replied: 'Why not?'[75]

So three British officers crossed the Rhine, for a parleyvoo. Montgomery's memoirs are silent on this venture, but a photograph is printed, showing a scratch lunch on the east bank of the Rhine, this time on 26 March, with the three officers in uniform: the CIGS, correctly turned out; Monty in battledress and double-badged beret; and Churchill, as throughout this visit – no doubt thanks to Sawyers – in the uniform of the 4th Hussars, in which he had served as a lieutenant at the turn of the century. Before lunch on the following day, the last of the triumphal visit, Brooke noticed that the 'late lieutenant', as he still described himself in *Who's Who*, walked over to the bank of the Rhine and pissed into it. 'I honestly believe,' Brooke wrote later, 'that he would really have liked to be killed on the front at this moment of success. He had often told me that the way to die is to pass out fighting when your blood is up and you feel nothing.'[76]

Triumph and Tragedy is the title Churchill chose for the final volume of his war memoirs. Its theme is set out prominently at the beginning: 'How the great democracies triumphed, and so were able to resume the follies which had so nearly cost them their life.' It is divided into two parts. 'The Tide of Victory' covers the period from D-Day, marching through Paris, Quebec, Moscow, to Christmas in Athens at the end of 1944. 'The Iron Curtain' deals with 1945, from Yalta to Potsdam. In general, then, it is the military progress that is triumphal, the political story that is tragic. In one of the drafts for the book – little of which Churchill actually wrote but all of which he directed – there is a more explicit statement of the theme. 'Berlin, Prague and Vienna were needlessly yielded to the Soviets,' said the draft. 'Here may be discerned the Tragedy in our hour of Triumph.'[77]

Although these exact words were neither written by him nor printed in the final text, they undoubtedly express Churchill's retrospective view. But it was prudent of him in 1953 (when he was once more Prime Minister, and Eisenhower now President) to tone down this assertion in *Triumph and Tragedy*. It was left to Sir Arthur Bryant, in publishing the Alanbrooke version in 1959, to state explicitly in print that the British were 'forced to witness at the dictate of one of their principal allies the needless subjection of the whole of Eastern Europe to the totalitarian tyranny of the other'.[78] What Bryant chose to publish, as much as what Churchill chose to omit, was governed by the perspectives of the 1950s rather than those of March 1945.

As Churchill watched the forces of the great democracies irresistibly surmounting the Rhine barrier, it was a triumph almost in the original Latin sense of the word: a moment formally recognizing the achievement of a victorious commander. The late lieutenant of Hussars knew this at the time. What is less clear is the moment at which the statesman who put the term 'iron curtain' into general circulation realized that his hopes at Yalta were to suffer tragic disappointment. Nor is it clear how far the Prime Minister's great friend in the White House, in the final stage of their celebrated relationship, checked him or failed him. And it is not even clear whether the continuing Anglo-American strategic differences really did represent – at the time, with the knowledge then available – such simple choices, least of all about Berlin.

Of course everyone had long assumed that the Allied advance aimed at getting to Berlin. The German capital was there; Hitler himself was now there; the Russians were nearly there. 'Clearly, Berlin is the main prize, and the prize in defence of which the enemy is likely to concentrate the bulk of his forces,' Eisenhower had told Montgomery. 'There is no doubt whatsoever, in my mind, that we should concentrate all our energies and resources on a rapid thrust to Berlin.'[79] Admittedly, that was written in mid-September, at the time of the Octagon conference in sunlit Quebec, before the autumn fogs of Arnhem and, above all, the wintry shock in the Ardennes. Nonetheless, in his war memoirs, Eisenhower follows his upbeat account of crossing the Rhine – 'The March 24 operation sealed the fate of Germany' – within a few pages with the statement: 'A natural objective beyond the Ruhr was Berlin.'[80]

This much was obvious. So was the fact that, until the crossing had been achieved in force in the last week of March, the Russians remained so much closer to Berlin. The British forces weekly, *Crusader*, had run a map of Germany as its front page on 11 March, with a circle of arrows centred on Berlin, showing that, to the east, the two Russian armies were respectively forty and seventy-five miles away; to the west, the distances were immensely greater – 290 miles from the Rhine at Cologne, between Bradley's and Montgomery's sectors; 365 miles from Strasbourg, in Patton's. Still, the unspoken implication that Berlin was the target was unmistakable. Nor did the Supreme Commander's press conference on 27 March suggest otherwise. Asked who would get to Berlin first, Eisenhower pointed to the respective distances (now 250 miles as against 33) and simply said: 'They have a shorter race to run, although they are faced by the bulk of the German forces.'[81] He did not discourage the current assumption of a race for Berlin, albeit one in which the Western Allies started with a severe handicap.

Hence the thrill when the breakout in the west dramatically changed these distances, as newspapers in all the Allied countries now blazoned on their front pages, day after day.

GEN. PATTON 175 MILES FROM BERLIN
(Melbourne, *Age*, 2 April)

BRITISH SWEEP MENACES FOES IN HOLLAND
PATTON'S TANKS 155 MILES FROM BERLIN
(*New York Times*, 3 April)

PATTON TANKS 150 MILES FROM BERLIN
(*Winnipeg Free Press*, 3 April)

YANKS 140 MILES FROM BERLIN
(Toronto, *Globe and Mail*, 4 April)

BRITISH BURST ACROSS WESER RIVER
DEMPSEY VANGUARDS 136 MILES FROM BERLIN
(*Winnipeg Free Press*, 6 April)

CANADIANS PACE ALLIED DRIVE
HUNS REPORT PATTON 90 MILES FROM BERLIN
(*Globe and Mail*, 7 April)

U.S. 1ST AND 9TH DRIVING ON FOR REICH CAPITAL
(*Chicago Tribune*, 11 April)

64 TO BERLIN, 125 TO LINK-UP
(London, *Daily Mail*, 12 April)

Triumphs breed triumphalism. 'The newspapers have won the war already,' Colville commented as early as 27 March.[82] But the race for Berlin that was headlined over the following fortnight – in London, New York, Chicago, Toronto, Winnipeg or Melbourne alike – innocently parted company with the war that the Supreme Commander, with his 4 million troops, had meanwhile decided to wage.

There was to be no race for Berlin because he decided otherwise. Montgomery was no more consulted about the new plans than he himself (rather unwisely) had previously consulted the Supreme Commander about his own. Having crossed the Rhine, Montgomery was abruptly relieved of the command of Simpson's 9th Army, which reverted to Bradley's 12th US Army Group. He was told by Eisenhower that Berlin had 'become, so far as I am concerned, nothing but a geographical location', and that the Allied forces would be heading towards Leipzig instead.[83] Stalin had been told much the same, in a direct communication from SHAEF. Then, and only then, Churchill was told that Stalin had been told.

This was an extraordinary way of making and communicating a major Allied decision; but it was not necessarily the wrong decision in itself. Eisenhower always claimed that it was simply a military decision: that there was no point in his risking perhaps 100,000 casualties in order to reach an objective which his Russian allies were determined to reach anyway, more quickly and more determinedly, and which lay centrally within their zone of occupation, as agreed between the Big Three. The irony was that, at Yalta, it had seemed more likely that the Red Army would overrun the demarcation lines than that the Western Allies would be able to do so, which is why the Americans had insisted on prior agreements confirming zone boundaries. If these agreements were now shackles, they had been forged by themselves for their own armies. The American zone was in the south – and so was the 'national redoubt', conjured up by Nazi propaganda as the site of a last stand in the mountains but given credence at the time by SHAEF intelligence. Again this was an argument for swinging south rather than driving east.

For Montgomery, any such considerations were secondary. The prospect was that, if Berlin were to be the Allied objective, it would naturally be with his 21st Army Group in the van, supported no doubt by Bradley's 12th Army Group on his right flank. Although Montgomery's memoirs go along with the cold-war pre-emption argument, for him it was surely the irresistible lure of glory that pointed to Berlin.

Just as surely, this was what the Supreme Commander was determined to deny him. The Americans had not fought this war so that Monty could ride on their shoulders into Berlin. Eisenhower accordingly gave Bradley the lead role by switching the advance to the south, towards Leipzig – with his left flank to be protected by Montgomery. In consequence, Bradley's 12th US Army Group was given Simpson's 9th Army, at Montgomery's expense, as part of this plan. 'Merely following the principle that Field Marshal Brooke has always emphasized, I am determined to concentrate on one major thrust,' Eisenhower told Marshall.[84] This was a final twist of the knife in the long-running strategic controversy. Eisenhower, who had claimed Brooke as a late convert to the broad front, now claimed himself to be a late convert to the pencil-like thrust that he had previously caricatured. Moreover, this message was apparently drafted by one of his British subordinates in SHAEF, where Monty's own behaviour had long ensured that he lacked friends quite irrespective of national considerations – an impartiality that it had always been Ike's mission to foster. They both reaped where they had sown.

These were the military considerations, spoken and unspoken, that made Eisenhower's decision rational, persuasive and popular – at least so far as the Americans were concerned. And they were quite unsurprised to find that, just as they had long suspected, it was the British who wanted a more political approach. For Churchill the argument, especially in hindsight, was that there was strategic advantage in capturing territory – notably Berlin – in order to bargain subsequently with the Russians. Did this mean that he could justify losing more British lives, or Roosevelt losing more American lives, simply for territory that would then be handed back to the Russians? Or did it mean that the two of them should flout the Big Three agreement? These were questions that went unanswered, mainly because Churchill never posed them to Roosevelt, who left it to his own chiefs of staff to affirm a purely military view of the issues.

In Washington it all looked different. Roosevelt's determination to sell the Yalta agreement to the American people, as he had sold the New Deal and Lend-Lease and Germany First before it, was shown by his decision to report personally to Congress. He had done this on 1 March, two days after disembarking from the *Quincy*, and, for the first time, did so openly seated in a wheelchair. The manner was indefatigable, first in seeking to quench alarm about his health, fired by unflattering newsreel images from Yalta. 'I was well the entire time' was the noble lie. 'I was not ill for a second, until I arrived back in Washington, and there I heard of all the rumors which had occurred in my absence.'[85] The forthcoming conference in San Francisco, with the United States represented by equal numbers of delegates from each political party, was depicted at the centre of his vision of a new international order. Thus the initial American image of Yalta was framed in terms tipped more towards idealism and less towards pragmatism than in Great Britain.

In particular, the President's credibility depended on his having squared Stalin. This was hardly the moment for Roosevelt to undermine his chiefs of staff and overrule the American Supreme Commander in order to pick a fight with the Red Army over Berlin, unless he were very sure of his ground and fired up for a decisive change in policy. The Prime Minister continued to send more messages to the President than he received, as had always been the case; and Churchill continued to believe that the responses were FDR's own. From the end of March, however, Roosevelt was no longer in the White House but at Warm Springs, Georgia, for rest and recuperation. Though there is no direct evidence that he was actually presented with the views of his chiefs of staff, which were endorsed in messages drafted for him, the faltering President certainly expressed no dissent from what was done in his name.

For Churchill, the slight was as great as for Montgomery. No Berlin, no British glory, no support from Washington: his 'hopeless mood' when he had first heard of Eisenhower's telegram to Stalin set the tone, as Brooke discovered. 'He drives me quite frantic and I can only just keep my temper nowadays,' he wrote on 29 March, exasperated by Churchill's failure to see the wood for the trees. 'Quite incapable to really grasp strategy and its implications. On those occasions I feel I just can't stick another moment with him, and would give almost anything never to see him again!'[86] Of course better-rested Brookie saw him again the very next day, which was Good Friday, and was to be summoned to a further meeting at Chequers on Easter Sunday, 1 April.

Large and small points, strategy and politics, pique and vanity, Allied co-operation and national rivalries were all wound up together. In one explanatory telegram from Eisenhower to Churchill, a signalling error had suggested that Montgomery, left protecting Bradley's flank with the British and Canadian Armies, would only be responsible for 'patrol tasks'.[87] Another explosion at Chequers. The truth was bad enough without error compounding the indignity of what Churchill described to Eisenhower as 'the relegation of His Majesty's forces to an unexpectedly restricted sphere'.[88] This barb, later omitted from *Triumph and Tragedy*, was repudiated by the Supreme Commander's well-justified appeal to his own record.

Brooke felt the same as the Prime Minister, albeit at a lower temperature. 'Most of the changes are due to national aspirations and to ensure that the USA effort will not be lost under British command,' he observed on 1 April. He did not like it, but he had long accepted that this was the way the war was going to end. After all, had it been different, he would have been Supreme Commander himself, as had originally been promised. As it was, Eisenhower was now commanding, as they all kept telling each other, three times as many American troops as the million British and Canadians in Germany. Even Churchill accepted this, and sought solace in one of his familiar maxims: 'There is only one thing worse than fighting with allies, and that is fighting without them!'[89]

8

Shadows of Death

March–April 1945

'For us it remains only to say that in Franklin Roosevelt there died the greatest American friend we have ever known, and the greatest champion of freedom who has ever brought help and comfort from the new world to the old.'

Churchill in the House of Commons, 17 April 1945

There were innumerable deaths in the Second World War, either directly caused by it or indirectly hastened: certainly not fewer than 50 million worldwide, mainly in the Soviet Union and China. In Europe, the Poles bore the brunt; 6 million died, including Polish Jews, doubly vulnerable. Poland thus lost over 20 per cent of its citizens, putting even the Soviet Union's loss of 4 per cent into perspective in this macabre arithmetic. These are subsequent estimates; the full scale of the Polish losses, as of the extent of the Jewish Holocaust, only emerged later. But enough was known at the time to make the British and the Americans particularly sensitive, albeit in different ways, about the fate of these prime victims of Nazism.

On the western front casualties were relatively low, though still appalling. When the Western Allies finally counted their own losses in the north-west Europe campaign since D-Day, these were substantially fewer than the half-million dead that the Red Army sustained in the same period. The US Army lost 110,000 men killed; the British, Canadian and Polish formations 42,000. These losses were broadly in line with the relative strength of the different armies under Eisenhower's command, though complicated by the fact that the proportion of American soldiers was continually increasing during that period from half to roughly three-quarters. 'Get me the best figures available of the losses sustained by the English in this war,' Churchill asked in April 1945. He was told that one in 165 Englishmen (meaning Britons presumably) had died.

This compared with a ratio of one in 175 New Zealanders, one in 385 for both Canadians and Australians, and one in 775 Americans.[1] Compared with a ratio of one-in-five for Poland, of course, both the British Empire and the Great Republic had come off lightly. Still, the British sacrifice (although the Prime Minister would never have put it so indelicately) was thus nearly five times as great as that of the Americans.

Blood and treasure: these historic accounting terms for measuring the costs of war remain pertinent. Historically, moreover, they have often been alternatives, especially for a privileged nation, as Great Britain had been for couple of centuries, which could provide 'the sinews of war' through its economic resources and financial dominance and thus pay its allies to put their troops in the field. Footing their bills was a cheap option compared with facing the grisly 'butcher's bill' of military carnage.

In this war, correspondingly, Lend-Lease was simultaneously the Americans' great contribution to Allied victory and – in the early years, at least – their substitute for doing more of the actual fighting themselves. Teasing questions were posed at the time by astute American critics. If British soldiers storm an enemy position in an American tank, should Great Britain be charged for the tank or the United States for the services of the crew? What price a tank that has been 'totalled'? What price the deaths of members of its crew? When Britons made such points, it was more seemly to do so by contrasting the sacrifices of the United States with those of its Russian ally than with their own: a comparison which in any case came naturally to Soviet sympathizers, like E. H. Carr of *The Times*. Thus when the paper offered an assessment of President Roosevelt's latest report on Lend-Lease and reciprocal Mutual Aid, the real bottom line was the impact of the Red Army. 'The plain impossibility of measuring these figures against the prodigious deeds and sacrifices of the Russians themselves is a sufficient demonstration that the material achievements of mutual aid provide no ground whatsoever for boastful or competitive claims between the allies' was the editorial comment, bringing out the point that the financial figures reflected where the fighting was actually taking place.[2] It followed that Britain had received most in Mutual Aid when its armed forces had necessarily borne the brunt of the fighting, while the United States's receipts, initially negligible, had grown since committing its own troops to combat in Europe.

The fact that expenditure of blood and treasure was often inversely related fitted nicely into the logic of the system of Mutual Aid established between the Allies. It provided the counterpart, once the United States had entered the war, to the previous one-way flow of Lend-Lease. It was a rational way of pooling resources, letting each Ally do what it could do best in the common cause, and doing so in ways governed by the current priorities of the war itself. If each country thereby contributed a similar proportion of its resources, the burden would be distributed equally and, as Roosevelt declared in June 1942, 'no nation will grow rich through the war effort of its allies. The money costs of the war will fall according to the rule of equality in sacrifice, as in effort.'[3]

This conception of Mutual Aid informed British relations with Canada in a broadly helpful way. Before Pearl Harbor, though Canada was at war and the United States not, the integration of the North American economies, based on geography and the dollar, became increasingly close as soon as Lend-Lease got under way. Mackenzie King played his cards well. Unlike Great Britain, Canada was not brought into Lend-Lease, thus suffering a possible disadvantage; but unlike Great Britain, it was not required to sell off investments in the United States, thus enjoying a tangible advantage. In fact, Canadian supplies for Britain were paid for with US dollars; so because their booming war production was charged against the British Lend-Lease account in Washington, the Canadians enjoyed the best of both worlds, and the British certainly had no cause for complaint. Instead, the wartime prosperity of the Canadian economy worked very much to reciprocal benefit, as was shown by the billion-dollar gift from Canada to the United Kingdom in 1942. 'Per head of population the Canadian gifts will cost Canada about five times what lend lease costs the United States,' commented one British official. 'Canada's income tax is already as high as ours; it may have to go higher.'[4]

To conclude that Canadians were, on this reckoning, five times as unsordid as the Americans would be naive. As with Lend-Lease, motives were mixed. Cabinet ministers in Mackenzie King's government quickly became embarrassed – not least in the eyes of their Quebec constituency – by public descriptions of the gift as soft-hearted generosity to Great Britain, and instead pointed to its hard-headed economic benefits at home. It was politically impossible to conceive of another gift; but functionally it was replaced by the Mutual Aid Act of 1943. Again a billion dollars was made available, this time to all the Allies in theory though in practice mainly to the British, allowing them to draw on these dollars for supplies that they were unable to finance in other ways. Various juggling acts were necessary to make the figures fit, with Canada taking over other war costs, notably the Royal Canadian Air Force squadrons overseas, previously paid for by the British Treasury. Essentially, however, Mutual Aid was the servant of a common commitment to defeating Hitler. Canada was using Mutual Aid as a balancing item, financing the dollars that supported the British war effort, which in turn supported Canadian industries, which in turn kept domestic employment and output high, which in turn paid the taxes to foot the bill.

Mutual Aid was an umbrella term. Under its auspices, Canada ended up financing the United Kingdom to the tune of a billion dollars a year, thus maintaining the rate established by the unique billion-dollar gift of 1942 while subsequently adopting the new name and principles. The Canadians did this for their own good reasons without any intention of claiming that these amounts ($3.4 billion to the sterling area as a whole) constituted a claim against the United Kingdom, to be settled at the end of the war. The fact that the war was eventually won by the Allies was sufficient justification.

But though the British likewise adopted the official term Mutual Aid in reciprocal relations with other Allies, the Americans continued to talk of Lend-Lease, after Pearl Harbor as much as before. This was significant in that it fostered the natural supposition that to lend implied being repaid. Moreover, the same accounting procedures that identified the extent of the reciprocal Mutual Aid ('Reverse Lend-Lease' supplied by Britain to the United States) also put a dollar value on Lend-Lease in the other direction. So much for Roosevelt's initial impulse to 'get rid of the silly, foolish old dollar sign'. Such book-keeping naturally gave the American public the impression that repayment of these dollars was in prospect. 'Somewhere, false expectations are being encouraged,' warned one economist in 1943. 'Here is material for first-class discord, unless steps are taken to clarify the situation.'[5]

Roosevelt, with his instinctive distaste for too much clarity, instead preferred to let Lend-Lease roll on for the time being, ambiguously but generously. In 1944, the United States poured out Lend-Lease supplies worth nearly $15 billion, over 70 per cent to the British Empire and the rest to the Soviet Union. The United Kingdom itself received 57 per cent of the Empire share, or over $6 billion.[6] This was before the spirit of Quebec had evaporated and before Roosevelt's notoriously bad memory for his oral promises let him down.

Keynes, who had been so central to all the Anglo-American financial negotiations, proved to be an unreliable judge of their outcome. British ministers who were beguiled by his silver tongue were accordingly mis-led. Thus Hugh Dalton, as President of the Board of Trade, thought himself well informed on the real position, having been told by Keynes in mid-December 1944 that 'we have got much more out of the last talks than we realise and than it is wise publicity to affirm.' The Board of Trade was particularly worried about the tight rules forbidding most British exports, maintained in case these contained commodities sup-plied by the United States under Lend-Lease. Yet these restrictions obvi-ously hampered Britain in earning the foreign currency that would have to replace Lend-Lease. Contrary to Roosevelt's earlier suggestions, any real change in this respect would have to await VE-Day, and meanwhile only raw materials would be liberated from restriction. Keynes made light of this to Dalton: 'We have really got all the export freedom we can use and we have *not*, as has been suggested, had our Lend-Lease supplies cut down, but are really getting even more than before.'[7]

Such expectations quickly proved false, since actual Lend-Lease deliv-eries for 1945 were sharply curtailed. It was the Americans' money, of course, and they had the obvious right to decide what to do with it. The British, however, bound by reciprocal obligations, were slow to read the signals. Public comment focused instead on those concessions that had been secured, applicable from 1 January. 'At least one major obstacle has been partially removed by the new Anglo-American agreement,' *The Times* rejoiced, with a series of reports on how 'with lend-lease problems settled, allocations of labour and materials for export sales are likely to increase.'[8] For example, American machine tools, previously supplied on Lend-Lease for war purposes, could now be retrospectively purchased for cash, thus permitting them to be used for manufacturing British exports. This was indeed a gain, though a modest one given the fact that the necessary target for post-war exports was 150 per cent of the 1938 figure, compared with current export capacity at about 30 per cent.

Much of what actually happened during 1945 was at variance with the warm words that Keynes remembered hearing in Washington in 1944. His own outlook was intermittently tinged with a sort of desperation, the response not only of a natural optimist but of a tired and sick man who was willing things to come right and would brook no discouragement. Even the achievements at the Bretton Woods talks the previous summer now seemed less sure, once the Americans embarked on the long process of turning its conclusions into legislation.

The problem was not just the likely reception from suspicious critics in Congress but a dispute between Keynes and Harry White about the interpretation of a clause on 'convertibility'. This was not only technically abstruse but also crucially important to Britain. The basic principle was that free exchange of goods should be paralleled by free exchange between currencies – if only to pay for the trade thus promoted. But a country (like wartime Britain) desperately short of dollars would naturally wish to protect its scanty currency reserves by controls on foreign exchange. The issue was thus how quickly and how fully free convertibility would be implemented after the war. During their last meeting, at the end of the Lend-Lease renegotiations in Washington in late November, White had promised to clarify the point in writing. 'No such reply has been, or is likely to be, received,' Keynes noted a month later. 'American autographs are very rare.'[9]

James Meade, now head of the economic section of the cabinet office, was drawn into this dispute. He thought the Americans correct on this occasion. 'Keynes has been in one of his silly moods,' he commented, surmising that a familiar process was at work. 'Within a week, I don't mind betting, he will be as violently in favour of accepting without amendment as he is at present against doing so.'[10] This prediction proved wrong. Keynes insisted that the Chancellor of the Exchequer, Sir John Anderson, take up the matter with Morgenthau, his opposite number in Washington. Another letter was thus despatched, at the highest level. The US Treasury, frightened of the response in Congress if it made any changes to the Bill, froze into immobility until this had been passed by the House of Representatives. As a delay of four months in answering the Chancellor demonstrated, Morgenthau's autograph had become as rare as White's.

If this was the American way of doing business, the British were hardly in a position to complain. In this instance, when they swapped notes about what had actually happened at Bretton Woods, it turned out that nobody could clearly remember. Had Keynes, at the critical moment, told a Treasury colleague that the Americans and Canadians could go to hell, or had he said: 'Oh, all right then'?[11] Whatever he had said could not be unsaid; and it was too late now to change, because of fears of reactions in Congress. Keynes was left reflecting that 'it does seem to me extraordinarily awkward for the Chancellor to have to tell the House that he does not understand the meaning of clauses so fundamental as those which determine our obligation of convertibility, and that he is signing something ambiguous or meaningless, in the hope that, at a later date, the meaning attached to it will be one which he will find satisfactory.'[12]

Such acts of faith, however, had characterized almost the entire history of wartime financial negotiations with the Americans. It was not the first time that the British signed what they were asked to sign, hoping that it would all turn out all right in the end, and meanwhile trusting to their defective memories of incoherent expressions of goodwill from American contacts who were subsequently handicapped by constitutional restraints, real or imagined. To the rational mind of James Meade, the current difficulties suggested an alarming threat to the achievement of Bretton Woods, especially the idea of an International Monetary Fund to lead the post-war world into prosperity. 'The prospect of a simultaneous attack on the Fund by MPs as being a capitulation to the Americans and the Gold Standard,' he reflected, 'and by Congressmen on the grounds that it is a clever plot of Lord Keynes to get money out of the Americans is not a very happy one.'[13] This was avoided, for the time being at any rate, by postponing the parliamentary scrutiny of Bretton Woods until after it had secured Congressional approval: a process that was to drag on until mid-July.

Everything seemed to depend on everything else, as so often when economic issues became enmeshed in the coils of international politics. The economists thought that they understood each other, despite different national pressures upon them, and could together devise plans that would serve the enlightened self-interest of all. Thus Meade had a genuine fellow-feeling for the Americans with whom he was currently negotiating on trade issues, especially the New Dealers with their enthusiastic adoption of Keynesian policies for avoiding a post-war slump. Looked at in this way, the liberal multilateral trade arrangements envisaged at Bretton Woods were the international aspect of full-employment policies that worked to general advantage. Hence the famous Article VII commitment under Lend-Lease – both to the elimination of trade discrimination and also to the reduction of tariffs – ought to hold no terrors, if fairly implemented. For Meade and Lionel Robbins – usually for Keynes too – this was axiomatically a better approach than the bilateral alternative still noisily championed by many supporters of imperial preference.

The fact was that imperial preference had decayed into a hollowed-out relic, left over from the early days of the century. Like much else in the panoply of British imperialism, it looked more potent from a distance, and the Canadian government was certainly worried at the beginning of 1945 about its apparent resurgence. The idea of solving the dollar shortage via imperial trade using sterling had little appeal for Canadians, who – outside the sterling area themselves – might find themselves discriminated against. Launched at the end of February, an unusual Canadian initiative for once received unusual attention in London, with Mackenzie King alerting Churchill to the significance of what was proposed. This was nothing less than an offer to help finance Britain's transition to post-war trade recovery – provided there were no measures of discrimination against Canadian exports.

One irony here is that the most prominent supporter of imperial preference was himself Canadian. Lord Beaverbrook, intermittently a member of the war cabinet and always welcome at Churchill's table, ran his *Express* group of newspapers on this ticket. He actually preferred the slogan of Empire Free Trade, and now scented a revival of his longstanding crusade. But this was exactly what his compatriots now feared, seeing no place for themselves within the sterling area. Instead the Canadian Government spoke of a credit of $1200 million, on easy terms, in the three years after the end of the Japanese war (or after Stage II of Lend-Lease). Here was an offer from Canada to help finance Britain's inevitable dollar shortage in the post-war period, just as it had during the war itself through Mutual Aid. Again the motives were generosity buttressed by self-interest, since Canada would thereby insure its own export trade by underwriting its finance.

The Canadian move came at an opportune moment. The war in Europe was plainly moving towards its close, giving the problems of transition to peace a new urgency; yet the prevailing stasis in Anglo-American economic negotiations left a policy vacuum. For once not wholly overshadowed by the United States, Canada found its concerns taken seriously. When Attlee was briefed by Meade and Robbins on

21 March, they stressed the advantage of using a Canadian loan as a means of facilitating the adoption of a non-discriminatory trade policy. The Deputy Prime Minister seemed receptive to their arguments: not only that 'Empire Unity would really be promoted by an Article VII policy' that did not exclude Canada from a sterling bloc, but also 'that North America as a whole would only give us the support which we should need after the end of the Lend-Lease and Mutual-Aid period if we played ball on Article VII'.[14]

Lend-Lease had by now become a continual source of contention in Washington. The Congressional debates on the legislation, which required annual renewal, elicited many anti-British and anti-Roosevelt sentiments in the course of March and April. An amendment restricting Lend-Lease to purely military items had been passed in the House and was supported by the Republican leaders, Taft and Vandenberg, in the Senate, where the vote tied 39–39 on 10 April. The casting vote fell to Vice-President Truman, presiding over the Senate, and he cast it in favour of the status quo, thus keeping the broader remit. He signed that the bill had been passed accordingly. Truman was shortly to sign the bill a second time, this time as President of the United States, thus bringing it into force; but he clearly appreciated which way the Lend-Lease tide was now flowing – out.

And meanwhile there was the Great American Meat Famine. Though this has largely escaped subsequent historical prominence, in mid-March it certainly claimed front-page attention in American newspapers, with stories that were incredulously picked up in the British press. True, the United States was now facing cuts of 12 per cent in civilian meat allocation for three months. The Associated Press news agency ran a story that 'the American horn of plenty is running out' and the American Meat Institute of Chicago, not to be outdone, claimed that the United States faced 'a near-famine of meat'. Who was to blame? Fingers pointed to Great Britain, where current stocks, run up under Lend-Lease, were the 'greatest unallocated supply of food in the world', or so US officials had assured the *Washington Post*. The plight of famine-stricken Chicago could thus be ended by an overdue cut in Lend-Lease to greedy London!

It was obviously psychology rather than hard facts that drove the story of the meat famine. The whole scenario might have seemed implausible from the outset, given that wartime prosperity had boosted American annual meat consumption to about 150 pounds per head, about five times the current British ration. But the story was enough to force Churchill to make a statement in the Commons on 21 March. He revealed that British food stocks were actually under 6 million tons.[15] This was less than 1 per cent of what had been claimed. Admittedly, flows through Britain to feed liberated Europe accounted for temporary fluctuations in the levels. 'The crisis has again uncovered the deep-rooted American suspicion of being fleeced by the rest of the world,' Isaiah Berlin commented. He had recently reported a Gallup Poll, asking Americans if they had had to make any real sacrifices for the war: 64 per cent said no, only 36 per cent yes.[16]

The fact that Americans were in a position to support their Allies without really hurting themselves, however, did not mean that they could be presumed upon to do so. Just as their generosity could not be taken for granted, still less could any feelings of guilt or remorse about not having entered the war sooner. The *Chicago Tribune* gave the strong version: 'Americans are not apologetic for what we have done or for what we are taking in the war.'[17] Not only had they done more than their share since Pearl Harbor, even before it they had borne the costs of supporting the British (and later the Russians). They kept hearing about Lend-Lease, but it seemed like lend, lend, lend – where would it stop? Though its alleged abuses might often have proved no more substantial than the meat famine, the Rooseveltian magic of the concept was fading fast. Little wonder that the American public remained over-whelmingly under the impression that Lend-Lease had now done its job and ought soon to be repaid – an impression that no President could ignore.

On 18 March, Keynes had finished the first draft of a paper with the forbidding title 'Overseas Financial Policy in Stage III'. It was to become the intellectual foundation of Britain's post-war financial negotiations with the United States. Keynes, still a Fellow of King's College, Cambridge, had retreated there for ten days in order to write it, as well as to rest; and though the document was to be circulated and revised before it went to the cabinet two months later, it spoke to the context of March 1945.

Keynes's central point was that the enlightened world order of Bretton Woods and multilateral trade, to which the United States was so strongly committed, required a prior settlement of unfinished business. He envisaged, as he had put it a few weeks earlier, no less than 'an appeal for a reconsideration of the sharing of the costs of the war'. Exactly how the Americans chose to respond would be, as much as Lend-Lease had been, a challenge to Roosevelt's political creativity. 'It ought to come as a *coup d'état* from the President,' Keynes enjoined, 'as a great surprise for everyone concerned.'[18] In writing his paper, Keynes built on this fundamental moral assumption, suggesting that Lend-Lease was a fine beginning, but really ought to have begun sooner. 'The President has often used words implying that he accepted in some sense the principle of equal sacrifice. We must ask him to let us take him at his word,' Keynes reasoned, in seeking a fair apportionment of costs in 'what afterwards became a common war'.[19] In writing this Keynes showed himself attuned to the familiar wartime rhetoric that had moved so many of his compatriots – and showed too that he was grotesquely out of kilter with American public opinion.

The Allies had one great bond of unity: the defeat of Hitler. The nearer they came to achieving this, the greater became the stresses making for disunity. 'The P.M. and Eden both fear that our willingness to trust our Russian ally may have been in vain and they look with despondency to the future,' noted Jock Colville as early as 7 March, himself commenting: 'but, God knows, we have tried hard to march in step with Russia towards the broad and sunlit uplands.' A couple of weeks later, he wrote in his diary that it might be 'easier to forgive our present enemies in their future misery, starvation and weakness than to reconcile ourselves to the past claims and future demands of our two great Allies'. He was thinking of the recent deterioration in relations with Russia, of course, but not only that. 'The Americans have become very unpopular in England,' he admitted.[20]

In Italy, Harold Macmillan confessed himself equally concerned about the current state of Anglo-American relations. 'I am afraid there are still a lot of people who want to make trouble between the U.S. and the U.K. or who harbour quite extraordinary suspicions of British foreign policy,' he reflected. 'This they believe to be extremely subtle, Machiavellian, even Jesuitical. If only they could realise (as I have learned in these last years) how amateurish, hand-to-mouth and incompetent a department the F.O. really is, they would be surprised indeed.'[21]

This pointed to a real quandary for the British, as became increasingly apparent in the course of March and early April. The optimistic view of

Yalta was crumbling in the face of obstruction and obfuscation by the Soviet Government. 'We're getting *nowhere* on Poland,' concluded Alec Cadogan, as the diplomatic impasse stalled the agreed moves towards a broad-based government and democratic elections.[22] Yet the Churchill Government was itself handicapped in enlisting support by many Americans' deepseated feeling that the British were simply up to their old game again. For Americans with this mind-set, their two Allies were almost equally reprehensible, sometimes almost indistinguishably so. This is why Robert Sherwood, when he reported a recent visit to General MacArthur's headquarters to the President on 24 March, alerted him to talk about a shadowy phalanx of 'Communists and British Imperialists' and to suspicions of their alleged influence in the White House itself.[23]

Senator Vandenberg was more pragmatic than paranoid. He now found himself torn. He was ready for once to believe that a British Foreign Secretary might be right when Eden voiced worries about Poland in the Commons on 7 March, and he himself echoed the same points in the Senate. Equally, Vandenberg was resigned to the reality that both Roosevelt and Churchill had given their stamp of approval to the Yalta decisions. Above all, the Senator was willing to serve on his country's delegation to the San Francisco conference of the United Nations – because the alternative was to see everything wrecked. 'What would *that* do for Poland?' he argued privately. 'It would simply leave Russia in complete possession of everything she wants.'[24]

Vandenberg's relations with the President, hitherto based on mutual aversion, had plainly taken a new turn by the time they met in the White House in mid-March. 'Just between us, Arthur,' FDR confided, 'I am coming to know the Russians better, and if I could name only one delegate to the San Francisco conference, you would be that delegate.'[25] Yet, within the space of a day or two, Roosevelt was criticizing the British rather than the Russians to his cabinet. 'In a semi-jocular manner of speaking,' so James Forrestal recorded, 'he stated that the British were perfectly willing for the United States to have a war with Russia at any time and that, in his opinion, to follow the British programme would be to proceed towards that end.'[26]

What FDR really thought, as so often, remains obscure. He intended to go to San Francisco himself, to preside at the inaugural United Nations conference, ready to exert his enormous influence and prestige. At his *tête-à-tête* with his new friend Arthur, he probably thought that the best thing was to humour a powerful man whom he would rather have with him than against him, deferring real decisions until later. This is, of course, exactly what he had done at Yalta in agreeing to support Stalin's claim for extra votes in the new United Nations body. Rumours were already in the air about 'secret understandings' between the Big Three. Here was one so sensitive that Stettinius referred to it by code in his diary, having told the President on 12 March of 'an intuitive feeling that it would be much better not to let the X-matter come up at San Francisco if we could possibly avoid it'. On this he found that they were in agreement: 'the president himself has made up his mind without my guiding it that he would like to get by at San Francisco without that coming up.'[27]

How could the President have believed this possible? How could the Secretary of State have hoped that his Soviet opposite number, Molotov, would not raise such an important point? Their handling of the X-matter, as much as of any Polish difficulties, points to some lack of political astuteness at this juncture. It took another week for the penny to drop. Stettinius then phoned the White House with the message that the President should summon the US delegates, in advance of San Francisco, 'and tell them the whole truth about this X-matter'.[28] Alger Hiss and Chip Bohlen should also be present, as the only State Department officials who knew the full facts.

The President briefed the delegates at the White House on 23 March. He was at his best and at his worst: spinning a story of how he had cajoled Stalin down from his extravagant claim for even more votes; purporting to have put forward an American counter-claim to forty-eight votes as a means of reducing the Soviets to three; offering a purely hypothetical view that, if he were a delegate at San Francisco, he personally would favour the Soviet proposal; and finally 'saying that that was all there was to that subject'. Stettinius listened uneasily, conscious that the delegates still did not appreciate 'the degree to which the United States government was committed'.[29] The fact that they had listened in silence did not, however, mean that they were so easily beguiled.

'This will *raise hell*,' Vandenberg wrote in his diary. He was angry not only at the secrecy but at the way the numbers had been justified – 'if it is important enough to cause Stalin to demand three votes, we will be asked by the country why we are stopped at "three" instead of "six" to match the British.' After talking to a fellow Republican, John Foster Dulles, a few days later, he came to the conclusion that this manoeuvre 'could easily dynamite San Francisco – or subsequent Senate approval of the entire Treaty'.[30]

The question was indeed explosive. It had been poorly handled by the Big Three, but was much more than a procedural defect. Its charge in the United States was so deadly because it managed simultaneously to excite the Russophobes and the Anglophobes. At just the time when events in Poland were bringing the good faith of the Soviet Communists into question, then, here was an issue with the potential to put the British Empire in the dock alongside them, at least in the eyes of the Mid-West constituency that Vandenberg understood so well.

The combustible trail had been laid by Roosevelt's confidential disclosure; it took less than a week for the inevitable spark to be struck in New York. On 29 March the *Herald Tribune* ran a leaked version of Roosevelt's comments, with a scathing editorial about the unworthy nature of the proposal. The White House was besieged with newspapermen demanding confirmation of the story, with not so much as a press release ready to appease them. The next day, with the deeply fatigued President already in transit to Warm Springs, Stettinius had to face prolonged and hostile questioning on matters evidently unknown even to his own Assistant Secretaries of State (though the fiasco was hardly his fault alone). Roosevelt, hitherto the consummate politician in his handling of American public opinion, showed that he had lost his touch, perhaps lost his grip. He left no strategy in place for news management on a point which was bound to emerge anyway and which abruptly revealed its capacity to derail his grand design.

A glance at the front pages of the *Chicago Tribune* over the next week provides graphic testimony that, if isolationism was mouldering in its grave, its soul went marching on. The tone is conveyed by the prominent cartoon on 2 April, 'Playing the Big Shot with the Family Funds', showing a gregarious FDR at the 'world bar' with bottles open, labelled 'Lend-Lease', flanked by John Bull with glass in hand and by Stalin. The next day's cartoon delivers the United Nations punch, with the point that three American votes, compared with six British, must obviously be a trick dreamt up by 'Winston' – a surmise not lacking in historical veracity, as we now know. 'As I anticipated,' Vandenberg consoled himself, 'the Yalta episode has stirred up the old (and heretofore) latent bugaboo about "six votes for Britain".' Now poacher turned gamekeeper, he cited 'ample evidence that our critics are already going to work on it with a vengeance'.[31] The best that Isaiah Berlin could make of it was to wonder 'why the dominions do not squawk more loudly than they do about being represented as obedient stooges to HMG'.[32]

It proved easier to get into such trouble than to get out of it. Roosevelt was damned if he did claim his derisory three votes and damned if he didn't. He thus embarrassed his own supporters while delighting his unregenerate opponents. It was predictable that Vandenberg should try to reserve his own position and natural that this should be seen as an early sign that the United States delegation was split – though fortuitous that this coincided with the news that Molotov was now declining to go to San Francisco at all. 'Mr Roosevelt's pretentious foreign policy is coming apart at the seams,' the *Chicago Tribune* exulted on 3 April. 'It was inevitable that it should fail because it was an attempt to organise the world under a series of falsehoods.' Worse, the next day's *New York Times*, previously so supportive, not only spoke of blunders at Yalta, notably on the votes issue, but commented: 'In these blunders President Roosevelt played a conspicuous part.'

Polemics aside, it was the taint of secrecy that did the lasting damage to the image of Yalta. What else would fall out of the Crimean closet? Initially, idealistic hopes had helped sustain belief that the Big Three had really shifted the world out of the era of power politics and secret diplomacy, but the mood was perceptibly souring. The State Department was left to wriggle out of the demeaning claim to extra American votes but Stettinius publicly acknowledged the Administration's obligation to support the Soviet Union's claim; so this, by default, became the American position. This new twist was simply new grist to the mill for the *Chicago Tribune*. Its front-page cartoon on 9 April shows FDR telling 'America's Internationalists', with pleasing directness for once: 'Give the British Empire six votes, Russia three votes, and America only one vote in the League Assembly!'

It may seem improbable that the ghost of the British Empire should have intruded so prominently into these debates of March and April 1945, usually characterized in hindsight as heralding the advent alike of the United Nations and of the cold war. Yet Vandenberg called the controversy over votes 'the major tragedy of Yalta (with the exception of Poland)'.[33] The effect was not only to distract attention from the Polish situation but also to vitiate the force of Churchill's pleas for a united Anglo-American response.

As over Lend-Lease, the British were presuming upon a closer ideological affinity than actually existed between the English-speaking peoples. Thus, given that Chicago sits on one of the Great Lakes and Toronto on another, it takes more than geography to explain the contrasting reactions in each city to the Allies' predicament at the end of the war. 'Must Share Our Food' was the headline on an editorial in the Toronto *Globe and Mail* on 2 April, commenting on the announcement of cuts in American meat exports to Britain. It argued that 'there is no acceptable explanation for us not doing more for our allies as long as we continue to go unrationed' and deplored the idea 'that the British people, having sacrificed so much to victory, should achieve with their victory the promise of thinner rations than war demanded'. The *Chicago Tribune*, fresh from unmasking the pretensions of the British Empire, was not so easily deceived. 'British to Get More Sugar in 1945 than U.S.' was one headline that week. An editorial on 11 April, defiantly headed 'America First', asserted that the American people 'are not ashamed to put American interests first and keep them there'.

The next day, Thursday, 12 April, saw the sudden death of President Roosevelt. In his last days at Warm Springs, Roosevelt had continued to attend to business somewhat fitfully, perhaps doing more than a man in his condition should, though probably less than the situation demanded. Churchill's long telegrams about the worrying situation in eastern Europe were not ignored but the President had not focused his remaining energies on formulating an effective response – if indeed one existed. He approved various replies drafted for him; but on the day before his death he wrote to Churchill himself, saying that he hoped to 'minimize the general Soviet problem as much as possible because these problems, in one form or another, seem to arise every day and most of them straighten out' – which was his own authentic posture when he could not predict what the morrow would bring.[34]

Nearly everyone in close contact with Roosevelt, certainly from the time of Yalta onwards and often from that of Quebec, seems to have harboured fears about his health. Yet nearly everyone was shocked when he died. The impressions of Sherwood, who had seen him less than three weeks earlier, were typical. Thus he told his wife 'that the President was in much worse shape than I had ever seen him before' and that he was 'unnaturally quiet and even querulous', failing to sustain his usual leading role in conversation. 'I thought it was a blessing that he could get away for a while to Warm Springs, and I was sure the trip across the country to San Francisco would do him a lot of good,' Sherwood wrote. 'The thought never occurred to me that this time he might fail to rally as he always had.'[35] He was far from alone in being unprepared for the news that reached Washington at 5 o'clock on the afternoon of 12 April. Two hours later, while waiting for the Chief Justice to administer the presidential oath of office to the Vice-President, so Stettinius recorded, 'I was sitting next to Truman and we had a rather intimate talk relative to the fact that he did not believe that this would happen.'[36]

One reason for choosing Harry S. Truman as Vice-Presidential candidate in 1944 had been in case of Roosevelt's death in office. In particular, he was thought safer than the left-leaning Henry Wallace, relegated by Roosevelt from Vice-President to Secretary of Commerce. Truman was a product of the party machine in Missouri, a border state (bordering the South) that could be relied upon to vote Democrat in that era. He had been an efficient, businesslike senator with a shrewd insider's understanding of Congressional politics; but in few other respects could he rival the gifts of his predecessor, whose charismatic appeal and patrician eloquence helped give him an extraordinary position as a world statesman. Death exaggerated the contrast by freezing Roosevelt's reputation at its apogee. 'Henry Wallace walked with me from the office to the White House,' Stettinius wrote on a day that could have seen President Wallace assume office, 'and said that from the standpoint of Roosevelt as a person in history that [sic] this was a good time for him to go.'[37]

'ROOSEVELT DIES ON EVE OF ALLIED TRIUMPHS' was how the *Daily Mirror* reported the news, which had reached London at midnight, too late for extensive comment in the British morning papers on 13 April. The Prime Minister was distressed, talking late into the night to his security man, Walter 'Tommy' Thompson, who remembered Churchill saying: 'No one realized what that man meant to this country.'[38] Judging by public reaction the next day, however, a lot of people thought that they realized. The editorial in *The Times* called Roosevelt's death 'a calamity for all the world', and added that Britons had 'good reason to love as well as honour him, for they knew him to be a friend', citing Lend-Lease and his part in bringing the United States into the war.

There is copious evidence that Roosevelt's death evoked more than decorous platitudes. It caused 'a great stir', Jock Colville recorded on

13 April, evidently surprised at the deep impact of the news.[39] 'In Great Britain particularly,' *The Times* stated, 'it has come to all with a sense, that was manifest everywhere yesterday, of acute personal loss.' This claim is borne out not only in the diaries of the political elite but by Mass-Observation, in a survey undertaken the same day.[40] 'I've been surprised by the depth of affection he seems to have inspired in all sorts of people,' said one middle-class man, aged forty. 'All the people I've talked to today seem to be genuinely sorry about his death. All classes.' Likewise a member of the upper classes, aged forty-eight: 'It is a tremendous tragedy' (this was Chips Channon, MP).[41] A fifty-year-old skilled worker said much the same: 'Well, I feel myself it's a real loss for everybody, his death. He wasn't all for self, and he wasn't all for his own country at the expense of others, he was a real good man, and there's not many of them.'

The marked expressions of esteem for Roosevelt voiced on British streets stemmed from his personal identification with policies of direct benefit to ordinary people. 'I don't know where we'd be if it wasn't for Roosevelt sending us food and ammunition on that Lend-Lease plan,' said a working-class woman of forty. 'It was all his idea.' And what worried many now was no longer the war itself but uncertainty over its aftermath. 'I'm afraid it will have serious repercussions on the peace,' said a middle-class woman of thirty-five. 'I had far sooner it was Churchill who had died.'

Fears about a policy vacuum fed on inevitable ignorance about President Truman. 'It is really a disaster,' commented an upper-class man, aged fifty-eight (Harold Nicolson, MP). 'Under that bloody American Constitution, they must now put up with the Vice-President who was actually chosen because he was a colourless and harmless man.'[42] A thirty-year-old working-class woman found this equally unsettling: 'I don't know anything about the new man they've put in Roosevelt's place. I should think it is going to be very difficult for him, because everybody liked Roosevelt.' The only consolation was that so much had already been agreed at Yalta. 'I mean, even if this other bloke – Truman – even if he wanted to, do you think Stalin and Churchill are going to listen to him and upset all their arrangements?' one middle-class man, aged fifty-five, reasoned. 'And as far as I know he hasn't any intention of upsetting things. I believe he's a very good bloke.'

On both sides of the Atlantic there was a reservoir of goodwill for

Roosevelt's successor. This went with a recognition that continuity was to be the watchword in international policy, if only because of the extraordinary – and irresponsible – state of ignorance about foreign affairs in which the Vice-President had been kept. The unique quality of Churchill's personal relationship with Roosevelt was often mentioned, though it is curious that a Prime Minister so ready to brave air flights, whether impulsively to hazardous Athens or sentimentally to the war zone on the Rhine, should not have been moved to attend the presidential funeral. In failing to seize the opportunity to meet the new President, if not to pay his last respects to the old one, Churchill was surely remiss, as he later acknowledged.

Obviously Roosevelt was a greater loss to the Americans than to the British. Churchill's public response nonetheless fostered the Roosevelt myth with unique authority. He yet again repeated familiar words when he told the House of Commons in his tribute to Roosevelt on 17 April that 'he devised the extraordinary measure of assistance called Lend-Lease, which will stand forth as the most unselfish and unsordid financial act of any country in all history.' Members cheered, perhaps unmindful that members of the US Senate had, only a week previously, taken a rather more jaded view of the current Lend-Lease legislation.

This was a big day for Churchill. He had been the focus of attention that morning at the memorial service for the President in St Paul's Cathedral. The 'Star-Spangled Banner' was sung as a negro spiritual, the Last Post was sounded. Chips Channon recorded that, as he left, he 'saw Winston standing bare-headed, framed between two columns of the portico and he was sobbing as the shaft of sunlight fell on his face and the cameras clicked'.[43] His grief was visibly displayed, whatever his inner feelings. Many of those who listened to his Commons speech that afternoon found the performance rather below his best, with Churchill too obviously straining for emotion, notably when he read from Long-fellow's 'Sail on, O ship of state'. But he himself sailed on regardless into his peroration, amid further cheers: 'For us it remains only to say that in Franklin Roosevelt there died the greatest American friend we have ever known, and the greatest champion of freedom who has ever brought help and comfort from the new world to the old.'[44]

Like others, Churchill sometimes succumbed in hindsight to the temptation to speculate on how much difference Roosevelt's death really made. In doing so he usually exaggerated the extent to which, at Yalta and afterwards, an ailing Roosevelt had failed to respond to his own prescient warnings about what was soon to be called an iron curtain across Europe. In this sense, the decisions of a dying President became the issue – one charged with abiding political passion in the United States. 'Now that death has claimed Franklin Delano Roosevelt,' the *Chicago Tribune* had said in breaking the news, 'the true story of his decline in health for more than a year is expected to be unfolded.' Republican critics of Yalta duly seized on such revelations, though it seems unlikely that the President, even if fully fit, would have behaved very differently.

What was distinctive about the Roosevelt myth in Britain was its focus on the effect of his removal from the scene. After the President's sudden death, evoking its unprecedented response among Britons, there was a natural inclination to see it as the adventitious cause of subsequent disappointments. In particular, when Lend-Lease was abruptly cut off some four months later, Mass-Observation again reported reactions on the street. 'Be different if only old Roosevelt had lived – he was a real friend to us,' said one middle-aged working-class woman. Because his pro-British image had so assiduously been built up, the underlying realities and continuities of American policy were often ignored, in newspapers as much as in government. Little wonder that a working-class man of similar age subscribed to similar sentiments: 'Pity Roosevelt's dead. It couldn't have happened like this in his time.'[45]

Preparations for the San Francisco conference continued throughout March and April regardless of the change of President in Washington. Truman, poorly briefed on the Yalta understandings, had no ambition to take charge of the conference personally and left everything to Stettinius, whose status was thus enhanced (at least temporarily). Indeed Roosevelt's death actually helped the conference get off the ground since it facilitated a change of stance by the Russians, who now pleaded their respect for the late President in agreeing to send Molotov after all. It was to be a foreign ministers' conference, then, and Eden was to lead the British delegation. This meant that Attlee had to serve under him, which troubled the self-effacing Deputy Prime Minister less than it did some members of the Labour Party who felt their Leader thereby slighted.

In London, the excuse for not letting the Viceroy come home to discuss the Indian situation had previously been the Yalta conference, because of which he been told that he must wait until March. But by 10 March, with no actual date yet forthcoming, Wavell had smelt a rat, writing in his diary that 'I don't think the PM wants me at all and will procrastinate as long as possible.' Five days later Wavell duly discovered that the excuse had changed, when he received a cable from Leo Amery saying 'that as Attlee would be busy with the San Francisco conference they must postpone my visit till June'. The Viceroy read this as more than a personal snub – 'Tell India to wait till it's more convenient.'[46] He protested with such indignation that Amery got the India Committee to change its mind and agree to an early visit. That left only one obstacle, albeit the greatest of all: the Prime Minister's rooted prejudices.

Amery's own plan, for giving India Dominion status on VE-Day while leaving democratization until later, had already been scuppered. Only Cripps would listen to him, though still preferring his own approach. So the agenda was to be that proposed by Wavell: a variant on the Cripps Offer of democratization as a preliminary to independence. Neither option, it is needless to say, had any attractions for the Prime Minister. When he heard of the India Committee's wish to allow Wavell to argue his case in person, he reluctantly assented, though speaking to Amery 'most bitterly and contemptuously of W. as never any real use as a soldier but who he had thought would at least carry on in India and not try and advertise himself by cringing to the Hindus etc.' Amery, well used to taking such diatribes in his stride, did not bother to argue back, having got the decision he needed. He was simply content to have engaged Churchill's attention for once: 'We had a few minutes more on India generally – the first talk on the Indian problem at large in five years!'[47]

These were not auspicious circumstances for Wavell's visit to London. He arrived on 23 March and was to stay in a suite in the Dorchester Hotel for the next couple of months. In the first week, preoccupied with pissing in the Rhine, Churchill was not directly involved over India. This was an advantage for the India Committee, meeting under Attlee's chairmanship, as had become usual since Churchill rarely attended. 'The atmosphere generally was friendly,' Wavell noted on 26 March, 'no one seemed to have any alternative proposals though they stressed the dangers and difficulties of making any move.' He did well, in Amery's opinion. Wavell's impression was that there was a lot of skirmishing, with Cripps playing a useful supporting role to Amery, and he thought the inscrutable chairman more dubiously cast. In the evenings the Viceroy saw a better quality of drama in John Gielgud's Hamlet and Laurence Olivier's Richard III. The present King, meanwhile, so the Viceroy suspected after an interview, had been 'told by PM that I was casting spanner into works over India', which left him somewhat worried.[48] 'I am afraid that he has good reason to be worried!' Brooke commented after talking to him, Field Marshal to Field Marshal. 'From what he told me he is quite prepared to resign if he does not get what he wants, and I should not be surprised if he was eventually driven to take such a course.'[49]

It did not come to that. Instead, Wavell found his patience taxed rather than his plans scouted. At their first meeting, on 29 March, Churchill explained to Wavell that he had been at the front and had then had to prepare an oration on Lloyd George, who had died three days previously. 'He said that he had had no time to consider India but eulogised the India Committee as a very strong and representative body who would advise him,' Wavell noted. 'He then said "you must have mercy on us", and proceeded to state all the problems they had to consider, and the reasons for delay in considering India, which he thought could be kept on ice.' After this dampening experience, it was at least more cheering to hear from Cripps that the India Committee – in the Prime Minister's absence of course – was largely persuaded of the need to make a move: 'Cripps seemed to think prospects were considerably brighter than they had been before I came home.'

So it was again a question of telling India to wait until it was more convenient. It was a familiar scenario and in 1943–4 had been gruesome in its effects, leaving 3 million deaths in the Bengal famine as damning evidence of Britain's neglect of the basic interests of its Indian subjects. Lord Cherwell provided statistics to bolster the Prime Minister's ingrained conviction that there was no overall shortage of food, which was true only to the extent that local social and economic forces governed who would starve and who would survive. Wavell, determined to allow no repetition on his watch, found the India Committee on 4 April still maintaining, 'on the basis of Cherwell's fatuous calculations', that no extra food and no extra shipping to provide it were necessary. 'An unsatisfactory meeting,' he noted tersely. 'Went straight on to see Gielgud's Midsummer Night's Dream, a fine performance.'

The Bengalis, of course, were not unique in their plight. This was the 'tulip winter' for the people of the Netherlands, trapped for months under Nazi oppression while the Allied advance had been checked. But here at least, action was belatedly forthcoming. After Wavell attended the cabinet on 9 April, he wrote that 'it brought home to me the very different attitude towards feeding a starving people when the starvation is in Europe.'[50]

Meanwhile the India Committee moved slowly forward, pleasing Amery as much that it was moving at all as it left Wavell frustrated by the slowness. The Viceroy's plans, which seemed too radical to the Tories, were paradoxically criticized as too undemocratic by Attlee, with his ideological antipathy to the bourgeois base of the Indian National Congress. 'Attlee's attitude really hardly differs from that taken by Winston 10 years ago,' Amery commented, 'namely that we cannot hand India over to Indian capitalists and exploiters.'[51] And all the while Cripps, whose actual knowledge of India was much fresher and more extensive than Attlee's, worked adroitly, draft by draft, to capture a workable consensus. Thus Leo Amery, the lifelong imperialist and last-ditch supporter of imperial preference, found himself colluding with Stafford Cripps, the pre-war advocate of alliance with the Communists as the only way of overthrowing capitalism and imperialism alike. A final draft on 12 April united the whole committee. 'It is an odd thing to think of Cripps and myself as the two main collaborators in this business,' Amery noted, while Wavell acknowledged, after hearing of the compromise, that 'we have got the India Committee a long step on the road.'[52]

The essential point was the turn towards a political rather than a purely military strategy. Since the Cripps Mission, India had been condemned alike to political stalemate and social polarization. The *Raj Quartet* of novels by Paul Scott, especially *The Day of the Scorpion* (1968), feelingly evoke the tensions within the different communities in these years, brutally stifling real communication or comprehension between them. Congress's withdrawal from a creative political role, initially self-inflicted, was perpetuated by the imprisonment of the very political leaders who were needed to broker a viable settlement. Though the precarious war situation, which had perhaps been enough to seal the fate of the Cripps Mission in 1942, had meanwhile been stabilized, military victory itself promised no panacea, as Wavell, the educated soldier, had the sense to see. Hence the importance of securing him a brief to open negotiations with the Indian political parties.

The Viceroy's handicap in such a scenario was that he did not suffer politicians gladly. But he steeled himself to patience. He found it odd that he was excluded from so much of the further deliberations of the India Committee (chaired by the Lord Chancellor after Attlee's departure for San Francisco) but was content to rely on Amery and Cripps to fight their corner. Indeed the three of them had a highly significant meeting on 24 April to settle their line in presenting these proposals to the cabinet. 'On the whole satisfactory, and we agreed that if we three stood pat on this, it would be difficult for the India Committee or the Cabinet to override us,' Wavell noted.[53] It was this message that Amery conveyed a couple of days later, tactically using Anderson, a member of the India Committee as well as Chancellor of the Exchequer, as the messenger 'to impress on Winston the seriousness of the position that would follow if Wavell were turned down and he, Cripps and myself resigned'.[54]

This was a serious threat, seriously meant. Amery, Wavell and Cripps – each from his own perspective – agreed that the prospect of victory gave Britain a unique moment to seize the initiative before the momentum of Indian politics gathered pace. Yet India still had to wait. 'I feel I have failed to make HMG realise the importance and urgency of the Indian problem or the real facts of the position,' Wavell wrote on 29 April. 'We have been talking for 5 weeks, in a very disconnected way.'[55] The cabinet meeting the following day was equally disconnected, as Amery soon enough discovered: 'For half an hour or more Winston talked away, alternately pouring contempt on the proposals as too trivial to have any effect anywhere and saying that the Indian problem could not be revolutionised in the last days of a dying Parliament.'

Disturbingly, the British cabinet now heard the pledge at the heart of the Cripps Offer repudiated by the Prime Minister. Amery's argument that the hour of victory was the right one to make such a concession was simply swept aside – 'Winston frankly takes the view that we made the offer when in a hole and can disavow it because it was not accepted at the time.'[56] So the post-dated cheque would not be honoured even though the bank itself had not failed. Perhaps Churchill, having recently saluted Roosevelt as the champion of freedom, was emboldened to follow the example of the only other surviving member of the Big Three,

Stalin, who plainly had no monopoly on choosing which fine promises of post-war democracy he would subsequently honour.

'In comparison with the main issue of winning the war, for which the soldiers are still risking their lives, all other issues appear to be of but secondary importance, to be judged on the basis of whether they speed or postpone victory,' declared an editorial in the *New York Times* on 2 April. This dignified reminder was felt necessary if only to deplore the effect of the controversy over votes at the United Nations in setting the Allies at loggerheads before their essential object had been achieved.

The paper's reporting of war news was itself an exemplary model of Allied impartiality, with three-decker headlines that allowed equal honours to all. Thus on 5 April:

US 3rd ARMY DRIVES TO BISECT THE REICH

BRITISH CROSS THE WESER, RACE TO PORTS

RUSSIANS WIN BRATISLAVA, SHELL VIENNA

In London *The Times* of the same date deployed its own typographical conventions to very similar effect:

British Armour across the Weser

Allies Break into Hanover Plain

Canadian First Army Closing on Arnhem

French Take Karlsruhe

Likewise on 10 April, the headlines in New York:

US AND BRITISH ARMIES DRIVE FOR ELBE

CANADIANS CUT OFF 80,000 IN NETHERLANDS

RUSSIANS CAPTURE THE HEART OF VIENNA

And on the same day in London, *The Times'* headlines (unlike its editorials) again failed only to celebrate the role of the Red Army:

Double Advance by Canadians

Drive towards Emden and the Zuyder Zee

Links with Parachute Troops

Big Gains by American First Army

Here was the war reported in the unexceptionable, *bien-pensant* terms that General Eisenhower liked to read. 'Ike was in an expansive mood today,' Harry Butcher recorded on 2 April, 'and, as usual, tossed bouquets of credit in all directions.' He was happy to concede that 'Monty had done a fine job in crossing the Rhine', but knew that this was hardly likely to go unnoticed. What he wanted was more credit for the efforts of Hodges and his 1st US Army and, as ever, that 'Bradley's magnificent contribution in this campaign' should get more attention. 'Patton, being colorful and audacious, drew the headlines in the American press,' Ike acknowledged, 'while Monty, likewise colorful and always "good copy", led the parade of black type in England.'[57]

Too true. 'MONTY'S TANKS "RUNNING WILD"' was one recent headline in the London evening paper *The Star* (28 March). 'BRITISH 100 MILES BEYOND THE RHINE' was the main news in the tabloid *Daily Sketch* on the same day as Ike's conversation with Butcher, fulfilling his predictions rather than his intentions about press coverage. 'Great news poured in from the Western Front all yesterday as General Eisenhower partially lifted the security "blackout",' the *Sketch* began its report. 'The most sensational break-out of the whole Rhine campaign took place on Field-Marshal Montgomery's front.' Though the small print, down-column, usually disclosed other successes by Eisenhower's forces, his own hopes for recognition of Bradley and Hodges, let alone Devers, Simpson or Patch, remained unmet, at least in Fleet Street. The fact that three out of four of Ike's troops were now Americans, and correspondingly dominating the advance, could well have escaped a reader of the British popular press.

This version, moreover, had surprisingly wide circulation throughout the Empire. When Canadians opened their newspapers, they found the war reported much as it was in London, partly because the Canadian army was part of Montgomery's 21st Army Group with Canadian special correspondents attached to it rather than to SHAEF. Admittedly, the *Globe and Mail*, the anglophone champion of the Ontario war effort, was scrupulous in giving only slightly enhanced attention to the current Canadian achievements. Its headlines on 3 April –

BRITISH 100 MILES IN REICH

HUNS FLEEING HOLLAND AS CANADIANS GAIN

– did not differ from that in *The Times* in its order of precedence, simply in sharper compression and language.

In Canada, moreover, indifference or hostility to the war, though not absent, could hardly be explained simply as a function of distance from Europe. Anti-war attitudes were to be found mainly in the east, flourishing in Quebec's unique cultural and linguistic climate, rather than in the west, as with isolationism in the United States. So out on the prairies – twice as far west of Toronto as Chicago – the *Winnipeg Free Press* told a common story, focused on Europe. Hence its banner headlines on 4 April: 'MONTY'S FORCES RACING FOR BREMEN', or the next day: 'NAZIS REELING UNDER ALLIED BLOWS', or a week later: 'YANKS CROSS ELBE IN LAST LAP DRIVE'.

The truth is that the British Empire lived on in sentiment well beyond its capacity to defend its own far-flung territories. In Melbourne, where the Japanese threat had bulked all too large ever since Singapore fell, the *Age* nonetheless had essentially the same focus as newspapers in London:

RAPID BRITISH DRIVE FOR GERMAN PORTS
(6 April)

ALLIES IN OUTSKIRTS OF GREAT NAZI CITIES
(9 April)

BRITISH ARMOUR IN DRIVE ON BREMEN

– though not forgetting 'AMERICANS IN ESSEN' (10 April). Even in the King's antipodean dominions, then, this was seen as a war still focused on the fighting in Europe and still disproportionately influenced by British feats of arms.

For more Americans than Allied propaganda ever admitted, however, this was a significantly different war. It was not just that readers of the *Chicago Tribune* were privileged to find otherwise unreported insights on the news from Germany, like the headline on 11 April giving the background to the 21st Army Group's difficulties: 'Nazi Hannover Home of British Ruling Family'. (The German spelling helped make the point.) Nor was it simply an understandable readiness to blazon the achievements of the US Army, ensuring that the name of Patton eclipsed that of Monty in the headlines. It was a different war in a more fundamental way. The priorities of the military conflict to which American isolationists had reluctantly been converted after Pearl Harbor are clearly illustrated by the layout of the *Chicago Tribune*'s front page on 2 April:

ADVANCE 3 Mi. on OKINAWA

162 Mi. to BERLIN; Push On

In its editorial on 12 April, 'The Facts Are Plain', the message was that the British had been unable to protect their possessions in Asia and did not deserve to keep them. Likewise, they now had (even with the Canadians) two armies in Germany, compared with more than five American – 'in the European war we have shown that Britain needs us, but we do not need Britain.'

Churchill himself was not unaware of the reality of the position, as was demonstrated in his table talk if not in his public rhetoric. On 6 April he was telling Field Marshal Smuts that 'there was no greater exhibition of power in history than that of the American army fighting the battle of the Ardennes with its left hand and advancing from island to island towards Japan with its right.'[58] This perception underpinned his own strong feeling that, however urgently the Americans now wanted to get on with the Pacific war, they had the capacity to take Berlin as well.

Such a strategy had already been ruled out by Roosevelt, supporting Marshall, supporting Eisenhower. By coincidence, it was not until the day of the President's death, 12 April, that Eisenhower first told Patton that the US armies would be halted on the line of the Elbe, which they had now reached. Patton was dismayed. His own immediate consolation was that his 3rd Army was now turned south towards Prague; his subsequent frustration was to be told that Prague too was to be left to the Red Army. Again, as Marshall put it, 'I would be loath to hazard American lives for purely political purposes.'[59]

The *Daily Mirror* on 13 April had not cleared the whole of its front page for the late news of Roosevelt's death, instead staying with the exciting war developments:

END IN A FEW DAYS, U.S. TOLD:

BRIDGEHEAD IS 6 MILES LONG OVER ELBE

The journalists were as unaware as the eager US troops who had reached the Elbe that it was less a bridgehead than a terminus. Still, with daily reports that the Third Reich was at last falling apart, there seemed to be only two significant figures who refused to believe that the end was near. One was Eisenhower, buoyed up by Bradley and Bedell Smith in his belief in a Nazi retreat to their supposed national redoubt; hence the logic of the new SHAEF decision to turn powerful US Armies to the south, where they in fact found only token resistance rather than any last-ditch Nazi fortress.

The only other person of comparable eminence to resist the evidence of his own eyes was, of course, the Führer, under siege in his bunker in Berlin. For him, Roosevelt's demise was the last good news of the war, with its meretricious promise that death would release Hitler – like Frederick the Great in the crisis of the Seven Years War – from the logic of destruction at the hands of an alliance that might now fragment.

The relative ease, and certainly the speed, of the Allies' advance on the western front contrasted with the stubbornly slow erosion of the German position on the eastern front. This fed Stalin's insatiable appetite for paranoia, provoking charges that some deal between the Western Allies and the Germans must be behind it. Churchill's reaction was violent, reinforcing his sense of a breach of faith on Stalin's part. Colville observed that 'it looks as if the Germans had succeeded in persuading the Russians that something sinister was afoot.'[60] But that, of course, was how Goebbels had persuaded the American high command of the existence of the national redoubt.

Propaganda thus had real effects on the campaign. The British had been indignant at being confined to a support role, on the left flank of the American-led strike force, in the SHAEF plan. But the sudden southern diversion of the American troops that Montgomery was meant to be supporting left him instead as the master of the north German plain, quite contrary to the Supreme Commander's previous plan. For this, Monty owed Goebbels an unacknowledged debt. Moreover, the crumbling confidence in Soviet intentions led Eisenhower to order Montgomery to use the 21st Army Group to reach the Baltic coast, thus sealing off the neck of the Jutland peninsula and pre-empting the Red Army in Denmark. Admittedly, Montgomery was denied the support of the US 9th Army, leaving his own forces thinly stretched; but this also had the effect of highlighting the British role.

Fleet Street thus had further opportunity to laud their hero. The *Sunday Dispatch*'s banner headline on 8 April dominated its front page:

MONTGOMERY ON LAST LAP:

120,000 TROOPS RACING FOR BERLIN

In fact, of course, Berlin was not to be the target but it was not until 21 April that this, and the consequent decision to halt on the Elbe, was confirmed to the press by Bedell Smith. Meanwhile, whatever the final destination, the pace maintained by the British tanks, which had often been unfavourably contrasted with the Americans, was certainly impressive. The *Daily Mirror*, with its huge tabloid circulation, followed up on 11 April: 'ALLIES CAPTURE HANOVER, MONTY RACES FOR HAMBURG'. Likewise on 16 April: 'MONTY REACHES NORTH SEA, FIGHTING IS BITTER'. The Liberal *News Chronicle* on 19 April kept its main focus on the advances of the 21st Army Group in the north-west with the banner: 'MONTY MOVING ON HAMBURG'.

The bad news came mixed with the good. It was the Allied advance into Germany that now exposed conditions in the Nazi prison camps to the Western press. Reports from Belsen, entered unwarily by the British 11th Armoured Division, brought harrowing stories, printed within days: accounts of starving inmates foraging for food and water among piles of corpses. 'Many lay or sat inert,' wrote the *News Chronicle* correspondent. 'Those who could move moved. They were filled with restless, feverish excitement.' He had nothing but cigarettes to give them, as unready for what he would actually find as the appalled troops. 'Jews, Jews, Jews,' cried one woman in German. 'All because we are Jews.'[61]

At this stage, however, the Jewish dimension was not pre-eminent. Neither Belsen nor Buchenwald, liberated by Patton's army, were central to the extermination policies of the Holocaust. Some of the camp victims in the early photographs were prisoners of war; one picture that became familiar showed emaciated British soldiers sitting or lying forlornly, unsmiling in their gaze. Liberation was doubtless welcome, seldom joyful, often too late. The British buried 23,000 at Belsen. As well as the press, both British parliamentary and US congressional delegations were given facilities, pre-empting any possibility that the atrocities would be dismissed as Allied propaganda. The point was often made at the time that though such images were shocking and such reports distressing, they represented an inescapable truth about the Nazis, and thus about the war.

By contrast, there was a good deal of disingenuous propaganda in the celebrations of the long-awaited 'link-up'. American and Russian soldiers had indeed met at Torgau on the Elbe on 25 April. Three days later a coordinated release of the news along with a carefully posed handshake between the troops – 'A picture the world will never forget' – inevitably became big news in all Allied countries. It happened, of course, not because the US forces were advancing – they had been stalled on the Elbe for the best part of a fortnight – but because units of the Red Army had succeeded in outflanking and encircling Berlin.

With such clear portents of the end of the European war, it seemed that the Allies could at last afford to relax. Stalin was confident that the doomed German capital would be taken by his forces, within days but without interference from his allies. Roosevelt had died before his great antagonist, Hitler, though with victory assured. Churchill lived on to savour, with mixed feelings, the moment on which all his energies had been fixed since 1940.

In London, the V2s had now stopped and the blackout ended on 23 April. Churchill, safely reinstalled in 10 Downing Street, was greatly impressed a few days later to receive a telegram from the Soviet leader – 'the most friendly U.J. has ever sent,' Colville thought – and spent several hours talking of nothing else. To his private secretary, appalled at the work piling up in the absence of both Eden and Attlee at San

Francisco, this was an unwelcome diversion of his master's attention: 'His vanity was astonishing and I am glad U.J. does not know what effect a few kind words, after so many harsh ones, might well have on our policy towards Russia.'[62]

Had Churchill become dispensable, now that his historic mission was on the point of fulfilment? A man of parts, he had always had his foibles indulged by weary subordinates or loyal colleagues who recognized their own forbearance as among the personal costs of victory. 'My God!' Sir Alan Brooke had written in his diary on 12 April, 'how little the world at large knows what his failings and defects are! And thank heaven they don't or we should not be where we are now!'[63]

A few days previously, Ernest Bevin had broken the Coalition spell, or at least its working conventions, by openly voicing dissent. 'I have a profound admiration for the Prime Minister as a war leader – unfettered' were his words. 'I gave him my loyalty in that position: I never gave it to him as leader of the Conservative Party.'[64] A public riposte from Brendan Bracken was prominently reported in Beaverbrook's *Evening Standard* – a copy of which Churchill theatrically read and then discarded at a cabinet meeting attended by all the offending ministers. Taxed in the House of Commons at this discord in his Government, he adroitly made a joke of it – 'but already (so Chips Channon thought) one smells the odour of dissolution about, though the country is against an unnecessary election at this time.'[65] What had been said had simply not been said since 1940; but it could not be taken back. Indeed Bevin reiterated his view of Churchill, more pungently if more privately, when he talked with Dalton a week later. 'He's all right as a National Leader,' Bevin claimed, 'but, when he turns into the Leader of the Tory Party, you can't trust him an inch. He just becomes a crook.'[66]

The recent death of Lloyd George had considerable resonance. Not only had he been the Prime Minister credited with achieving victory in the First World War, but he had also notoriously cashed in on his reputation by perpetuating his wartime coalition at the 1918 General Election. When Churchill had delivered his eulogy of Lloyd George in the House of Commons at the end of March, it seemed to many a more convincing tribute to an old friend and comrade in arms than that he paid to Roosevelt only a couple of weeks later. 'As a man of action, resource and creative energy he stood, when at his zenith, without a rival,' Churchill had said of Lloyd George, in words which inevitably implied some introspection.[67] He too was being hailed as the man who won the war; he too would need to cash in electorally when the war in Europe ended – and with it, as the Labour Party had already made clear, the Coalition Government.

Thursday, 26 April, was polling day in the Chelmsford by-election. Although the political parties which formed the Coalition observed an electoral truce during the war, a new centre-left party calling itself Common Wealth had taken to putting up candidates in Conservative constituencies that fell vacant and had already won a couple of seats, both well before D-Day. Now on the very threshold of victory over Hitler, Churchill's Conservative Party, which had won 70 per cent of the vote in Chelmsford in 1935, lost the seat to Common Wealth, which now polled 57.5 per cent. To a true-blue Tory MP like Channon – 'I'm in despair about England,' he wrote – this was the writing on the wall.[68] His own constituency at Southend was nearby and his own poll in 1935 had been 65 per cent. Whatever did it portend? In faraway San Francisco, Eden was 'so upset by the Chelmsford election that he thinks he'll be out of office in a couple of months' (so Cadogan recorded).[69] At Downing Street, as Colville noted when the result came in, 'the clouds descended' as Bracken and Beaverbrook joined 'a lengthy conclave'.[70]

These were not the sort of problems that had ever beset Stalin, as he had maliciously made clear at Yalta. Hitler in his prime had had his own methods for securing legitimacy at the polls; but he too would never have to face the electorate again. Holed up in his bunker under the Reich Chancellery, with Soviet troops fighting their way through a terrorized Berlin, street by street and rape by rape, Hitler at last faced the reckoning. The defection of Himmler, broaching talk of an armistice through the Swedes, was a final demoralizing blow to the Führer.

'A most peaceful day, ending with thrilling news,' Harold Macmillan wrote in his diary at Assisi on 29 April, en route from Rome to Alexander's headquarters at Caserta. He was aware not only of Himmler's inept peace feelers but of a possible military armistice on the Italian front; he wanted to keep out of the way so as to deny the Russians any excuse to think of this as a separate political surrender. 'In the evening,' he recorded, 'we heard the news that the partisans of Milan had seized and hanged Mussolini and other Fascists.'[71] Photographs of Mussolini and his mistress hanging upside-down were widely published the next day.

On 1 May there was an irrepressible buzz of talk about a possible German surrender. Expectations were stoked up that Churchill might have a statement to make to the Commons that day. It was rather an anti-climax when all he could say, attempting a joke, was that the war situation was better than five years previously. Patience was rewarded. 'In the middle of dinner,' Colville recorded late that night, 'I brought in the sensational announcement, broadcast by the Nazi wireless, that Hitler had been killed today at his post at the Reichs Chancery in Berlin and that Admiral Doenitz was taking his place.' Dönitz did not inherit the unique title of Führer but such sovereignty as the Third Reich still exercised now devolved upon him at his Baltic headquarters near Kiel. Colville shrewdly commented that much in this report might have been fabricated in order to protect the Hitler myth. In fact the Führer had died the day before, and in a far from glorious suicide, deserting his people when the game was up. But Nazi propaganda scored a final triumph with that great military romantic, the Prime Minister, who said: 'Well, I must say I think he was perfectly right to die like that.'[72]

On the west coast of North America, thanks to the time difference, the story hit the streets at once. 'HITLER IS DEAD' was the hot news in the final edition of the *Vancouver Daily Province* for 1 May. It reported the Nazi claim that Hitler had died in battle but also that the BBC had suggested that he may have died of a stroke. Associated Press already carried speculation about whether he was really dead at all. Still, it was obviously the world's biggest story and, in probably the world's largest printing font, 'HITLER DEAD' took up half the front page of the *Daily News* in New York on 2 May, the day that most American and all British newspapers broke the epic news.

In Downing Street, the Prime Minister sat up late into the early hours of 2 May, savouring the moment of his historic triumph in inspiring a united people to resist the Nazi tyrant. And then the leader of the Tory Party got down to his crooked business. To Colville, as 3 a.m. saw his master still conferring with his crony Beaverbrook about electoral tactics, and 4 a.m. loomed with government business still undone, bathos dawned with the new day. Colville found himself 'cursing politics and all politicians, staring with exasperation at a box crammed with important unlooked-at papers and rather hoping that at the coming election the sovereign people follows the recent example of the electors of Chelmsford'.[73]

9

Justice?

May 1945

'For a hundred good reasons, we have had to accept during the war a post-war financial burden entirely disproportionate to what is fair.'

Keynes, paper for the cabinet, May 1945

When the San Francisco conference opened at the end of April few expected it to last for two months. It had been envisaged as an opportunity for Roosevelt to exercise his unrivalled political skills upon a wider audience than the Big Three, and to inaugurate a world organization among the United Nations who had waged war against the Nazis. Beginning before the war in Europe had ended, the conference was indeed the bridge to peace, though a much longer and more rickety bridge than many had hoped. But at least its load-bearing capacity proved sufficient to survive its initial stresses and it did not collapse, as at several times seemed likely.

The new President had at once asked all the cabinet to stay in post, which they agreed, though none except James Forrestal was to survive for long. On 14 April, Truman had seen Morgenthau, who explained to him that 'we have moved the financial capital from London and Wall Street right to my desk in the Treasury.' Truman responded: 'That's where I want to keep it.'[1] He assured Morgenthau of his support. These initial promises of continuity in policy were substantially kept but, as the President learnt more about the job that he had inherited, he moved to stamp it with his own style and began to assemble his own team.

Truman had to start from cold in his handling of international relations. He had seen Europe as a soldier in the First World War; he had been an alert and conscientious Senator; he had chaired committees on Lend-Lease; but as Vice-President he had been kept in the dark. On the day after Roosevelt's death Stettinius 'told the president that our relations with the Soviet Union since Yalta had deteriorated. He said he understood this, but asked why.' The Secretary of State attributed the problem less to Stalin himself than to the pressures upon him within the Soviet Union and recorded that Truman's immediate inclination was to stand up to the Russians – 'he gave me the impression that he thought we had been too easy with them.'[2]

'Stettinius is now Secretary of State in fact,' Vandenberg wrote that same day. 'Up to now he has been only the presidential messenger.'[3] It was soon to be rumoured, however, that Truman had other plans: that he wanted instead to appoint James Byrnes, a seasoned politician who had already accompanied Roosevelt to Yalta. Upset and undermined, Stettinius confronted Truman, who fobbed him off with a half-truth: 'Jimmy Byrnes is not going to San Francisco, and we are counting upon you to carry through.'[4] The decision to appoint Byrnes, a paid-up Democrat, had nonetheless been made, partly on the grounds that the Secretary of State was constitutionally next in line to succeed to the presidency now that there was no Vice-President. Throughout the San Francisco conference the rumour mill ground on regardless, as did Stettinius – a Secretary of State in fact, perhaps, but only on an ill-concealed interim basis.

In the absence of the President, at San Francisco the US delegates assumed greater power and authority, as Vandenberg was quick to realize. He welcomed the fact that they were now able to 'wash the slate clean of whatever undisclosed commitments FDR has made to Stalin or Churchill'.[5] Already a formidable figure within the Delegation, he now became pivotal in determining the American line, supported by his confidant Foster Dulles, ready to work with the biddable Stettinius, and by extension with the inexperienced Truman, but in no sense overawed in developing his own agenda.

Vandenberg was there to ensure that whatever the US Delegation agreed at San Francisco would be sabotage-proof in Congress, unlike the unhappy experience over the League of Nations in 1919–20. If he were to be responsible for delivering Republican support, he had told Anthony Eden, when they met at Lord Halifax's embassy in Washington on 17 April, 'I would have to insist on three "musts".' They were interrelated and all had an ethical dimension. He insisted that the pledges of the Atlantic Charter be specifically mentioned; he also insisted on a retrospective application to a case like Poland. 'The distinct and specific inclusion of *justice* as an objective' was how Vandenberg expressed his primary imperative. He commented in his diary on his talk with Eden and Halifax, in which he had thus established his own diplomatic credentials: 'I think we shall work very well together at Frisco.'[6]

Eden was in Washington, having attended Roosevelt's funeral. He was joined by Alec Cadogan, who, having been present at both Dumbarton Oaks and Yalta, was the Foreign Office's anchorman on United Nations business, of which he was to get more than his fill during the coming weeks. Both of them were by now on easy terms with the gregarious and publicity-conscious Stettinius, with Cadogan's phlegmatic mien providing a nice foil. 'I'm afraid that wherever Ed. is,' he commented wryly in his diary, 'we shall have brass bands, and shall have to inspect the Fire Brigade and open the flower show.'[7] Eden took the opportunity to see some other members of Truman's cabinet. He told Forrestal of his belief 'that the chief pivot of Russian policy today was an effort to drive a wedge between England and the United States'.[8]

Molotov too passed through Washington on his way to San Francisco. He met Stettinius and Eden for preparatory talks, hearing from them that they regarded Poland as the crucial issue. They got nowhere. Whether it was even worth holding the conference came into question, now that relations were rapidly becoming so poor, for which the blame was generally put on Molotov himself rather than Stalin. When Forrestal attended a cabinet meeting on 23 April, he heard Stettinius's bleak report that 'the Russians had receded from their agreement at Yalta with President Roosevelt on the Polish question' and were instead demanding a seat for the Lublin Poles at San Francisco. President Truman heard much support around the table for taking a strong line. But Chip Bohlen's notes also show that General Marshall reminded the cabinet of the need to secure the promised Soviet participation in the war against Japan – 'The Russians had it within their power to delay their entry into the Far Eastern war until we had done all the dirty work.'[9]

The President opted for firmness rather than conciliation when he received the Soviet Foreign Minister later that afternoon. His crash course on the Yalta minutes had left him feeling that they were regrettably hazy, as he had told Stettinius, but they agreed that now was the moment to draw the line. In Truman's recollection, when he bluntly said that he expected the Yalta agreements to be carried out, Molotov responded that he had never been talked to like that in his life. 'Carry out your agreements, and you won't get talked to like that again' was the undiplomatic riposte, straight from Kansas City, Missouri – or perhaps these words from Truman's memoirs remained unspoken, if Bohlen's official notes are to be trusted.[10]

The force of Truman's utterance, however, was clear enough. This was retailed to the assembled US delegates in San Francisco as soon as Stettinius arrived there the next day. It came as 'a thrilling message', Vandenberg noted. Moreover, he applauded the news that Truman had sent Stalin a blunt demand for co-operation: 'Stettinius said Eden could scarcely believe his eyes when he saw a copy – and cheered loudly.' The old isolationist's inveterate suspicion of British foreign policy showed remarkable signs of breaking down. 'This is the best news in months,' he enthused. 'FDR's appeasement of Russia is over.'[11]

Eden himself did not arrive until 2.30 a.m. on 25 April, the day the conference opened. 'Despite the hour,' Cadogan observed, 'Ed. had arranged a brass band and a guard of honour!' The American Secretary of State was formally the host of the conference. Stettinius was in any case one of nature's hosts and the penthouse suite that he had been loaned at the top of the Fairmont Hotel was the gum-chewing, smoke-laden, cigar-strewn cynosure for martini-shaking and deal-making alike. San Francisco struck Cadogan at once as 'a wonderful town', built on seven hills, thus agreeably like Rome; and thankfully unlike Yalta, not least in its accommodation and conveniences. Cadogan did not have to share the Foreign Secretary's bathroom this time but instead marvelled at Stettinius's abilities as impresario, quickly shown in the opening session at the Opera House: 'Quite fantastic, with orchestral accompaniment.'[12] The inevitable military band had duly introduced Stettinius and the dignitaries.

The real business began the next day, plunging the conference into prolonged and tedious wrangling about procedural issues which became the pattern for much of the next two months. Truman's tough line on Poland had won him enough credibility with the hawks among the US delegates to persuade all except Vandenberg that they should immediately honour Roosevelt's pledge to support granting the Soviet Union three votes in the new Assembly. Indeed, if the American position was that the promises of Yalta ought to be observed, it was tactically unwise to go back on this one, however unwisely tendered in the first place.

Vandenberg actually saw the point of this but asserted his own hard-won independent status in recording symbolic dissent.

So the X-matter inevitably surfaced at San Francisco, though occluded in unexpected ways. It was overshadowed, almost as soon as the delegates left the festivities at the Opera House, by Molotov's unexpected demand that the chairmanship of the conference itself should rotate rather than being exercised by the United States, as the hosts. At the steering committee on 26 April, so Vandenberg was led to believe, there was a sinister turn of events. 'Eden was *supposed* to move *one* Chairman and support Stettinius,' he noted. 'Instead, without any notice to our people, Eden moved for four Chairmen with Stettinius to be the presiding Chairman (a sort of compromise with the Russian view).' Worse, the ghost of the British Empire, with its automatic six votes, was seen flitting round the conference table: 'Smuts of South Africa and Fraser of New Zealand both supported the Eden compromise – to the shocked amazement of our people.'[13]

Averell Harriman had been brought from his Moscow embassy to assist at this conference, much as he had previously at Yalta. When he went to complain to the perfidious British, he found a different story about the chairmanship. His charge that they had 'let Ed. down' seemed to Cadogan at variance with what Stettinius himself had agreed with them – 'it had all been fixed with him beforehand.'[14] Harriman evidently accepted this. Back in the US Delegation, however, Vandenberg persisted in 'finding out whether Eden and the British had double-crossed us' and would not let go – 'If we can't count on *them* we'd better find it out.' Though the Senator acknowledged that 'Harriman was particularly insistent in the view that Eden acted in good faith and that it was all the result of a misunderstanding', he wanted to bring the matter to a head. 'I continue to believe,' he wrote in his diary, 'that *this* is the point at which to line up our votes (with a last chance for the British to prove good faith) and *win* and *end this appeasement of the Reds now before it is too late.*'[15]

In fact the main difficulty about the X-matter was the way it now became entangled with pan-American politics. This was the United Nations Conference on World Organization, and the United Nations, in the sense that Roosevelt had used that term, meant the anti-Nazi coalition. The test for the forty-six countries originally invited had been a declaration of war on Hitler. It was a test that some passed rather doubtfully, with comical belatedness, especially in South America; and

Argentina, whose regime neither Roosevelt nor Truman had wanted to be present, was not invited at all, though it refused to take no for an answer. Then came a linkage to the vote on the two extra Soviet republics. 'The Latin Americans will probably vote against,' Cadogan noted with surprise, 'unless Molotov agrees to the admission of Argentina! The regular old Geneva "marchandage".'[16] As a veteran of League of Nations politicking, he could recognize these games, with their bargaining chips and dominoes. The United States obviously wanted to keep on good terms with its southern neighbours; and though its support for the Argentinian proposal would serve to sharpen the question of why semi-fascist Argentina should be seated if the anti-fascist credentials of the Lublin Poles were rejected, at least Latin American support for the two extra Soviet votes would thereby be secured. It had the makings of a deal.

There were many dominoes that duly fell into place at San Francisco, day by day. Thus when Molotov accepted the chairmanship compromise, sensing his isolation, he simultaneously cleared the decks for the X-matter. 'Stettinius read Truman's letter agreeing to carry out FDR's tragically unfortunate pledge at Yalta,' Vandenberg observed on 27 April, now reconciled to the hard politics of these compromises, as he noted the assenting votes of the American and British delegates alike: 'A picture of Anglo-Saxon nations *keeping* faith – altho we all hated what we had to do.' Step by step, the old isolationist was subordinating his suspicion of the British Empire in favour of the necesssary unity of the English-speaking peoples. And then came the inevitable Soviet proposal to admit the Lublin Poles, with Stettinius now pleading that it would be bad faith to do so when the promises of Yalta remained unfulfilled, followed promptly by a supportive statement from the British Foreign Secretary. 'I forgive Eden for what happened yesterday,' Vandenberg wrote. 'He backed us up today magnificently.'[17]

What came out of this confrontation was an Anglo-American political rapprochement that left the British Foreign Office much relieved. Cadogan was left to do the backstairs business on Saturday, 28 April. 'Molotov said he wouldn't admit the Argentines unless we admitted his beastly sham Polish Government,' he recorded, 'Ed. and I flatly refused this, so we parted in a nice deadlock, which a new committee will try to resolve tomorrow morning.' Resumption of business on Monday brought no alleviation in the bestiality. 'Molotov being tiresome,' wrote

Cadogan, with distaste. 'We admitted his 2 beastly Republics, and he then opposed the admission of Argentina, arguing that if Argentina were admitted, his beastly Warsaw Poles shd. be admitted.'[18] But the point was that the Soviet Union was now isolated and could be heavily outvoted, given that the Latin American block vote had been squared. It was a piece of jobbery well done. 'The *net* of all this battle,' as Vandenberg put it, 'is that Molotov won only at those points where he had a commitment from the dead hands of FDR.'[19]

The conference finally declared that there were fifty United Nations – newly liberated Denmark was also added – but its proceedings showed them to be significantly disunited. The premise of Dumbarton Oaks had been agreement between the great powers. Roosevelt's vision was that the Big Three would act together under his personal influence, that China too would be brought in as one of four world policemen (and perhaps that France could again be accepted as a fifth great power). Thus the security council was to be the all-important executive forum, with an assembly of smaller powers intermittently summoned to applaud. This concept was broadly endorsed at Yalta. But though the Big Four kept meeting privately at San Francisco, the Soviet Union was now plainly bent on its own course and Chiang Kai-shek's rickety regime in China was only a client of the United States (and France, still with only a provisional government, was in limbo). Lacking unity, the supposed great powers lacked authority. The other forty-five exploited the situation, realizing that their votes needed to be courted rather than simply dragooned. As a result, the Assembly was inflated in its role at the expense of the Security Council, where the Russians had to fight hard to retain the veto power on which they insisted.

It was a sort of politics in which veterans of Capitol Hill, familiar with the techniques of horse-trading and log-rolling, had more relevant skills and experience than apparatchiks from the Kremlin, schooled in pleasing a single despot. But the Russians initially seemed receptive to the American approach. 'Molotov was in great good humour,' Vandenberg wrote after one evening session in Stettinius's penthouse. The Soviet foreign minister had now 'learned the American phrase "OK" and he used it with obvious amusement whenever he agreed to a proposal', which seemed encouraging.[20] To Attlee the good humour seemed only superficial. 'We used to sit there,' he recalled, 'and old Senator Vandenberg would say "Okay" and Molotov would say "Okay" and I would say "Okay" and everything would go as merrily as a marriage bell – until we came to something that mattered, or that the Russians thought did.'[21]

On 4 May, hard realities intruded on a drafting session on self-determination. Vandenberg had been congratulating himself that 'everything I want in respect to "justice" and "human rights" and "fundamental freedoms" is in.' But then, at about 5 o'clock, Eden was called to the phone in the penthouse, to be told that sixteen Polish political leaders, in Moscow to discuss broadening the provisional government, had been arrested. 'This is bad business,' Vandenberg admitted.[22]

This prompted a confrontation that evening. 'After dinner Ed. and Anthony sat Molotov down,' Cadogan recorded, 'and cross-examined him about the arrest by the Soviet Government of the Polish leaders – a perfectly disgraceful performance.' What was new was the official story that these men, whose whereabouts had already caused concern, were being treated as war criminals rather than as potential ministers in a broad-based government. 'There was some quite plain speaking,' Cadogan wrote, 'and Molotov looked more uncomfortable than I've seen him look before.'[23] Plainly this was no longer OK. But what could be done except – unthinkably – scupper the conference?

A week later, as Eden and Attlee prepared to leave San Francisco, the conference had already moved beyond the assumptions of wartime alliance with the Soviet Union and towards post-war realignment. The British Foreign Secretary was now 'a great guy' in the eyes of his unlikely admirer, Senator Vandenberg: 'I have come to have a deep affection and a profound respect for him. We have become great friends.'[24] As when Churchill and Roosevelt had become great friends, their instinct for mutually compatible aims fostered the warm personal feelings. Vandenberg's first steps in international diplomacy at San Francisco confirmed his own changed outlook. When he dwelt feelingly on the impact of one of his speeches in defence of the world organization, Stettinius pointed out that he had himself said much the same. 'But I am talking about *me*,' Vandenberg replied, 'because I am the old isolationist.'[25]

In Britain, early reports of the conference did not inspire confidence. 'The usual ball-up of major powers playing against each other' was how one young skilled worker put it to Mass-Observation. Obviously much remained confidential but the confrontations in formal sessions told their own story and Stettinius's regime ensured that there were few real secrets. Another artisan in his thirties was more specific in attributing blame. 'The Polish question is the biggest snag,' he said, 'and it can't reach a solution till Russia is prepared to do a bit of give and take.' Obviously attitudes towards the Soviet Union varied. Even those who wanted more co-operation were often pessimistic about achieving it. 'We're so far apart ideologically,' said a young working-class woman. 'Not that Russia has any cause to trust us.' Another woman, middle class and fifty, was more decisive: 'Unless we make some kind of a stand, we've got to agree with a Russian domination over the whole of Eastern Europe.' There was already a widespread feeling, as voiced by a middle-class man of forty, that confrontation had become inescapable: 'America and the United Kingdom are being pushed into each other's arms by Russia's suspicious attitude.'[26]

By the middle of May 1945, then, the United Nations already appeared largely as a theatre for continuing power politics by other means. In San Francisco the conference had lost its sense of urgency and expectancy. Stettinius continued to preside and important business still had to be settled, but the ground-rules had now been established in an incrementally slow negotiating process, obviously polarized by the Polish impasse. For Cadogan, now to be left minding the United Nations portfolio for the British Foreign Office, there was time to attend Attlee's farewell cocktail party (and to seize the opportunity for a little lobbying of the Saudi Arabians and the Turks). He thought the British delegation had got on well, given that they were drawn from different parties. 'Anthony leaves tomorrow,' he noted on 12 May. 'The P.M. has been consulting him as to the election, whether to have it now (i.e. end of June) or October.'[27] Great Britain was about to become another disunited nation.

News that the German forces in Italy, numbering nearly a million, had surrendered to Field Marshal Alexander, as Allied Supreme Commander in the Mediterranean, came through on the evening of 2 May. This had been expected almost hourly; Churchill had been frustrated that afternoon at having nothing to say to the Commons but returned at 7.30 p.m. with confirmation. Harold Nicolson, a great diner-out, was already at a dinner party at the Ritz when he heard. 'I feel quite ecstatic,' he wrote in his diary. 'It is almost incredible.'[28] But he had special reason to rejoice, with a son on the Italian front. To Chips Channon, who had stayed in the House and seen the Prime Minister return, 'flushed and pleased', the moment was almost an anti-climax: 'This was a tribute indeed to General Alexander, but most members were disappointed as they expected that his rather dramatic appearance meant the end of the war.'[29] Alan Brooke, likewise confessing himself 'completely unmoved' by the overnight announcement of Hitler's death, could not quite explain his lack of emotion – 'I think I have become so war weary with the continual strain of the war that my brain is numbed, and incapable of feeling intensely.'[30]

'DEATH OF THE GERMAN ARMY' was the *Evening Standard*'s banner headline on the streets of London the next afternoon. Montgomery had taken Hamburg without a fight. 'The rout of the *Wehrmacht* has assumed tremendous proportions in the face of the British advance,' reported its special correspondent. There were strong hints of more to come in the news summary: 'More big and sensational news is forecast from Montgomery's HQ.'

It was by now apparent that an overdue military surrender was imminent. Montgomery had authority to accept it on behalf of the Supreme Commander. Friday, 4 May, was set for the signature of the surrender document at the 21st Army Group's tactical headquarters at Lüneburg Heath, south-east of Hamburg, where Montgomery's caravan was now sited. Tension mounted at SHAEF in Rheims, where the Supreme Commander impatiently awaited a phone call from Lüneburg. 'Why don't you wait just another five minutes?' Kay Summersby implored her boss when he seemed impatient to leave at 6.55 p.m. The wait was rewarded; the call finally came through at 7 o'clock. Harry Butcher eavesdropped on the conversation. 'Fine. Fine,' he heard Ike say. 'That's fine, Monty.'[31] Perhaps the Supreme Commander's cordiality was enhanced not only by relief but by the thought that it was the last of his subordinate's high-profile engagements that he would have to sanction.

This was the famous hour of victory that everyone had been waiting for, not least in Fleet Street. The next day's *Daily Mirror* had a front-page photograph (in fact taken on 3 May) of Montgomery, in his usual beret and battledress, walking to meet the representatives of the *Wehrmacht* in their long military greatcoats and high-peaked caps.

TRIUMPH DAY FOR MONTY'S MEN:

ANOTHER MILLION IN GREATEST SURRENDER

'This is the moment, says Monty' was the down-column headline on the left side of the page, balanced on the right side by 'Germans stupid to fight on, says Ike.'

Photographs of Monty, seated in a military tent, reading the surrender document to the Germans, were widely published and established an abiding image of this as the real end of the war. The version in Montgomery's war memoirs helpfully annotates the presence of Chester Wilmot, watching intently. 'This was the decisive act,' Wilmot later explained, 'for within the area covered by this capitulation, the new Führer [meaning Dönitz] and the Supreme Command of the *Wehrmacht* had established their last headquarters in the border town of Flensburg.'[32] This served to legitimate the *Wehrmacht*'s wish to avoid surrendering to the Red Army. Thus it was Montgomery to whom the effective surrender of the Third Reich was made, and in the British sector at Lüneburg rather than on the Soviet front in Berlin, still less in the mythical national redoubt to the south, in the American sector. In fact, fighting still continued against the Red Army in Czechoslovakia.

Visiting Downing Street, even Brooke's blood was now stirred. He found the Prime Minister 'seriously affected by the fact that the war was to all intents and purposes over so far as Germany was concerned'. A tearful Churchill paid unaccustomed thanks to the chiefs of staff for all their efforts 'from El Alamein to where we are now'.[33] In this narrative, the turning-point in the Western Desert had eventuated in a German surrender, with pleasing symmetry, to the very British commander who had brought about their defeat (under Churchill's leadership, of course).

As with the German surrender in Italy, it was not official until accepted by the relevant Allied Supreme Commander. This necessary process, coming after the Lüneburg surrender had apparently settled the issue, was further denuded of theatrical impact by Eisenhower's own scrupulous behaviour. He was determined not to fall for any delaying ploys by the *Wehrmacht*, aimed at allowing the Germans to continue resistance against the Red Army and thus to breach Allied unity. Moreover, he deputed the actual signature of the documents to Bedell Smith as his chief of staff, whose own instinct to avoid publicity he shared. 'The damned war room looks like a Hollywood setting' was Ike's comment, or so Butcher heard, much to his consternation in trying to secure media coverage adequate to the event's importance.[34] In the end, his biggest headache was over a breach of the press embargo by Edward Kennedy of Associated Press, whose story ran in North American newspapers on 7 May, the same day that the surrender had been signed (at 2.41 a.m. British Double Summer Time). This too served to give the official confirmation of the news by Eisenhower a sense of anti-climax.

The ill-fated embargo was put in place mainly out of consideration for the Soviet Union. Once the Associated Press had the story in the United States, much to Butcher's chagrin, there was little that could be done to retrieve the situation. The news was officially confirmed in Britain on Monday evening and Tuesday, 8 May, was declared VE-Day. There was to be a second public holiday on Wednesday, which was the day observed by the Russians, who insisted that a further surrender ceremony be conducted in Berlin. This was legally unnecessary but psychologically imperative for the Red Army, which had actually conquered the city.

There was a good deal of press comment on the unsatisfactory way that the news had broken, with premature celebrations taking the edge off the long-anticipated joy of the occasion. But by 8 May the magnitude of the event spoke for itself. 'This has been the true crusade in which men of many nations have united to fight and overcome the power of evil, each according to its powers,' commented the *Manchester Guardian*. 'It has fallen to Russia to fight the greatest battles, to America to forge the weapons of victory, to Britain to maintain the the hope of the world in its darkest hour, and these three played the biggest parts in the final triumph.' Liberal not only in its own politics but in its even-handed praise of all the combatant Allies – not forgetting the Brazilians fighting in Italy – this famous newspaper took a magnanimous view which tried to put the British contribution into a fairly realistic perspective.

For every reader of the *Guardian*, however, there were fifty of the *Daily Mirror*, which had enjoyed a wartime boost of its circulation to over 4 million. The *Mirror* plainly touched a chord not only among its working-class readers at home but among British troops. Its VE-Day edition carried different messages. One was in its cartoon by Zec, showing a wounded soldier struggling through the débris with the laurel wreath of victory, saying: 'Here you are – don't lose it again.' Another kind of message was in the famous strip cartoon 'Jane', showing the adventures of a personable young woman in the forces, often caught with her clothing in mild disarray. The VE-Day instalment has often been celebrated for the fact that Jane was uniquely seen naked – but only after what looks to a modern eye like a mass asssault on her by soldiers pillaging her garments as souvenirs. 'You've said it, Jane!' says a grinning squaddy in the final frame. 'You've been demobbed already! Ha! Ha! – Joke! – Get it?' This was an age of innocence, not least about politically correct responses – an age far removed from our own assumptions, as we need to remember.

The main message of the *Daily Mirror* on 8 May was surely its double-page centrefold spread. 'A DIARY OF THE WAR' was the headline: 'being an account of the victorious emergence of the British Empire and its Allies from the black waves of Fascism with which Germany and Italy engulfed Europe and threatened the world for six years.' The summary of key dates admittedly includes inset photographs of the heads of Stalin and Eisenhower. Above them, twice as large, is that of Alexander, with the bold caption, 'beat them "hands up" Burma to Italy'. To the right, his face at least twice as big again, and wearing the trademark double-badge beret, is Montgomery – 'beat them from Egypt to Denmark'. The news in millions of working-class households was that – as the Beatles were to sing twenty years later – 'the English army had just won the war.'

VE-Day itself lived up to expectations. It was a good day to be in London. By mid-afternoon, the streets were packed with good-humoured crowds, civilians and armed forces alike, determined to fete the victory that they had long been promised. At 3 p.m. Churchill spoke from Downing Street, relayed by loudspeakers and by the BBC. 'It was a short, factual statement, arranged by a man of letters, though ending with a tinny sound,' wrote Lord Moran, who found its ending forced. 'Advance, Britannia,' Churchill concluded. 'Long live the cause of freedom. God Save the King.'[35] But it went down well enough, and the Prime Minister then struggled through the Whitehall crowds to repeat it in the Commons.

An expectant House was kept waiting for him. 'At last, Winston, smiling and bent appeared, and had a tremendous reception,' wrote Chips Channon. 'Everyone (except the recently elected cad for Chelmsford) rose and cheered and waved handerchiefs and Order Papers.'[36] The House then passed a motion, as it had in November 1918, to process to the parliamentary church of St Margaret's across the road for a service of thanksgiving. Churchill led the MPs through the dense crowds, accompanied – in Attlee's absence at San Francisco – by the Deputy

Leader of the Labour Party, Arthur Greenwood. It was an ecumenical and forgiving moment not only for the procession of elected Members but evidently for their constituents on the pavement. 'I had expected some jeers or tittering, since politicans are not popular and in the mass seem absurd,' wrote Nicolson. 'But not at all. Cheers were what we received, and adulation.'[37]

This mood was sustained throughout the rest of the day. Even Sir Alan Brooke was caught up in it when he went through the crowded streets from the War Office to Buckingham Palace for a joint meeting with the war cabinet and the chiefs of staff (whom he still thought inadequately recognized for their contribution to victory, of course). The King remembered to thank them, however, and Brooke later wrote about the Prime Minister in his diary with rare detachment and object-ivity. 'The difficulties with Winston have been of almost unbearable proportions, at times I have felt that I could not possibly face a single other day,' he admitted. 'And yet I would not have missed the last 3½ years of struggle and endeavour for anything on earth.'[38]

The crowds were still thick in the Mall and Whitehall. Churchill went onto the balcony of the Ministry of Health in response to calls for him to appear. 'This is your victory,' he told them – an irresistible cue for those who replied that it was his. Even after dinner, there was clamour for him to return, which he did at 10.30 p.m. in his one-piece, zip-up 'siren suit'. He reminded his compatriots that they were 'the first to draw the sword against tyranny'. He reminded them that they had endured alone for a whole year. 'There we stood, alone,' he declaimed. 'Did anyone want to give in?' Again the crowd assured him, no, of course not. That night, perhaps for the last time, he spoke for England. 'My dear friends, this is your hour,' he had reiterated. 'This is not a victory of a party or of any class. It's a victory of the great British nation as a whole.'[39]

All this might be true but it was hardly the whole truth. Partisan loyalties, increasingly poorly disguised or suppressed for several months, were both a cause and a result of the imminent end of the wartime Coalition. There was much talk, even before VE-Day and certainly immediately after it, of whether a General Election should be held in June or October. The sooner the better from Churchill's point of view, while his heroic status remained untarnished: or so it seemed both to Tories who quietly assumed that they could ride on his coat-tails, and to the Labour Party, which naturally preferred October. At any rate, Churchill knew perfectly well that since the Coalition's historic objective had now been achieved, the Labour Party had no mandate to participate further in his Government. Moreover, he himself had told the Commons the previous October that 'it would be wrong to continue this Parliament beyond the period of the German war.'[40]

Yet VE-Day came and went with the Coalition still in place. For one thing, both Attlee and Eden were away in San Francisco, where the British had taken the bar on the nineteenth floor of the Mark Hopkins Hotel, with its magnificent views over the city, for a celebration that was somewhat inhibited by a city ban on alcohol for twenty-four hours. Attlee was leader of the second party in the Coalition, Eden the second-in-command (and heir-in-waiting) of the majority party. Until their return nothing could be settled; and this in itself helped to rule out a snap election on the Lloyd George model. In 1918 the General Election had been announced post-haste, only three days after the Armistice, with polling day a month later, endorsing a 'coupon' for the man who won the war. This had made sense for a Prime Minister without a party, though also with cross-party support, making him a coalition leader *faute de mieux*, with no other real option. The position in 1945, though superficially similar, was crucially different.

Winston Churchill, seventy years old, five years into his premiership on 10 May, and leader of the Conservative Party for over four, seemed temporarily baffled about his next step. Sawyers the butler was to lament to a concerned Lord Moran: 'He's keeping dreadful hours, sir, these days.'[41] With a sudden release of much of the tension upon him, Churchill was understandably suffering some reaction, with exhaustion compounded by late nights. 'He sounded very tired,' observed Hugh Dalton when he heard the prime ministerial broadcast on 13 May.[42] The next day's cabinet revealed similar signs, 'with Winston in one of his worst moods', Brooke noted. 'Kept rambling on and on and failed to arrive at any conclusions.'[43] Amery's judgement was similar – 'Winston more rambling than ever' – as he watched his own party leader fail once more to get to the Indian business before them.[44] These were seasoned critics, but even to the tolerant Jock Colville things seemed bad that day: 'The PM looks tired and has to fight for the energy to deal with the problems confronting him.' Churchill went to bed leaving piles of government papers unattended, telling Colville 'that he doubted if he had the strength to carry on'.[45]

Clement Attlee's return on 16 May brought the election question to a head. It had already been arranged for the Labour Party Conference to convene at Blackpool five days later. On the afternoon of 17 May, he told Dalton that the Prime Minister seemed undecided but that 'the Tory pressure on him for a quick election was very strong.'[46] When Attlee was later summoned to a midnight meeting with Churchill, however, he found a new proposal: to go on to the end of the Japanese war. Churchill had long contemplated this as a possibility. But the duration of hostilities was currently estimated at up to eighteen months; the current Parliament, already ten years old, would expire in October; and a 'coupon' or blank cheque election was already ruled out; so the status quo was not an option. Churchill therefore offered a referendum to prolong the Parliament, or failing that, a July election, but definitely not October.

Attlee was himself ready to commend the proposal for a continuing war coalition. Indeed he secured an insertion in Churchill's formal letter to himself about it, committing such a coalition not only to the defeat of Japan but also to implementation of post-war schemes for social security and full employment, obvious Labour priorities. 'Attlee was in favour of going on,' Dalton noted on Friday, 18 May. 'Bevin and I were inclined to agree. But we doubted whether the Conference would take it.'[47] All three left for Blackpool that weekend, prior to the conference's official opening on Monday.

There was a real dilemma here for Labour ministers, well aware that vital national problems remained after VE-Day. On 12 May, Churchill had sent a telegram to Truman outlining reasons for continuing apprehension about the Russians. 'An iron curtain is drawn down upon their front,' he wrote. 'We do not know what is going on behind.'[48] Not only did he put a famous phrase into circulation (at first privately): he took steps to see if words could be matched with action, secretly ordering the military planners to examine Operation Unthinkable. This examined how British and American forces might be mobilized against the Soviet Union, which Churchill saw as a last chance of securing justice for Poland. The plan was ready by 22 May. The following day Brooke noted that 'Winston insists on retaining that portion of the Russian zone which we have been able to occupy in our advance as a bargaining counter with the Russians.' The CIGS personally dismissed this as 'fundamentally wrong', as between Allies whose joint actions had conquered Germany. 'But this is a political matter,' he concluded, 'and politics are as crooked as rams' horns!'[49]

The CIGS was absorbed with his own tasks, the most immediate of which over the next couple of days was to examine Operation Unthinkable as instructed. 'The idea is of course fantastic and the chances of success quite impossible,' he concluded. 'There is no doubt that from now onwards Russia is all powerful in Europe.' These were profoundly secret and important matters that he confided to his own diary, and did so with only the most fleeting reference to the ram's-horn political crisis that had meanwhile grabbed his master's attention: 'For the present he is absorbed in this mad election and for the next few months he will be unable to devote much attention to war plans!'[50]

Rather than a mad election eclipsing the war plan, however, it might surely have been the other way around, had Churchill been serious about the equally mad war plan. Had it been seriously contemplated or justified, an approach to Attlee and Bevin, Churchill's invaluable supporters over Greece, might have been his trump card for continuing the Coalition – but again, only had they been more open to persuasion than Field Marshal Sir Alan Brooke about the plan's military merits, let alone its acceptability to the Labour Party. The fact is that Operation Unthinkable would have demanded a degree of political assent from both the United States and from his Coalition partners that Churchill could no longer command. Little wonder that it lapsed with the demise of the Coalition.

Moreover, as Churchill fully realized that crucial weekend, it was not his Coalition colleagues whom he needed to win over for prolongation of coalition, so much as the ordinary members of the Labour Party, now assembling at Blackpool. 'But they wouldn't look at it,' he later told Moran. 'Boiling with hate.'[51] Boiling with a kind of accumulated political frustration that Blackpool decisively vented, perhaps. The party was impatient to debate its manifesto, *Let Us Face the Future*, with bold commitments in social policy that cynics dismissed as New Jerusalem or Brave New World. Though Attlee had put the case for continuing the Coalition to the party's National Executive, he found virtually no support. After a private session, the conference was reported to have rejected the Coalition plan by 1100 votes to 2. It was turned down as a Tory dodge, tainted with Beaverbrook's influence, rather than as a personal reflection on Churchill. 'It is clear,' Dalton had written, 'that the Old Boy has been hustled along by Max and Bracken and by the Tory Head Office.'[52]

The leaders of the two main parties in the Coalition were soon at loggerheads. Harold Macmillan was thrilled to have a ringside seat, staying at Chequers over the long Whit weekend, with Churchill and his son Randolph. 'Winston was hurt at the unnecessarily waspish and even offensive tone of Attlee's reply,' Macmillan noted when it arrived over dinner on 21 May.[53]

Stung, the Prime Minister started buzzing himself. 'At once all was swept aside and electioneering became the only topic, while the PM, Macmillan and Randolph all tried their hands at drafting a reply to Attlee,' Colville observed. With the successive exchanges of letters, released to the media on that and the following day, the Coalition's fate was sealed. 'So tomorrow the PM resigns,' wrote Colville on 22 May, 'and the Government which has won the war is at an end.' Churchill went to Buckingham Place the following morning to tender his formal resignation and was promptly invited to form a new Government until the General Election could be held on 5 July. He thus became the head of a Conservative Government and, like the Leader of the Labour Party, bowed to the pressures from his own party whatever his personal inclinations. His war record was inevitably conscripted for partisan ends, as in his final letter to Attlee. 'Lord Beaverbrook persuaded him to leave out the last paragraph,' Colville observed, 'which had contained generous references to the help of his late Labour colleagues.'[54]

Yet Churchill evidently still thought his appeal as a national leader would see him through. 'There's pretty universal gratitude to you,' Moran advised him, 'and there's a notion about that you aren't very keen on this brave-new-world business.' Churchill replied: 'The desire for a new world is nothing like universal; the gratitude is.'[55] His hypothesis could only be tested by how the electorate responded: whether still in thrall to their great war leader or now preoccupied with post-war problems.

For five years, the media had flourished on hot war news. With the end of the European war, things were different. 'I don't bother reading the news since VE-Day,' a young working-class woman told Mass-Observation. 'I'm fed up.' More than half of the respondents likewise claimed to have stopped reading the papers – 'They've got very dull and

I can't be bothered with them,' said one young artisan.[56] Yet buoyant circulation figures suggest that the newspaper habit persisted strongly into the post-war period. The *Daily Mirror* is the prime example of unprecedented wartime penetration into strata of British society which had been simply unfamilar with national newspapers on a daily basis (rather than just on Sundays). Its undisguised sympathy for the Labour Party was paralleled by the Tory allegiance of its main rival in circulation, Beaverbrook's *Daily Express*. Admittedly, each had at times riled the Churchill Government: the *Mirror* for its populist voicing of grievances, in Zec's cartoons as much as editorially, and the *Express* for its campaign in favour of an early Second Front. But both newspapers had vigorously supported the war effort, exploiting a degree of independence to sustain a broad consensus that could not be dismissed as simply propaganda.

This consensus did not suddenly end on VE-Day. On many international issues it prevailed, especially among rival party leaders who – uniquely in this election – shared a recent experience of ministerial office. The real 'opposition' was not the Labour front bench but the delegates at Blackpool who had heard their Leader, fresh from San Francisco, trying to educate his party. 'It is just as well to remember that all who shout for democracy are not democrats,' Attlee told the conference, in his non-polemical vein, 'and that both on the Right and on the Left in some of these countries are people who seek to enforce the will of the minority on the majority by force.'[57] Obviously he had Poland on his mind – and perhaps on his conscience, as had Churchill. But the expiring Coalition Government, still less the prospective Conservative Government, was in no position to do much about it.

The last days of the Coalition saw another major issue sidelined, at least until after the General Election. With VE-Day, Stage II of Lend-Lease began. Agreement on this had already been reached, of course, following the Quebec conference; though the inexperience of President Truman again showed when he unquestioningly signed orders for an immediate cutback of supplies that even saw the recall of ships at sea. Roosevelt's abhorrence of writing anything down had been intended to make the Allies reliant on his goodwill; but the goodwill died with him. The effect on the British, the largest beneficiary of Lend-Lease, was actually most telling. 'I don't want to give them everything they ask for,' Truman told Morgenthau, who replied: 'I never have; in fact they have complained about it.'[58] Such complaints were silent, or at least went unheard, whereas the impact on the Soviet Union was most conspicuous at the time. On 14 May *The Times* reported that all supplies to Russia had been suspended. 'This is because Russia is no longer at war,' it explained, with deceptive simplicity. True, VE-Day implied this – since Stalin had not yet fulfilled his Yalta pledge to enter the Japanese war – just as VJ-Day would imply the equally sudden cessation of supplies to Great Britain. But this further implication seems to have been ignored subsequently by the British themselves.

As it turned out, Lend-Lease was actually to be restored to the Soviet Union at the end of June. Stalin's belated declaration of war on Japan, as Truman knew, was forthcoming and supplies related to the Pacific war were therefore sanctioned. Great Britain, of course, was in a different position as a belligerent ally of the United States, thus assuring continued military supplies. But the test was now that each Lend-Lease consignment should be specifically relevant to British fighting capacity in the Pacific, rather than to the more general needs of an ally, the spirit of Quebec notwithstanding. Stage II was thus less beneficial in practice to the United Kingdom than Keynes had expected.

The real problem, however, was Stage III. It would inevitably be triggered by VJ-Day just as Stage II had been triggered by VE-Day. That left another eighteen months to sort out a huge problem of transition from war to peace – or so everyone assumed. Even on this timetable, Keynes was worried, with his extensive experience of the rigours of Anglo-American financial negotiations, that time might be short. He had prepared his paper on the topic, 'Overseas Financial Policy in Stage III', in March. After much discussion by Treasury colleagues, it was ready for presentation to the war cabinet on 15 May.

This was a week after VE-Day, so the timing seemed excellent. But it was also the eve of Attlee's return from San Francisco, which led, day by day, to the end of the Coalition Government a week later. The Coalition could, in principle, have formulated an agreed policy on overseas financial policy, just as it had on Keynes's ideas for sustaining high employment at home in 1944. Conversely, whichever party formed the government when Japan surrendered and Stage II thus ended would necessarily require a policy for Stage III. But the end of the Coalition paralysed decision-making since Churchill's new 'caretaker' Government, as the press dubbed it, was only a holding operation.

Keynes thus found serious consideration of his proposals postponed until after the General Election. They became another 'unthinkable' scenario, or at least little thought was given. Week by week, the problem loomed nearer but no solution was discussed by the British cabinet, still less with the Americans. Six weeks into Stage II, with doubts now arising about the duration of Japanese resistance and hence about the date of VJ-Day, Keynes warned the Treasury: 'If the end catches us without our having made any serious progress with Stage III finance, it will be awkward.'[59]

Keynes's paper 'Overseas Financial Policy in Stage III' had not dated at all well since its composition in March. In particular, there had been a strong unspoken assumption that the political clout and creativity of President Roosevelt would serve to make a radical assault on the economic problem politically feasible. Even in early April, as R. H. Brand, the Treasury's Washington representative, well realized, there was reason for caution. 'The President is immensely overburdened,' he had warned Keynes, 'and he is ill.' Writing two weeks after Roosevelt's death, he acknowledged that Truman's inexperience and background would enhance the role of Congress. 'It would have been important even with the old President,' he told Keynes. 'It is likely to be much more important now.'[60]

The reams of good advice that Keynes received from his old friend Bob Brand provoked elaborate answers and useful technical amendments, but no real change in the thrust of his Stage III paper, which remained the same in May as two months previously. It was an eloquent plea, cogent too, provided one accepted its fundamentally moral premises about the war.

The need for post-war economic assistance from the United States appeared an inescapable conclusion of Keynes's logic. Great Britain had waged war to the limit of its capacity, but had minimized external borrowing (unless Lend-Lease were to be thought of as a repayable loan, of course). Britain's liabilities had thus been limited, but were still frightening. At the end of 1944 they totalled £3 billion (or $12 billion at the prevailing exchange rate), of which much the biggest item consisted of the 'sterling balances' that were owed to the Dominions and to India. Keynes projected that by the end of the Japanese war these balances themselves might total £3 billion – and no less than half of this sum was owed to India.[61]

Or was it? Readers of Churchill's war memoirs would hardly think so. 'No great portion of the world population was so effectively protected from the horrors and perils of the World War as were the peoples of Hindustan,' he wrote. Financially, he claimed, supplies needed for the defence of India had been charged by zealous British officials of the Raj to Great Britain itself, provoking his response that 'we reserved the right to set off against this so-called debt a counter-claim for the defence of India.'[62]

Whether India would have needed defending at such expense from Japanese attack but for the fact that it was a part of the British Empire was, of course, another matter. Indeed the problem went further back. In 1939 it had been agreed that India would only be responsible for its own immediate defence costs and that the British Government would be charged for Indian troops used outside India. And since Burma had been separated from the Raj in 1935, this meant that the burgeoning costs of the Burma campaign fell mainly on Britain, thus running up the sterling balances that measured what Britain owed. Admittedly, the Indian Army came cheap at the price – obviously cheaper than equipping an equivalent number of British troops. Keynes tried to put the Indian costs into perspective by showing that, over three years, they amounted to less than half of overseas military expenditure. Still, the total was obviously beyond Britain's current capacity to repay, even if it wished to do so.

It thus emerged that the British Empire did not pay for itself. Though many critics of imperialism assumed that it must constitute a great economic resource which Britain unfairly exploited, Keynes's examination of defence costs during this great imperialist war suggested the opposite. With a single exception – 'Canada is doing her full duty' – the other constituent parts of the Empire and Commonwealth had profited from the war at British expense. 'In 1944 Australia made a net overseas profit out of the war of £94 million,' Keynes asserted, as one example. Liabilities had been accumulated during the war under arrangements that now needed radical restructuring since 'this small country is carrying a burden of Imperial Defence which she cannot continue to carry by herself.' Hence the foundation for Churchill's later claim about the Indians: 'They were carried through the struggle on the shoulders of our small Island.'[63]

If the sterling balances represented the deadweight costs of victory, there was also an ongoing cost to be borne: that of adjustment to a peacetime equilibrium. The war economy, dependent on Lend-Lease to cover its external deficit, had to be replaced by sufficient British exports to balance the books. And while this was happening, Keynes estimated, an accumulated balance of payments deficit of up to $8 billion was likely, even on the assumption of a long Stage II to begin this process. He pointed, then, to the stark alternatives that would herald the arrival of peace in Stage III. Could Britain perhaps go it alone, as in 1940? This option Keynes called Starvation Corner, with the necessity of intensifying the existing policies of austerity, Soviet-style, and planning foreign trade on a bilateral basis (especially in the sterling area and the Empire). Obviously this would involve repudiating plans for multilateral trade, on the Bretton Woods scenario, as favoured by the United Sates and Canada.

An alternative, which Keynes called Temptation, was to seek as many dollars as the Americans were ready to lend, on such terms as they stipulated. Perhaps they would lend as much as $8 billion, simply as a business proposition. 'It is interesting to note that the total war burden we should be carrying,' Keynes observed, adding this figure to the $12 billion already owing (in sterling balances chiefly), gave a total of 'exactly the same figure, namely $20 billion, that the Russians think appropriate in the case of Germany' – that is, the total demanded at Yalta. It would be the difference between the war reparations exacted under coercion from a vanquished nation by one superpower and those due under contract from a victorious nation to the other superpower (and to its own Empire). Keynes dismissed such an outcome as 'an outrageous crown and conclusion to all that has happened'.

Inventive as ever, Keynes produced a third alternative – 'which I shall venture to call Justice' – that ought to govern the post-war reckoning. 'For a hundred good reasons,' he argued, 'we have had to accept during the war a post-war financial burden entirely disproportionate to what is fair.'[64] Only action by the United States and Canada could put this right, and thus put Britain in a position to work with them in making a success of a multilateral international economy. By offsetting the deadweight costs of 1940 in 1945 dollars, the temporary gap in the British balance of payments could be closed and the transition to peace made possible. This ought to be good business for everyone concerned; but the way that the case was put all too plainly involved more than business considerations.

Keynes was, in short, mounting the familiar British exercise of cashing in on the Finest Hour. 'What you propose that the United States should do for us may well be Justice on the assumption that she *ought* to have come into the war when we did,' Brand had cautioned from Washington. 'But that will never be a popular argument here or one that it is desirable to stress or one that we can carry without provoking serious reactions.' Perceptions were simply so different. He quoted one American official concerned with Lend-Lease and Mutual Aid: 'All Americans knew that they had saved the United Kingdom from absolute destruction, whereas the opposite was not the truth, and this made the two cases not in the least comparable.' Brand drew the conclusion, at least as a matter of tactics: 'The American political leaders might well put a scheme forward before their own people as an act of Justice to us, but we could not do so, however true it might be.'[65]

Excellent advice all, and delivered with authority from Washington, where the real decisions would be made. But Keynes was not really listening. On 16 May, the day after his paper went to the war cabinet, the Canadian delegation that had been promised in February arrived to talk about their ideas about a possible post-war loan to Britain. Keynes took them to Cambridge over the Whit weekend and opened amicable discussions. He was in top form, on his home ground. After dinner one evening in King's College, they all walked to the sylvan banks of the Cam, past the meadow where cattle grazed in an evocation of English pastoral, to the Fellows' garden. One of the Canadians remarked on the beauty of the scene. 'Yes, it is beautiful, isn't it?' Keynes responded. 'And we want to keep it, you know. That is why you are here!'[66]

This was the same weekend that saw the unravelling of the Coalition, which in turn stalled decisions on Keynes's Stage III proposals. But discussions continued in the Treasury, where one young official, R. W. B. ('Otto') Clarke, was undeterred by his awe of the great Lord Keynes from taking a critical stance. The proposed treatment of the sterling balances struck Clarke as fundamentally flawed. With a flourish of the pen, Keynes had suggested that in the cases of India, Egypt, Palestine and Iraq, 'we should be entitled to write down their balances by at least a third', because of inflated exchange rates.[67] For India alone this would mean sacrificing £500 million or $2 billion – a contribution towards British solvency of a quarter of the amount to be asked from the United States itself. Clarke simply cited Sir Archibald Rowlands, the recently appointed Finance Member of the Viceroy's Executive Council: 'Rowlands advises that we would be unwise to talk about justice to the Indians because we shall never get past that point.'[68]

Rowlands knew what he was talking about. The son of a Welsh grocer, a scholarship boy at Oxford, a high-flying civil servant on secondment in India, he was alert to the tides of Indian nationalism and a firm supporter of Wavell's reform agenda. 'British Government officials in India,' Churchill might complain, 'were wont to consider it a point of honour to champion the particular interests of India against those of Great Britain whenever a divergence occurred.'[69] So long as he was responsible for Indian finances, Rowlands would act accordingly. The Viceroy too saw his duty in similar terms, having told the Chancellor of the Exchequer in April that 'a statement about the balances, i.e. that we would not repudiate them, and an early discussion with Indian representatives were desirable.'[70]

'The Wavells have now been here for over six weeks,' Chips Channon had noted on 2 May. 'Will they never return?' He enjoyed meeting them socially, especially Lady Wavell, whom he found 'enchanting – amusing and provocative'.[71] The Viceroy was another matter: as widely admired as both a scholar and a soldier as he was manifestly and proudly lacking in the skills of a politician. Yet the paradox of his position was that he was trying to broker a political solution and succeeded (in London at least) for highly political reasons.

The fact that the Government had only accepted the Viceroy's visit under duress was thrown back in his face whenever he complained at the lack of attention he received. He was then told that he should have waited until June; but he himself was acutely aware that by then the moment might have been lost. 'Talk with Archie,' wrote Amery in early May, 'very cross with having to wait till next week for any decision and at the general lack of courtesy with which he has been treated.'[72] The fact that VE-Day saw him still in London initially seemed an unmitigated blow to Wavell: 'Peace in Europe is very welcome but has come too soon for my plans in India, or rather HMG has been so slow that the opportunity has been missed.'[73]

The belated mitigation for Wavell, however, was that the consequent end of the Coalition unexpectedly strengthened his own political clout. 'He has been blundering and a bore to both Winston and the Cabinet,' Channon had concluded shortly before VE-Day. 'I am sorry for him but he is in real jeopardy.' Week by week, however, and lunch by lunch, it dawned on Chips that his old friend Archie, despite thinking that 'the PM has treated him shabbily', had actually been put in a strong position by the course of events. 'Were he to resign now, on the eve of an election,' Channon reflected on 16 May, 'Winston would be embarrassed.'[74] The immediate effect of the change of government was the loss of sympathetic Labour ministers, notably Cripps and Attlee but also Bevin; yet the possibility of India becoming an election issue was obviously something that Churchill now wanted to avoid. This was the new factor which gratuitously gave Wavell a hold over the Conservative Government, and his own stoked-up wrath made him ready to use it.

It was the day after the Coalition ended that Wavell's diary first noted signs of change. 'A long day but some movement at last or hope of movement,' he wrote on 24 May. 'I began the day by writing to the PM to point out that I had been 8 weeks at home, that I had had nothing from India Committee for 4 weeks or from himself for 7 weeks, and asking for a decision.'[75] Leo Amery was shown his 'very aggrieved and rather truculent letter to Winston' and persuaded him to tone it down. What Wavell needed to understand was how to channel his anger in the new political situation. Amery was reappointed as Secretary of State for India the next day, noting without surprise Churchill's quixotic and inconsequential attitude: 'He added that I was the only person who could handle it, though he also went on to say, apropos of the statement which he agrees should be made in order to keep India out of the election, that he thinks it all wrong.'[76]

Churchill, however, could no longer have it both ways. If he wanted to sanitize Indian policy for electoral purposes, he had to accept terms agreeable to Amery and Wavell.

At the first meeting of the new cabinet on 30 May, Amery was gratified to find India, for once, taken as the first subject. Moreover, he found that the Prime Minister, despite his usual ignorance and unfamiliarity with the papers, 'was in amiable mood and agreed that it was worth while keeping India out of party politics'. Only on reflection that afternoon did the price strike Churchill as too high. 'Presently he rang up,' Amery noted, 'and told me that his conscience smote him at the idea of doing the wrong thing about India merely in order to avoid party trouble.' Dismissing this as nonsense, Amery discussed the situation with the Viceroy, whom he now found resolute. 'I said that PM could not expect me to return to India empty-handed,' Wavell recorded, 'and that surely it would be unfortunate if from an electioneering point of view India came into party politics, which could hardly be avoided if I was turned down since Attlee, Cripps and Bevin all knew of the proposals.'[77] This was one barrel of the gun, and one with repercussions. Amery supplied a second barrel by agreeing that if Wavell went, he would have to resign too.

Although the Prime Minister remained obdurate when the cabinet reconvened that evening, his position was now untenable. He faced the prospect not only of the Viceroy's resignation but also that of his Secretary of State for India – and with full knowledge of the reasons inevitably in the hands of Attlee, Cripps and Bevin during an election campaign. It was exactly what Churchill had tried to avoid. He had to agree that the Viceroy should have his chance to address the cabinet personally the next day.

Wavell prepared carefully for the vital meeting on 31 May. 'Cabinet began with a long polemical statement by PM against my proposals,' he noted afterwards. But he himself had made a good impression, ready for once to engage Churchill in discussion, face to face. An adjournment while the India Committte tinkered with the drafting allowed time for further reflection before the cabinet was again summoned late that evening.

'The climax of my visit was an extraordinary one,' Wavell wrote. 'At the meeting of the Cabinet at 10.30 p.m. the PM made just as forcible an address in favour of my proposals as he had made in their damnation this morning.' The manner of the proceedings seemed to him quite bizarre but the basic reason not hard to find: that 'with the Election looming up he could not possibly risk India becoming a party issue, and decided to give way with a good grace. What an extraordinary man he is!'[78]

If Amery, equally relieved at getting what they both wanted at long last, was less amazed, it was because he drew on longer experience of these performances. 'As sometimes happens,' he commented, 'after beginning with unreasoning opposition and refusal even to realise what is intended, all that is said has a way of sinking in subcutaneously and eventually comes out as his own. The whole Wavell scheme was then warmly expounded by him as his own inception.'[79] A proposed conference of Indian political leaders was duly sanctioned. The Viceroy was thus free the next morning to settle his very large bill at the Dorchester Hotel – offset against the Indian sterling balance presumably – and to depart from Victoria Station, en route to Delhi.

10

Peace, Politics and Potsdam

June–July 1945

*'I regret our domestic situation has caused delay in the Conference. We are
willing to sit as long as necessary.'*

Attlee at Potsdam, 28 July 1945

The end of the European war presumably entailed a European peace
treaty. Everyone agreed on that. The First World War had led to the
Paris conference, which spawned a series of peace treaties, the most
important being that signed at Versailles. In one sense, nobody wanted
a repetition of Versailles, which currently enjoyed a very bad press; it
was blamed for betraying the hopes of the heroic Allied soldiers, for
imposing an unworkable system of reparations, for creating a League
of Nations that was crippled by lack of American participation, and
ultimately for failing to keep the peace. Roosevelt and Churchill, both
in subordinate office at the time of Versailles, had shown themselves
determined not to make the same mistakes again; likewise the men to
become their successors, Truman and Attlee, who had both served in
the trenches as junior officers. Yet they all expected another Versailles,
in the sense of a final peace treaty legally ending the war. As it turned
out, though such a treaty was eventually to be signed (and again in Paris)
this did not eventuate until November 1990, and all that happened in
1945 was a final meeting of the Big Three in an outer suburb of the
capital of their defeated enemy, and with only one of the leaders who
had attended the conference at Yalta still present for the conclusion of
that held at Potsdam.

It was Churchill who had begun pressing for the Big Three to meet
from the moment that the German surrender was in the bag. He was
worried about the 'iron curtain' and, if Operation Unthinkable remained just that, still reluctant to surrender control of those parts of the

assigned Soviet zone currently occupied by British trooops. As a potential bargaining counter against Stalin, this had to be played soon or not
at all.

Truman, still feeling his way, was less anxious for haste. There was a
widespread American view, not only in the press but also within the
administration, that the British were using the current difficulties in
Poland to drive a wedge between the United States and the Soviet Union.
Isaiah Berlin reported from Washington: 'The myth of Mr Roosevelt as
a great and wise mediator between the powerful figures of Mr Churchill
and Marshal Stalin, whose policies might otherwise have come into
open collision seems to be deeply embedded in the popular consciousness
of the American people.'[1] Nobody had been more closely identified
with FDR's foreign policy than Harry Hopkins, who now told James
Forrestal that 'it was of vital importance that we be not manoeuvred
into a position where Great Britain had us lined up with them as a bloc
against Russia to implement England's European policy.'[2]

The suspicion died hard, even among his American friends, that
Churchill would use any ploy to prop up the power of the British Empire.
In such matters Truman was Roosevelt's successor in more than name
(and initially relied on many of the same advisers, of course, from the
quizzically Anglophile Hopkins to the frankly Anglophobe Admiral
Leahy). In a re-run of Roosevelt's manoeuvres before Yalta, the new
President played for time and in particular resisted the suggestion that
he might visit Great Britain first, using the well-worn argument that no
impression of 'ganging up' on Stalin should be given in advance.

Truman wanted to be assured of a successful conclusion to the San
Francisco conference before the Big Three met. He wanted this in itself
but also because it would free him of his obligations to Stettinius, and
thus allow him to take James Byrnes instead as his new Secretary of
State to the projected summit meeting.

In parallel moves in late May, Truman sent two personal representatives to talk to Stalin and to Churchill respectively. For Moscow, the
choice was deft: Hopkins, despite frail health, was persuaded to pick up
the threads with Stalin, trading on the residual amity of Yalta to try to
resolve outstanding difficulties. In their talks (again fully recorded by
Chip Bohlen) Stalin blamed any Polish difficulties on the conveniently
absent British – 'he was speaking only of England and said that the
British conservatives did not desire to see a Poland friendly to the Soviet

Union.' When Harriman, also present as US ambassador, took the opportunity to assert that 'it was obviously desirable that the United States and the Soviet Union should talk alone', Stalin agreed that this was 'correct and very much to the point'. One assertion that Stalin repeatedly made to Hopkins – along with suggestions that Hitler was still alive – was that 'he did not intend to have the British manage the affairs of Poland.'[3]

Nor were they given any chance to do so. A renegotiation of the Yalta stipulations about the future government of Poland, affecting its composition, was completed without British assistance. And the fate of the sixteen Polish prisoners? 'I am doing everything under heaven to get these people out of jug' were Hopkins's soothing words to Churchill.[4] But the real message, that the prisoners' fate was a side issue, was one accepted by Britons and Americans alike. After Hopkins's departure, Stalin put the sixteen through a brisk show trial; some were condemned simply for using radios to communicate with London, where *The Times* on 22 June nonetheless hailed the sentences as an example of Soviet forbearance. The new agreement offered the London Poles minority representation in a provisional government, which they were induced to accept. 'How right you were to take the momentous decision you took in my room,' Churchill later assured a doubtful Mikolajczyk.[5] The Prime Minister himself, however, had only assented to it as a done deal that was better than deadlock. In a notably gloomy disquisition to the cabinet on 11 June he concluded that 'never in his life had he been more worried by the European situation than he was at present.'[6] His own marginal role in this essentially bilateral settlement on Poland starkly demonstrated his position as a charter member of the Big Three whose subscription had lapsed.

The eclipse of Great Britain's great-power status was signalled by Truman's rebarbative choice of his emissary to England. Joseph Davies had been American ambassador to the Soviet Union, of which he had formed a benignly favourable impression. His wife was a major contributor to the Democratic Party. Joe Davies was the sort of regular party loyalist with whom Truman felt comfortable. But he was not held in any esteem in London, where the best Alec Cadogan could say of him on one occasion was: 'J.D. didn't give himself away and said nothing startlingly stupid.'[7] At any rate, Davies was hardly the ideal person to break the news to Churchill that the American President proposed to meet the Russian leader – and that perhaps the British Prime Minister might care to join the two of them at some later point.

This, at any rate, was the proposal as Churchill understood it in the course of an after-dinner discussion on 26 May that lasted deep into the night at Chequers. He later summarized the position in a minute which he obviously intended for the President's benefit. 'It must be remembered that Britain and the United States are united at this time upon the same ideologies, namely, freedom, and the principles set out in the American Constitution and humbly reproduced with modern variations in the Atlantic Charter,' Churchill wrote, explaining his refusal 'to accept the idea that the position of the United States is that Britain and Soviet Russia are just two foreign Powers, six of one and half a dozen of the other, with whom the troubles of the late war have to be adjusted'. Specifically, he made clear his refusal to attend any such meeting except as a full participant, adding with aggrieved formality: 'The Prime Minister does not see that there is any need to raise an issue so wounding to Britain, to the British Empire and Commonwealth of Nations.'[8]

Far from falling about in confusion or embarrassment, Joe Davies was not impressed, least of all by the Prime Minister's anti-Soviet rhetoric. As he put it in his own report for the President, Churchill 'was now express-ing the doctrine which Hitler and Goebbels had been proclaiming and reiterating for the past four years in an effort to break up allied unity and "Divide and Conquer" '.[9]

Truman clearly did not find, in the reports from either of his chosen emissaries, any encouragement for giving the British a central role. But the concept of the Big Three unexpectedly received artificial resuscitation from Moscow, perhaps because Soviet diplomacy was accustomed to proceed like a very slow tram following a very old schedule along very familiar tramlines. On 27 May an invitation arrived from Moscow for a Big Three meeting. So at least the Russians recognized Britain's right to attend. Churchill thus found himself rescued by an independent initiative from Stalin, launched just before the latter's talks had begun with Hopkins. The Russian motivation was that this proposed meeting of the Allies was to be held in the Berlin area, in territory currently occupied by the Soviet Union, thus focusing the attention of the world on the Red Army's liberating role. After waiting for Davies to report back to him in person, Truman acquiesced.

The planned meeting of the Big Three thus had something for everyone. Churchill, despite a nasty moment along the way, was relieved to be invited at all. Stalin succeeded in making himself host in all but name. Truman was content that his wishes were respected in deferring the summit until 15 July. He had his own reasons for this choice of date. By then, as it turned out, all British and American troops had withdrawn within their own zones of occupation, thus allowing the Russians, as Churchill later put it in his 1946 Fulton speech, 'to occupy this vast expanse of territory which the Western democracies had conquered'.[10]

But sticking to the assignment of zones, as agreed at Yalta, cut both ways. For it needs to be remembered that the Western democracies were meanwhile allowed to occupy their assigned three sectors of Berlin, which the Red Army had conquered. It was made clear to Eisenhower, when he negotiated with his Russian opposite number, Marshal Zhukov, that the status of Berlin and the Allied control commission would not be settled until and unless the British and US forces withdrew from the Russian zone. Neither Eisenhower nor his own commander-in-chief (Truman) nor any senior presidential advisers saw any point in prolonging this stand-off, especially since it would be a direct breach of the same Yalta agreements which they were currently trying to make the Russians honour. Again Churchill found himself forced to retreat from an isolated position. The parallel troop movements on all sides were in fact to be completed only ten days before the start of the conference.

Monday, 28 May, had found a cheerful Prime Minister, his invitation to Berlin in his pocket, presiding over a reception at 10 Downing Street. This was attended by both his present Conservative ministers and his former Labour and Liberal colleagues: a triumphant funeral wake for the Coalition Government that had won the war. Churchill addressed them all, with tears running down his cheeks, as he recalled their historic achievement: 'The light will shine on every helmet.' He went on to say that he was sure that, 'if ever such a mortal danger threatened, we would all do the same again.' Hugh Dalton, the likeliest choice as Foreign Secretary if Labour were to win the election, recorded this remark in his diary with evident puzzlement. 'I wondered whether this meant anything. If so, it could only have meant Russia,' he commented. 'Probably it was only a phrase.' Anything else seemed unthinkable at the time. Churchill's own goodwill and good spirits were unambiguous in his announcement that 'when he went to meet Stalin and Truman, he wanted to take with him "My good friend, Clem Attlee" to show that, whatever happened in the election, we were a United Nation.'[11]

Exactly a week later, Churchill made his first election broadcast. What attracted almost all the attention and comment at the time, as subsequently, was his warning against what a socialist government would mean: 'They would have to fall back on some form of Gestapo, no doubt very humanely directed in the first instance.'[12] It would be directed, presumably, by his good friend, Clem Attlee. 'I met Attlee in the lavatory, and he seemed shrunken and terrified, and scarcely smiled,' Chips Channon reported the next day from Westminster, and was himself in no doubt at the boost to Tory prospects – 'Everyone is cock-a-hoop.'[13]

Not quite everyone. Jock Colville, amused to watch the Prime Minister delivering his broadcast from Chequers like an old-fashioned hustings orator, realized that it had not been a success. Lord Moran, listening with a group of academic colleagues in Birmingham, was disappointed: 'It was plain that it had not gone down with anybody.'[14] Leo Amery, beginning his own campaign for re-election as a Conservative candidate, was 'greatly depressed by it'; he thought that 'Winston jumped straight off his pedestal as world statesman to deliver a fantastical exaggerated onslaught on Socialism' and, like many others, he blamed Lord Beaverbrook and Brendan Bracken, with their reputation as the Tory attack dogs.[15] It did not really matter whether these two were personally responsible for the tone – Colville thought not. The next evening, in his reply for the Labour Party, Attlee struck home when he said that 'the voice we heard last night was that of Mr Churchill, but the mind was that of Lord Beaverbrook.'[16]

Again, there was general agreement about the impact of the broadcast, this time favourable. 'I fear he scored off Winston,' Harold Nicolson wrote, while to Amery it was 'a very adroit reply to Winston's rodomontage'.[17] What Attlee had done was to congratulate his opponent for demonstrating 'the difference between Winston Churchill the great leader in war of a united nation, and Mr Churchill the party leader of the Conservatives'. He delivered his reprimand with a magisterial authority not hitherto familiar to many outside the cabinet room (or even, like Chips Channon, inside the House of Commons lavatory). 'Attlee, the "poor Clem" of the war years, did his piece tonight, and did it well,' Moran acknowledged, going on to reflect that Churchill seemed on the wrong track: 'For the first time the thought went through my head that he may lose the election.'[18] To the few who took any notice of it, the Gallup Poll suggested that Moran was right, but for the wrong reason. Labour had long been ahead, with its vote steady since February at 45–47 per cent, against a Conservative figure in the range 27–33 per cent. A poll in mid-June, after the 'Gestapo' exchanges, showed the Labour vote stationary but the Conservatives rising to 37 per cent.

Churchill's preoccupation with getting re-elected in 1945 was no greater than Roosevelt's had been in 1944; it was a condition of democratic government. There is nothing surprising or discreditable in the way that his attention now focused primarily on the campaign. 'No sign of Winston today – I suppose he was busy with his broadcast for tonight,' Cadogan noted on 21 June. 'Nothing is in his mind – or anyone else's – but the Election.'[19] It was at this point that the antics of the party leader of the Conservatives intersected with the plans of the great leader in war. Not only did he reconsider his invitation to Attlee to attend the Big Three meeting in July but also whether the conference should take place as agreed.

And all because of the Laski affair. Churchill, bereft of any better plan, had no intention of abandoning his robust right-wing approach, and found his efforts inadvertently encouraged from the left. Professor Harold Laski of the London School of Economics was one of the Labour Party's leading intellectuals and was currently serving as chairman of its National Executive Committee, an influential but hardly commanding position. Already discontented with the parliamentary leadership – his recent suggestion to Attlee that he should make way for a more charismatic figure had received a terse and cutting dismissal – Laski intervened immediately after the announcement that Attlee would be attending the Big Three. In a statement published in the press on 15 June, Laski insisted that Attlee could go only as an observer. Again Attlee asserted himself, this time through a public exchange of letters with Churchill, defining to mutual satisfaction the active though non-governmental role proposed. Laski backed down on the immediate point he had raised.

This was not, however, the end of the matter. Bracken and Beaverbrook may not have been behind the Gestapo broadcast but they were directly responsible for inflating the Laski affair. Bracken used an election broadcast to demand whether continuity in foreign policy had now been abandoned. Cadogan dismissed this broadcast as 'very bad.

Imitating Winston's style, and no stuff.'[20] Even to a senior diplomat of Conservative outlook, then, this sounded like empty bluster. If Sir Alec had deigned to read the *Daily Express* over the next few days he would have found Beaverbrook in full cry. 'SOCIALIST SPLIT: ATTLEE REPUDIATES LASKI ORDER' on 16 June, with a photograph captioned 'Laski on the throne', and on 19 June publicity for the phrase (coined by Harold Macmillan) 'Gauleiter Laski'.

Yet it would be wrong to think that this was simply a Tory election stunt, of the kind that the Labour Party customarily expected. For one thing, nobody knew how the foreign policy of a majority Labour government would turn out; perhaps Attlee would be merely the Kerensky of a socialist takeover, Laski its Lenin; perhaps it was not such a good idea for Churchill to take Attlee to Berlin as a human shield. At any rate, Alan Brooke was disconcerted to learn on 19 June that the Prime Minister was contemplating a further step over the Laski affair. 'As a result,' the CIGS noted with dismay, 'the Big Three meeting is now to be put off from July 15th to August 15th, with all the incumbent disadvantages to the war by delaying the decisions of our badly wanted [Combined] Chiefs of Staff meeting!'[21] Cadogan heard the same news and, in attendance at the following day's cabinet meeting, listened to 'a long rambling talk about desirability of postponing Big 3 meeting in view of the Attlee–Laski imbroglio'. The preparation of draft messages to Stalin and Truman testifies to the seriousness of this possibility, though Cadogan's private view remained cynical – 'I think in these days everyone, at the back of their mind, is searching how to turn everything to party advantage.'[22]

The idea of postponing the Big Three proved to be a passing whim for Churchill. Maybe he blenched at the enormity of asking Stalin and Truman to throw over all the arrangements, in effect to propitiate Professor Laski. Maybe it struck Churchill that he risked being absent from a meeting that they might nonetheless hold without him. It may even have occurred to him that he could not count on being Prime Minister on 15 August. More likely, having put himself in the hands of Bracken and Beaverbrook, he probably thought that the Conservatives were doing nicely in exploiting these events. The *Daily Express*, confident that the Conservatives were winning, saw no reason to change tack. At any rate, with polling day now only a couple of weeks away, the political temperature was rising in Britain.

There was a last-minute scramble to make ready for the Big Three conference. The Russians chose exactly where in the Berlin area it would meet: not within the ruined city, for obvious reasons, but about fifteen miles south-west, in Potsdam and its neighbouring suburb of Babelsberg. There each delegation could be given suitably dignified if cramped quarters. The former crown prince's Cecilienhof Palace – described by Attlee as a 'Stock-Exchange-Gothic mansion'[23] – was chosen for the plenary sessions. To veterans of Yalta, the scenario was familiar. 'In some ways I think this is odder,' wrote Cadogan on arrival. 'Here we are, in the midst of this devastated and denuded country, living in a little town of our own, consisting of villas set amidst trees (not unlike Le Touquet) with more or less every comfort of a somewhat rough and ready kind.'[24]

The name of Potsdam, then, was to join those of Teheran and Yalta. Nominally at least, the Americans and British went in their own right, not as the guests of the Russians. The French, although now an occupying power, were piqued at not going at all and tended to blame the British for such snubs. This was a backhanded compliment to the abiding prestige of perfidious Albion. Actually, the Big Three was less likely to have been turned into the Big Four than into just the Big Two.

Field Marshal Lord Wavell returned to Delhi on 5 June. He was determined to make up for lost time in broaching his plan for democratization of the Indian government from above, by using his viceregal powers to reconstruct his Executive Council on a broadly representative basis. This would give it a legitimacy plainly lacking in existing arrangements. In San Francisco, Mrs V. L. Pandit, Nehru's sister and herself a considerable figure in the Indian National Congress, had made a strong moral impression in campaigning against the seating of an Indian delegation composed of the Viceroy's nominees. There is no need to accept that the Indian members of the Executive were simply stooges of the British, nor to suppose that its British members, like Sir Archibald Rowlands, failed to urge the Indian position on matters like the sterling balances. The problem was not personal but structural.

Wavell had imagined that his proposals might offer a way forward, if not to immediate independence, then to full self-government. Belatedly, he had been given his chance by Churchill, who was readier to run the risk of a settlement than risk dragging India into the election campaign. The fact that only 6 per cent of candidates mentioned India in their election addresses (8 per cent of Labour, 4 per cent of Conservatives) shows that the ploy worked in Britain. Whether it would work in India was more to the point, as Wavell was well aware; and he set to work at once. 'Met Council in evening and disclosed the proposals; they met with a very cold reception, and no one except Archie Rowlands fully supported them, and hardly any Member had a good word to say for them,' he noted. 'What it really amounts to is that, as at home, nobody really wants to move at all.'[25] The discouraging beginning was compounded by an immediate press leak of this discussion from within the Council, with the minor consolation that some nationalists concluded that the proposals could not be all bad if the oligarchic Council opposed them.

Wavell's next big step was to appeal more widely for support. In a broadcast that drew favourable press comment he announced the release of the members of the Congress Working Committee, imprisoned since the 'Quit India' protests of 1942. Their crime, of course, had been to undermine morale and security at home through political agitation while the Allied forces they ought to have been supporting were engaged in a desperate conflict at the front: much like the dissident Poles, though the comparison did not apparently occur to Churchill. However, at just the moment when the sixteen Poles were being locked up, the Viceroy was (as Hopkins might have put it) doing everything under heaven to get the Congress leaders out of jug. After a thousand days in a British gaol, Jawaharlal Nehru emerged into the political spotlight, uncertain of his next steps. Meanwhile, Mohammad Ali Jinnah, leader of the Muslim League, which had obviously benefited from Congress's withdrawal from active politics, entered into public exchanges with Wavell, as did Gandhi, who made an early plea for the word 'independence' to be used.

A key issue was the Viceroy's proposal that there should be an equal number of Hindus and Muslims on the new Council. This was a lot for Congress to swallow. It was not just that the Muslims were obviously a minority of the population – that is exactly why they felt vulnerable – but Congress prided itself on its secular appeal and its own ability to attract Muslims. Indeed its president, Maulana A. K. Azad, was a prominent Muslim, albeit a mere 'poster boy' in the eyes of the Muslim League, which now claimed to be the sole channel for Muslim representation. Congress tended to dismiss these communal difficulties as the product of a divide-and-rule strategy on the part of the British Raj and likely to disappear with it. But whether the League's claim for a

'Pakistan' as a safe haven for Muslims could be countered by an offer of security for Muslim fellow citizens within a united India was now the pivotal issue. Thus Congress and the League each claimed nationalist credentials and both identified British imperialism as their enemy; but whether they could agree between themselves about post-imperial India still had to be put to the test. Deadlock in Delhi already seemed likely.

In San Francisco, meanwhile, another set of apparently intractable negotiations were belatedly moving towards resolution. Stettinius had felt a mounting sense of frustration and urgency. 'Here we've been in San Francisco a month,' he told the US delegates, 'and we haven't begun to swing our weight around yet.'[26] From the perspective of the delegation as a whole, including independent-minded Republican politicians like Arthur Vandenberg and Harold Stassen, the main problems were caused by the irrepressible assertiveness of the forty-five smaller countries and, above all, by the protean obduracy of a single great power: not Great Britain this time but the Soviet Union. Thankfully for the British, this meant that the Americans needed a reliable ally among the Big Five, and there was only one available.

The debates on colonialism and the former mandated territories were conducted in this context. Hence a new American readiness to abandon an outright commitment to 'independence' for all, in favour of simply asking for 'self-government'. Surely, Stassen now argued with colleagues, he and his fellow US delegates 'did not wish to find ourselves committed to breaking up the British empire'.[27] Whether this San Francisco logic would more generally work in Britain's favour depended as much on American perceptions of the Soviet Union as on anything the British themselves did.

The conference had again ground to a standstill at the beginning of June. The problem was whether an international organization of equals ought to admit that a few great powers should exert a veto over any of its business. At any rate, this demonstrated the fallaciousness of the assumption that the British Empire had six votes locked up, since the Australian and New Zealand delegations, championing the rights of smaller countries, took a principled stand against the veto. But the pragmatic reality was that, without some sort of veto, the Soviet Union would never have signed up; and the other so-called great powers (China and France as well as Great Britain and the United States) had an obvious self-interest too. The American position (supported by the British) was that the Yalta agreement granted each of these five permanent members of the security council a veto over its actions – but not over whether an issue could be brought before the council in the first place, which was the Russian position. Given that each move here had to be referred to Moscow, progress was glacial.

Stettinius, conscious that the President needed results, found himself stymied, the more so when a leak to the *New York Times* made the story public and thus raised the stakes. Picking up a suggestion from Lord Halifax, Stettinius suggested to Truman that Hopkins, still in Moscow, be asked to raise the issue. It was in this situation that Hopkins scored his great coup on 6 June, at his final meeting that day with Stalin, who coolly accepted the American reading of Yalta, leaving his own ambassador, Gromyko, to scramble for cover in San Francisco. '*America Wins!*' Vandenberg exclaimed, though luckily only in his diary on 7 June, prudently telling himself the next day: 'We did not *gloat* over a victory.'[28]

The Secretary of State, even more determined not to gloat, at last had his moment. He found his own infectious affability sufficient to disarm Gromyko's last diplomatic reservations over the necessary documents. 'But, Andrei, that's awfully small,' Stettinius enjoined at one point, 'you can't find fault with that.'[29] And so it turned out, despite the familiar last-minute drafting crises. The US delegates felt that they had indeed won essential points. Vandenberg delighted at working closely with Halifax – 'Hi, Ed!' – now that he was on first-name terms with the austere and aristocratic British ambassador.[30] The other Ed, Edward J. Stettinius, was able to vindicate his tenure at the State Department by steering the conference to unanimous acceptance of the United Nations Charter. President Truman, one of his pre-Potsdam objectives achieved, went to San Francisco himself for the occasion on Monday, 25 June.

On this same day that the San Francisco conference concluded, Lord Wavell opened the first session of the conference he had summoned at Simla. His big success lay in simply getting all the Indian parties to attend it. Simla was a very good place to escape the stinging heat in Delhi, often 40°C in June, which is why the Viceroy's summer residence was sited there, amid the foothills of the Himalayas. The Viceregal Lodge, in all its imposing incongruity with its setting, housed the conference sessions, with well-appointed chalets nearby to accommodate the different delegations, in a manner reminiscent of Yalta and foreshadowing Potsdam.

Like Yalta and Potsdam, the final results proved disappointing. Admittedly, Wavell had his first face-to-face meeting with Gandhi, who was in his prolix and anecdotal mood: benign enough, but refusing to participate officially on the grounds that (officially again) he was not a member of the Congress Party. Jinnah, flexing his muscles as master of the Muslim League, lent little credence to the Mahatma's protestations, saying: 'it was another trick of Gandhi's, he pretended not to belong to the Congress when it suited his book, but when necessary appeared as the Dictator of Congress which everyone knew he was.'[31] This was pejorative but not inaccurate. It was a relief that Jinnah put the same point more politely in talking to the press. So Gandhi remained at Simla only for consultation, yet with a charismatic presence rivalled only by Nehru, who attended later and likewise on a non-official basis.

It became apparent within days that Congress and the League could not agree in direct talks. Nor could they when they negotiated indirectly by sending Wavell lists of names for possible inclusion. The crunch was that Congress insisted on including some Muslim names on its list while Jinnah was equally insistent that only he could nominate Muslims, asserting his role as their sole spokesman. 'I ask you not to wreck the League,' he pleaded with Wavell, who suspected that his main motivation by this stage was a well-founded fear of being made the scapegoat for failure.[32] Eager to protect himself in American eyes, Jinnah decided that he could no longer refrain from provocative public comment. He gave a statement on 11 July to the United Press accusing Congress of 'a flank movement', designed to 'reduce Muslim effectiveness by securing Congress and Muslim quislings'.[33]

By this point, Wavell faced impasse and had to report the conference's breakdown to London. 'I am sorry to say the Cabinet mostly seemed pleased,' Amery recorded on 12 July. The Prime Minister was absent from this cabinet meeting, on holiday before going to Potsdam. But when Amery re-read his diary more than two years later he added a retrospective note: 'The immediate wrecker was Jinnah, but the real wrecker perhaps the long delay before Archie was allowed to try, and so Winston.'[34]

Churchill, much to his doctor's relief, was taking a much-needed rest from his electoral exertions on the Basque coast of France. Even before leaving, he had been reading few government papers. 'I am worried about this damned election,' he told Moran. 'I have no message for them now.'[35] The main issues in which voters were interested, as he had come to realize, concerned domestic policy: housing far the most important, followed by full employment and social security. Labour was identified with a series of proposals that seemed all the more credible because many of them had been worked out under the Coalition Government, notably the Beveridge Plan for a welfare state, published at the end of 1942, and the commitment to Keynesian policies to sustain a high and stable level of employment, declared in 1944. Here Churchill indeed had little to say. Instead he had reverted to the sort of partisan knock-about that he had abjured since the 1930s. In the process he not only cheapened his appeal as a national figure but also identified himself more closely with the Conservative Party, which was still associated not only with pre-war unemployment but with pre-war appeasement of Hitler – a policy that virtually everyone condemned in hindsight.

It is not the case that Labour was uninterested in foreign policy, which was mentioned by 84 per cent of its candidates in their election addresses, compared with 71 per cent of Conservatives. Nor, as newspapers as different as the *Daily Telegraph* and the *Manchester Guardian* both acknowledged, were there sharp partisan differences in outlook on the world. True, whereas 16 per cent of Labour candidates stressed working closely with Russia, only 2 per cent of Conservatives said the same. But 49 per cent of Conservative and 28 per cent of Labour candidates talked of working closely with both Russians and Americans alike. Simple arithmetic tells us that more Conservative candidates (51 per cent) than Labour candidates (44 per cent) said that they wanted to work closely with the Soviet Union. And only 2 per cent of Conservatives (and no Labour candidates) said the same of the United States alone. The real point is surely that, even in late June 1945, such invidious choices between wartime allies seemed unnecessary to most people. Hence too the fact that 60 per cent of Labour candidates, and 27 per cent of Conservatives, mentioned the world organization for peace, made topical by the San Francisco conference.[36] Continuity of foreign policy (Laski notwithstanding) was a widespread assumption; and if it was, it did not depend upon electing Churchill when the votes were cast on 5 July.

Still Prime Minister until the votes were counted – a delay of three weeks was necessary to collect the forces' ballots – Churchill took his French holiday. Then he would put in an appearance at Postdam and

conclude the Big Three's business before going home. 'I shall be only
half a man until the result of the poll,' he intimated to Moran. 'I shall
keep in the background at the conference.' In that case, there was little
point in wasting time on prior homework. Instead, the paints were
called for. 'Where is the cobalt?' Churchill demanded of the admirable
Sawyers.[37]

Leisured days unfolded, at the table as at the easel. Plainly this was a
deeply fatigued man, long overworked in the service of his country, and
craving a few days of complete relaxation. The briefs that the Foreign
Office had compiled remained an unopened book. On 12 July, the
breakdown at Simla evoked no response – not even the favourable news
that the *New York Times* and other American papers blamed Jinnah
rather than the Viceroy (just like the British papers and indeed most
Indian observers). There was little talk of the Big Three meeting, though
Churchill perked up at the thought that Attlee would be there, saying
mischievously: 'We don't know whether we are on speaking terms until
we meet at Berlin.'[38] He had, however, shown his concern that the leader
of the Labour Party should properly represent his country by providing
him with a valet.

President Truman, still fresh to the job, still learning the ropes, still
reorganizing his own team, prepared for Potsdam differently. With the
success of the San Francisco conference, he had felt free to reward his
Secretary of State appropriately. On 21 June Stettinius was clumsily
informed through an intermediary that the President now had other
plans for him. He was to be left in charge of United Nations business
but Truman's long-rumoured, long-denied intention to appoint Byrnes
as Secretary of State was at last confirmed. Stettinius saw at once that
'there was no use taking me to Berlin.' Inevitably the news leaked out
before Truman's arrival in San Francisco for the final ceremonies. 'Mr
President,' Stettinius asked him when they eventually met, 'do you really
believe that you can do this thing and put Byrnes in without its appearing
publicly like a kick in the pants for me?' Truman replied: 'I sincerely
believe it can be done that way.'[39]

Truman's sincerity, of course, was hardly the point in an act he found
personally distasteful but politically necessary. 'I think it was grossly
unfair,' Vandenberg commented privately. 'It must have startled the
foreign ministers of the other forty-nine nations who saw Stettinius
make a spectacular success of his job at San Francisco only to be "shot

at sunrise" as his reward.'[40] The overriding factor was Truman's decision to have Byrnes at his side: a self-made Irish-American Democratic politician of proven loyalty and public standing. 'It would be his object to return home with a reputation for having found a lasting *via media* for such divergent trends as may there seem likely to divide Great Britain and the Soviet Union,' Isaiah Berlin commented, adding: 'He tells excellent Southern stories.'[41]

The new president was growing into his job and, with poll ratings even higher than Roosevelt had achieved, plainly wished to begin remodelling the administration in his own image. Several cabinet changes had already been made. Morgenthau, whose relations with Truman were never close, had a declared antipathy to Byrnes; so it was logical that Byrnes's appointment to the State Department should prompt a further change at the Treasury.

It had long been apparent, at least to those not oblivious to the signals, that Lend-Lease was in trouble. In particular, the Quebec offer on Stage II, which Churchill had once thought 'beyond the dreams of justice', seemed to be a dead letter in Washington – as dead as the President who had once volunteered it. By definition, it was only since the beginning of Stage II on VE-Day that the issue had acute practical importance. Throughout late May, all of June and early July, Churchill found that his appeals to Truman over this agreement were simply brushed aside. Morgenthau, nursing his own hurt feelings over the praise given to Keynes for negotiating the terms, refused to carry the can for these lapses, as he had in the past. 'I'm not going to take it,' he complained at one point. 'I was willing to take it from Roosevelt because I was his friend, but I want a little more now.'[42]

Morgenthau and Stettinius, when given the responsibility for implementing the Quebec offer, had found it hard enough trying to remind the previous president of his own promises to Churchill. Whether the new president could be expected to honour the undertakings of his late predecessor was another matter – it was like Yalta, only worse. Nobody in Washington seemed to be working from the same documents. Each agency involved had its own interpretation, supported, like biblical disputes, with texts that were themselves of uncertain provenance or meaning. Morgenthau alone had been there at every crucial step. With unique credentials but declining authority, he maintained that Truman's belated response should say to Churchill: 'what you and Mr Roosevelt agreed on, bingo, I carry out.' But the drafts in circulation did no such thing, refusing the British without any justification and thus putting the President in an invidious position. Or so Morgenthau believed – 'He gives no reason why he's welching.'[43]

There was to be no official answer to the British before Potsdam. This was hardly a promising basis on which to launch Anglo-American discussions on Stage III. When it dawned on Morgenthau that the President would not back him, that Lend-Lease had been taken out of his hands, that the State Department was taking control of Stage III planning, and that the famous (or infamous) Morgenthau Plan was now a dead letter, he virtually threw in his hand. He told his staff that he did not now want 'to be part [sic] in helping to finance England'.[44] Morgenthau's outburst to this effect came on 3 July, the same day that Byrnes was sworn in as Secretary of State. The previous day, Hopkins, now mortally ill, had sent his own letter of resignation. He was to receive ungrudging thanks for his services from Truman. Nonetheless, the Roosevelt old guard was palpably on the way out.

Morgenthau had initially hoped to go to Potsdam himself. Truman ruled this out, ostensibly because, with the President and Secretary of State abroad, the Secretary of the Treasury, as next in line, should stay in Washington, with power to convene the cabinet. After all, this was not unflattering, and the same arrangement that the great Roosevelt had made when he went to Yalta. A conversation on 5 July, however, put all this in a new light. 'Oh, I am going to say that you are the man in charge while I am gone,' said the President, while Morgenthau persisted in inquiring about his own tenure, asking: 'Well, I would like to know whether you want me to stay until V-J Day.' That was conventionally supposed to be more than a year away, of course. 'Well, I don't know,' was Truman's only response. 'I may want a new Secretary of the Treasury.'[45]

Morgenthau drafted his letter of resignation that same day. As with Stettinius, dignity was outwardly maintained, though everyone in Washington could sense how things really stood. As with Hopkins, a long-serving intimate of FDR departed with mutual felicitations. But with these changes, Great Britain lost three powerful and sympathetic voices in Washington. The spirit of Quebec finally evaporated on the eve of Potsdam.

Hopkins said that he was writing his memoirs. He died before he finished – indeed before he really started, but some fragments from the summer of 1945 were rescued by his friend Robert Sherwood. 'I believe that the British have saved our skins twice – once in 1914 and again in 1940,' Hopkins wrote, adding about the second occasion: 'This time it was Britain alone that held the fort and they held that fort for us just as much as for themselves, because we would not have had a chance to have licked Hitler had Britain fallen.' But he well realized why so many of his compatriots took another view. 'When the Prime Minister said that he was not selected to be the King's Minister to liquidate the Empire,' Hopkins wrote, 'every isolationist in America cheered him.'[46] Two men whom he had learned to respect or even revere, Roosevelt and then Churchill, had given the necessary leadership in a broadly successful war against fascism; but there remained an unresolved tension between its rationale and that of the generally unsuccessful imperialist war that Churchill was still intent on waging.

'Nothing will be decided at the conference at Potsdam,' Churchill had predicted privately.[47] At the time, this is how it seemed. All the big questions on the agenda, notably the interlocked fate of Germany and Poland, had been on the agenda at Yalta. It was never likely that Potsdam would provide new answers.

Churchill arrived on Sunday, 15 July, having flown from Bordeaux. 'I followed him,' wrote Moran, 'through two bleak rooms with great chandeliers to the opposite side of the empty house, where french windows that had not been cleaned for a long time, opened upon a balcony, and there, without removing his hat, Winston flopped into a garden chair, flanked by two great tubs of hydrangeas, blue, pink and white.' He was clearly weary and in need of refreshment. 'Where is Sawyers?' he demanded.[48] A whisky was procured. It was all very familiar.

The British occupied a series of lakeside villas in Babelsberg. It was an oasis of peace, its air of make-believe enhanced by the fact that this had been the German Hollywood. 'I spent the afternoon settling in and in the evening tried for pike in the lake,' wrote Brooke, housed with the chiefs of staff, three doors away from the Prime Minister.[49] In between was 'a drab and dreary little building destined to house Attlee!' noted Cadogan, who could not resist adding: 'Very suitable – it's just like Attlee himself!'[50] The rival party leaders had ten hot sticky days ahead of them before the votes were counted at home. Yalta had taken eight days. The initial expectation was that Potsdam would be over before they had to depart.

There was bound to be a different style in the absence of the inimitable FDR, the man who had taken the United States into the war and who alone knew his own exit strategy. Moran brooded about the effect on Churchill – 'now Roosevelt was dead he found himself at Potsdam without any policy, except the vague idea of smashing Germany and Japan into unconditional surrender.'[51] If there was a post-Roosevelt vacuum, it was on the British rather than the American side.

The approach of the Big Three at Yalta had been to reach agreements on virtually everything, often couched in ambiguous terms to which everyone could assent. This suited Churchill on a tactical level, since he relished his ability to hit upon sonorous phrases and much admired his own literary handiwork. It suited Roosevelt on a strategic level, since he relied in all his political dealings upon exploiting ambiguity to achieve his own ulterior ends. And it suited Stalin on a pragmatic level, since he got what he wanted by genially nodding at those abstractions about democracy by which his Anglo-American allies seemed to set such great store. Yalta thus looked good at the time but the results did not prove lasting.

Potsdam was the opposite. The differences between the Big Three were not so determinedly concealed and there was less effort to paper over the cracks. Instead, the formula was to defer contentious matters 'until the full peace conference', thus agreeing to disagree. Especially after the experience of San Francisco, where the 'forty-five' had proved so tedious, none of the Big Three wanted to convene a full-scale, Paris-type conference until they had themselves reached agreement on how to run it. Moreover, once Truman knew that both San Francisco and Bretton Woods would be ratified by the Senate, he had most of what he wanted – and what Roosevelt had wanted, of course.

There was never any chance that, simply through seniority within the Big Three, Churchill would exert as much influence as the new President, who knew his own limitations but also, by now, the strength of his political position. Truman, so the Washington embassy reported, 'has the sympathetic backing of almost all sections of the country – far more than President Roosevelt could have commanded were he now at Potsdam'.[52] During the Potsdam conference, the Senate approved the

Bretton Woods legislation by 61–16; and its approval of the United Nations Charter – supported by two-thirds of Americans according to Gallup – was by now a formality. The final vote was to be 89–2. Though by now a foregone conclusion, this was still a striking contrast with the Senate's repudiation of the League of Nations after Versailles.

Rather against expectations, Truman commanded the stage at Potsdam with an authority that Wilson lacked at Paris in 1919. Despite his modest manner, Truman was determined to exert this leverage to the full. He was the new factor in the Big Three, necessarily destabilizing the personal dynamics established through long sessions at Teheran and Yalta. He was nonetheless nominated to preside over the Big Three sessions, like his predecessor. It soon became clear that Truman's preference for an early night clashed with the nocturnal habits of both Churchill and Stalin, and the presidential parties ended more abruptly than in the bad old days of Yalta, though there was no avoiding the inevitable three formal dinners, with dozens of toasts in the Russian style. In the Potsdam photographs, Generalissimo Stalin (a recent promotion but no surprise) usually appears in his new white-jacketed uniform and the late lieutenant of Hussars in the ancient uniforms into which Sawyers squeezed him. But the American commander-in-chief looks more comfortable than either in the July heat, wearing his well-pressed, double-breasted, summer-weight suits – a touch of Washington, DC, rather than Ruritania.

Churchill wanted to meet Truman as soon as possible. He did so after his first night in Babelsberg, on the morning of Monday, 16 July, and told everyone how delighted he was. 'He takes no notice of delicate ground, he just plants his foot down firmly on it,' Churchill explained to Moran while changing for dinner that night; and in case his physician was baffled by these anatomical references, he jumped and brought down his bare feet to demonstrate.[53] This early impression of Truman was reinforced as the conference proceedings developed and was widely shared on the British side. 'On the whole I liked him,' Brooke commented later, 'not the same personality as his predecessor, but a quick brain, a feeling of honesty, a good business man, and a pleasant personality.'[54]

Businesslike is the word that almost everyone used about Truman. Efficient and businesslike, quick and businesslike, affable and businesslike: but always focused on mastering and settling the business in hand. In this he had an able lieutenant in James Byrnes, on his first outing as

Secretary of State, short on political rhetoric but long on negotiating skills. Like the President, he was a pianist who could make a decent stab at Chopin. Significantly, Byrnes was the bearer of the American memory of what had happened at Yalta. The preparations this time pleased him better, the voyage out aboard USS *Augusta* having been used for systematic briefing sessions. In support, 'Chip' Bohlen and 'Doc' Matthews, also veterans of Yalta, were joined this time not by Alger Hiss but by another State Department colleague, Ben Cohen. A bachelor in his fifties, slouching in posture, careless in his dress and table manners, this new boy at Potsdam lacked both Hiss's panache and his finesse in espionage. But Cohen had a renowned facility on paper which makes the notes he took the most faithful record of the words actually spoken around the table at the Cecilienhof Palace.

Potsdam was news. In particular, a large American press corps was camped outside the gates. 'BIG 3 PARLEY BEGINS TODAY' was the banner headline in the *Chicago Tribune* on 16 July. Yet there was actually little hard news to sustain all the large type. The next day's papers reported equally prominently that the start of the conference was delayed because of Stalin's mysterious absence; but beyond that, the efforts of the press met with frustration. 'When we were at Teheran, there were no journalists. At Yalta there were few,' Churchill happily reminisced before proposing a helpful solution at the second Big Three plenary. 'If my colleagues are willing,' he suggested, 'I am willing to have a talk with them and explain as a newspaperman the need for secrecy.' Truman did not see any need to subject his elderly colleague to the unwelcome glare of publicity by making him their sole spokesman before the world's journalists. 'Most of them are Americans,' he said. 'Your election is over and so is mine.'[55]

So the tight security around Potsdam and Babelsberg was paralleled by a press embargo as effective as that at Yalta. In Britain, where city lights had gone on that week for the first time, this new blackout in the media met with impatience. 'I think the lack of news is very annoying, I must say,' one woman told Mass-Observation. 'I suppose it's the Russian influence.'[56] The newspapers lost interest accordingly and focused on other stories. The Japanese war, where the British and US Navies mounted their first combined operation, now received comparable attention in the press of both countries, with rare unanimity in the news columns of both the *Chicago Tribune* and the *Daily Mail*; and both papers likewise offered frequent reminders that Lend-Lease was a simmering issue, albeit temporarily on the back burner.

Stalin's absence until the first plenary on Tuesday, 17 July, apparently on health grounds, had given Churchill and Truman a free day on Monday. After their cordial meeting that morning, they later went their separate ways to see the sights, which for once justify the word awesome. Moran, after a morning visit, had already tried to convey this to an initially unresponsive Prime Minister, who suddenly decided in late afternoon to see for himself. 'As we drove to Berlin,' Moran noted, 'no one on the road seemed to recognize him, until we came to the centre of the city, where a workman looked hard at us and pointed after the car.' It was one of the few places in Europe where Winston Churchill could have travelled incognito. He saw the ruins of the Chancellery, the ruins of the bunker. 'Hitler,' he reflected, 'must have come out here to get some air, and heard the guns getting nearer and nearer.' They drove back in silence, Churchill's thoughts evidently elsewhere. As he was undressing for bed he said to Moran: 'The Socialists say I shall have a majority over all other parties of thirty-two.'[57]

The next day the leader of the British Labour Party had an amicable lunch with the leader of the Conservative Party. It was obviously prudent that Churchill and Attlee should mend their fences in private before appearing together that day at the first plenary. With his remarkable capacity for underplaying his hand, Attlee reverted to type after his recent self-assertion in the election campaign. It quickly became apparent to all that he could be relied upon to support Churchill whenever necessary in the conference proceedings, and likewise relied upon to say little; he was to speak on only a handful of occasions during the nine plenary sessions held before the British General Election results. What really signals their mutual confidence on major issues is the fact that Attlee was immediately made party to the extraordinary news brought by their American guest for lunch that day, Henry Stimson, the Secretary for War.

On the previous day an atomic bomb had successfully been exploded in New Mexico. The impact was at the very highest end of expectations, of the order of 20,000 tons of TNT. Two further bombs were operational. British consent to their use against Japan had already been given, in accordance with prior understandings. The question at Potsdam was what use President Truman should make of the new weapon. It offered a means of finishing off Japan without delay – how much it would shorten the war depended on differing estimates of how near the Japanese were to surrender (and whether that surrender had to be unconditional). It offered, too, a means of finishing off Japan without the Russians. It offered, in short, much food for thought as the conference opened.

Churchill himself, on his French sojourn, had disclosed his low-profile strategy for keeping in the background at Potsdam. This was abandoned shortly after 5 p.m. on 17 July, as soon as the first plenary opened. Truman chaired it and did so in his own brisk style, even forgetting the opening civilities of welcome in his evident desire to get down to business. As topics were raised in an effort to establish an agenda, Churchill was irrepressibly stimulated to speak on each item, but found himself treated less indulgently than in the past. It was happily agreed that future meetings should begin at 4 p.m. Churchill was happy at the prospect of an extra hour of his own oratory. Truman's idea was to wrap up the business sooner and was pleased to bring the next day's session to a close by 6 o'clock, while Churchill clearly thought it extraordinary to curtail these fine, free-wheeling, unscripted, unrehearsed opportunities for talk at large, simply because that day's agenda had been concluded. What the Foreign Office feared, since the Prime Minister had read none of the briefs, was that he would give away their case inadvertently, rather than leave matters in the experienced hands of Eden and Cadogan.

The three foreign ministers were to play a bigger role at Potsdam than they had at Yalta. Molotov was an old hand; Byrnes a new one but more of a heavyweight than Stettinius. Eden laboured bravely under the shadow of the loss in action of his son (whose death was confirmed during the conference). When matters kept being referred to this Little Three, Stalin commented: 'As all the questions are to be discussed by the foreign ministers, we shall have nothing to do.' Ben Cohen recorded the laughter at this point, and then the exchanges about how to proceed next. 'The secretaries should give us three or four points – enough to keep us busy,' said Churchill, confident that he would find enough to say. 'I don't want just to discuss, I want to decide,' Truman rebuked him. 'You want something in the bag each day,' Churchill blandly agreed, with unaccustomed docility.[58]

Churchill was well aware that at Potsdam he needed to nobble the

President on unfinished business of his own. A private lunch on Wednesday, 18 July, with nobody else present at the table, provided the ideal opportunity for Churchill to prepare the ground for the talks on Stage III of Lend-Lease, covering the period after victory over Japan. Time was suddenly pressing, now that he knew about the atom bomb test. Instead of being more than twelve months away, VJ-Day might well be upon them in only a few weeks. So Keynes's proposals for renegotiating a sort of retrospective Lend-Lease, which the cabinet had stalled until after the General Election, assumed a new urgency. It was necessary to impress on this new president, so impressively quick on the uptake, that not all debts could be measured simply in dollars.

'I spoke of the melancholy position of Great Britain,' Churchill recorded immediately afterwards, 'who had spent more than one-half her foreign investments in the time when we were all alone for the common cause, and now emerged from the War the only nation with a great external debt of £3,000 millions.' (He meant the sterling balances, totalling $12 billion at current exchange rates.) What Britain needed was time to get on its feet. 'The President then spoke of the immense debt owed by the United States to Great Britain for having held the fort at the beginning.' The President's response was almost too good to be true. 'If you had gone down like France,' said Truman, 'we might well be fighting the Germans on the American coast at the present time.' Churchill paraphrased the President's conclusion: 'This justified the United States in regarding these matters as above the purely financial plane.'[59]

Did Truman really say this? Did he really mean it? Churchill dictated this *aide mémoire* the same afternoon, intended for the cabinet, and Moran transcribed much of it as it stood, so its provenance as an accurate record is good. The mutual appreciation fostered at Potsdam between Churchill and Truman is obvious. But this exchange, so reminiscent of the spirit of Quebec, was more significant for Churchill, desperately conscious of the forthcoming British plea for Justice, than for Truman, anxious to be polite.

Above all, it should be remembered that the President was a long way from home. Suppose he had called for a copy of the *Chicago Tribune* after lunch that day; it might well have been two days old; and if so, he could have benefited from its pertinent editorial, 'A Poorer Country' – a title that did not refer to Britain's plight. If the American people seemed to have more money to spend, the *Tribune* cautioned, this was only because of government spending, mainly in Europe. 'Our government officials and others who look only at the statistics of our liquid assets and conclude that we can give unlimited help to others are blind and foolish,' it admonished. 'If there are nations which have gotten rich out of the war, the United States is not one of them.'[60]

Similar warnings can be found, virtually every day of the week, in the *Tribune*'s files. One front-page cartoon shows Uncle Sam doing the real work in the Pacific, with Britain and Russia making token efforts only. Blood and treasure are explicitly linked. 'I want Russia in the war against Japan,' one Senator demands. 'I want England as fully in the war against Japan as we were in the war against Germany. Money's the only thing we've got left that they need!' In the editorial columns, 'the New Deal theory that it is America's duty to put all its assets into a global basket and permit all comers to pick out what they need and desire' is duly exposed. A couple of days later, in case any reader still cannot see the connection to 'Our Bedfellows' at Potsdam, the cartoon shows the Big Three sitting down to a lavish meal with dishes labelled 'Lend-Lease'.[61]

Here was an issue with a special ambiguity at Potsdam. The British and American chiefs of staff began their talks before Stalin's arrival. 'An easy meeting with no controversial points!' wrote a relieved Brooke.[62] Japan was the obvious focus. Whatever was said in the press or in Congress, behind closed doors there was no suggestion of the Americans making pleas for more extensive participation in the Japanese war, still less of the British resisting them: almost the reverse. Thus Field Marshal Brooke was pleased that General Marshall was so ready to accept the British offer to provide as much as a quarter of the projected invasion force. One complication was the proprietorial attitude of Admiral King about US Navy operations. 'His war is in the Pacific,' Moran observed, 'and the conflict with Germany has been to him only a tiresome distraction.'[63] King's longstanding reluctance to allow the intrusion of the Royal Navy into his ocean was well known. In fact, all these arguments were to be eclipsed by a new factor: the atomic bomb.

As more information from New Mexico became available via Stimson, the implications of the new weapons of mass destruction were debated by the small number of Americans privy to the secret, and the even smaller number of Britons. The initial question was whether to tell Stalin, and if so, what and when and how. That he should be told, but only at a late stage in the conference, was agreed between Churchill and Truman. Meanwhile, they had to meet him day by day with the great unspoken matter hanging in the air. There is little doubt that Churchill's imagination was increasingly fired by what he heard, especially after receiving a detailed briefing on the results of the test on 22 July. 'Stimson, what was gunpowder? Trivial,' he declared. 'What was electricity? Meaningless. This atomic bomb is the Second Coming in Wrath.'[64]

'The Marshal was very amiable,' the British Prime Minister told his doctor, using the adjective three times, after a long dinner at the Russian headquarters on 18 July. They had exchanged gifts of cigars and had sat smoking and talking for five hours at the table. Churchill heard what he wanted to hear: 'I think Stalin wants me to win the election.' Evidently well briefed from Communist sources in Britain, Stalin pontificated that Labour would win 220 or 230 seats, that the soldiers would support strong government – no red army in Britain – and hence Churchill's majority might be about 80. Moreover, this sudden enthusiasm for the democratic process seemed infectious. 'Stalin gave me his word there will be free elections in the countries set free by his armies,' Churchill reported, apparently impressed. 'We must listen to these Russians,' he told a sceptical Moran. 'They mobilized twelve million men, and nearly half of them were killed or are missing.' For his part, Churchill was more than ready to talk about opening access more freely to the Black Sea. 'I think,' he said, 'that Stalin is trying to be as helpful as it is in him to be.'[65]

Churchill had been wooed by Stalin before. If he was susceptible, he was also ready to use any personal rapport as licence for plain speaking. He had already signalled his interest in Poland. 'The burden of this matter rests on Britain,' Churchill maintained. 'We received the Poles when they were driven out by the Germans.'[66] He continued in this vein the day after his amiable dinner, telling Moran afterwards: 'I don't think Stalin was offended at what I said. He doesn't mind straight speaking.'[67] They had just tangled on whether intervention in Franco's Spain was justifiable, then on whether Tito's Yugoslavia was carrying out the Yalta agreements – a contentious issue. 'Let us drop it,' Truman suggested. 'It is very important,' Churchill rejoined. 'We are dropping it,' Truman explained from the chair, 'only for the day as we did with Franco.' Churchill grumbled: 'I had hoped that we could discuss these matters frankly.'[68] But he blandly took the credit later, telling Moran: 'When you come to a stony place, you adjourn. You have a conversation, carry it a certain distance, and then drop it.'[69]

The one thing on which it was easy to agree at Potsdam was to set up a permanent council of foreign ministers, meeting quarterly. They were charged with preparing for a peace conference that would not take place unless the great powers could meanwhile agree among themselves. 'I think the meeting place should be London,' Churchill had maintained. 'London is the capital city most under fire of the enemy and the longest in the war.'[70] Attlee was symbolically wheeled out in support. Proximity rather than sentiment prevailed in getting London agreed.

Fed by the foreign ministers, who met earlier each day, the plenary sessions proceeded on this principle: looking difficulties boldly in the face and then deferring awkward decisions, sometimes to another day and sometimes to a full peace conference. 'The feelings of revenge and retribution are poor guides in politics' was one of the uplifting maxims that Stalin introduced. 'Democracy is Democracy the world over' was another.[71] Everyone could agree with such sentiments but they did not lead to concrete conclusions. Time and again the outstanding problems of Germany and Poland resurfaced, especially the border between them and reparations; time and again they were stalled.

'I shall be glad when this election business is over,' Churchill told Moran. 'It hovers over me like a vulture of uncertainty in the sky.'[72] His own inner misgivings began to sap his confidence, both in Stalin's amiability and in Truman's capacity – and both were necessary to clinch the business in hand. By Saturday, 21 July, after six full days at Potsdam and five plenaries, the lack of progress was evident. 'It looks as if we may not finish on Wednesday,' wrote Cadogan. 'If we don't, Winston and Anthony will fly back on that day and be back here on Friday.'[73] No mention of Attlee, of course.

That afternoon's plenary had revealed increasingly open conflict about Germany and Poland, with Truman no longer prepared to defer the awkward issues. At Yalta, Poland's eastern border had been settled as the Curzon line, thus ceding a large slice of Polish territory to the Soviet Union, with the promise of compensation for Poland in the west. The Oder–Neisse line, though often mentioned at Yalta, had not been agreed as the new border between Germany and Poland; but the Red Army subsequently treated it as such, driving out the German population in the course of its advance and allowing the Lublin Poles to take over government of this territory. Yet when the occupation zones of Germany had been decided at Yalta, the 1937 frontiers had been used; so part of the eastern zone assigned to the Russians had meanwhile unilaterally been handed over by them to the Poles. This was what Truman objected to. 'I wanted the administrations in the four zones to be as we have agreed,' he said. 'We can not agree on reparations if parts of Germany are given away.' This link was crucial. The point was not so much the irregularity of creating a *de facto* fifth zone under Polish occupation as the effect on Germany's resources (which were thereby diminished) and its population (thereby displaced).

'On paper it is formerly German territory but in fact it is Polish territory,' Stalin countered. 'There are no Germans left.' Truman asked: 'Where are the nine million Germans?' 'They have fled,' was the laconic answer. 'How can they be fed?' Churchill asked, turning to the problem that the displaced Germans, evicted from the arable east, would pose for the industrial west – 'It is apparent that a disproportionate part of the population will be cast on the rest of Germany with its food supplies alienated.' The British zone, of course, was centred on the Ruhr. Would it simultaneously be asked to provide reparations (for the Russians) while having to feed the refugees displaced from the east (by the Russians)? 'If the Germans have run out they should be encouraged to return,' Churchill continued. 'The Poles have no right to create a catastrophe in the feeding of Germany.' He put the issue bluntly to Stalin: 'We do not wish to be left with a vast German population on our hands deprived of its food supply.'[74]

At Yalta, Churchill had tried, half-heartedly, to support the Poles in resisting encroachment on their borders in the east. At Potsdam he changed sides, this time ranged against Polish claims. Admittedly, even at Yalta he had warned against stuffing the Polish goose with too much German food; at Potsdam he realized that he himself needed this food for the Ruhr. And Poland, of course, was now hardly 'mistress in her own house and captain of her soul', as Churchill had hoped at Yalta. The whole situation was a product of the way the Red Army had conducted its advance, sweeping out the Germans like dust before a broom; and the Russians were calling the shots. But at least the Americans were now roused to the dangers, much to Churchill's relief. 'I had a most fruitful hour with the President,' he told Moran on 22 July. 'We not only talk the same language, we think the same thoughts.' What he did not tell his doctor (until the next morning) was what he had also learned from the Americans about the atom bomb.

That afternoon's plenary saw battle resumed. In private Churchill was already counting the days before 'this bloody election' was determined.[75] In public he said: 'We must hope that the Polish question will become ripe for discussion before we leave.' He claimed that the present Polish territorial proposal was not to Poland's own advantage. 'I have grave moral scruples regarding great movements and transfers of populations,' he said. 'Nine million people are involved.' No, Stalin countered: 'There are neither eight nor six nor three million Germans in this area.' How many, of course, depended partly on how the area was defined. When the Russians talked of the Oder–Neisse line, they meant the area up to the western Neisse. But the river that the British had in mind was the eastern Neisse, and between the two had lived some 3 million people. If this became Polish territory, this population was likely to be added to the Germans already displaced. When Churchill talked up the numbers, and when Stalin talked them down, the dispute was rather unreal. The smaller the number of Germans who remained in the east, the larger the number already heading west as displaced persons.

The Big Three all came out with their well-rehearsed lines at this juncture. 'We must not be accused of settling the frontier without hearing the Poles,' Stalin piously insisted. 'I cannot see the urgency,' Truman responded from the chair. 'The question can be settled only by the peace conference.' But Churchill's immediate rejoinder – 'There is urgency, Mr President' – pointed to the danger of simply letting the Poles dig themselves in, adding to their own territory while diminishing what ought to be a German zone. 'The burden falls on us, the British in particular,' he argued. 'Our zone has the smallest supply of food and the greatest density of population.'[76] It was agreed to consult the Poles, which obviously entailed further delay.

Meanwhile Churchill was ready to digress on some favourite themes, like imperial possessions. After San Francisco, existing British mandates were protected, as Truman reminded him. 'Eden said Italy lost her colonies,' Stalin interjected. 'Who gets them?' Churchill supplied an answer of sorts: 'The British alone conquered the Italian armies.' 'Alone?' queried Truman, no doubt mindful of the American role in the Italian campaign. 'But Berlin was taken by the Red Army,' Stalin then reminded them. 'I meant the Italian colonies, Mr President, were taken by us,' Churchill explained, triggered by these remarks to expound the purity of his country's motives. 'We do not seek territorial aggrandizement,' he claimed. 'We have suffered grievous losses, though not so great in human life as has Russia. We come out of the war a great debtor.' Britain, in its 'rectitude and complete disinterestedness', made no claim for these North African colonies.

'Who wants them?' he asked, only to be quickly assured that Truman did not – 'We have enough "poor Italians" to feed in the United States.' Churchill ruminated on the options. 'We considered them for Jewish settlement, but the Jews are not attracted to them,' he said. 'Of course, we have great interest in the Mediterranean.'

That at least would have come as no surprise to American critics of British imperialism, who had long suspected no less. What surprised Churchill – not having read the relevant papers of course – was to sense Russian interest: 'I am frank to say I have not considered the possibility of Russia claiming territory in the Mediterranean.'[77] But for Stalin, the grand master, all the pieces on the board were in play. Thus Churchill's move to talk about Soviet troop concentrations in Bulgaria was to be countered the next day by Stalin's assertion: 'Russia has very few troops in Bulgaria, but the British have more in Greece.'[78] The 'naughty document' they had agreed nine months previously had, of course, played off British preponderance in Greece against Russian preponderance in Bulgaria. On Stalin's theory, rights of conquest should be mutually respected.

The spoils of war seemed rather inequitably apportioned: for the British, an option on former Italian territory which even Churchill did not want; for the Russians, former Polish territory which Stalin really did want; and for the Poles, gains and losses engineered alike by their Soviet masters.

Churchill sometimes spoke as though the news of the atomic test transformed everything: explaining Truman's new-found confidence, animating Anglo-American solidarity, and tipping the balance of power. Yet Churchill's own mood fluctuated almost by the hour. At dinner on the very day that he learned of the Second Coming in Wrath he nonetheless seemed reconciled to Soviet supremacy in Europe. 'The idea of Germany as a single unit has vanished,' he concluded. 'Instead, we have Russian Germany divided from British Germany by a line drawn by God knows whom, on no economic or historic grounds.' Yet the Russians still demanded reparations from the whole of Germany. 'They will grind their zone, there will be unimaginable cruelties,' Churchill concluded. 'It is indefensible, except on one ground: that there is no alternative.' Yet at the next night's formal dinner, a revived Prime Minister was to propose a toast to Stalin the Great. To his doctor, the sad reality was that of an exhausted man, too tired to prepare, improvising on the spot, and resigned to cutting his losses: 'In fact – he makes no bones about it – he intends to shelve the really big decisions until he knows what has happened in the poll.'[79]

As breakfast was slowly cleared away on Monday, 23 July, Moran found the Prime Minister impatient for a confidential talk – 'That will do, Sawyers; you can do that later' – and heard his first of the atomic secret. 'We put the Americans on the bomb,' Churchill declared. 'We fired them by suggesting that it could be used in this war. We have an agreement with them.' He was referring to the informal understanding over the atom bomb reached with Roosevelt at the first Quebec conference in 1943. 'We thought it would be indecent to use it in Japan without telling the Russians, so they are to be told today,' Churchill continued. 'It has come just in time to save the world.'[80]

Not everyone agreed, especially about the effect on the Russians. When the chiefs of staff were told at lunch that same day, Brooke thought the Prime Minister's reaction much exaggerated. 'Now we had a new value which redressed our position (pushing his chin out and scowling), now we could say if you insist on doing this or that, well we can just blot out Moscow,' said Churchill, and responded angrily to any criticism. 'I was trying to dispel his dreams and as usual he did not like it,' Brooke recorded. 'But I *shudder* to feel that he is allowing the half baked results of one experiment to warp the whole of his diplomatic perspective!'[81]

Yet the news of the bomb left little mark on the proceedings of the conference. The final plan was for Truman to tell Stalin about it after the eighth plenary on 24 July. It was the last full day before Churchill's departure and one that caught him on very mixed form. It was a bad decision – had Sawyers slipped up? – to choose a tropical Air Force uniform for a morning visit to the President, since the weather suddenly turned cold, but the successive effect of two stiff whiskies, a brandy, a restorative lunch, and an afternoon sleep did the trick. 'I feel quite different,' said Churchill as he awoke, though Sawyers, aware of the 5 o'clock meeting, kept chivvying: 'You're going to be late, sir.'[82] Instead, Churchill hit top form in a demob-happy display.

There was certainly plain speaking but within conventions that were now established. All the Big Three played in character, with Truman sometimes like a patient schoolteacher, trying to find procedural dodges to rescue the business from the jocular banter of the bad boys who were showing off in front of the class. One issue was whether it was right for Italy to be recognized when the Soviet-friendly governments of Bulgaria, Rumania, Finland and Hungary were not. Churchill pointed to difficulties in gaining access and information about the latter, citing the restrictions placed on diplomats in Rumania and Bulgaria. 'An iron curtain has been rung down,' he claimed.[83] 'They are all fairy tales,' said Stalin. 'Statesmen may call one another's statements fairy tales, if they wish,' Churchill responded. 'The same condition prevails in Italy,' Stalin countered. 'That is not accurate,' Churchill riposted. 'You can go where you like in Italy.'

It still remained unclear, however, whether peace treaties could be prepared, still less concluded, if these countries were not recognized. 'May I suggest that we again refer the matter to the Foreign Ministers?' Truman suggested. 'Mr Churchill is not right,' said Stalin. 'Peace treaties can be prepared even though governments are not recognized.' 'Then we should provide for the conclusion of treaties *for* not *with* these countries,' Churchill responded and had the satisfaction of acknowledging Stalin's approval for this adroit verbal distinction. 'Thank you, Marshal.' 'Don't mention it.'[84]

As the session broke up, Truman cornered Stalin for an informal exchange with only their interpreters. The President was deliberately pitching his recital of the development of unspecified new weapons in the key of a Chopin nocturne rather than a Wagnerian overture. In *Triumph and Tragedy* there is a vivid cameo of the scene, as Churchill watched from a distance to gauge Stalin's reaction: 'He seemed to be delighted. A new bomb! Of extraordinary power! Probably decisive on the whole Japanese war! What a bit of luck!'[85] Churchill clung to the idea that this showed that Stalin had little sense of the significance of what he was now being told. The fact is that Stalin had already been told most of this by Soviet agents.

And then everyone went on pretending that nothing had happened.

The Americans pretended that they still needed their Allies' help in finishing the Japanese war (whereas covertly this was now the last thing they wanted). The British pretended that they could make a contribution in the Pacific on a scale that they would have found crippling (and made this empty offer patently in order to reassert their imperial power and prestige in Asia). The Russians pretended that they had similarly disinterested motives for accelerating their long-promised declaration of war against Japan (and did so manifestly in order to claim a share of the spoils).

Churchill had summoned the Supreme Allied Commander in South East Asia, Lord Louis Mountbatten, to Potsdam. Just ahead of Stalin, Mountbatten was told (by Marshall) about the plan to use the new atomic weapon against Japan and dined with Churchill on 24 July. 'It was a mournful and eerie feeling,' Mountbatten wrote in his diary, 'to sit there talking plans with a man who seemed so confident that they would come off, and I felt equally confident that he would be out of office within 24 hours.'[86] Two days later, release of news of his visit made a rare breach in the wall of secrecy. The *Daily Mail's* banner headline was 'LORD LOUIS TALKS WITH STALIN', fuelling speculation that the Soviet Union was near to war with Japan.

A Polish delegation had duly arrived in Potsdam, led by the Communist Bierut, and including the long-suffering Mikolajczyk in a subordinate position. Churchill was reluctant to be drawn in to what he saw as another pantomime. 'I'm sick of the bloody Poles,' he told Moran. 'I don't want to see them.'[87] Nonetheless he had two sessions with them. Each side rehearsed its points. Churchill told the familiar story of how Britain had gone to war for Poland and still wished to protect its interests so long as no threat was posed to Russia. Bierut, supported by Mikolajczyk, asserted the Polish claim to all territory up to the line of the western Neisse, from which only 1.5 million Germans remained to be displaced. Churchill warned that this was too much and too many, and pressed for free elections, as in Britain. Theirs would be even more democratic, replied Bierut (a claim about which Mikolajczyk privately expressed scepticism). The Polish leaders did not make a good impression – 'dreadful people all of them, except Mikolajczyk', according to Cadogan.[88]

Churchill had had to get up at an unaccustomed hour in order to see Bierut for the second time at 10 a.m. on Wednesday, 25 July, his own last day at Potsdam and the eve of the election results in Britain. The morning had not begun well. 'I dreamed that life was over,' he told Moran. 'I saw – it was very vivid – my dead body under a white sheet on a table in an empty room.'[89] Churchill then saw Bierut for the best part of an hour – or the worst part perhaps – before attending the plenary at 11 o'clock.

The first business in this ninth plenary was to hear Churchill report back on the Poles. 'They all agree that there are about one and a half million Germans in this area,' he said. 'The issue is all mixed up with the reparation issue, and the four power zones of occupation.' If no agreement were reached on either the Polish border or the impact on the occupation zones, he warned, 'it would mark the breakdown of the conference.' The usual inconclusive, point-scoring wrangle with Stalin then developed. 'We were only exchanging views,' said Churchill. 'I am finished.' 'What a pity,' said Stalin. 'We shall adjourn until Friday at five p.m.,' Truman intervened, seeking to close the proceedings within the allotted hour. 'I hope to be back,' Churchill rejoined. This gave Stalin his opportunity: 'Judging from the expression on Mr Attlee's face, I do not think he looks forward avidly to taking over your authority.'[90]

The British party leaders then flew home. So did Field Marshal Brooke, whose business was over, having attended a joint chiefs of staff meeting the previous day (which gave discouraging news about Lend-Lease supplies). To put him in the picture, he had been given access to the official British record of the Big Three's plenary sessions to date – 'and they are very interesting reading, the one fact that stands out more clearly than any other is that nothing is ever settled!!'[91] Cadogan, left minding the shop in Potsdam, attended a foreign ministers' meeting ('at which I impersonated A.') and later reflected on the virtue of having a mid-conference break like this, to take stock, while the shape of the British Government hung in the balance. 'Personally, I have an instinctive feeling that there may be some shocks for the Conservatives,' he wrote, 'but that's based on nothing.'[92] The election forecasts that Churchill had been fed by Beaverbrook, however, continued to predict a Conservative majority of up to a hundred. Lord Moran had sometimes provoked irritation by querying such confidence; but actions speak louder than words. 'I was so sure that we should return to Berlin,' he later wrote in his diary, 'that I left my baggage there.'[93]

*

The results of the 1945 General Election blew nearly all the forecasts sky high. Yet the opinion polls were within about 1 per cent of the actual result. For two years Gallup had found Labour invariably leading the Conservatives in voting intentions; its final poll, taken between 24 and 27 June, a week before votes were cast, showed the Conservatives at 41 per cent and Labour at 47 per cent. Apart from the fact that most commentators did not trust the science of such findings, they faced a real problem in predicting the relationship between votes cast and seats won; and this was complicated by the fact that the emergence of a new two-party system made maxims derived from the pre-war period misleading. On 4 July the *News Chronicle*, which published the final Gallup Poll, offered an extrapolation from the 1929 General Election which suggested that Labour's 47 per cent vote might produce as many as 370 seats – but hedged this with an alternative extrapolation from 1935 showing that it could produce as few as 200.[94] In fact Labour won 393 seats, the Conservatives 210, the Liberals 12 and others 25. It was one of the biggest landslides in British electoral history, giving Labour a majority for the first time, and a large one at that.

The results flooded in on the morning of Thursday, 26 July. A landmark was reached at 10.25 a.m. with the defeat of the first cabinet minister: Harold Macmillan at Stockton. Brendan Bracken's defeat came within half an hour, as did Leo Amery's. Churchill himself was returned at Woodford, Essex, where neither the Labour nor Liberal parties had put up a candidate against the Prime Minister. It was not really a personal rebuff, though it obviously felt like it at lunch that day at 10 Downing Street. But at least there was the consolation of a vintage aphorism, later to adorn the pages of *Triumph and Tragedy*. 'It may well be a blessing in disguise,' Clementine Churchill had ventured, stimulating the reply: 'At the moment it seems quite effectively disguised.'[95]

In theory, the Prime Minister could have carried on until he met the new House of Commons, returning to the unfinished business of the Big Three as a lame duck. Instead he decided immediately to resign. As the results reached Potsdam, Sir Alec Cadogan pondered the outcome: 'It certainly is a display of base ingratitude, and rather humiliating for our country.'[96] When Lord Moran called at Downing Street late the same afternoon, Churchill greeted him: 'Well, you know what has happened?' Moran knew well enough and mumbled likewise about the ingratitude of the people. 'Oh no,' Churchill answered, 'I wouldn't call it that. They have had a very hard time.'[97] The following day there were farewells at Downing Street to the wartime chiefs of staff, led by the CIGS (who had written a little over a week previously: 'Abusive minutes from PM based on false facts and bearing no relation to realities'). Now Brooke shifted, as he had done so often, to another perspective: 'It was a very sad and very moving little meeting at which I found myself unable to say much for fear of breaking down. He was standing the blow wonderfully well.'[98] Churchill's hour of greatness as war leader was over and it would be for others to meet the costs of victory.

In theory, too, Attlee could have put the Labour Party through its formal procedure for a leadership election. This is what his old rival Herbert Morrison, backed by Laski, thought should happen, for obviously self-interested motives. Instead, as soon as the King asked him, Attlee moved promptly to form a new government. In this the position of Ernest Bevin was critical. His immediate support for Attlee was decisive – and predictable given his strong antipathy towards Morrison. This also exacerbated Attlee's problem in cabinet-making. Morrison was to be denied not only the premiership but the consolation prize of the Foreign Office, for which Hugh Dalton was the favourite. But if Morrison was to be given a major role in domestic policy it meant that Bevin ought not to be, and therefore could not have the Treasury, as had been generally expected. The solution was to switch Dalton to the Treasury and Bevin to the Foreign Office.

These key cabinet appointments were announced on the morning of Saturday, 28 July. Though Attlee was working quickly, he had already put off his departure for Potsdam until that afternoon and told Stalin and Truman that he 'and a colleague' would be ready for a Big Three meeting after dinner.[99] Otherwise, the British delegation of thirty-five was kept intact, to the surprise of Americans as well as Russians. The appointment of Bevin as Foreign Secretary was neither untoward nor unwelcome in the Foreign Office. Cadogan, who had thought this likely from the moment the election result was known, wrote: 'I think he's broadminded and sensible, honest and courageous' and added the obvious departmental consideration: 'He's the heavyweight of the Cabinet and will get his own way with them, so if he can be put on the right line, that may be all right.'[100] It must be a possibility that Attlee, after confronting Stalin across the table for nine days, saw the point of installing at his side a figure of Churchillian presence and pugnacity (not to mention physical bulk).

Attlee and Bevin duly arrived at Potsdam on Saturday evening. They talked first with the American President and Secretary of State, who explained the Soviet claim to make the Oder–Neisse line the German border. 'Mr Bevin immediately and forcefully presented his strong opposition to these boundaries,' Byrnes recalled. 'His manner was so aggressive that both the President and I wondered how we would get along with this new Foreign Minister.'[101] This was before the mandarins of the Foreign Office had had any time to ensure that Bevin was 'put on the right line'; he clearly had his own line and his own longstanding suspicions of Soviet policy. At 10 p.m. the Russian Generalissimo received the representatives of the British proletariat and immediately resumed his electoral research, demanding explanations of such an unexpected result, and suggesting that the voters were no longer interested in a faraway American war on Japan. 'We would not let down the Americans,' Attlee responded and Bevin underlined the British commitment in Asia by observing that 'Britain had become a debtor to India to the extent of one thousand million pounds.'[102]

It was a long Saturday for Attlee and Bevin. At 10.30 p.m. that evening the deferred tenth plenary opened after a break of two clear days, with Attlee in Churchill's place, Bevin in Eden's, and everyone else as they were. 'I regret our domestic situation has caused delay in the Conference,' Attlee apologized. 'We are willing to sit as long as necessary.' They picked up where they had left off. Byrnes reported on his efforts to secure agreement on the admission of Italy and others to the United Nations. 'Unfortunately, we find when we agree with the Soviets the British disagree and when we agree with the British the Soviets disagree,' he explained. 'If the British and the Soviets can get together it is satisfactory to us.' Cadogan was asked by Attlee to state the British position, as laid down by Churchill. Stalin then reiterated his claim that there was no difference between Italy and the countries of eastern Europe. Bevin spoke for the first time: 'We know about the Italian government, but we don't know about the others.'[103] It was as though Churchill had never left.

What had changed, however, was the Americans' determination to wrap up this conference by summarily striking the best deal possible with the Russians. The President, anxious to leave before the atom bomb was used in Japan, put the business in the hands of Byrnes, who had already begun bilateral meetings with Molotov before Churchill's departure. The temporary British absence simply facilitated moves towards resolving outstanding issues between the Big Two.

Byrnes's strategy was simple. If the major issues on which the conference was deadlocked could not be solved separately, perhaps they could be solved together. Stalin was in a position to get his own way on the Polish border, even if this had adverse effects on the other zones of Germany. But he could not simultaneously succeed in exacting Soviet reparations from the whole of Germany (which he had thereby disrupted) unless the Western occupying powers co-operated. Here lay a possible trade-off: concessions by the Americans on the Oder–Neisse line in return for restriction of the Russians' reparations claim. As a side issue, Italy and its admission to the United Nations was to be made part of the package.

Reparations had been central to the Versailles treaty. Potsdam produced no peace treaty but neither did it produce a retributive settlement – at least, not for the western zones of Germany since both Britain and the United States were more concerned with restoring economic viability. That left reparations for the Soviet Union, which had been agreed in principle at Yalta and set at half of a notional total of 20 billion dollars. The Potsdam twist was that if the Soviet Union could extract reparations in kind worth up to 10 billion dollars *from its own zone*, the sums would add up. Admittedly, a sweetener would have to be thrown in, specifying some extra contribution from the rest of Germany. This would have to be provided in practice from the production of the Ruhr, where Britain's interest as the occupying power made it reluctant to mortgage more than a small percentage of the resources available.

Such was the thinking behind Byrnes's deal, of which the British were informed, on which they were consulted, but over which they had marginal influence. Was it worth having? Was it better than nothing? The Morgenthau Plan was plainly dead; western Germany at least could be rehabilitated rather than ravaged; there would be no general, Versailles-style ongoing reparations to sour the post-war world. The division of Europe, in short, would be recognized as a fact of life, politically and economically. Failing to agree on an amicable peace, as they had still hoped at Yalta, the Big Three could at least agree to leave Potsdam without sowing the seeds of a new war.

On his first morning back, Sunday, 30 July, Attlee held a staff conference for the British delegation: a typically businesslike innovation. He chaired it and, as in the plenaries, left the Foreign Secretary to make the running. 'He effaces Attlee,' Cadogan noted, 'and at Big 3 meetings he does all the talking while Attlee nods his head convulsively and smokes his pipe.'[104] Bevin now outlined his own ideas for seeking a bargain that included reparations, withdrawal of Soviet troops from the Polish zone, early elections in Greece and, of course, some agreement on the Oder–Neisse line. When the British ambassador to Moscow said that territory up to the western Neisse was likely to be taken willy-nilly, Attlee intervened to say that 'there was a difference between our accepting a *fait accompli* and becoming accessories *before* the fact.'[105] Over the next couple of days such nice distinctions and moral scruples were steadily eroded.

There was no plenary on either Sunday or Monday – Stalin pleaded a cold – so Byrnes was left unimpeded to market his three-part bumper bundle. The British staff conferences continued each morning. On Tuesday, Bevin summarized the progress made by the foreign ministers. Molotov seemed ready to buy the offer on reparations, Byrnes to offer concession on the western Neisse in return, with only Bevin holding out. At a subsequent meeting that morning with Mikolajczyk, Bevin suggested that he might become more accommodating towards Poland over the border in return for satisfactory assurances about internal conditions and elections; but the obvious difficulty was not whether Mikolajczyk agreed but whether he could deliver. Bevin finished a busy morning with a working lunch given by Molotov, who was assured of the continuity of British foreign policy – in substance if not in style. When he asked when the conference would end, Bevin replied that 'it would end as soon as M. Molotov had agreed to all his proposals.'[106]

All the strands at Postdam came together in the eleventh plenary at 4 p.m. on Tuesday, 31 July. Byrnes presented his three-part proposal. 'The questions are not connected,' said Stalin but he implicitly acknowledged that they now were. There was a lot of bargaining across the table about what percentage of western German resources could be earmarked for reparations to Russia. Bevin, the old trade-union negotiator, haggled away – 'Take out paragraph 4 and I will give you 12½ and 10 per cent' – before clinching with Stalin. Then, inevitably, borders. 'I have been instructed to hold out for the eastern Neisse,' said Bevin. But again he was negotiating, and from weakness, and without American support. The best he could do was to concede the western Neisse as a provisional boundary for administrative purposes, subject to a peace conference, with the proviso that Soviet troops would be withdrawn accordingly. 'I will do all I can,' said Stalin. 'That settles the Polish question,' said Truman.[107]

There were thirteen plenaries in all at Potsdam, four more than at Yalta. The last two had little substantive business, focused chiefly on drafting issues, with a final communiqué approved at the final session on 1 August, finishing half an hour after midnight. When it came to signing, there was a dry joke from Attlee. 'I favour alphabetical order,' he said; 'that is where I would score over Marshal Zhukov.'[108] He wrote a friendly letter to Churchill that night, bringing him up to date on Uncle Joe and his changeable moods: 'We have, of course, been building on the foundation laid by you, and there has been no change of policy.' He commended Bevin's performance and reached for a well-worn – but irresistibly apt – metaphor: 'I think that the results achieved are not unsatisfactory having regard to the way the course of the war had dealt the cards.'[109]

In *Triumph and Tragedy* Churchill later wrote that 'neither I nor Mr Eden would ever have agreed to the Western Neisse being the frontier line.'[110] He did not, however, explain how he would have stopped this happening. 'Joe has got most of what he wants, but then the cards were mostly in his hands,' Cadogan wrote. As for playing the hand, he thought Bevin was doing well, ready to read all his briefs, take them in, and then make up his own mind. 'I think he's the best we could have had.'[111] Bevin now held the post of British Foreign Secretary; but the Red Army held Warsaw, Berlin, Prague and Vienna. Facts on the ground militated for the status quo. This was decision by default.

Potsdam never had the glamour or notoriety of Yalta and even at the time this final Big Three meeting was seen as rather an anti-climax. 'I must admit I take no interest in it whatsoever now that Churchill isn't in it,' one woman told Mass-Observation.[112] If the very term Big Three seemed less appropriate than in the Churchill–Roosevelt era, it was still given its last airing. 'BIG THREE SPEAK' was how the *Daily Mail* reported the communiqué on 3 August, seizing on the point: 'The spirit of this Declaration is preventive not punitive.' Most of the American press was polite, even hopeful, and perhaps with better reason than after Yalta.

In the long run Potsdam turned out to mark a success of sorts. After the downfall of Napoleon in 1815, the victorious powers, initially in the guise of a Holy Alliance, succeeded in keeping the peace in Europe for forty years, until the Crimean War. After the downfall of Kaiser Wilhelm in 1918, the victorious powers maintained the Versailles peace for only twenty years. After the downfall of Hitler in 1945, the victorious powers settled into a far more permanent European peace (albeit under the umbrella of a 'cold war' until 1989). What Potsdam produced was not agreement between the great powers but agreement to disagree: much less than had been hoped, obviously, but better than the hot war that had just ended in Europe or the war in Japan that was about to generate heat on a scale never before imagined in human history.

What Potsdam obviously failed to do, however, was to ensure that the life of the world would move forward into broad, sunlit uplands. This was to disappoint American as much as British hopes. 'Nobody won but Russia at Potsdam,' concluded an unimpressed *Chicago Tribune* on 4 August. The judgement was predictable, the line of reasoning familiar. 'It was a mistake for President Truman to go to Potsdam,' it said. 'The greater mistake was for America to have gone into Europe's war.' As usual, the implications of refusing to do so were not spelled out.

Such judgements, and from such a quarter, have easily been scorned as the last gasp of isolationism and kneejerk Anglophobia. Yet not everything that the choleric Colonel McCormick and his newspaper said was nonsense. After all, he was not so much an Anglophobe as a hater of American Anglophiles. The *Tribune* showed mixed feelings about Britain's position, internally and externally alike. It did not gloat over Churchill's electoral downfall but took a sober view of the Labour Government's inheritance in its mission to ameliorate the lot of the working man: 'This task will be undertaken at a moment when there is a shortage of houses, food, clothing, and almost everything else that enters into the standard of living; when Britain's industrial plant is in need of immense capital investment; when her domestic debt is greater than ever; and when Britain owes more money abroad and has less coming in from foreign debtors than at any time in her modern history.'[113] In 1945 others nurtured greater illusions than this, especially in Britain.

Hollow victories, in some ways, for Churchill and Attlee alike (albeit obviously preferable to defeat in either case). Germany had been thwarted in 1940 by a single undefeated enemy, the British Empire, which had gone to war to protect Poland (and with guilty feelings about Czechoslovakia). Churchill had truly expressed national unity at this juncture. But by 1945 the British role in finally defeating Germany was minor – about one in ten of the troops on the ground. One result was that British concerns about Poland ultimately counted for little (and those about Czechoslovakia for even less). Whatever was settled at Potsdam depended on the two superpowers: the United States with its unexampled capacity to wage war simultaneously in both Europe and the Pacific, and the Soviet Union, manifestly in control of the contested territory in Europe, as was apparent to anyone at the Potsdam conference who ventured outside its heavily armed security ring. 'From now on Britain lives among the faded glories of the past,' the *Chicago Tribune* commented. 'She fought to prevent the unification of Europe under Germany, only to see the same objective accomplished under Russian leadership.'[114] The greatest illusion, however, would surely be to suppose that a better alternative had been available in 1940 and that victory at all costs could have been achieved in any other way.

PART 4

The Liquidation of the British Empire

11

Hopes Betrayed

August–October 1945

'Keep a bit of India.'
Churchill to Wavell, 31 August 1945

The British Empire was rather like a great country estate: its acres and its assets supporting the power and prestige of its proprietors through several generations. The Second World War proved to be a great leveller. The Churchills were the last to live in the big house, in the style to which they were accustomed, albeit with nagging thoughts about the unpaid bills. When the Attlees took over in 1945, they shut up the big house, through a mixture of choice and necessity, and moved to more modest accommodation on the residue of the estate, which they conscientiously set about improving as farmland. But everyone could see that the game was up.

India, of course, was the big house and Africa the hobby farm. Within two years, the British Empire was to undergo liquidation, not only in India but also in Palestine, manifestly unable to sustain Britain's traditional great-power pretensions. This was accepted, as the reorganization of Europe was at Potsdam, under constraint. Ernest Bevin was the dominant presence both in international policy-making and in the public eye; the number of references to him in *The Times* in these years easily outscores those to either the Prime Minister or Churchill (or indeed President Truman). Though he often bemoaned the fact that Britain's reduced resources limited his initiative, Bevin asserted a strong foreign policy which showed that he had no wish to abdicate a world role. The Middle East was promoted to the sort of strategic position formerly occupied by India, with informal influence now preferred to formal control, and appealing, as Bevin put it, to peasants rather than pashas. Moreover, the Labour Government's commitment to economic development in Africa showed an aspiration to reinvent a sort of welfare-state colonialism. Yet it remains only a clever paradox to talk of the revival of imperialism under Attlee and Bevin. The British Empire was indeed finished as any real rival or equal to the new superpowers, the Soviet Union and, above all, the United States.

In Britain, many people did not see the outcome of the war in this way in 1945. They just thought that they had won. Understandably, they lived for the moment – and had lived for this moment during long years of anticipation. 'London went crazy last night,' the *Daily Mail* reported when VJ-Day finally came on 15 August. It said that 'the rollicking thousands who turned out to celebrate made the biggest and noisiest crowd London ever saw.'[1] The Leader of the Conservative Opposition in the House of Lords, Lord Cranborne, heir to the Marquess of Salisbury and a key supporter of Churchill since Munich, improved the day by reading the minds of his countrymen. 'In this moment of victory, their first thoughts would go to God, who had brought them through this great danger; and next to their King, the corner stone of that great Empire of which they were proud to be citizens,' he told his fellow peers. 'He had passed through the Valley of Death; long might he live to guide them through the sunny uplands of prosperity and peace.'[2]

Many American observers, however, were not too blinkered to see what was happening – and the *Chicago Tribune* was not too polite to offer its own opinion. Its valedictory tribute to Churchill as a British statesman – 'the greatest of his age' – turned on his ability to summon the New World in support. 'In the classic British tradition, he has husbanded the manpower of England and skilfully shifted the heavier burden of fighting to the allies,' it commented. 'In a changing and developing world, he has not lost sight of the only thing that is eternal in British foreign policy, the interests of the empire, and has skilfully used every weapon at his command to protect them.' Hence a subsequent warning for Britain that 'we have no interest in maintaining her oppressive empire, and we are certainly not going to allow her domination of our foreign policy to continue, which is the only way in which that empire can be maintained.' The losing imperialist war that the British had fought in Asia, on this reading, had been subsumed in a bigger, better war that the United States had won. 'Who, then, would dispute our title to the victory?' another editorial demanded. 'The British, defeated in Hong Kong, Malaya, Burma, and Borneo, and driven from all their colonial possessions?'[3]

These territories were to be retrieved, at least for the time being. Churchill's insistence on fighting in Burma and the Malayan peninsula, rather than committing British forces against Japan itself, had long been a sore point with the Americans, who rightly suspected that the prime objective was imperialist. Relations between Allied commanders in this theatre made Ike and Monty seem like brothers, with the American General ('Vinegar Joe') Stilwell egregious in his views. The Supreme Allied Commander in South East Asia, 'Glamour Boy' Mountbatten, was only the worst of the hated Limeys who appear in Vinegar Joe's diary – 'the bastardly hypocrites do their best to cut our throats on all occasions. The pig-fuckers.'[4]

From 1943, the tide had turned against Japan, and thus in favour of the British, relieving pressure on India. The 14th Army, commanded by General Sir William Slim (whom even Stilwell respected), successfully concluded the protracted Burma campaign, and belatedly achieved the recognition deserved by this 'forgotten army' – a paradoxical kind of fame. By mid-September, Singapore and Hong Kong were to be back in British hands. In *Triumph and Tragedy* Churchill suggested that rogue Japanese might still have carried on fighting, making occupation 'a matter of urgency'.[5] The real urgency, of course, was for the British to pull this off before the Americans obstructed a restoration of imperial control that had never been part of Roosevelt's plan (as was shown by his actions against French efforts to retrieve Indo-China or his talk of ceding Hong Kong to China). After San Francisco, after Potsdam, Truman had his own priorities and simply shrugged as the Union Jack was raised again over these territories.

The fact was that, though the British Empire might have survived the war, it had not really won the war. Its finest hour was behind it. It was hardly likely to last for a thousand years. It was actually well into its last thousand days.

By August 1945 decisive changes in the position of the British Empire had already been determined. It no longer constituted a united force capable of acting as a superpower; and the consequences were now inescapable. It was what Attlee, in his matter-of-fact language, had called at Potsdam 'the way the course of the war had dealt the cards'. In particular, it was the prime task of his Labour Government to meet the costs of victory, as incurred – with Labour's full concurrence – under the wartime Government of his illustrious predecessor. 'Read Keynes' paper today on our financial outlook,' Sir Alec Cadogan wrote on the morning after VJ-Day. 'It is certainly grim reading! There are terrible times ahead of any Govt. in this country.'[6]

If there is a different kind of story to be told about the two years between the end of the Second World War and the moment when the King–Emperor lost his Empire, it correspondingly needs telling in a different way. What happened in the heroic age of Churchill and Roosevelt is made more humanly accessible for us today through the personal records kept by a number of men – only men unfortunately – who were conscious that they were watching history happen from a privileged vantage-point. Cadogan's sense that 'I've lived through England's greatest hour' was not his alone.[7] Some of the most faithful diarists happily continued into the post-war era: in Britain, Hugh Dalton, now with new eminence as Chancellor of the Exchequer, the economic adviser James Meade and, for a short time, his colleague Lionel Robbins; in the United States, James Forrestal, a lonely survivor in Truman's cabinet, and Arthur Vandenberg, still pivotally influential in the Senate; in India, Lord Wavell as Viceroy.

But when the tumult and the shouting dies, and the captains and the kings depart, Kipling failed to remind us that the chroniclers and courtiers often push off too. 'Charles, will you transfer your services to Attlee?' Churchill had teased his doctor at an anxious moment.[8] Lord Moran, of course, did no such thing, but his diary abruptly declines in significance with the break-up of Churchill's court. Jock Colville, at thirty, with his career to make, soon left Downing Street for the Foreign Office, where Alec Cadogan was now serving his final months before becoming Britain's first permanent representative at the United Nations. Sir Alan Brooke handed over as Chief of the Imperial General Staff (to Montgomery) as soon as he could. He was made a mere baron by Churchill – Haig had been given no less than an earldom by Lloyd George – but became Viscount Alanbrooke under Attlee. Between them, these four diarists did for the Churchill of 1944–5 what Boswell had done for his eloquent, irascible, fallible hero, Dr Johnson. The new Prime Minister, for obvious reasons, never found his Boswell – never even found his Sawyers (who was to leave Churchill's service in 1946).

Leo Amery, Harold Macmillan and Harold Nicolson all lost their seats in Parliament in 1945. Only Macmillan was to come back later.

Amery instead went into retirement, plagued by the trial and execution of his son John as a Nazi collaborator. Nicolson continued his diary but dearly missed the thrilling access to the great and famous that the House of Commons had given him, and never succeeded in getting into the House of Lords. Chips Channon held his seat, 'stunned and shocked by the country's treachery, and extremely surprised by my own survival', and was much disappointed by the new Parliament – 'never have I seen such a dreary lot of people.'[9]

Harry Butcher went home to the United States with the hugely popular General Ike in the summer of 1945 and quickly realized that his diary was a potential goldmine, with an obliging publisher on hand to unlock the gold as soon as 1946. Henry Morgenthau and Edward Stettinius, rich men who felt their dismissal by Truman more keenly than any financial incentive, left the diaries of their days of power locked up for future academics to edit.

Isaiah Berlin's time at the Washington embassy had effectively come to an end in June 1945, when he had been sent to San Francisco for the end of the conference. Excluded from the British delegation to Potsdam by Eden – 'I can't have Isaiah chattering round the place' – Berlin was to spend some months at the Moscow embassy before gravitating back to academic life.[10] The reports to the Foreign Office that Lord Halifax, the British ambassador, continued to sign in Washington were never the same again. But though the post-war style was certainly less rhetorical, the events usually less dramatic, and the personalities often less colourful, the agenda inherited from the war was actually little changed.

'ATOMIC BOMB: JAPS GIVEN 48 HOURS TO SURRENDER' was the *Daily Mail* headline on 7 August. The detonation over Hiroshima was the big news worldwide. Its immediate significance in speeding the end of the war was well recognized even if its long-term effects were not. Eye-witness reports brought home the horrors, with initial suggestions of up to a quarter of a million killed; at least 80,000 died that day. Opinion in Britain was divided from the outset. 'A shocking thing,' one young working-class woman said. 'I don't think myself they ought to have made it.' Another woman of virtually the same age and class said: 'Well, I think nothing on earth's too bad for the Japs. I was very glad it was them got it, because there's no good ones.'[11]

A statement from Downing Street, drafted by Churchill and released by Attlee, accompanied the first news, naturally stressing the British contribution to the project. 'Japan is faced with obliteration by the new British-American atomic bomb' was how the *Daily Mail* began its report, and photographs of half a dozen of the British scientists involved in its development appeared on the front page. It was true that the Manhattan Project (the American code-name) or Tube Alloys (as the British called it) had benefited from British co-operation, especially in the early stages of the alliance. A typically informal understanding between Churchill and Roosevelt had been formalized in the Quebec Agreement of 1943, giving Britain a veto over the use of atomic weapons. One informed American estimate was that without British co-operation there would have been no atomic bomb available during 1945.[12] Though the Quebec Agreement was not to be revealed even to the relevant joint congressional committee in Washington until May 1947, its gist was hinted at in the London press, with the confident British assumption that Truman was bound by assurances tendered by his predecessor. This was becoming a familiar story.

The end of the Japanese war was an American business. The news that the Soviet Union had declared war (not until 8 August) came now as an anti-climax, overshadowed and overtaken by news of a second bomb, dropped on 9 August, which blasted Nagasaki and finally broke the dogged Japanese resistance. The surrender was made to Americans, on terms devised by Americans. Unlike the long-delayed downfall of Hitler, all this happened within days. It was obviously an immense relief for the overstretched British forces serving in Asia, spared the prospect of participating in a final assault upon the Japanese home islands. This was the immediate British interest, colouring immediate reactions at home; but there was another effect, with fundamental importance for British economic prospects.

VJ-Day arrived a hundred days after VE-Day. Stage II of Lend-Lease – which had conventionally been expected to last for over 500 days – thus ended with no agreement in place on Stage III, which had now begun. This was Keynes's 'awkward' possibility – in spades. Even when the British had had the President's assurances at Quebec that Stage II of Lend-Lease would continue in the same spirit as previously, these had turned out to count for little, and promises 'beyond the dreams of justice' amounted to even less. Lacking any agreement on Stage III, the British now pinned their hopes on the goodwill of the Americans, relying upon them to see the problem in the same light as themselves. Disappointment was thus inevitable, and feelings of betrayal too.

The only top-level contact on this matter had been at Potsdam, just before Churchill left, at a meeting of the joint chiefs of staff. Churchill had been focused on the immediate problem of easing restrictions on Lend-Lease supplies to the British in the Japanese war. Truman responded that 'he was handicapped in his approach to this matter by the latest renewal of the Lend-Lease Act' and asked for patience 'as he wished to avoid any embarrassment with Congress'. These Stage II problems were virtually to solve themselves with the sudden end of the war; the real problem was Stage III. But all that Truman had said on Stage III at Potsdam was that 'he was not quite clear how far he could accept liability for reconstruction and rehabilitation of the United Kingdom under existing United States law.'[13]

These matters were all the more sensitive because they were already being openly debated in the United States – by all the usual suspects. Indeed, if this debate is counter-pointed with the British claims, some idea can be gained of the chasm that existed between the incompatible assumptions of the two allies, well before they belatedly sat down to negotiate Stage III. 'The British have recently made much of the poverty the war has brought them,' commented the *Chicago Tribune*, just after the Hiroshima bomb, warning that such stories were being 'told with the obvious purpose of getting 14 billion dollars of lend-lease indebtedness and 4½ billion dollars of World War I debts wiped off the books. There is also talk of further large gifts.'[14] A public tutored to be watchful of the wily British was being put on its guard.

In London, informed people knew perfectly well that Lend-Lease must end with the Japanese war. But they held their breath, as though fearing to precipitate the impending avalanche. Two days after VJ-Day, Hugh Dalton resumed his diary, now that he was nicely installed at 11 Downing Street, the Chancellor's official residence. 'I am conscious of having some mountainous problems in front of me, especially with "overseas financial liabilities",' he wrote privately: 'Lend-Lease may be stopping any time now and the resulting gap will be terrific.'[15] Earlier that week (13 August) *The Times* had talked discreetly of the Government's need, 'with the end of lend-lease now in prospect', to prepare for a financial accord with the United States. Keynes's much-redrafted paper was now before the new cabinet, which it warned of 'a financial Dunkirk'. This was still on the assumption that Lend-Lease 'would continue to the end of 1945'.[16] In the American press, reports that Lend-Lease would be ended very much sooner were already appearing. They turned out to be well founded.

On Monday, 20 August, a formal letter was handed over in Washington, terminating all Lend-Lease supplies at once except against cash payment. Dalton and Bevin, with their advisers, looked at its terms the same evening, dismayed and shocked. Perhaps they should have recalled that this was virtually a repeat of what had happened to Russia after its war ended on VE-Day: a lesson that the British had not absorbed and treatment from which they had imagined themselves in some special way exempt. It seems to be a legend, though one often repeated, that Truman later repented what he had done; he certainly says no such thing in his memoirs.[17]

True, there were personal reasons to explain the abruptness and the narrow legalism of the decision. It reflected not only the determination of Leo Crowley, as administrator of Lend-Lease, to pre-empt congressional criticism but also his opportunism in securing presidential authority for immediate action in the absence of key State Department officers. Dean Acheson, who took a more accommodating view, was celebrating his promotion to Under-Secretary with a short holiday in Canada. William Clayton, Byrnes's Assistant Secretary, was in London.

Will Clayton was in a difficult position. A tall Southerner of forceful personality, he was an ideological free trader and thus axiomatically in favour of giving teeth to the free-trade aspirations in Article VII of the Lend-Lease agreement. This was likely to pit him against the British if they tried to hang on to imperial preference; but he was certainly no Anglophobe and was quite ready to argue against tariffs in his own country. The real answer, as he saw it, lay in free multilateral trade, aided by the flexible multilateral currency arrangements to finance it that had been agreed at Bretton Woods. In all of this, of course, there was much common ground between him and British multilateralists like Lionel Robbins, James Meade and (usually) Keynes. On his visit to London, Clayton had already been sounded out informally about Stage III assistance to Britain, on which he was ready to smile in principle – if it meant that Britain signed up to the multilateral agenda – coupled with the warning that there were bound to be strings. Keynes noted the smile, ignored the warning. Then Clayton heard of the precipitate ending of Lend-Lease, in his absence, behind his back, upsetting his strategy. He was appalled, not because he was in the pocket of the British but because he needed more time to bring them to terms.

The news made a slightly delayed public impact. The Labour movement's own paper, the *Daily Herald*, close to Bevin, ran the announcement as only the third story on 22 August (first was the Japanese occupation and second a statement from the President of the Board of Trade, Sir Stafford Cripps, on clothes rationing): 'Lend-Lease Stops But Food Safe'. The following day it reported, this time as the second story, that Lord Halifax was to return from holiday to the Washington embassy, thus continuing negotiations with Clayton, who was obviously seeking to soften the suddenness of the blow – and was just as obviously therefore singled out for reproof by critics in the United States. None of this reporting, however, signalled a major crisis in Anglo-American relations.

It was the Government's decision to raise the temperature in the House of Commons on 24 August that made the difference. As Prime Minister, Attlee made a statement which bluntly regretted the lack of prior consultation. In paying tribute to Lend-Lease for enabling maximum Allied mobilization, he also offered an exposition of its rationale. 'The very fact that this was the right division of effort between ourselves and our allies leaves us, however, far worse off when the sources of assistance dry up than it leaves those who have been affording the assistance,' he explained. 'If the role assigned to us had been to expand our exports so as to provide a large margin over our current needs which we could furnish free of charge to our allies, we should, of course, be in an immeasurably stronger position than we are today.' This was very well put (as newspaper comment agreed) and for the very good reason that it closely paraphrased Keynes's 'Financial Dunkirk' paper for the cabinet.[18]

The essence of Britain's difficulty was that Lend-Lease was not a series of gifts but a system of flows. It did not have a one-off effect: simply on consumption, like a Christmas present. Instead it was meant to work upstream into production, thereby distorting the dynamics of the British economy. So the supply process, deliberately geared to aiding the Allied war effort, necessarily required time for adjustment to Britain's peacetime needs – especially the need to export. Put in these terms, the Keynes–Attlee point might seem irrefutable. But when, on 23 August, the *Chicago Tribune* ran an editorial, 'Santa Claus Dies Hard', it was defining the problem in quite different terms. The British had got used to expecting handouts and evidently believed 'that the way to get capital is to get America to donate'. Now they wanted more. 'Strangely enough, there are Americans willing to give it to them,' the *Tribune* commented. It advised Mr Clayton to come home.

Back in the House of Commons, speaking as Leader of the Opposition, Churchill was notably supportive of the new British Government. 'I cannot believe that this is the last word of the United States,' he declared; 'I cannot believe that so great a nation, whose lend-lease policy was characterised by me as "the most unsordid act in the history of the world", would proceed in such a rough and harsh manner as to hamper a faithful ally, the ally who held the fort while their own American armaments were preparing.' To the *Chicago Tribune*, of course, this was 'the familiar refrain of the war debt defaulters thru the last two decades, that our allies were fighting America's war until we were induced to come to their aid'. And Britain's problems? 'Those are their problems.' The editorial was headed: 'The Dining Room is Closed'.[19]

The termination of Lend-Lease closed a chapter in Anglo-American relations – and with an unhappy ending. The fine print of the agreements may have been impenetrably arcane, the legal advice disputable, the economics beyond the reach of many people: but each side of the story seemed essentially simple on each side of the Atlantic. The House of Commons had been told that Keynes would be joining Halifax in negotiations in Washington, and pious remarks were made about saying nothing to prejudice a settlement and avoiding recrimination. But the *Daily Mail* of 25 August was not alone in its judgement: 'On the face of it the American action would seem to be harsh and almost callous.' The British myth of the most unsordid act was simple and compelling. 'President Roosevelt devised the Lend-Lease system to take the dollar sign out of inter-Allied transactions and help win the war,' a further *Mail* editorial claimed three days later. 'It would be ironical if, with the war won, the grand object achieved, the dollar sign should be put back in.'

This was certainly the reaction that Mass-Observation reported in Britain, with two out of three people critical of what Truman had done. There were two main theories: that Roosevelt would have acted differently (a popular view) and that the move was ideologically motivated. 'I'm not up on the details,' said a young working-class woman, 'but everybody's saying they've done it against our Labour Government

– that's the long and short of it.' Some defended the United States. 'I think she is right,' said a working-class man in his mid-forties. 'It's her money – we can't expect to have it put in our hands.' But more felt the other way: either confirmed in their prejudices ('Well, I never did like them much') or recoiling from unjust treatment ('oh, it's not right at all, it's taking a wicked advantage'). One middle-aged working-class man thought it put wartime German propaganda in a new light: 'They were always saying we'd sold out to America and we'd find ourselves bankrupt at the end of the war. And it looks to me they were right.'[20]

Keynes had made some changes to his brief before the Labour cabinet saw it, but chiefly in presentation. If the financial Dunkirk was to be avoided, three things were essential. Two of them rested in Britain's own hands: intense expansion of exports and drastic cuts in overseas spending. The third, though, was substantial aid from the United States. Keynes had given up the bright idea of asking for retrospective Lend-Lease for the period of American neutrality; in its place was a simple, bold, cheeky suggestion that the United States should make a grant-in-aid of perhaps $5 billion to Britain. Justice remained the core of his approach, though the labels he had previously used were now abandoned. Temptation, in the sense of a big loan on ordinary business terms, made no appearance, in deference to Treasury criticism. Austerity, therefore, remained as the only ostensible alternative, yet as unattractively represented as ever.

This meant, of course, that there was no real fallback position. There had been, earlier in the summer, an attempt to prepare one in the Treasury, through the efforts of the young Otto Clarke, under the sponsorship of Sir Wilfrid Eady, the Joint Second Secretary. They wanted to explore a humdrum alternative to the visionary dream of Justice – a bit of hand-to-mouth borrowing within the sterling area, which itself might be expanded to include Britain's trading partners in Europe, where other countries faced similar problems; an acceptance of unavoidable austerity; and bilateral trading arrangements to conserve precious dollars, thus delaying the free convertibility of sterling, as ultimately required by Bretton Woods. All of this had been simply brushed aside by Keynes, who, in one of his less prescient predictions, denied that dollars would prove scarce in the post-war world and thus that the United States was likely to run a big trading surplus.

The essence of their differences, however, was as much political as it was economic. What Clarke and Eady envisaged (rather more presciently in their case) was 'the atmosphere of secrecy and leakage which will be inevitable in Washington', in which the British negotiators must be in a position 'to break off, knowing that there was some Plan II, which could be used to keep us going'. They did not deny the grandeur of appealing to Justice, but suggested that 'we must look at it as it might appear to the U.S.A., from the other end of the telescope.'[21]

Here was one foreseeable difficulty in Keynes's approach, duly foreseen within the Treasury. In the Economic Section of the Cabinet Office, another foreseeable difficulty was identified by its Director, James Meade, when he learnt that trade experts, like Lionel Robbins, were deliberately excluded by Keynes from the British negotiating team. Meade's problem was not with the central argument of Keynes's 'really brilliant' analysis, which he welcomed for its commitment to multilateral trade, just as Article VII had long required.[22] 'We can't do without American asssistance in Stage III,' Meade argued. 'We shan't get such assistance except in return for implementing Article VII.' Thus concessions on trade policy, especially over imperial preference, were inevitably the quid pro quo. 'Meanwhile Keynes and the financial pundits are to go to Washington to try to negotiate a financial arrangement for Stage III,' Meade noted at the end of August; 'and the commercial policy pundits are only to follow later if the Americans refuse (as I am willing to bet they will) to talk about other financial assistance without simultaneously talking about the implementation of Article VII.'[23] This was another bet that Keynes was to lose.

There is little doubt that Keynes had left cabinet ministers with a very optimistic view of the prospects. Uneasily conscious of his own deteriorating health, he needed to believe for many reasons: because the case was intrinsically good, because it would complement the grand design of Bretton Woods, because it would vindicate his faith in Anglo-American co-operation, and because, if he were going out on the high-wire without a safety net, he simply needed to believe in himself. 'When I listen to Lord Keynes talking,' so Bevin was reputed to have said, 'I seem to hear those coins jingling in my pocket; but I am not so sure that they are really there.'[24]

In the British press, and hence in the eyes of its British readers, the story began in hope. After all, the war had seen so many problems and misunderstandings sorted out between the Allies. *The Times* was soon canvassing the idea of a loan at a nominal rate of interest. 'This solution would be entirely in accord with the spirit of President Roosevelt's declared principle that the United Nations should share equitably the burden of the war,' it argued on 29 August, 'for it is as a direct consequence of the way in which the allied war effort has been financed that both the British deficit and the sterling debts have arisen.' Such analysis, though rightly pointing to the only sort of solution likely to prevail, was oblivious to the fact that Keynes's brief excluded the option of an interest-bearing loan; and it demonstrated the common British fallacy that the magic of Roosevelt's name could still unlock doors, even Treasury doors, in Washington.

The only objective cause for British optimism was the new President's own report to Congress on Lend-Lease. 'TRUMAN SAYS "WIPE THE SLATE CLEAN"' was the *Daily Mail*'s front-page headline on 31 August on a move that 'brought the Roosevelt touch back into world politics last night'. True, the President seemed to be suggesting that Lend-Lease had been repaid in victory and should be written off. But Byrnes quickly backtracked, obviously fearful that the President's manifestly popular move in unilaterally withdrawing Lend-Lease would be spoilt if he unilaterally withdrew any claim for repayment. Many Americans saw this as a bargaining chip in their hands, not to be relinquished except for British concessions. The *Mail* later printed a centre-page article by Henry Morgenthau (14 September) under the title 'Make a Bonfire of all books that record war debts', arguing for post-war aid to Britain. Only a couple of months previously he had been the long-established master of the US Treasury; now he was an old man speaking the language of a suddenly distant era.

The formal negotiations in Washington opened on Tuesday, 11 September. On Wednesday, Halifax and Keynes held a defiant press conference, replete with the Dunkirk spirit. Thursday's *Daily Mail* led with 'HALIFAX SAYS "BRITAIN ASKS NO FAVOURS"'; the *Daily Herald* had 'BRITAIN "NOT A SUPPLICANT" IN AMERICA'. But it soon became apparent that the reception for their remarks was cool where it really mattered, in the United States. Keynes had seized the opportunity for laying out in public the lines of a case that had now become familiar in private: the sacrifices in a common cause and the greater adverse effect on the British economy justifying a faithful ally in seeking mutual co-operation to ease the transition to peace. It was a theme that he went on to develop in private; but the leak of his analysis in the *New York Times* on 21 September was the real test of how far such arguments carried. The next day's British papers duly picked up the story, proudly showing how outstandingly the country had contributed to victory. 'Britain and America have fought together, suffered together, triumphed together,' the *Daily Mail* declared: hence its bewilderment that the war had enriched America while impoverishing Britain.

As the reception in the American press showed, however, such claims were read as implicit reproaches to the United States and slights upon its own record. *The Times*, in a magnificent display of transatlantic tone-deafness, chose this moment (22 September) to run a story canvassing the obvious solution: 'Retrospective Lend-Lease'. This was defunct as a proposal. Indeed, within the negotiations, claims for retrospective compensation for purchases made before Lend-Lease were dubbed 'half-dead cats', which sufficiently indicates their moribund status.

Keynes had told the Treasury at the outset 'that the atmosphere is perhaps rather too good. One's experience in Washington has always been that when things look beastliest all will be glowing three months hence, and vice versa.'[25] This was the best forecast he made, especially the bit about *vice versa*. What was reported in Britain depended partly on whether it was in the Labour loyalist *Daily Herald*, anxious to sustain the Government's bargaining strategy, or the Tory imperialist *Daily Mail*, readier to credit American offers. The headlines rode a switchback of expectations, initially ranging from good to not so good, and latterly reaching consensus on bad to very bad.

FREE LOAN TO BRITAIN IS PLANNED BY U.S.
(*Daily Herald*, 15 September)

U.S. MAY GIVE BRITAIN ALL THE AID SHE NEEDS
(*Daily Mail*, 29 September)

EMPIRE PREFERENCE MUST GO, SAYS U.S.
(*Daily Herald*, 5 October)

TRUMAN PLANS THANKSGIVING GIFT TO AID BRITAIN
(*Daily Mail*, 6 October 1945)

BRITAIN WILL ANSWER 'NO' TO WASHINGTON
(*Daily Herald*, 6 October)

AGREEMENT ON LOAN TO BRITAIN – OFFICIAL
(*Daily Mail*, 10 October)

ANGLO–U.S. TALKS IN PERIL OF COLLAPSE
(*Daily Herald*, 23 October)

How to pay for the war – he had used this as the title of a pamphlet in 1940 – was once Keynes's big problem. Now there was a new question: how to pay for the peace? Pending demobilization, and with occupied countries to feed, the costs of the peace were not very different from the costs of the war – except that there was no Lend-Lease to help cover them. In this situation, the urgency of the Washington negotiations was matched only by their protracted length, and the acute public concern over their outcome only by the sparsity of reliable information. Behind closed doors, in London as in Washington, the story was often no less baffling.

As so often in Anglo-American relations, the British Empire was a thorn in the flesh. The Americans knew that the British ambassador in Washington, Lord Halifax, had himself served as Viceroy of India from 1926 to 1931, and though they may not have grasped exactly why he had been known as Lord Irwin at that time, it was exactly what was to be expected of such a manifestly aristocratic grandee (whom Senator Vandenberg was probably the only person in the world to call 'Ed'). Being an ex-Viceroy was not Halifax's only claim to notoriety. He had also been Chamberlain's Foreign Secretary, and thus forever tarred as one of the men of Munich. Further, he had famously been passed over in favour of Churchill as Prime Minister in 1940, a decision that nobody now regretted. Sent to Washington, almost in exile, his talent for appeasement and personal ingratiation was let loose upon the Americans, with Churchill's full backing this time. In between the financial negotiations themselves, Halifax had his work cut out in seeking to fend off the imperial and international complications that threatened to spoil Britain's case.

Leo Crowley, the villain of Lend-Lease termination, bulked large in

British demonology. His face, Keynes once said, reminded him of the 'buttocks of a baboon' and British insiders started calling him the Baboon.[26] Indeed they went so far as to code-name their copious telegrams to Washington BABOONS (the even more numerous answering telegrams were NABOBS) – an amazing indiscretion for Halifax to permit since any such leak in leaky Washington to the news-hungry American press would surely have created an embarrassing diplomatic incident and further diminished British prospects.

While Keynes and Halifax negotiated in Washington, their every move was to be laboriously reported by telegram to the core ministerial team in London: Dalton as Chancellor, Bevin as Foreign Secretary and Cripps as President of the Board of Trade. All three were, in the end, converts to Bretton Woods, Bevin the hardest nut to crack because of his initial suspicion that fixed currencies might herald a new Gold Standard. 'Any danger of a settlement tonight?' he would ask with a grin as he marched into the cabinet room.

In London, night by night, these three busy cabinet ministers read the rapidly accumulating NABOBS that Keynes usually drafted himself. They found their NABOBS replete with wit, insight and, above all, detail, such as only a mind fully engaged with the tortuous course of the negotiations could fully appreciate. The three met frequently to sanction the hundreds of BABOONS that were fired off to Washington. Asked on one occasion if he had the relevant telegram, Bevin replied: 'I've got 'undreds.'[27] Their minds then switched, day by day, to their other pressing tasks.

The Washington negotiations, though important, were not all-important; they did not take place in a vacuum or insulated from other issues that affected Anglo-American relations. Bevin obviously had other problems on his plate, like the London conference of foreign ministers which he hosted for three weeks in September. Likewise, Dalton had to concentrate on his first budget, presented in late October. And Cripps, as well as running the Board of Trade, was heavily involved in the work of Attlee's cabinet committee on India and was conducting a copious correspondence with his contacts in the Indian National Congress, notably Jawaharlal Nehru.

In an Anglo-American context, India turned out to present less of a political problem than in Churchill's day, simply because of Churchill's removal from power. Even the *Chicago Tribune* acknowledged that the election of a Labour Government brought independence appreciably nearer. Leo Amery, the outgoing Secretary of State for India, magnanimously sought consolation for the abrupt ending of his own political career. 'From the point of view of the things we both agree about so far as India is concerned, I am by no means sure that the change is not all for the good,' he had written to the Viceroy. 'The last few weeks of the late Government made me feel that I might have even greater difficulties with Winston, and less support, than I had during the Coalition.'[28] Wavell was inclined to agree: 'I think Labour is likely to take more interest in and be more sympathetic towards India, but will have some weird ideas about it.'[29] He was soon to have the opportunity of finding out more at first hand, summoned home for the second time that year.

In place of Amery at the India Office stood the unimposing figure of Lord Pethick-Lawrence, long seen as an idealistic friend to Congress and, at seventy-three, only slightly younger than Gandhi, whom he much admired. But it was the more recent political experience and greater political weight of Attlee and Cripps that really drove policy within the India Committee. Not surprisingly, a revival of the Cripps Offer, with its phased plan for constitution-making on a representative basis, became Government policy. To Wavell, in London from late August, this looked like a concession to Cripps's vanity in wanting a quick settlement with his name to grace it, whereas the emergence of the demand for Pakistan counselled delay in reaching independence. 'I agreed the time-lag would be considerable and might amount to 5 or 6 years,' Wavell told Pethick-Lawrence.[30] Such thinking was regarded as reactionary by Cripps and Attlee.

The Viceroy recorded a rather more congenial response when he met Bevin, 'who I thought was very sensible about Palestine', among other matters. 'He was anxious,' Wavell noted on 31 August, 'to get some announcement out about progress on the Indian political situation before Sept 10, when he meets Foreign Ministers of U.S.A. and Russia.' This was to be the first of the meetings set up at Potsdam; if Bevin could signal a policy change to two allies both critical of British imperialism, this would obviously ease the pressure on Great Britain. That such moves would not have been countenanced by the previous government was made clear to Wavell later the same day when Churchill, in 'his usual jeremiad about India', depicted himself as the anchor that had now been cast off. His final injunction echoed in the Viceroy's ears as he left: 'Keep a bit of India.'[31]

It is little wonder that this visit confirmed Wavell's self-image as the sole repository of disinterested common sense. Not reactionary, like Churchill, certainly not, but ready now to implement cautious changes in the Indians' own best interests – maybe even independence by 1951? Although seeing that a purely military approach would no longer work, Wavell was inhibited in exploring political initiatives by his own distaste for politicians. Through these spectacles, the honest soldier could see that Attlee 'made it clear, without intending to do so, that the Cabinet was thinking more of placating opinion in their own party, and in the USA, than of the real good of India'. And the discerning Viceroy found Cripps just as easy to decode over dinner when Cripps 'revealed in what he said that at the back of his mind was pledges to the party tail and fear of their pressure, instigated by Congress propaganda, rather than the real good of India'.[32] Still, he recognized a better atmosphere in the India Committee; previously he had needed to use the accelerator, now he needed to apply the brakes, but at least he was allowed to stay in the driving seat for the time being. He left London better satisfied than on his previous visit, after little more than a couple of weeks rather than a couple of months, and with agreement on an announcement to take back to India.

Wavell's statement was made in Delhi on 19 September. It had all the marks of compromise. The Viceroy spoke of the early realization of self-government yet tempered this with phrases that left his future options open. 'It is now for Indians to show that they have wisdom, faith and courage to determine in what way they can best reconcile their differences,' he said.[33] In India, this left an aftertaste of disenchantment, a taint of procrastination. It reopened the scars of the propaganda war over the failure of the Cripps Mission, not least for Nehru, who wrote: 'I have not yet got over Stafford Cripps' behaviour just after his visit to Delhi in 1942.'[34] Whether Congress, still less the Muslim League, were prepared to trust a Labour Government remained to be seen, given the way that their earlier hopes had been blighted.

In the London press, however, the tone was generally positive and non-partisan. 'BRITAIN MAKES NEW OFFER TO INDIA', proclaimed the *Daily Mail*, which presented it as a renewal of the Cripps Offer, while the *Daily Herald*, anxious to proclaim the novelty of

Labour's approach, had an upbeat banner headline: 'CABINET OFFERS INDIA NEW DEAL'. Perhaps this verbal homage to Roosevelt was the right way to win American approval. Certainly Wavell, for all his aversion to politics and salesmanship, had done his best to oblige on this occasion by repeating his announcement for an American film crew in Delhi. Though the news came too late to help Bevin through his London conference, which, after a week, was already heading towards deadlock, in Washington India was already on the agenda.

The British Empire was a central issue in the financial negotiations because of the sterling balances. That meant, above all, India, because Britain owed more to India than to the rest of its sterling creditors. From the first, Keynes had linked the amount of American assistance that Britain would need at the end of the war with its existing indebtedness to wartime creditors in the sterling area. Confidentially, in his advice to the Treasury, he had contemplated writing down these sterling debts by about a third – in effect, a partial default. Any such cut, discounting a debt in this way, was normally something for a creditor rather than a debtor to determine. Yet the Indians, as creditors, were hardly likely to agree; and the British, as debtors, and as trustees of the Raj, did not want to propose such a default directly. But if the Americans proposed it, that would be another matter, of course, strengthening the British hand in bargaining with India (and others) for relief later.

The Americans could safely be relied upon to make such a link. To many of them it seemed outrageous that, if they made dollars available to the British, these might simply be recycled into paying off the sterling balances. For these balances had been run up to finance British war purchases of a very similar kind to those supplied by the United States under Lend-Lease. Why, then, should the Americans alone contemplate wiping the slate clean on what they had supplied to Britain – still less contemplate providing more dollars to pay for what others had supplied to Britain on a cash basis? And especially when all this had happened within the wretched Empire, which was thus being privileged as a creditor over the Great Republic!

Lord Halifax found himself in the thick of these developing arguments. The American team was now pressing the British to come out with it, say what they meant, and actually tell them how much they were thinking of cutting the sterling balances. 'This put us in a little difficulty, as we have to be very careful not to give our sterling creditors away behind their back,' Halifax noted in his diary on 19 September. 'The Americans plainly thought that we should tell India where she got off, and that this little financial pill could be well covered up with the sugar of Wavell's political announcement.'[35]

There were some nice moral issues here. The British delicacy about not doing anything behind the Indians' backs was partly for fear of getting found out. Then again, was it right to default on debts to under-developed countries simply because they were in the Empire? 'Did we really intend to be negotiating independence with India and Ceylon with one hand and holding out the begging bowl with the other?' Otto Clarke later demanded. He commented that it was 'remarkable that the Americans were pressing us, for if we had proposed such things ourselves we should have been submerged with cries of "British Imperialism" '.[36] As Halifax put it: 'one can imagine the howl that American public opinion would set up, if their own interests were not engaged, over such unilateral action on our side.'[37] At any rate, the idea of trading political concessions to the Indians in exchange for financial concessions from them was ruled out.

On the sterling balances, though, embarrassment apart, the British were ultimately on the same side of the fence as the Americans. Their interests coincided – but not with those of the Indians. At one point, the whole Washington negotiation became sidetracked in exploring this imperial morass. Harry White, Keynes's old sparring partner in the US Treasury (where he was now under suspicion as a Soviet agent), made his last fling: an ingenious plan for the United States itself to take over the sterling balances. It would then write off one third (as Britain would) but its own unique financial strength meant that the United States could afford to offer creditors ready cash on the remainder (as Britain could not). The twist was that these dollars would naturally come at a price, discounted for cash payment by no less than 50 per cent – a second cut. The arithmetic and the transfers were all forbiddingly complex. India was to remain, in British eyes, 'the stumbling block to this (and perhaps to any) scheme'.[38] The fact that, on this White Plan, Indian and other sterling creditors would have lost about 70 per cent of their balances could itself not be discounted as a reason for killing this plan.

Meanwhile the London conference had been concluded. It was sup-posed to follow up on the substantive issues unresolved at Potsdam but proved unable to agree even on a communiqué, and had dispersed amid discord. Held at Lancaster House, with Bevin in the chair as host, it was not a happy inauguration into the world of diplomacy. Formally, what broke up the conference was failure to agree on whether the Big Three foreign ministers of Britain, the United States and the Soviet Union should be joined on their council by those of France and China as the Big Five. The silky prevarications of Molotov on this issue failed to disguise a more visceral conflict with Bevin on wider issues. Molotov said (as the interpreter translated it): 'Eden is a gentleman, Bevin is not.'[39] Bevin said that Molotov's repudiation of his own earlier agreement over the Big Five was 'the nearest thing to the Hitler theory I have ever heard'.[40] There was a threatened walk-out, first provoked and then averted by Bevin, and a memorable sing-song after a banquet, improvised by Bevin, with renderings of 'Cockles and Mussels' and 'Roll Out the Barrel'.

Most MPs, especially on the Labour benches, had been elected only weeks earlier amid professions of Anglo-Soviet friendship. Such hopes were not dramatically dashed but now suffered a process of erosion. As early as 24 September the *Daily Herald* was running bleak headlines: 'MOLOTOV IS FORCING SOVIET BLOC ISSUE – Wants to Build up Two-Zone Europe'. On 3 October it was 'BIG FIVE TALKS COLLAPSE: SOVIET STAND'. Yet its editorial stance was simply to profess bafflement at the failure of the foreign ministers to work out their problems in a spirit of conciliation. The same day's *Daily Mail* went no further than commenting: 'One of the most unfortunate things about it is the resultant loss of faith in Russian political integrity.'

A cold-war perspective might suggest that Russian behaviour had now succeeded in driving the British and Americans into each others' arms. But this was not – or certainly not yet – the case. Whether Rumania and Bulgaria were to have democratic elections was the key isue for Byrnes. For Bevin, it was more evidently Russia's designs in the Mediterranean, notably its claim to the Italian colony of Tripolitania. 'It was not a question of power politics,' he told Molotov, 'but it would cause great uproar if any new miltary power were to come across the lifeline of the British Empire.'[41] Churchill could not have put it more clearly, or in terms less likely to overcome ingrained American suspicions of British motives.

All told, the breakdown of the London conference failed to mark an epoch. Truman showed as little concern over it as he did over Mackenzie

King's tip-off that the defection of a Soviet agent, Igor Guzenko, had exposed a spy ring in Canada. Neither event brought about any fundamental change in the USA's policy towards the Soviet Union, which was to play a waiting game. Though the temperature may have been falling, no cold-war priorities intervened to influence, still less divert, the course of the Loan negotiations.

Palestine was seen as a more immediate problem than Russia in the autumn of 1945. Lionel Robbins, taking a weekend off from Washington to visit his sister in Philadelphia, found her 'very gloomy about the anti-British propaganda now being carried on by the New York Zionists', which was indeed now overshadowing the negotiations.[42] For example, the well-publicized intervention of the financier Bernard Baruch, denouncing loans that would be used to subvert free enterprise, came after prompting by American Zionists keen to enlist financial muscle in favour of their current agenda. Rabbi Abba Hillel Silver, their leader, told Baruch: 'President Truman must be "stiffened up" to insist upon the admission of one hundred thousand immigrants into Palestine which he requested.'[43]

The demand that Britain should admit 100,000 Jewish refugees to Mandate Palestine had become the crux, and was to remain crucial until the end of the mandate itself. It made the link between the horrors of the Jewish holocaust under the Nazis, the fate of the Displaced Persons of eastern Europe – many housed in DP camps in the west – and the dream of a Jewish national home as enshrined in the Balfour Declaration.

For Churchill, Zionism had always been British imperialism by other means. That he should lose faith in the means was an appalling setback for the Weizmann strategy of using moderation to win British support. When Churchill refused to take the Zionist case to Potsdam in July, it had come as a further blow to Weizmann. 'He has lost much of his old enthusiasm and vitality and I think he is losing grasp of events,' Richard Meinertzhagen noted after they dined together.[44] Advised by Halifax of the potency of the issue in the United States, where criticism without responsibility appeared an easy option, Churchill had been moved to some apostate reflections in his last days in power. 'I do not think we should take the responsibility upon ourselves of managing this very difficult place while the Americans sit back and criticize,' he wrote in a minute to the Foreign Office. 'I am not aware of the slightest advantage which has ever accrued to Great Britain from this painful and thankless task,' he ruminated. 'Somebody else should have their turn now.'[45]

By the time that Baffy Dugdale attended the World Zionist Conference, held in London at the beginning of August, she could see most of her long-held assumptions tottering like a house of cards. The electoral landslide that swept away Churchill was the biggest since the landslide that had swept away her Uncle Arthur in 1906. The historian Lewis Namier, helping to revise Weizmann's speech in the light of events, offered her an uncomfortable perspective: 'Lewis thinks that as a Governing Class we are finished.'[46] Events seemed to bear this out.

The great consolation seemed to be that the Labour Party had a strong Zionist plank in its platform. This claimed, citing Nazi treatment of the Jews as its justification, that there was 'neither hope nor meaning in a "Jewish National Home", unless we are prepared to let Jews, if they wish, enter this tiny land in such numbers as to become a majority'.[47] Hugh Dalton had been instrumental in getting this declaration adopted the previous autumn, and had, of course, expected to be Foreign Secretary in a Labour Government, well placed to push through a policy that he acknowledged would mean a transfer of the Arab population. It was all a wonderful piece of Fabian demographic engineering: Jews would find a new home in Palestine while Palestinians would have to look for one elsewhere in the Arab world. Dalton was close to Weizmann, who had been delighted at the sweeping nature of a commitment initially made before Moyne's assassination but not subsequently amended during the months before Labour fought the 1945 election.

The Zionist conference thus took place at a moment when Weizmann's hopes of Churchill had been betrayed but not yet his hopes of a Labour Government. As with the Indian National Congress, more radical figures were not so trusting; David Ben Gurion's suspicion of the British was already well formed (and well founded as it turned out). Baffy Dugdale sensed the vulnerability of Weizmann's position. Rabbi Baeck, the Chief Rabbi of Berlin until 1943, got an understandably emotional reception on the first day, as did the Director of the Department of Immigration in the Palestinian Jewish Agency, with his 'report on his recent visit to the Camps, where the Jews are still living in scandalously bad condition'. To Dugdale the great gulf was between European suffering, on the one side, and the Americans and British on the other. 'There is great (and perhaps unreasonable) feeling that the latter have not done enough,' she wrote, with some understatement of an anti-British reflex that most Americans at the conference clearly shared.[48]

The demand for admission of 100,000 Jews – the apparently obvious, simple and just remedy staring everyone in the face – was to be taken to the Colonial Office by a delegation led by Ben Gurion. In his view, there could be no co-operation with the British Government until it abandoned the White Paper of 1939, restricting immigration. Weizmann's failure to gauge the conference's more radical mood was apparent to the loyal Baffy. Into the second week, she wrote of 'a big row in the morning, which led to Rabbi Silver putting himself at the head of the extremists', which graphically demonstrated a shifting balance. The new prominence and confidence of American Zionists made them the dynamic force in a new situation.

President Truman could not afford to insulate himself from such pressures. He too thought it right to ask for the admission of 100,000 Jews to Palestine, and had advice to this effect from a confidential investigation of the camps (the Harrison Report) which he asked Byrnes to deliver personally to the British Government at the start of the London meeting of foreign ministers in September. Meanwhile Truman made his general thinking clear enough to the Washington press: although ruling out the commitment of American troops, he wanted agreement on increased immigration. 'This revelation,' a worried British embassy reported, 'has, of course, put new fight into the assorted Zionist battalions, who seem to see more hope in Truman's more simple and direct approach to their problem than in his predecessor's delicate man-oeuvrings.'[49]

Roosevelt's calculated ambiguity combined with Churchill's post-Moyne loss of interest in Zionism had made it relatively easy to maintain a front of unity over Palestine. Truman did not directly repudiate Roosevelt's policy: he just seemed unsure of what it actually was, unsure of what Ibn Saud had been told, but quite sure that some plain speaking would do no harm. To Attlee and Bevin, on the other hand, the responsibility of power had a sobering effect in detaching them from the innocent simplicities of the Dalton policy. 'Let the Arabs be encouraged to move out, as the Jews move in,' the Labour Party Declaration had read.[50] That the new Foreign Secretary had meanwhile discovered the problem to be rather more complex became apparent in the course of September. In particular, the pledges on immigration – giving the Arabs themselves a say in the matter – were not repudiated.

This obviously came as a shock to Zionists. Dugdale wrote that 'of course there is black despair, they had hoped so much from the change of Government!'[51] If the British Government was unwilling to commit itself, what about the Americans? Zionists seized on rumours of Truman's support for the 100,000 plan as at once a rebuke to the British and a potent counter-weight. They seized too on rumours of a split in the cabinet, perhaps involving Dalton; though in fact these proved insubstantial, if only because the Chancellor, besieged by NABOBS, had other pressing concerns.

Weizmann was hardest hit. Others were disappointed by the British, but took it as predictable. Weizmann, however, was also disappointed in them, having believed for so long that they would yield to his entreaties. His Zionist critics had half expected any misplaced hopes to be betrayed and resorted readily enough to other methods: direct action on the ground in Palestine and exploitation of the political process in the United States, where power really lay. Weizmann himself contemplated resignation but instead resigned himself to an almost Gandhian abdication of practical politics. 'Weizmann's present idea is to demand that the British clear out of Palestine, having failed to administer the Mandate,' Meinertzhagen recorded at the end of September. 'He thinks once we are out, he can come to a working arrangement with the Arabs.'[52] In this perspective, if only the British would quit Palestine, their divide-and-rule tactics would be exposed as a sham, and peace would ensue.

It was Truman himself who escalated the crisis. He was pushed by the imminence of the first elections he had faced during his presidency: admittedly, only for mayor of New York but a contest that he wanted the Democrats to win under his leadership and where the Republicans were bidding for the support of the large Jewish vote. Alerted by Byrnes in London that a public statement on Palestine was coming, presumably confirming his support for the 100,000 demand, Bevin warned that the Americans would in that case face a public statement from himself, asking them to commit large numbers of troops. Attlee too warned of the inflammatory consequences, citing the presence of 90 million Muslims in India as a relevant consideration.

The President gave a promise to keep silent until the end of the

London conference. He then went back on it when he met the press on 29 September, giving them an inevitably partisan view of the frustration by the British of his efforts on the 100,000 agenda. This came, moreover, some five weeks before polling day. That this was the reason was candidly acknowledged by Byrnes when, still in London, he tried to explain the facts of life to Bevin. It did not wash. Bevin's anger was ignited with a high-octane mixture of right-minded moral indignation and wrong-footed political embarrassment.

Britain was now publicly in the dock. Any delay was read as a callous refusal to help 100,000 Jewish refugees, when the means lay in its hand to rescue these prime victims of the war from their post-war sufferings in the camps. As Halifax reported from Washington, the issue was politically explosive, not only in New York, but in the Senate, with both parties vying for position. An influential Republican Senator, Robert Taft, was explicitly linking Palestine with the outcome of the Loan negotiations.[53]

Obviously the British case did not go by default, but it was heard mainly at home. The *Daily Mail*, for example, acknowledged the plight of the refugees. 'Nothing would please this country more than to let them in,' it asserted. 'But the British people, unlike President Truman, have been living with the Palestine problem for 25 years, and they know that such a solution is impracticable.' Arab hostility to a unilateral lifting of the agreed immigration quotas would leave Britain vainly trying to hold the balance in Palestine itself and set the Middle East ablaze. Britain would be blamed for the outcome and it was 'easy to imagine the protest about "British Imperialism" and "power politics" 'that would doubtless ensue.[54]

Hitler had proved an invaluable common enemy in enforcing common wartime priorities, thus helping to mitigate differences between Zionist activists and the British Government. But Hitler also served to raise the stakes for Zionism, judged as a response to the Jewish holocaust he had perpetrated. After Hitler, a suppressed antagonism between Zionism and British policy was thus unleashed. With world power slipping from the British Empire to the United States, it was natural that American views on the future of Palestine should assume more importance. In parallel, an older, genteel, elitist Zionism, compatible with the interests of the British Empire, was plainly giving way to a newer, rawer, populist Zionism, driven by the priorities of American politics. It was in this context that Zionism emerged as a major complication in Anglo-American relations, political and economic alike.

There were many hopes betrayed in the first weeks of peace. For most Zionists, the fact that Bevin proved even less prepared than Churchill to further their aims was an acute blow. For many Indian nationalists, the election of a Labour government was likewise perceived as disappointing in its impact on policy, as seen in its conspicuous failure to employ the word independence. For British voters who had hoped for good relations with both the United States and the Soviet Union, the London conference proved disturbing – without even the consolation of American friendship, it seemed, now that the lifeline of Lend-Lease had been abruptly cut with nothing to replace it.

Perhaps it is not surprising that Mass-Observation found many British people frankly unhappy, once peace had finally arrived. One survey at the end of August showed only 32 per cent saying they were cheerful and 57 per cent depressed. Specific comments evoked feelings of unease about the Russians after Potsdam, of resentment towards the Americans after the termination of Lend-Lease, of reproach to the British themselves for the way that 'united effort ceased' as soon as the fighting ended. 'Perhaps it is a reaction,' was one response; 'perhaps a sense of the futility of it all; perhaps the feeling which practically every one has, that the peace problems are going to be as great as the war ones.'

No single voice speaks for all. Some comments focus on material difficulties that faced nearly everyone: 'Crowded round me are discontented folks waiting for more food, clothes and liberty in work.' But others remain poignant in their confessional anonymity, hinting at a dimension of tragedy which, though it may have been widely shared, was individually experienced. 'I have lost my youth, and to what end?' one woman lamented. 'I was happier when I lay listening to bombs and daring myself to tremble; when I got romantic letters from abroad; when I cried over Dunkirk; when people showed their best sides and we still believed we were fighting for something.'[55]

12

The Costs of Victory

October 1945–April 1946

In Washington Lord Halifax
Once whispered to Lord Keynes.
'It's true they have the money bags
But we have all the brains.'

Anonymous lines about
Anglo-American negotiations.[1]

This piece of doggerel was never more apt than in the Loan negotiations of late 1945. Its beauty rests in the fact that its authorship could be either British or American; that it can just as easily be taken as a satire on the naivety of American brute power as on the self-deceiving superciliousness of the British. Whether Halifax and Keynes were the best pair of negotiators to lead the British team was to be often debated. But at least they got on well personally. Halifax played a bigger part in the negotiations than has usually been appreciated, not least in handling a colleague whose genius he ungrudgingly recognized, whose impulsiveness he tactfully restrained, and whose precarious health he sought to safeguard.

In the event Maynard Keynes told his friends (and his doctor) that he felt much better than he had expected, at least for the first two of nearly three long months in Washington. With Lydia in constant attendance, he bounced resiliently through the early confrontations, with his famous aptitude for sloughing off his former opinions like the skins of a snake, as Lionel Robbins was to discover. Belatedly summoned to Washington as one of the trade experts, Robbins arrived at the end of September and caught up on the gossip from the British civil servants: 'Many valuable sidelights on the opening weeks of the negotiations at which Maynard appears to have been incomparably eloquent and persuasive.'[2]

Yet Keynes's three-day exposition of the British case, designed to prompt an immediate offer of American help, had failed – if not in its rhetoric then in producing the desired effect.

The problem was not that the American negotiators were anti-British – at least not after Crowley's political demise at the end of September. Keynes's initial response was to crow that 'the Baboon is dead' but on reflection he saw that any jubilation could easily backfire: 'It is unfortunate that the British Press is highlighting this epiosde as being a victory of our friends over this particular enemy since that is being cabled back to the American Press.'[3] A settlement commended to Congress by Crowley would have carried more weight; as it was, the Baboon was left free to grunt his disapproval. Even so, far more welcome on the other side of the table was the familiar figure of Will Clayton, for the State Department, who had heard most of Keynes's well-rehearsed lines before: common cause, finest hour, faithful ally, unequal burden, sweet breath of justice, etc. The new Secretary of the Treasury, Fred Vinson, was a typical Truman appointment: a Kentucky Democrat, no economist, a lawyer filling in at the Treasury on his way to the Supreme Court. Above all, he was always ready to profess his awe of Congress and to appeal to the reaction of the ordinary voter. 'Mebbe so, Lawd Keynes, mebbe so,' was the line from Judge Vinson, 'but down where I come from folks don't look at things that way.'[4]

Bretton Woods had sometimes been like this, as Robbins had reason to remember, meaning that these were arguments that could not be won by argument alone. As he now perceived, 'this is not a matter of dialectic success, it is a matter of high politics; and it will take a great deal to shift Clayton and Vinson from their conviction that an outright surrender of Imperial Preference is the price necessary to get the financial arrangements through Congress.'[5] If Clayton played ball, it would be because the British delivered on his multilateral trade agenda, despite the Empire; and if Vinson played ball, it would be because he was sure that it was the kind of package that he could sell to Congress. A Gallup Poll in late September showed that 60 per cent of the folks disapproved of a loan to Britain – let alone of the outlandish notion of simply giving the dollars away.[6] For all Keynes's golden words and his unrivalled mastery of a complex brief, his clever stratagems were never going to prevail.

Indeed Robbins's presence, along with the Board of Trade officials sent with him, testified to the abject failure of the ploy for avoiding detailed trade talks. Clayton simply demanded that parallel negotiations take place about ending commercial discrimination; the British had signed up to Lend-Lease long ago on the basis of Article VII; for him this was the hinge of the whole business, as the British ought to have foreseen. They must agree to dismantle imperial preference in favour of steps toward multilateral free trade; and they must agree to dismantle exchange controls so as to let the money finance that trade – free convertibility of sterling into dollars.

So when Robbins (who had foreseen this linkage) arrived, he decided to heal his bruised relations with Keynes (who had not) by pretending when they met again that 'nothing had ever happened'. 'Result excellent,' he noted. 'Maynard could not have been more cordial.' An invitation was immediately proffered to a lunch made more agreeable by further demonstration of Keynes's lack of rancour and his blissful ability to rethink his position. After three weeks in Washington, he now realized that any sort of grant-in-aid was a hopeless non-starter. 'But I perceive that we shall have great difficulty in dehypnotising London,' Robbins commented; 'and I think that Maynard will have to be told that, having himself made the magic passes that now hold the King's Treasurers entranced in rapturous contemplation of ideal "justice", it will be up to him, sooner or later, to use quite special arts to reverse the process and bring them back to considering soberly nice questions of more or less day-to-day convenience and expediency.'[7]

In the end, this is virtually what happened, though it did not happen all at once, still less without difficulty. If there is one telegram, of the hundreds that were exchanged between London and Washington, that captures the story, it is NABOB 177, sent by Keynes to Dalton on 18 October. Clayton had offered Britain a loan of $5 billion, but bearing interest, albeit at the low level of 2 per cent, and repayable over fifty years. A press conference had publicized the offer; the assumption was that it would provide the basis for agreement. Instead, the British cabinet turned it down flat, still fixated by Keynes's talk of the sweet breath of justice.

Yes, Keynes tried to explain to them, such had been their hopes in seeking a broad and generous settlement from their ally. 'If we are to believe what we are told by Vinson and Clayton repeatedly and with great emphasis the American Administration has rejected any such settlement,' NABOB 177 informed Dalton. 'They have done this not because they themselves would resist but because of their honest and considered judgement that Congress and the public are not in the mood to stand for it.' What was needed was a trade, or 'at least the appearance of a trade', in order to satisfy American public opinion. 'Thus precisely those elements which will spoil the flavour to us are necessary to make the result palatable here.' He wrote wistfully of the way that Roosevelt might have invented a solution. As things stood, however, 'we must think again substituting prose for poetry.' Pragmatism demanded making a different response to the well-meaning Clayton, because 'from his own point of view and from ours too when once we have accepted the inevitability of prose, Clayton is generous and not unreasonable.'[8]

Justice, as the British understood it, simply would not sell to Congress, which demanded a *quid pro quo*. This was the trap in which Keynes now found himself caught. He had, of course, helped spring it for himself by wilfully neglecting the politics of the mission. Perhaps he should have started from different premises; or perhaps he was simply the wrong negotiator to send to Washington. Perhaps the presence of a Labour Government, mistrustful and mistrusted, made things harder; perhaps Keynes would have done better with Churchill still in power, perhaps with Roosevelt too. Yet such speculations miss the main point.

This was an unfolding drama with a plot of tragic ineluctability for British pride and pretensions. It was Churchill and Roosevelt who, between them, had been largely responsible for putting Britain's financial fate into American hands. It was Roosevelt who had insisted on Article VII as the consideration for Lend-Lease; Roosevelt who had deliberately maintained this system even when Britain and the United States became Allies. It was Churchill who had proclaimed the unique unsordidness of the transaction, thereby suggesting that there was no *quid pro quo*, and hence no deferred cost to be met. Lend-Lease, the solution to Britain's crisis in 1940–41, had thus become the prime cause of Britain's crisis in 1945.

Keynes was not blind to the broader logic of the situation. As he had put it in the peroration of his opening statement, Britain's wartime achievements in mobilization, which even the Nazi technocrat Albert Speer now lauded, 'were the direct consequence of the perils of 1940; but they would have their own consequences in the inevitable financial and economic difficulties which the U.K. would face during the immediate post-war period'.[9] This was the moment when Keynes had left the unspoken plea for Justice hanging in the air, appealing for an even more unsordid act of deliverance. This was the moment, alas, when his advocacy failed and Britain was instead asked to deliver.

This was a trade-off that the Americans exacted with consistency and a good conscience. As Robbins noted: 'there has been no change in the attitude which Clayton developed in London. Preference must be extinguished as a price for financial assistance.'[10] Clayton knew that the British had signed up to these terms and was not going to allow them to default on commitments which he believed were the right thing in any case.

On the British side, it should be said, there was an element of play-acting in the tragic assassination of imperial preference. The scale of the duties agreed at Ottawa in 1932 had been modest, their impact unremarkable, their net benefit to the British economy disputable, their continued desirability debatable. Again it is Robbins's diary that catches this note, for, like most economists, he had never liked the Ottawa Agreement. 'But it was one thing to wish it had not been introduced,' he explained to an American colleague. 'It was quite another to accept the obligation of unilateral abolition, especially under financial duress.'[11] This goes a long way towards explaining the huffy reaction in London. 'The Labour Ministers discovered the Empire,' Meade observed with due scepticism at one point.[12] True, the idea of the Commonwealth had a strong pull for Labour; and there was a historic political resonance in imperial preference, which true believers like Lord Beaverbrook and Leo Amery made the basis of their noisy opposition to the loan negotiations.

There was an inherent difficulty in playing to two audiences simul-taneously. In Washington, the British game was firstly to talk up their own concessions so as to impress Congress with how much was being conceded to the Americans, and secondly to talk them down again so as to persuade London of how small each concession really was. Very similar difficulties surfaced over Palestine, which kept intruding into the financial negotiations and which was in any case a more acutely poli-ticized issue, as Bevin discovered when he had been apprised of the diplomatic significance of the New York election.

What Bevin did, once his just wrath had subsided, was not to shut out the Americans, as having no right to speak on the problem, but to bring them into play as part of the solution. Throughout October and the first half of November, a plan was developed for setting up an Anglo-American committee on Palestine.

Byrnes was unexpectedly ready to tolerate the idea provided that he had the whip hand in setting the terms of reference. This meant that the 100,000 proposal had to have pride of place in considering the fate of European refugees, now flooding into the American and British Displaced Person camps. Bevin remained of the opinion that for the Americans 'to play on racial feeling for the purpose of winning an election is to make a farce of their insistence on free elections in other countries'.[13] So Byrnes, wearily, repeatedly and unabashedly, had to educate the British in the importance of such issues; as Halifax reported home at the end of October, any tardiness 'would inflame the million or so Jewish voters as also their sympathies and altogether destroy the prospects of the Democratic candidate whose Republican rival for Mayor was, he reminded me, a Jew'.[14]

On Tuesday, 6 November, as was widely expected, the Democrats easily won the New York election. The way was thus clear for an announcement seven days later setting up an Anglo-American committee (which was to be given a brief to report within 120 days). All of this happened on American terms, driven by the American electoral process; but the British at least succeeded in drawing the United States into participation in the search for a viable policy. Bevin's relief and confidence buoyed him into making two brash remarks that day. His boast to the House of Commons – 'I will stake my political future on solving this problem' – was manifestly bold, albeit qualified in his other remarks. The boldness was to be remembered when the qualifications had long been forgotten. His second hostage to fortune was an unwary summary of Government thinking made to a press conference: 'that I want the suppresssion of racial warfare, and therefore if the Jews, with all their sufferings, want to get too much to the head of the queue, you have the danger of another anti-Semitic reaction through it all'.[15]

To Bevin, this was a rough demotic allusion to the experience of ordinary British people in queueing for rations, as for much else. To Zionist critics in the United States, it was a sly invocation of the manifest anti-semitism that drove British policy on Palestine. Once Bevin had been identified as their enemy, in short, the imputation of motive naturally followed, either in good faith or in bad, duly compounded by transatlantic differences of nuance and sensitivity. It may be significant that a British Zionist like Meinertzhagen, who read Bevin's statement twice and hated every word – 'It is a complete surrender to the Arabs, every word of the speech denoting fear of the Arabs' – nonetheless did not make anti-semitism one of the many charges he levelled.[16]

At any rate, Bevin's tone exacerbated a difficulty that the Loan negotiations could have done without at that stage. Zionists were the more angry with him because they naturally saw the new committee as a success for his diplomacy and feared it as a means of ensnaring the United States. All the reasons for welcoming it in the House of Commons had become reasons for fearing the reactions of Congress, as Byrnes and Truman made clear (as usual).

The simultaneous announcement about the committee in Washington coincided with the visit of the British Prime Minister. Like Churchill before him, Attlee addressed both Houses of Congress on 13 November. Everything else was unlike: the lack of the thrilling wartime context, the lack of stirring rhetoric, the lack of much public attention. If Palestine was the particular topic of the day, the general theme was the downbeat defence of an ordinary, democratically elected British government whose alleged socialist excesses were much exaggerated. 'We in the Labour Party,' Attlee told anyone who was listening, 'declare that we are in line with those who fought for Magna Carta and habeas corpus, with the Pilgrim Fathers, and with the signatories of the Declaration of Independence.'[17] His public mission was obviously to counter Baruch-style invective against the Loan just as the Anglo-American committee was designed to counter the anti-British force of Zionist propaganda.

As well as this barely hidden agenda, there was a top-secret agenda. Under the guise of consultations with Truman and Mackenzie King – the Not-So-Big Three even further diminished – Attlee was in Washington to talk about atomic collaboration. Truman had been making statements, to popular approval, about the exclusive rights of the United States to nuclear weapons and technology, under the auspices of what a very small number of privileged Americans knew as the Manhattan Project. Conversely, awkward questions had been raised in the House of Commons about the secret agreement made at Quebec in 1943. Was this really a 'British-American atomic bomb' or what? It turned out that nobody in Washington was at all impressed by the Quebec Agreement – indeed nobody could find a copy because it had been filed in FDR's papers at Hyde Park under 'Tube Alloys', the British code-name.[18] Mackenzie King, who thought he had come to Washington to talk about the Guzenko affair, found this ignored for the time being; but it had an

indirect effect in increasing American concern about sharing any information. Attlee was vehemently assured that of course the agreements
made by the dead President could not be revealed – politically impossible, Byrnes said, with the customary wise nod towards Congress – but
vehemently assured also that of course they would be honoured.

Attlee had to accept this for the moment. He said goodbye to his host
at the embassy, Lord Halifax, and had barely said hello to Lord Keynes.
They were left to get on with the job, however unpromising the prospects
of Anglo-American accord.

The final deal was simple. The sterling balances – now over £3 billion
or $13 billion – were left hanging over Britain's head, with only vague
talk about somehow reducing them. And having turned down an
interest-bearing loan of $5 billion from the United States, the British
cabinet had to settle for one of $3.75 billion.

The reason the cabinet settled was also simple. 'We are playing for
very big stakes,' Keynes telegraphed, warning of the stark and forbidding
alternatives. 'There is no way out remotely compatible with the present
domestic policy of the Government except on the basis of substantial
American aid,' he told the Chancellor. 'Indeed, the fact that some Americans are becoming aware of this is one of the hidden, unmentioned snags
in our path.'[19] As Dalton could now see, 'those who represent us out
there and we here at home have drifted into a condition of mutual
incomprehension.'[20] Once understanding of the real position was
brought home to ministers, however, further resistance within the
Government collapsed. Bevin, who had not much liked Bretton Woods,
decided that he preferred it to Starvation Corner.

The last fence had to be jumped in early December; otherwise the
deadline for achieving parliamentary approval of Bretton Woods by the
end of the month could not be met; and if not, all bets would be off.
The Secretary of the Cabinet, Sir Edward Bridges, was despatched by
air to Washington at three hours' notice. This was obviously a rebuke
to Keynes, implicitly questioning his leadership and his judgement. But
when Bridges saw for himself how things stood, any personal interpretation of the British failure to get better terms became unsustainable.
Admittedly, Keynes was under acute stress by this stage; and when he
relieved his feelings through sardonic sallies at Vinson's expense, it was
not helpful. Yet this was not the nub of the difficulty. It is a tribute to

Vinson's magnanimity that he now defended Keynes, not least by refusing to concede anything further to Bridges.

The cabinet's final qualms were not about the size of the Loan. If this was to be smaller, so was the burden of servicing it. And repayment was not only deferred until 1951 but the terms were elastic, with waiver provisions to be triggered when payments could not be afforded. Likewise, the undertakings to negotiate on imperial preference allowed a good deal of latitude – almost as much as the Americans reserved for themselves in promising to negotiate away their own tariffs. In fact, all that the British were publicly pledged to do was to enter negotiations in good faith, thus making abolition of any preferential access to the British market dependent on the agreeement of those Dominions which stood to lose the advantage. Only in private was a further assurance given to Clayton that, 'if the Dominions were to adopt an unreasonable position', the British Government would override it.[21] As so often before, the British and American negotiators took away conflicting views of what had actually been agreed and ambiguity was to store up future trouble.

The point that the cabinet resisted until the last in 1945 was the use of the Loan to enforce the early convertibility of sterling. Instead of the long transitional period that Bretton Woods envisaged for dismantling exchange controls, a fixed timetable was specified for Britain: a mere twelve months after the ratification of the Loan agreement. Here the cabinet's objections were not so much misplaced as irrelevant in the face of American determination.

Given the fermenting contention, perhaps the most remarkable feature of the agreement is the easy settlement of Lend-Lease itself. Since August, Britain had been drawing on continuing supplies from the United States, albeit at a much reduced rate; and there was a huge inventory of stockpiled goods that had been supplied at one time or another. The simple analogy had always been that what had been lent – like a garden hose – would be returned after use. Moreover, once Mutual Aid accounting put the dollar sign back, an extreme reading was that everything might have to be repaid. Lend-Lease to Britain had totalled $27 billion (and Reverse Lend-Lease $5 billion). In the event, all British commitments under Lend-Lease were written off at only $650 million, to be added to the amount loaned.

This gave Dalton some good news to spice his announcement of the agreement in the Commons on 12 December. 'Lend-lease, a great scheme, a great idea – (cheers) – begun by the late President Roosevelt – (cheers) – the most unsordid act in history, as it had been aptly called – had had a fine, clean end which we should welcome. (Cheers).'[22] There was rather less to cheer when he turned to the Loan itself.

Nobody pretended it was a triumph. Churchill claimed that a Conservative government could have got better terms – an unwise remark, provoked by Bevin, who seized on it to say that this was a slur on the political impartiality of the US Administration. The Loan was agreed by 345–98; Bretton Woods by 314–50 half an hour later. Churchill's advice to his followers to abstain on the Loan, though much derided, reflected divisions in his party: not only the fact that seventy Conservative MPs nonetheless voted against the Government in the Commons but also the danger of a revolt in the Conservative-dominated Lords.

Hence the unusual significance of the following week's debate in the House of Lords, in which Keynes spoke. Fresh from docking at Southampton, he first commented that 'two days in Westminster are enough to teach one what a vast distance separates us here from the climate of Washington.' This was the theme of his speech – 'I give the American point of view' – thus advancing many of the arguments that he had himself contested for the last three months.[23] Keynes used the full register of his oratory to suggest that Justice had always been a chimera, and that the grand design of Bretton Woods could only be implemented through the admittedly imperfect Anglo-American agreement he had brought home. Beaverbrook proved ineffective; the Conservative revolt did not materialize; the Lords accepted the agreement by 90–8, with many abstentions.

The financial costs of victory were fast becoming clear. In the course of the New Year, the US loan was to be supplemented by a loan on similar conditions from Canada. Even in the professionally sceptical eyes of the Treasury, the Canadians had a record of being helpful; and, sotto voce, the message that 'so far we have always managed to see Britain through' remained reassuring.[24] But the Mackenzie King Government's overriding political concern, not to be seen as softer than the Americans, inevitably shaped the settlement. The fact that the Canadian loan was for $1.25 billion – a third the size of the American loan from a country and an economy more like a tenth the size – spoke for itself, not only of old imperial sentiment but also of the Canadian trade interests at stake in sustaining the British market.

What, then, did the residual benefits that accrued from the British Empire really amount to? It was integral to the financial settlement that the sterling balances somehow be scaled down. Keynes had proposed cancelling about one-third of the debt; Harry Dexter White had proposed cancelling, in effect, at least twice as much. After all, in net terms, the Americans could claim to be out of pocket by about $22 billion under Lend-Lease and generously wrote this down to $650 million, barely 3 per cent. But when it came to the sterling balances, instead of cancelling 97 per cent of the wartime liability (on the Lend-Lease model), or 70 per cent (on the White model), or even 33 per cent (on the Keynes model), the cuts ultimately achieved by the British were to amount to about 1 per cent. A grand total of only £38 million was to be actually cancelled – all by Australia and New Zealand, and again with a mixture of sentimental and trading concerns.

Thus the only tangible contribution to the costs of victory came from three members of the Commonwealth that were already fully independent. For the rest, the paradox was that nominal imperial control delivered so little financial return to Britain. No real cuts were made in the sterling balances, what with British banking scruples about honouring liabilities on the one side and, on the other, nationalist hostility to the mere idea of paying for Britain's war. India's sterling balances in 1946 stood at over £1300 million.[25] The British thus owed their own Raj more than they owed the Great Republic.

To those of Churchill's cast of mind, it might seem extraordinary that 'this small Island', having carried India to safety on its back, should now have Indian creditors on its back too. What he ignored, of course, was the fact that there was no common cause to which Indian representatives had committed themselves, just a declaration of war on Hitler by the Viceroy, long before Japanese attacks. The old slogan from the American struggle for independence, 'no taxation without representation', still had its pertinence, as FDR would doubtless have enjoyed pointing out. So perhaps it was a lesson in the folly of holding an Empire that both provoked predatory aggression and then saddled Britain with the costs of its defence – a self-defeating form of imperial exploitation.

The costs of victory could be measured by the loss of British assets abroad and the accumulation of external liabilities instead – a net loss of 28 per cent of the country's total wealth. British net overseas investments of over £1 billion (or $4 billion) had been wiped out. Moreover,

Britain now had to face financial liabilities of much the same order that Keynes had estimated in advising the cabinet in May. Then he had toyed with the idea of a US loan of up to $8 billion, to be added to sterling balances estimated at that time at another $12 billion. As it actually turned out, by the end of 1945, the two loans from North America (including the Lend-Lease settlement) added up to $5.6 billion and the sterling balances now amounted to £3.6 billion or $14.4 billion, giving a total of $20 billion. The figures were slightly different, the total exactly the same. Yet this had been Keynes's totally unthinkable scenario only months previously, summoned up only to be dismissed as outrageous.[26] His point that it was the same sum that Russia had thought right for German reparations at Yalta could likewise be modified to say that it was double what Germany was ostensibly asked to pay at Potsdam.

The *Sunday Times* of 16 December voiced the opinion that 'as victors we are being asked to pay reparations', echoing the sentiment in the previous day's issue of *The Economist*, that 'our reward for losing a quarter of our national wealth in the common cause is to pay tribute for half a century to those who have been enriched by the war.' As Keynes explained it privately to Halifax: 'The general public was upset solely because they were being told by those who ought to know, that, after all their past *and present* sufferings, they were being given a raw deal by their old comrades in the U.S.'[27]

The financial burdens were, in the end, less important than the moral effect. After all, the Indians and other holders of sterling balances might indignantly refuse to scale down their claims; but they could not freely draw on their funds, locked and blocked in cash-strapped London. The American Loan itself, though a huge notional liability, was coupled with technical conditions that alleviated its real impact. When Keynes told the House of Lords that 'I shall never so long as I live cease to regret that this is not an interest-free loan', he did so not because of the money at stake but, rather, 'what a difference it would have made to our feelings and to our response!'[28] The provision for a waiver of British payments was likewise intended to ease possible difficulties for Britain as debtor (as well as protect the creditor from outright default, of course). But this very process of monitoring was seen as vexatious and demeaning. Even convertibility, though its potential effects were more deadly, was mainly resented because it was to be implemented, willy-nilly, on a timetable prescribed for Britain alone by the United States.

The Loan, in short, though presented as an Anglo-American agreement, lacked the reciprocity of a true partnership. Those who opposed it in Britain were wrong about many things but not about the fact that it marked the humiliation of the British Empire, not least by requiring unconditional British consent in advance of any American commitment. At the beginning of 1946 the British debate was over but the debate on the Loan in Congress was only just beginning.

Richard Crossman had been elected as Labour MP for Coventry at the age of thirty-seven in July 1945. Three months later, still a new boy at Westminster, taking any chance to learn the ropes – as he had hoped, by making use of his fluency in German to join a parliamentary delegation to Vienna – he first heard from the Labour Chief Whip that 'Ernest Bevin has got another job for you, something about Palestine.'[29] Like Dalton, Crossman was a traitor to his own privileged class and took a tough-minded delight in arguing for a sort of Fabian socialism in which the intellectuals tended to know best. Certainly he was an intellectual himself: a classical scholar who had thrown up an Oxford Fellowship to become deputy editor of the left-wing weekly the *New Statesman*. He had soon become a wartime recruit to government service, enjoying his efforts in 'black' propaganda as much as he relished the Machiavellian insights on Anglo-American relations of Harold Macmillan, for whom he had worked in the Mediterranean.

Crossman agreed to serve on the Anglo-American committee of inquiry regarding the problems of European Jewry and Palestine, as set up in mid-November 1945. It met from early January to late April 1946. Not content with inspiring much of its report, Crossman then set about publishing his own highly subjective account of it, *Palestine Mission* (1947). Finished by September 1946, on a schedule that permitted little hindsight to intrude, the book's journalistic immediacy is further increased by the incorporation of a diary (much of it originally written for his wife). This reveals Crossman as a superb diarist, as telling in his eye for detail as in his command of an argument. He went on to have a political career that took him into the British cabinet in the 1960s but he is best remembered today for the volumes of his later diaries as a cabinet minister, which give a compellingly vivid picture of how government power is actually exercised. Indeed the television series *Yes, Minister*, with its portrayal of the hidden influence of the senior civil servant, Sir Humphrey, with his suavely deployed expertise, owed much to Crossman's diary.

If Crossman later became the great connoisseur of the workings of the political process at the highest level, his apprenticeship began with the story told in *Palestine Mission*. The plot is fairly simple. It tells how a young British socialist politician was converted to Zionism through the impact of what he saw and heard in these 120 days of intense inquiries, and how the committee's benign and unanimous recommendations fell victim to the wiles of American politics and, above all, of British officialdom. It is thus the story of the triumph of Sir Humphrey – or rather of Sir Humphrey as a composite stage villain who evidently manipulates a strangely inert British Foreign Secretary in nefarious ways that the diarist has not yet quite fathomed.

In this sense the author of *Palestine Mission* exhibits a degree of naive innocence that his subsequent political career served all too well to cure. But the author already knew full well what he was doing as an opinion-forming journalist, so in another sense it is not an innocent document at all. It is a tract, compiled in haste in the summer of 1946 with the manifest intention of educating its readers about the merits of the case for Zionism. And since Crossman could never resist an argument himself, he presented the case against it too, and did so with a fullness and a candour that was an inherent part of his dialectical approach. Selective quotation from his diary can easily render a pro-Arab Crossman. 'If I was a mountain Arab,' he writes when in the hills of Palestine, 'I would shoot any Jew who came into Nablus at sight.' And he prints this in the book, only omitting 'at sight' and saying that he would 'want to' do this.[30] What *Palestine Mission* best shows us, however, is the appeal of Zionism for the British left: for the sort of people quite unimpressed by, say, Colonel Richard Meinertzhagen's embarrassingly atavistic enthusiasm for the Old Testament plus the British Empire.

'The British Press at this time showed no interest in the Jewish problem,' wrote Crossman, 'and in the little space which it gave to it, no very violent partisanship.'[31] The second part of this statement is truer than the first. Both *The Times* (with middle-of-the-road scepticism) and the *Manchester Guardian* (with passionate liberal sympathy) carried news and comment on Zionism, and the issue was by no means ignored in the popular press, despite acute shortages which often reduced newspapers to only four pages. For instance the front page of the *Daily Mail* on 5 October 1945 was dominated by a banner headline: 'ARABS WARN: "WAR IF MORE JEWS ENTER PALESTINE"'. A month later, on the same day as another front-page banner, 'BRITISH TROOPS FIRE ON TEL-AVIV MOB', the *Mail* devoted its leader page to full statements by protagonists of the Zionist and Arab cases. This replicated what the *Daily Herald* had already done in devoting its centre page to a debate: '100,000 Homeless Jews for Palestine?'[32] What is true, then, is that both Conservative and Labour newspapers self-consciously treated Palestine as an issue outside normal party politics.

The basic contentions have changed surprisingly little in the subsequent sixty years. Zionism was presented as the obvious response to the Nazi experience. 'A hundred thousand Jewish people, broken, destitute, hopeless, remain in the concentration camps into which Hitler threw them' was how the *Mail*'s anonymous writer put it, making out an appealing case for immigration and, what went with it, development: 'Palestine, before the arrival of Jews in any numbers, was a barren wilderness.' This was countered by the 'simple and straightforward' claim that for thirteen centuries this had been an Arab country, albeit one capable of accepting its existing population of 600,000 Jews. 'As long as immigration continues,' this argument went, 'the threat of an ultimate Jewish majority and the establishment in the country of an alien national state, in which Arabs will be either reduced to a minority in their own land or compelled to leave it, remains.'

The two Labour members who had debated in the *Herald* displayed virtually the same contrasting scenarios. There was agreement only that Jews were currently outnumbered by two to one in Palestine, which pointed either to the self-evident necessity or to the self-evident folly of admitting substantially more. 'The persecutions in Europe are not the Arabs' fault,' argued Richard Stokes, MP for Ipswich, 'and it is as stupid as it is illogical to attempt to force them to solve the problem for us.' If to him any large departure from exisiting immigration policy was ruled out because it would be 'disastrous', Barbara Gould, MP for Hendon North, implicitly questioned his tender-minded perspective. 'Let us be realist and face the the facts – there is no easy way out,' she argued. '*Bloodshed in Palestine is inevitable.* Let no one doubt that.'

The stark realities of the DP camps understandably fuelled emotional responses. Refugees had flooded into them, bearing out the worst fears of Churchill, Attlee and Bevin at Potsdam, that redrawing the map of eastern Europe would have a horrendous human cost – and that the British would end up footing the bill for much of it. Only a small proportion of DPs were initially Jews but they attracted disproportionate attention because of their disproportionate suffering under the Nazis. Moreover their numbers had grown as the British hope that many of them could safely return to their countries of origin was increasingly mocked by events. Polish Jews may have suffered a double penalty during the war – for their nationality as well as their religion – but that did not mean they were doubly welcome if they returned to Poland, where disfiguring post-war pogroms were only the worst of the hostile actions they faced when they tried to reclaim their former homes. Jewish refugees were warned accordingly and sat in the camps pondering the limited options open to them.

The British line was that to segregate Jews was to allow Hitler a posthumous victory. From August 1945, however, the Americans had begun setting up special camps in their zone for Jewish DPs, and generally offered better conditions, with the natural result that increasing numbers of Jewish refugees gravitated to American camps. The Harrison Report, given to President Truman in August and subsequently leaked to the *New York Times*, suggested that Palestine was pre-eminently where these Jews wished to emigrate. Hence the centrality of the 100,000 issue. The paradox was that those Jews whose sole priority was early admission to Palestine would have done better to opt for the British camps since their inmates naturally enjoyed priority in claiming immigration certificates. These were to be issued at the rate of 1500 a month throughout 1946 (though the number available for distribution in the camps was cut by the British policy of offsetting illegal immigrants against the quota). Moreover, those committed Zionists who had the strongest incentive to get to Palestine simultaneously had the strongest incentive to choose to be with their fellow Jews in the American camps. Still, at the time of the Harrison Report, there were no more than 50,000 Jews in the American camps – it was not until the summer of 1946 that a further wave was to arrive from Poland – so initially a target of 100,000 immigrants to Palestine might actually have been difficult to fulfil. As time passed, what Zionists feared was that zeal rather than numbers would prove insufficient, if the vulnerable morale of long-term DPs shifted the focus from Palestine to finding a safe haven anywhere else.

Jewish immigration to the United States was thus the great unvoiced issue. The British certainly hinted at it as one solution; this was behind the drafting difficulties of the terms of reference for the Anglo-American committee. Everyone was long familiar with the entreaty inscribed on the Statue of Liberty; and surely, in 1945–6, none were more tired, or more poor, or yearning more keenly to breathe free than the huddled masses of displaced Jews. Yet US immigration policy remained, as it had throughout the Nazi period, as firmly against admitting Jews to the United States as British policy was against admitting them to Palestine. Zionist propaganda in the United States naturally focused on the second rather than the first of these restrictions. Indeed, in the camps themselves, Zionist agitation had an even stronger motive for maintaining this focus: if it was taken as given that American immigration was simply not an option, this would obviously recruit potential immigrants, as well as political sympathy, for the remaining option of Palestine. It is easy to see why some people regarded the 100,000 campaign as a sacred cause and others as an unholy alliance, and why Anglo-American relations were often preserved by some politic silences.

Even before the *Queen Mary* docked in New York, carrying the British members of the committee for its initial meetings in early January 1946, Crossman had decided that the big question was not what to do about the Jews of Europe but what to make of Zionism itself. 'In my view we cannot assist the Jews in Palestine in any way they would call assistance without violating Arab rights,' he wrote in his diary. '*We must in fact either accept or reject Zionism as such*, putting the awkward, incompatible alternatives clearly before our Governments.'

Crossman remained faithful to this view, temperamentally ready to accept that the great forces making for political progress in the world often involved injustice to those who had the bad luck to be standing in the way. 'Having started on the *Queen Mary* very pro-Arab, I am now swinging to the Jewish side,' he claimed as the first days of evidence unrolled before the committee in Washington. Not, of course, that he had stupidly failed to see through the case that was stridently being put to them. 'By shouting for a Jewish state, Americans satisfy many motives,' he commented. 'They are attacking the Empire and British imperialism, they are espousing a moral cause, for whose fulfilment they will take no responsibility, and most important of all, they are diverting attention from the fact that their own immigration laws are the basic cause of the problem.'[33]

Jewish immigration was the key issue: capable of mobilizing wide-spread American support if channelled towards Zionism, capable of alleviating the problem of the refugees if British restrictions were lifted, capable of altering the demography of Palestine in favour of the Zionists, capable of igniting the hostility of Arabs throughout the Middle East if their land were to be appropriated. This seemed, in British eyes, an intractably difficult problem. What was resented – even by Zionist sympathizers like Crossman – was the common American assumption that it was fundamentally simple, morally or practically.

A couple of passages in *Palestine Mission* make this point well enough. The first cites those American witnesses who pointed to their country's black record on immigration in the years 1933 to 1944. 'Despite the Nazi persecution the number of Jewish immigrants was only 160,000 in these eleven years, about half the number of Jews who entered America in the 1920's,' Crossman wrote. 'The record of Canada and Australia was no better, whereas Great Briatin, despite her density of population, admitted 200,000 refugees in the same period.' To the British members of the committee, it seemed provoking that it was their country which, having fought alone against Hitler and offered so many Jews a refuge, should now be arraigned by self-righteous American Zionists. Yet everyone said that no modification of US restrictions could be entertained; and in a later passage Crossman shows how he came to dismiss this as 'academic' when he talked to the DPs themselves in the camps: 'They knew and I knew that America was not prepared to open its doors.'[34]

Another ten days of testimony in Washington reinforced such perceptions without really changing them. 'The Zionists are terrific, especially Rabbi Wise, their leader, who speaks like and looks like the prophet Micah, and feels himself the leader of the people of the ghetto,' Crossman observed. 'They are passionately anti-British and have obviously organized nearly all the American Jews and all the Press.'[35] That this was not far from the truth was obviously worrying, not least for the British Embassy, all too aware that the unfolding debate on whether to approve the British Loan did not need this sort of freight. Rabbi Stephen Wise, though less extreme than his rival Rabbi Silver, was quite ready to use the obvious weapons to hand. 'Can't tell you how happy I am with your statement over Lend-lease,' he had promptly assured Truman the previous August.[36] The job of the presidential adviser on minority affairs, David Niles, was to ensure that future statements achieved the same happy effect.

The committee's adjournment to London at the end of January saw the temperature drop. Hearings took place at the Royal Empire Society (nowadays the Royal Commonwealth Society) in Northumberland Avenue. Maybe this had the right ring about it though unfortunately not the right heating system, which was broken. The American members of the committee had a taste of British post-war austerity. To 'Texas Joe' Hutcheson, the judge who was co-chairman, it was one of many difficulties to be borne patiently before he could go home, his duty done.

Sir John Singleton, his fellow chairman, his fellow judge, was as quintessentially British in his well-cut suits and his sense of affront that his country should be put in the dock. As well as Crossman, there was an ex-Labour MP, Lord Morrison, and a very Tory MP, Reginald Manningham-Buller, an able lawyer who had been Singleton's pupil (and who rose eventually to be Lord Chancellor under Macmillan, inevitably lambasted for a Bullying Manner). Sir Frederick Leggett had a lifetime's experience as an industrial conciliator, and was thus well known to Bevin; and Wilfrid Crick, an economist at the Midland Bank, made six in all.

It was not the intellectual capacity of the British members so much as their lack of real political clout that could be questioned; and the American team had even less political standing. No serving member of Congress had been induced to sit. Again, intellectually their team could boast the Director of the Institute of Advanced Study at Princeton, Frank Aydelotte, as well as the formidable and dispassionate former envoy to India, William Phillips. His colleague James McDonald, later first US ambassador to Israel, was openly Zionist, as was Frank Buxton, former editor of the *Boston Herald*, with its hereditary scorn for British imperialism; and so was Bartley Crum, the only American member with obvious political ambitions, a lawyer with close links to the White House through Truman's adviser Niles.

The committee, rather against predictions, did not split along national lines. This was partly a tribute to the goodwill of the senior Americans, like Phillips, clearly uneasy at the biased testimony in Washington. Indeed, by the time they shivered together in London, some camaraderie developed under Texas Joe's genial eye. Here there was no Zionist lobby on the American scale to steal the show, though Baffy Dugdale attended every day, having helped prepare the Zionist case. She consoled herself for not having been summoned as a witness by relishing the testimony of the veteran Leo Amery: 'He revealed that he drafted the Balfour Declaration!'[37] It was almost like having Moses intervene in a discussion of the Ten Commandments. But these were arguments that had moved beyond the world in which a mere national home rather than a state would appease Zionist ambitions – or in which Hugh Dalton's drafts of a Labour policy could offer a convincing alternative. The Labour Party's Zionist commitment was now considered by Crossman 'about as half-baked and ill thought out a policy as I could conceive' – a comment in his diary that he prudently chose not to reprint.[38]

In London the committee had its only meeting with the British Foreign Secretary. Entertaining them at the Dorchester Hotel, Bevin made himself agreeable, especially to the Americans, and tried to dispel any notion that the committee was simply a stalling device. Indeed Crossman wrote in his diary that 'he made an excellent speech at a Dorchester lunch in which he promised to carry out whatever we recommended.'[39] Crossman was later to use this statement, seemingly rather casually given, to bring the committee to compromise in its report, perhaps believing that unanimity in itself would guarantee results. At any rate, this Bevin Declaration proved as flexible as the Balfour Declaration; it probably amounted to no more than the truism that Bevin would naturally be ready to act if whatever the committee recommended was agreed – not only between its own membership, but between the British and American governments. Baffy Dugdale, an experienced political operator on the backstairs, had her own view: 'I do not believe this Committee are sufficiently heavyweight to cut much ice, whatever they report.'[40]

Sitting on the committee, Crossman came to share some sense of team spirit and to think that a common view might yet emerge. After London, the membership dispersed over Europe in an investigation of the camps. There they found some 98,000 Jewish DPs, desperate to move somewhere and aware that it would not be the United States; about 70 per cent of them seemed ready to get to Palestine at all costs, and to fight the Arabs once they got there if necessary. 'It is the destiny of my nation to be lords of Palestine,' one Polish lad told Crossman, explaining: 'It is written in the Balfour Declaration.'[41]

Bartley Crum seized the moment to press for an interim report, simply endorsing the 100,000 proposal. This was obviously what the American Zionists wanted out of the committee and hence what Truman wanted too. True, there was already agreement on this. As Crossman put it:

'The fact had to be admitted – shameful as it was – that Palestine was the only country where 100,000 Jews could be absorbed in the immediate future.'[42] But this was simply to treat Palestine as a dumping-ground for a European problem, and this the committee was unprepared to do – at least not before visiting the lands in question.

Cairo and Palestine provided instructive contrasts for Crossman. 'Our arrival in Cairo coincided with a general strike to protest against the presence of British troops,' he wrote, knowing full well how Egypt's subservience to Britain rankled as a nationalist issue.[43] High British officials strutted around in pro-consular mode while a nominally independent Egyptian government proclaimed only its own decadence. Thinking of its hundreds of millions of sterling balances, some awkward questions arose about the viability of such arrangements. 'How do we propose to reply to the Egyptian demand that we should take our troops out of Egypt?' Keynes was asking at the time of the committee's visit. 'Is it appreciated that we are paying the cost of keeping them there by *borrowing it from Egypt*?'[44]

Crossman was always least impressed by witnesses who appeared content to wish away the conflict and brush aside objections in a state of blinkered self-righteousness. In this sense, the Arabs presented the worse case, with intransigent statements on behalf of the newly formed Arab League and a refusal, on the model of King Ibn Saud, to enter into the give and take of real discussion. Even so, the secretary of the Arab League, Azzam Pasha, put forward a cogent explanation of why the new Zionism excited such resistance from a people traditionally free of anti-semitism: 'the Jew, our old cousin, coming back with imperialistic ideas, with materialistic ideas, with reactionary or revolutionary ideas and trying to implement them first by British pressure and then by American pressure, and then by terrorism on his own part – he is not the old cousin, and we do not extend to him a very good welcome.' Here was a perspective that Crossman could well comprehend: 'Jewish colonial settlement in Palestine – from the Arab point of view – is simply another variant of the western imperialism which they are determined to discard.' To a Meinertzhagen, the imperialist pedigree of Zionism was part of its charm; to a Crossman it was an unfortunate provenance. 'The Jews might long to return to Zion,' as he commented, 'but they were white men like ourselves.'[45]

It was not until the committee reached Palestine itself that Crossman's

Fabian synthesis was fully formed. He set out the advantages and disadvantages of what he called a Jewish solution alongside those of an Arab solution. And he did so, of course, as a supporter of a Labour Government in Britain currently needing American assistance in facing its financial Dunkirk. Hence the first advantage of a Jewish solution: 'Acceptable to American public opinion.' Hence too the first disadvantage of an Arab solution: 'It is certain to intensify anti-British and isolationist influences and might even endanger the Loan.'[46]

Crossman, moreover, was now among white men like himself. He was introduced to his fellow socialist, David Ben Gurion, increasingly spoken of as Weizmann's successor. Ben Gurion immediately said that he had read Crossman's book *Plato To-Day*, and they began a congenial discussion on whether Plato was a fascist. The next day, Friday, 8 March, the venerable Weizmann himself gave evidence. 'He is the first witness who has frankly and openly admitted that the issue is not between right and wrong but between the greater and the lesser injustice,' Crossman wrote in his diary. 'Injustice is unavoidable and we have to decide whether it is better to be unjust to the Arabs of Palestine or to the Jews.'[47] Mrs Dugdale, now his house guest, heard Weizmann with equal and more predictable respect: 'His mind was like a giant's among the pigmies (which is all this Committee is).'[48]

That weekend Weizmann entertained more house guests at his comfortable home in Rehovoth: both Crossman and Crum. There was talk from 5 p.m. to midnight. 'Crum is openly 100% on Jewish side,' Dugdale observed. 'I am less sure of Crossman, but he is an intelligent man.'[49] It was at this point that Crossman seems to have been converted to the partition of Palestine, into Zionist and Arab states, as his own preferred solution. After midnight, as they walked outside and 'the scent of orange blossom streamed up from the grove below like a sweet mist', Weizmann told his guest of how he had seen the site of his house for the first time as a member of General Allenby's forces in 1918. 'Then it was a bare hill in a swamp.'[50] It was an epiphany of the Zionist promise.

The door that Weizmann had gently prised ajar was pushed wide open by the vigorous efforts of younger Zionist leaders. Crossman had met the economist David Horowitz in the United States. He and Golda Meyerson (later Meir) proved wonderful guides during 'a solid day of socialist sightseeing' in new Zionist settlements, 'where these people are ten times as efficient as their neighbours'. Then there was an evening with Ben Gurion, who advised him: 'Imagine that we're Englishmen fighting for our national existence, and calculate that we shall behave as you would behave if you were in our situation.'[51]

Relations with the Arabs were inevitably different. Crossman had publicly confronted Jemal Husseini, cousin of the Mufti of Jerusalem, with wartime photographs of the Mufti consorting with the Nazis. This cross-questioning, not unnaturally, gave offence to the Arabs and it had taken determined efforts to bring Crossman together with Jemal socially. Crossman's diary sought to convey Jemal's summing-up of the essence of the situation: 'I appreciate that your country has been greatly weakened by the war and that you will need American support to keep your Empire together.' Crossman clearly acepted much of this, though without admitting such narrow alternatives. 'If Arab policy was so inept as to compel us to choose between American and Arab friendship,' he warned Jemal, 'I myself as a realist would have to choose American.'[52]

The perceived ineptitude of Arab politics reflected the backwardness of Arab society. In the end, Crossman rejected both, not least because both were fostered by the patronizing policies of the British proconsuls whom he so disliked. In this regard, his attitudes were much closer to those of kneejerk American anti-imperialists like Crum than to most of his fellow Britons. And Crossman sympathized too with the American idealization of the heroic settler in conquering a new land.

In the end, Crossman chose to follow Weizmann in advocating the line of least injustice. He did so for the positive reason that 'if I believed in social progress I had to admit that the Jews had set going revolutionary forces in the Middle East which, in the long run, would benefit the Arabs.' The Zionist ends thus justified means that were admittedly inequitable. It was hard cheese on the Arabs. 'I do not think I would have reached this conclusion if the national home had been merely a national home,' Crossman concluded. 'In Palestine I had come to realise that it was something more – a socialist commonwealth, intensely democratic, intensely collectivist, and strong enough to fend for itself.'[53]

This in turn induced a more indulgent view of the armed insurrection that branded Zionism in British eyes. Cross-questioned by Manningham-Buller on whether the Jewish Agency would assist in suppressing terrorism, Ben Gurion had said: 'We cannot do it because, as I told you, it is futile, sir, it is futile.' On the day, Crossman had thought there was no excuse for this response but later came to extenuate it as 'a statement of fact'.[54] The fact, for him, was that the Zionists were ready to fight for their beliefs and fight for their lives; fight the British and fight the Arabs; fight on the beaches and fight in the hills. This seemed to Crossman the final validation of their claim to be a nation. More than once, in slightly different forms, he quoted the words with which Ben Gurion had left him on parting: 'Make up your minds one way or the other, and remember that either way we shall fight our Dunkirk.'[55]

The committee's report was a compromise. The Zionists did not get what they wanted; they had to agree to a binational state or, as Texas Joe Hutcheson kept saying, 'No Arab, No Jewish State.' It was his triumph to secure this compromise and it provided a non-Zionist context for endorsing the immigration of 100,000 Jews. Maybe it was naive to think that the humanitarian case for doing this could thus be decoupled from the Zionist political dynamic of using further immigration to take over the country; but that was the package deal, presented as such, and only viable as such. What would thwart such a proposal would be to untie the package by competitive cherry-picking among the recommendations. Thus Baffy Dugdale, who got hold of an advance copy, saw that it was impossible to say yes and no at the same time (as Ben Gurion wished). 'As for tactics – much depends on whether the publication of the Report is accompanied by announcement of its acceptance by the Governments,' she wrote on 29 April. 'I think it *must* be so.'[56] It was a reasonable expectation.

Nonetheless, it is not what happened. Prompted by Crum and McDonald, who squared Rabbi Silver on how to finesse the report, Niles had already prepared a statement to be issued by Truman. This simply snatched at the 100,000 recommendation, without offering American assistance on the rest, and was issued on the same day as the report's publication, 30 April. For the second time in six months, the President acted irrespective of the British, provoking Attlee's equal and opposite reaction the next day, which emphasized instead the need to disarm 'private armies' in Palestine.

As Crossman saw it, the extremists had won, not for the first or the last time in Palestine. Once his anger subsided, he found time to learn some subsequently valuable lessons. He learnt how the report had been submitted to the cabinet along with relevant advice on each point from British officials. 'Now, at the moment of decision, the officials gave judgment on our judgment,' he commented as the truth dawned on him.[57] He thus came belatedly to see that he should have paid more attention to the role of civil servants like Harold Beeley, Bevin's key adviser on Palestine, who had been seconded to the committee and whose significance – 'I think Beeley the Secretary is biased against us' – Baffy Dugdale had quickly discerned from the outset of the London hearings.[58] There was nothing unusual here, no conspiracy, no skul-duggery; but Crossman's appreciation of the role of Sir Humphrey was under-researched in 1946.

Palestine was a difficult enough problem in itself. It was made more difficult because of the dire position of the Jews of Europe after the Nazi horrors. Britain's own difficulty in dealing with any of this was obviously not helped by its post-war weakness, military and economic alike. Yet American political involvement, which might have been hoped to remedy some of these deficiencies, only seemed to add to these pre-existing difficulties in 1945–6. Attlee privately told Crossman: 'My annoyance is with the Americans who forever lay heavy burdens on us without lifting a finger to help.' In *Palestine Mission* Crossman recognized that popular support for the British Government's policy was driven by popular resentment against the United States at this juncture: 'The British people felt that it had been very badly used.'[59]

The British and American positions, which the work of the Anglo-American committee had been intended to reconcile, had as a result become even more sharply polarized. This fiasco, with manipulation maximizing mutual misunderstanding, could hardly have been worse – until Ernest Bevin rekindled the controversy a few weeks later with some more plain words of his own. At the Labour Party conference in June, he showed himself still smarting over the use made of the 100,000 proposal. 'I hope I will not be misunderstood in America if I say that this was proposed with the purest of motives,' he commented sarcasti-cally. 'They did not want too many Jews in New York.'[60] The remark was not well-judged, if only because of the huge offence it created in the United States. This in turn was all the greater, as is often the case, because what was said came so near to the truth. Bevin had said the unsayable and done so, moreover, while the fate of the Loan was still undecided.

When Mass-Observation asked people in Britain how they felt about the Americans, the replies had generally been favourable, running at about 45 per cent in the years 1941–4 (with a dip in 1943) and rising to 58 per cent in 1945. By March 1946, however, only 22 per cent took a favourable view and the figure fell slightly later in the year.[61] Given the verbal responses to related questions, a link with the end of Lend-Lease and the Loan negotiations seems overwhelmingly likely. In the United States, attitudes were complementary (though hardly complimentary). In February a State Department poll had found, for the first time, a majority approving the British Loan (by 44 per cent to 37 per cent) but by June the proportion offering any degree of approval had slipped to 38 per cent, as against 48 per cent disapproving.[62] The English-speaking peoples were not speaking well of each other.

'Back of all this,' Keynes told Bob Brand at the end of January, 'England is sticky with self-pity and not prepared to accept peacefully and wisely the fact that her position and her resources are not what they once were.' He offered this as a psychological insight on the public mood, but what immediately worried him was the associated drift in Government policy, where 'the mixed chauvinism and universal benevolence of the F.O. and other departments and the weakness of the Chancellor in these matters are slopping away on everything and everybody in the world except the poor Englishman the fruits of our American loan.'[63]

In one of his final state papers, Keynes tried to quantify his warning. The problem was not that the likely proceeds of the Loan would be squandered by the British people, financing their New Jerusalem on tick: in fact there was 'not a single bean of sustenance for themselves' and the problem was one of external finance. Keynes wrote that 'we shall require, on balance, the whole of it, and, unless we change our ways, much more, to feed and sustain Allies, liberated territories and ex-enemies, to maintain our military prestige overseas, and, generally speaking, to cut a dash in the world considerably above our means.'[64]

Here was the real problem with which any post-war British Government was inexorably faced. Keynes's examples make the point. Maintaining an army of 100,000 Poles in Italy – out of a total of 220,000 for the total exiled Polish armed forces – was a cost to be met on Britain's external account. How? The British forces in Greece needed to be maintained, and even a new Greek Army was to be supplied with British equipment. Again, how? Relief and rehabilitation needs in Italy, Austria and Greece too had to be paid for across the foreign exchanges, as did imports into the British zone in Germany. Yet again, how? British forces outside Europe had been over 800,000 on VJ-Day – and were still likely to number 650,000 during 1946. Keeping them in India would thus require £125 million and in the Middle East another £75 million: a total of £200 million or $800 million, in one year alone – not far short of a quarter of the US Loan itself. These were just some of the costs of victory.

Litttle wonder that Keynes called for drastic cuts. 'It seems monstrous,' he argued, 'that we should first de-industrialise and thus bankrupt the Ruhr to please Russia and then hand over the territory, or at any rate the industries, to an international body to please France, but that we alone should remain responsible for feeding the place.'[65]

The food shortage in the British zone was a major problem. It led to the introduction of bread rationing from 1946 to 1948, a measure that had been avoided during the war. In March and April 1946 Mass-Observation asked people in Britain how they felt about giving up some of their food for Europe. Some drew the line at what Keynes called paying reparations to Germany. 'If it came to it, I suppose I'd do it as willing as the next,' said a middle-aged working-class man. 'But not to help Germany. Only the countries that have been overrun. I wouldn't care what happened to the Germans – they've asked for it.' But for every response like this, there were others like the working-class woman of forty who said: 'I shouldn't *like* it, but I'd be willing if things were desperate.' Indeed this latter view seems to have been twice as common: an unillusioned, unheroic magnanimity in sharing the sort of hardships which war had made all too familiar. 'Well, if we must we must,' said one working-class woman of sixty. 'But we are so short ourselves it would be very bad if they cut us down worse.'[66]

Such responses should be borne in mind before simply reproaching the British people for seeking to avoid an intensification of existing austerity by turning for further help to their American allies, who had admittedly already given so much. The welfare state, which the Labour Government was committed to building, was a political and economic option of another kind altogether. The Beveridge Plan for universal social insurance was the main domestic agenda in 1946. Here was a choice about how to allocate resources within the country, with very little impact on its external finances. Keynes, a supporter of Beveridge's proposals, had made the essential distinction time and again. 'Anything we can actually *do* we can afford,' he had told a radio audience in 1942. 'We shall, in very fact, have built our New Jerusalem out of the labour which in our former vain folly we were keeping unused and unhappy in enforced idleness.'[67] Keynes had a reputation for changing his mind; but here he was utterly consistent in simultaneously encouraging properly costed social investment at home while urging drastic cuts in overseas spending.

In the United States, such distinctions were not always made. The fact that the Loan was sought by a Labour Government was the elephant in the room – as deliberately unmentioned by the administration itself as the electoral nuances of Jewish immigration. But it was nonetheless a factor throughout the negotiations and, even more so, the subsequent debates on ratifying the Loan. One Congressman pithily said it would 'promote too damned much Socialism at home and too much damned Imperialism abroad'. When another Representative asserted that he would not vote for it as long as the British had the crown jewels, he was at least making a relevant point since the value of these baubles could in principle have been realized for foreign currency. When other Congressmen asked why the British Government could not borrow from its own public, however, they had failed to grasp that, while the Chancellor of the Exchequer could in principle raise any amount of pounds sterling, the problem was to find dollars.[68] And since British exports were meanwhile too low to finance dollar imports, there was a gap in the balance of payments, which convertibility would only make worse by quickly exhausting the inadequate British currency reserves.

Senator Vandenberg was again in a key position and a quandary. 'The British loan is a tough conundrum for me and for my Republican colleagues,' he had acknowledged. Partly he was worried about the financial trade-off, since the British, he wrote on the day after the House of Lords debate, 'are already beginning to "shylock" us even before the papers are signed'. They were plainly insufficiently grateful: 'If we are not going to get good will what are we going to get?' But his deeper concern was political, fed by the logic of having to deny to other Allies what was granted to one. Hence his 'doubt whether a majority of this Congress would vote a postwar loan to Russia – at least not until the "iron curtain" reels up for keeps'.[69]

What initially complicated, but also later unlocked, the issue for

Vandenberg was thus the context of relations with the Soviet Union. He came to appreciate this the more keenly since he was one of the US delegates to the United Nations Organization at its inaugural meeting in London in January. Here he applauded Bevin's forthright challenges to the Russian Vyshinsky, as a wholesome contrast to the more equivocal approach of his own Secretary of State. Some members of Truman's cabinet had similar doubts, notably the hawkish James Forrestal, who recorded a comment from Churchill, now on a long holiday in the United States, that he found 'considerable consolation in the victory of Bevin because Bevin was able to talk more firmly and clearly to Russia than he could have, by virtue of being a Labour government'.[70] And Bevin seemed Churchillian not only in his robust foreign policy but in the levels of approval he currently enjoyed from the British public. Gallup already showed that 47 per cent thought he was doing a good job in December but this jumped to an extraordinary 73 per cent by February 1946.

James Byrnes had been running US foreign policy with as much of a free hand as Ernest Bevin ran British foreign policy. The difference was that Bevin had Attlee's full support whereas Byrnes provoked Truman's increasingly restive irritation. It had been Byrnes's idea to try to recoup on the failure of the London meeting of foreign ministers in October by himself going to Moscow in December, to exercise his skills as dealmaker; and whether the British Foreign Secretary, with his reputation for truculence, chose to accompany him was left very pointedly for Bevin to decide, without prior consultation. It was like the prelude to Potsdam, only worse, in establishing a Big Two axis. In the event, while the Russians kept on talking, and kept on trying to isolate the imperialist British from the surely more reasonable Americans, Moscow produced little sign of real progress, especially over Iran, where Soviet promises of post-war withdrawal remained unfulfilled.

It was on Byrnes's return that Truman made it clear that he now felt it time for a tougher line to replace the endless search for unavailing compromises. 'I'm tired of babying the Soviets,' he allegedly told Byrnes.[71] The deadline passed on 31 December for the Soviet Union to sign up for Bretton Woods – by default, establishing rival economic as well as political systems in the world. Within the State Department itself, the interpretation of Stalin's policy was given a sharp twist with the receipt in February of a 'long telegram' from a key official in the Moscow embassy, George Kennan, who spoke influentially of the need for long-term containment of Soviet ambitions.

The context in which Winston Churchill's speech at Fulton, Missouri, was delivered on Tuesday, 5 March 1946, was fortuitously helpful in gaining it worldwide attention. With the President proudly taking him to his home state, the distinguished visitor could speak for himself, yet also in a sense that he knew was privately welcome not only to Truman but to the British Government. Churchill's tone was not aggressive – he entitled the speech 'The Sinews of Peace' – but he drew a parallel between the appeasement of pre-war Germany and the dangers in appeasing post-war Russia. He established two sound-bite phrases with which Fulton was to become synonymous. One was the warning about an 'iron curtain', which he had first introduced in prime-ministerial correspondence with Truman and had then voiced across the table at Potsdam; though this did not steal the headlines the next day.

'BRITAIN AND AMERICA IN PEACE,' proclaimed The Times in London on 6 March, 'Mr Churchill Apeals for "Special Relationship".' Here was the real thrust of the Fulton speech, with its plea for 'the fraternal association of the English-speaking peoples' in what Churchill called 'the special relationship between the British Commonwealth and Empire and the United States'. Truman sat and nodded, though carefully distancing himself when subsequently pressed for an official comment. In London, likewise, Attlee and Bevin kept their distance in public from a trial balloon, unofficially launched by a fellow citizen while on a well-deserved recuperative holiday in the United States.

It was Fulton that made 'special relationship' into a term of art: the first time that the phrase had been specifically applied in this sense. When Churchill had made a parliamentary speech in November he had dwelt on the forces making for agreement between 'the English-speaking peoples of the world' and stressed the naturalness of the process by which Britons and Americans concurred. 'They can hardly help agreeing on three out of four things,' he had asserted. 'They look at things the same way. No policies, no pacts, no secret understandings are needed between them.'[72] But he did not call this far-fetched fantasy a special relationship. It is a form of words which The Times had previously employed in quite other contexts: in 1942 impartially about either the United States and Argentina, or about France and Algeria, or about Britain and the Dominions (quoting H. V. Evatt, the Australian foreign minister); in 1943 about Britain and Europe; in 1944 about Canada and the United States (quoting the minister, Richard Law) as well as about Britain and Portugal (quoting Anthony Eden).

It was now the 'special relationship' that prompted an initially ambiguous reception of Fulton in the United States. The subtext of potential alliance with Great Britain often met with hostility or at least suspicion of British motives. Yet, within days, Stalin's personal denunciation of Fulton helped recruit support for Churchill from quarters traditionally scornful of British imperialism. Since these were often the strongest opponents of the Loan, this was a significant intrusion of a further issue into that argument – not, for once, Palestine and its attendant Zionist protagonists but the Soviet threat. It became common by the end of March to talk about the Loan as 'an investment against Russian imperialism' and the new factor was bringing round some truly dubious supporters. 'This may well be the first fruit of Fulton' was the sour comment in *The Economist* on 23 March. 'It is an unpalatable coating for the pill.'[73]

It was not that Churchill unintentionally aided the Labour Government here: he fully intended to weigh in, given the national interest at stake. His action in abstaining in the parliamentary vote on the Loan had produced natural confusion about his real views and licensed opponents of the Loan like Bernard Baruch. What Churchill did throughout his American visit was to act virtually as an agent of the British Government in staving off the possibility that the Loan would collapse, and with it his hopes of a rekindled special relationship.

On 10 March, five days after the Fulton speech, Lord Halifax hosted a dinner for Churchill at the Washington embassy. Vandenberg was one of nine Senators and Congressmen to attend and, according to the note kept by a British official, took the lead in getting Churchill to explain his position. Churchill obliged, making clear that convertibility was an economic drawback but that the 'deeply humiliating' aspect lay in the fact that the Loan would bear interest and that imperial preference had been entangled in the negotiations.

His political analysis, however, was the key. 'There were fears of British socialism in this country,' Churchill acknowledged, 'but he would point out that most of the leaders of the present Government had been members of the Wartime Coalition Government; were men of experience and understanding and were certainly not rash doctrinaire socialists, liable to go to extremes.' The fact that many of Labour's domestic measures were the same as those of the Conservative Party showed the non-partisan nature of the British case. Churchill emphasized the point to his dinner guests: 'In foreign policy the agreement was almost complete.'[74]

Russian Communism rather than British socialism was thus the issue. In the following month, Vandenberg's announcement that he would support the Loan was to have a decisive impact on the Senate's approval. The British embassy reported after the final vote that 'an unspoken fear of Soviet Russia was at work to induce many Senators, otherwise opposed, to support the Administration.'[75]

Keynes had been in the United States for the first meetings of the International Monetary Fund and the World Bank, as set up at Bretton Woods. 'I judge the American loan to be quite safe unless some quite unexpected factor develops,' he advised senior ministers on his return home aboard the *Queen Mary* at the beginning of April. He admitted that the economic argument had only weighed with those already converted. 'With the unconverted, on the other hand,' he reported, 'the changed situation in regard to Russia has been fairly decisive.' Churchill's interventions, both public and private, came in for special credit: 'He told all his friends that he was in favour of the Loan, that we needed it and that the argument against lending to a Socialist Government was a wrong and invalid argument, with which he would have nothing to do.'[76] Since Churchill had also travelled back on the same trip of the *Queen Mary*, Keynes's sources were particularly good, not least for his story of how Baruch had finally been persuaded to withdraw his opposition.

After Fulton, it seemed, even the Zionists could be out-trumped in Washington. Under pressure from the State Department, and explicitly not 'as a matter of favor to the British Government', Rabbi Stephen Wise was induced to give public support to the Loan before the final vote.[77] In May it was carried by 46–34 in the Senate.

The final debate in the House in July was to be crucial. One Representative – Clare Booth Luce, well known not only in her own right but as the wife of the owner of *Time-Life* – commented that 'if that famous alien the man from Mars, had been in the gallery, he might well have concluded that we were discussing a loan to some treacherous enemy recently defeated by us in a battle.'[78] A climactic moment, two days before the vote, came when two Massachusetts Representatives (one of them the Majority Leader, McCormack) repudiated a large advertisement in the *Boston Globe* – 'Kill That Loan' – which had used their names without authorization, simply on the strength of their previous support for Zionism. Their plea for each issue to be settled on its merits, however, masks the fact that it was an alternative issue that was now linked with the Loan in securing it a margin of 219–155.

Not only supporters of the Truman administration but, crucially, many Republican isolationists simply found this the best way to vote against Stalin and the iron curtain. They were not voting for Keynes and Bretton Woods, nor for Churchill and the special relationship, still less for Attlee, Bevin and the New Jerusalem (not to mention the old one in Mandate Palestine). The fact that the proceedings proved so dilatory was a testament to the reluctance with which Congress had been persuaded to come to the aid of its erstwhile 'faithful ally'. It also meant that the President was not to sign the legislation until 15 July 1946, which in turn meant that, since convertibility was required twelve months afterwards, a sterling crisis was thus ordained for the summer of 1947.

13

Sabotage?

April–November 1946

> '*You will have to choose between the two, the Muslim League and the Congress, both your creations. Every day you pass here coquetting now with the Congress, now with the League and again with the Congress, wearing yourself away, will not do.*'

Gandhi to Cripps, June 1946

The Labour Government's way of dealing with India showed some parallels with its way of dealing with Palestine. Over India too it established a parliamentary-style delegation of inquiry to advise on the incompatible claims of different factions, each claiming to be more representative than it was; and here too this rather low-powered body was largely ignored, out-trumped at a higher level of decision-making in the politics of a fluid situation.

There were important differences. One was that, whereas over Palestine Labour ministers quickly decided that their party's simplistic pledges to the Zionists could hardly be honoured, over India Labour's longstanding affinities with the aspirations of the Indian National Congress continued to shape Government policy. The latent threat of political opposition at home admittedly raised the stakes. But the commitment of key ministers, especially Attlee and Cripps, to the goal of rapid independence nonetheless prevailed – despite untoward developments in India. Indeed the upshot was that Indian independence, albeit accompanied by partition, came sooner rather than later.

Britain's sheer power to impose its imperial will had not survived the war. The Attlee Government recognized this. It therefore counted on the goodwill of natural allies, who professed to share its aims, in reaching workable solutions to difficult problems. In Palestine it looked to the United States for assistance while in India it hoped that Labour's sympathy for Congress – all too obvious in Conservative eyes – would correspondingly help to achieve results. Yet, over Palestine, ministers repeatedly found that the American President could not be relied upon to put the goal of facilitating an agreed settlement ahead of his immediate political worries at home. This came as a shock, a disappointment, a breach of good faith; but whether it can be called sabotage raises the question of whether the intention was to wreck or intentionally destroy an otherwise viable project. The same criteria need to be applied in judging events in India, where the role of Gandhi remained inescapably pivotal in determining the attitude of the Indian National Congress.

In India the American dimension did not bulk so large as in Palestine. The reason was surely that in the United States the Indian dimension did not bulk so large as did Zionism. In the index to the *New York Times* for 1946, references to Palestine take up thirty-nine columns (not to mention another nine on Zionism, and two on Jews and Jewish organizations). In total this is about one per cent of the indexed stories in the paper – almost exactly the same proportion as in *The Times* in London for references to Palestine and Jews ('Zionism, see Jews'). But whereas *The Times* carried nearly 60 per cent more coverage of India than of Palestine, in the *New York Times* almost the exact opposite was the case: nearly 60 per cent fewer stories on India than on Palestine.

Not that public opinion in the United States was wholly uninterested in the Indian cry for self-determination. But, once the Cripps Offer had been rejected by the Indian National Congress in 1942 and the Simla proposals had been rejected by the Muslim League in 1945, the problem had appeared rather more complex than simply one of British imperial possessiveness. The United States, once seen as a saviour by Congress, was now regarded by many Indians as complicit in British imperialism. On 18 February, for example, the *New York Times* duly printed Gandhi's and Nehru's expressions of popular hostility towards Great Britain but on the next two days carried reports of an Indian mob in Bombay tearing down the Stars and Stripes from the US Information Service. Moreover, the fact that Attlee's Government had displaced Churchill's thereby removed a notable obstacle to Anglo-American understanding – a specially dysfunctional relationship on this particular issue. Furthermore, when Cripps himself again emerged in 1946 as the most prominent member of a ministerial delegation to India, this was also reassuring in the eyes of informed Americans.

It was obvious by 1946 that Cripps, the country-house radical, had somehow emerged from the war as a reformist politician of the centre-left: a champion of multilateral trade and the American loan in external policy, and at home the personification of high-minded austerity. Moreover, his experience during the Cripps Mission had reinforced his view that a Marxist analysis could not unlock the involuted problems of imperialism and communal conflict in India. The point is important because Cripps, along with Attlee, was the major influence on British policy in bringing the Indian Empire to an end. Certainly they wanted to see India stay in the Commonwealth if possible; certainly they wanted economic links to be maintained; certainly they wanted to reconcile India's new role with traditional British strategic concerns. But all this was now premised on Indian self-determination, in the hope that politics could resolve conflicts that would otherwise result in bloodshed.

The belief that doing the right thing might turn out to be expedient may, of course, be dismissed as naive. This was hardly how Churchill would have acted if he had been in power after the war, as his decisions in government amply suggest and his actions in opposition explicitly confirm. But the fact that leading Conservatives, like Rab Butler and Harold Macmillan, subsequently adroitly distanced themselves from their contemporary criticisms of British policy perhaps tells its own story – hindsight implicitly commending foresight. It did not take sixty years to vindicate the big decisions over India. Where there is still justifiable room for some historical revision, however, is over the role of Cripps himself, which was arguably more important than even that of Attlee.

Despite his heavy involvement in the Loan negotiations as President of the Board of Trade, it was Cripps who kept pressing for a more conciliatory stance on India in the autumn of 1945. He succeeded in getting agreement to sending a parliamentary group of two peers and eight backbench MPs to investigate (though little came of this in the end). He failed to persuade Attlee to summon Jinnah and Nehru to talks in London, but in consolation the idea was hatched of sending out a representative of the British cabinet. By mid-January this had become a plan for a delegation of three cabinet ministers, including Cripps himself, to visit India, with a wide brief to achieve a mutually agreed settlement.

Lord Pethick-Lawrence, as Secretary of State for India, was naturally a member of this cabinet delegation. So was Albert Alexander, First

Lord of the Admiralty under both Churchill and Attlee: a patriotic working-class figure who struck Lord Wavell as 'the very best type of British Labour, the best we breed'.[1] The Viceroy was less keen on the presence of Cripps, his fellow Wykehamist, whose influence throughout he rightly perceived as dominant.

There were many problems to overcome. One was a direct hangover from the war. Prominent Indian Army officers, captured by the enemy, were prosecuted for defecting to the Japanese-sponsored Indian National Army. This created tension, if only because Congress leaders, though longstanding rivals of the INA, could not afford to let their own nationalist credentials be compromised. Equally, Wavell could not forget how the war effort had been undermined and he reacted straightforwardly as a soldier, in supporting disciplinary measures, rather than as one of his despised politicians. Readers of the later novels in Paul Scott's *Raj Quartet* will recall how this issue festered in the background throughout the post-war months. It surely manifested the need for a political approach that this honest but obtuse Viceroy was incapable of providing.

The political problems of India were diverse; but two interlocked issues were salient in shaping the context for the negotiations of 1946. Jinnah had indicated the nub of the difficulty in December 1945: 'The deadlock in this country is not so much between India and the British. It is between Hindu Congress and the Muslim League.'[2] This was an analysis totally rejected by the Congress leaders. They bridled at being called Hindu when they had made heroic efforts to establish a secular nationalist party. They resented being put on a par with the Muslim League and its absurd scheme for Pakistan. They remained committed to the view that these supposed difficulties were themselves only the effects of British rule and would accordingly disappear with it – if only the British were really intent on yielding power rather than mouthing their endlessly deceptive words about it.

When Cripps resumed a private correspondence with Nehru, what it revealed was the rigidity of the Congress mind-set. Nehru may have been right to blame a century of British rule for preventing 'the internal forces from establishing an equilibrium among themselves'; he might have had a point when he called the introduction of separate electorates (for minorities like the Muslims) 'the seed of the poisonous tree that has grown now to poison all our national life and prevent progress'. But in projecting this interpretation of history straight onto the political divisions in India in 1946 he was surely showing himself out of date and out of touch.

The fact that Nehru, like most Congress leaders, had been in prison from the repression of the Quit India agitation of 1942 until June 1945 was rather more than a regrettable personal incident. It was a symptom of Congress's debilitating wartime paralysis, exacerbating the already damaging effects of its political withdrawal from government since 1939. The fault lay mainly on the British side but some of the wounds on Congress were self-inflicted. The point was that the Muslim League, previously little more than a shell, had meanwhile established a dynamic that had transformed the political situation. Yet Nehru still took for granted the political backwardness of the Muslims; he idly explained the success of League organization as 'strikingly similar to the Nazi technique'; he disparaged the cry for Pakistan as 'a sentimental slogan which they have got used to'. He thus assured Cripps that talk of direct action could be dismissed – 'I do not think there is much in Jinnah's threat' – and that the imposition of a unitary constitution based on majority voting was still the obvious way forward. 'There may be some petty riots in some cities,' Nehru conceded.[3]

Hence the Congress insistence that there was no real deadlock between itself and this upstart, reactionary Muslim League. The only deadlock that mattered was between India, represented by Congress itself, and the British. The results of the provincial elections, still coming in while the cabinet delegation began its business, merely confirmed the new balance. In winning around 90 per cent of the vote in the reserved Muslim seats, the League had now established a legitimacy as commanding as that of Congress elsewhere. This lent political cogency as well as personal animosity to the League's contention that Congress was posturing in keeping a Muslim, Maulana Azad, as its president when he was a mere poster-boy. Though this was slighting to Azad's own achievements, it was true enough in identifying the real power in Congress as now lying outside its formal structure. On the threshold of Indian self-government, the chief contenders for the Congress leadership were two Hindus: not only the charismatic intellectual Nehru but also the tough, pragmatic party manager, Vallabhbhai Patel.

Congress's unresolved internal stresses centred on an undeclared war for the Gandhian succession. If Nehru can rightly be called charismatic, what word is left to describe the extraordinary and abiding appeal of the Mahatma himself? If he no longer held any formal position within Congress, it was because he did not want to and did not need to. The danger all along was that the pragmatic political deals hammered out within the formal structures of negotiation would in the end be at the mercy of appeals to values, judgements and slogans that were deemed not negotiable at all.

Above all, Gandhi was bound by his own almost mystical conception of India. He had talked in 1942 about a 'vivisection of India' – not as a description of the (abhorrent) proposal for Pakistan but of the (equally objectionable) constitutional devices that were being discussed as a means of avoiding partition. For all the impressive strength of its position, which Gandhi had been largely responsible for building, Congress still lacked an effective political realism; and for this deficiency Gandhi was also largely responsible. It refused to face facts; it hid behind tired excuses and ancient alibis. This helps explain its deep-seated reluctance to believe mounting evidence – like the provincial election results – of the changes brought about by the war.

Whereas Jinnah had no difficulty in accepting that the British really were intent on leaving India, Nehru still needed persuading. He voiced understandable qualms about failure to use the term 'independence', which helped spur Cripps to secure approval for a brief far wider than he had been given by Churchill's cabinet in 1942. This was made apparent in Attlee's parliamentary statement about the cabinet delegation in March. 'The temperature of 1946 is not the temperature of 1920 or of 1930 or even of 1942,' the Prime Minister declared, with reference to the options between which India was now asked to choose. 'The British Commonwealth and Empire is not bound together by chains of external compulsion,' he argued, and so, if India 'elects for independence, in our view she has a right to do so'.[4] For Attlee, it might be concluded, the Commonwealth was a substitute for Empire, whereas for Churchill it was a euphemism for Empire. And in working so hard to keep India within the Commonwealth, Attlee and Cripps readily conceded independence, thus squaring with their own longstanding commitment to the principle of self-determination.

The parliamentary Conservative party, in Churchill's absence, proved notably supportive of sending the delegation, if only for want of a better alternative. It was, as Sir John Anderson said from the Opposition front bench, 'an interesting debate, entirely free from party or sectional controversy'.[5] But this marked a highly conditional kind of approval, subject to the delegation's ability to secure agreement among the Indian parties – and dependent on Churchill himself keeping out of the way, whether in Florida or in Fulton. On arrival in Delhi, Cripps was able to tell a press conference on 1 April 1946: 'We want to give independence to India as quickly and as smoothly as we can.'[6] The chips were down, the final attempt at deal-making about to begin.

Pethick-Lawrence, Cripps and Alexander sat alongside the Viceroy, day by day, through a series of over 400 interviews that lasted from 26 March until 17 April. Though an official record was kept throughout, Cripps sat busily writing his own notes, which became the basis of his diary, and his colleague Alexander did likewise. It was Cripps rather than Pethick-Lawrence who was spokesman at most of the press conferences, on a variety of bland pretexts which certainly did not fool Alexander, who felt some sensitivity about his status as the 'silent man'.[7]

Cripps, of course, had been here before. He privately blamed failure in 1942 on the previous Viceroy, Lord Linlithgow, and this time wanted to keep his distance from Wavell, showing reluctance to stay even for a couple of nights at the Viceregal Lodge on arrival. But Wavell proved accommodating and Cripps wrote on 25 March of 'a preliminary chat with the Viceroy last night which seemed successful since there was no great divergence of opinion'.

Cripps staked a good deal on employing an informal approach. His methods in 1946, much criticized at the time and subsequently, stemmed from his determination to avoid making the same mistake (even if this ultimately led him to make the opposite mistake). Above all, since he attributed the failure of the Cripps Mission to Gandhi, this time Cripps went to great lengths to win him round, both directly and indirectly, rather than work through Azad. But it is not true that he only consorted with Congress; instead he likewise tried to establish an effective network with the Muslim League and the Sikhs.

This was the task assigned to two young personal assistants, Major Woodrow Wyatt and Major John McLaughlin Short. Wyatt was an ebullient Labour MP, whose political career was to describe a long arc from the *Tribune* left to the Thatcherite right, and whose recent experience as a member of the parliamentary delegation to India made him a well-connected aide for Cripps. Wyatt's main job was to keep open the line to the Muslim League. Short, currently working for the Ministry of Information, was an expert on the Punjab. He had met Cripps in 1942 and bombarded him with memoranda throughout the winter of 1945–6, educating him on the Pakistan issue. As eccentric in his methods as he was idiosyncratic in expression, Short was difficult to pin down, but his main job was to talk to the Sikhs. The 'two majors' set to work with a relish, providing much entertainment in more senses than one. Their wine bill alone for a month was of the order of £5000 at today's prices. Yet Cripps, personally uncensorious about alcohol, thought that he was getting good value and defended this lapse from austerity against Treasury scrutiny.

For Cripps the real work was behind the scenes, especially in mending his fences with Congress. 'We had some intensely interesting talks and I ended up with a long talk with Jawaharlal in the garden,' he wrote after a reception given for the Working Committee. 'I think the whole atmosphere was most promising and there did not seem to be any suspicions about us as there were last time.' On the surface, relations with the Viceroy remained harmonious, and even friendly, but Cripps was somewhat naive in supposing that 'we have, I think, quite got over the slight suspicions that were in his mind when we came out.'[8] Wavell in fact harboured a jaundiced view of the 'hole-and-corner' methods adopted by 'Cripps and his minions (Wyatt and Short)'.[9]

There were other supporting characters like Sudhir Ghosh, whose role as 'Gandhi's emissary' offered him eagerly exploited opportunities to inflate his own position. The youthful Ghosh, Cambridge-educated and purposefully ingratiating, was now an employee of the Tata industrial conglomerate, which seemed happy to finance his apprenticeship as a spin doctor. Already known to Wyatt, whose talents were not dissimilar, Ghosh used him to send a warning to Cripps: 'When Sir Stafford came to India in 1942, the old man described his offer as a "a post-dated cheque" and that was the end of it. So beware of the old man.'[10] This turned out to be good advice.

Cripps had concluded from his early conversations 'that the one effective way of settling the matter was to get Jinnah and Gandhi to agree'. This was easier said than done, but he made sure that his first courtesy call – 'and so a great compliment' – was thus upon the Quaid-i-Azam (the honorific title bestowed on their leader by his devoted Muslim followers). Cripps found Jinnah reasonable. 'To use the common language, he had got rid of his inferiority complex.' He assured Cripps that he was ready to meet Gandhi. 'I suggested that if they got stuck,' Cripps recorded, 'I might perhaps help as a friend of both – unofficially.'[11] Jinnah was, of course, far readier to meet Gandhi, whom he regarded as the dictator of Congress, than to consort with its Muslim president. Cripps clearly now hoped that his inevitably well-publicized first visit to Gandhi would be perceived as a further step in mutual conciliation rather than as any kind of snub to the Muslim League.

'GANDHI CHOOSES TO LIVE WITH "UNTOUCHABLES"' was the *Daily Herald* headline in Britain on 1 April. Gandhi had arrived in Delhi on an officially commissioned special train (towards the cost of which Ghosh was duly sent to press a third-class fare upon the Viceroy's secretary) and on arrival took up residence in the Harijan sweepers' quarter, where a camp had been set up. The simplicity of the Mahatma's hut was juxtaposed with the installation of electricity, loudspeakers and telephones. Here, within a week of his own arrival in Delhi, Cripps had his initial informal meeting with Gandhi, first joining over 3000 people for prayers before retreating, shoeless, to the hut for forty minutes of private talk. Cripps then whisked Gandhi off in the official car to meet Pethick-Lawrence. 'We both asked him to act as our adviser with all frankness and this he promised to do and to help as best he could,' Cripps recorded in his diary on 1 April. 'Old Gandhi seemed physically very fit,' he concluded. 'I am really fond of the old man though he is no child at negotiation! He's got an unassailable position in the country and knows it . . .'

It is obvious that Cripps hoped for more than spiritual uplift from the Mahatma. It was Gandhi's proven ability to thwart a settlement that made his position pivotal and thus made efforts to propitiate him worthwhile. The alternative strategy was to keep the old man at arm's length – as the Viceroy clearly wished – and to rely on Azad's diffuse professions of goodwill or Nehru's subtle rhetoric or Patel's brute exercise of authority in carrying Congress. But Cripps felt that he had tried all this in 1942, only to be disappointed. Believing that the Muslim League was bluffing about the irreducibility of its demand for an independent Pakistan, Cripps thought that Congress could be induced to acquiesce in an acceptable compromise if only Gandhi did not feel his *amour propre* slighted in the process. No trouble was to be spared in courting the old man. Wavell confessed himself 'frankly horrified at the deference shown to Gandhi' during his first official meeting with the delegation on 3 April, when a delay in supplying him with a glass of water meant that 'Cripps hustled off himself to see about it.'[12]

The round of interviews continued, day by day. By the middle of April, press reports began to speak increasingly of a deadlock. Backed by the final election returns, Jinnah was becoming increasingly intransigent in his public demands for Pakistan. It was an explosive atmosphere. 'We can't leave this country without a settlement of some kind,' Cripps wrote in his diary on 7 April. 'If we did there would be bloodshed and chaos within a few weeks.'

The time had come to lay down a timetable and to make hard choices, especially about Pakistan. Cripps drew up a statement, to be put to the parties, posing two alternatives: either Scheme A for union or Scheme B for partition. Scheme A suggested the most flexible form of union, while Scheme B stipulated the possible extent of an independent Pakistan in rigorous terms. If Jinnah's 'two-nation theory' justified Muslim separation, Cripps argued, it would be 'wholly inconsistent with this theory if non-Muslim majority areas should be added to Pakistan'.[13] The idea was obviously to make union as appealing as possible, and partition as unappealing. To this extent the proposal was simply an extension of Labour's traditional pro-Congress approach; and British interests in the region, both economic and strategic, predisposed against 'balkanization' and thus against Pakistan.

Cripps, however, was clearly intent on telling both sides equally that neither could have everything it wanted. Jinnah might champion the Muslim minority in India as a whole, but a Scheme B Pakistan could only offer salvation to Muslims in those parts of northern India where Muslims were already relatively secure in their majority status. Faced with an agonizing choice, could Jinnah be tempted into some form of federation under Scheme A? Cripps's information was that Vallabhbhai Patel, the strong man of Congress, stood for the hard line on a unitary solution in which the Hindu majority would naturally prevail. Could he be persuaded by Gandhi to offer the olive branch of Scheme A, so as to avert partition?

Before the Indians could be confronted with a delicately poised choice, the British Government had to face its own moment of truth. Cripps's negotiating strategy demanded that Scheme B be specified in a form unattractive to the Muslim League. So Pakistan's consequent economic and strategic weakness would likewise make Scheme B an unattractive option from the point of view of British defence interests in the region. The cabinet and the chiefs of staff in London therefore had to be won over. Attlee cabled back that even Scheme B was 'better than no agreement at all as this would lead to widespread chaos'.[14]

'Crucial Week in India: attempt to bring parties closer,' *The Times* reported on 15 April. On the same day, Cripps received a private letter from Azad, who knew that the delegation's plan was to put a proposal to both parties and then leave them to chew it over while the cabinet ministers left Delhi for a break in Kashmir over Easter. Azad suggested that he should himself first receive an informal briefing, so as to anticipate likely objections from Jinnah and help secure the backing of the Congress Working Committee.

Any hopes that the League would enter into informal negotiations with Congress were promptly dashed by Jinnah. Twenty minutes of 'photographing and cinematographing a fake meeting' on 16 April did not help his official interview with the delegation to get off to a good start. 'I am afraid it yielded no useful results,' admitted the usually indomitable Cripps. The tone of the meeting had been set, much to the Viceroy's chagrin, by the Secretary of State's insistence on the 'velvet glove', which in his hands was liable to become a woolly glove of unravelling platitudes. But the ministers seem to have been agreed in relying on personal appeals to Jinnah rather than a sterner confrontation with him. 'This is the really critical time and I feel personally that I must leave no stone unturned to get a favourable result for the future of 400 million people hangs in the balance in the next few days,' Cripps wrote in his diary on 16 April. 'May God give us wisdom to do what is right. I have never felt a heavier responsibility on my shoulders than just at this moment.' He spared himself no effort. On the next day he spent a long evening with Jinnah, not getting home until nearly one o'clock, only to rise at 5.45 a.m. for a meeting at Gandhi's camp in the sweepers' colony.

Jinnah seemed locked into a posture of total inflexibility. 'He isn't quite big enough to take the plunge, though he realises the immense dangers if there is no agreement,' thought Cripps. 'I told him that his attitude tended to throw us into the arms of Congress and appealed to him to make some advance to a compromise – but I could not get anything out of him.' At this point, neither Scheme A nor Scheme B was regarded by Jinnah as any basis for negotiation with Congress. If only by comparison, Gandhi appeared more forthcoming. 'As always he was charming and wanted to be helpful,' Cripps noted; and he seized on the suggestion that if anyone were to meet Jinnah, it should be Nehru.[15]

Throughout the visit of the cabinet delegation, a contest was taking place for the presidency of Congress, thus virtually settling who would shortly become prime minister of India. In declaring to Cripps that 'the real man to consult was Jawaharlal' – rather than Patel, still less Azad – Gandhi gave a highly significant indication of his own preference, which turned out, as usual, to clinch the matter. What apparently weighed with Gandhi was, above all, Nehru's qualifications as a sophisticated negotiator – someone 'who was educated at Harrow and Cambridge and became a barrister' – who could stand on level terms with any British opposite number.[16] In effect, Nehru was chosen because he was a match for Cripps.

Cripps heard what he wanted to hear from both Jinnah and Gandhi in one further respect: that, although each party was fearful of being seen by its own supporters to proffer the necessary concessions, a compromise solution that was imposed by the British might actually be accepted on both sides. At the delegation's meeting with Wavell on 18 April, Cripps opportunely tabled his own proposal. Though there is no evidence that this document was shown in advance to either Jinnah or Gandhi, Cripps's diary that day does hint that, when he went on from the Viceregal Lodge to meet Nehru for lunch, he was more open: 'We discussed the merits of various compromises and it didn't look as if the Working Committee were going to give very much either!'

Yet Cripps's own attempt to square the circle, it quickly emerged, was not acceptable to Congress. Admittedly, his draft award rejected partition as impracticable, on the ground that if Pakistan were to be extensive enough to be viable, its claim to non-Muslim areas would be unjustifiable. Cripps proposed instead to accommodate the Muslim demand for some kind of self-government by means of a three-tier structure, in which provinces could opt for 'grouping' into Hindustan or Pakistan at an intermediate level below that of a Union of All India, which would be responsible for certain common functions, including defence.

Here was the origin of the proposal on which everything turned in 1946 – in effect, the last moment to avert partition and bloodshed in

India. The exact scheme kept changing, the consequent arrangements for the transition kept changing, the venues in which discussion took place kept changing; but the essence of the choice henceforth dominated every phase of these complex and protracted negotiations. For some such exercise in federalism was the only chance of weaning the Muslim League from the Pakistan option. Yet Congress remained reluctant to grant grouping the sort of legitimacy necessary to entice the League into such constitutional arrangements.

Since the League would only participate if it were persuaded to trust Congress, their mutual perceptions became the real issue at every stage. As Cripps told Nehru at one point: 'If there was confidence and goodwill, it would work anyway; if there wasn't, it wouldn't – and he more or less agreed.'[17] Everything in the end turned on trust or its absence; but not, as in 1942, mistrust of Cripps himself, or of the Viceroy, or of the British Government, so much as mistrust between Congress and the League.

In Britain, India did not provide the main headlines as people celebrated their first post-war Easter, which fell that year on Sunday, 21 April. Worries nearer home – housing, rationing, shortages of all kinds – had more attention. Yet the Labour Government was still riding high. Opinion polls and by-elections alike confirmed that it was holding its support. Success bred success in winning unlikely converts. Harold Nicolson, who badly wanted a peerage, had told the Lord Chancellor earlier that week that he would be prepared to take the Labour whip in the Lords – 'I said I was heart and soul with the government in its foreign policy and that I also agreed with its domestic policy.'[18] John Maynard Keynes, with a peerage already and rather more forebodings about future policy, was spending Easter at his house below the Sussex Downs, where he died peacefully on Easter Sunday morning. India's sterling balances would trouble him no more.

In the London Sunday papers, reports from India were sobering, with rising communal tension and a total impasse in the talks. 'Indian leadership has failed dismally to bridge the ever-widening gulf between Muslims and Hindus,' commented the *Observer*, a Conservative newspaper in those days. 'The great Congress hoax of India's "oneness" has been exposed, as Mr Jinnah always maintained it would be, as a pure myth.' 'IT MAY BE A LONG JOB', conceded the *Daily Herald* a few days later, loyally seeking to make the best of it.[19] The cabinet delegation, now taking a short holiday in the mountains of Kashmir, took stock of a worrying position amid innocent recreations: trout-fishing for Cripps, snooker for Alexander and Pethick-Lawrence (who unexpectedly displayed more aptitude at the billiards table than at the negotiating table).

On their return to Delhi, the heat was on, in every sense, as temperatures steadily soared to around 40°C. Jinnah was wary of the latest compromise plan that Cripps put to him. 'However I went on and on (like casting a fly over a fish that won't take),' Cripps wrote, though clearly finding him as difficult to play as any Kashmir trout. This proved not to be crucial since, as Cripps admitted the following day, 'Jawaharlal turned it down flat! So that was that.' No sooner was one scheme rejected by one party than Cripps tried an alternative on the other side; dining privately with Jinnah that night, Cripps detected the first signs of concession towards the idea of a federal centre. 'The plot thickens!' he wrote as he pondered his tactics, deciding what to say and to whom.[20]

At last there came a corresponding sign from Congress of a willingness to engage in face-to-face talks. Much oppressed by the Delhi heat, Azad pined for escape to another Simla conference; he determined to ignore his evidently divided Working Committee in seeking out Cripps on 26 April. Azad said to him – none of this was on paper – that he was confident that Congress would, after all, enter negotiations on the basis of a three-tier approach; Jinnah could be told as much. Cripps reported back to his colleagues and, despite the Viceroy's growing wish 'to stop all this to-ing and fro-ing by Cripps', secured their approval.[21] Cripps respected Azad's confidences when he met Gandhi and also played on Jinnah's fear of being held responsible for a breakdown (again) to bring him into line.

The upshot of Cripps's efforts was thus an agreement, if only an agreement to leave Delhi for the first face-to-face negotiations between the parties since the breakdown of the 1945 Simla conference. 'This important move, at a time when negotiations were threatened with deadlock,' reported the *Sunday Times* on 28 April, 'is a major triumph for Sir Stafford Cripps.' The delegation's invitations to a second Simla conference specified its agenda: to consider a constitution for a union government, as Congress wished, balanced with the creation of two groups of Hindu and Muslim provinces, respectively – the essential concession to win Jinnah's acceptance. Azad had just been induced by Gandhi to stand aside as president of Congress and to nominate as his successor not Patel, the self-appointed hammer of the Muslims, but Nehru. This move made Jinnah's participation in the tripartite talks easier for Cripps to secure.

As in the previous summer, Simla was again an attractive refuge from baking Delhi in May 1946. This was the first meeting between the parties since the end of the war. There were twelve official participants in the tripartite talks: four each from Congress and the Muslim League, three ministers plus the Viceroy. Gandhi orbited the conference, eccentrically. He was not an official delegate but he had been officially invited and accommodated. Seclusion was part of the plan. Journalists, denied any hard news, competed in their evocative word-pictures and speculated, with increasing tetchiness, on the hopes of a settlement.

The signs were mixed. Jinnah made a point of arriving late; his clothes got lost in transit; he refused to shake hands with Azad. Congress's other Muslim representative, the gigantic Ghaffar Khan, 'the frontier Gandhi', spoke no English; his role was to bulk uncomprehendingly large as a symbol of Congress's hold on the North West Frontier Province, within the territory claimed for Pakistan. Nehru thus did most of the talking for Congress, if only as interpreter. The brooding Patel, so recently slighted in his political ambitions, was hardly an encouraging influence as Congress's fourth representative.

The talks provided moments of optimism. When, on 6 May, Jinnah offered to come into a union if Congress would accept grouping – the essence of any conceivable bargain – Cripps's spirits rose. Nehru's response was encouraging. 'The atmosphere, except for Vallabhbhai Patel's scowls, was good and helpful,' Cripps noted on 7 May. 'Patel is just anxious to break the thing up and doesn't want anything but a Congress dictatorship with himself as dictator!' Cripps, ever more convinced that the way to outflank the Congress hardliners was to enlist Gandhi's influence, accordingly arranged for him to meet the Viceroy and the delegation that evening. The stratagem backfired. Gandhi was in his uncompromising mood – 'we must choose between the two parties and then hand the matter over to one or the other of them to do entirely in their own way' – a course which he followed to the logical conclusion of calling the three-tier plan worse than Pakistan. In sparring with Cripps, however, Gandhi did throw out a challenge for him to come up with a workable scheme; and this, despite everything, Cripps set about doing. 'The *only* chance now of getting anything agreed is the old man.'

Cripps was adroit in drafting a nicely balanced compromise. In effect the Muslim League was asked to work within the framework of an All-India Union Government, while Congress was asked to accept Hindu–Muslim parity within it and the legitimacy of provinces entering groups, which might set up their own legislatures and executives. Having cleared his draft with his colleagues, while the Viceroy saw Jinnah, Cripps met Gandhi and 'we went through it word by word and line by line'. Cripps thought that he had 'convinced him that it was fair' and wrote that the meeting was 'wholly successful I think and as he left he said he went with a light heart'. Cripps accepted not only Gandhi's minor drafting amendments but his advice on postponing formal meetings for twenty-four hours. The two men of God were in apparent communion. 'I prayed hard for guidance before it and I am sure that I got all that I asked for,' Cripps recorded on 8 May. 'I felt more in harmony with him than ever before.'

Nor did Cripps conceal his jubilation from his colleagues. Wavell had qualms about whether the proposed deal was fair to the Muslims, and still disliked this whole style of negotiation. Unaware of the Viceroy's private opinion – 'I do not quite trust Cripps and wholly mistrust Gandhi' – Cripps may have been guilty of some complacency: 'I must say that we really have been an excellent team!'[22]

Disillusionment soon came, in the form of a letter from Gandhi with the fairly predictable caveats that he wished to enter, having talked with the four official Congress delegates. They could not be bound by the proposed constitutional arrangements for grouping and, above all, could not accept parity with the Muslims. Gandhi reiterated: 'This is really worse than Pakistan.'[23]

Nothing dismayed, Cripps decided to work on Azad and Nehru instead. This was negotiation by attrition, closing the gap by inches – much as in 1942, as all of them must have been well aware. Cripps's tactics consisted of patient informal conciliation to outflank the formal gestures of confrontation. 'Each time they break away and write letters saying they can't do this or that, we draw them back again!'[24] Wyatt brought back encouraging news that Gandhi was, after all, prepared to let Congress accept Cripps's proposal, provided two points were met. First, that Congress should remain free to argue against grouping upon entering a constituent assembly. Secondly, that though parity for Hindu–Muslim representation was unacceptable as a principle, if the issue were left specifically to Nehru and Jinnah, then something practically amounting to parity might emerge.

Here was the pivot of the whole Simla conference. On 9 May, Nehru proposed talks between the two parties, along with an umpire to adjudicate on differences. If Jinnah's slighting riposte, that he was ready to meet any *Hindu* member of Congress, was intended to provoke uproar and breakdown, it failed. Azad magnanimously did not rise to the insult; the restraint on the Congress side was notable; after a silence, Nehru simply suggested an adjournment while he talked with Jinnah. The two withdrew for forty minutes while most of the rest spilled out into the gardens. The upshot was an adjournment for two days, to allow Jinnah and Nehru to get down to business.

The cabinet delegation had been in India for seven weeks now. Alexander was surely justified in writing in his diary on 9 May of 'a sudden dramatic turn' which gave rise to 'feelings of greater optimism than we had experienced at any time since we had been in India'. Cripps and Gandhi relaxed together by plying each other with compliments. 'We mustn't become a mutual admiration society!' the Mahatma declared at one point. 'He is a great dear and I am really fond of him – though sometimes he is difficult to understand because of the way his mind works,' Cripps enthused in his diary on 9 May. 'He appears to be quite irrational but that is because he acts sometimes inspirationally.'

The proposed Jinnah–Nehru summit talks certainly gave the press its most positive news. 'MORE HOPE FOR INDIA TALKS' proclaimed the Conservative *Daily Mail* on 10 May. The crucial point was that the leading Indian politicians themselves – facilitated by British mediation but at last free of British tutelage – were getting to grips with the problems of resolving their own fate. Had some form of compromise between Congress and the Muslim League ultimately flowed from these exchanges, the vision of Indian unity through non-violence might not have perished through a deficiency in the political skills necessary to implement it.

The second Simla conference, like the first, ultimately broke down. On the surface, the reason was much the same: Jinnah's insistence on himself nominating any Muslim representatives. Thus he could again be blamed. But underlying this largely symbolic issue was a more fundamental issue about power. Here the onus lay with Nehru to satisfy Jinnah that

Congress really did accept the premise of grouping of provinces, since only such an undertaking – and evidence of its good faith – could possibly persuade the Muslim League to set aside its demand for Pakistan.

The position of Maulana Azad, the outgoing Congress president, was only the personal aspect of this conflict. The new point, feeding on old resentments about how Muslims had been excluded from provincial power after 1937, was that Jinnah sought to make it a principle that Congress should not choose any Muslim representatives. Faced with this demand at Simla, Nehru's posture changed from one of negotiation and flexibility to one of equally principled defiance. 'We simply cannot agree to this, even temporarily, for it means a negation of what we have stood for all these long years,' Nehru explained to Cripps. 'It would be a dishonourable act on our part which is bound to be deeply resented.'[25]

Here was a sinister portent of a dispute that returned to dog subsequent negotiations. Congress and the League were engaged in a broader and finally intractable struggle for representative legitimacy. Nehru's position was that both sides had agreed to accept arbitration, necessarily accepting thereby the final decision of an umpire. Jinnah's position, by contrast, was that Congress first had to accept grouping: otherwise the Muslim League's essential demand for recognition would itself be subject to arbitration. He reiterated that 'if the Congress would agree to Groups of Provinces as desired by the Muslim League he would seriously consider a Union.'[26] The result was again impasse.

In Britain, the breakdown at Simla marked the re-emergence of India as a party political issue. In May 1946, the reinvigorated hero of Fulton was back on fighting form; and the news from Simla licensed him to break the party truce, now that the Indians themselves were in such obvious disarray.

Churchill had sometimes spoken despondently of the Raj. 'India must go,' he had told one visitor while on holiday on Lake Como the previous September: 'We were now in their debt – was 1200 million the figure? – which we owed to them for the privilege of having saved them from conquest by the Japanese.'[27] He had been on the other side of the Atlantic, with the emollient Rab Butler leading for the Opposition, when the House of Commons had endorsed the decision to send out the cabinet delegation. What really moved him was the link he perceived between the Government's decision to evacuate British troops from

Egypt, its policy in Palestine, and the options it was now contemplating in India.

Churchill had already drafted a letter to Attlee. In it he minimized the degree of bipartisan acquiescence and warned that its continuance depended on 'an Agreement between the great forces composing Indian life'. A couple of days after the news from Simla came through, the letter was sent: 'I must resume my full freedom to point out the dangers and evils of the abandonment by Great Britain of her mission in India.' Churchill did not deny the latent right to independence implicit in Dominion status. But he claimed that this merely acknowledged a remote contingency. 'If, at the present time, you reach immediately a solution of independence, I should not be able to support this,' he told Attlee. 'I may add that the dangers of civil war breaking out in India on our departure are at least as great as those which are held by the Anglo-American Commission on Palestine to make a continuance of British or Anglo-American Mandate necessary.'[28] Was this danger to keep Britain in India too?

The bipartisan front in Britain on Indian policy, uneasily but successfully maintained since 1939, was thus threatened by the return of the unregenerate imperialist. The cabinet was clearly worried. In London they focused on references to Indian independence in the draft of the long-awaited, much-revised statement to be issued by the cabinet delegation. In drafting it, Cripps had seized on Attlee's 'historic words' in the House of Commons, and throughout made frequent and unvarnished use of the term independence, appreciating that its introduction had dispelled longstanding suspicions, which its subsequent qualification would simply rekindle with renewed force.

Yet Attlee suddenly had cold feet, having just learnt of Churchill's views. Attlee told the delegation that he was reluctant to 'give ammunition to critics of the Government here' but, far from imposing his own view at this juncture, he ultimately gave way to the united expertise of the cabinet delegation and Viceroy, backed by their refusal otherwise to take responsibility for the statement.[29] The fact that Wavell joined the ministers in taking this stand shows the seriousness of the issue and in fact produced a degree of unity between them otherwise lacking.

Insofar as Cripps did not attribute the outcome of the Simla conference to God, he attributed it to Jinnah. In the conference's final stages, Cripps had struck Wavell as deplorably partisan in seeking to pin the blame upon the Muslim League. Both he and Alexander thought that the chances for acceptance of the delegation's own solution, on which work had steadily been proceeding, had been prejudiced.

Cripps undoubtedly wanted Gandhi to remain involved in the negotiations. 'I think that more than ever he holds the key to the situation,' Cripps wrote, reflecting his private view of the bottom line in these negotiations. No Gandhi meant no Congress, no Congress meant no settlement, no settlement meant no transfer of power – which was unthinkable at this point. 'My own view is that we *must* at all costs come to an accommodation with Congress,' Cripps wrote on 14 May. 'We can get through I believe without the League if we have Congress with us but not without Congress even if we have the League.' Cripps saw here the threat of a split in the delegation. Wavell and Alexander, after golfing together in Simla, had taken to dining together in the air-conditioned luxury of the Viceregal Lodge, and were plainly hostile to further 'appeasement' of Congress. Indeed Wavell was now talking of resignation if there were concessions: Cripps if there were not.

The cabinet delegation's statement was presented to the press on Thursday, 16 May, 'our D-Day', as Cripps called it. Simultaneously published as a White Paper in London, it was essentially Cripps's attempt to build on the measure of agreement revealed at Simla and to erect this into a system of government. At its heart was the historic compromise necessary to secure political acceptance: an All-India Union sufficiently strong to appease Congress, balanced against a system of provincial grouping with sufficient legitimacy to win the acquiescence of the Muslim League. In drafting and redrafting it, Cripps had walked on eggshells around Gandhi's susceptibilities so that he might have no excuse for branding this scheme as 'worse than Pakistan'. The name Pakistan was not used and a dichotomous 'vivisection' of India was avoided by proposing three groups – in essence, today's Pakistan, today's Bangladesh, and today's Republic of India. These were not to be constituted on an explicitly communal basis but through the consent of the provinces. 'A United India,' the *Manchester Guardian*'s headline called it on 17 May, adding: 'Pakistan Claim Rejected'. The chances of a settlement and the possibility of forming an interim government suddenly appeared closer.

In a remark almost as widely quoted as that about 'a post-dated cheque' in 1942, Gandhi abandoned banking metaphors in favour of horticulture: the proposals contained 'a seed to convert this land of sorrow into one without sorrow and suffering'. What attracted less attention at the time was his assertion that, since the constituent assembly was necessarily a sovereign body, it was open to it to vary any of the provisions in the statement, notably on grouping.[30]

What now consumed Gandhi's attention was the small print of the statement, which could, with the requisite ingenuity, be construed as providing an escape clause from the acceptance of grouping. Yet what Congress surely had to understand was the political reality of striking a bargain with the Muslim League. And what that meant was – rather than outwitting the discredited and obsolescent British Raj – offering their fellow Indian citizens a *quid pro quo* that they could decently accept. It was this kind of problem that Cripps and Gandhi, however often they met, failed to resolve. It simply slipped between the other levels at which their exchanges took place.

On 20 May the delegation sat with the Viceroy, considering a letter from Gandhi about grouping. The meeting was already becoming acrimonious; but the real drama came with the delivery of a second letter from Gandhi, this one replete with uncorroborated allegations of what had been privately said to him by Cripps and Pethick-Lawrence. Unlike 1942, when similar discrepancies had emerged about his assurances to Congress, Cripps was not without a witness. No one now doubted Pethick-Lawrence's veracity nor mistook his indignation at being misrepresented – indeed it was his idea to restrict any future contact to recorded interviews with all three ministers. 'I have never seen three men taken more aback by this revelation of G. in his true colours,' noted the Viceroy, who took special care to observe Cripps's outraged reaction – 'shaken to the core' and 'quite *ahuri*'.[31]

Cripps felt undermined because he had staked so much on Gandhi's influence. When Cripps found himself confined to bed the following day, though the symptoms were those of his recurrent colitis, it was also true (as Alexander put it) that 'undoubtedly he had also received a very severe shock from the line taken by Mr Gandhi in his letters.'[32] Cripps had driven himself hard, living off his reserves of nervous energy as he chased the elusive prospect of agreement, persuading himself each day that one more arduous session with Gandhi would do the trick. With so much invested in this process, and used to getting his own way, Cripps was vulnerable to the sort of rebuff he received on 20 May, when his overstretched body rebelled.

Cripps attended no official meetings from 21 May until 3 June. He was missed by everyone. Even the Viceroy noted the loss of 'our chief drafter' and Alexander, despite their disagreements, called it 'a great loss to the delegation to be without his fertile suggestions as regards courses of action'.[33]

While Cripps was ill, he was sent a personal letter by Gandhi, enclosing an advance copy of his public response to the cabinet delegation's Statement. It larded a compliment to 'the best document the British Government could have produced in the circumstances' with the characteristic reflection that 'what is best from the British standpoint' might, from the Indian, 'possibly be harmful'.[34] Cripps, after a week away from official business, sent an appropriately providential reply. 'I have naturally wondered why it was just at this critical time that I should have been withdrawn,' he wrote; 'but no doubt there must be some purpose in it.' Cripps expatiated on how much he had relied upon Gandhi over the previous couple of months and tried to shake his insistence that independence would be a farce unless Britain simply quit India, leaving no troops to maintain peace and order, and with no provision that a constitution should first be made. 'I feel that the moment has come for the supreme act of Faith or Trust on all sides,' he wrote, adding: 'I also believe that you, my dear friend, can do more in this direction than any other man in the world.[35] Unmoved by mere words, Gandhi showed himself set in another direction altogether.

In Cripps's absence, Wavell had initially made good progress towards the formation of an interim government, which Congress wanted settled before they would give a decision on the constitutional proposals. Meetings between the Viceroy and Nehru inspired a degree of mutual confidence, not least in Wavell's readiness to observe a convention of non-interference; and in fact Congress was already satisfied on this point.

The real trouble arose on other issues. The Muslim League was edging, with frustrating slowness, towards acceptance of the statement; Congress swaying, with frustrating indecisiveness, between acceptance and rejection. Back on the job, Cripps wrote on 4 June that 'it is very tense and exciting for these next few days to see how things develop – when one remembers that the future of this great continent of 400 millions depends upon it for its future.' His colleague Alexander, just off for another game of billiards at the club, was more forthright, jovially observing: 'Truth is they are all B—rs.'[36]

Jinnah now held the key. He had been playing a hard tactical game all along, never disclosing his bottom line even to his own awed followers. Was it irreducibly an immediate demand for an independent Islamic state based on severance of the Muslim-majority provinces? If so, no real negotiation was possible. As the authoritative edition of the Quaid-i-Azam's papers now makes clear, Jinnah left no diary divulging his inner thoughts. But Cripps, who did, based his own strategy on a reading of the highly intelligent Jinnah that surely has much historical cogency.

Cripps now sensed that 'Pakistan', a fine slogan and an elastic concept, might itself be a negotiating ploy allowing Jinnah to settle for something less – but something that he himself valued more. For it could be used as a tool to entrench the Muslims' position throughout India, notably in provinces where they would always be a minority and thus potentially vulnerable. For example, Jinnah himself lived in a fine house in Bombay, which would be outside Pakistan. To a Bombay Muslim, grouping was a real safeguard whereas the sort of Pakistan on offer was a distant symbolic notion. Conversely, a Muslim in those parts of the Punjab where Muslims were already in a clear majority had less need of Pakistan in this respect. And Muslims in the parts of Bengal that we now know as Bangladesh, while a majority, are self-evidently no longer united with their co-religionists as citizens of modern Pakistan.

Jinnah thus had to educate the League into accepting the delegation's Statement of 16 May, which rejected Pakistan in favour of Indian unity. 'I advised you to reject the last Simla Conference formula,' he told his followers on 6 June. 'But I cannot advise you to reject the British Cabinet Mission's proposals.'[37] He secured the League's acceptance by a large majority, which, Cripps thought, ought to make it easier to persuade Congress too. 'I think Jinnah has been very good and helpful in the way he has put it across to the League – though from his speeches one might imagine that the Cabinet Mission were halfwits and not his best friends!' Cripps wrote that day, pleading indulgence of Jinnah's tactics: 'That was I think to get the majority with him!' The League's demand for parity in an interim government now became crucial.

Gandhi had joined the Congress Working Committee in withdrawing from Delhi into the northern hills and only returned on Sunday, 9 June, for further deliberations. The next day the cabinet delegation received an informal message 'that Mr Gandhi was feeling neglected and somewhat hurt that he was not being contacted'. When Pethick-Lawrence and Cripps said that there was no way out except by seeing Gandhi, Alexander invoked their experience of 18–20 May and warned that unless the whole delegation were formally involved, he would have to consider leaving for home.[38]

The agreed plan was twofold. First for Wavell to see Jinnah and Nehru together, building on his success so far, with a view to reaching agreement on the personnel of an interim government that would in practice embody parity, while not conceding it as a principle. Secondly, for Pethick-Lawrence alone to see Gandhi. If both initiatives failed, Cripps would demand 'to have a shot at it myself', whatever his colleagues thought: 'The Viceroy and First Lord particularly seem terrified lest I should give something away and don't understand the need for frank and free *personal* talks – as against formal interviews – for getting this sort of business through.'[39] Gandhi was reported in the *Manchester Guardian* on 12 June as saying: 'If the negotiations break down it is God's will.'

The upshot was that Nehru and Jinnah negotiated separately with the Viceroy. The crisis centred on the formation of an interim government. Wavell's transparency about his intentions had helped him to secure agreement for participation under the existing conventions; but his lack of finesse in playing his hand was now a handicap in the keen bargaining, and bluffing too, that took place over personnel.

For the first time in six weeks, Cripps dined out. Over a cordial dinner with Nehru – 'Jawaharlal was his dear and charming self and in very good form' – Cripps received new information. Nehru gave him to understand that agreement on an interim government was unlikely; 'but he clearly contemplated we should go ahead with the constituent assembly and perhaps ask the Muslim League to form a Government.' Nehru thought that no communal trouble was imminent. 'I definitely asked him what his advice was,' Cripps recorded on 13 June, 'and it was to go ahead with our scheme even if there were a refusal by Congress.' Here was a new twist: possibly a more hopeful one. The indication that Congress could still contemplate accepting the constitutional scheme, even if it rejected the government posts currently on offer, came as news to Cripps.

By this point, even Cripps was aware that the real threat to the search for political compromise came from Gandhi himself. 'You will have to choose between the two, the Muslim League and the Congress, both your creations,' Gandhi now told Cripps. 'Every day you pass here coquetting now with the Congress, now with the League and again with the Congress, wearing yourself away, will not do.' In advising Cripps to catch his boat home to England, Gandhi's stance was that of the prophet: 'Stick to your dates even though the heavens may fall.' This time it was Cripps who was unmoved, calling this 'a most ridiculous letter from the Old Man'.[40]

A compromise on the make-up of a provisional government remained the aim. On 16 June, a second statement was duly issued, exactly a month after the first. Drafted by Cripps, it announced that invitations to serve in a coalition government had gone out to fourteen named individuals. These comprised six Congress Hindus, five Muslim League members and three from the minorities. 'HAND-OVER TO FOURTEEN INDIANS ON JUNE 26' ran the banner headline in next day's *Daily Herald*. For a couple of days, press reports were full of optimism, only to be confounded yet again by events.

The next move by Gandhi came as a last-minute upset: a proposal to substitute a Muslim for a Hindu as one of the Congress representatives in order to affirm the latter's non-communal character. This was an admirable principle; its effect otherwise. 'Of course he must know – as we pointed out – that this would be like a red rag to Jinnah and would make a settlement out of the question,' Cripps wrote on 17 June.

The debates over the next couple of days began to realize his worst dreams, as the potency of Gandhi's influence was felt and those who had favoured compromise, like Nehru, appeared to buckle. 'It really is rather maddening that after these three months the whole scheme long and short term looks like being broken down by a completely new stunt idea introduced by Gandhi, and apparently the Working Committee haven't the guts to disagree with him!' wrote Cripps on 18 June. For him the issue was not one of principle but one of tactics; for Gandhi perhaps both.

Everything was now up in the air. The crucial figure was Vallabhbhai Patel, hitherto invariably depicted by Cripps as a brooding, scowling Hindu nationalist, resentful of Nehru's access to the British elite. Yet, as both men came to sense, Patel's hard-nosed realism made him an ally. Was this, Cripps reflected on 19 June, to be the moment of truth when the politicians asserted themselves against the moralists? 'I feel that now

Congress are embarking on a constructive share of the Government and are no longer to be oppositional,' Cripps commented; 'this divorce was almost inevitable though its repercussions, if it persists, may be difficult and dangerous.'

Congress's rejection of the government posts was sealed when Patel decided that it was impossible for the Working Committee to repudiate Gandhi on such an issue. Partly because of Nehru's current absence in Kashmir, Patel had become the pivotal figure and now sought to ensure that Congress's decision would not exclude it from participating in any other government that the Viceroy formed. The point was that the only parties eligible to participate would be those that had accepted the 16 May constitutional statement – which Congress had not yet done. The contention over the interim government had meanwhile spilled over into the press, mainly through Jinnah's agency, thus exacerbating tension. At this point Cripps envisaged complete breakdown and an early return home for consultation: 'It is no good blaming anyone for it – it arises from the long and deep communal division and perhaps it was too much to expect that we should be able to overcome it.'[41]

As Congress, having rejected places in the interim government, moved towards formal acceptance of the constitutional statement of 16 May, Gandhi again broke loose. He seized on the stipulations over grouping to raise the temperature; and also evinced indignation at learning that Azad had assured the Viceroy that Congress would not prejudice his formation of an interim government through insistence on nominating a Muslim. It was eventually settled that all three ministers should see Gandhi with Patel.

The interview took place early in the morning of 24 June. Alexander, 'roused from my wet and sticky bed at 6 o'clock', prepared for the worst and duly found that 'Gandhi who was enjoying his weekly 24 hours of silence, had removed all but his loin cloth and then sat right up in a divan chair, with his legs crossed, nodding and waggling his head as the case might be!'[42] Cripps did much of the talking, while Gandhi laboriously scrawled his comments on small pieces of paper, to be read out by his attendant, Sudhir Ghosh. The proceedings left Cripps apprehensive. 'I really believe that at 77 he is not able always to take things in,' he wrote that day, 'and consequently he sticks to what is in his mind and so muddles it – with alas disastrous results to everybody.' It was Patel who struck everyone as the man of business. After seeing him, Cripps knew what he wanted from Congress – or at least what he could get.

At 8 o'clock that evening, ten minutes after the end of Gandhi's period of silence, he came with Patel to the Viceroy's Lodge for a formal interview. The atmosphere was false for many reasons. It is not surprising that Wavell thought Cripps and Pethick-Lawrence disingenuous in the assurances they now gave Gandhi about grouping. They certainly dissimulated a goodwill towards him that they no longer genuinely shared. The strategy, as Cripps described it, was to 'let the Old Man talk all the time', to bear with his 'long references to his S. African experiences', and generally to humour him. 'Patel seemed to be with us practically throughout the interview,' Cripps noted pointedly on 25 June, 'and we thought it had gone off pretty well and at any rate nothing had come up of any real importance to prevent them accepting the long-term scheme.'

Despite all blandishments, Gandhi was intent on advising rejection of both official statements: that on the constitution as much as that on the provisional government. 'I must not act against my instinct,' Gandhi told Cripps, acknowledging that he 'had nothing tangible to prove that there were danger signals'.[43] His influence was nonetheless potent. 'It really is the most devastating way of conducting negotiations,' Cripps commented in his diary on 25 June. 'Twice we have had complete agreement with the Working Committee, once about 5 days ago on the whole thing and yesterday on the long term proposals alone.' Hearing that the latter had indeed been accepted, he wrote warily: 'I only hope that they have not filled it up with qualifications and reservations so that it really amounts to a rejection!!' This was a shrewd if discouraging hunch.

Gandhi had thus been overruled – in form at least – and Congress's ostensible acceptance secured. Cripps was nonetheless right to wonder whether the scheme would not be rendered nugatory by Congress's insistence on holding to its own interpretation of the provisions on grouping. Both he and Pethick-Lawrence had refrained from pressing the point in the final interview with Gandhi, so they subsequently explained to the Viceroy, because 'it might have kept the Congress from agreeing to the long-term plan'. In asking his colleagues to 'bear in mind that a lot of this trouble about the sections and grouping was due to Mr Gandhi personally', Cripps hinted that the Working Committee might well come around – 'but they could not throw Mr Gandhi over completely'.[44] The fudged proposals could be justified as a means of buying time.

The door was thus left open for Congress to be invited, after all, into some future interim government, which was undoubtedly what Cripps wanted. The Viceroy, however, felt that he had been outmanoeuvred and put into a false position vis-à-vis the Muslim League. Now aggrieved, Jinnah went back to his Working Committee and obtained a vote to accept the posts on offer in the coalition – posts that were no longer on offer in a coalition-that-never-was. Such manoeuvres duly increased the Viceroy's embarrassment over unresolved problems, left for him to face after the delegation finally left for home at the end of June.

The constitutional arrangements were never to be implemented, basically because Congress failed to evince its willingness to accept the provisions on grouping. Yet this was not really a matter of untidy drafting nor legalistic interpretation, with the British Government in the position of negligent or treacherous arbitrators. The Muslim League, despite its commitment to Pakistan, had been induced by the delegation into a constitutional scheme providing for a united India – on certain conditions, the most important of which was a recognition of grouping. Cripps and Pethick-Lawrence trusted Congress, one way or another, to make good that inducement; the League was soon to conclude that the behaviour of the Congress leaders left it with no basis for such trust, and thus with no reason to compromise its own aim of Pakistan.

'SUCCESS OF A MISSION' – so loyal readers of the *Daily Herald* were blandly assured on 27 June. 'The successful conclusion of the Indian talks is more than just a diplomatic triumph for Labour Party policy,' wrote its correspondent. 'It is the first great victory of the peace and a sign that there are still men of good will on earth.' This was as misleading about the failure to clinch a settlement as was the accompanying comment on Cripps's role: 'Perhaps it is because they are both vegetarians, but he seemed best able to understand the mysteries of the Mahatma's mind.' On this reasoning, both would have been on the same wavelength as Hitler.

Cripps was by now used to being called 'the English Gandhi' – seldom intended as a compliment. Abstention from meat and alcohol, indifference to personal comfort, a susceptibility to uplifting moral rhetoric, a relish for the stratagems of a clever lawyer, a belief that religion offered the true path in life – such affinities undeniably existed. They helped to foster mutual regard, especially on Cripps's side for a man against whom he never uttered any public reproach.

Gandhi's image is rightly inseparable from the whole story of the struggle for Indian emancipation. Cripps was to call him 'the Prophet who gave his work and life to accomplish this very end'.[45] True, his all-or-nothing utterances had often served a prophetic function, asserting an ethic of ultimate ends as he simply insisted on doing what seemed right, regardless of the consequences. Naked, he had challenged the panoply of British imperialism, with courage and with guile, and left the British to face the consequences. But an ethic of responsibility, accepting second-best solutions for fear of worse, was perhaps what Indian politicians needed in 1946. In this respect, Nehru showed some of the necessary discernment, Patel some of the necessary ruthlessness – but both were still inhibited by deference to the Mahatma.

What Gandhi could not countenance was not so much any particular compromise as compromise itself. This is surely why he deliberately, and with a good conscience, moved to sabotage the negotiations of late May and June 1946 – from the very moment that Jinnah was bringing the Muslim League to the table. 'Whatever we get, will be our deserts, not a gift from across the seas,' Gandhi declared. His message had a strong tincture of fatalism. Pethick-Lawrence confided at the time that 'he was coming to believe Gandhi did not care whether 2 or 3 million people died & would rather that they should than that he should compromise.'[46] Pethick-Lawrence, like Cripps, came to this view sadly and ruefully. But it was Gandhi's incapacity to abide any imperfect solution that now struck them as fatal in this final attempt to reach a negotiated settlement.

During the second half of 1946, both in Britain and in the United States, attention shifted towards Palestine rather than India.[47] Yet these were fraught months in India – far from dull, alas. An awkward situation turned into one that shook the nerve even of the imperturbable and soldierly Viceroy. He had an unenviable task and it is difficult to blame him for venting his frustration at the way that the cabinet delegation had avoided a showdown with Congress before themselves departing. Feeling close to Alexander, Wavell reproached Pethick-Lawrence and, above all, Cripps. 'The fatal weakness of the Mission in their abject attitude to Congress, and the duplicity of Cripps,' Wavell privately concluded, 'left behind a legacy which it was beyond my power to counter-act.'[48] This was true in its own terms but it avoided the issue of how far political finesse – a face-saving formula here, an adroit form of words there – may be necessary in brokering a peace process that could not tie up all the historically generated loose ends at once. In the House of Commons in mid-July, Cripps tried to hint delicately at the parallel need for Congress to accept grouping in good faith and for the League not to abuse such provisions. He pleased nobody.

Nehru, elected president of Congress in July, was not helped by his own noble assumption that a free India would not be divided on communal lines. For this perhaps induced some complacency about the possibility that the Muslim League would simply back off from the historic compromise to which Jinnah had led them – and which Gandhi's opposition had jeopardized. In this delicate situation, Nehru's speeches in July showed him focused on his new tasks as party leader, faced with followers whom Gandhi himself had refused to lead towards conciliation. Thus Nehru ducked the challenge of assuaging the League's apprehensions that it had offered concessions in vain. His contemptuous references to grouping at a press conference on 10 July likewise pleased nobody.

In particular these left the Quaid-i-Azam explosively displeased. When he spoke to his restive supporters on 29 July at the council of the Muslim League, the fuse of partition was finally lit. 'The League, throughout the negotiations was moved by a sense of fair play,' Jinnah claimed, 'and sacrificed the full sovereign state of Pakistan at the altar of the Congress for securing the independence of India.' Yet their sacrifice, in seeking to avoid 'bloodshed and civil war', had been 'treated with defiance and contempt', so he now argued. 'There was no sign of the slightest gesture of compromise from them.'[49] Hence the crucial steps that he announced: to withdraw agreement on the constitutional scheme, to press for Pakistan instead, and to adopt a strategy of direct action, beginning on 16 August.

The result, as had long been feared, was an outbreak of communal violence, beginning in Calcutta, in divided Bengal, with deaths measured in thousands. In the ensuing weeks, the realities of power in India were determined by the politics of the street, rather than by the eventual formation of an uneasy interim government under Nehru in September, still less by the constitutional road-map left by the cabinet delegation.

The Viceroy accordingly felt it time to prepare a 'breakdown plan' for phased withdrawal by the British towards the north. In Delhi, this now seemed a prudent worst-case scenario. In London, it struck ministers as paving the way to disaster. 'Civil war would come upon us at once,' Cripps was to argue at a Downing Street meeting in late September.[50] His view prevailed in determining the Government's response: to maintain the momentum towards a transfer of power, in spite of the slide into violence.

It is too easy to see this outcome as predetermined – as though there is nothing to explain because there were no alternatives (though admittedly there were few good ones). The Labour Government had played its best card in giving the cabinet delegation its wide brief to facilitate agreement on a path to independence that would have avoided the obvious hazards of partition. After Gandhi's critical intervention, even the second-best solutions of compromise had been fatally disabled. So the British Government was faced with the pragmatic, unglamorous options of the next-best-in-the-circumstances. And if we look beyond India itself, it is by no means obvious that deterioration in the Indian situation made out the case for granting independence.

It should be remembered that the Conservative Opposition, previously quiescent over India, was now becoming raucous about developments in the Middle East. In particular, there were denunciations of the Government for capitulation to Egyptian nationalism when it decided to evacuate troops from Egypt (and send them to Palestine instead). In a speech at the end of May by the Conservative frontbencher Oliver Lyttelton, a significant extrapolation had been made from Egypt to India: 'If we scuttle and skedaddle there we shall have reasons to hang our heads in shame if that country is plunged into all the horrors of internal strife and civil war.'[51] On this line of reasoning – one highly familiar in imperialist rhetoric – the threat to the peace was always the clinching reason for staying, not for leaving; and internal divisions among nationalist successor groups tended to reinforce this time-honoured logic, which remained Churchill's lodestar.

In Palestine, indeed, the Government's stance was more in keeping with this traditional line of thinking. How delighted the British would be to leave if only the Arabs and the Jews could agree between themselves! The obvious catch was that this was such a difficult condition to fulfil. What it meant in practice was that agreement would have to be reached between the Palestinians' international patrons, all of whom tended to treat actual Palestinian Arabs and Zionist settlers as mere clients, childishly unable to determine their own future. The Arabs' lack of political sophistication thus made their cause the plaything of exactly the caste of pashas and princes whom Bevin professed to despise. Conversely, though the Jewish Agency was undoubtedly more effective in articulating the aspirations of the pioneers who constituted the 'Yishuv', the fact that Zionism had an international outreach also made the United States into its surrogate champion (and paymaster).

One paradox of Zionism was that it was nothing if not an international movement, yet one dedicated to the support of what was nothing if not a national claim. Another paradox was that Zionism in the 1940s was patently a result of anti-semitism, as the prime response to the Nazi atrocities, yet it was also patently a cause of anti-semitism – not only among Palestinian Arabs who felt immediately threatened but also in the country that actually had the responsibility for the Palestine mandate.

We naturally tend to describe all this as happening under the shadow of the Holocaust. But this usage is not how contemporaries talked. The Nazis' Wannsee conference which decisively established the extermination policy was held in January 1942; and if *The Times* is searched electronically from then until 1950, only thirty-nine uses of the word 'holocaust' are revealed. In 1943 there is 'the holocaust at Stalingrad' and the holocaust when a village in the Ukraine is set on fire; in 1944, during the Normandy campaign, German troops duly 'fall under the holocaust from our waiting guns'; and in 1945 first Cologne and then Berlin experience 'the holocaust' of Allied bombing. At the end of August 1946 'the Calcutta holocaust' exercised much attention; and in the next couple of years the dozen or so uses of the word are mainly directed to the possibility of atomic warfare.

On 2 July 1946 *The Times* reported a statement from the Chief Rabbi of Jerusalem, employing a new semantic twist. For Rabbi Herzog deplored the retreat from the recommendations of the Anglo-American Committee on Palestine by calling for 'the immediate migration to the Holy land of 100,000 of the survivors of the Nazi holocaust'. His creative imagery did not catch on at the time but the force of his plea was evident. The impasse between the British and American governments had brought a sense of frustration in Palestine. Zionist terrorism was stepped up in June and five British officers were kidnapped, which in turn prompted the British High Commissioner to ask his Government to break off negotiations about the 'hundred thousand'.

Bevin was determined not to do this. Though angry at Truman's pre-emptive statement on the 100,000 in May, he still wanted to draw the Americans into taking part in the search for a solution and insisted that talks 'should not (repeat NOT) be even partially suspended'.[52] Yet the incoming Chief of the Imperial General Staff, Montgomery, was restive after his recent visit to Palestine, where his official diarist had recorded his impatience with 'a state of affairs in which British rule existed only in name, the true rulers being the Jews whose unspoken slogan was "You dare not touch us".'[53] The CIGS insisted on action as only a Field Marshal, still freshly garlanded from victories in the field, was able to do. What could a mere Labour cabinet say – steady on, Monty, you can't talk to us like that? Instead they sanctioned a move on the night of 29–30 June to occupy the headquarters of the Jewish Agency, arresting about 2000 people, including members of the Agency's executive, notably Moshe Shertok, though not Ben Gurion, who was abroad.

It was not a clever move. True, evidence was seized proving the Agency's complicity in the activities of Haganah, the 'home army', and showing links between Haganah and terrorist groups; but most of those arrested were trade unionists, political agitators and idealistic cranks – the sort of people who joined the Labour Party in Britain. The real terrorists were in the Stern Gang, which had murdered Moyne, and in Irgun, led by Menachem Beigin (a spelling later modified to Begin). Above all, the political effect, in alienating the moderates, both among the Yishuv and among their Zionist patrons, undoubtedly outweighed any supposed military advantage. Monty no more had the magic key in Palestine than Wavell did in India; but at least Wavell knew it.

'What imbecility as well as what evil this Government is capable of!' Baffy Dugdale wrote as soon as she heard the news in London. The move was indeed a body blow to Chaim Weizmann. Already under pressure because of his trust in British-style constitutionalism – and in the British themselves – he saw himself further eclipsed by more radical American Zionists. 'Irreparable harm has been done,' Dugdale sadly concluded.[54] Richard Meinertzhagen, internally torn because of his inbred allegiance to the British Army, still reacted emotionally by blaming the Government: 'And still we continue Hitler's policy of extermination against these unfortunate people. Have we no shame or pity?'[55] This sort of rhetoric, moreover, was now used in the House of Commons by Richard Crossman, smarting from the way his own stratagems had been thwarted: 'As the Nazis found, as we have found in the past, as history has always proved, as we found in Ireland and with the Boers in South Africa and as we shall find in this case, where we are fighting against the people's natural rights, those people will be determined to die for those rights.'[56]

American Zionists had already shown themselves less squeamish about terrorism – as long as it was in a good cause. In the tit-for-tat escalation of violence that ensued, the British could now be blamed for whatever retribution fell upon them. Visiting Palestine, Weizmann found himself a lonely voice arguing for a peaceful solution. 'He thinks only his presence has so far restrained "rivers of blood",' Dugdale noted after her guru's return to England on 19 July.[57]

Any such restraint ended three days later, at 12.37 p.m. on Monday, 22 July, when the King David Hotel in Jerusalem was blown up. The seven-storey building was the British headquarters. The casualties included Arabs and Jews as well as British. Initial reports unofficially put the dead at 39 with another 53 missing; after a couple of days it was said that 47 were dead, 55 injured and 72 missing. 'Death Roll of 123 Feared in Jerusalem,' reported *The Times* on 25 July (ultimately it was to be put at 91). In an editorial, 'The Shadow of Terrorism', it commented on the outrage, now acknowledged as the work of Irgun under the leadership of Beigin, once a corporal in the British Army (later, as Prime Minister of Israel, awarded the Nobel Peace Prize in 1978). 'When every allowance has been made for the emotions aroused among the Jews in Palestine by the sufferings of their co-religionists in Europe,' said *The Times*, 'it is impossible to acquit the Agency of failure to recognize and avert the peril which terrorism presents to the interests not only of the national home but of Jews in every country.'

There is little doubt that such sentiments were widely shared in Britain, or that they were shared less widely among Americans. To the British Government, the discovery of plans to extend Zionist terrorism to the United Kingdom, with Bevin as one obvious target for assassination, was a chilling reality, with MI5 more concerned about the Zionists than about the Soviets. Yet even in the *New York Times*, famed for the objectivity of its reporting, the King David Hotel had been pushed off the front page by 24 July and thereafter competed for coverage on the inside pages with other Palestine stories. When it came to terrorism, the Atlantic remained wide, New York not vulnerable.

Moreover, within a week of the explosion, the moral high ground was adroitly seized by the Zionists. They were able to capitalize on a non-fraternization order issued by the British military commander, Sir Evelyn Barker. He had included a phrase saying that this step aimed at 'punishing the Jews in a way the race dislikes as much as any – by striking at their pockets and showing our contempt for them'.[58] Since Haganah intelligence got hold of a copy of this letter, with its anti-semitic taint, and publicized it very effectively, the Palestinian Jews were quickly able to reclaim their victim status. This was obviously important in deflecting American opinion, though the lack of prominence given to the bombing itself meant that this item too was buried away in the small print of the inside pages; and its effect can easily be exaggerated. Still, after Herbert Morrison had apologized in the House of Commons for the terms of the General's order, the *Washington Post* showed itself convinced that 'the Goering model' (*sic*) prevailed in British policy and that this was the real point: 'A history of broken promises accounts for the rise of extremism.'[59] The British were thus left counting the cost of this blunder while still counting the bodies exhumed from the ruins of the King David Hotel.

Morrison was involved because of the eponymous 'Morrison–Grady Plan'. This became the designation of new Palestine proposals, produced in London during July as a result of the resumed Anglo-American talks; and it fell to Morrison to present them to the House of Commons in the absence of Attlee (who was in turn in Paris, substituting for the Foreign Secretary while Bevin recuperated from a heart attack). Morrison, whose only relevant sin was pro-semitism, had been picking up the pieces in co-operation with Henry Grady, representing the State Department. Grady was genuinely co-operative – his sin in the eyes of the American Zionists who were soon to scrutinize his handiwork. The Morrison–Grady plan was based on provincial autonomy within a binational Palestine: balancing the claims of a Jewish as against an Arab province, acting as scrupulously and delicately as the cabinet delegation had done in India a few weeks earlier; and the plan was to meet with the same fate at the hands of intransigent but well-placed opponents.

The Morrison–Grady plan was ready on 24 July, two days after the explosion at the King David Hotel. It went to the British cabinet the next day and was approved. It went to the American cabinet on 30 July, four days after General Barker's remarks on non-fraternization. None of this was ideal. But President Truman knew that he did not live in an ideal world and he was becoming exasperated with the relentless pressure from the Jewish lobby. 'Jesus Christ couldn't please them when he was here on earth,' he told his cabinet, 'so how could anyone expect that I would have any luck?'[60] As political realities in New York as much as in Palestine intruded further into the discussion on 30 July, the State Department was left isolated in its support for the plan.

Morrison was in fact parading a dead duck when he brought the plan the next day before the Commons. But it provoked some reflections of wider significance from the Leader of the Opposition. Churchill's pro-Zionist reputation, though as spurious as Bevin's anti-semitic reputation, has sometimes disguised the fact that they actually agreed on first principles. 'Almost any solution in which the United States will join us could be made to work,' Churchill declared.[61] Certainly the converse was true: that any solution in which the United States would not join was thereby doomed.

Remarkably, Churchill went on to explore such a possibility. He said that if the United States would not play its part, the mandate should be returned to the United Nations and Britain relinquish 'a thankless, painful, costly, laborious, inconvenient task'. He claimed to speak as a friend of Zionism, but a candid friend, rather as he had after Moyne's assassination. 'If in the Jewish movement or in the Jewish Agency there are elements of murder and outrage which they cannot control,' he warned, 'and if these strike not only at their best but at their only effective friends, they and the Zionist cause must inevitably suffer from the grave and lasting reproach of the atrocious crimes which have been committted. It is perfectly clear that Jewish warfare directed against the British in Palestine will, if protracted, automatically release us from all obligations to persevere as well as destroy the inclination to make further efforts in British hearts.'[62]

The reaction to the debate of Colonel Richard Meinertzhagen, in rural Wiltshire, though unimportant in itself, catches the note of disillusion that now permeated old-fashioned imperialist Zionism. 'Abandon Palestine to anarchy and bloodshed!' he wrote incredulously. 'Same as Egypt and India. It is a glaring admission of failure, unprecedented in the history of our Empire.'[63]

Amid all the rhetoric, the wretched DPs sat in their camps. Their plight, which had made the 100,000 issue so politically emotive, had hardly been relieved by either British or American policy on immigration. The British were legally admitting only about 350 Jewish DPs a month to Palestine. The Americans admitted 5718 Jews to the United States between May 1945 and September 1946 – on average, this was also about 350 a month.[64] At this rate, the job would take 143 years. The small chances of legal immigration for Jewish DPs had to be weighed against the risks of attempting illegal immigration, which simultaneously offered a back door into Palestine and closed the front door even further – because the British deducted the illegals who settled from the monthly quota of 1500. Yet all that changed was that the camps continued to receive further refugees from eastern Europe. Everyone could see that an effective solution depended on breaking the deadlock and securing Anglo-American agreement.

This was the logic of the Zionist shift of position on partition. Nahum Goldmann of the Jewish Agency was instrumental in softening the Zionist line here. Accepting partition into separate Jewish and Arab states meant surrendering the biblical claim to the whole of Palestine in face of the fact that the Arabs were in a clear majority. It also meant accepting the fact that the brouhaha of the 100,000 demand had done so little to help the actual situation. Goldmann's access to David Niles in the White House went a long way to converting the President to the merits of partition as a pragmatic goal, to which the Morrison–Grady plan might be seen as a stepping stone. Since Bevin, who had cordial discussions with Goldmann, was plainly ready to continue the search for compromise, hopes now centred on the conference including Jewish and Arab representatives that the British Government proposed to hold in London.

Though this conference formally opened on 9 September, it proved frustratingly difficult to begin real talks. Not only were the Arab states reluctant to attend, because they feared any kind of Jewish state, but many of the appropriate representatives of the Yishuv had been locked up by the British since the end of June. Patience was clearly going to be necessary in achieving any results; after all, the cabinet delegation in India had spent a couple of months waiting for a breakthrough. On 1 October, Bevin spoke to a group headed by Weizmann, who evidently conveyed to Baffy Dugdale that 'Bevin is obviously full of goodwill, but as far as ever from understanding the elements of the Jewish case.'[65]

Bevin told this Jewish Agency deputation of how deeply the King David Hotel incident had embittered British public opinion. 'Great Britain had accepted more people as refugees in proportion to its size than any other country,' he pointed out, suggesting that Jewish terrorism was poor recompense. 'Ever since he had taken office he had been trying to create an atmosphere conducive to final settlement,' he enjoined. 'But his task was made very difficult by the acts of the Jews.'[66]

His task was about to be made very much more difficult by the acts of the Americans. On 4 October, under pressure from Rabbi Silver, Truman issued a statement, allegedly made urgent by the fact that this was the eve of Yom Kippur, the Day of Atonement. The statement can be read, not as an outright endorsement of partition, but as a plea for compromise between this and the Morrison–Grady plan, which is what the State Department still wanted. This would have diluted the autonomy of the Jewish as of the Arab entities. But, as Goldmann was told by the Jewish Agency's representative in Washington, 'not a single newspaper has pointed up this part of the statement and all the headlines carried by the papers read "Truman's Support of a Jewish State".'[67] In the age of the spin doctor, the reason will hardly seem mysterious, with Niles ready to brief with a Zionist interpretation – scorning Grady's efforts – that his master was certainly not going to disavow only a month before the congressional elections. As Forrestal bitterly commented later: 'It amounted to a denunciation of the work of his own appointee.'[68]

For Attlee, the scenario was familiar. He had just asked Truman for delay in issuing a statement at such a delicate moment; but he should have remembered what had happened in September 1945 over the 100,000 and in May 1946 over the Anglo-American report. Thrice denied, Attlee was in no mood to leave the President unrebuked: 'I have received with great regret your letter refusing even a few hours grace to the Prime Minister of the country which has the actual responsibility for the government of Palestine in order that he might acquaint you with the actual situation and the probable results of your action.'[69] As usual, Palestine did not show the special relationship at its best.

Whether the failure of the London conference can be attributed solely to the Yom Kippur statement can be disputed. Whether Truman's words had been misconstrued can be debated. Whether he intended to disable the conference is doubtful; but disabled it was, now that the Americans appeared simply as partisans of one side rather than honest brokers.

Anti-semitism was undoubtedly a factor in British policy. Not, however, because it had inspired it all along, in accordance with the devil-theory about Ernest Bevin, but because its growth in Britain was now such an obvious result of the deteriorating situation in Palestine. Most people, admittedly, did not care very deeply about Palestine, as surveys by Mass-Observation confirmed. By November 1946, however, those who expressed views blamed the Jews rather than the British Government, let alone the Arabs.

The King David Hotel cast a sombre shadow and anti-semitism lurked within it. But this hardly accounts for the explicitly pro-Arab tone often adopted. 'I don't agree with British policy in Palestine,' said one middle-aged skilled worker. 'I think the Arabs should be left in possession of the country.' Another man, a few years younger, likewise said: 'I look at it from the Arabic point of view really – it's their country – feel sorry for the Jews – but I think the Arabs ought to have more say.' What most respondents voiced, however, was a more straightforward revulsion against a violent situation, for which Zionist terrorism was held mainly to blame, but for which Britain ought no longer to bear responsibility. 'Leave them there to scrap it out,' as a lower-middle-class man of sixty put it. 'It's one of those dead end problems with no possible way out.'[70]

14

Scuttle?

December 1946–August 1947

'The British Empire seems to be running off almost as fast as the American Loan. The haste is appalling. "Scuttle" is the word, and the only word, that can be applied.'

Churchill in the House of Commons, 20 December 1946

By December 1946 it had become obvious to the British Government that it needed a shift in policy over India as much as over Palestine. Attlee and Cripps, who really determined the Government's stance on India, accordingly opted for bringing the British Raj to a speedy end under a new Viceroy entrusted with this task. Churchill, who had already publicly voiced the case for handing the Palestine mandate back to the United Nations, found an exasperated Labour Government ready to pick up this suggestion (or ploy) in default of American support. The making of a new consensus between Government and Opposition, however, was thwarted by Churchill's continued refusal to accept the inevitability of independence for India. The threat that he might intervene, which had some effect in prompting policy moves by the Government, had even more in shaping the rhetorical contest over the end of Empire.

The agreed settlement for India envisaged by the cabinet delegation – the constitutional statement of 16 May plus the interim government statement of 16 June – was as dead as the Morrison–Grady Plan. But nobody wanted to be the first to say so. Thus the British Government went on pretending that a constituent assembly might still work, and Congress was determined that it should still be convened, with only the Muslim League ready to state the obvious and declare that the moment for an historic compromise had now passed. Indians meanwhile went on killing other Indians in Bengal and Bihar. Gandhi was naturally distressed and courageously went to Bihar himself. His self-appointed spin doctor, Sudhir Ghosh, despondently told Cripps: 'We have been dragged down to the level of beasts.'[1]

True, Wavell had brought representatives of the Muslim League into the interim government. This proved as unreal as Congress's acceptance of grouping. Though Jinnah himself stood aside, his influence was exerted through his faithful lieutenant, Liaquat Ali Khan. Liaquat was personally far from abrasive but claimed an independence of action for the Muslim League ministers that obviously vitiated any real sense of cabinet responsibility and undercut Nehru's position as First Minister. Preparations for the constituent assembly went ahead, despite the fact that it was premised on a statement only nominally accepted by Congress in June and repudiated by the Muslim League since August.

All the characters in this charade were frozen into their habitual postures, at a time when decisive action was more necessary than ever. Though Cripps was busy enough running the Board of Trade, he was again relied upon by Attlee for strategic advice and was instrumental in getting Nehru to come to London for direct talks with Jinnah.

The ensuing London conference was convened on 4 December. Maybe it too was a charade but at least a consequential charade this time. Jinnah, visibly a sick man, was accompanied and supported by the urbane Liaquat; Patel declined to accompany Nehru, his rival and usurper. Party divisions in India now mirrored those in Britain. Jinnah's presence in London meant that Churchill could open a private line to the Muslim League: an ominous development since, as Wavell now learned from Rab Butler, 'Winston was anxious to make it a party issue.'[2] Likewise, Nehru's presence meant that he and Cripps could resume their informal discourse in private as well as spar with each other in formal sessions over the interpretation of the contested constitutional statement. The Viceroy meanwhile had produced another variant of his breakdown plan, this time as a pre-emptive strategy, stating that the British would withdraw in their own way and in their own time. Wavell was surprised to find an unanticipated ally in Cripps, who was also moving towards the idea of setting a date for independence.

After three days, it was the familiar deadlock – in London, as in Delhi, as in Simla (twice). Congress wanted to take over a united India and the Muslim League wanted to take over an independent Pakistan. Faced with this, Cripps unveiled his thinking to his colleagues on 5 December, arguing that 'there was a strong case for a declaration now that we would only stay a year or 18 months in India. We should have to hand over to a government set up by the Constituent Assembly.' This evaded the question of what would happen if no such government could be set up; but in that event, Cripps argued, 'we should have to hand over piecemeal to such authorities as we thought best at the time.'[3] And since the official communiqué at the end of the conference went on to say that there was no question of forcing a constitution on unwilling parts of the country, a new logic was now emerging. British withdrawal was no longer to be dependent on an agreed settlement between the Indian parties; the default position in the absence of agreement was, in effect, partition of some kind; and setting a date for withdrawal injected the requisite note of urgency in bringing matters to a head.

Simply on the desirability of a deadline, Wavell and Cripps were in unlikely agreement. But they disagreed about Wavell's military plan, with its abdication from political responsibility; and a further dimension of Cripps's thinking was kept from the Viceroy – the need for a new Viceroy. Cripps, moreover, having toyed with the remarkable notion of going out himself as the last Viceroy, had hit upon the perfect candidate: someone of high profile, charismatic presence, flexible views and proven acceptability to the Congress leadership. Evidence is now available to confirm what has long been suspected: that Cripps covertly reached an understanding with Nehru during the London conference that Wavell should be replaced by Admiral Lord Louis Mountbatten, who may indeed have met discreetly with the two of them at this time.

Cripps had tried his best to bring the Muslim League into an agreed settlement. Indeed in June 1946 he had really been closer to Jinnah than to any of the Congress leaders, faced with sabotage from Gandhi. Attlee later held to the extraordinary belief that the cabinet delegation 'broke down on the absolute refusal of the Moslems to come in'.[4] Whether he operated on this misperception in 1946 is unclear but it may help explain his conduct. Certainly Cripps, who obviously knew better, changed tack following the League's resort to direct action in its renewed campaign for Pakistan; and he henceforth lived up to his prior reputation as a partisan of Congress.

Hence Cripps's deal with Nehru over the change of Viceroy. Their intermediary, as during the negotiations with Gandhi the previous summer, was Ghosh – a man with the mien of a stage villain but one whose testimony on this occasion, almost in spite of himself, turns out to be well founded. Thus when Cripps later wrote to Ghosh of 'the two suggestions I made to Jawaharlal', he was surely alluding to a highly confidential proposal on 4 or 5 December that Wavell be replaced by Mountbatten.[5] It was plainly Cripps rather than Attlee who originated this idea. Nehru went home knowing of the plan nearly two weeks before Attlee put it to the King – and two months before Wavell himself knew of it.

It had been part of the Government's strategy – or at least its hand-to-mouth tactics – to ensure that India had not been debated in the House of Commons for several months. But Churchill insisted that a debate take place on 12 December, a few days after the London conference broke up. 'It would be a pity,' he claimed, 'if the British Empire in India passed out of life into history, without the House of Commons seeming to take any interest in the affair, and without any record, even in Hansard, of the transaction.' The debate duly broke the conspiracy of silence in bringing the Raj back into the news in Britain. 'INDIA: CHURCHILL ATTACKS CRIPPS' was the banner headline in the tabloid *Daily Graphic* the next day. Churchill adopted a controversial tone in scorning the legitimacy alike of the Indian election results and of the constituent assembly, currently in session despite the Muslim League boycott. It was at this point, stung by Labour interventions, that he not only turned directly on Cripps but for the first time reopened the history of the Cripps Mission of 1942, claiming that 'we had to pull him up because' – at which point Hansard records an interruption, followed by a challenge from Cripps to disclose all or nothing of what had happened on that occasion. Churchill prudently declined, amid laughter.[6] It was widely known that Churchill had never really been behind the Cripps Offer but he hardly wanted this shown up in public. The debate marked the end of the increasingly uneasy bipartisanship that had hitherto been maintained. Instead India became the subject of Churchill's fitful but influential interventions, in which he adopted a strikingly contentious rhetoric to cloak the Conservative Party's lack of a viable alternative strategy.

Churchill's interventions were fitful mainly because of his other commitments. The most important of these was the writing of his war memoirs, the six volumes eventually published as *The Second World War* (1948–54). This was a huge undertaking, with a correspondingly huge advance payable; the aim was to secure both Churchill's historical reputation (already high by ordinary standards) and his finances (hitherto precarious, given his expensive lifestyle). After his American expedition – memorable for the Fulton speech – Churchill had settled down to work in the latter months of 1946, discovering in the process that the five chapters he had planned on the 1930s had expanded to eleven by January 1947 and to seventeen by the time he had a presentable draft of the whole volume ready by July.[7] The final text of the first volume, published as *The Gathering Storm*, runs to 260,000 words – about one-third longer than the book you are reading at this moment – and although Churchill had considerable assistance, it remains true that big books do not write themselves without trenching heavily on an author's time, energy and ability to pursue other activities.

It is not surprising, then, that Churchill gave his duties as Leader of the Opposition only intermittent attention during the last twelve months of the Raj. But, as Fulton had shown, when he chose to speak the world still listened. His warnings about a cold war could claim justification from the train of events during 1946–7, just like his pre-war warnings on Nazi Germany, about which he was currently writing; his warnings on India, likewise stuck in the mindset of the 1930s, attracted similar attention. On 12 December he talked of the 'confusion, uncertainty and gathering storm, which those who have studied the Indian problem over long years might well have foreseen'.[8] Eight days later, getting into his stride, he spoke again in a debate on the cabinet's offer of independence to Burma. 'The British Empire seems to be running off almost as fast as the American Loan,' he told the House. According to *The Times* report the next day, he added: 'The haste is appalling. "Scuttle" is the word, and the only word, that can be applied.'[9]

It was not the first application of the word. But what this great connoisseur of words had now done, in his spare time from dictating the war memoirs, was to invest it with a connotation that was henceforth canonical. A search of *The Times* shows that it had printed this versatile word only a dozen times in the previous eighteen months, not only as a noun (as in coal scuttle, real or metaphorical) but as a verb, chiefly with reference to birds that scuttle – the *Oxford English Dictionary* suggests the usage, to scuttle away or to scuttle off. But to scuttle also specifically meant deliberately to sink vessels, notably naval vessels, as the German Navy had famously done at Scapa Flow after the Great War. That was an action obviously within the ken of Captain Arthur Marsden, a former

Royal Navy officer, now an obscure Conservative backbencher, who had spoken in the Egypt debate on 25 May 1946. 'People are getting bothered,' he had reflected, 'about all this scuttle and run and the surrender of what so many hold dear and sacred.'[10] Whatever the etymology, the pejorative force of the term was unmistakable. Two days later, Marsden's front-bench colleague Oliver Lyttelton had picked it up in his speech about 'scuttle and skedaddle' in both Egypt and India.

Maybe it is true that run-of-the-mill orators plagiarize but great orators steal. Certainly Churchill had felt no inhibition, a couple of months later, in himself purloining what Lyttelton had cribbed from Marsden, and 'the scuttle from Egypt' was held to show how Britain was 'falling in influence and authority in the world'.[11] At any rate, when Churchill again hit upon 'the only word' that could be applied to the Government's India policy after the London conference, he indelibly made it his own. Lord Cranborne, leader of the Opposition in the House of Lords, rallied to the cause after the Christmas recess with a speech bemoaning the taunts about 'the Big Two and a Half' that were now directed at his nation. 'The reason for that change was simple,' said Cranborne. 'Ever since the Government had come into office they had pursued a policy of undignified scuttle from one country after another.'[12]

As yet, of course, the Government's new India policy had not been announced. A White Paper had been drafted by Christmas Eve, in the presence of the innocent Wavell, who then returned to Delhi, unaware that he would not have the responsibility of implementing its proposals. The publication of the White Paper had to be deferred until 20 February 1947, and in it the date set for British departure from India was fixed as June 1948.

The cabinet faced a political crisis: not only what to do but also how to justify it. Scuttle, in short, had now entered the lexicon and Bevin was not alone in not liking the concept at all. At a fraught meeting on 31 December, Attlee and his colleagues, prompted by their potential political vulnerability, developed a new ideological robustness. The end of bipartisanship, which had previously constrained them in every cautious consensual utterance, in fact liberated them to counter the taunts about scuttle with arguments that Labour actually believed in (as did liberals in other parties too).

'The general feeling of the Cabinet was that withdrawal from India need not appear to be forced upon us by our weakness nor to be the first step in the dissolution of the Empire,' ran the minute. 'On the contrary this action must be shown to be the logical conclusion, which we welcomed, of a policy followed by successive Governments for many years.' Attlee was therefore asked to frame the statement, with which he would introduce the White Paper, along such lines. 'There was, therefore, no occasion to excuse our withdrawal,' it was suggested: 'we should rather claim credit for taking this initiative in terminating British rule in India and transferring our responsibilities to the representatives of the Indian people.'[13]

As in the construction of any political myth, the generalizations were edited so as to skirt many awkward questions. In particular, this version sought to give credence – far more than historical scholarship would sanction – to the dissembling utterances of some frankly reactionary Viceroys and British governments in the past. But Attlee was in a position to deliver his lines with a straight face, in a way that Churchill simply could not have got away with: just as Churchill in 1940 could construct the necessary and inspiring myth of national salvation in a way that Neville Chamberlain could not have done. As with many myths, it was the more persuasive the closer it stuck to the truth. The political record of Attlee and Cripps, as longstanding supporters of Indian claims, thus gave them credentials that were henceforth to prove valuable in winning over public opinion for their Indian policy.

The rhetoric of the end of Empire had found its paradigm – or rather each rival version had found its voice and its cry. The fact that scuttle became a cliché was in fact a tribute to Churchill's continuing ability to shape the terms of debate – as was the fact that its catchphrase salience belatedly stirred the Attlee Government into arguing for its own convictions in Indian policy.

Churchill threw into one of his speeches in April the remark that 'we were living to a large extent upon the American loan, and he had been shocked to see the rate at which it was flowing out because a great part of it was being spent on tobacco and films.'[14] This was an unexpectedly edifying and austere reflection from a man whose favourite after-dinner relaxation was a private showing of the latest Hollywood movie while he smoked a big cigar.

Everyone knew that the North American loan underpinned Britain's financial position; few at the time claimed to know precisely how; and what they thought they knew often turned out later to be wrong, or at least misleading, once the official statistics were subjected to subsequent revision. In *The Times* of 14 February 1947 Lionel Robbins, with the authority of a former head of the Economic Section, publicly warned of bankruptcy unless increased British exports filled the gap in the balance of payments before the American loan was exhausted. This came not from an opponent of the loan but from a supporter, who understood the assumptions on which it had been framed.

When Keynes negotiated it in Washington, he had put the cumulative deficit on the British balance of payments for the three years 1946–8 at a total of £1250 million. This married nicely with the final amount advanced by the United States and Canada: $5000 million (with the exchange rate at just over four dollars to the pound). The first published estimates put the cumulative deficit at £1245 million. It looked as though Keynes had scored a posthumous bullseye.

Not so. Virtually everything was worse than it looked at first sight – and was made worse by the faulty signals that the available figures initially gave. The underlying problem was that Keynes had guessed completely wrong about the post-war strength of the dollar. He thought that once the British balance of payments came into equilibrium, there would be no shortage of dollars; and he did not live to see himself refuted on this point. During 1946 Britain was struggling along with a net current account deficit of £230 million, corresponding almost exactly to the gold and dollar deficit of £225 million. The one explained the other, or so it seemed. During the transition period to a peacetime economy, this was just the sort of predictable financial gap that the loan negotiations had envisaged. Drawing down the best part of a billion dollars from the loan to finance it presented no problem.

Privileged by hindsight, we can see where it all went wrong in 1947. The root cause was not the deficit for that year of £380 million on the balance of payments; this amounted to another billion and a half dollars, which could again easily be covered by the loan – still, on this arithmetic, leaving half of it untouched. And since we now know that the British balance of payments was indeed to be brought into balance by the end of 1948, it looks as though Keynes's scenario ought to have coped with the problems of transition. But the reality is that, because he had been wrong about the dollar, the deficit in 'hard currencies' (gold and dollars) zoomed above one billion pounds in 1947, or 4 billion dollars – thus exhausting what was left of the loan a year ahead of time. And there was no way of meeting this 'dollar gap' through the export surplus (including invisible earnings) that Britain was notching up in soft currencies, which holders of dollars would not accept.[15]

It was thus not until 1947, and fairly suddenly, that the British cabinet became aware of the warning signs. Dalton had writen in his diary before Christmas 1946: 'as I constantly tell my colleagues, we shall be on the rocks in two years' time, if we have exhausted the Canadian and U.S. Loans, unless we have severely cut down our overseas expenditure (military and other) and built up our exports to a much higher level than now.'[16] This was a reasonable analysis, given what the Treasury then knew. It is true that American tobacco and films cost dollars; but not every Briton consumed them on a Churchillian scale. These were petty luxuries in a bleak world, whereas the maintenance of the pretensions of the British Empire was more evidently a luxury that the country could no longer afford.

By March 1947, evidence of the dollar drain was immediate and unmistakable. Post-war American prosperity was part of the problem since it fuelled an unanticipated rise in dollar prices which, so Dalton estimated, reduced Britain's spending power by a billion dollars. The other main reason was 'our ever rising dollar bill to feed the Germans' – the costs of victory again. The Chancellor had already told the cabinet that 'we were racing through our United States dollar credit at a reckless, and ever-accelerating, speed.' He went on to warn his colleagues that 'if we continue from now on to draw these dollars at the same rate at which we have been drawing them since 1st January, i.e., at the rate of $700 millions a quarter, the United States Credit will now be exhausted in February 1948.'[17] This was his best prediction; the true position turned out to be worse.

What could be done about it was less easy to see. Consumption of imports had already been cut to the bone, with the British people subsisting under austere conditions: ill-housed, ill-clothed, ill-fed. In the New Jerusalem, milk and honey were among the few foodstuffs not to be rationed. Even bread was to remain rationed until the summer of 1948. Yet defence expenditure still accounted for 40 per cent of the budget in 1947, with the amount spent overseas a direct drain on the precarious balance of payments. Dalton's efforts secured a cut of 5 per cent in military spending – half of what he had sought.

Almost every aspect of the looming crisis had an American dimension. Not only was it a dollar loan, but the main call upon it was specifically to finance the dollar gap, and this would be made worse once convertibility of sterling into dollars was enforced, under the loan agreement, within a few months. Cuts in British dollar imports would offend not only the British electorate but the Virginia tobacco lobby and the media moguls of Hollywood, who had influence and means of retaliation. Any cuts in military expenditure also affected US interests, maybe not so much in India, but politically in Palestine and strategically in Greece, if there were to be a British military withdrawal.

Relations with the United States during the past year had not engendered mutual confidence, still less blossomed into the sort of special relationship advocated in the Fulton speech. Decisions over atomic energy exemplified the friction between the self-confident, self-reliant, self-absorbed Americans and the touchy, exasperated and importunate British. The Quebec Agreement of 1943 was not worth the paper it was written on (and the United States administration, as we know, had mislaid the paper anyway). Its provisions for granting Britain an ongoing partnership over nuclear weapons were simply ignored. Senator Brian MacMahon, chairman of the Senate Committee on Atomic Energy, was unaware of the Agreement; the eponymous MacMahon Act was passed in the summer of 1946, prohibiting the sharing of nuclear secrets. The British Government's response was covertly to sanction a programme of their own in October 1946, clearly aimed at producing atomic weapons. Bevin's intervention was later recalled as crucial, notably his claim, which made up in fervour what it lacked in syntax, that 'I don't want any other Foreign Secretary of this country to be talked at, or to, by the Secretary of State in the United States as I have just had in my discussion with Mr Byrnes.'[18]

The British atomic bomb was thus commissioned for two reasons. One was that Bevin's assertive reflexes about the British Empire were much the same as Churchill's: it simply should not be pushed around. And the other was mutual mistrust between Britain and the United States. The lack of personal empathy between Bevin and Byrnes was only one manifestation of an underlying tension.

Bevin's six weeks in New York in November and December 1946 proved sobering. He was there mainly for another foreign ministers' conference, which was not the lowest point in the Byrnes–Bevin relationship if only because they had the common problem of dealing with the obdurate Molotov. Byrnes had his own troubles. He was not well (the excuse offered when he resigned at the end of the year) but then neither was Bevin (by whom resignation was considered neither a virtue nor an option). Byrnes no longer had Truman's confidence; and the President himself suddenly faced a hostile Congress, following the Republicans' success in winning both Houses in November 1946. Though Vandenberg, now Chairman of the Senate's Foreign Relations Committee, held to an internationalist line (and a generally good opinion of Bevin) and though the Republicans had already developed a mythology of betrayal over Yalta, they were unreliable cold warriors. The fact that they were mainly focused on reining in what they saw as the free-spending ideology of the New Deal, both at home and abroad, left the United States reluctant to take up such a burden if it meant sending forth either troops or dollars.

In this context, the Greek situation took on a new significance. Bevin had always been as strong a supporter of British intervention as Churchill; but Churchill, of course, had simply been denounced for his pains, at least in the United States, as an unreconstructed imperialist. Admittedly, after Fulton, after the barren disputes with Molotov at successive international conferences, after a succession of incidents signalling Soviet ambitions in Europe and the Middle East, American public opinion was no longer set in this mould. Conversely, Soviet propaganda shifted from its chiefly anti-British focus, and the arrival of the US Navy off Athens was now denounced by Moscow Radio as the work of 'American imperialists'. But when Bevin told Byrnes that economic necessity might force Britain to withdraw its troops, still trapped in action against the Communist guerrillas in northern Greece, there was certainly no offer of US forces. Instead, the British continued for the moment to borrow dollars from the Americans in order to defray the costs of keeping troops in Greece.

Bevin was shaken by evidence of his own unpopularity in New York, where this former leader of the British dockers found that American dockers would not handle his baggage. A meeting with President Truman was another matter. It was agreed that Palestine might be easier to handle now that the American elections were over. Bevin acknowledged that the British had given conflicting pledges – 'so have we,' Truman interjected. They were not friends but they could be friendly: men of a similar age, experience and outlook, happy to exchange reminiscences of how, forty years previously, the one had been selling mineral water in Bristol while the other was selling corn in Missouri. Neither of them was anti-semitic but they talked together about the Jews in a stereotyped way, commiserating about how difficult they were. That Rabbi Silver, said Harry, 'he thinks everything I do is wrong.' Yes, yes, yes. 'They sometimes expect me to fulfil all the prophecies of all the prophets,' said Ernie. 'I tell them sometimes that I can no more fulfill all the prophecies of Ezekiel than I can those of the other great Jew, Karl Marx.'[19]

While he was away, Bevin got a candid insight into the Prime Minister's thinking, which, probably responding to party feeling, was now set on a different tack from his own. Attlee typed the letter himself on 1 December; he did not want anyone else to see it; he did not want to undercut a Foreign Secretary of whom he thought so highly, and on whose backing his own leadership of the Labour Party often depended. But in Greece, as in India and in Palestine, it seemed to Attlee a time for ruthless reappraisal. 'The Middle East position is only an outpost position,' he told Bevin. 'I am beginning to doubt whether the Greek game is worth the candle.' Indeed he went further in wondering how far such commitments were viable in the absence of more effective support from the United States. 'There is a tendency in America to regard us as an outpost,' he concluded, 'but an outpost that they will not have to defend.'[20]

Facing Labour backbench criticism in his absence, Bevin already realized that he was getting out of touch. He returned to London just before Christmas and had a proper talk with Attlee for the first time in a couple of months. Attlee confirmed his own wish to withdraw British troops from Greece and to hand over the Palestine mandate. Moreover, only days later, Attlee brought Bevin into line on the exit policy for India.

The Foreign Secretary had played no part in any of the Indian negotiations and seemed not to be fully abreast of recent developments. He showed it when he wrote to the Prime Minister on New Year's Day, saying that in India the Government appeared 'to be trying nothing except to scuttle out of it, without dignity or plan' and adding that he was against fixing a date. What Bevin was evidently slow to grasp was the difference between Wavell's 'breakdown' timetable for piecemeal military evacuation, which the cabinet had repeatedly rejected, and the Attlee–Cripps idea of using a fixed date to achieve a kind of political handover otherwise unattainable or indefinitely postponed. Attlee there-fore responded to Bevin the next day that 'a scuttle it will be if things are allowed to drift' and – always at his best when laconic – concluded: 'If you disagree with what is proposed, you must offer a practical alternative. I fail to find one in your letter.'[21] Bevin was not used to being reprimanded in this way; but he henceforth accepted Attlee's lead. The Foreign Secretary had come home chastened, not to say chastized.

And a cold coming he had of it, with the weather sharp and the days short in the very dead of winter. December was already severe. Coal stocks were desperately low, with the minister responsible, Emanuel Shinwell, seemingly oblivious of the danger should the weather get worse. As it happened, this was the worst winter for over sixty years. The snow of mid-December, after a short thaw, returned at the end of January, when record low temperatures were recorded. On 7 February, Shinwell told the House of Commons that there would be no electricity for industrial production over much of the country; by mid-February coal stocks at the power stations were down to ten days' supply; 2 million workers were laid off; the supply of newsprint was restricted for two weeks. Little improvement was felt throughout the month and at the beginning of March renewed blizzards were still piling up ten-foot snowdrifts.

It would be frivolous to suppose that most British people spent these weeks worrying about the British Empire. It is not even true that the public turned against the Labour Government as a result of these hard-ships. Labour's opinion poll lead over the Conservatives was already down to 3 or 4 per cent in January – the same as in the previous May – and Gallup polls in March, June and July 1947 all showed the parties (remarkably) in an exact dead heat. Nonetheless, the fuel shortage, and the failure of socialist planning to cope with it, could obviously be used against the Government by an Opposition that had now found its voice. The Conservative grandee Lord Swinton told the Lords that the crisis was not due to 'an act of God, but the inactivity of Emmanuel' (sic).[22] If Churchill wanted to be prime minister again, once he had got his memoirs written, there were tangible, populist issues of government competence nearer to home than India and Palestine.

The chronology, as usual, is worth bearing in mind. On Friday, 14 February, Bevin announced that Britain would refer the Palestine mandate to the United Nations; on Tuesday, 18 February (just after London's coldest day for eighteen years), the cabinet agreed to withdraw

British troops from Greece; on Thursday, 20 February, Attlee made the dramatic announcement of the Government's decision to quit India.

Wavell knew what was coming – by then. A fortnight previously he had been entertaining Harold Macmillan, currently an Opposition front-bencher, in the Viceregal Lodge. Macmillan disclosed that Patel reminded him of Bevin, and opined that the 'charming but nervy' Nehru 'would not stand the racket of great events'. (When Nehru died in office in May 1964, he had been prime minister of India for nearly seventeen years, whereas Macmillan had resigned as British prime minister the previous October after six and a half years.) 'Just after lunch,' Wavell noted that day, 'I had a letter from the P.M. by special messenger, dismissing me from my post at a month's notice. Not very courteously done.'[23] True, but Wavell had refused to go to London (where Attlee would have told him personally). The old soldier still went like a gentleman, confessing his own failure and wishing his successor well.

There were three historic arguments about India and its place in the British Empire. One was strategic. The defence of India remained a priority for the chiefs of staff, just as it had for generations of their predecessors. Indeed this concern had largely governed 'the official mind of imperialism' during the nineteenth-century era of annexation: not only to protect India itself but the route to India, which had given Suez and the Nile valley and much of Africa such a high strategic priority. But the chiefs of staff had already been overruled in 1946 during the negotiations of the cabinet delegation; they would have to make the best of whatever settlement emerged; and the experience of the Second World War suggested that the defence of India was a strategic liability beyond Britain's current capacity.

This sense of fundamental change interlocked with the second argument: economics. The traditional view again was that possession of India was a great boon to Great Britain; and not only committed imperialists but also their anti-imperialist critics took this for granted. Whichever of these species he can be assigned to, Ernest Bevin had been in no doubt on this score. 'When I say I am not prepared to sacrifice the British Empire, what do I mean?' he had demanded in the Commons in February 1946. 'I know that if the British Empire fell . . . it would mean that the standard of living of our constituents would fall considerably.'[24] This was an axiom or an assumption rather than an established fact, especially in relation to India, which may be why little was subsequently heard of the contention. For the measures of self-government already instituted in India had made it politically impossible to extract substantial commercial advantages for British interests, as evidenced in the collapse of the Lancashire cotton trade. Financially, too, the boot was on the other foot. As long as India was a debtor, fear of default had been an argument against trusting an independent government to honour its obligations. But the the war had left India a creditor on a vast scale, with Britain owing it huge sums in the form of the sterling balances.

When India emerged as a party cry in British politics during the winter of 1947, both of these historic aspects of the issue were already moribund. Instead the debate turned on a third argument: the alleged moral dimension. Here the Conservatives made their final stand on the principle that it was not right for the British to abandon the cause of good government in India in face of the obvious dangers of communal unrest. Hence it was unworthy of their own best traditions to scuttle. These were sentiments that had widespread appeal, certainly within a governing class raised to respect such ideals, and this included high-minded anti-imperialists. As Sudhir Ghosh had told Cripps at one point: 'this extraordinary sense of moral responsibility which our British friends feel for everyone else' was itself a final barrier to quitting India.[25]

For the Labour cabinet, the moment of truth had been delayed until December 1946. For it was then that the preliminary decision to expedite independence in Burma cleared the way for the crucial decision on India (to which Burma had been attached until the 1930s). When this was coupled with the failure of the London conference, it plainly demonstrated to the cabinet that moral absolutes had to yield to the second-best solutions that might prove viable in an imperfect world. In this sense it was a replay of the arguments between Cripps and Gandhi some six months previously, and tough-minded politicians like Hugh Dalton had taken a relish in putting the choice in the starkest of terms. 'It is quite clear that we can't go on holding people down against their will, however incompetent they are to govern themselves,' he had written in his diary, 'for the whole pace, as determined in the East, has quickened over the war years, and it would be a waste both of British men and money to try to hold down any of this crowd against their will. They must be allowed to find their own way, even through blood and corruption and incompetence of all kinds, to what they regard as "freedom".'[26]

It is evident, then, that a number of strands came together in the making of the Government's new policy on India. It was to be officially published on 20 February 1947, after further adjustments, notably in settling the transfer date as June 1948. Mountbatten played some part in tinkering with the exact date but certainly did not write his own ticket, as he subsequently liked to claim, and some of his recollections in fact confirm that it was Attlee and Cripps who were firmly in control. Thus Mountbatten reminisced about putting to them his demand for 'plenipotentiary powers' as Viceroy and doing so during an interview where no notes were taken: 'But Cripps nodded his head and Attlee replied, "All right, you've got the powers and the job".'[27]

Where Cripps went too far was in making a quixotic offer to go out as a member of the new Viceroy's staff. Mountbatten graciously declined, privately telling the King: 'I don't want to be ham-strung by having to bring out a third version of the Cripps offer!!!'[28] Instead he suggested that Cripps take the India Office; but Attlee demurred, intent now on adopting an active role himself (and consequently replacing Pethick-Lawrence with his deputy, the pliant Lord Listowel, as the last Secretary of State for India).

When he spoke in a cold and dimly lit House of Commons on 20 February, the Prime Minister publicly set a timetable for Indian independence under the Viceroyalty of Mountbatten. He justified this with an authority that impressed his hearers, balancing the claims of morality and expediency, at once talking about a mission fulfilled in India and delicately scorning Churchill's views as half a century out of date. 'It is a fact that in spite of all the declarations we have made there are still people in India who think they can hang on and let things drift,' he asserted. 'We are against drift.' Naturally, Opposition laughter greeted this claim and a Conservative member duly called out: 'Scuttle.'[29]

Churchill himself took up the cry. When the Indian proposal was debated a fortnight later, he asked whether Mountbatten's mission was 'merely "Operation Scuttle" on which he and other distinguished officers have been dispatched? (Opposition cheers)'. His peroration was pre-ordained: 'Let them not add by shameful flight, by premature hurried scuttle – let them not add to the pangs of sorrow that they all felt – the taint and smear of shame. (Loud Opposition cheers).'

After this, it was downhill all the way, as the tired tropes succumbed to repetitive strain injuries through over-exercised metaphors. It is a blessing to posterity that *The Gathering Storm* took off the cream of Churchill's eloquence, leaving the House of Commons with a thin diet of curds and whey. Churchill's speech in the three-day debate in mid-March 1947, supposedly on economic affairs, managed to get back to the familiar lines: 'Scuttle everywhere was the order of the day: Egypt, India, Burma.' Then, only three weeks later, there was the Government's new plan to reduce the period of conscription to twelve months – 'another example of the the policy of scuttle before anything that looks difficult or fierce which has characterized the Socialist Government adminis-tration, and which in less than two years has reduced us from our victory day to our present confusion and disrepute.'[30]

Churchill ploughed on unabashed. When the formal motion on the national service cut was debated a month later, he again worked himself up about 'this sudden volte face, change and scuttle', this time provoking the intervention of a young backbench Labour MP, James Callaghan. 'Mr Churchill had used the words "demoralize", "squalid", and "scuttle" in the last three debates in the House,' Callaghan observed, to ministerial laughter. 'He was sure that Mr Churchill, with the richness of his language, could find some other words. (Ministerial laughter).'[31] Jim Callaghan had not yet learnt – more than thirty years before 'the winter of discontent' – that repetition is the essence of a successful soundbite.

Palestine and India had already been linked, not least by Churchill, who was ready to attack Government policy on each – from opposite flanks. And on Palestine a lot of flank was exposed. The final attempt by the British to find an agreed solution was by now faltering towards impasse, as yet another London conference was soon to confirm. This time it was the Arabs who agreed to attend, the Jews who refused. Previously, key representatives of the Jewish Agency, gaoled by the British, could not come to London; but now they would not, following the decision of the World Zionist Congress, at its meeting in Basle in December 1946, to boycott negotiations in favour of direct action.

This had been a body blow to Chaim Weizmann. The split in Basle, as Baffy Dugdale recorded it, was that 'broadly speaking the Americans and the Palestinians oppose the Conference. Chaim says that if they do not enter the Conference, Zionism is dead as a constructive political movement for a generation.' For entering the forthcoming conference necessarily meant considering an agenda for partition of some kind –

something that most pragmatic Zionists would now settle for, but which the hardliners were unprepared to avow. Hence the dramatic moment (which Dugdale's diary catches) when Rabbi Silver 'threw down the gauntlet – against partition and in favour of "resistance" – but not one word to distinguish it from terrorism'.[32] As she could well see, Weizmann's re-election as President of the World Congress meant little in this context – it was exactly because he was perceived as pro-British that he faced defeat. Though Nahum Goldmann bravely put the case for partition, as he had done for four months now, the American delegates were set on rejection.

Long foreshadowed, the American takeover of the Zionist movement now put it on a course that repudiated the axioms on which British Zionism had worked for thirty years. Weizmann's eloquent speech, as always making clear his own abomination of terrorism, was well received in the hall but Dugdale saw on the following day how it was dismissed by many delegates: 'Too flippant – too pro-British, etc.' This marked Weizmann's eclipse, and with it the withdrawal of Dugdale from her life's work – 'I cannot work for or with any Executive that is pursuing a policy of non-cooperation with Britain.'[33]

Churchill has too readily been co-opted in indulgent accounts as a lifelong Zionist. This is to ignore the integral link that he, even more than Weizmann, had always seen between the Jewish national home and British imperialism. The new nexus of Jewish terrorism in Palestine plus American pressure-group politics had little appeal for either of these old men; but Weizmann, as a Jew, could hardly jump ship whereas Churchill, despite professions of personal regard, instigated a personal as well as a political breach. The stark fact is that he never again met Weizmann after Moyne's assassination in November 1944. In the House of Commons, moreover, Churchill's tone was surely that of a former rather than a current adherent. 'All my hon. Friends on this side of the House do not agree with the views which I held for so many years about the Zionist cause,' he told the House at the end of January 1947. 'But promises were made far beyond those to which responsible Governments should have committed themselves.'[34]

It was now that Churchill modified his earlier suggestion that Britain might hand back the mandate to the United Nations within twelve months by saying that this should be done within six months. Although he was to mock Attlee for announcing a deadline over India (and then shortening it), he did much the same himself over Palestine. This was Churchill's own policy of scuttle.

The London conference meanwhile hobbled along against a background of mounting terrorist activity in Palestine. Its co-chairman with Bevin was the new Colonial Secretary, Arthur Creech Jones, a conventional Labour Zionist. He began as an advocate of partition; the Arab delegates rejected any mention of partition; the Zionists were only unofficial participants and were anyway officially opposed to partition. None of this was at all promising. Creech Jones himself soon decided that partition was unworkable. 'It would be very difficult to establish a viable Jewish State without prejudicing the vital interests of the Arabs,' he advised the cabinet on 7 February; 'and wherever the frontiers were drawn, large numbers of Arabs must inevitably be left under Jewish rule.'[35] Creech Jones therefore joined with Bevin in putting forward a final set of proposals: trusteeship under the United Nations as the prelude to a binational state, which would be based on both Jewish and Arab cantons. The plan proposed to admit 96,000 Jewish immigrants over two years. Again a time-limit was to be applied – this time a five-year transition period under the mandate before independence.

The Bevin Plan, as it became known, found no takers. As Ben Gurion put it: 'They were first and foremost Jews and they wanted a Jewish state in Palestine in which the Jews would be a majority.'[36] So while the Arabs thought the Bevin Plan looked too much like a Jewish state in embryo, the Zionists maintained that it did not look enough like one. Hence Bevin's announcement to the last session of the conference on 14 February that Palestine would now be referred to the United Nations.

The Zionists thought that this must be a trick. Their reasoning was that partition, and hence a Jewish state, would require a two-thirds majority in the General Assembly – which was inconceivable unless not only the United States but also the Soviet bloc supported it, as the clever British must have realized. True, there was an inescapable logic in the situation. What the Foreign Office feared was that Arab hostility over a possible partition would stoke anti-British sentiment if it were Britain that imposed this solution. So if Palestine were to end up partitioned, why not let the United Nations itself incur the odium, especially since its members were so free with their advice and criticism? And the two-thirds threshold for varying the mandate in this way, giving the Arab states their leverage at the United Nations, was indeed built into the internationally agreed procedures. Why not let the people who were so ready to play politics with this issue instead play their share in finding the solution?

Even so, Bevin still shied away from evacuation of Palestine at this stage, if only because of its strategic importance. Admittedly, the safe-guarding of vital British oil interests in the Middle East always militated against upsetting the Arab states that now controlled these resources. And, unless the old Italian colony of Cyrenaica (Libya) were to fall to British trusteeship, the lack of an alternative base to support British troops in the Canal Zone was a problem, even if Palestine was not much of an answer to it. As a Machiavellian ploy in great-power politics, however, reference of Palestine to the United Nations left much to be desired. Far from being an adroit move to shift responsibility onto others, it still left Britain meanwhile with the increasingly burdensome task of actually administering the mandate – responsibility without power.

That this was not an ideal solution was readily apparent; whether it was even a second-best solution, failing American support, was doubtful. Bevin's own apprentice boast to do better in Palestine, advanced in more hopeful days, was now hung round his neck. Critics on the Labour left, like Richard Crossman, were scathing; when he and his friends Ian Mikardo and Michael Foot (ultimately to become leader of the Labour Party himself, against Margaret Thatcher) published their pamphlet *Keep Left* in May, its main target was the Government's alleged subservi-ence to American foreign policy – but Crossman's fury over Palestine was an obvious ingredient. Yet even at this low point in Bevin's fortunes, the Gallup poll in February 1947 had shown that 58 per cent of the British people thought that he was doing a good job as Foreign Secretary. This speaks of some realism about their view of Britain's influence in the world, or perhaps just of low expectations.

In Churchill's 'Operation Scuttle' speech of 6 March, a cogent point lurked behind the rodomontade. His contrast of the Indian decision with the unresolved situation in Palestine obviously had the immediate aim of identifying Bevin's hand – 'I do not know who it is, I only have my surmise' – in maintaining a residual British commitment. 'The sustained effort we are making, if applied to India,' Churchill argued, 'would have enabled the plan of the Cripps Mission to be carried out and be fully discussed with full deliberation.' Churchill made the connection, as he had done before, because he thought the Government's policy was wrong in both Palestine and, above all, in India. 'Two bottles of powerful medicine had been prepared, but they had been sent to the wrong patients. (Laughter).'[37]

He worked for his laugh and got it; but if his argument was serious, it was because it deftly identified some contradiction in analysis. After all, from the British point of view, both the Indian and the Palestine problems exhibited many similar features: deep-seated conflict between intermingled ethnic groups, a claim by one militant religious minority for partition and its own state, a growing resort to violence, and the confident but contradictory assertions that bloodshed would either cease or escalate if the British withdrew. Churchill's inherent difficulty was that when he built on the maintenance of an expensive British presence in tiny Palestine to argue for the desirability of deploying such resources instead in vast India, he was using a weak lever to support a strong policy. The unspoken converse seemed more to the point: that if there was no profit for Britain in trying to maintain its ongoing presence in Palestine, where it sought ineffectually to hold down fewer than 2 million fractious inhabitants, there was certainly no case for trying to do likewise on the scale required in India, with a population two hundred times bigger.

Perhaps his line of thought was best revealed, not in the Commons, but in a speech at Wanstead at the end of April 1947. 'The Government, always ready to scuttle away from any difficulty, had evidently cast away our mighty Indian Empire,' he claimed. 'In Palestine a different processs was at work in the minds of the Government. There we had to go on fighting at all costs.' So far, so familiar. Yet what was the practical, constructive conclusion to be drawn about future British policy? It was all very well to satirize the Government's propaganda: 'We must carry on this "squalid war on terrorism". We were fighting the Jews in order to give the country to the Arabs.' But Churchill was not actually soft on terrorism himself, as his waning support for Zionism testified. Thus when he argued that 'Palestine was not a twentieth part of the importance of India to us, and was an immense source of expense and worry, and was bringing upon us a great deal of disapprobation from many countries', the implicit thrust of his argument was surely to propose an 'Indian' solution for Palestine rather than to press the lost cause of a 'Palestinian' policy in India.

One way or another, once it became clear that British policy was to leave India sooner rather than later, the logic of applying this thinking to Palestine too became more appealing. All it needed was for events on the ground in Palestine to render the option of staying sufficiently odious. In this sense, the final decision on India was to carry Palestine too – and after a fairly short time-lag – on this occasion with Churchill anticipating rather than resisting what the Government eventually proposed.

General George Marshall, who had played such an outstanding role in achieving victory as Roosevelt's wartime chief of staff, was the surprise nominee to replace Byrnes as Secretary of State in January 1947. Truman had thus found a man whom he could trust and Marshall's bipartisan support was shown by the way that Vandenberg stage-managed the nomination through the Senate in a single day. The appointment was well received both at home and abroad, giving Marshall unique authority in determining American policy. He was no stranger to the British, who had found him firm but fair, and always as good as his word, in resolving such conflicts as arose; but he and Bevin had had little personal contact and the first major crisis to be handled between them arrived unpropitiously in February.

Marshall remembered well enough how Greece had often surfaced as a problem in Anglo-American relations, from the days of its liberation by the British in the autumn of 1944. At that time it had been an axiom in Washington that British troops were only in Greece to further Churchill's atavistic imperialist ambitions; and Lend-Lease itself had been imperilled because of Roosevelt's suspicions on this score. Yet Bevin, who had played a key role in mobilizing political support for British intervention, now faced an entirely different situation. Far from the Americans welcoming the suggestion that Britain might pull out, they were appalled at the very thought of it; and far from the British showing a dogged determination to stay the course, they now seemed ready to cut and run.

There was a further twist to the way that Greece was perceived by the great powers. It was, of course, one of the countries listed on the 'naughty document' which recorded Churchill's confabulations with Stalin in October 1944 (again annoying Roosevelt). Crudely, their deal had been that Britain was to have 90 per cent influence in Greece in return for Soviet influence of 90 per cent in Rumania; but in practice the reciprocity turned on a different hinge. Whenever Churchill subsequently asked pointed questions about Soviet control of Poland, Stalin would respond by talking about British activity in Greece. And initially the Americans stayed out of such exchanges.

Their purported indifference did not, however, represent the real view of influential figures in the State Department, notably Dean Acheson, now acting as Marshall's chief of staff. Not only was there increasingly overt American concern to safeguard Greece from Communist insurrection but, on the other side of the balance, the situation in Poland had now deteriorated in an alarming way. All too steadily, the political influence of Mikolajczyk's Peasant Party was being undercut by Communist control of state machinery; the elections of January 1947 were blatantly rigged, in a way that made a mockery of the democratic phrases of the Yalta and Potsdam agreements, this time provoking protest from the United States. Hence the new imperative for some further response by the Western powers, either through idealism, in order to protect Greek democracy, or through realism, in order to compensate in the Balkans for what was now lost on the Baltic.

Bevin had had no change of heart about Greece. But, in the same week that the Government's new policies on India and Palestine were declared, the cabinet agreed to withdraw the remaining British troops (already in the process of being scaled down to 8000, a tenth of the original force). Britain's financial plight was pressing, Greece a strain too great. It was left to a rueful Foreign Secretary to settle for the best terms he could get from the Chancellor of the Exchequer, short of an immediate unilateral withdrawal – 'that we should put up a strong telegram to the United States asking them what they were going to do and on the other hand telling the Greeks that we could not continue' – in order to prompt urgent joint action.[38]

Consternation in Washington! Acheson had got the news on Friday, 21 February, and tried to spare his boss, enjoying a much-needed weekend away (though it seems that Bevin nonetheless managed to get through to Marshall by telephone on the Sunday). James Forrestal was at the cabinet luncheon on Monday: 'Marshall said that this dumped in our lap another most serious problem – that it was tantamount to British abdication from the Middle East with obvious implications for their successor.'[39] Truman quickly agreed with Marshall and Acheson that the United States would have to provide the necessary resources. Meanwhile, over lunch at his club with a journalist, Acheson was apocalyptic about the possibilities that now opened up for further Soviet expansion. 'There are only two powers left,' he said. 'The British are finished. They are through.'[40]

The problem for the administration was to get the necessary funds from a Congress elected on the Republican platform of cutting expenditure. Congressional leaders at the White House, faced with a sombre assessment from Marshall and a more fervent appeal from Acheson, gave key pledges of support. The most important came from Vandenberg, now not only chairman of the Senate Foreign Relations Committee and majority leader but also president of the Senate, in the absence of a Vice-President since Truman's elevation. For him, as for others, Greece suddenly had a new significance. 'But I sense enough of the facts to realize that the problem of Greece cannot be isolated by itself,' he wrote in early March. 'On the contrary, it is probably symbolic of the world-wide ideological clash between Eastern Communism and Western democracy; and it may easily be the thing which requires us to make some very fateful and far-reaching decisions.'[41]

It was in such terms that Truman made his historic speech to a joint session of Congress on 12 March – twelve months after Fulton. 'At the present moment in world history nearly every nation must choose between alternative ways of life,' he declared, making this the ground for giving a specific commitment to Greece (and also Turkey). He asked for $400 million to back his pledge of American support against 'subjugation by armed minorities or by outside pressure'.[42] Here was what became known as the Truman Doctrine, with the might of the United States thus guaranteeing the future of a strategic part of the eastern Mediterranean, hitherto regarded as a purely British concern. In telling newsmen of his full support, Vandenberg was evidently concerned about how the new stance might look. 'We should evolve a total policy,' he explained. 'It must clearly avoid imperialism.'[43]

Of course it must. If Churchill had gone into Greece for the sake of the British Empire, nobody must be allowed to think that Truman had gone in for equivalent motives. Subtle and astute, Acheson was well aware of such nuances when he went to give evidence before the relevant congressional committees. Nonetheless it is little wonder that Churchill concluded the chapter on British intervention in Greece in *Triumph and Tragedy* by quoting Acheson's testimony on the security threat to the

United States that a Communist government in Greece would pose. 'If Greece has escaped the fate of Czechoslovakia and survives to-day as one of the free nations,' Churchill commented, 'it is due not only to British action in 1944, but to the steadfast efforts of what was presently to become the united strength of the English-speaking world.'[44]

By the time Truman spoke, his Secretary of State was in Moscow. The council of foreign ministers set up at Potsdam had had conferences in London, Paris and New York; now its fourth meeting began in Moscow on 10 March. There were forty-three sessions between then and 25 April; and, as at previous conferences, there was excruciatingly little progress to report, with wearisome recriminations in which Molotov and Bevin played the leading roles.

Some wondered whether this might be the final appearance of the British Foreign Secretary, who had set out for Moscow in poor shape. 'Bevin is in no fit condition to go on much longer,' Dalton had noted after one of their meetings at the end of February, adding: 'Just how he will fare in Moscow is anybody's guess. It is quite on the cards, I fear, that he may not come back.'[45] Unable to fly because of his heart, constantly accompanied by a personal physican, exposed to bleak views of eastern Europe from the windows of a slow train, Bevin nonetheless benefited from the trip. He found Moscow reinvigorating, and not just because of the frequent satisfaction of giving Molotov a piece of his mind. The new factor was the presence of Marshall, offering plenty of time to establish a personal relationship between the British and American Secretaries of State. Here was an opportunity to foster closer co-operation, given the combination of Russian obduracy and the Truman doctrine.

When Bevin got back home, everyone noticed the difference. Among the first to feel the force of his renewed confidence and vigour were the authors of *Keep Left*, especially since this was now answered in kind from a pro-Government standpoint. The rival pamphlet, *Cards on the Table*, was written by the Labour Party's able and combative International Officer, Denis Healey (within twenty years to become Secretary of State for Defence). He offered a cogent analysis of the need to check Russian ambitions in central and eastern Europe. This was not simply a matter of rival national interests, with their own historic legitimacy. Rather, Healey pointed to the concentration of power within the Soviet system, with its lack of responsibility to public opinion giving a sinister turn to a ruthless foreign policy executed in the name of international socialism. Published just before the Labour Party conference, *Cards on the Table* disclosed the intellectual justification for a social democratic foreign policy, while what Dalton described on 29 May as 'the tidal wave of the Bevin speech' ensured a personal triumph over left-wing critics. 'He has a most astonishing – and unique – conference personality,' Dalton commented in some awe. 'There was no come-back.'[46]

The real come-back was Bevin's own. He felt on top of his job; he felt vindicated by events in his longstanding wariness of the Soviet Union; and he felt, after seven weeks together in Moscow, that he had an intuitive understanding of Marshall, notoriously not a man to wear his heart on his sleeve. All of this was just as well in view of the looming crisis.

The costs of victory were still being totted up. The country was pledged under the terms of the Loan Agreement, as signed by Truman in July 1946, to make sterling freely convertible into dollars within twelve months (at least for current transactions) on the expectation that the Loan would sufficiently cushion this shock. Convertibility was now only weeks away. Yet the drain of dollars meant that the cushion was getting smaller while the gap between sterling and dollar prices was getting bigger. Britain's great war leader had the occasional pang about this (before taking partisan advantage of the Government's predicament, of course). Churchill declared in May that 'he was extremely glad to hear Mr Dalton say the other day that he was going to raise the question of why Britain should be the only debtor country in the world, while those she had rescued and those she had conquered went into the future without having to drag a terrible chain of war debts behind them.'[47]

Dalton repeatedly went back to his cabinet colleagues asking for more cuts. He had already made this a resigning issue and reiterated at the end of May 'that we were racing through our United States dollar credit at a reckless pace, and that they should be prepared to take hard and difficult, but necessary, decisions in the early future'. Further cuts in food imports were high on the list of remedies: economically feasible if politically damaging. 'Our overseas income is insufficient for our overseas needs,' the Treasury warned, while pointing out that even a general rise in British exports would not be sufficient to do the trick: 'Superimposed on this is the hard currency problem which can be solved only by a recovery of the non-dollar world; this is not yet in sight.'[48]

The dislocation of the European economy was an obvious result of the war, just as much as the prosperity of the American economy. The disparity between them was thus an outstanding post-war problem. With a smaller economy than Britain's, France was running up a visible trade deficit of nearly a billion dollars with the United States in 1947, almost exactly the same as the eventual British figure; and, though much smaller, Belgium and Luxembourg together had a dollar deficit of nearly half this size, as did the Netherlands. These were certainly symptoms of big anomalies in international finance, compounded in Britain's case by the complexities of handling the sterling balances. Yet the European economy, based on soft-currency transactions, was already recovering; it was actually on the low slopes of the trajectory that was to deliver thirty years of unprecedented growth. Indeed, as throughout Europe, what distorted the British visible trade balance was the import of American capital equipment. The dollar deficit was really due not to consumption of tobacco and films but to investment in the machinery that would provide higher levels of both production and productivity as the recovery gathered momentum.

What needs explaining, then, is the temporary setback of 1947. The severity of the north European winter was a large part of the story. This was especially so in Britain, where the dependence of the economy on coal, and on its movement by an antiquated rail network to the power stations, had been cruelly revealed. Power interruptions brought a sharp fall in output for February. Since coal, railways and electricity supply were all high on Labour's list for nationalization, the political charge was pretty obvious. The vesting date, bringing the coalmines into public ownership, amid much publicity, had been 1 January 1947; the country's acute coal shortage was blatantly apparent six weeks later.

All of this was dramatic, especially in American eyes. When Will Clayton, still assistant secretary for economic affairs at the State Department, returned home from Europe in May he struck a note of alarm. 'Europe is steadily deteriorating,' he told the State Department, asserting that successive political crises resulted from 'grave economic distress', with millions of people 'slowly starving', in a scenario of impending general collapse – 'The modern system of division of labour has almost broken down in Europe.'[49] To Clayton, the true believer in the efficacy of free markets in providing for mankind's salvation, it was obvious what was needed: hardly more nationalism, certainly not more nationalization, but instead action to push these benighted people into acting more like a united states of Europe.

Such ideas enlisted some generous economic impulses in Washington. But the context was inevitably political, shaped by the analysis of Kennan's long telegram of February 1946 and the public declaration of the Truman Doctrine. Clayton thus caught a sense that, if alternative ways of life were at stake, the Soviet model was the standing alternative if the United States were to fail in sustaining its own ethic of freedom in beleaguered Europe.

Charles Bohlen, who had sat with the Big Three at Yalta, was told to draft a speech for the Secretary of State, who was to receive an honorary degree at Harvard University. In it Marshall was to propose a recovery programme for 'Europe as a whole', backed by the United States, but dependent on an initiative from the Europeans themselves. Two murky issues were deliberately not made explicit: nothing about European integration and a private decision to 'play it straight' in ostensibly inviting Soviet co-operation.[50] British participation was simply taken for granted. The British embassy in Washington was given a prior briefing by Acheson but the official who wrote it up for the Foreign Office sent his comments to London by surface mail and they only arrived on 5 June, the day of the Harvard commencement ceremony.

The BBC at least had been given the right spin on Marshall's message, but the reaction of the Foreign Secretary depended unusually upon his own hunch in making sense of what he heard. The story goes that Ernest Bevin, after tuning in his portable wireless on the morning after the speech, was immediately seized with a vision of what Marshall's plan might achieve – a story that may have been improved in the telling but still seems basically correct. Given the American reluctance to act on the assumptions of a special relationship in which Britain had privileged access, but given also that Bevin now felt that he could read Marshall, the prompt British response undoubtedly helped to turn rhetoric into policy. Bevin not only replied warmly to the American initiative but made arrangements to fly to Paris himself to begin putting together a joint European response, including a formal invitation to the Russians to a forthcoming conference, also in Paris.

The Marshall Plan was merely a phrase, or at most an aspiration, in June 1947. It was, however, from the outset an idea with wings. 'The terms of the offer to finance European recovery on a continental plan,'

The Times commented on 16 June, 'inevitably suggest a parallel with those of the lend-lease agreement. That "most unsordid act", it seems, is not to stand alone.' This elevated comparison was taken up by Anthony Eden, acting as leader of the Conservative Party. 'It is indeed a generous action,' he told the Commons, 'and one which deserves to rank with the most unsordid act in history.'[51] Yet, like Lend-Lease, Marshall Aid was naturally predicated on American self-interest – if only to make it politically feasible in Congress – and had clear policy objectives which the language of philanthropy and good works failed to capture.

Any misconceptions that the British may have entertained about their own role were soon dispelled. At talks in London at the end of June, Will Clayton was accompanied by the American ambassador, Lew Douglas. For the British Government, Attlee, Dalton and Cripps supported Bevin, who did most of the talking. A central issue was what was meant by 'Europe' in Marshall's proposal. Did it include Russia? Not really, seemed to be the answer, but it was politic to let the Soviet Union exclude itself (as was shortly to happen at the Paris conference on the plan). Did it include Britain? Yes, of course, Clayton was happy to clarify, but he did so in accordance with his own conception of Britain as one of an integrated group of recipients on one side of the table rather than in any special position on the other side of the table where the American paymasters sat.

These exchanges have an element of pathos. When he looked back on the Marshall initiative, as Bevin was to tell American journalists a couple of years later, 'it was like a life-line to sinking men' in offering hope, generosity, the inception of a mutual effort – 'I think you understand why, therefore, we responded with such alacrity and why we grabbed the lifeline with both hands.'[52] This is a valid perspective on how Marshall Aid came to alleviate Britain's dollar crisis in the nick of time and fostered the economic recovery of western Europe. As an imaginative exercise in enlightened self-interest, it was indeed the true successor to Lend-Lease.

The record of the first Anglo-American talks of June 1947 freezes the moment when the patriotic British Foreign Secretary had to get used to this new dispensation. 'If the UK was considered just another European country,' he argued with Clayton and Douglas, would it not 'fit in with Russian strategy' and put Britain at the mercy of the Russians? As it seemed to Bevin, if Britain were thus 'lumped in' and regarded 'as merely another European country', it would sacrifice 'the little bit of dignity we have left'. Clayton, so Bevin expostulated, surely could not be seeking to treat Britain like the Soviet Union treated Yugoslavia – 'Britain with an Empire is on a different basis.'[53] The new basis, however, was simply that the United Kingdom, with whatever qualms about its European identity, could afford neither to spurn Marshall Aid nor to maintain the British Empire.

Wavell's last day as Viceroy had been 22 March, when he received the Mountbattens in the Lodge for the briefest of briefings, before departing the next day. After his modest soldierly farewell, Delhi had to get used to the flamboyant style of Admiral Lord Louis Mountbatten, who had all the obsession with punctilio of a minor member of the royal family yet had been selected by the austere Cripps and the dowdy Attlee as the agent of a socialist government's great act of imperial abnegation.

'Dickie' to his intimates, Mountbatten was well suited to play the part, with a theatrical talent all his own and a canny sense of political realism. He was supported, as he had been as Supreme Commmander in South East Asia, by a huge entourage known in Delhi as 'Dickie Birds'. A key appointment was that of General Sir Hastings Ismay as his chief of staff, a role in which he had served Churchill as wartime Minister of Defence – and one in which he was currently again helping the author of the six volumes of the *The Second World War*, from which labours 'Pug' Ismay took a sabbatical to go to India.

The new Viceroy, with his outgoing and sexually vibrant wife Edwina at his side, signalled a new order. This was at once immensely grand and engagingly informal. Under Wavell, admittedly, the Congress leaders had already been dined in the Lodge, overcoming their own principled refusal to be suborned; but under the Mountbattens Indians were welcomed as never before. It was no accident that, as the months unfolded, the lonely widower Jawaharlal Nehru came to find a close confidante in Edwina Mountbatten – a relationship which shocked some at the time for its supposed impropriety and which has affronted Pakistani historians for its breach of impartiality, but which would have been inconceivable in the time of Viceregal predecessors as recent as the Linlithgows. What the Mountbattens brought to the extraordinary challenge of this posting, in short, was an equally extraordinary mixture of qualities, attributes and instincts. Their response to near-famine conditions in Bengal was to implement rationing in the Viceregal Lodge. A lot of this was symbolic; but the British Raj had been ruled by symbols and would be wound up likewise.

Mountbatten presided over one last effort with the Indian parties to find an agreement that might have averted partition. Gandhi, though shaken by his first-hand experience of communal violence in Bengal and Bihar, which his own presence helped to temper, still abhorred any vivisection of India. He thus maintained to the new Viceroy that he 'considered it wicked of Sir Stafford Cripps not to have recommended the turning over of paramountcy to the Central Government representing the sovereignty of the Indian nation'.[54] But the British Government, for all its sympathies with Congress, was simply unprepared to impose a unitary settlement in the absence of consent from the Muslim League – which was itself now bent on achieving Pakistan at all costs. Nehru and Patel, breaking from Gandhi's tutelage at last, tacitly accepted the inevitability of partition, provided that the two disputed provinces of Bengal and Punjab were themselves partitioned. Gandhi himself belatedly came round to the merits of the cabinet delegation scheme, which he had effectively killed a year before and now ineffectively championed.

The outcome was not independence on the terms that either the Congress had long desired or the Muslim League had more recently demanded; nor on those that the British Government had earlier envisaged. But it was what was feasible in 1947. Mountbatten drew up proposals for an accelerated transfer of power on the basis of Dominion status, which was a legally expeditious antechamber to independence; but he suddenly ran into unexpected trouble from Nehru, horrified by what he saw as a Balkanization of India. Moving fast to repair this temporary breach in their growing mutual confidence, Mountbatten produced a second plan – only to find that meanwhile the cabinet in London had approved his first plan and were now understandably confused.

At the end of May, therefore, the new Viceroy was summoned home to London for ten days of consultation. He knew that he had the backing of Attlee and Cripps. Unlike Wavell, then, Mountbatten found the politicians amenable to Viceregal guidance; and since he himself was in turn guided by the work of his Reforms Commissioner, V. P. Menon, a close ally of Patel, the final plan was virtually assured of acceptance by Congress. In effect, the Indians were at last writing their own ticket for independence. The package deftly combined Dominion status and a quick handover – within months – to two central governments in India and Pakistan, with the option of choosing partition for Bengal and the Punjab. Congress got the degree of centralism that it wanted in inheriting sovereignty over the bulk of India; the Muslim League got Pakistan, albeit on a scale much reduced from their original claim; the British got a transfer to two governments which would remain members of the Commonwealth, initially as Dominions. The position of the princely states was left to be determined, but under conditions which made their accession to either India or Pakistan a foregone conclusion for most (and ultimately for all).

Mountbatten's personal achievement lay in securing assent to this plan. He did so in London through successive meetings with Churchill, who, apparently bemused by the Dominion concept, agreed with deceptive readiness to give bipartisan support to the necessary legislation. Even more important, Mountbatten secured acceptance of the plan in Delhi on 3 June, within days of his return. Nobody was entirely happy; few were irreconcilably hostile; most were ready to make the best of it. At a press conference the Viceroy revealed that independence could be as near as 15 August.

This left a mere ten weeks to prepare. In London legislation had to be drafted at breakneck speed. In the Commons, Churchill had waxed benign about how 'the many nations and States of India may find their unity within the mysterious circle of the British Crown, just as the self-governing Dominions have done for so many years after all other links with the mother country, save those of sentiment, have been dissolved.'[55] Such rhetoric, of course, bore almost no relation to what was going on in India. Hence the shock to Churchill, if no one else, that the legislation was to be called simply the Indian Independence Bill. The old man's understanding of the constitutional development of the Commonwealth had plainly not taken in the implications of the Statute of Westminster. The inherent principle of self-determination appeared to have passed him by; yet, as Attlee put it in a firm reply, this provided 'a most valuable counter to the demands for independence outside the Commonwealth as it shows that this demand can be satsified within it'.[56]

It was actually left to the pragmatic and widely trusted Ismay, now on a visit to London, to save the day for bipartisanship. On 8 July, prompted by Attlee, Ismay went down to Chartwell, where work on *The Gathering Storm* was in full spate. Nobody was better placed than 'Pug', an off-duty member of 'the Syndicate' that was actually composing the work, to persuade a besieged author, up against a pressing deadline, that he need worry no further about India, which was now in good hands.

Churchill was absent when the Indian legislation went through the Commons without opposition on its second reading on 10 July, making the third reading a mere formality. 'By passing this Bill,' said Cripps, 'we shall be firmly and finally establishing our honesty of democratic purpose.'[57] He at least had a right to say this. Nobody contradicted these *bien-pensant* claims; nobody mentioned scuttle. 'An Emperor of India no longer rules from London,' declaimed the *New York Times* when the legislation received the royal assent. 'Victoria's great-grandson has cast aside that empty title. The Raj is dead.'[58] And, within a month, its territory was to be subjected to a hasty partition between the two successor states.

Partition was an expedient that had often been peddled as the solution to rival claims for self-determination, in Palestine as much as in India. One difference was that it was demanded by a religious minority in India with the price to pay of receiving a 'moth-eaten' Pakistan; whereas partition was demanded by a religious minority in Palestine with the evident ambition of leaving the moth-eaten fragments to the Arab majority. Britain's decision to submit the problem to the United Nations had meanwhile stalled any decision: on immediate issues of immigration as much as on the ultimate future of the country. In May 1947 the infant world organization showed its early addiction to acronyms by setting up UNSCOP (United Nations Special Committee on Palestine). Comprising members from eleven supposedly impartial countries, UNSCOP arrived in Palestine in mid-June.

In theory UNSCOP was to be left in tranquillity to come up with the internationally acceptable answer that had eluded the imperialist British. In practice its deliberations were conducted amid a propaganda assault aimed at influencing international opinion by any means that served. In this the Zionists proved more adept than the Arabs. Richard Crossman, though bested by Bevin in the Labour Party's foreign policy debates, managed to catch the UNSCOP delegates in Geneva, with apparent success in heading them off from a Bevin-style binational state and pointing them towards partition. In New York, where the profits of the musical *A Flag is Born* went to Irgun, its author, Ben Hecht, had a widely quoted message to his terrorist friends published in the *Herald Tribune* on 15 May: 'Every time you blow up a British arsenal, or wreck a British jail, or send a British railroad sky high, or rob a British bank, or let go with your guns at the British betrayers and invaders of your homeland, the Jews of America make a little holiday in their hearts.'[59]

In Palestine itself, Irgun and the Stern Gang were plainly a small minority within the Yishuv. Haganah, by contrast, enjoyed widespread support in its campaign for direct action on immigration. Declining morale in the camps was stoking fears that not enough Jewish DPs might persist in their commitment to reach Palestine; and the British policy of housing intercepted 'illegals' in Cyprus simply created another set of camps. Both sides now raised the stakes: Haganah by organizing the purchase of bigger, better ships in the United States, the British by deciding that any future illegals would be returned to their port of embarkation.

A small news item appeared in the *New York Times* on 7 March: 'Palestine-Bound Mystery Ship'. It was enough to alarm the British Foreign Office since the *President Warfield*, which shortly set out for Europe with an American crew, obviously presented a challenge on a new scale, with its capacity to carry up to 5000 passengers. An old flat-bottomed ship, now newly repaired, the *President Warfield* had seen service in the Second World War, notably in approaching the Normandy beaches – a problem not unlike that of making a clandestine landing on the Palestine coast.[60]

What happened on the high seas in late July was actually rather an anti-climax. The *New York Times* on 18 July interjected into an already obscure report of the UNSCOP sittings in Palestine a statement that the *President Warfield* was nearing the coast with 4500 illegals, embarked from Marseilles. The next day the ship's attempt to resist boarding by the Royal Navy (while still actually outside Palestinian waters) made the front page, though only down-page in column 6: '3 Slain on Zionist Vessel As Refugees Fight British'. Rabbi Silver was quoted: 'The assault in force by the British navy against a ship carrying Jewish refugees to their internationally promised homeland, reported in today's press, fills right-thinking men and women everywhere with indignation and horror.'

Messages from the ship said that Haganah had renamed it *Exodus 1947*. It was the early blossoming of a potent exercise in Zionist propaganda, which later flowered luxuriantly in Leon Uris's novel *Exodus* (1958; filmed 1960), which bears much the same relation to the actual history of the episode as Dan Brown's *The Da Vinci Code* does to biblical scholarship. True, *Exodus 1947* was the usage employed by the Zionist Labour MP Sidney Silverman when he raised the matter in the House of Commons a few days after the boarding. But this renaming did not catch on in Britain, where news of the *President Warfield* was soon overtaken by reports of two more immigrant ships. These were different in that both sides backed down: Haganah ordered them to turn back peacefully and the British did not persist in sending the illegal immigrants back to their port of embarkation.

The big story from Palestine that week had a different focus. Three Irgun terrorists were due to be hanged, despite threats that two British sergeants, captured a fortnight previously as hostages, would be subject to reprisals. Beigin's hard line was also seen in his deliberately embarrassing revelation that Haganah had been party to planning the King David Hotel blast twelve months previously; he now called Haganah 'a militia protecting the British'. On 29 July the hangings were duly reported, as was Irgun's promise that 'the streets will run red with British blood'.[61] In London two days later, *The Times* gave prominence to an unconfirmed report that the two British sergeants had been executed. For the *New York Times*, this was a minor item, barely making a down-column slot on the front page: 'Hostages Hanged, Irgun Announces'.

On 1 August the contrast between American and British reporting was stark. 'BRITISH SERGEANTS FOUND MURDERED' was *The Times* headline; 'Bodies Hanging from Tree Near Nathanya; Palestine Shocked by Crime'. Any shock was muted by the time it reached the *New York Times* – and now directed as much at the alleged response of the British troops as at the terrorists, in a report confined to column 8: 'Incensed Britons Kill 5 in Tel Aviv To Avenge Hanging'. The *Washington Post* had the same angle in its down-column story: 'Troops Avenge Hostages Deaths: 5 Jews Are Slain in Tel Aviv After Hanging of Two Britons'. *The Times* meanwhile was scornful of Irgun's propaganda in justifying action against 'a terrorist organization called the British Occupation Army' and lamented 'the harm done to Jewish aspirations' by this outrage. It certainly reported the rioting in Tel Aviv but echoed official denials that any British troops had been involved (though it later became clear that some had).

These were different news values, formed by different viewpoints and different prime loyalties. The naive British reaction against terrorism as such was countered by a sophisticated American extenuation of the circumstances in which terrorism had arisen. The leader in *The Times* of 1 August, 'Murder in Palestine', was thus reciprocated next day by an editorial in the *Washington Post*, 'Competition in Terror', which blandly equated the two sides. Both the British and 'the underground' might be guilty, but the thrust of its conclusion was clearly in one direction: 'Presumably the British authorities will take prompt measures to punish the men who exacted such a barbaric revenge.' The *Post* did not have Menachem Beigin and his colleagues in mind.

American Sunday newspapers, with their copious use of newsprint, were a marvel to British readers in those days of rationing. In its section on the news of the week on Sunday, 3 August, the *New York Times* laid out a big map of Palestine: 'As Terror and Counter-Terror Mount in the Holy Land'. Next to it, two large photographs were juxtaposed. One showed a train, 'wrecked by Jewish extremists', while the other was a shot of 'the refugee ship *Exodus 1947* after it was rammed by a British destroyer' (which had not happened, though damage was sustained). The subsequent decision to ship the remaining illegals to Germany, since most of them refused to land in France when taken back to Marseilles, was an easily exploited propaganda gift to international Zionism. Only in Britain was it felt (in the words of *The Times*) that 'this attempt at moral blackmail has failed and will continue to fail.'[62]

This was a war that the British could not win. Mass-Observation surveys had consistently shown that over half of the people interviewed in the street (57 per cent) either were not interested in Palestine or said that they harboured a vague feeling of 'horror, regret or dismay'. Who to blame and what to do? In the whole sample, 13 per cent were angry with the Jews and another 5 per cent with both Jews and Arabs. While 7 per cent blamed the British, none blamed the Arabs alone. With whatever motives or biases, 26 per cent said that Britain should withdraw, only 5 per cent that Britain should be 'firm' – and a baffled 44 per cent did not know.

It is evident that Zionism had failed to enlist popular support, or even understanding, in Britain. Talking about a 'Jewish national home' evoked more support, though the Balfour Declaration was little known and quite often supposed to be pro-Arab. The hanging of the two British sergeants at this point, and the booby-trapping of their bodies, made a raw impact which undoubtedly heightened anti-semitism in Britain. In some cases the incident confirmed pre-existing prejudice against British Jews – 'They're for them, the buggers,' as one working-class woman put it. But this was a minority feeling – only 20 per cent approved of the demonstrations, generally regarded as anti-semitic, that took place in London, Manchester and Liverpool on 2 August. Terrorism in Palestine was another matter. 'It's a disgraceful way to fight,' said a young middle-class man, and the sense of weariness came out in other responses, like that of an artisan-class housewife: 'It doesn't matter what we do out there, they just fight and fight and fight.'[63]

A parliamentary debate on 12 August echoed such feelings. The formal end of the mandate was not to come until after further dispiriting months of occupation, in May 1948; but the British will to continue collapsed in August 1947. Within weeks of the two sergeants' deaths, the British cabinet decided to leave Palestine.

The reasons were many. Failure to reconcile the claims of Jews and Arabs made a mockery of the original mandate. The absence of American support, when combined with the absence of American restraint from interference, unleashed a new phase in Zionist politics which made a difficult situation impossible. It seems inescapable to conclude that terrorism clinched the matter for the British. Lack of political will to continue combined with lack of economic resources to do so. Faced with an economic crisis at the end of July, the cabinet had already been under pressure from the left to make an immediate reduction in British forces in Palestine. A backbench petition to Attlee was signed, of course, by Ian Mikardo, Michael Foot and Richard Crossman of the Keep Left Group, but also attracted signatures from other MPs whose left-wing leanings were later less conspicuous, including Jim Callaghan and Woodrow Wyatt.

The Government was in trouble. It was not just the Keep Left Group but Labour loyalists who sensed a lack of leadership, amply documented from the inside in Dalton's diary. A backbench move to substitute Bevin as prime minister in place of Attlee testified to the seriousness of a crisis that now revived memories of the collapse of a Labour Government in 1931, when faced with a financial panic which party mythology blamed on American bankers. It was a situation in which rumours that Bernard Baruch was on the line from New York to Tory MPs, talking of a change of government, could be given undue credit when taken in conjunction with the mounting partisan hostility of the Tory press.

This run on the pound had begun in early July, anticipating the formal establishment of convertibility on 15 July. Though Dalton could claim to have issued warnings which his cabinet colleagues had not taken seriously enough, when the storm broke it revealed Bevin and Cripps as the strong ministers among Labour's Big Five. The two of them had to overcome a past history of mutual distrust, going back to Cripps's fellow-travelling period. So when Bevin and Dalton spent a long journey together in the back of a heavily guarded ministerial car – 'These Jews have made all this fuss necessary,' the pro-Zionist Chancellor noted – Bevin's outdated opinion of Cripps as 'more than half-way to Moscow' was still an obstacle to closer co-operation.[64] This may indeed have helped Attlee to hang on to his job when Cripps, in a resigning frame of mind, later pressed the proposal that Bevin should instead take over.

The optimistic view was that the market had already discounted the effect of convertibility. The pessimistic view, that this was only the beginning, was steadily confirmed as the dollar drain went from bad to worse. At a meeting called to rally the Parliamentary Labour Party on 30 July, Dalton used a line given him by Bevin: 'I think it will be a pity if they are left under the impression that I led anyone to believe that the Marshall Plan was a solution.' Equally, Dalton roundly declared to nervous backbenchers that this would be no 1931: rather, 'that Socialism did best when it marched in step with the rules of arithmetic'. That night the Big Five appeared to rather less advantage when Morrison, infuriated at Bevin's post-prandial prolixity, walked out of their conclave saying that he had 'had enough of this drunken monologue'. Attlee showed little grip. The meeting broke up well past midnight. To members of the wartime Coalition, it was all too familiar. 'Anyhow it was often worse with Winston,' Dalton assured the top civil servants in attendance.[65]

On 31 July, the same day that *The Times* first reported the Irgun claim to have hanged the two sergeants, its lead story was 'GOVERNMENT PLANS TO MEET CRISIS', with all eyes now set on a promised prime-ministerial statement in the following week. The cabinet agreed to make cuts in food imports and in supplies to Germany – putting victors and vanquished alike on short rations – and, despite opposition from Bevin and Alexander, to make large cuts in overseas military expenditure. This was the package unveiled by Attlee in the Commons on 6 August.

Attlee's speech was a characteristic performance. Dalton privately termed it 'most disappointing', though the 'very fine winding-up speech' from Cripps the next day retrieved the position.[66] But the Chancellor acknowledged that the Prime Minister's statement had real substance, painfully crafted as it was within the Treasury, which may be why it reads better than it sounded. As so often in his career, Attlee's political forte was to counter Churchill's rich rhetoric with a deflationary appeal to hard fact. A few days previously the Leader of the Opposition had made a great oration at his birthplace, Blenheim Palace, dwelling amid its architectural splendours on the sorry state to which a socialist government had reduced the country after two years in which they had 'blithely cast away India and Burma, regardless of what may happen in the near future after our slowly-built-up Empire has passed away'.[67]

Attlee put it differently. 'The suggestion that the Government had frittered away the American loan was not true,' he said to ministerial cheers, and proceeded to lecture the House on the true position. 'We got through the world war with the help of Lend-Lease, which was rightly described by Mr Churchill as "the most unsordid act in history",' he explained. 'But it left us in a most vulnerable position. We had to face the task of reconstruction, involving the whole remodelling of our economy and what we wanted essentially was time to effect the change-over.'[68] No, the Loan had not proved big enough, as some had suspected all along. But, as Attlee liked to say, those were the cards that had been dealt at the end of the war.

'After the 15th August all the "postwar problems" will loom as great out here as they did in Europe,' Mountbatten confided to the Governor of Madras.[69] Not until 8 August, with only a week to go, was the Viceroy's secretariat informed where the boundary commission proposed to draw the line partitioning the Punjab. The task of implementing partition had been given to a British judge, Sir Cyril Radcliffe, working under a deadline that allowed only a month to prepare his recommendations. These were obviously imperfect; indeed, the inherent impossibility of a clean, clear, fair and amicable partition had been a prime reason for going to such lengths to avoid it. Everyone knew that bloodshed was inevitable; it was lessened in Bengal by Gandhi's presence. None of this diminishes the tragedy that at least 200,000 people, and perhaps as many as a million, were to die. Even so, in 1946 talk of two or three million possible deaths had been common. Whatever Radcliffe proposed was bound to be wrong and catch unhappy people of the wrong ethnic identity on the wrong side of the line at the wrong moment.

What he actually proposed for the Punjab on 8 August was altered by 12 August. This fact is clear amid many conflicting charges as to effect, agency and intent. The crucial change affected the Sikh city of Amritsar (a famous name in imperial history) and it certainly made the city viable as a part of India by eliminating a salient that would otherwise have gone to Pakistan. It seems unlikely that Mountbatten knew as little as he claimed of this last-minute amendment; but his main concern was now to defer wider publicity of the award until immediately after the independence celebrations. Again, there are good reasons that can be cited on both sides of this decision. It was hardly the cause of the communal atrocities that were to disfigure independence; partition was the reason at one level and deep-seated issues of ethnic and religious identity a causal factor lying deeper still. What Mountbatten achieved was a transfer of power that maximized the goodwill at the hour of independence, midnight on 14–15 August.

'Long years ago we made a tryst with destiny,' declared Nehru, 'and now the time comes when we shall redeem our pledge, not wholly or in full measure, but very substantially.' This was indeed a memorable speech and it caught a real sense of the significance of what was taking place. 'A moment comes, which comes but rarely in history, when we step from the old to the new, when an age ends, and when the soul of a nation, long suppressed, finds utterance,' he claimed.[70] Like Churchill, with whom he had so often clashed, Nehru was able to speak for his nation, giving its experience a historical resonance while history was actually happening, and thus helping to shape that history. And like Churchill, he told the truth – but not the whole truth and nothing but the truth.

For others the end of the Indian Empire naturally meant different things: hopes, triumphs, pathos or bathos. 'Down comes the Union Jack,' wrote Radcliffe in a letter home, 'and up goes – for the moment I rather forget what, but it has a spinning wheel or spiders' web in the middle.'[71] V. P. Menon, who was, though not the architect, the clerk of works of Indian independence and soon to be the author of the Indian constitution, later wrote of the British whom he had hitherto served: 'They left of their own will; there was no war, there was no treaty – an act without parallel in history.'[72]

The King had to get used to signing himself George R. and not George R. I., like his father. He did so a few days later to his mother, Queen Mary, who noted on the back of the envelope: 'The first time Bertie wrote me a letter with the *I* for Emperor of India left out, very sad.'[73] But for most British subjects, the event seems to have been a happy relief from the dispiriting news coming out of Palestine and the alarming news that they heard daily about sterling (with convertibility soon to be abandoned on 20 August). Kipling, the great poet of empire, was currently unfashionable, and his hard-pressed compatriots could not spare much time for mutual commiserations that all their pomp of yesterday was one with Nineveh and Tyre.

Epilogue

The headlines in *The Times* for Wednesday, 15 August 1947, read:

POWER HANDED OVER IN INDIA

Birth of Two New Dominions

Lord Mountbatten on a Friendly Parting

This occupied columns 1 and 2; in column 3 the story was already more sombre: 'High Death Roll in Punjab'. Its editorial, 'The End of an Era', picked up on the Viceroy's speech to rejoice that India and Pakistan 'derive from their own ancient and lofty civilizations their title to the full sovereign privileges implicit in Dominion status'.

Here was no talk of the dissolution of the British Empire but an adroit form of words to square the circle: not simply ending empire but redeploying the concept of the Commonwealth so as to provide a status that simultaneously fulfilled an inherent right to self-determination. If this line of argument expressed another myth, perhaps this was no bad thing. This, some might well think, was what the Atlantic Charter had intended. Some might even think that it was not inconsistent with the finest hour of the British Empire and Commonwealth, when, beguiled by the rhetoric of the great imperialist Churchill, it fought on against the Nazis and sought victory – at all costs, including its own supersession.

The concept of the Commonwealth as we know it today was not formulated until 1949, largely as a response to the problem of accommodating the independent republics of India and Pakistan within an international body of equals, replacing the previous ambiguous terminology of 'British Commonwealth'. Thus the Commonwealth was a free association of independent countries – but territories, of course, which

505

happened to have formed Britain's imperial possessions in an earlier age. The sleight of hand involved in this transition left many baffled about the constitutional niceties; but there was nothing new about the imperial misapprehensions of the British people.

In the Mass-Observation archive there is a revealing survey of popular attitudes towards the British Commonwealth and Empire, undertaken in 1948.[1] As it explains, in the course of carrying out the pilot surveys, 'it became clear that there was some confusion in the minds of many people as to the precise meanings of the terms "Empire" and "Commonwealth".' Britons were still comfortable with the term British Empire, using it as Churchill did, in a sense that embraced Britain and the Dominions as well as colonial territories – and in a way that was infused with more sentiment than accuracy.

Most Britons in 1948 could not offer a satisfactory explanation of the difference between a colony and a Dominion. Not only did 52 per cent admit that they did not know but another 17 per cent offered wrong definitions. 'One's more populated,' claimed an electrical fitter from Fulham. 'A colony is something that's founded, a dominion's sort of there,' suggested a plumber's wife from Tooting, only to be contradicted by a butcher's wife from Liverpool: 'A colony is just a small island.' We can probably see what a polisher from Birmingham was driving at when he offered: 'A colony is where we settled – a dominion is where people were born.' All told, though, the survey points to some failings in imperialist indoctrination. This was an Empire on which, for seven people out of ten, the right question was never set – or answered correctly, at any rate.

About a quarter of the population had contact with friends or relatives in the Empire. Overwhelmingly such communications were maintained with persons living in Canada, Australia and New Zealand, and these were the countries of which people knew most. When 42 per cent of those asked said that they were still hopeful about the future of the Empire (as against 24 per cent not) it was obviously the Old Commonwealth of which they were thinking. 'We cannot manage without them' was the most frequent line of response and 84 per cent said Britain would be worse off without the Empire. 'We couldn't live for five minutes without the Empire,' said a painter and decorator from Rochdale. 'No, we are very small,' the wife of a paint operator from Leatherhead reflected. 'We would get sat on, I suppose. They do want an Empire behind them.' If we wonder for whom Winston Churchill and Ernest Bevin spoke, we need look no further.

The fact that the Dominions had proved Britain's key allies in a recent struggle for national survival speaks to the authenticity of this largely inarticulate assumption. Indeed it underpins the residual notion of the Empire sustaining Britain's power in the world – a world that had actually ended, despite appearances, at Yalta or at latest Potsdam. Great Britain still played a major international role, but no longer the determining role which was the premise of imperial power. Churchill's declarations about not presiding over the liquidation of the British Empire were thus on a par with his promises about the sunlit uplands. It is clear that he himself had great difficulty in adjusting to the new scheme of things and, spared the responsibility of power after July 1945, often hit out at the iniquities of a socialist government in betraying the hopes of the British people.

These were matters fiercely debated at the time and, like many issues raised in this book, have been revisited by distinguished historians with whom I do not always agree. Thus I dissent from the case argued with customary bravura by Correlli Barnett, that the pursuit of a New Jerusalem, based on the welfare state and full employment, represented a self-inflicted mortification for the British people.[2] There were indeed costs to be borne, in financing both the Beveridge-style expansion of social security and later the National Heath Service, just as there were benefits to be enjoyed. But these were predominantly transfers between different members of the population of the United Kingdom – a matter quite distinct from the need to finance the United Kingdom's post-war external liabilities, especially in dollars. The real economic crisis came because of the costs of victory, incurred under Churchill's own leadership.

Indeed some historians then turn the argument back upon Churchill himself. They rightly sense irony in the fact that the dissolution of the British Empire, against which he railed, was hastened by his own actions. And John Charmley, who has pursued this line of analysis with most vigour, is surely right in suggesting that many of the dilemmas that Churchill faced – especially over Poland – arose from the same intractable difficulties that Neville Chamberlain had confronted earlier.[3] In both cases, to be sure, the fundamental problem was an over-extension of British commitments in an era of declining British power. The next step, however, is one where I part company from such revisionists, in disparaging Churchill's essential historical role.

In short, should Churchill himself be blamed? Not surely for resisting Hitler in 1940; not for doing whatever he could to stop the Nazis in their tracks; not for mobilizing the British people – and the British Empire – to resist the blandishments of a negotiated peace; and not, therefore, for employing a rhetoric that submerged their immediate cause in an appeal to instincts of freedom and decency that may indeed claim to be universal. If the principles of democracy that Churchill evoked had a special appeal for Americans, this also disclosed an inherent contradiction with his own ideas about the British Empire. But what mattered in 1940 was the purposeful creation of a national myth that was itself a historical force in giving the British people a story about the war that they could believe in, by believing in themselves. The fact that the story, as historians tell it today, is somewhat more complex, nuanced and ambivalent is another matter. Today we can dispense with much of the rhetorical self-deception that Churchill and his countrymen needed in order to endow us with that privilege.

Like Churchill, this book acknowledges a tragedy of sorts for the British people in their hour of triumph in 1945. They suffered some ineluctable consequences of the war, not through folly or wickedness but because they found themselves trapped in historical processes which they could not fully control. Even to use the word tragedy in relation to Great Britain, however, requires some care – and humility. Churchill was told shortly before VE-Day that one in 165 of the British population had died in the war – over 300,000, which is in line with later estimates. But we know that one in five Poles perished; and we know that 6 million Jews were exterminated; and we know that Polish Jews suffered worst of all, the victims not only of the Nazis but often of their own compatriots. There are tragedies and tragedies.

One tragedy, moreover, may well engender others. The Polish experience during the Second World War is one which Norman Davies has done more than any other recent historian to illuminate.[4] He captures the enormity of Polish losses, in a population trapped between the gigantic war machines of Nazi Germany and the Soviet Union, brutally directed by Hitler and Stalin alike. Yet it remains important to recognize just as fully that the sufferings of the mainly Catholic Poles did not inspire them to magnanimity about the fate of their fellow citizens, the

Jews of Poland, who faced sporadic wartime persecution and more widespread post-war pogroms when they tried to reclaim their ancestral lands.

It was the Polish Jews who were most determined to flee eastern Europe, as it was left after Potsdam, and to make a new life for themselves. Who can possibly blame them? And if they accepted the advice proffered in Zionist propaganda, that immigration to Palestine was their best bet, who would say that they were wrong? And if they saw British restrictions on legal immigration as vexatious, who would not in their position? And if they exploited the workings of the arrangements for Displaced Persons to use illegal channels in getting to Palestine, what other options did they have? Finally, if they saw their arrival as Zionist settlers as a triumph over anti-semitism, British imperialism and American lassitude, little wonder that they established a powerful narrative of their providential deliverance. Meanwhile, however, Palestinian Arabs lost the land on which their families had lived, often for generations, sometimes for centuries.

Neither the British nor the Americans come very well out of the story in Palestine. There could be no clearer example of the shift of power after the war from the British Empire to a new dispensation where the United States could call the shots whenever it chose to do so. The end of the mandate in Palestine was thus the most blatant signal of the dissolution of the British Empire. When the mandate was referred back to the United Nations in 1947, few expected the Zionists to succeed in mobilizing a two-thirds majority for the creation of their own state within Palestine. Yet this had happened by 1948 and, after the Arabs had lost the war as well as the vote, the result was the establishment of the state of Israel, as Zionists had long hoped. Though the full reasons for their success were complex, the main one is simply that the United States exerted its power and influence to bring about this outcome.

Both the British and the Americans had found that it was easy to make promises to both sides about Palestine. But often it is only possible to keep promises to one side, and it becomes necessary to choose which. In the end the British generally chose the Arabs and the Americans chose the Jews. That is surely why there is now a Zionist state in Palestine but no Arab state.

India was not as bad as this. Here at least the British Government belatedly took a grip on a situation that threatened to slip beyond its control. It was not an ideal solution, if only because there are no ideal solutions in such intractable conflicts. Churchill certainly had no answers that spoke to the condition of India in the 1940s (or the 1930s for that matter). Once he was out of power, however, the Attlee Government played the few cards in its hand with some of the skill and ruthlessness that the situation demanded. In particular, the work of the cabinet delegation in 1946, which has usually been derided, surely offered the Indian parties independence on the basis of a historic compromise which they would have to make themselves. It was, by definition, hardly the best solution in the eyes of either side; but each side needed to reconcile itself to a second-best solution if hasty partition and predictable bloodshed were to be avoided. Unfortunately, this is not how Gandhi, still the most powerful man in India, looked at the world. His failure to rise to the political challenge in 1946 emerges as the most significant missed opportunity in the whole story.

Perhaps no scheme for Indian union would have survived in the long run. The conventional Congress theory that communal division was purely a function of British rule was certainly tested to destruction. In the twenty-first century, the authenticity of Islamic identity is immediately recognizable in a way that still seemed disputable in the 1940s. But even if partition had eventually come in India, it surely need not have come in the way it did in 1947. In the final months, Gandhi's response was heroic on a personal moral level, but that need not blind us to the degree of his own responsibility for engendering this situation. Here, as in Palestine, prophetic moral certainties, driven by religion, have more obviously fuelled ongoing conflict than paved the way to utopia. People seeking peace may suffer from too many prophets and not enough politics.

The last thousand days of the British Empire thus saw the emergence of the world that we live in today, with fewer glimpses of the broad, sunlit uplands than had once been hoped. Yet any sense of disappointment needs to be measured not just against hopes that were betrayed but against the actual historical alternatives, which may have been almost unimaginably worse than what actually happened. The threat that the Nazis and their allies posed to civilized values was met with the requisite force, as it had to be: by the Soviet Union, whom Churchill determined to accept as Britain's ally from June 1941, and above all, from December 1941, by the United States, whom Churchill welcomed with long-anticipated relief. Churchill's Grand Alliance thus played a necessary and beneficial historical role.

One aspect of the myth that Churchill created, however, has had a curiously long afterlife: the notion of a special relationship between the English-speaking peoples. The work of Churchill's biographer, Martin Gilbert, strikes me as far too indulgent towards the great man's myth-making and, especially in dealing with Churchill and the Americans, far too uncritical in its perspectives. Likewise, the history of the English-speaking peoples that Churchill took to the end of the nineteenth century now finds a twentieth-century sequel in the narrative supplied by Andrew Roberts, more tendentiously than persuasively argued in my opinion.[5]

Again, there is no call to disparage the real achievements of both Churchill and Roosevelt in creating a uniquely efficacious Anglo-American wartime partnership. Nor is there need to cavil at each of them for inimitably supporting it in language that exceeds the test of strict veracity. Lend-Lease, which was a great piece of American statesmanship, ought indeed to be hailed as an expression of enlightened self-interest, given the dearth of such comparable measures in the ordinary, dispiriting round of international relations. But whether it was the right vehicle for relations between allies in a common cause, as Britain and the United States became after Pearl Harbor, is still a question worth asking. All told, hyperbolic language about unsordid motivation is not adequate for historical analysis.

What the British call the American Loan and what the Americans call the British Loan similarly needs some demystification. In strict economic terms, it was indeed necessary if the United Kingdom were to maintain an austere but acceptable standard of living while its external balance of payments was put on a viable peacetime basis. And the famous 'consideration' exacted in return for Lend-Lease – a British pledge to relinquish imperial preference – came into the reckoning here. In the end, the consideration became the *quid pro quo* not for Lend-Lease but for the Loan. Yet Commonwealth preference mysteriously survived into the post-war world – because its abolition was again a pledge, which the British subsequently claimed to honour simply by negotiating with the Dominions (who were the very people least likely to agree to end their preferential access to the British market). Only with Britain's entry into the European Economic Community in 1973 did the system expire. In 1945, then, any termination of preferences was more symbolic than economic.

Likewise the terms on which the Loan was granted. In 1945 the cabinet agonized over what Britain could afford in future repayments, and in debate the emotive language of 'reparations' was used. Yet the actual terms proved relatively easy to meet. Not only were there no repayments until 1950 but the 'waiver' clause allowed Britain to defer payments in 1956, 1957, 1964, 1965, 1968 and 1976 – years when the balance of payments was in trouble. Meanwhile, economic growth and inflation whittled down the real cost, even with the (very low) interest charges of 2 per cent. When the final payments of $83.25 million to the United States and $22.7 million to Canada were made at the end of December 2006, these actual sums were small change measured by the scale of today's international financial transactions.[6] But to conclude simply that this was the real impact, rather than the associated rhetoric, may miss the point.

Churchill is in many ways the central figure in the story told in this book. If he emerges from it as a fully plausible human being, fallible and inimitable, he is not thereby diminished. His elevated language has often been quoted, and sometimes contrasted with his low sallies in private; but again, this is not to say that the public utterances can be dismissed – rather that their function needs to be understood. Many were moved by Churchill's words, not least himself.

Britain's great wartime leader usually knew what he was doing; yet he was also in thrall to his own eloquence in projecting an ongoing Anglo-American relationship as the lodestone of post-war British policy. Britons who have continued to take this too literally have left themselves as open to disillusionment as any who once believed in the sunlit uplands – and with far less justification or excuse. It is not at all anti-American to recognize the necessarily different priorities of a superpower on a continental scale and those of a middle-sized ex-imperial European country. Such an alliance may often be expedient. But, as its history shows, it is not an alliance of equals and its efficacy depends more on mutual needs and pragmatism than on sentimental bonds.

I end this book as I began it: still learning about the history that frames my own life, from being a child in the 1940s to making sense of the apparently very different world of the early twenty-first century. Yet we are still confronted, to a surprising extent, with the legacy of the developments surveyed in this book: in Anglo-American relations, in the Indian subcontinent, and obviously in historic Palestine. This book would be presumptuous if it pointed to any simple solutions; but I conclude it more confident than ever that these are problems which we can understand better if we know a bit more history.

Abbreviations

5 HC Debs	House of Commons debates, 5th series (Hansard)
5 HL Debs	House of Lords debates, 5th series (Hansard)
CT	*Chicago Tribune*
DBPO	*Documents on British Policy Overseas*, ed. Rohan Butler and M. E. Pelly, with H. J. Yasamee, Series 1, vol. i on Potsdam (London, 1984)
DM	*Daily Mail*
FDR–WSC	*Roosevelt and Churchill : their secret wartime correspondence*, ed. Francis L. Loewenheim, Harold D. Langley and Manfred Jonas (London, 1975)
FRUS	*Foreign Relations of the United States*, esp. vols. for the conferences at Malta and Yalta (Washington, DC, 1955) and Potsdam (Washington, DC, 1960)
G&M	*Globe and Mail* (Toronto)
Gilbert	Martin Gilbert, *Winston S. Churchill*, vols. v–viii (London 1976–88)
JMK	*The Collected Writings of John Maynard Keynes*, 30 vols., ed. Donald Moggridge (London, 1971–89)
MA	*The Age* (Melbourne)
MO	Mass-Observation, with archive file number
Nation's Voice	*The Nation's Voice: speeches, etc by Mohammad Ali Jinnah*, ed.Waheed Ahmad, vols. iv–vi, 1944–7 (Karachi, 2000–2002)
NC	*News Chronicle*
NYT	*New York Times*
ODNB	*Oxford Dictionary of National Biography* (digital edn, 2004–)
PM	Crossman, R. H. S., *Palestine Mission* (London, 1947)
SWW	Churchill, Winston S., *The Second World War*, 6 vols., (London, 1948–54)
TOP	*India:The Transfer of Power*, 1942–7, 12 vols., editor-in-chief Nicholas Mansergh (London, 1970–83)
TT	*The Times* (London)
WD	*Washington Despatches 1941–1945 : weekly political reports from the British Embassy*, ed. H. G. Nicholas; introduction by Isaiah Berlin (London, 1981)

The Diarists

Alanbrooke   *War Diaries, 1939–1945, Field Marshal Lord Alanbrooke*, eds. Alex Danchev and Dan Todman (London, 2001)

Alexander diary   A. V. Alexander papers, Churchill Archives Centre, Cambridge

Amery   *The Empire at Bay: the Leo Amery diaries, 1929–45*, eds. John Barnes and David Nicholson (London, 1988)

Baffy   *Baffy: the diaries of Blanche Dugdale, 1936–1947*, ed. N. A. Rose (London, 1973)

Butcher   Harry C. Butcher, *My Three Years with Eisenhower* (New York, 1946)

Cadogan   *The Diaries of Sir Alexander Cadogan, 1938–1945*, ed. David Dilks, (London, 1971)

Chips   *Chips: the diaries of Sir Henry Channon*, ed. Robert Rhodes James (paperback edn, Harmondsworth, 1970)

Colville   *The Fringes of Power: Downing Street diaries of John Colville, 1939–1955*, vol. ii (paperback edn, Sevenoaks, 1986)

Cripps diary   Stafford Cripps papers, Bodleian Library, Oxford

Dalton   *The Second World War Diary of Hugh Dalton 1940–45* and *The Political Diary of Hugh Dalton, 1918–40, 1945–60*, ed. Ben Pimlott (both vols.) (London, 1986)

Forrestal   James Forrestal, *The Forrestal Diaries* (London, 1952)

King   Mackenzie King diary, Public Archives of Canada; excerpts in J. W. Pickersgill and D. F. Foster (eds.), *The Mackenzie King Record*, vol. ii (Toronto, 1968)

Macmillan   Harold Macmillan, *War Diaries* (London, 1984)

Meade   *The Cabinet Office Diary of James Meade, 1944–46*, eds. Susan Howson and Donald Moggridge (London, 1990).

Meinertzhagen   Richard Meinertzhagen, *Middle East Diary, 1917–1956* (London, 1959)

Moran   Lord Moran, *Churchill at War, 1940–1945*, introduction by John, 2nd Lord Moran (paperback edn, London, 2003)

Morgenthau   John Morton Blum, *From the Morgenthau Diaries*, vol. iii (Boston, Mass., 1967)

Nicolson   *Diaries and Letters of Harold Nicolson*, ed. Nigel Nicolson, 3 vols. (London, 1966–8)

Robbins   *The Wartime Diaries of Lionel Robbins and James Meade, 1943–45*, eds. Susan Howson and Donald Moggridge (Basingstoke, 1990)

Stettinius   *The Diaries of Edward R. Stettinius, Jr., 1943–1946* eds. Thomas M. Campbell and George C. Herring (New York, 1975)

Vandenberg   *The Private Papers of Senator Vandenberg*, eds. Arthur H. Vandenberg, Jr and Joe Alex Morris (London, 1953)

Wavell   *Wavell: the Viceroy's journal*, ed. Penderel Moon (London, 1973)

Bibliography

This includes full publication details for all citations given in footnotes only by author's surname and short title; and works to which I am particularly indebted are asterisked thus *.

Addison, Paul, *Churchill: the unexpected hero* (Oxford, 2005)

Aldrich, Richard J., *Intelligence and the War against Japan* (Cambridge, 2000)

Annual Register (London, 1947)

Bailey, Thomas A., *A Diplomatic History of the American People* (New York, 1955)

Barnett, Correlli, *The Desert Generals*, new edn (London, 1983)

—, *The Lost Victory: British dreams, British realities, 1945–50* (London, 1995)

Bayly, Christopher and Tim Harper, *Forgotten Armies: the fall of British Asia, 1941–1945* (London, 2004)*

Bedell Smith, Walter, *Eisenhower's Six Great Decisions* (London, 1956)

Beevor, Antony, *Berlin: the downfall, 1945* (London, 2002)

Berlin, Isaiah, *Flourishing: letters, 1928–1946*, ed. Henry Hardy (London, 2004)

Bethell, Nicholas, *The Palestine Triangle: the struggle between the British, the Jews and the Arabs, 1935–48* (London, 1979)*

Black, Conrad, *Franklin Delano Roosevelt: champion of freedom* (New York, 2003)

Blake, Robert, and William Roger Louis, *Churchill* (Oxford, 1993) for essays by Michael Carver, Sarvepalli Gopal and Norman Rose

Blumenson, Martin (ed.), *The Patton Papers*, vol. ii: *1940–45* (Boston, Mass., 1974)

Bradley, Omar N. and Clay Blair, *A General's Life: an autobiography* (New York, 1983)

Brasted, H. V. and Carl Bridge, 'The transfer of power in South Asia', *South Asia*, xvii (1994), 93–114

Brower, Charles F. (ed.), *World War Two in Europe: the final year* (London, 1998) for essays by Warren Kimball, David Reynolds and David Eisenhower

Brown, Judith M., *Gandhi: prisoner of hope* (New Haven, Conn., 1989)

—, *Nehru: a political life* (London, 2003)

Brown, Judith M., William Roger Louis and Alaine Low (eds.), *The Oxford History of the British Empire*, vol. iv: *The twentieth century* (Oxford, 1999)

Bryant, Arthur, *Triumph in the West, 1943–1946* (London, 1959)

Bullock, Alan, *The Life and Times of Ernest Bevin*, 3 vols. (London, 1960–83)*

Butler, David and Gareth Butler, *British Political Facts, 1900–1994* (Basingstoke, 1994)

Butler, R. A., *The Art of the Possible: the memoirs of Lord Butler* (paperback edn, Harmondsworth, 1973)

Byrnes, James F., *Speaking Frankly* (London, 1947)

Cain, P. J. and A. G. Hopkins, *British Imperialism: crisis and deconstruction, 1914–1990* (London, 1993)

Cairncross, Alec, *Years of Recovery: British economic policy, 1945–51* (London, 1985)

Cannadine, David, *Ornamentalism: how the British saw their empire* (London, 2001)

Chace, James, *Acheson* (New York, 1998)

Charmley, John, *Churchill: the end of glory* (London, 1993)

—, *Churchill's Grand Alliance: the Anglo-American special relationship, 1940–57* (London, 1995)

Churchill, Winston S., *Blood, Sweat and Tears: speeches 1938–40*, ed. Randolph S. Churchill (New York, 1941); British title: *Into Battle* (London, 1941)

—, *End of the Beginning: speeches 1942*, ed. Charles Eade (London, 1943)

—, *The Unrelenting Struggle: speeches 1940–1*, ed. Charles Eade (London, 1942)

—, *The World Crisis, 1911–18*, 2-vol. edn (London, 1938)

Clarke, Peter, *The Cripps Version: the life of Sir Stafford Cripps* (London, 2002)*

Clarke, Peter and Clive Trebilcock, *Understanding Decline: perceptions and realities of British economic performance* (Cambridge, 1997) for essays by Charles Feinstein, Peter Clarke and Jose Harris

Clarke, Richard, *Anglo-American Economic Collaboration in War and Peace, 1942–1949*, ed. Alec Cairncross (Oxford, 1982)

Cohen, Michael J., *Palestine to Israel: from mandate to independence* (London, 1988)*

Dallas, Gregor, *Poisoned Peace, 1945* (London, 2005)*

Dalton, Hugh, *High Tide and After: memoirs 1945–1960*, (London, 1962)

Davies, Norman, *Europe at War, 1939–45: no simple victory* (London, 2006)

D'Este, Carlo, *Eisenhower* (New York, 2002)*

—, *Patton: a genius for war* (New York, 1995)

Dilks, David, *The Conference at Potsdam, 1945* (Hull, 1996)

Dobson, Alan P., *The Politics of the Anglo-American Economic Special Relationship, 1940–1987* (Brighton, 1988)*

Edmonds, Robin, *The Big Three: Churchill, Roosevelt and Stalin in peace and war* (London, 1991)

Edwards, Jerome E., *The Foreign Policy of Col. McCormick's Tribune, 1929–1941* (Reno, Nevada, 1971)

Elstob, Peter, *Hitler's Last Offensive* (London, 1971)

Farago, Ladislas, *Patton: ordeal and triumph* (New York, 1963)

Feis, Herbert, *Between War and Peace: the Potsdam Conference* (Princeton, NJ, 1960)*

Ferguson, Niall, *The War of the World* (London, 2006)

French, Patrick, *Liberty or Death: India's journey to independence and division* (London, 1997)*

Fussell, Paul, *Wartime: understanding and behavior in the Second World War* (New York, 1989)

Gallagher, John, *The Decline, Revival, and Fall of the British Empire*, ed. Anil Seal (Cambridge, 1982)

Gallagher, John and Ronald Robinson, 'The imperialism of free trade', *Economic History Review*, 2nd ser., vi (1953), 1–15

Gandhi, *The Collected Works of Mahatma Gandhi*, vol. lxxxiv (New Delhi, 1981)

Gardner, R. N., *Sterling–Dollar Diplomacy in Current Perspective* (New York, 1980)

Gilbert, Martin, *Churchill and America* (New York, 2005)

Gopal, Sarvepalli, *Jawaharlal Nehru: a biography*, vol. i: *1889–1947* (London, 1975)

— (ed.), *Selected Works of Jawaharlal Nehru*, vols. vii–xv (New Delhi, 1975–80)

Gormly, James L., *From Potsdam to the Cold War: Big Three diplomacy, 1945–1947* (Wilmington, Delaware, 1990)

Granatstein, J. L., *How Britain's Weakness Forced Canada into the Arms of the United States* (Toronto, 1989)

Halamish, Aviva, *The Exodus Affair* (Syracuse, NY, 1998)

Hamilton, Nigel, *The Full Monty* (paperback edn, London, 2002)

—, *Monty*, 3 vols. (paperback edn, Sevenoaks, 1984–7)

Harris, Kenneth, *Attlee* (London, 1982)

Harrod, Roy F., *The Life of John Maynard Keynes* (London, 1951)

Hastings, Max, *Armageddon: the battle for Germany, 1944–5*, paperback edn (London, 2005)*

Heller, Joseph, *The Stern Gang* (London, 1995)

Hennessy, Peter, *Never Again: Britain, 1945–51* (London, 1992)

Hogan, Michael J., *The Marshall Plan* (Cambridge, 1987)

Howard, Anthony, *Crossman: the pursuit of power* (London, 1990)

Ignatieff, Michael, *Isaiah Berlin: a life* (London, 1998)

Jalal, Ayesha, *The Sole Spokesman: Jinnah, the Muslim League, and the demand for Pakistan* (Cambridge, 1985)

Jay, Douglas, *Change and Fortune: a political record* (London, 1980)

Jenkins, Roy, *Churchill* (London, 2001)

Kazimi, Muhammad Reza, *Liaquat Ali Khan: his life and work* (Oxford, 2003)

Keegan, John, *The Battle for History: refighting World War Two* (Toronto, 1995)

Kennedy, Paul, *The Parliament of Man: the United Nations and the quest for world government* (London, 2006)

—, *The Rise and Fall of the Great Powers* (paperback edn, London, 1988)

Kershaw, Ian, *Hitler, 1936–45: nemesis* (London, 2000)

Kimball, Warren F., *Forged in War: Roosevelt, Churchill, and the Second World War* (New York, 1997)*

—, *The Most Unsordid Act; Lend-Lease, 1939–1941* (Baltimore, Maryland, 1969)

— (ed.), *Churchill and Roosevelt : the complete correspondence*, 3 vols. (Princeton, NJ, 1984)

Lane, Ann and Howard Temperley (eds.), *The Rise and Fall of the Grand Alliance* (London, 1995) for essays by Kathleen Burk, Correlli Barnett and Norman A. Graebner

Louis, William Roger, *The British Empire in the Middle East, 1945–1951* (Oxford, 1984)*

—, *Imperialism at Bay, 1941–1945: the United States and the decolonization of the British Empire* (Oxford, 1977)*

MacDonald, Charles B., *A Time for Trumpets: the untold story of the Battle of the Bulge* (New York, 1997)

Mackenzie, Hector, 'Justice denied: the Anglo-American loan negotiations of 1945', *Canadian Review of American Studies*, xxvi (1996) 79–110

Macmillan, Harold, *The Blast of War, 1939–1945* (London, 1967)

McCallum, R. B. and Alison Readman, *The British General Election of 1945* (London, 1947)

McCullough, David G., *Truman* (New York, 1992)

McJimsey, George, *Harry Hopkins* (Cambridge, Mass., 1987)

Mclachlan, Donald, *In the Chair: Barrington-Ward of The Times, 1927–1948* (London, 1971)

Meachem, Jon, *Franklin and Winston: a portrait of a friendship* (London, 2004)

Mee, Charles L., *Meeting at Potsdam* (London, 1975)

Menon, V. P., *The Transfer of Power in India* (London, 1957)

Milward, Alan S., *The Reconstruction of Western Europe 1945–51* (London, 1984)

—, *The Rise and Fall of a National Strategy, 1945–63* (London, 2002)

Mitchell, B. R., *British Historical Statistics* (Cambridge, 1988)

Moggridge, D. E., *Maynard Keynes: an economist's biography* (London, 1992).*

Montefiore, Simon Sebag, *Stalin: the court of the Red Tsar* (London, 2003)

Montgomery, *The Memoirs of Field Marshal Viscount Montgomery of Alamein* (London, 1958)

Moore, R. J., *Escape from Empire: the Attlee government and the Indian problem* (Oxford, 1983)*

Morgan, Sir Frederick, *Overture to Overlord* (London, 1950)

Morris, Benny, *The Birth of the Palestinian Refugee Problem Revisited* (Cambidge, 2004)

Murray, G. E. Patrick, *Eisenhower versus Montgomery: the continuing debate* (Westport, Conn., 1996)

Nobécourt, Jacques, *Hitler's Last Gamble: the battle of the Ardennes* (London, 1967)

Ovendale, Ritchie, *Britain, the United States, and the End of the Palestine Mandate, 1942–1948* (London, 1989)*

Overy, Richard, *Why the Allies Won* (London, 1995)

Owen, Nicholas, 'The Conservative party and Indian independence, 1945–7', *Historical Journal*, xlvi (2003), 403–36.*

—, 'The Cripps Mission of 1942', *Journal of Imperial and Commonwealth History*, xxx (2002), 61–98

Pelling, Henry, *Britain and the Marshall Plan* (London, 1988)

Pimlott, Ben, *Hugh Dalton* (London, 1985)

Porch, Douglas, *The Path to Victory: the Mediterranean theater in World War II* (New York, 2005); British title: *Hitler's Mediterranean Gamble**

Porter, Bernard, *The Absent-Minded Imperialists* (Oxford, 2004)

Pressnell, L. S., *The Post-War Financial Settlement* (London, 1986)*

Reid, Robert R., *The Front Page Story of World War II* (Vancouver, BC, 1994)

Reynolds, David, *The Creation of the Anglo-American Alliance 1937–41* (London, 1981)*

—, *Rich Relations: the American occupation of Britain, 1942–1945* (London, 1996)

—, 'The Origins of the Two "World Wars"', *Journal of Contemporary History*, xxxviii (2003), 29–44

—, *In Command of History: Churchill fighting and writing the Second World War* (London, 2004)*

Reynolds, David, Warren F. Kimball and A. O. Chubarian (eds.), *Allies at War: the Soviet, American, and British Experience, 1939–1945* (Basingstoke, 1994)

Roberts, Andrew, *The History of the English-Speaking Peoples in the Twentieth Century* (London, 2006)

Rose, Norman, *Churchill: an unruly life* (London, 1994)

Sayers, R. S., *Financial Policy, 1939–45* (London, 1956)

Schofield, Victoria, *Wavell: soldier and statesman* (London, 2006)

Sherman, A. J., *Mandate Days: British lives in Palestine, 1918–1948* (London, 1997)

Sherwood, Robert, *Roosevelt and Hopkins* (New York, 1948)*

Singh, Anita Inder, *The Origins of the Partition of India 1936–1947* (Delhi, 1987)

Sissons, Michael and Philip French (eds.), *Age of Austerity, 1945–51* (London, 1963) for essays by David Leitch and John Higgins

Skidelsky, Robert, *John Maynard Keynes*, vol. iii: *Fighting for Britain, 1937–1946* (London, 2000)*

Stafford, David, *Roosevelt and Churchill: men of secrets* (London, 1999)

Staley, Eugene, 'The economic implications of Lend-Lease', *American Economic Review*, xxxiii (1943), 362–76

Strawson, John, *The Battle for the Ardennes* (London, 1972)

Thomas, Hugh, *Armed Truce: the beginnings of the Cold War, 1945–46* (paperback edn, (Sevenoaks, 1988)*

Thompson, John A., 'Another look at the downfall of "Fortress America"', *Journal of American Studies*, xxvi (1992), 393–408

—, 'Conceptions of national security and American entry into World War II', *Diplomacy and Statecraft*, xvi (2005), 671–97

Thompson, W. H., *Assignment Churchill* (London, 1955)

Thorne, Christopher, *Allies of a Kind: the United States, Britain and the war against Japan 1941–1945* (Oxford, 1979)*

Thorpe, D. R., *Eden: the life and times of Anthony Eden* (London, 2003)

Tippett, Maria, *Portrait in Light and Shadow: the life of Yousuf Karsh* (Toronto, 2007)

Tiratsoo, Nick (ed.), *The Attlee Years* (London, 1991) for essay on India by Nick Owen

Toland, John, *The Last 100 Days* (New York, 1965)

Tomlinson, B. R., *The Political Economy of the Raj, 1914–1947* (London, 1979)

Toye, Richard, 'The Attlee government, the imperial preference system, and the creation of the GATT', *English Historical Review*, cxviii (2003), 912–39

—, 'Churchill and Britain's "Financial Dunkirk"', *Twentieth Century British History*, xv (2004), 329–60*

—, *The Labour Party and the Planned Economy, 1931–1951* (Woodbridge, 2003)

Truman, Harry S., *Memoirs*, vol. i (Garden City, NY, 1955)

Vaughan-Thomas, Wynford (introduction), *Great Front Pages: D-Day to victory, 1944–5* (London, 1984)

Walton, Calder, 'British intelligence and the mandate of Palestine', *Intelligence and National Security*, xxii (2007)

Watt, Donald Cameron, *How War Came* (London, 1989)

—, *Succeeding John Bull: America in Britain's place 1900–1975* (Cambridge, 1984)

Wheeler-Bennett, John, *King George VI* (London, 1958)

Williams, Francis, *A Prime Minister Remembers: the war and post-war memoirs of the Rt. Hon. Earl Attlee* (London, 1961)

Wilmot, Chester, *The Struggle for Europe* (London, 1952)*

Woods, Randall Bennett, *A Changing of the Guard: Anglo-American relations, 1941–46* (Chapel Hill, NC, 1990)*

Wybrow, Robert J., *British Political Opinion 1937–2000: the Gallup polls*, ed. Anthony King (London, 2001)

Ziegler, Philip, *Mountbatten* (New York, 1985)

References

PREFACE

1. To the House of Commons, then broadcast, 18 June 1940. Churchill, *Blood, Sweat and Tears*, p. 314; *Into Battle*, p. 234.
2. Kennedy, *Great Powers*, p. 475.
3. Churchill, *Blood, Sweat and Tears*, p. 314, cf. p. 307; *Into Battle*, p. 234, cf. p. 227.
4. Churchill, *End of the Beginning*, p. 215 (10 November 1942).
5. Brown, Louis and Low (eds.), *Oxford History of the British Empire*, iv, 5.
6. Cadogan, 23 May 1945, p. 745.
7. Robbins, 11 Oct. 1945, p. 233.
8. I paraphrase Gallagher and Robinson, *EHR*, vi, 15; cf. Gallagher, *Decline, Revival, and Fall of the British Empire*.

PROLOGUE

1. Churchill, *World Crisis*, ii, p. 1122.
2. Jenkins, *Churchill*, p. 457.
3. Gilbert, viii, pp. 1122-3.
4. Tippett, *Karsh*, ch. 7.
5. Churchill, *Blood, Sweat and Tears*, p. 276; *Into Battle*, p. 208.
6. Churchill, *Blood, Sweat and Tears*, p. 297; *Into Battle*, p. 223.
7. Churchill, *Blood, Sweat and Tears*, p. 351; *Into Battle*, p. 262; cf. Reynolds, *Creation of the Anglo-American Alliance*, pp. 129-31.
8. *FDR–WSC*, 4 June 1944, p. 10.
9. Thorne, *Allies of a Kind*, p. 119.
10. *SWW*, i, p. 345.
11. Reynolds, *In Command of History*, p. 52.
12. Morgenthau, Aug. 1944, p. 337.
13. Reynolds, *Creation*, p. 165.
14. Text of Atlantic Charter in Cadogan, pp. 400-401.
15. 9 September 1941, Reynolds, *Creation of the Anglo-American Alliance*, p. 259.
16. Louis, *Imperialism at Bay*, p. 125.
17. Morgenthau, 17 Dec. 1940, pp. 208-9.
18. Kimball, *Forged in War*, p. 72.
19. Churchill, *Unrelenting Struggle*, p. 60.
20. *TT*, 3 Nov. 1941.
21. Churchill, *Unrelenting Struggle*, pp. 296, 298; 'the most unsordid act in the history of

any nation' in *SWW*, ii, p. 503, cited as a speech to Parliament; cf. Reynolds, *Creation of the Anglo-American Alliance*, p. 161, citing PREM notes.

22. *JMK*, xxiii, pp. 87–8.
23. ibid., xxiii, p. 106.
24. ibid., xxiii, p. 86.
25. Cadogan, p. 400.
26. Gardner, *Sterling–Dollar Diplomacy*, pp. 58–9.
27. Kimball, *Most Unsordid Act*, pp. 207, 217.
28. Black, *Roosevelt*, p. 595.
29. Vandenberg, 28 October 1944, p. 123.
30. Edwards, *Foreign Policy of McCormick*, pp. 176–85, 189; cf. Kimball, *Forged in War*, pp. 75–6, 124
31. *SWW*, iii, p. 538.
32. ibid., p. 539.
33. Reynolds, *Creation of the Anglo-American Alliance*, p. 221.
34. Staley, *AER*, xxxiii, 367n; Thorne, *Allies of a Kind*, pp. 111, 506.
35. Thorne, *Allies of a Kind*, p. 138.
36. *SWW*, iv, p. 185.
37. Kimball (ed.), *Churchill and Roosevelt*, i, pp. 400–402.
38. *FDR–WSC*, 4 March 1942, p. 184.
39. *SWW*, iv, p. 190.
40. *TOP*, i, pp. 403–4.
41. Gilbert, vii, p. 78.
42. Clarke, *Cripps*, p. 305.
43. *FRUS* 1942, i, p. 631.
44. *FDR–WSC*, 11 April 1942, pp. 202–3.
45. Kimball (ed.), *Churchill and Roosevelt*, i, p. 448.
46. *NYT*, 13 April 1942.
47. Thorne, *Allies of a Kind*, p. 358.
48. *JMK*, xxiii, pp. 224–5.
49. 10 January 1942, Pressnell, *Post-War Financial Settlement*, p. 51.
50. Facsimile, 5 Feb. 1942, in ibid., pp. 384–6.
51. *WSC–FDR*, p. 176.
52. Gardner, *Sterling–Dollar Diplomacy*, p. 65.
53. Kennedy, *Great Powers*, tables 34 and 38, pp. 455, 458.
54. Mitchell, *British Historical Statistics*, pp. 840–41.
55. £1 = $4.03. Simplified from Sayers, *Financial Policy*, table 12, p. 501, which includes other items that complicate the accounts – and also make them balance exactly.
56. 13 Aug. 1945, *JMK*, xxiv, p. 399.
57. Robbins, 13 May 1943, p. 19.
58. Robbins, 2 June 1943, p. 52.
59. Robbins 15 June 1943, p. 72.
60. Robbins, 23 June 1943, p. 84.
61. Gardner, *Sterling–Dollar Diplomacy*, p. 97.
62. *JMK*, xxvi, p. 10 (23 May 1944).
63. ibid., pp. 27–9.
64. Gardner, *Sterling–Dollar Diplomacy*, p. 111.
65. Robbins, 24 June 1944, pp. 158–9.
66. Robbins, 30 June 1944, p. 166.
67. Robbins, 22 July 1944, p. 193.
68. Reynolds, *Creation of the Anglo-American Alliance*, pp. 191–2.
69. Porch, *Path to Victory*, pp, 328, 280.
70. Kimball, *Forged in War*, p. 153
71. *SWW*, iv, p. 59; House of Commons, 27 Jan. 1942.

72. *TT*, 24 Oct. 1945.
73. Wilmot, *Struggle for Europe*, p. 341.
74. Butcher diary, 3 June 1943, quoted in Hamilton, *Monty*, ii, p. 333.
75. *SWW*, iv, p. 662.
76. *TT*, 21 Sep. 1944.
77. Dalton, 1–2 Jan. 1944, *War Diary*, p. 693.
78. Porch, *Path to Victory*, pp. 680–81.
79. Dalton, 9 May 1945, *War Diary*, p. 857.
80. Kimball, *Forged in War*, p. 170.
81. Thorne, *Allies of a Kind*, p. 275.
82. Cadogan, p. 400.
83. Butcher, 9 Aug. 1944, pp. 637–8.
84. *NYT*, 1 Aug. 1944.
85. *TT*, 5 Aug. 1944; *NYT* 2 Aug. 1944.
86. *NC*, 22 and 23 Aug. 1944.
87. *DM*, 25 Aug. 1944.
88. Chips, 23, 25 and 31 Aug. 1944, pp. 478–9.
89. *SWW*, vi, p. 124.

CHAPTER 1: THE SPIRIT OF QUEBEC

1. *G&M*, 12 Sep. 1944.
2. Gilbert, vii, p. 968.
3. *SWW*, vi, p. 58.
4. Kimball, *Forged in War*, p. 182.
5. Gilbert, vii, p. 852.
6. Butler, *Art of the Possible*, p. 91.
7. Gilbert, viii, p. 468.
8. Amery, 4 Sep. 1944, p. 998.
9. Colville, 14 Aug. 1944, p. 130.
10. Alanbrooke, 14 Aug. 1944, p. 580.
11. Alanbrooke, 15 Aug. 1943, p. 441.
12. Amery, 6 Sep. 1944, p. 998.
13. Morgenthau, 17 Aug. 1944, p. 340.
14. Cadogan 15 Sept., p. 665.
15. Alanbrooke, 8 and 9 Sep. 1944, pp. 589–90; cf. Bryant, *Triumph in the West*, pp. 269–70.
16. Alanbrooke, 8 Sep. 1944, p. 589.
17. Kimball, *Forged in War*, p. 246.
18. Porch, *Path to Victory*, p. 629.
19. King, 12 Sep. 1944, *Record*, p. 71; cf. *SWW*, vi, pp. 57, 65.
20. Alanbrooke, 10 Sep. 1944, p. 590.
21. Colville, 7 Sep. 1944, p. 139.
22. *SWW*, vi, p. 131.
23. King, 11 Sep. 1944, *Record*, pp. 65, 67.
24. Moran, p. 219.
25. King, 12 Sep. 1944.
26. Gilbert, vii, p. 969.
27. King, 11 Sep. 1944, *Record*, p. 67.
28. *SWW*, vi, pp. 132–3.
29. Moran, 20 Sep. 1944, p. 224.
30. King, 13 Sep. 1944.
31. *SWW*, vi, p. 133.

32. ibid., p. 129.
33. Alanbrooke, p. xlviii.
34. Alanbrooke, 12, 13, 14 and 15 Sep. 1944, pp. 591–3.
35. King, 14 and 12 Sep. 1944.
36. King, 11 Sep. 1944, *Record*, pp. 65, 67.
37. King, 12 Sep. 1944, *Record*, p. 72.
38. King, 14 Sep. 1944, *Record*, p. 75.
39. Alanbrooke, 14 Sep. 1944, p. 593.
40. King, 14 Sep. 1944, *Record*, p. 82.
41. Amery 4 Sep. 1944 p. 998; cf. Dalton, p. 787.
42. Colville, 5 and 6 Sep. 1944, pp. 137–8.
43. Colville, 14 Sep. 1944, p. 144.
44. King, 14 Sep. 1944.
45. Berlin, 25 Jan. 1945, *Flourishing*, p. 523.
46. Moran, 13 Sep. 1944, p. 216.
47. *New York Post*, 24–9 Nov. 1947, in Morgenthau, p. 369.
48. Moran, 13 Sep. 1944, p. 217.
49. Morgenthau, 15 Sep. 1944, p. 370.
50. Morgenthau, 29 Sep. 1944, p. 379.
51. Morgenthau, 17 Aug. 1944, p. 341.
52. Butcher, 19 Sep. 1944, p. 669.
53. Morgenthau, 23 Aug. 1944, p. 344.
54. Gilbert, vi, p. 798.
55. ibid., p. 1035.
56. Morgenthau, (23) Aug. 1944, p. 336.
57. Morgenthau, 19 Aug. 1944, p. 308.
58. King, 11 Sep. 1944, *Record*, p. 67.
59. Reynolds, *Creation of the Anglo-American Alliance*, p. 117.
60. ibid., p. 136.
61. Morgenthau, 19 Aug. 1944, p. 309.
62. Morgenthau, 25 Aug. 1944, p. 310.
63. Agreed record, 14 Sep. 1944, *JMK*, xxiv, pp. 126–7.
64. Colville, 14 Sep. 1944, p. 145.
65. Morgenthau, p. 373.
66. Colville, 15 Sep. 1944, p. 145.
67. King, 14 Sep. 1944, *Record*, p. 78.

CHAPTER 2: SETBACKS

1. Macmillan, 8 Oct. 1944, p. 544.
2. Colville, 8 Oct. 1944, p. 156.
3. Moran, 9 Oct. 1944, p. 236.
4. Alanbrooke, 10 Oct. 1944, p. 603.
5. Gilbert, vii, p. 991.
6. Moran, 8 Oct. 1944, p. 234.
7. Gilbert, vii, pp. 991–2.
8. Ian Jacob, 26 Oct. 1944, in Gilbert, vii, p. 992n.
9. Reynolds, *In Command of History*, pp. 458–9.
10. *SWW*, vi, p. 203.
11. Gilbert, vii, p. 1002.
12. ibid., p. 1008; cf. Dallas, *Poisoned Peace*, pp. 81–3.
13. Gilbert, vii, pp. 1013–14.
14. ibid., p. 1028.

15. Moran, 16 Oct. 1944, p. 248.
16. Alanbrooke, 12 Oct. 1944, p. 604.
17. *SWW*, vi, p. 175.
18. *DM*, 1 Sep. 1944; cf. Butcher, p. 653.
19. Eisenhower, *Crusade in Europe*, p. 243.
20. Butcher, 18 April 1944, p. 525.
21. Morgan, *Overture to Overlord*, p. 275.
22. Wilmot, *Struggle for Europe*, p. 338.
23. ibid., p. 468.
24. Butcher, 7 Sep. 1944, p. 657.
25. Bradley and Blair, *General's Life*, p. 31.
26. Butcher, 20 Nov. 1944, p. 702.
27. Eisenhower, *Crusade in Europe*, p. 306.
28. Reynolds, *Rich Relations*, pp. 393–4.
29. Wilmot, *Struggle for Europe*, p. 489.
30. Blumenson, *Patton Papers*, p. 539.
31. ibid., p. 550.
32. ibid., p. 533.
33. Butcher, 24 Sep. and 29 Oct. 1944, pp. 671–2, 694.
34. Blumenson, *Patton Papers*, p. 548.
35. Eisenhower, *Crusade in Europe*, p. 312.
36. Butcher, 24 Sep. 1944, p. 675.
37. Montgomery, *Memoirs*, pp. 297–8.
38. Wilmot, *Struggle for Europe*, p. 518n.
39. Alanbrooke, 5 Oct. 1944, p. 600.
40. Cadogan, 30 Oct. 1944, p. 676.
41. Alanbrooke, 9 Nov. 1944, p. 620.
42. Alanbrooke, 20 Oct. 1944, p. 612.
43. Gilbert, vii, p. 1047.
44. Chips, 7 Nov. 1944, p. 483.
45. Cadogan, 6 Nov. 1944, p. 678.
46. Meinertzhagen, 28 April 1944, pp. 190–91; cf. p. 204.
47. Rose, *Churchill*, p. 157.
48. Gilbert, v, p. 847.
49. Amery, p. 364.
50. Gilbert, v, p. 847.
51. Gilbert, v, p. 1070
52. Gilbert, vii p. 1049.
53. Alanbrooke, 6 Nov. 1944, p. 618.
54. Amery, 6 Nov. 1944, p. 1018.
55. Sherwood, *Roosevelt and Hopkins*, p. 830.
56. Vandenberg, p. 124.
57. *Economist*, 11 Nov. 1944, pp. 631–2.
58. 5 HL Debs., cxxiii, 199 (9 June 1942).
59. Gilbert, vi, p. 1163.
60. 5 HL Debs, cxxiii, 199 (9 June 1942).
61. *TT*, 18 Nov. 1944.
62. Berlin, *Flourishing*, p. 690.
63. Berlin, 9 Aug. 1943, ibid., pp. 443–51, at pp. 449, 450.
64. Ignatieff, *Isaiah Berlin*, pp. 117–18.
65. Baffy, ?7 Nov. (misdated 5 Nov.), 9 Nov. 1944, pp. 217–18.

CHAPTER 3: BAD TO WORSE

1. Colville, 26 Nov. 1944, p. 162.
2. Morgenthau, mid-Nov. 1944, pp. 319–20.
3. Morgenthau, 17 Nov. 1944, p. 382.
4. Cadogan, 21 Nov. 1944, p. 682.
5. Alanbrooke, 17 Nov. 1944, pp. 626–7.
6. Macmillan, *Blast of War*, p. 246.
7. Dalton, 1–2 Jan 1944, *War Diary*, p. 693.
8. Cadogan, 23 Nov. 1944, p. 682.
9. Amery, 23 Nov. 1944, p. 1020.
10. Alanbrooke, 24 Nov. 1944, p. 628; cf. Bryant, *Triumph in the West*, p. 338.
11. D'Este, *Eisenhower*, p. 489; cf. pp. 324–6.
12. Alanbrooke, 26 Nov. 1944, p. 629.
13. Alanbrooke, 27 Nov. 1944, p. 629.
14. Alanbrooke, 28 Nov. 1944, pp. 629–30.
15. Dalton, 28 Nov. 1944, *War Diary*, p. 810.
16. Amery, 28 Nov. 1944, pp. 1010–11.
17. Macmillan, 28 Nov. 1944, p. 593.
18. Amery, 30 Nov. 1944, p. 1021.
19. Colville, 30 Nov. 1944, pp. 163–4.
20. Cadogan, 1 Dec. 1944, p. 684.
21. Alanbrooke, 2 Dec. 1944, p. 631.
22. *FDR–WSC*, 3 Dec. 1944, p. 615.
23. *JMK*, xxiv, pp. 167–8.
24. Morgenthau, 18 Nov. 1944, p. 320.
25. Stettinius, 21 Nov. 1944, p. 175.
26. Morgenthau, 21 Nov. 1944, p. 320.
27. Stettinius, 21 Nov. 1944, p. 176.
28. Thorne, *Allies of a Kind*, pp. 111, 145, 279, 392, 506n.
29. Forrestal, 23 Nov. 1944, pp. 36–7.
30. Colville, 25 Nov. 1944, p. 162.
31. *FDR–WSC*, 28 Nov. 1944, p. 610.
32. Stettinius, 26 Nov. 1944, pp. 278–80.
33. *JMK*, xxiv, p. 188.
34. ibid., p. 204.
35. *TT*, 1 Dec. 1944.
36. Stettinius, 22 Dec. 1944, p. 204.
37. *TT*, 1 Dec. 1944.
38. Baruch letter, 1 Dec. 1944, Morgenthau, p. 323.
39. Morgenthau, 27 Nov. 1944, p. 392.
40. Stettinius, 27 Nov. 1944, p. 184.
41. *WD*, 27 Nov 1944, p. 465.
42. Cadogan, 26 Nov. 1944, p. 684.
43. Gilbert, vii, 994.
44. Macmillan, 28 Nov. 1944, p. 593.
45. *WD*, 2 Dec. 1944, p. 467.
46. Alanbrooke, 4 Dec. 1944, p. 632. This offensive comment was clearly directed at Eisenhower, not Bradley, as Bryant's eviscerated version of 1959 ambiguously implied; *Triumph in the West*, p. 346.
47. Macmillan, 4 Dec. 1944, p. 596.
48. Colville, 4 Dec. 1944, pp. 166–7.
49. *SWW*, vi, 252–3.

50. Colville, 4 Dec. 1944, pp. 166–7.
51. Nicolson, ii, 415 (5 Dec. 1944).
52. Alanbrooke, 5 Dec 1944, p. 632.
53. Colville, 5 Dec. 1944, p. 168.
54. Macmillan, 5 Dec. 1944, p. 597.
55. Dalton, 5 Dec. 1944, *War Diary*, pp. 810–12.
56. Sherwood, *Roosevelt and Hopkins,* pp. 838–9.
57. *FDR–WSC*, pp. 619–21.
58. ibid., pp. 616–19.
59. Macmillan, 7 Dec. 1944, pp. 598–9.
60. Amery, 7 Dec. 1944, p. 1021.
61. Colville, 7 Dec. 1944, p. 168.
62. Cadogan, 8 Dec. 1944, pp. 685–6.
63. Colville, 8 Dec. 1944, p. 168.
64. Nicolson, ii, p. 417 (8 Dec. 1944).
65. Macmillan, 8 Dec. 1944, p. 599.
66. Nicolson, ii, p. 416 (8 Dec. 1944).
67. Amery, 8 Dec. 1944, p. 1022.
68. Dalton, 8 Dec. 1944, *War Diary*, pp. 813–14.
69. Commons, 8 Dec. 1944, *SWW*, vi, pp. 256–8; cf. Sherwood, *Roosevelt and Hopkins*, p. 839.
70. MO 2454; cf. Reynolds, *Rich Relations*, pp, 103, 393.
71. MO 2229 (April 1944).
72. Sherwood, *Roosevelt and Hopkins*, p. 840 (10 Dec. 1944).
73. Alanbrooke, 11 Dec. 1944, p. 634.
74. Sherwood, *Roosevelt and Hopkins*, p. 841.
75. *WD*, 10 Dec. 1944, p. 473.
76. Alanbrooke, 12 Dec. 1944, pp. 634–5.
77. Alanbrooke, 13 Dec. 1944, p. 635.
78. Butcher, 16 Dec. 1944, p. 723.
79. Macmillan, 8 and 9 Dec. 1944, p. 600.
80. Colville, 11 and 12 Dec. 1944, p. 169.
81. Dalton, e.g. 27 Feb. 1941, *War Diary*, p. 167.
82. Amery, 13 Dec. 1944, p. 1022.
83. Dalton, 13 Dec. 1944, *War Diary*, p. 816.
84. Bullock, *Bevin*, ii, pp. 344–5.
85. *FDR–WSC*, 15 Dec 1944, p. 630.
86. *WD*, 17 Dec. 1944, pp. 476–7.
87. Colville, 14 and 15 Dec. 1944, pp. 170–71.
88. *SWW*, vi, pp. 263–4, cf. Sherwood, *Roosevelt and Hopkins*, p. 842.
89. Stettinius, 18 Dec. 1944, p. 200.
90. *WD*, 24 Dec. 1944, pp. 481–3.
91. Macmillan, 15 Dec. 1944, p. 607.
92. Butcher, 16 Dec. 1944, p. 722.
93. Alanbrooke, 13 Dec. 1944, p. 635.

CHAPTER 4: BATTLES OF THE BULGE

1. To Albert Speer, Kershaw, *Hitler*, ii, p. 732.
2. 11–12 Dec. 1944, Kershaw, *Hitler*, ii, p. 743.
3. Cadogan, 18 Dec. 1944, p. 688.
4. Nicolson, ii, p. 419 (18 Dec 1944).
5. Alanbrooke, 18 Dec. 1944, p. 636.

6. Nicolson, ii, 419 (19 Dec. 1944).
7. Butcher, 23 Dec. 1944, p. 730.
8. Butcher, 22 Dec. 1944, p. 724.
9. Alanbrooke, 20 Dec 1944, p. 637.
10. D'Este, *Eisenhower*, p. 648.
11. Butcher, 26 Feb. 1945, p. 763.
12. Butcher, 23 Dec. 1944, p. 730.
13. Wilmot, *Struggle for Europe*, p. 592.
14. Bryant, *Triumph in the West*, p. 367; Hamilton, *Monty*, iii, p. 219.
15. Alanbrooke, 30 Dec. 1944, p. 638.
16. Hamilton, *Monty*, iii, p. 279; D'Este, *Eisenhower*, pp. 656–7.
17. Cadogan, 16 Dec. 1944, p. 687.
18. Cadogan, 17 Dec. 1944, p. 688.
19. Macmillan, 19 Dec. 1944, p. 611.
20. Colville, 19 and 20 Dec. 1944, p. 171.
21. Nicolson, ii, p. 421 (20 Dec. 1944).
22. *SWW*, vi, pp. 255, 266.
23. Macmillan, *Blast of War*, p. 518.
24. Cadogan, 21 Dec. 1944, p. 689.
25. Eden diary, 21 Dec. 1944, in Cadogan, p. 689.
26. Macmillan, 21 Dec. 1944, p. 613.
27. Colville, 22 Dec. 1944, p. 172.
28. Gilbert, vii, p. 1115.
29. Macmillan, 25 Dec. 1944, p. 616.
30. Moran, 25 Dec. 1944, p. 256.
31. Colville, 26 Dec. 1944, p. 175.
32. *SWW*, vi, pp. 274–6.
33. Macmillan, 26 Dec. 1944, p. 617.
34. Colville, 26 Dec. 1944, p. 176.
35. Moran, 26 Dec 1944, p. 258.
36. Macmillan, 26 Dec. 1944, p. 618.
37. Moran, 26 Dec. 1944, p. 259.
38. Colville, 26 Dec. 1944, p. 180.
39. Macmillan, 26 Dec. 1944, p. 619.
40. Moran, 26 Dec. 1944, p. 260.
41. Moran, 27 Dec. 1944, p. 261.
42. Colville, 27 Dec. 1944, p. 182.
43. 26 Dec. 1944 but misdated 27 Dec. in *SWW*, vi, p. 273 (probably receipt date).
44. Macmillan, *Blast of War*, p. 525.
45. Macmillan, 27 Dec. 1944, p. 620.
46. Macmillan, 28 Dec. 1944, p. 629.
47. Nicolson, ii, p. 423 (30 Dec. 1944).
48. *WD*, 31 Dec. 1944, p. 487.
49. Cadogan, 3 Jan. 1945, p. 692.
50. Macmillan, 31 Dec. 1944, p. 631.
51. Alanbrooke, 30 Dec. 1944, p. 638.
52. Dalton, 21 Dec. 1944, *War Diary*, p. 821.
53. Amery, 28 Dec. 1944, p. 1023.
54. Cadogan, 27 Dec. 1944, p. 691.
55. Meade, 31 Dec. 1944, p. 21.
56. *WD*, 31 Dec. 1944, pp. 486, 488.
57. *WD*, 7 Jan. 1945, p. 494.
58. Thorne, *Allies of a Kind*, p. 108.
59. Berlin, 1 Feb. 1945, *Flourishing*, p. 528.

60. *Economist*, 30 Dec. 1944, pp. 857–8.
61. *WD*, 7 Jan. 1945, p. 494.
62. *NYT*, 7 Jan. 1945.
63. *WD*, 7 Jan. 1945, p. 493.
64. *NYT*, 7 Jan. 1945.
65. *Economist*, 7 Jan. 1945, p. 1.
66. *DM*, 2 Jan. 1945.
67. *G&M*, 6 Nov. 2004.
68. MacDonald, *Time for Trumpets*, p. 614.
69. Butcher, 1 Jan. 1945, p. 737.
70. Alanbrooke, 13 Nov. 1944, p. 623.
71. Alanbrooke, 2 Jan. 1945, p. 641.
72. Colville, 2 Jan. 1945, p. 185.
73. Amery, 2 Jan. 1945, p. 1023.
74. Colville, 5 Jan. 1945, p. 186.
75. Alanbrooke, 3 Jan. 1945, p. 642.
76. Strawson, *Battle for the Ardennes*, p. 134; Hastings, *Armageddon*, p. 235. Davies, *Europe at War*, p. 25, gives 38,000 deaths overall (compared with 132,000 for OVERLORD, nearly a million at Stalingrad, and 4650 at El Alamein).
77. Eisenhower, *Crusade*, p. 356.
78. Bradley, *General's Life*, p. 382.
79. Montgomery, *Memoirs*, p. 311.
80. *WD*, 14 Jan. 1945, p. 497.
81. Colville, 9 Jan. 1945, p. 187.
82. Alanbrooke, 8 Jan, 1945, p. 644.
83. Bryant, *Triumph in the West*, p. 377.
84. Wilmot, *Struggle for Europe*, p. 611n.
85. Ingersoll in Murray, *Eisenhower versus Montgomery*, p. 21.
86. Butcher, 9 Jan. 1945, p. 740.
87. Hamilton, *Monty*, iii, p. 301.
88. *MA*, 9 Jan. 1945.
89. Hamilton, *Monty*, iii, p. 304.
90. Colville, 9 Jan. 1945, p. 188.
91. Hamilton, *Monty*, iii, p. 301.

CHAPTER 5: AWAITING THE BIG THREE

1. *FDR–WSC*, 19 Nov. 1944, p. 602.
2. Gilbert, vii, p. 1138.
3. Cadogan, 4 Jan. 1945, p. 692.
4. Colville, 10 and 11 Jan. 1945, pp. 188–9.
5. Macmillan, 11 and 12 Jan. 1945, pp. 643, 645.
6. Alanbrooke, 12 and 18 Jan, 1945, pp. 645–6.
7. Amery, 9 and 12 Jan. 1945, pp. 1023–4.
8. Forrestal, 11 Jan. 1945, p. 41.
9. Stettinius, 30 Dec. 1944, p. 208.
10. Vandenberg, 10 Jan. 1945, pp. 132–5.
11. *WD*, 14 Jan. 1945, pp. 498–9.
12. Louis, *Imperialism at Bay*, p. 383.
13. ibid., pp. 438–40.
14. ibid., pp. 431, 434.
15. Black, *Roosevelt*, p. 1039.
16. Cadogan, 17 Jan. 1945, p. 696.

17. *WD*, 21 Jan. 1945, p. 500.
18. Butcher, 19 Jan. 1945, p. 743.
19. Colville, 18 Jan. 1945, p. 192.
20. *SWW*, vi, p. 245.
21. Nicolson, ii, p. 429 (18 Jan. 1945).
22. McLachlan, *In the Chair*, pp. 252–3.
23. Moran, 14 Feb. 1945, p. 292.
24. Commons, 18 Jan. 1945, Gilbert, vii, p. 1151.
25. Thorne, *Allies of a Kind*, p. 515.
26. *DM*, 19 Jan. 1945.
27. Alanbrooke, 20 Jan. 1945. pp. 647–8.
28. Harris, *Attlee*, pp. 241–3.
29. Colville, 20 Jan. 1945, p. 192.
30. Colville, 21 Jan. 1945, p. 193; Gilbert, vii, p. 1156.
31. Alanbrooke, 22 Jan. 1945, p. 648.
32. Amery, 22 Jan. 1945, p. 1026.
33. Colville, 23 Jan. 1945, p. 194.
34. Reynolds, *JCH*, xxxviii, 39.
35. Wavell, 31 Dec. 1944, p. 108.
36. Louis, *Imperialism at Bay*, p. 283n.
37. Amery, 10 Sep. 1943, p. 938.
38. Wavell, 31 Dec. 1944 p. 108.
39. Amery, 13 Dec. 1944, p. 1023.
40. Amery, 15 Jan. 1945, p. 1025.
41. Amery, 19 Jan. 1945, p. 1026.
42. Wavell, 20 Jan. 1945, p. 111.
43. Amery, 19 Jan. 1945, p. 1026.
44. Wavell, 25 Jan. 1945, p. 111.
45. *WSC*, 1 Feb. 1945: Gilbert vii, p. 1166.
46. *FDR–WSC*, 21 Jan. 1945, p. 651.
47. Butcher, 27 Jan. 1945, p. 751.
48. Sherwood, *Roosevelt and Hopkins*, p. 847.
49. Butcher, 27 Jan. 1945, p. 750.
50. *FRUS* Yalta, p. 541.
51. Sherwood, *Roosevelt and Hopkins*, p. 848.
52. Alanbrooke, 31 Jan. 1945, p. 652.
53. Alanbrooke, 1 Feb. 1945, p. 653.
54. Moran, 30 Jan. 1945, pp. 264–5.
55. Cadogan, 30 Jan. 1945, p. 699.
56. Moran, 30 Jan. 1945, p. 265.
57. Cadogan, 31 Jan. and 1 Feb. 1945, pp. 700–701.
58. Alanbrooke, 1 Feb. 1945, p. 652.
59. Cadogan, 2 Feb. 1945, p. 701.
60. Stettinius, 1 Feb. 1945, pp. 231–3.
61. *FRUS* Yalta, p. 459.
62. Moran, 2 Feb. 1945, p. 266.
63. ibid.
64. Dalton, 2 Feb. 1945, *War Diary*, p. 827; *FRUS* Yalta, pp. 830–31.
65. Alanbrooke, 2 Feb. 1945, p. 654.
66. *FRUS* Yalta, pp. 541–6.
67. Alanbrooke, 3 Feb. 1945, p. 655.
68. Stettinius, 2 Feb. 1945, p. 234.
69. Thorpe, *Eden*, p. 304.
70. Gilbert, vii, p. 1169.

CHAPTER 6: YALTA

1. Moran, 3 Feb. 1945, p. 267.
2. Alanbrooke, 3 Feb. 1945, p. 655.
3. Cadogan, 4 Feb. 1945, p. 703.
4. Moran, 4 Feb. 1945, p. 270.
5. *SWW*, vi, p. 304.
6. *FRUS* Yalta, p. 486.
7. Alanbrooke, 4 Feb. 1945, p. 655.
8. Berlin, 24 Jan. 1945, *Flourishing*, p. 521.
9. *FRUS* Yalta, p. 570.
10. *FRUS* Yalta, pp. 572–3.
11. *FRUS* Yalta, p. 574.
12. Alanbrooke, 4 Feb. 1945, p. 655.
13. Alanbrooke, 5 Feb. 1945, p. 656.
14. ibid., p. 657.
15. Moran, 4 Feb. 1945, p. 273.
16. *FRUS* Yalta, p. 590.
17. Moran, 5 Feb. 1945, p. 274.
18. *FRUS* Yalta, p. 590.
19. Moran, 4 Feb. 1945, p. 272.
20. Moran, 7 Feb. 1945, p. 276.
21. Moran, 5 Feb. 1945, p. 274.
22. *FRUS* Yalta, p. 619.
23. Moran, 5 Feb. 1945, pp. 274–5.
24. *FRUS* Yalta, pp. 620–62. Bohlen's minutes say 'founded' (p. 622) but 'foundered' is obviously what Maisky meant.
25. Cadogan, 6 Feb. 1945, p. 704.
26. Cadogan, 7 Feb. 1945, p. 705.
27. *FRUS* Yalta, p. 673.
28. Stettinius, 6 Feb. 1945, p. 245.
29. *FRUS* Yalta, p. 675.
30. Moran, 6 Feb. 1945, p. 275.
31. *FRUS* Yalta, p. 723.
32. *FRUS* Yalta, p. 743.
33. *SWW*, vi, pp. 313–14.
34. *FRUS* Yalta, p. 747.
35. *FRUS* Yalta, p. 724.
36. Sherwood, *Roosevelt and Hopkins*, facsimile, p. 863.
37. Cadogan, 8 Feb 1945, p. 706.
38. Moran, 8 Feb. 1945, p. 277.
39. *FRUS* Yalta, p. 795.
40. Sherwood, *Hopkins and Roosevelt*, p. 870.
41. Moran, 7 Feb. 1945, p. 277.
42. Gilbert, vii, p. 1209.
43. *FRUS* Yalta, p. 668.
44. *FRUS* Yalta, pp. 669–70.
45. *FRUS* Yalta, p. 725.
46. *FRUS* Yalta, p. 911.
47. *FRUS* Yalta, p. 973.
48. *FRUS* Yalta, pp. 788–91.
49. Sherwood, *Roosevelt and Hopkins*, p. 870.
50. *SWW*, vi, p. 352.

51. Cadogan, 9 Feb. 1945, p. 707.
52. Alanbrooke, 8 Feb. 1945, p. 660.
53. *FRUS* Yalta, pp. 797–8.
54. Churchill, *Blood, Sweat and Tears*, p. 337.
55. *TT*, 27 March 1944.
56. *FRUS* Yalta, pp. 798–9.
57. *FRUS* Yalta, p. 844.
58. Byrnes, *Speaking Frankly*, p. x.
59. *FRUS* Yalta, p. 856.
60. *FRUS* Yalta, p. 858; Louis, *Imperialism at Bay*, pp. 459–60.
61. Moran, 9 Feb. 1945, p. 279.
62. Wilmot, *Struggle for Europe*, p. 639.
63. Moran, 9 Feb. 1945, p. 279.
64. Stettinius, 4 Feb. 1945, p. 237.
65. *FRUS* Yalta, p. 565.
66. Alanbrooke, 9 Feb. 1945, p. 661.
67. Gilbert, vii, p. 1207.
68. Sherwood, *Roosevelt and Hopkins*, p. 860; *FRUS* Yalta, p. 983.
69. *SWW*, vi, p. 342.
70. *FRUS* Yalta, p. 906.
71. Byrnes, *Speaking Frankly*, p. 22.
72. Stettinius, 2 Dec. 1944, p. 187; Sherwood, *Roosevelt and Hopkins*, p. 871.
73. Moran, 11 Feb. 1945, p. 281.
74. Sherwood, *Roosevelt and Hopkins*, p. 871.
75. Moran, 11 Feb. 1945, p. 281.
76. *FRUS* Yalta, pp. 970, 977–8.
77. Moran, 11 Feb. 1945, p. 282–3.
78. Cadogan, 11 Feb. 1945, pp. 708–9.
79. Moran, 11 Feb. 1945, pp. 284–5.
80. Reynolds, *In Command of History*, p. 473.
81. Moran, 11 Feb. 1945, p. 282.
82. Gilbert, vii, p. 1213.
83. Moran, 12 Feb. 1945, p. 286.
84. Addison, *Churchill*, p. 202.
85. Colville, 24 Feb. 1945, p. 204.
86. Moran, 11 Feb. 1945, p. 285.

CHAPTER 7: FALTERING AND ALTERING

1. Cadogan, 13 Feb. 1945, p. 711.
2. Colville, 15 Feb. 1945, p. 199.
3. Amery, 12 Feb. 1945, p. 1029.
4. Cadogan, 13 Feb 1945, pp. 710–11.
5. Moran, 13 Feb. 1945, pp. 287–8.
6. ibid., p. 289.
7. Macmillan, 5 Feb. 1945, p. 678.
8. Moran, 14 Feb. 1945, p. 291.
9. Macmillan, 14 Feb. 1945, pp. 692–3.
10. Cadogan, 15 Feb. 1945, p. 712.
11. Macmillan, *Blast of War*, p. 547.
12. Nicolson, ii, p. 437 (27 Feb. 1945).
13. Macmillan, 14 Feb. 1945, p. 693.
14. Moran, 14 Feb. 1945, p. 293.

15. Stettinius, 2 Jan. 1945, p. 211.
16. Sherwood, *Roosevelt and Hopkins*, p. 872.
17. Moran, 17 Feb. 1945, p. 294.
18. *SWW*, vi, p. 348.
19. *WD*, 11 Feb. 1945, p. 512.
20. Macmillan, 8 and 9 Feb. 1945, pp. 680–82.
21. *WD*, 11 Feb. 1945, p. 514.
22. Byrnes, *Speaking Frankly*, p. 45.
23. *WD*, 17 Feb. 1945, pp. 515–16.
24. Vandenberg, 13 Feb. 1945, p. 148.
25. Vandenberg, 17 Feb. 1945, p. 151.
26. Macmillan, 17 Feb. 1945, p. 697.
27. Nicolson, ii, p. 434 (15 Feb. 1945).
28. Colville, 19 Feb. 1945, p. 200.
29. Cadogan, 20 Feb. 1945, pp. 717, 719.
30. Colville, 21 Feb. 1945, p. 201.
31. Cadogan, 21 Feb. 1945, p. 719.
32. Gilbert, vii, pp. 1228–30.
33. Cadogan, 22 Feb. 1945, pp. 719–20.
34. Dalton, 23 Feb. 1945, *War Diary*, pp. 835–7.
35. Colville, 23 and 24 Feb. 1945, pp. 202–5.
36. Nicolson, ii, pp. 435–6 (21 and 26 Feb. 1945).
37. Chips, 26 April 1939, p. 241.
38. Thorpe, *Home*, p. 124.
39. Nicolson, ii, p. 436 (27 Feb. 1945); Gilbert, vii, pp. 1234–5.
40. Gilbert, vii, p. 1235.
41. Colville, 27 Feb. 1945, p. 205.
42. Nicolson, ii, p. 437 (27 Feb. 1945).
43. Chips, 28 Feb. 1945, pp. 485–6.
44. Nicolson, ii, pp. 439–40 (28 Feb. 1945).
45. Cadogan, 1 March 1945, p. 721.
46. Gilbert, vii, 1234.
47. *TT*, 2 March 1945.
48. Butcher, 28 March 1945, p. 780.
49. D'Este, *Eisenhower*, p. 668.
50. Hastings, *Armageddon*, p. 343.
51. Butcher, 14 March 1945, pp. 770–71.
52. Butcher, 7 March (entry written 11 March), 1945, p. 768.
53. Wilmot, *Struggle for Europe*, p. 677.
54. Cadogan, 8 March 1945, p. 722; Colville, 8 March 1945, p. 211.
55. Alanbrooke, 4 March 1945, p. 669.
56. Alanbrooke, 2 March 1945, p. 667.
57. Colville, 4 March 1945, p. 209.
58. Alanbrooke, 6 March 1945, p. 669.
59. Amery, 12 March 1945, p. 1031.
60. Colville, 15 March 1945, p. 214.
61. Black, *Roosevelt*, p. 1094.
62. Cadogan, 12 March 1945, p. 722.
63. Nicolson, ii, p. 441 (13 March 1945).
64. Colville, 20 March 1945, pp. 215–16.
65. Alanbrooke, 22 March 1945, p. 673.
66. Chips, 23 March 1945, p. 488.
67. Colville, 23 March 1945, p. 216.
68. Alanbrooke, 23 March 1945, p. 673.

69. Alanbrooke, 23 March 1945, pp. 673–4.
70. Butcher, 24 March 1945, p. 776.
71. Colville, 25 March 1945, p. 220.
72. Eisenhower, *Crusade*, p. 372.
73. Alanbrooke, 25 March 1945, p. 676; cf. Bryant, *Triumph in the West*, pp. 436–7.
74. Butcher, 1 April 1945, p. 792.
75. *SWW*, vi, p. 365.
76. Alanbrooke, 26 March 1945, note on p. 678.
77. Reynolds, *In Command of History*, p. 476.
78. Bryant, *Triumph in the West*, p. 441.
79. Montgomery, *Memoirs*, p. 277.
80. Eisenhower, *Crusade in Europe*, pp. 391, 396.
81. Butcher, 28 March (conf. 27 March) 1945, p. 788.
82. Colville, 27 March 1945, p. 222.
83. Hamilton, *Monty*, iii, p. 455.
84. Eisenhower, *Crusade in Europe*, p. 400.
85. Black, *Roosevelt*, p. 1088.
86. Alanbrooke, 29 March 1945, p. 679.
87. Reynolds, *In Command of History*, p. 471; *SWW*, vi, p. 402.
88. Gilbert, vii, p. 1275.
89. Alanbrooke, 1 April 1945, p. 680.

CHAPTER 8: SHADOWS OF DEATH

1. Hastings, *Armageddon*, pp. 380, 490.
2. *TT*, 25 Nov. 1944.
3. 5th Report on Lend-Lease; Staley, *AER*, xxxiii, 366.
4. Granatstein, *Britain's Weakness*, p. 39.
5. Staley, *AER*, xxxiii, 368.
6. Sayers, *Financial Policy*, p. 529.
7. Dalton, 14 Dec. 1944, *War Diary*, p. 818.
8. *TT*, 2 and 22 Jan. 1945.
9. *JMK*, xxvi, p. 146.
10. Meade, 14 Jan. 1945, pp. 29–30.
11. *JMK*, xxvi, p. 170.
12. ibid., p. 174.
13. Meade, 20 Jan. 1945, p. 33.
14. Meade, 25 March (for 21 March) 1945, p. 57.
15. *TT*, 19–21 March 1945.
16. *WD*, 26 March 1945, p. 530; cf. p. 521.
17. *CT*, 3 April 1945.
18. *JMK*, xxiv, p. 249.
19. ibid., pp. 280–81.
20. Colville, 7 and 20 March 1945, pp. 211, 215.
21. Macmillan, 7 March 1945, p. 710.
22. Cadogan, 21 March 1945, p. 723.
23. Sherwood, *Roosevelt and Hopkins*, p. 878.
24. Vandenberg, 7 March 1945, p. 156.
25. Vandenberg (mid-March), p. 155.
26. Forrestal, 16 March 1945, p. 53.
27. Stettinius, 12 March 1945, p. 297.
28. Stettinius, 19 March 1945, p. 306.
29. Stettinius, 24 March 1945 (for 23 March), pp. 306–7.

30. Vandenberg, 23 and 27 March 1945, pp. 159–60.
31. Vandenberg, 5 April 1945, p. 163.
32. Berlin, 9 April 1945, *Flourishing*, p. 547.
33. Vandenberg, 5 April 1945, p. 163.
34. *FDR–WSC*, 11 April 1945, p. 709.
35. Sherwood, *Roosevelt and Hopkins*, p. 880.
36. Stettinius, 12 April 1945, p. 315.
37. ibid., p. 316.
38. Thompson, *Assignment Churchill*, p. 303.
39. Colville, 13 April 1945, p. 233.
40. MO 2229, 13 April 1945.
41. Chips, 13 April 1945, p. 489.
42. Nicolson, ii, p. 447 (13 April 1945).
43. Chips, 17 April 1945, p. 490.
44. *TT*, 18 April 1945.
45. MO 2281, 3 Sep. 1945.
46. Wavell, 10 and 15 March 1945, pp. 115, 117.
47. Amery, 16 March 1945, p. 1032.
48. Wavell, 26 and 28 March 1945, pp. 119–120.
49. Alanbrooke, 28 March 1945, p. 679.
50. Wavell, 29 March, 4 and 9 April 1945, pp. 120–23.
51. Amery, 10 April 1945, p. 1035.
52. Amery, 12 April 1945, p. 1036; Wavell, 15 April 1945, p. 124.
53. Wavell, 23–5 April 1945, p. 126.
54. Amery, 26 April 1945, p. 1038.
55. Wavell, 29 April 1945, p. 127.
56. Amery, 30 April 1945, pp. 1039–40.
57. Butcher, 2 April 1945, p. 793.
58. Colville, 6 April 1945, p. 227.
59. Hastings, *Armageddon*, p. 486.
60. Colville, 5 April 1945, p. 226.
61. *NC*, 19 April 1945.
62. Colville, 26 April 1945, p. 239.
63. Alanbrooke, 12 April 1945, p. 683.
64. 7 April 1945, Bullock, ii, p. 369.
65. Chips, 10 April 1945, p. 489.
66. Dalton, 19 April 1945, *War Diary*, p. 852.
67. Gilbert, vii, p. 1271.
68. Chips, 27 April 1945, p. 491.
69. Cadogan, 28 April 1945, p. 735.
70. Colville, 27 April 1945, p. 240.
71. Macmillan, 29 April 1945, p. 746.
72. Colville, 1 May 1945, p. 242.
73. ibid.

CHAPTER 9: JUSTICE?

1. Morgenthau, 14 April 1945, p. 422.
2. Stettinius, 13 April 1945, p. 318.
3. Vandenberg, 13 April 1945, p. 167.
4. Stettinius, 16 April 1945, pp. 322–3.
5. Vandenberg, 13 April 1945, p. 167.
6. Vandenberg, 17 April 1945, p. 170.

7. Cadogan, 20 April 1945, p. 730.
8. Forrestal, 21 April 1945, p. 63.
9. Forrestal, 23 April 1945, pp. 64–6.
10. McCullough, *Truman*, p. 376.
11. Vandenberg, 24 April 1945, pp. 175–6.
12. Cadogan, 25 April 1945, p. 733.
13. Vandenberg, 26 April 1945, p. 178.
14. Cadogan, 27 April 1945, p. 734.
15. Vandenberg, 26 April 1945, pp. 179–80.
16. Cadogan, 28 April 1945, p. 735.
17. Vandenberg, 27 April 1945, pp. 181–2.
18. Cadogan, 29 (for 28) and 30 April 1945, pp. 736–7.
19. Vandenberg, 30 April 1945, p. 182.
20. Vandenberg, 2 May 1945, p. 183.
21. Williams, *Prime Minister Remembers*, p. 60.
22. Vandenberg, 4 May 1945, p. 183.
23. Cadogan, 5 May 1945, p. 739.
24. Vandenberg, 13 May 1945, p. 191.
25. Stettinius, 15 May 1945, p. 368.
26. MO 2249, 16–17 May 1945.
27. Cadogan, 12 May 1945, p. 741.
28. Nicolson, ii, p. 454 (2 May 1945).
29. Chips, 2 May 1945, p. 492.
30. Alanbrooke, 2 May 1945, p. 686.
31. Butcher, 4 May 1945, p. 821.
32. Wilmot, *Struggle for Europe*, p. 705.
33. Alanbrooke, 4 May 1945, p. 687.
34. Butcher, 6 May 1945, p. 828.
35. Moran, 8 May 1945, p. 305.
36. Chips, 8 May 1945, p. 494.
37. Nicolson, ii, pp. 457–8 (8 May 1945).
38. Alanbrooke, 8 May 1945, p. 689; Bryant, *Triumph in the West*, p. 458, omitted most of this.
39. Gilbert, vii, pp. 1347–8.
40. Williams, *Prime Minister Remembers*, p. 62.
41. Moran, wrongly dated 20 May (?23 May) 1945, p. 306.
42. Dalton, 12–14 May 1945, *War Diary*, p. 859.
43. Alanbrooke, 14 May 1945, p. 691.
44. Amery, 14 May 1945, p. 1041.
45. Colville, 14 May 1945, p. 246.
46. Dalton, 17 May 1945, *War Diary*, p. 860.
47. Dalton, 18 May 1945, *War Diary*, p. 861.
48. *SWW*, vi, p. 498.
49. Alanbrooke, 23 May 1945, p. 693; cf. Reynolds, *In Command of History*, pp. 476–7, 492–4.
50. Alanbrooke, 24 May 1945, p. 693.
51. Moran, wrongly dated 20 May (?23 May) 1945, p. 306.
52. Dalton, 19 May 1945, *War Diary*, p. 862.
53. Macmillan, 21 May 1945, p. 762.
54. Colville 22 May 1945, pp. 248–9.
55. Moran, wrongly dated 20 May (?23 May), 1945 p. 306.
56. MO 2249, 16–17 May 1945.
57. McCallum and Readman, *1945 General Election*, p. 129.
58. Morgenthau, 23 May 1945, p. 448.

59. *JMK*, xxiv, p. 362.
60. ibid., pp. 309, 320.
61. ibid., pp. 284–5.
62. *SWW*, iv, pp. 181–2.
63. *JMK*, xxiv, pp. 265, 269–70; *SWW*, iv, p. 181.
64. *JMK*, xxiv, pp. 278, 280.
65. ibid., pp. 307–8.
66. Moggridge, *Keynes*, p. 790.
67. *JMK*, xxiv, p. 286.
68. Clarke, *Anglo-American Economic Collaboration*, p. 128.
69. *SWW*, iv, p. 181.
70. Wavell, 16 April 1945, p. 124.
71. Chips, 2 and 16 May 1945, pp. 493, 496.
72. Amery, 7 May 1945, p. 1041.
73. Wavell, 8 May 1945, p. 129.
74. Chips, 2 and 16 May 1945 pp. 493, 496.
75. Wavell, 24 May 1945, p. 131.
76. Amery, 24 and 25 May 1945, p. 1043.
77. Amery, 30 May 1945, pp. 1043–4; Wavell, 30 May 1945, p. 134.
78. Wavell, 31 May 1945, pp. 135–6.
79. Amery, 31 May 1945, p. 1045.

CHAPTER 10: PEACE, POLITICS AND POTSDAM

1. *WD*, 2 June 1945, p. 572.
2. Forrestal, 20 May 1945, p. 73.
3. Sherwood, *Roosevelt and Hopkins*, pp. 890, 892, 909.
4. *SWW*, vi, p. 507.
5. Reynolds, *In Command of History*, p. 479.
6. Alanbrooke, 11 June 1945, p. 697.
7. Cadogan, 11 July 1945, p. 760.
8. *SWW*, vi, pp. 503–4.
9. Feis, *Between War and Peace*, p. 125.
10. Edmonds, *Big Three*, p. 428.
11. Dalton, 28 May 1945, *War Diary*, p. 865.
12. Gilbert, viii, p. 32.
13. Chips, 5 June 1945, p. 497.
14. Moran, 4 June 1945, p. 308.
15. Amery, 4 June 1945, p. 1046.
16. McCallum and Readman, *1945 General Election*, p. 143.
17. Nicolson, ii, p. 468 (5 June 1945); Amery, 5 June 1945, p. 1046.
18. Moran, 5 June 1945, p. 308.
19. Cadogan, 21 June 1945, p. 755.
20. Cadogan, 15 June 1945, p. 753.
21. Alanbrooke, 19 June 1945, p. 698.
22. Cadogan, 20 June 1945, p. 755.
23. Williams, *Prime Minister Remembers*, p. 70.
24. Cadogan, 15 July 1945, p. 761.
25. Wavell, 6 June 1945, pp. 138–9.
26. Stettinius, 22 May 1945, p. 377.
27. Louis, *Imperialism at Bay*, p. 537.
28. Vandenberg, 7 and 8 June 1945, pp. 208–9.
29. Stettinius, 7 June 1945, p. 394.

30. Vandenberg, p. 216.
31. Wavell, 24 June 1945, p. 147.
32. Wavell, 9 July 1945, p. 153.
33. *Nation's Voice*, iv, p. 176.
34. Amery, 12 July 1945, p. 1048; and p. 1045n.
35. Moran, 22 June 1945, p. 310.
36. McCallum and Readman, *1945 General Election*, pp. 23, 97–8.
37. Moran, 8 July 1945, p. 313–14.
38. Moran, 12 July 1945, pp. 321–3.
39. Stettinius, 21 and 25 June 1945, pp. 400, 404.
40. Vandenberg, n.d. (end June 1945), p. 225.
41. *WD*, 1 July 1945, p. 585.
42. Morgenthau, 29 May 1945, p. 449.
43. Morgenthau, n.d (but June 1945), p. 450.
44. Morgenthau, 3 July 1945, p. 451.
45. Morgenthau, 5 July 1945, p. 465.
46. Sherwood, *Roosevelt and Hopkins*, p. 921.
47. Moran, 8 July 1945, pp. 313–14.
48. Moran, (15) July 1945, p. 329.
49. Alanbrooke, 15 July 1945, p. 705.
50. Cadogan, 15 July 1945, p. 761.
51. Moran, (July 1945), p. 328.
52. *WD*, 22 July 1945, p. 593.
53. Moran, 17 July 1945, p. 336.
54. Alanbrooke, 24 July 1945, p. 710.
55. *FRUS* Potsdam, pp. 94–5.
56. MO 2290, 19 July 1945.
57. Moran, 16 July 1945, pp. 332–3.
58. *FRUS* Potsdam, p. 63.
59. *DBPO*, I, pp. 368–9 is the official version. Moran, 18 July 1945, pp. 336–7, had seen an earlier draft. Unlike either, *SWW*, vi, pp. 546–7, runs together both of the last two sentences as direct speech by Truman, which strengthens their effect, of course, but not necessarily their veracity.
60. *CT*, 16 July 1945.
61. *CT*, 18, 20, 22 and 24 July 1945.
62. Alanbrooke, 16 July 1945 p. 705.
63. Moran, 23 July 1945, p. 347.
64. *FRUS* Potsdam, p. 225.
65. Moran, 19 July 1945, p. 339.
66. *FRUS* Potsdam, p. 97.
67. Moran, 19 July 1945, p. 339.
68. *FRUS* Potsdam, p. 136.
69. Moran, 19 July 1945, pp. 339–40.
70. *FRUS* Potsdam, p. 178.
71. ibid., p. 180.
72. Moran, 20 July 1945, p. 341.
73. Cadogan, 21 July 1945, pp. 767–8.
74. *FRUS* Potsdam, pp. 217–18.
75. Moran, 22 July 1945, p. 343.
76. *FRUS* Potsdam, pp. 262–3.
77. ibid., p. 265.
78. Cohen notes, 23 July 1945, p. 312.
79. Moran, 22 July 1945, pp. 343–4.
80. Moran, 23 July 1945, p. 345.

81. Alanbrooke, 23 July 1945, p. 709.
82. Moran, 24 July 1945, p. 349.
83. *DBPO*, i, p. 649.
84. *FRUS* Potsdam, p. 372.
85. *SWW*, vi, p. 579.
86. Mountbatten diary, 24 July 1945, Ziegler, *Mountbatten*, p. 299.
87. Moran, 24 July 1945, p. 349.
88. Cadogan, 25 July 1945, p. 771.
89. Moran, 25 July 1945, p. 351.
90. *FRUS* Potsdam, pp. 388–9.
91. Alanbrooke, 23 July 1945, pp. 709–10.
92. Cadogan, 25 July 1945, pp. 771–2.
93. Moran, 26 July 1945, p. 352.
94. McCallum and Readman, *1945 General Election*, p. 277.
95. *SWW*, vi, p. 583.
96. Cadogan, 26 July 1945, p. 772.
97. Moran, 26 July 1945, p. 352.
98. Alanbrooke, 27 July 1945, p. 712; cf. 18 July, p. 706.
99. *DBPO*, i, p. 939.
100. Cadogan, 28 July 1945, p. 776.
101. Byrnes, *Speaking Frankly*, p. 79.
102. *DBPO*, i, p. 957.
103. *FRUS* Potsdam, pp. 467–9.
104. Cadogan, 31 July 1945, p. 778.
105. *DBPO*, i, p. 968.
106. ibid., pp. 1062–4.
107. *FRUS* Potsdam, pp. 528, 532–4.
108. ibid., p. 601.
109. *DBPO*, i, pp. 1143–4.
110. *SWW*, vi, p. 581.
111. Cadogan, 31 July 1945, p. 780.
112. MO 2290, 3 Aug 1945.
113. *CT*, 27 July 1945.
114. *CT*, 4 Aug. 1945.

CHAPTER II: HOPES BETRAYED

1. *DM*, 16 Aug. 1945.
2. *TT*, 16 Aug. 1945.
3. *CT*, 7, 20 and 16 Aug. 1945.
4. Thorne, *Allies of a Kind*, p. 453.
5. *SWW*, vi, p. 558.
6. Cadogan, 16 Aug. 1945, p. 782.
7. Cadogan, 15 Aug. 1945, p. 782.
8. Moran, 24 July 1945, p. 349.
9. Chips, 28 July and 1 Aug. 1945, p. 499.
10. Berlin, *Flourishing*, p. 583.
11. MO 2281, 3 Sep. 1945.
12. Edmonds, *Big Three*, pp. 399–402.
13. *FRUS* Potsdam, pp. 339–44.
14. *CT*, 8 Aug. 1945.
15. Dalton, 17 August 1945, *Political Diary*, p. 362.
16. *JMK*, xxiv, pp. 377, 410.

17. Truman, *Memoirs*, i, pp. 227–30, 475–6.
18. *TT*, 25 Aug. 1945; cf. *JMK*, xxiv, 399.
19. *TT* and *CT*, 25 Aug. 1945.
20. MO 2281, 3 Sept. 1945; cf. MO 2278, Aug. 1945.
21. Clarke, *Anglo-American Economic Collaboration*, pp. 126–36, at 126–7.
22. Meade. 1 July 1945, p. 103.
23. Meade, 26 Aug. 1945, p. 120.
24. Harrod, *Life of Keynes*, p. 596.
25. *JMK*, xxiv, p. 453.
26. Moggridge, *Keynes*, p. 799.
27. Jay, *Change and Fortune*, p. 137.
28. Amery, 28 July 1945, p. 1016.
29. Wavell, 26 July 1945, p. 159.
30. Wavell, 27 Aug. 1945, p. 165.
31. Wavell, 31 Aug. 1945, pp. 167–8.
32. Wavell, 4 Sep. 1945, p. 169.
33. Schofield, *Wavell*, p. 341.
34. Gopal (ed.), *Works of Nehru*, xiv, p. 81.
35. Halifax diary, 19 Sep. 1945 (courtesy Dr Richard Toye).
36. Clarke, *Anglo-American Economic Collaboration*, p. 56.
37. Halifax diary, 19 Sep. 1945.
38. Pressnell, *External Economic Policy*, pp. 290–92.
39. Bullock, *Bevin*, iii, p. 134.
40. Byrnes, *Speaking Frankly*, p. 105.
41. Bullock, *Bevin*, iii, p. 135.
42. Robbins, 14 Oct. 1945, p. 234.
43. Woods, *Changing of the Guard*, pp. 355–6.
44. Meinertzhagen, 3 July 1945, p. 194.
45. Cohen, *Palestine to Israel*, p. 177.
46. Baffy, 26 July 1945, p. 223.
47. Pimlott, *Hugh Dalton*, p. 389.
48. Baffy, 1 Aug. 1945, pp. 223–4.
49. *WD*, 27 Aug. 1945, p. 610.
50. Pimlott, *Hugh Dalton*, p. 389.
51. Baffy, 20 Sep. 1945, p. 225.
52. Meinertzhagen, 28 Sep. 1945, p. 197.
53. Cohen, *Palestine to Israel*, pp. 182–5; Bullock, *Bevin*, pp. 175–6.
54. *DM*, 1 Oct. 1945.
55. MO 2278, Aug. 1945.

CHAPTER 12: THE COSTS OF VICTORY

1. Gardner, *Sterling–Dollar Diplomacy*, p. xiii, says it was 'found on a yellowing piece of paper salvaged from the first Anglo-American discussions during World War II about postwar economic arrangements'.
2. Robbins, 30 Sep. 1945, p. 224.
3. *JMK*, xxiv, pp. 509, 511.
4. Gardner, *Sterling–Dollar Diplomacy*, pp. 199, 201.
5. Robbins, 2 Oct. 1945, p. 226.
6. Pressnell, *External Economic Policy*, p. 269.
7. Robbins. 29 Sep. 1945, pp. 223–4.
8. *JMK*, xxiv, pp. 547–8, 551.
9. ibid., p. 484.

10. Robbins, 1 Oct. 1945, p. 225.
11. Robbins, 4 Oct. 1945, p. 228.
12. Meade, 3 Nov. 1945, p. 164.
13. Ovendale, *End of the Palestine Mandate*, p. 95.
14. Louis, *British Empire in the Middle East*, p. 391.
15. Bullock, *Bevin*, iii, pp. 179, 181.
16. Meinertzhagen, 14 Nov. 1945, pp. 199–201 at 200.
17. Harris, *Attlee*, p. 281.
18. Thomas, *Armed Truce*, p. 634.
19. Dalton, *High Tide and After*, p. 77.
25. Dalton, ?6 Nov. (misdated 7 Dec.) 1945, *Political Diary*, p. 365.
21. Toye, *EHR*, cxviii, 919.
22. *TT*, 13 Dec. 1945.
23. *JMK*, xxiv, pp. 605, 610.
24. Clarke, *Anglo-American Economic Collaboration*, p. 39.
25. Moore, *Escape from Empire*, p. 29; Tomlinson, *Political Economy of the Raj*, p. 140.
26. Compare above, ch. 9.
27. *JMK*, xxiv, p. 627; cf. Bullock, *Bevin*, iii, p. 202.
28. ibid., p. 613.
29. *PM*, p. 11.
30. Diary, 15 March 1946, Ovendale, *End of the Palestine Mandate*, p. 116; cf. *PM*, p. 144.
31. *PM*, p. 59.
32. *DH*, 18 Oct. 1945, *DM* 15 Nov. 1945.
33. Diary, 30 Dec. 1945–1 Jan. 1946, 3 Jan. 1946, *PM*, pp. 26, 46.
34. *PM*, pp. 54, 88.
35. Diary, 13 Jan. 1946, *PM*, p, 47.
36. Woods, *Changing of the Guard*, p. 322.
37. Baffy, 30 Jan. 1946, p. 230.
38. Diary, Jan. 1946, Louis, *British Empire in the Middle East*, p. 407.
39. Diary, n.d., Howard, *Crossman*, p. 110.
40. Baffy, 29 Jan. 1946, p. 230.
41. *PM*, p. 89.
42. *PM*, p. 184.
43. *PM*, p. 114.
44. *JMK*, xxvii, p. 480.
45. *PM*, pp. 118–19, 109.
46. *PM*, pp. 128–9.
47. Diary, 8 March 1946, *PM*, p. 133.
48. Baffy, 8 March 1946, p. 231.
49. Baffy 9 March 1946, p. 232.
50. Diary, 10 March 1946, *PM*, p. 138.
51. Diary, 26 March 1946, *PM*, pp. 170–72.
52. Diary, 15 March 1946, *PM*, p. 146.
53. *PM*, pp. 176.
54. Diary, 11 March 1946; *New Statesman*, 11 May 1946, *PM*, pp. 139, 244.
55. Diary, 26 March 1946, *PM*, p. 172.
56. Baffy, 29 April 1946, pp. 235–6.
57. *PM*, p. 200.
58. Baffy, 29 Jan. 1946, p. 230.
59. Howard, *Crossman*, p. 125; *PM*, p. 204.
60. Louis, *British Empire in the Middle East*, p. 428.
61. MO summary, 1941–Dec. 1946.
62. Woods, *Changing of the Guard* p. 376; Gardner, *Sterling–Dollar Diplomacy*, table 2, p. 236.

63. *JMK*, xxvii, pp. 463–4.
64. ibid., pp. 466.
65. ibid., p. 479.
66. MO summary March–April 1946.
67. *JMK*, xxvii, p. 270.
68. Gardner, *Sterling–Dollar Diplomacy*, pp. 237–40.
69. Vandenberg, 19 Dec. 1945, pp. 230–31.
70. Forrestal, 10 March 1946, pp. 149–50.
71. Thomas, *Armed Truce*, p. 198.
72. *TT*, 8 Nov. 1945.
73. Gardner, *Sterling–Dollar Diplomacy*, p. 249; Toye, *TCBH*, xv, 350.
74. Judson note, 14 March 1946 (courtesy Dr Richard Toye).
75. Pelling, *Marshall Plan*, p. 5.
76. *JMK*, xxvii, pp. 482–3.
77. Woods, *Changing of the Guard*, pp. 292–3.
78. *Congressional Record* (House), 12 July 1945, col. 8877.

CHAPTER 13: SABOTAGE?

1. Wavell, 1 July 1946, p. 310.
2. *Nation's Voice*, iv, p. 346.
3. *TOP*, vi, pp. 852–3, 856, 857.
4. Text, *Nation's Voice*, v, pp. 686–92 at pp. 687, 689.
5. *Nation's Voice*, v, p. 706.
6. Clarke, *Cripps*, p. 406.
7. Alexander diary, 12 April 1946.
8. Cripps diary, 13 and 17 April 1946.
9. Wavell, 15 and 24 April 1946, pp. 245, 251.
10. Clarke, *Cripps*, p. 410.
11. Cripps diary, 30–31 March 1946.
12. Wavell, 3 April 1946, p. 236.
13. *TOP*, vii, p. 179.
14. ibid., 260.
15. Cripps diary, 18 April 1946.
16. French, *Liberty or Death*, pp. 262–3.
17. Cripps diary, 18 April 1946.
18. Nicolson, iii, p. 57 (16 April 1946).
19. *Observer*, 21 April 1946; *Daily Herald*, 25 April 1946.
20. Cripps diary, 24 and 26 (for 25) April 1946.
21. *TOP*, vii, pp. 345–6; Wavell, 26 April 1946, p. 253.
22. Wavell, 7 May 1946, p. 261; Cripps diary, 9 May 1946.
23. *TOP*, vii, pp. 465–6.
24. Cripps diary, 9 May 1946.
25. Clarke, *Cripps*, p. 428.
26. *TOP*, vii, p. 508.
27. Gilbert, viii, p. 141.
28. ibid., p. 230.
29. *TOP*, vii, p. 562.
30. ibid., pp. 613–15.
31. Wavell, 20 May 1946, p. 274.
32. Alexander diary, 21 May 1946.
33. Alexander diary, 22 May 1946.
34. Gandhi, *Collected Works*, lxxxiv, p. 181.

35. Clarke, *Cripps*, p. 438.
36. ibid., p. 414.
37. *Nation's Voice*, v, p. 46.
38. Alexander diary, 10 June 1946.
39. Cripps diary, 11 June 1946.
40. Gandhi, *Collected Works*, lxxxiv, 330–31; Cripps diary, 13 June 1946.
41. Cripps diary, 23 June 1946.
42. Alexander diary, 24 June 1946.
43. *TOP*, vii, pp. 1029–30.
44. ibid., pp. 1042–3.
45. Clarke, *Cripps*, p. 390.
46. ibid., pp. 438–9.
47. In the index to *The Times* for January to June, India takes up 23 columns as against 8 columns for Palestine; but the index for July to December shows them almost equal in coverage (21 and 20 columns respectively). The same sort of relative shift can be seen in the *New York Times* index, where the number of references to Palestine now doubled, which meant – given that it already enjoyed 60 per cent more American coverage than India in January to June – that in July to December there were three stories about Palestine for every one about India.
48. Wavell, 30 Oct. 1946, p. 367.
49. *Nation's Voice*, v, pp. 166–7.
50. *TOP*, viii, p. 570.
51. *TT*, 27 May 1946.
52. Bullock, *Bevin*, iii, p. 292.
53. Hamilton, *Monty*, iii, p. 636; cf. Montgomery, *Memoirs*, p. 423.
54. Baffy, 29 June and 4 July 1946, p. 237.
55. Meinertzhagen, 1 July 1946, p. 212.
56. House of Commons, 1 July 1946, *PM*, p. 250.
57. Baffy, 19 July 1946, p. 238.
58. *NYT*, 28 July 1946.
59. *Washington Post*, 2 Aug. 1946.
60. Louis, *British Empire in the Middle East*, p. 436.
61. Bullock, *Bevin*, iii, p. 253.
62. Gilbert, viii, p. 251.
63. Meinertzhagen, 2 Aug. 1946, p. 215.
64. Ovendale, *End of the Palestine Mandate*, pp. 141–2; Halamish, *Exodus Affair*, p. 4.
65. Baffy, 1 Oct. 1946, p. 240.
66. Bullock, *Bevin*, iii, pp. 303–4.
67. Louis, *British Empire in the Middle East*, p. 439.
68. Forrestal, 4 Sep. 1947, p. 299.
69. Ovendale, *End of the Palestine Mandate*, pp. 165–6.
70. MO 2432, 6 Nov. 1946; cf. MO 2515 (compiled Sep. 1947).

CHAPTER 14: SCUTTLE?

1. Clarke, *Cripps*, p. 461.
2. Wavell, 5 Dec. 1946, p. 390.
3. *TOP*, ix, pp. 276, 279.
4. Williams, *Prime Minister Remembers*, p. 209.
5. Clarke, *Cripps*, pp. 467–71.
6. 5 HC Debs, 12 Dec. 1946, col. 1368.
7. Reynolds, *In Command of History*, pp. 68, 82.
8. 5 HC Debs, 12 Dec. 1946, col. 1369.

9. *TT*, 21 Dec. 1946; cf *OHBE*, p. 337.
10. *TT*, 25 May 1946.
11. *TT*, 20 July 1947.
12. *TT*, 24 Jan. 1947. 'Scuttle' had an august pedigree. The *OED* is again helpful, in disinterring the political slang of the 1880s, when Lord Randolph Churchill was making his name in attacking the Liberals' alleged lack of enthusiasm for Empire and when 'scuttle' thereby acquired a new sense: 'To withdraw in a precipitate and undignified manner from the occupation or control of a country.' This is exactly how the term was now re-established, sixty years later; and Cranborne was grandson of the great Lord Salisbury (the Conservative prime minister who had briefly made Lord Randolph his chancellor of the exchequer).
13. Singh, *Origins of Partition*, p. 208; Owen in Tiratsoo, *Attlee Years*, pp. 180–81.
14. *TT*, 24 April 1947.
15. Cairncross, *Years of Recovery*, pp. 79, 102, 152ff.
16. Dalton, 20 Dec. 1946, *Political Diary*, p. 389.
17. Clarke, *Anglo-American Economic Collaboration*, pp. 156–7.
18. Hennessy, *Never Again*, p. 268.
19. Ovendale, *End of the Palestine Mandate*, pp. 181–2.
20. Bullock, *Bevin*, iii, pp. 339–40.
21. ibid., pp. 360–61.
22. *Annual Register*, 1947, pp. 7–8.
23. Wavell, 4 Feb. 1947, p. 417.
24. Feinstein in Clarke and Trebilcock, *Understanding Decline*, pp. 216–17.
25. Clarke, *Cripps*, p. 457.
26. Dalton, 20 Dec. 1946, *Political Diary*, p. 389.
27. Clarke, *Cripps*, p. 471.
28. *TOP*, ix, p. 453.
29. *TT*, 21 Feb. 1947.
30. *TT*, 7 and 13 March, 7 April 1947.
31. *TT*, 8 May 1947.
32. Baffy, 9 and 10 Dec. 1946, p. 243.
33. Baffy, 17 Dec. 1946 and 4 Jan. 1947, pp. 244, 247.
34. Gilbert, viii, p. 296.
35. Louis, *British Empire in the Middle East*, p. 461.
36. Ovendale, *End of the Palestine Mandate*, p. 195.
37. *TT*, 7 March 1947.
38. Bullock, *Bevin*, iii, p. 369n.
39. Forrestal, 24 Feb. 1947, p. 242.
40. Chace, *Acheson*, p. 165.
41. Vandenberg, 5 March 1947, p. 340.
42. McCullough, *Truman*, pp. 547–8.
43. Vandenberg, 13 March 1947, p. 343.
44. *SWW*, vi, p. 266.
45. Dalton, 24 Feb. 1947, *Political Diary*, p. 391.
46. Dalton, 29 May 1947, ibid., p. 393.
47. *TT*, 9 May 1947.
48. Clarke, *Anglo-American Economic Collaboration*, pp. 157, 161.
49. Milward, *Reconstruction of Western Europe*, p. 2.
50. Hogan, *Marshall Plan*, pp. 43–4.
51. *TT*, 20 June 1946.
52. Bullock, *Bevin*, iii, p. 405.
53. Hennessy, *Never Again*, pp. 294–5.
54. *TOP*, x, p. 121.
55. Gilbert, viii, p. 334.

56. Moore, *Escape from Empire*, p. 336.
57. *DM*, 16 July 1947.
58. *NYT*, 20 July 1947.
59. Louis, *British Empire in the Middle East*, p. 466.
60. Halamish, *Exodus Affair*, pp. 15–21.
61. *NYT*, 27 and 29 July 1947.
62. *TT*, 22 Aug. 1947.
63. MO 2515 (compiled Sep. 1947).
64. Dalton, 26 July 1947, *Political Diary*, p. 397.
65. Dalton, 30 July 1947, ibid., pp. 403–4.
66. Dalton, 8 Aug. 1947, ibid., pp. 406–7.
67. Gilbert, viii, p. 336.
68. *TT*, 7 Aug. 1947.
69. Ziegler, *Mountbatten*, p. 416.
70. Brown, *Nehru*, p.175.
71. French, *Liberty or Death*, p. 330.
72. Menon, *Transfer of Power*, p. 444.
73. Wheeler-Bennett, *George VI*, p. 716n.

EPILOGUE

1. MO 3046 (compiled Oct. 1948).
2. Barnett, *Lost Victory*.
3. Charmley, *Churchill: the end of glory* and *Churchill's Grand Alliance*.
4. Most recently in Davies, *Europe at War*.
5. Gilbert, *Churchill and America*; Roberts, *History of the English-Speaking Peoples*.
6. Ashley Seager, *Guardian*, 29 Dec. 2006; see also Christopher Meyer, *Sunday Times*, 31 Dec. 2006.

Acknowledgements

This is not a work of academic history, written looking over my shoulder at historiographical controversies, but I am confident that the scholarly foundations of the work are secure. My footnotes simply identify the sources of direct quotations (and a few statistics not easily verified elsewhere). The bibliography includes all works cited. But it also represents an acknowledgement of my debts to my fellow historians, especially the authors of the works asterisked. I ask them to accept this small tribute in payment of a large debt.

I have received help from various libraries and archives. Newspaper research was largely undertaken in the Macpherson Library of the University of Victoria, British Columbia; in the Suzzallo Library of the University of Washington, Seattle; and in the Cambridge University Library. Mass-Observation sources are used with permission of the Curtis Brown Group Ltd London on behalf of the Trustees of the Mass Observation Archive copyright © The Trustees of the Mass Observation Archive. I am grateful to Helen Langley of the Bodleian Library, Oxford, on behalf of Nuffield College, Oxford, and the Cripps family for permission to reproduce items from the Cripps archive. Likewise I thank Mrs Estrellita Karsh and Mr Jerry Fielder, on behalf of the Karsh Estate, for facilitating my request to include four of Karsh's incomparable portraits. I am grateful to Mrs Jennifer Hunt for permission to quote from the diary of her grandfather, A. V. Alexander (later Earl Alexander of Hillsborough), whose papers are held at the Churchill Archives Centre, Churchill College, Cambridge; and the Director of the Centre, Allen Packwood, not only helped here but also provided background information on one of the most elusive minor characters in my story: Churchill's butler, Frank Sawyers.

At Penguin UK, Stuart Proffitt backed this book from the outset, kept me on course throughout, made constructive criticisms of the penultimate draft, and retained a steely confidence that together we could meet an unforgiving deadline for publication. Others at Penguin UK rose to this challenge with superb professionalism: notably Phillip Birch, Richard Duguid and Mark Handsley (who saved me from blunders at the copy-editing stage). Cecilia Mackay brought a great sense of style to the picture research and layout. My agent in Vancouver, Sally Harding, proved indefatigable in her efforts on my behalf; and I have received heartening support from the team at Penguin Canada.

In Cambridge, St John's College (where I was a Fellow for twenty years) and Trinity Hall (where I was a Master for four) continued to provide generous hospitality during my research visits to the incomparable University Library. Three Cambridge friends, Stefan Collini, John Thompson and Richard Toye, read the whole manuscript, to my immense benefit. The book was actually written on Pender Island, British Columbia, in the house that Maria Tippett and I have built; her responsibility for shaping and sustaining this project is greatest of all.

My story remains the same on either side of the Atlantic, and no substantive changes have been introduced into this first American edition. But I gladly seize the opportunity of expressing my debt to Peter Ginna at Bloomsbury Press in New York for valued support and wise counsel.

Peter Clarke
Pender Island, January 2008

Index

Acheson, Dean 372, 486–7, 491
Africa xxvi–xxvii, 91, 365, 477; Italian
  colonies 349; North African campaign
  34–8, 50, 55, 69, 175, 183
Age (Melbourne) 158; quoted 158, 179,
  254, 285
Alexander, Albert (Earl Alexander of
  Hillsborough) 186, 502; and cabinet
  delegation (1946) 427–8, 431, 438,
  443–4, 453; diarist 431, 445, 446,
  450
Alexander, Field Marshal Sir Harold (Earl
  Alexander of Tunis), Allied
  Commander in Italy 76, 96, 111, 291,
  301–2, 305; and Churchill 182, 196,
  227; possible move 134, 152, 182,
  187, 248; and Greece 120, 122, 135,
  138, 139; and Macmillan 96, 162,
  235
Amery, Leopold (Leo): and imperial
  preference 14, 25, 107, 396; and
  Zionism 84, 86–7, 409–10; and
  Atlantic Charter 93; and India, 20,
  23, 88, 144, 145, 163, 176–8,
  278–82, 316, 318–19, 332; career
  ends, 354, 368–9, 381; diarist xxiii, 52,
  53, 59, 97, 99–100, 114, 115, 116,
  123, 151–2, 162, 173, 226–7, 248,
  325
Anders, General Wladislaw 43, 72, 235,
  237
Anderson, Sir John (Viscount Waverley)
  264, 282, 430
Antonov, General A. I. (Soviet chief of
  staff) 193
Antwerp 42, 78, 81–2, 105, 128
Arabs: and Palestine 84–88, 91, 461, 480;
  plans for resettlement 231, 388–9;
  British attitudes towards 397–8, 406,

463, 499; conflict with Zionism 411,
  455–6, 482, 500; inferior propaganda
  412, 414, 456, 496, 509
Arnhem (1944) 66, 73–4, 80–82, 95, 220,
  243, 250, 253
Associated Press (news agency) 267, 292,
  304
Athlone, Earl of (Canadian Governor
  General) 47, 64
Atlantic Charter (1941) 9–10, 13, 19, 49,
  124, 187, 232–3, 323, 505; and British
  Empire, 9–10, 13, 19, 91, 164; and
  Poland 40, 147, 164, 208, 294; and
  Palestine 91; and Greece 141, 147, 149,
  164
Attlee, Clement 186, 320; as leader of
  Labour Party 20, 59, 99, 123, 307–12;
  as Churchill's deputy 73, 138, 248,
  266, 341; rebukes Churchill 137,
  173–4, 205, 310, 325; and self-
  determination principle 10, 20, 311,
  398, 430, 469–70; and India (1944–5)
  145, 163, 281, 318–19, 365–6; and
  Cripps on India (1945–7) 381–2,
  425–7, 435, 443, 464–7, 470, 479,
  493–4, 496; at San Francisco 278–9,
  282, 289–90, 299–301, 305, 307–8;
  and General Election (1945) 325–8; at
  Potsdam 320, 325–8, 334, 337, 341,
  346, 353, 355–9; as Prime Minister
  355–9, 368, 369–70, 406; and Bevin
  on foreign policy 355–6, 358, 420–21,
  475–7, 492; and American Loan 373,
  398–9, 424; and Zionism 388–9,
  406–7, 415–16, 459, 462; and atomic
  secrets 369–70, 398–9; and sterling
  crisis (1947) 500–502; plays losing
  hand xx, 359, 367, 502, 510
Augusta, USS 8, 340

549